Programming BASICS

Using Microsoft Visual Basic, C++, HTML, and Java

Todd Knowlton
Karl Barksdale
Stephan Collings
E. Shane Turner
CEP, Inc.

Australia • Canada • Mexico • Singapore • Spain • United Kingdom • United States

Programming BASICS Using Microsoft Visual Basic, C++, HTML, and Java

by Todd Knowlton, Karl Barksdale, Stephen Collings, E. Shane Turner, CEP, Inc.

Publisher:
Kristen Duerr

Sr. Product Manager:
Dave Lafferty

Development Editor:
Jean Findley, Custom Editorial Productions

Marketing Manager:
Kim Wood

Editorial Assistant:
Jodi Dreissig

Print Buyer:
Denise Sandler

Production:
Karen Jacot

Design:
Julie Malone

Compositor:
GEX Publishing Services

Printer:
TransContinental

Printed in Canada

2 3 4 5 6 7 8 9 TC 04 03 02

For more information, contact Course Technology, 25 Thomson Place, Boston, Massachusetts, 02210.

Or find us on the World Wide Web at: www.course.com

ISBN 0-619-05803-X
ISBN 0-619-05801-3

How to Use This Book

What makes a good programming text? Sound instruction and hands-on skill-building and reinforcement. That is what you will find in Programming BASICS. Not only will you find an inviting layout, but also many features to enhance learning.

Objectives — Objectives are listed at the beginning of each lesson, along with a suggested time for completion of the lesson. This allows you to look ahead to what you will be learning and to pace your work.

SCANS — (Secretary's Commission on Achieving Necessary Skills) — The U.S. Department of Labor has identified the school-to-careers competencies. The eight workplace competencies and foundation skills are identified in exercises where they apply.

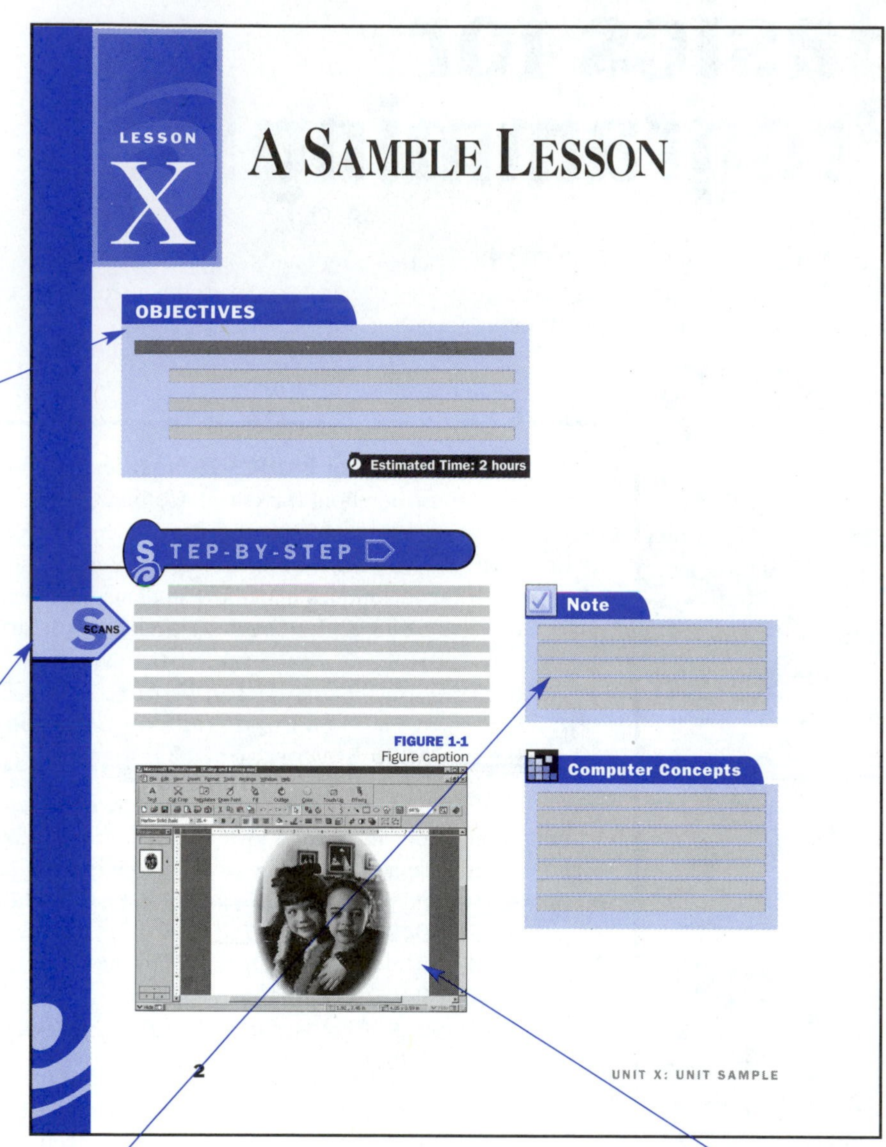

Marginal Boxes — These boxes provide additional information about the programming language in the lesson.

Code Lists — Code lists display entire programs or components of a program to emphasize conceptual discussion.

Screen Shots — Numerous screen shots help clarify the text.

How to Use This Book

Summary — At the end of each lesson, you will find a summary to prepare you to complete the end-of-lesson activities.

Review Questions — Review material at the end of each lesson and each unit enables you to prepare for assessment of the content presented.

Lesson Projects — End-of-lesson hands-on application of what has been learned in the lesson allows you to actually apply the techniques covered.

End-of-Unit Projects — End-of-unit hands-on application of concepts learned in the unit provides opportunity for a comprehensive review.

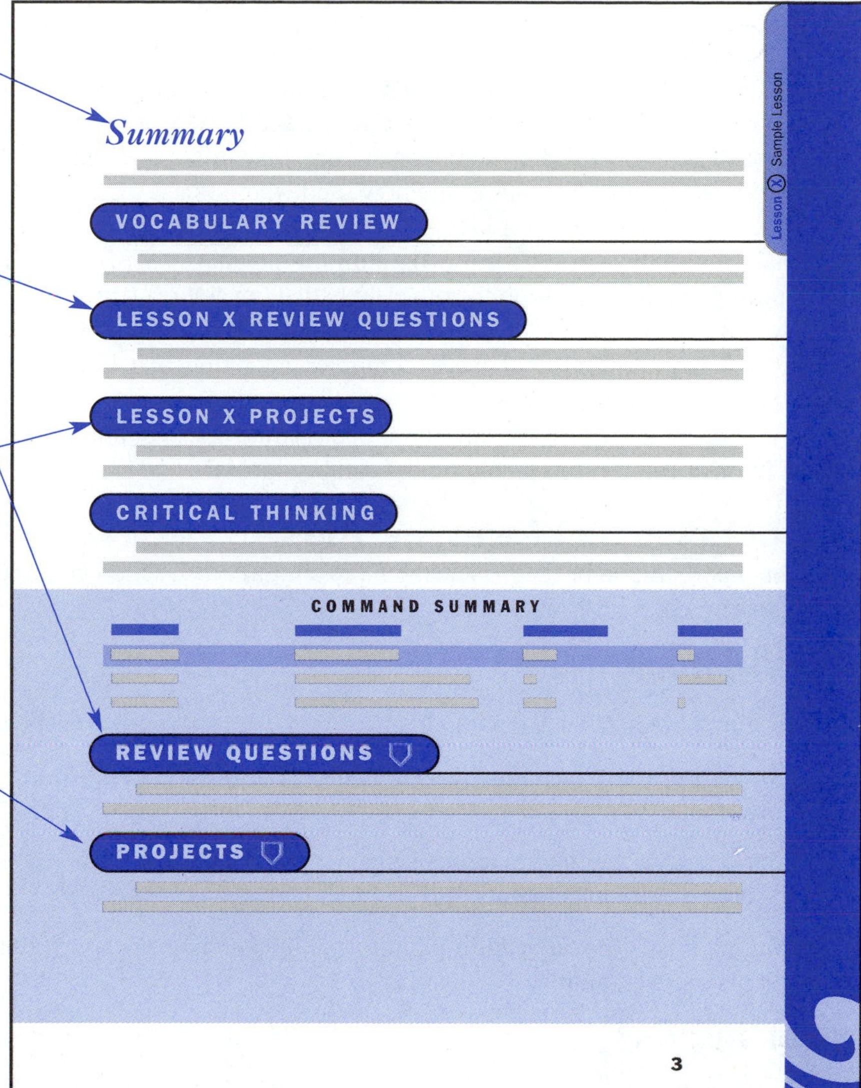

PREFACE

This book introduces computer programming in four of the most popular computer languages in use today: Visual Basic, C++, HTML/JavaScript, and Java. Most professional programmers have worked with various languages to gain an understanding of the differences that exist among them. The smart programmer knows the available tools and how (and when) to use them.

This book can be used for any programming survey course or computer lab where there is a need for a basic foundation in different programming languages. These lessons are a good introduction to programming and a preparation for other texts that cover each language in greater detail.

The lessons in this book do not assume you have had any previous programming experience. You do need to have knowledge of basic computer operations, such as how to use a mouse and how to manipulate windows and menus.

The units in this book are self-contained. If time does not allow working through the whole book, units of interest can be chosen and others can be skipped.

Instructional and Learning Aids

This instructional package is designed to simplify instruction and to enhance learning with the following learning and instructional aids:

The Textbook

- Learning objectives listed at the beginning of each lesson give users an overview of the lesson.
- Step-by-Step exercises immediately follow the presentation of new concepts for hands-on reinforcement.
- Illustrations, including numerous screen captures and code samples, explain complex concepts and serve as reference points.
- Marginal boxes provide additional information and note special features or information to enrich students' understanding.

END OF LESSON

- Lesson summaries provide quick reviews reinforcing the main points in each lesson.
- Written questions guage learners' understanding of lesson concepts and software operations.
- Projects offer minimal instruction so learners must apply concepts previously introduced.
- Critical thinking activities stimulate the user to apply analytical and reasoning skills.

END OF UNIT

- Review questions provide a comprehensive overview of unit content and help in preparing for tests.
- Unit applications for reinforcement ask the user to employ all the skills and concepts presented in the unit.
- A glossary follows each unit, providing a collection of the key terms from each lesson in the unit.

END OF BOOK

- A rich set of appendices provide additional information.
- A comprehensive index supplies quick and easy accessibility to specific parts of the book.

Other Components

- The Activities Workbook provides additional exercises and activities to reinforce each unit.
- The Instructor Resource Kit package is a CD-ROM that includes features such as guidelines for scheduling, lesson plans, data files necessary to complete the exercises and activities in the lessons, and solutions for exercises, projects, and activities.
- ExamView testing software, also included on the Instructor Resource Kit CD-ROM, allows the instructor to generate printed tests, online exams, and an instructor gradebook.

START-UP CHECKLISTS

Visual Basic

This unit has been tested with both Visual Basic 5.0 and Visual Basic 6.0. Microsoft Visual Basic is available for the Microsoft Windows operating system only.

Please note that at press time, Microsoft Visual Studio was still in development and not available, and thus beyond the scope of this text.

The minimum hardware requirements for the two versions of Visual Basic are as follows:

Visual Basic 5.0 — Learning Edition

- ✓ PC with a 486DX/66 MHz or higher processor (Pentium or higher processor recommended)
- ✓ Microsoft Windows 95 or later operating system, or Microsoft Windows NT operating system version 4.0 (Service Pack 2 recommended), or Microsoft Windows NT Workstation operating system version 3.51 with Service Pack 5
- ✓ 8 MB of RAM for Windows 95 or Windows NT Workstation 4.0 or 16 MB of RAM for Windows NT 4.0
- ✓ Hard disk space required: 37 MB
- ✓ CD-ROM drive
- ✓ VGA or higher-resolution monitor; Super VGA recommended
- ✓ Microsoft mouse or compatible pointing device

Visual Basic 6.0 — Learning Edition

- ✓ PC with a 486DX/66 MHz or higher processor (Pentium or higher processor recommended)
- ✓ Microsoft Windows 95 or later operating system, or Microsoft Windows NT operating system version 4.0 with Service Pack 3 or later
- ✓ 16 MB of RAM for Windows 95 or later or 24 MB of RAM for Windows NT 4.0
- ✓ Hard disk space required: 52 MB
- ✓ CD-ROM drive
- ✓ VGA or higher-resolution monitor; Super VGA recommended
- ✓ Microsoft mouse or compatible pointing device

For up-to-date hardware requirements on the latest Visual Basic compiler and for the requirements of other editions of the compiler, go to: http://www.programvb.com/basics/aboutvb.htm

C++

C++ is a language that is used on various types of computers and operating systems. The compiler software required to write C++ programs is available from a variety of software publishers, including Microsoft, Inprise, and Metrowerks. This checklist will help you ensure that you have the items necessary to successfully complete this text.

- A compiler or development environment capable of compiling standard C++ source code is required. Use the most recent version available for your operating system. Check your compiler's system requirements before installing the compiler. Also, verify that the compiler you are using supports template classes.
- If you need help using your compiler, consult your compiler's documentation.
- You will need the data files supplied for this unit. These files are primarily text files containing C++ source code for students to compile in the activities and exercises in the unit.

HTML/JavaScript

This unit may be used with any computer system that supports a compatible Web browser. In order to be compatible, the browser must support version 1.1 of the JavaScript language specification.

Compatible browsers include:

- Netscape Navigator 3.0 or higher
- Microsoft Internet Explorer 3.0 or higher

Computer systems that support these Web browsers include:

- PCs running Microsoft Windows
- Macintosh systems
- UNIX workstations

Additional software requirements are simply a text editor or word processor for creating HTML and JavaScript source code such as Notepad (Windows), SimpleText (Macintosh), Microsoft Word, WordPerfect, WordPro, ClarisWorks, or Microsoft Works.

Java

For this unit, you may use any Java compiler that adheres to the proposed Java standard. The programs in the text have been extensively tested with Borland, Microsoft, and Sun compilers. Testing was done with compilers that support Version 1.1 of Java as specified by Sun Microsystems.

It should be noted that Microsoft's Visual J++ version 1.1 does not adhere completely to Sun's specifications for Java 1.1. Several of the programs in this unit would not compile cleanly using the standard release of Visual J++, version 1.1.

Many of the programs were also tested with Symantec's Visual Cafe Java 2.0 for the Macintosh. However, programs requiring console input will not compile or run correctly due to the lack of console input support in the Macintosh platform.

Because Java was written to be a portable language, the programs in this unit can be run on DOS or Windows, with few exceptions.

TABLE OF CONTENTS

UNIT 3 INTRODUCTION TO C++

UNIT 4 Introduction to Web Programming with HTML and JavaScript

UNIT 5 Introduction to Java

INTRODUCING PROGRAMMING LOGIC AND LANGUAGES

UNIT 1

lesson 1 — 1 hr.

Introducing Programming Logic and Languages

Estimated Time for Unit 1: 1 hour

LESSON 1 INTRODUCING PROGRAMMING LOGIC AND LANGUAGES

OBJECTIVES

Upon completion of this lesson, you should be able to:

- Describe the various types of programs.
- Describe the role of the operating system.
- Describe how a computer gets instructions.
- Describe the role of a programming language, high- and low-level languages, interpreters, and compilers.
- Describe how to select a programming language.

Estimated Time: 1 hour

VOCABULARY

algorithm
assembly language
compiler
executable file
graphical user interface (GUI)
high-level language
interpreter
linker
low-level language
machine language
object code
object file
operating system
programming language
source code

What Is a Computer Program?

Computers are complex machines. They are, however, just machines. Think of a computer as a machine that follows instructions. From the moment a computer is turned on, it begins executing instructions, and it does not stop until you turn it off. These instructions are put into a logical sequence to create *programs*.

When you perform a particular task with your computer, such as using a word processor, a computer program provides the instructions to the computer. Programs such as word processors and games are called *application programs*. Figure 1-1 shows an example of an application program. But even when you are not running a particular application program, the computer is still executing programs.

When a computer is first turned on, it follows instructions that are embedded in its hardware on chips called *read-only memory* or *ROM*. On some computers, these instructions are called the *BIOS* or *basic input/output system*. The programs in ROM perform very basic operations and help the computer start its operating system.

FIGURE 1-1
Microsoft PhotoDraw is an example of an application program.

Operating Systems

The ***operating system*** is a set of programs that takes charge of fundamental system operations. Application programs rely on the operating system to handle the details. Let us look at some of the things an operating system does.

1. **The operating system manages the hardware resources.** The operating system allocates memory to programs and system operations. It also can allocate processor time when multiple programs are running.

2. **The operating system maintains the system of files.** The operating system organizes programs and files into directories.

3. **The operating system controls input and output operations.** Keyboard input, mouse movements, displaying items on the screen, and printing all involve the operating system.

4. **The operating system loads programs and supervises their execution.** When you issue a command to start a program, the operating system loads the program into memory and allows it to begin executing. The operating system regularly interrupts the program so that other programs can run and housekeeping chores such as updating the system date and time can take place.

Some operating systems you may be familiar with are Microsoft Windows, the Mac OS, Unix, and MS-DOS.

Many operating systems use graphical user interfaces as a control center from which programs are loaded. A ***graphical user interface*** is a system that allows the computer user to interact with the computer through pictures. Graphical user interface is often abbreviated as GUI, pronounced "gooey."

An example of an operating system with a graphical user interface is Microsoft Windows, shown in Figure 1-2. Modern operating systems such as Microsoft Windows do more than allow you to see your files and launch programs. They allow multiple programs to be run at the same time and provide resources that programs can share. They allow computers to network with each other and the Internet. They also make it easier to learn new programs, because each program has the same look and feel.

FIGURE 1-2
Microsoft Windows is an operating system with a graphical user interface.

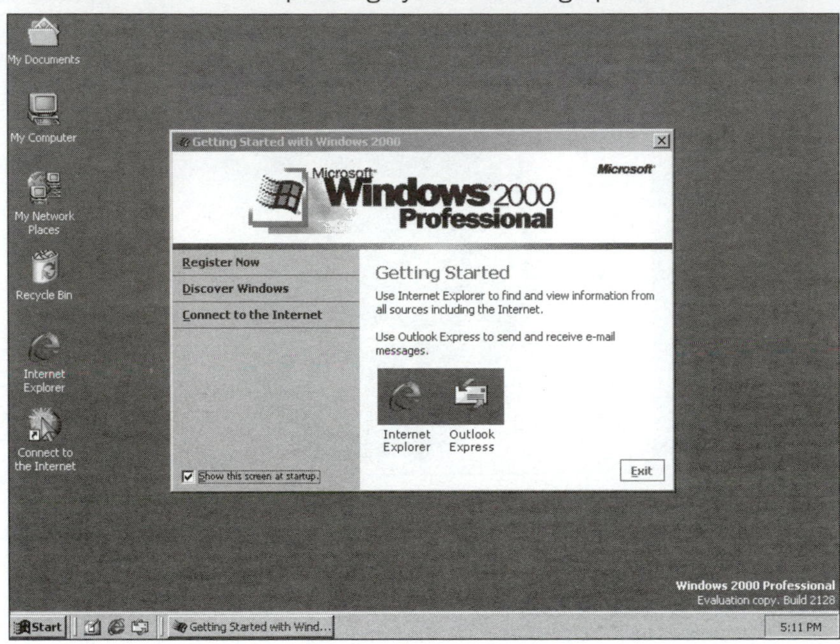

The Computer's Language

The device in the computer that actually processes the instructions provided by ROM, the operating system, and application programs is the *microprocessor*. Figure 1-3 shows an example of a microprocessor. A microprocessor is designed to "understand" a set of commands called an *instruction set*. Although there are similar instructions among different microprocessors, each model has its own instruction set. Microprocessors can only accept and carry out operations that are written in the format of their own unique instruction set. This is one reason why software written for one kind of computer does not automatically work on another kind of computer.

You may have learned that computers use a system of on and off circuits to represent all data and instructions. To learn more about how computers represent data and instructions, and to learn more about the binary number system, read Appendix B.

All instructions must be provided to the microprocessor in its native language, called ***machine language***. Machine language is actually a combination of circuits that can be either on or off. The number system commonly used to represent this world of ons and offs is called the *binary number system*. In the binary number system, ones and zeros are used to represent the on and off conditions.

FIGURE 1-3
The Intel Pentium III processor is an example of a popular microprocessor.

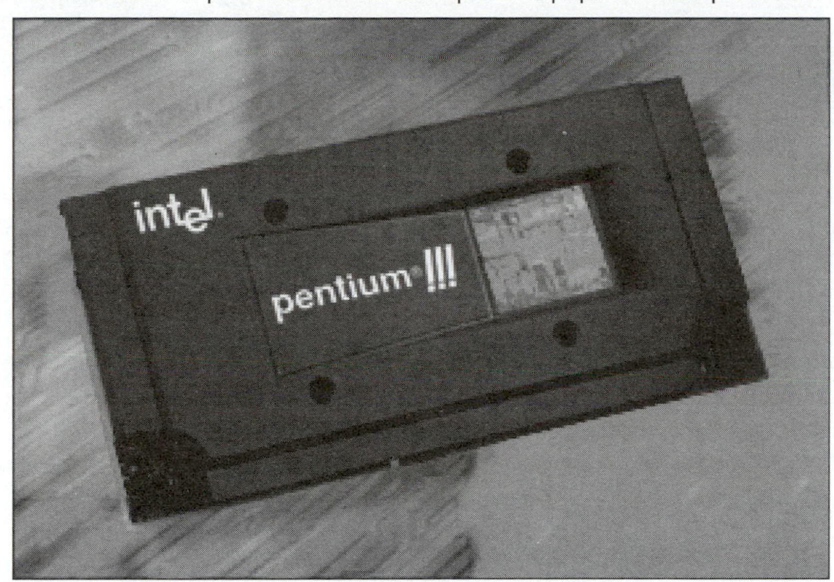

Programming a computer in machine language means programming in the combinations of ones and zeros that the microprocessor understands. Writing a program in machine language is difficult because even a simple program requires hundreds or even thousands of microprocessor instructions. Another problem is that the numbers used to represent the instructions are difficult for people to understand. Figure 1-4 shows a short machine language program. Each line is one instruction to the microprocessor.

FIGURE 1-4
Machine language is the language of the microprocessor. This machine language program adds 3 + 2 and stores the result.

```
01010101
10001011 11101100
01001100
01001100
01010110
01010111
10111111 00000011 00000000
10111110 00000010 00000000
10001011 11000111
00000011 11000110
10001001 01000110 11111110
0101111
01011110
10001011 11100101
01011110
11000011
```

Introduction to Programming Languages

Supplying instructions to computers would be extremely difficult if machine language were the only option available to programmers. Fortunately, special languages have been developed that are more easily understood. These special languages, called ***programming languages***, provide a way to program computers using instructions that can be understood by both computers and people.

Like human languages, programming languages have their own vocabulary and rules of usage. Some programming languages are very technical, and others are made to be as similar to English as possible. The programming languages available today allow programming at many levels of complexity.

Assembly Language

The programming language most like machine language is ***assembly language***. Assembly language uses letters and numbers to represent machine language instructions (see Figure 1-5). However, assembly language is still difficult for novices to read.

Assembly language programming is accomplished using an assembler. An *assembler* is a program that reads the codes the programmer has written and assembles a machine language program based on those codes.

FIGURE 1-5

In assembly language, each microprocessor instruction is assigned a code that makes the program more meaningful to people. It is still difficult, however, for the untrained person to see what the program will do.

Machine Language	Assembly Language
01010101	PUSH BP
10001011 11101100	MOV BP, SP
01001100	DEC SP
01001100	DEC SP
01010110	PUSH SI
01010111	PUSH DI
10111111 00000011 00000000	MOV DI, 0003
10111110 00000010 00000000	MOV SI, 0002
10001011 11000111	MOV AX, DI
00000011 11000110	ADD AX, SI
10001001 01000110 11111110	MOV [BP-02], AX
01011111	POP DI
01011110	POP SI
10001011 11100101	MOV SP, BP
01011110	POP BP
11000011	RET

Low-Level versus High-Level Languages

Machine language and assembly language are called ***low-level languages***. In a low-level language, it is necessary for the programmer to know the instruction set of the microprocessor in order to program the computer. Each instruction in a low-level language corresponds to one or only a few microprocessor instructions. In the program in Figure 1-5, each assembly language instruction corresponds to one machine language instruction.

Most programming is done in ***high-level languages***. In a high-level language, instructions do not necessarily correspond one-to-one with the instruction set of the microprocessor. One command in a high-level language may represent many microprocessor instructions. Therefore, high-level languages reduce the number of instructions that must be written. A program that might take hours to write in a low-level language can be done in minutes in a high-level language. Programming in a high-level language also reduces the number of errors because the programmer does not have to write as many instructions, and the instructions are easier to read. Figure 1-6 shows a program written in four popular high-level languages. Like the machine language and assembly language programs you saw earlier, these high-level programs add the numbers 3 and 2 together.

Another advantage of programs written in a high-level language is that they are easier to move among computers with different microprocessors. For example, the microprocessors in Macintosh computers use an instruction set different from that for microprocessors in most computers running Microsoft Windows. An assembly language program written for a Windows computer will not work on a Macintosh. However, a simple program written in a high-level language can work on both computers with little or no modification.

FIGURE 1-6
The same program can be written in more than one high-level language.

BASIC

```
10 I = 3
20 J = 2
30 K = I + J
```

Visual Basic

```
Private Sub cmdCalculate_Click()
  Dim intI, intJ, intK As Integer
  intI = 3
  intJ = 2
  intK = intI + intJ
End Sub
```

Pascal

```
program AddIt;

var
  i, j, k : integer;

begin
  i := 3;
  j := 2;
  k := i + j;
end.
```

C++

```
int main()
  {
   int i, j, k;
   i = 3;
   j = 2;
   k = i + j;
   return 0;
  }
```

So why use a low-level language? It depends on what you need to do. The drawback of high-level languages is that they do not always provide a command for everything the programmer wants a program to do. Using assembly language, the programmer can write instructions that enable the computer to do anything the hardware will allow.

Another advantage is that a program written in a low-level language will generally require less memory and run more quickly than the same program written in a high-level language. This is because high-level languages must be translated into machine language before the microprocessor can execute the instructions. The translation is done by another program and is usually less efficient than the work of a skilled assembly language programmer. Table 1-1 summarizes the advantages of low- and high-level languages.

TABLE 1-1
Low- and high-level languages

ADVANTAGES OF LOW-LEVEL LANGUAGES	ADVANTAGES OF HIGH-LEVEL LANGUAGES
Better use of hardware's capabilities	Require less programming
Require less memory	Fewer programming errors
Run more quickly	Easier to move among computers with different microprocessors
	More easily read

Interpreters and Compilers

Programmers writing in a high-level language enter the program's instructions into a text editor. A *text editor* is similar to a word processor, except that it saves files in a basic text format without the font and formatting codes that word processors use. The files saved by text editors are called *text files*. A program in the form of a high-level language is called ***source code***.

Programmers must have their high-level programs translated into the machine language that the microprocessor understands. The translation may be done by interpreters or compilers. The resulting machine language code is known as ***object code***.

INTERPRETERS

An ***interpreter*** is a program that translates the source code of a high-level language into machine language. It translates a computer language in a way similar to the way a person might interpret between languages such as English and Spanish. Each instruction is interpreted from the programming language into machine language as the instructions are needed. Interpreters are normally used only with very high-level languages. For example, the versions of BASIC that were included with early computers were interpreted languages.

To run a program written in an interpreted language, you must first load the interpreter into the computer's memory. Then you load the program to be interpreted. The interpreter steps through the program one instruction at a time and translates the instruction into machine language, which is sent to the microprocessor. Every time the program is run, the interpreter must once again translate each instruction.

Because of the need to have the interpreter in memory before the program can be interpreted, interpreted languages are not widely used to write programs that are sold to the public. The buyer of the program would have to have the correct interpreter in order to use the program.

COMPILERS

A ***compiler*** is another program that translates a high-level language into machine language. A compiler, however, makes the translation once, then saves the machine language so that the instructions do not have to be translated each time the program is run. Programming languages such as PASCAL and C++ use compilers rather than interpreters.

Figure 1-7 shows the steps involved in using a compiler. First, the source code is translated using the compiler to a file called an ***object file***. An object file, however, is incomplete. A program called a ***linker*** is used to create an executable program. The linker combines the object file with other machine language necessary to create a program that can run without an interpreter. The linker produces an ***executable file*** that can be run as many times as desired without having to be translated again.

Although using a compiler involves more steps than using an interpreter, most C++ compilers automate the task and make it easy for the programmer to use. Most compilers allow you to compile and link in a single operation. In fact, most modern compilers are part of a complete programming environment that helps you create source code, compile, link, run, and *debug* your programs. An example of a complete software development environment is Microsoft Visual C++, shown in Figure 1-8.

FIGURE 1-7
Compiling a program involves a compiler and a linker.

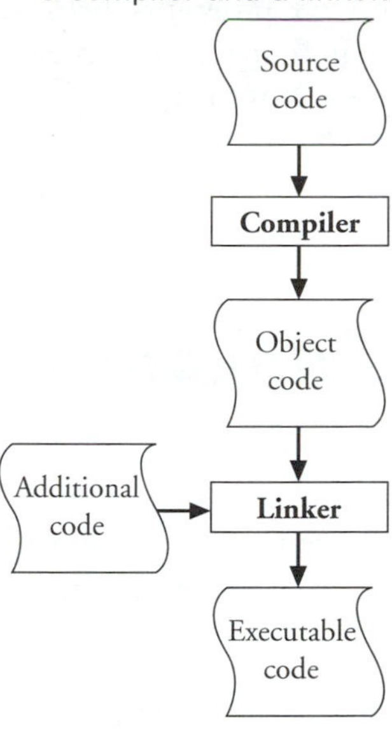

FIGURE 1-8
Microsoft Visual C++ is one example of a software development environment that includes a compiler.

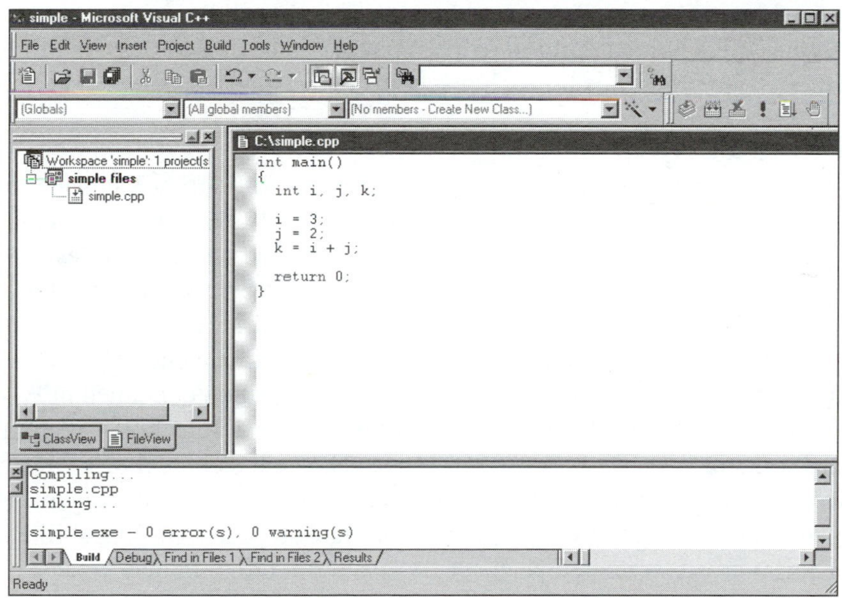

Programs you use regularly, such as word processors and games, are examples of programs written with a compiler. Compiled programs require less memory than interpreted programs because a compiled program does not require that an interpreter be loaded into memory. Compiled programs also run faster than interpreted programs because the translation has already been done. When a compiled program is run, the program is loaded into memory in the machine language the microprocessor needs.

Computer Concepts

Debugging a program refers to correcting programming errors. These errors, known as bugs, can be mistakes in keying source code or faulty logic, for example.

Languages to be Discussed

This text will introduce you to four of the most common programming languages in use today. Each language has its own syntax and characteristics that distinguish it from other languages. Each language is unique, and they are not all suitable for all programming projects. When creating a new system or program, the programmer must evaluate the project and determine which language is best suited to the requirements of the project. Four languages will be covered in this text.

Visual Basic

Visual Basic offers one of the quickest and easiest ways to create very powerful application programs to be used in the Microsoft Windows operating system. Visual Basic makes it easy to create powerful GUI applications. Visual Basic provides many tools to create the various components required to develop a GUI application. When creating an application using Visual Basic, the programmer creates the graphical user interface by drawing graphical representations of the objects required for the program and then assigns and refines the properties for each object to control their appearance and behavior.

HTML and JavaScript

HTML, which stands for Hypertext Markup Language, is a scripting language that is most commonly used to create Web pages. HTML was originally developed as a text-based language used to provide links to reference papers. It soon grew in stature and ability, and now it provides support for multiple media types, including text, graphics, audio, video, and other objects. HTML enables a programmer to provide a nonlinear approach to information presentation and retrieval. The use of hyperlinks allows someone viewing a Web page to jump to another page or object with the click of a mouse button. HTML uses a series of tags and attributes to format and display the information contained in Web pages.

JavaScript is another scripting language used in Web pages. Using JavaScript, programmers can create scrolling messages or banners within a Web page, validate the content of forms, perform calculations, display interactive messages to users of the Web page, create animated images, and retrieve information about the browser viewing the Web page to tailor the Web page to the capabilities of the browser. Like HTML, JavaScript is an interpreted language. A JavaScript program may consist of a single line of code, or it could have many lines that create a full-fledged application program within the Web page.

The C++ Programming Language

C++ is a full-blown, compiled programming language. C++ is called an object-oriented programming language. The entities created and controlled within the program are created as objects. The properties and behaviors of objects are clearly defined by the programming statements that create and manipulate the object. C++ is very similar to the C programming language, but has added syntax and functionality unique to an object-oriented language. An object created for one program can be modifed and used by other programs without having to completely rewrite the original program code. When a

C++ program has been written, it is compiled into object code, which is another term for machine code. Multiple object code files can then be linked together to create an application program. If any of the code within the application is modified, the changed module must be recompiled and the application relinked before the changes are evident to the user.

The Java Programming Language

Java is another object-oriented programming language. Do not confuse Java with JavaScript; they are completely different. Java is somewhat similar to C++, in that it can be used to create very large and powerful application programs. It can also be used to create small programs called applets that can then be loaded and run within Web pages. However, a Java applet is a compiled "class" file run within a Web page, not a simple text script created using the JavaScript language and contained within the HTML statements themselves. Java is partially a compiled language and partially an interpreted language. A Java program is compiled into something called pseudo-code, and that pseudo-code is then interpreted by a Java Virtual Machine running on the computer where the application is to be run. This makes Java programs very easy to migrate from a PC to a mainframe, to a Macintosh, or whatever platform it needs to run on. The Java Virtual Machine is responsible for converting the pseudo-code into machine code for the particular operating system running the program.

Choosing and Using a Language

How do you know what programming language to use? The choice of programming language is sometimes a complex decision. When choosing a language, you should consider the needs of the program you are creating. How important is speed? Will the program do anything that may require features that are not available in some of the higher-level languages? Who will maintain the program? Experience is the best preparation for making this decision. That is why most professional programmers work with various languages to gain an understanding of the differences that exist among them.

Hot Tip

To learn more about algorithms and the programming process, read Appendix C.

You should not become so accustomed to working in one or two languages that you begin to believe no other languages are necessary. Think of programming languages as tools. Some languages are appropriate for a wide range of tasks; some are appropriate for specific tasks only. The smart programmer knows the available tools and how (and when) to use them.

After a language has been chosen, how do you use a programming language to actually make the computer do something you want it to do? Computers operate by following a set of steps, called an ***algorithm***. A programming language allows you to provide the computer with algorithms that will produce the results you desire.

Summary

In this lesson, you learned:

- Computers are complex machines that follow instructions called programs.
- Application programs are programs that perform tasks for the user.
- Input and output operations and loading of executable files are handled by the operating system. The operating system loads a program and turns over control of the system to the program. When the program ends, the operating system takes control again.
- At the heart of the work a computer does is a device called a microprocessor. The microprocessor responds to commands called machine language.
- High-level programming languages allow programmers to work in a language that people can more easily read. Machine language and assembly language are low-level languages because each instruction in the language corresponds to one or only a few microprocessor instructions. In high-level languages, instructions may represent many microprocessor instructions.
- An interpreter or compiler must translate high-level languages into machine language. An interpreter translates each program step into machine language as the program runs. A compiler translates the program before it is run and saves the machine language as an object file. A linker then creates an executable file from the object file.
- There are many factors to consider when choosing a programming language. Experience will teach you what language is appropriate for a specific task.

VOCABULARY REVIEW

Define the following terms:

algorithm
assembly language
compiler
executable file
graphical user interface (GUI)
high-level language
interpreter
linker
low-level language
machine language
object code
object file
operating system
programming language
source code

LESSON 1 REVIEW QUESTIONS

TRUE/FALSE

Circle T if the statement is true or F if the statement is false.

T F 1. A word processor is an example of an application program.

T F 2. The programs in a typical computer's ROM provide programs such as spreadsheets and video games.

T F 3. The operating system controls input and output operations of a computer.

T F 4. An instruction set is a system for interacting with computer users through pictures.

T F 5. A compiler creates a source code file.

T F 6. The programming language most like machine language is C++.

T F 7. Programs written in low-level languages usually require less memory than those written in high-level languages.

T F 8. High-level languages are more difficult to read than low-level languages.

T F 9. An interpreter creates an object file that a linker makes into an executable file.

T F 10. Most modern compilers are programs that must be run separately from the linker.

WRITTEN QUESTIONS

Write a brief answer to the following questions.

1. What does the acronym ROM stand for?
2. List three operations managed by operating systems.
3. What device processes the instructions in a computer?
4. What number system is commonly used to represent the state of being on or off?
5. Give an example of a low-level programming language.
6. List three examples of high-level programming languages.
7. List two advantages of a low-level language.
8. Describe the process involved when using a compiler to program a computer.

9. Describe one advantage that compiled programs have over interpreted programs.

10. Why is it important for professional programmers to have worked with various programming languages?

LESSON 1 PROJECT

Make a chart of at least 12 high-level languages. Include a brief description of each language that tells the primary use of the language or its historical significance. If you can find the date the language was created, include that on your chart. Some languages to consider are Ada, ALGOL, BASIC, C, C++, COBOL, FORTRAN, Java, LISP, Logo, Oberon, PASCAL, PL/I, Scheme, and Smalltalk.

CRITICAL THINKING

Given that the following languages are listed in order from highest level to lowest level, answer the questions that follow.

BASIC, PASCAL, C++, assembly language

1. What language would be most appropriate for writing a quick, temporary program with the least effort and shortest code?
   A. BASIC
   B. C++

2. What language would be most appropriate for writing a program that must control the flow of data through a custom-built hardware device?
   A. PASCAL
   B. assembly language

INTRODUCTION TO VISUAL BASIC

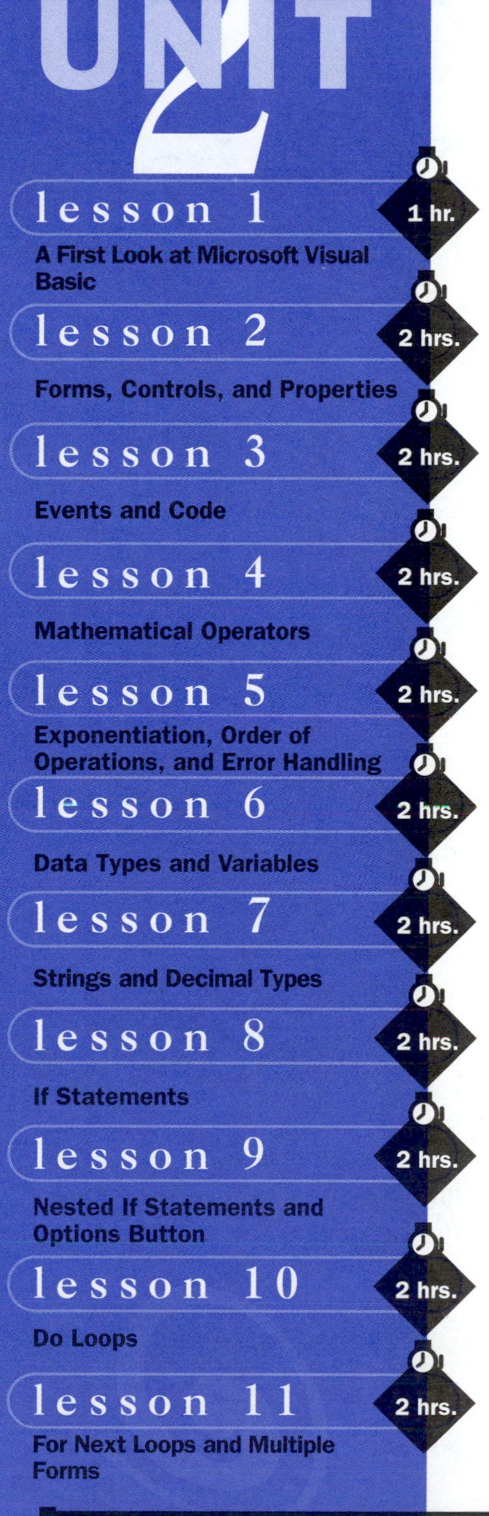

A First Look at Microsoft Visual Basic

OBJECTIVES

Upon completion of this lesson, you should be able to:

- Explain the purpose of Microsoft Visual Basic.
- Start the Visual Basic compiler.
- Open an existing Visual Basic project.
- Explain the purpose of the components on the compiler screen.
- Run a Visual Basic program.
- Position a form in a Visual Basic program.
- Exit Visual Basic.

Estimated Time: 1 hour

Introduction to Microsoft Visual Basic

Microsoft Visual Basic is a *software development tool*, which means it is a tool that allows you to create programs. One of the reasons that Visual Basic is so popular is because it allows you to easily create complex programs.

Visual Basic combines a graphical interface and programming code to make program development as rapid as possible. With Visual Basic, you use common graphical tools to create the user interface for your program. Then, an easy-to-use programming language provides "behind the scenes" functionality for the program.

You will learn much more about Visual Basic as you progress through the lessons in this book. In this lesson, you will take a quick tour of Visual Basic, identify the components of the Visual Basic environment, and run an existing Visual Basic program.

Starting Visual Basic

Like other Windows programs, Visual Basic can be started from a shortcut on the desktop or from the Start button and Programs menu. Depending on the version of Visual Basic you have installed, the exact name and location of the shortcut or folder containing Visual Basic may vary.

STEP-BY-STEP 1.1

1. Click the **Start** button.

2. Position the mouse pointer on the **Programs** menu. The Programs menu opens.

3. On the Programs menu, position your mouse pointer on the menu that leads to the Microsoft Visual Basic compiler. This menu may be named Microsoft Visual Basic or Microsoft Visual Studio.

4. When the menu opens, click the **Visual Basic** icon. The Visual Basic compiler starts and the New Project dialog box opens. Your screen should appear similar to Figure 1-1, although your dialog box may be sized differently and may contain fewer items.

5. Leave Visual Basic open for Step-by-Step 1.2. If the New Project dialog box did not appear when Visual Basic started, leave Visual Basic open and proceed.

FIGURE 1-1

The Visual Basic compiler starts with the New Project dialog box.

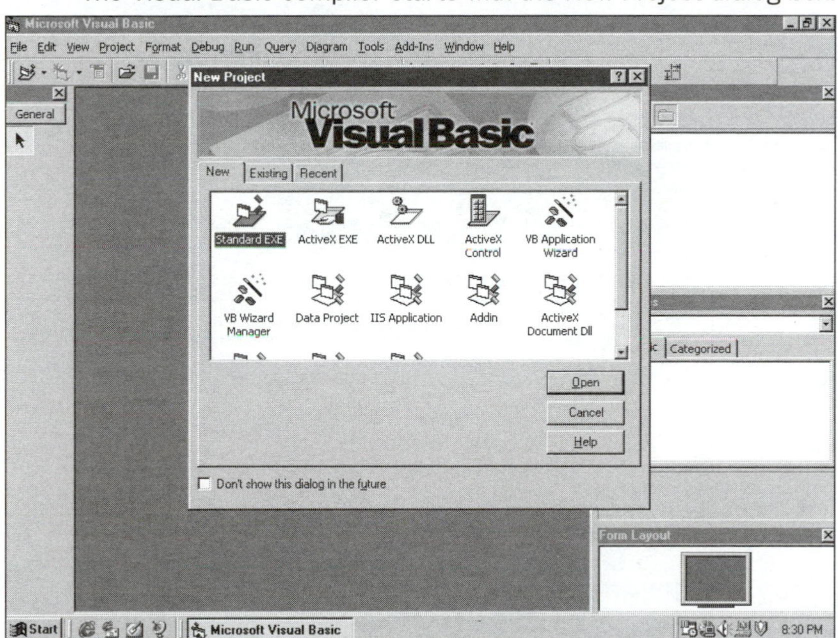

Opening an Existing Visual Basic Project

Visual Basic stores programs in a group of files called a *project*. The main project file has a VBP extension. To open an existing Visual Basic project, click the Existing tab, then open the VBP file that corresponds with the project you wish to open.

STEP-BY-STEP 1.2

1. From the New Project dialog box, click the **Existing** tab.

2. Click the **down arrow** in the **Look in** drop down list box to open a list similar to that shown in Figure 1-2.

3. Click the **up** or **down scroll bar arrows** to scroll as needed, then click the item that identifies the disk or drive that holds the data files for this book. A list of files and folders contained on the disk appears in the dialog box.

4. Navigate to the folder containing your data files, and find the **SnakeGame** filename. (Note that the filname will be **SnakeGame.vbp** if you have the file extensions turned on.)

5. Click **SnakeGame**, then click the **Open** button. Leave the project open for Step-by-Step 1.3.

Note

If the New Project dialog box did not appear when you started Visual Basic, choose Open Project from the File menu.

FIGURE 1-2
The Existing tab from the New Project dialog box allows you to open Visual Basic programs.

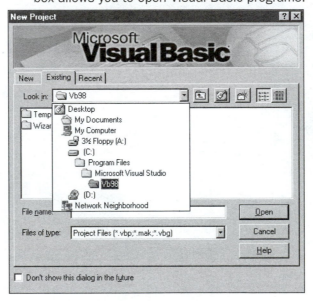

Components of the Compiler

When you run Visual Basic, you will notice that it looks similar to other programs you have run in Windows. The screen includes a menu bar, toolbars, and various windows. There is even a toolbox with tools that allows you to draw command buttons, scroll bars, and much more.

Figure 1-3 shows the components of the Visual Basic screen. Do not be concerned if your screen does not show all these components at this time.

FIGURE 1-3
The Visual Basic programming environment has components that are similar to other Windows programs.

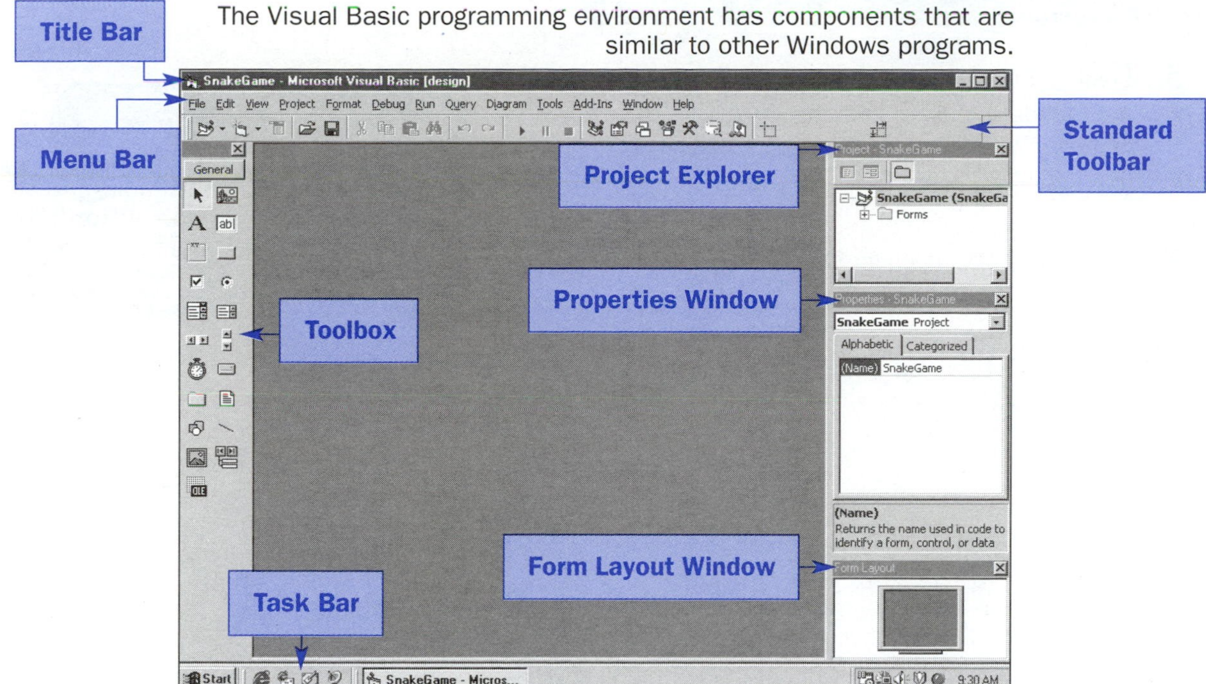

Menus and Toolbars

The Visual Basic menu bar has some menus found in other Windows programs (such as File and Edit) and some menus that are unique to this programming environment (such as Project and Debug). Like some other Windows programs, Visual Basic has more than one toolbar available. The toolbar that appears by default and that has the standard toolbar buttons is called the *standard toolbar*. Items on the toolbar may vary depending on which version of Visual Basic you have installed.

Note

Depending on which version of Visual Basic you have installed, you may see either a blank screen next to the toolbox (as shown in Figure 1-3) or you may see the SnakeGame form. If the SnakeGame form is not displayed, you will learn how to open it later in this lesson.

STEP-BY-STEP 1.3

1. Click the **File** menu on the menu bar. The File menu drops down as shown in Figure 1-4 (items shown may vary). Notice that many of the commands in this menu (such as New, Open, Save, and Print) are similar to File menu commands of other Windows programs.

2. Click the **File** menu again. The File menu disappears.

3. Open the other menus from the menu bar and look at some of the commands that are unique to Visual Basic (such as the List Properties/Methods command in the Edit menu).

4. Position the mouse pointer on the first button of the standard toolbar. A tool tip appears below the button with the name of the button, as shown in Figure 1-5.

STEP-BY-STEP 1.3 CONTINUED

5. Position the mouse pointer on each button on the standard toolbar. Like the menu bar, the standard toolbar contains many common Windows commands.

6. Leave the project open for Step-by-Step 1.4.

Hot Tip

For help identifying the toolbar buttons, position the mouse pointer on the toolbar button and pause. A *tool tip* will appear with the name of the button.

FIGURE 1-4
The File menu has many commands similar to those of other Windows programs.

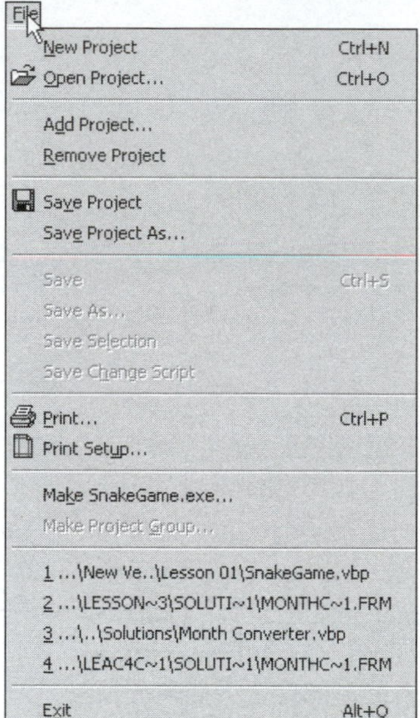

FIGURE 1-5
The standard toolbar contains buttons for frequently used Visual Basic commands.

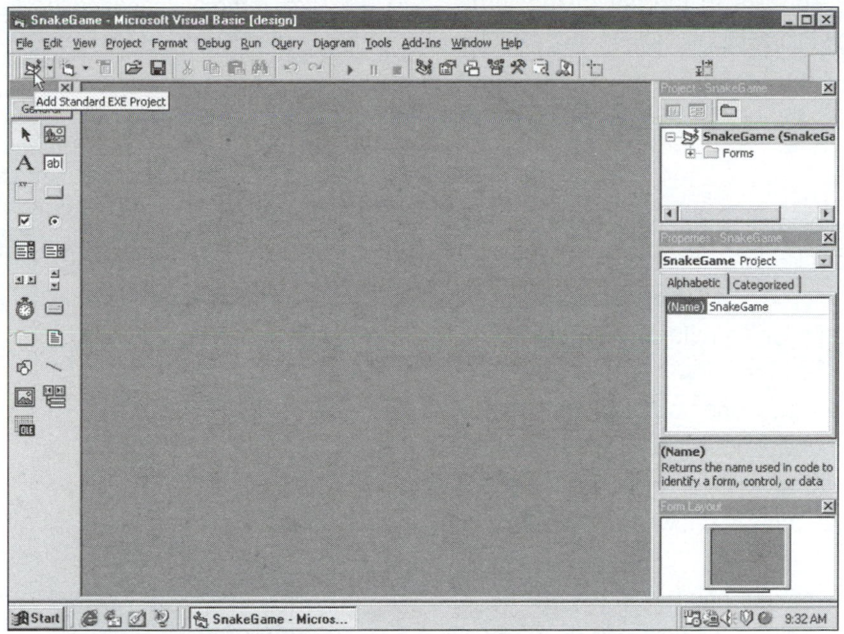

The Project Explorer

Another important component of the Visual Basic screen is the Project Explorer. The *Project Explorer* allows you to see the forms and files that make up your program. You will use the Project Explorer to access the forms on which you want to work.

STEP-BY-STEP 1.4

1. Click the title bar of the Project Explorer window, as shown in Figure 1-6. The Project Explorer window becomes active. If you do not see the Project Explorer window, choose Project Explorer from the View menu.

FIGURE 1-6
By default, the Project Explorer window is docked at the upper-right corner of the screen.

2. If a + sign appears to the left of the Forms folder in the Project Explorer window, click the + sign to open the Forms folder. The Forms folder opens and one form is listed, as shown in Figure 1-7.

3. If the SnakeGame form is not already displayed, double-click the only form in the Project Explorer list (**frmMainForm**). Your screen should look similar to Figure 1-8.

4. Double-click the title bar of the Project Explorer window. The Project Explorer window becomes undocked and is moved to the middle of the screen, as shown in Figure 1-9.

5. Position the mouse pointer on the title bar of the Project Explorer window and drag it back to the right side of the screen, just below the toolbar. The Project Explorer window becomes docked again.

6. Leave the project open for Step-by-Step 1.5.

FIGURE 1-7
The Project Explorer window organizes the forms used in a Visual Basic program.

Note

If you do not see the Forms folder, click the Toggle Folders button.

FIGURE 1-8
The form appears when it is double-clicked from the Project Explorer window.

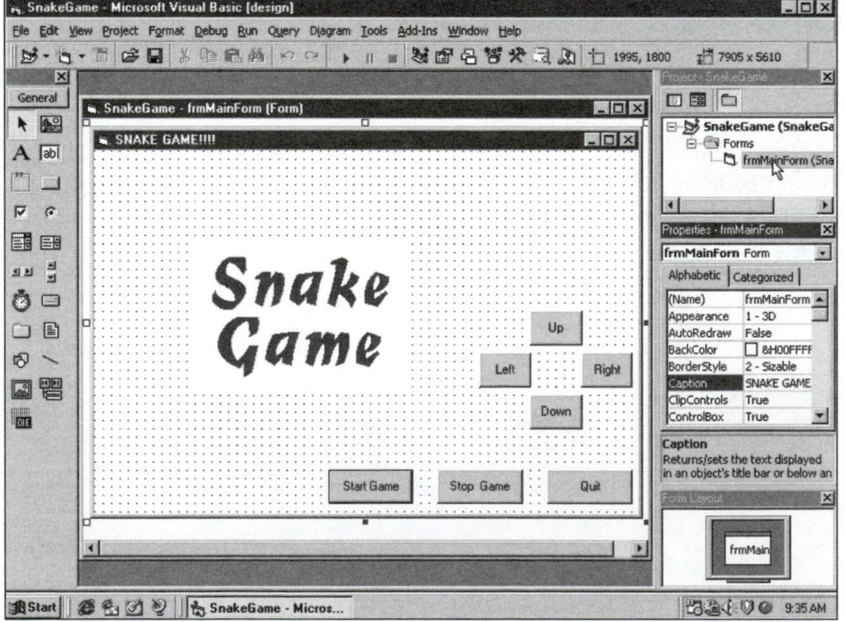

FIGURE 1-9
The windows on the right side of the screen can become undocked by double-clicking the title bar of the window.

The Properties Window

The pieces that make up a Visual Basic program are called *objects*. Windows, command buttons, text boxes, and scroll bars are all examples of objects. Objects placed on forms, such as command buttons and text boxes, are also known as *controls*. Each object has characteristics that can be customized. These characteristics are called *properties*. To see the properties of an object, select the object and view the properties in the *Properties window*. The properties of the object can also be changed from the Properties window. You will learn how to use the Properties window in the next lesson.

Note

If you cannot see all the command buttons on the form, choose Tile Vertically or Tile Horizontally from the Window menu. If you still do not see all the command buttons on the form, you can resize the form when you run the program later.

STEP-BY-STEP 1.5

1. Click the title bar of the Properties window. The Properties window becomes active, as shown in Figure 1-10. If the Properties window is not displayed, choose Properties Window from the View menu.

2. Click the **BackColor** property. A description of the property appears on the bottom of the Properties window, as shown in Figure 1-11. Do not change the current setting.

FIGURE 1-10
The Properties window displays the characteristics of the selected object.

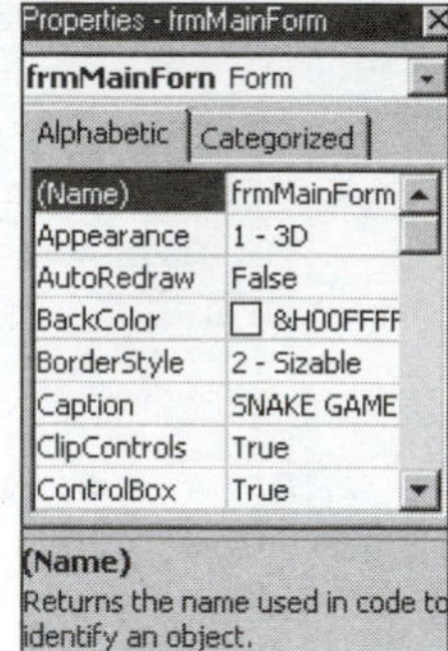

FIGURE 1-11
The bottom of the Properties window displays a description of the selected property.

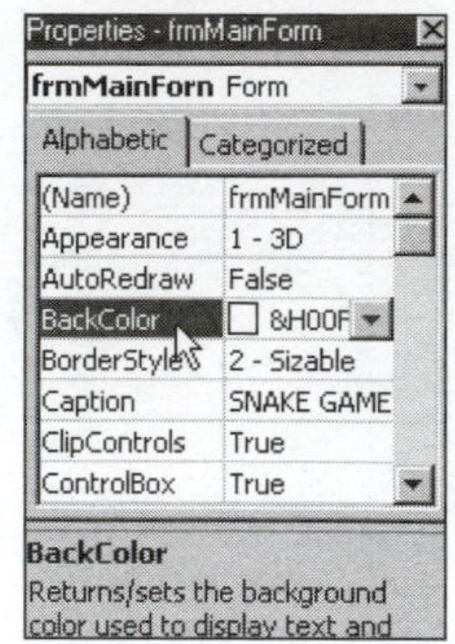

3. Click the **down arrow** on the scroll bar of the Properties window to browse through the list of properties.

4. Click the **Categorized** tab from the **Properties** window. The list of properties becomes grouped by the functions the properties perform, as shown in Figure 1-12.

5. Click the **Alphabetic** tab. The list of properties becomes grouped alphabetically.

6. Leave the project open for Step-by-Step 1.6.

FIGURE 1-12
Properties can be grouped by function.

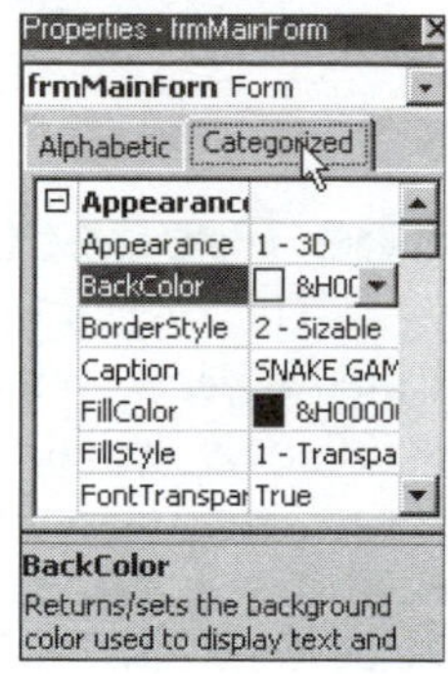

Note

The position of the Project Explorer window may vary when it is undocked.

The Toolbox

The last part of the Visual Basic screen to visit is the toolbox. The *toolbox* is the collection of tools that allows you to add objects (controls) to the forms you create in Visual Basic. The toolbox has tools for creating objects such as command buttons, text boxes, check boxes, option buttons (also known as radio buttons), picture boxes, and scroll bars. You will use the toolbox in the next lesson to create your first Visual Basic program.

STEP-BY-STEP 1.6

1. Position the mouse pointer on the top right tool in the toolbox. The name of the control that the tool creates will appear below the pointer, as shown in Figure 1-13.

2. Position the mouse pointer on each of the tools and read the names.

3. Leave Visual Basic open for Step-by-Step 1.7.

FIGURE 1-13
Positioning the mouse pointer on the tools in the toolbox will provide the name of each tool.

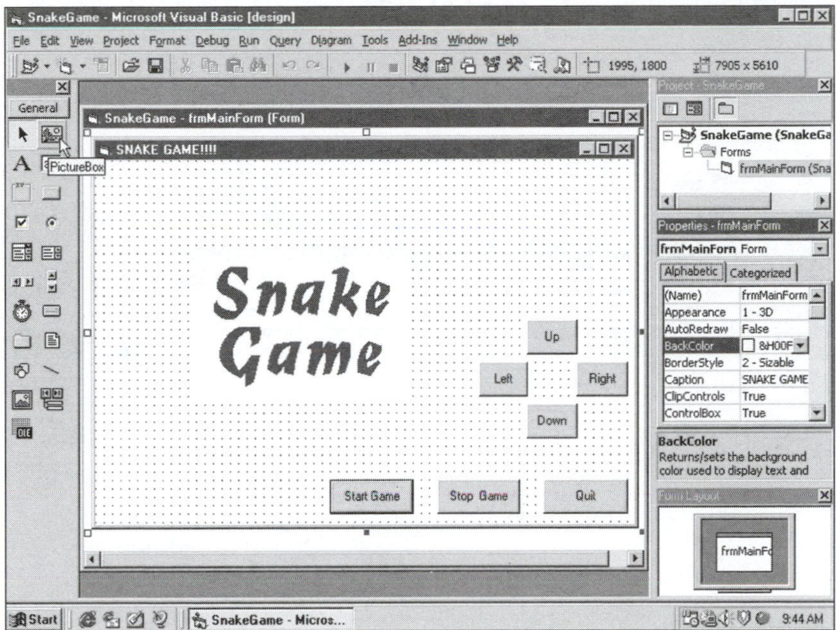

Running a Visual Basic Program

To run a Visual Basic program, click the Start button from the standard toolbar.

STEP-BY-STEP 1.7

1. Click the **Start** button from the standard toolbar. The SnakeGame program appears on the screen, as shown in Figure 1-14. If you cannot see all the command buttons shown in Figure 1-14, drag a corner or side of the SnakeGame window to resize it.

2. Click the **Start Game** button. A box appears on the screen and a line (the snake) begins growing toward the bottom of the box.

FIGURE 1-14
The Start button from the standard toolbar runs a program.

3. Before the line reaches the bottom of the box, click the **Right** button. The line will turn to the right and continue toward the right edge of the box.

4. Continue to click the **Up**, **Down**, **Left**, and **Right** buttons to steer the path of the line. When the line hits the edge of the box or crosses its own path, the game is over.

5. When the game is over, click the **OK** button to dismiss the Game Over message.

6. Click the **Quit** button to exit the program. The Visual Basic environment is again active.

7. Leave Visual Basic open for Step-by-Step 1.8.

Positioning a Form in a Visual Basic Program

The *Form Layout window*, which appears in the lower-right corner of the screen, shows the position the form will take when the program runs (see Figure 1-15). You can change the position of the form by dragging the form's representation in the Form Layout window.

FIGURE 1-15
Moving the form changes the position when the program runs.

STEP-BY-STEP 1.8

1. Click the title bar of the Form Layout window. The Form Layout window becomes active. If you do not see the Form Layout window, choose Form Layout Window from the View menu.

2. Position the mouse pointer on the representation of the form in the Form Layout window. The pointer changes to a four-way arrow, as shown in Figure 1-16.

3. In the Form Layout window, drag the form to the bottom right corner of the screen icon.

FIGURE 1-16
Moving the form sets the position at which the form will appear.

4. Click the **Start** button on the standard toolbar. Notice that when the program runs, the form appears in the bottom-right corner of the screen.

5. Click the **End** button on the standard toolbar. The program ends.

6. Leave the project open for Step-by-Step 1.9.

Note

Only the Form Layout window can change a form's placement when the program runs. Moving the actual form in the Visual Basic environment will not affect the form's placement when the program runs.

Exiting Visual Basic

Like other Windows programs, you can exit Visual Basic by choosing Exit from the File menu, or by clicking the Close box at the right end of the Visual Basic title bar.

STEP-BY-STEP 1.9

1. Choose **Exit** from the **File** menu. Because you moved the form in the Form Layout window, you will be asked if you want to save the project and form files.

2. Click **No**. Visual Basic closes.

Summary

In this lesson, you learned:

- Microsoft Visual Basic is a tool that allows you to create Windows programs.
- Visual Basic allows you to easily create complex programs.
- Visual Basic can be started from a shortcut in the Programs menu or from the desktop.
- Visual Basic projects are stored in files with a VBP extension. To open a Visual Basic project, you simply have to open the VBP file.
- Visual Basic has some menus found in other Windows programs and some menus that are unique to Visual Basic.
- The standard toolbar appears by default and contains buttons for frequently used Visual Basic commands.
- The Project Explorer allows you to see and open the forms and other files that make up a project.
- The Properties window lets you view the characteristics, or properties, of the objects that make up a Visual Basic program. The Properties window also allows you to make changes to those properties.
- The toolbox holds the tools that allow you to add objects such as command buttons to a form.
- To run a Visual Basic program, click the Start button from the standard toolbar.
- The Form Layout window allows you to set the position at which the form window will appear when the program runs.
- Exit Visual Basic by choosing Exit from the File menu or by clicking the Close box on the Visual Basic title bar.

LESSON 1 REVIEW QUESTIONS

TRUE/FALSE

Circle T if the statement is true or F if the statement is false.

T F 1. Microsoft Visual Basic allows you to create programs.

T F 2. Unlike other programs, you cannot start Visual Basic using a shortcut on the desktop.

T F 3. Visual Basic stores programs in groups of files called projects.

T F 4. The Form Layout window allows you to add objects to the forms you create in Visual Basic.

T F 5. The standard toolbar appears by default.

T F 6. Positioning your mouse pointer on a toolbar button will produce a list of properties for that button.

T F 7. You cannot change the properties of an object.

T F 8. An object's properties can be displayed alphabetically and by category.

T F 9. A scroll bar is an example of a property.

T F 10. The Start button on the standard toolbar runs your program.

WRITTEN QUESTIONS

Write a brief answer to the following questions.

1. What is the purpose of a software development tool?
2. What file extension is given to Visual Basic project files?
3. What is the purpose of the Existing tab of the New Project dialog box?
4. Which window lets you modify the characteristics of an object?
5. Which window lets you view the forms and files that make up a project?
6. Which tab shows properties grouped by the functions the properties perform?
7. What is contained in the toolbox?
8. Which command in which menu is used to close Visual Basic?
9. How do you undock a window?
10. What standard toolbar button exits a program that you are running?

LESSON 1 PROJECT

PROJECT 1-1

1. Start Visual Basic.
2. Click the **Existing** tab and open the project named **LoanAnalysis**. The project is located in the same folder in which the SnakeGame project is stored.
3. If necessary, click the + sign in the Project Explorer to open the Forms folder, then double-click the form.
4. Click some of the objects on the form and view two or three properties of the objects by clicking the property names in the Properties window.
5. Drag the form in the Form Layout window to the upper-left corner of the screen icon.

6. Click the **Start** button on the standard toolbar to run the program.

7. Enter the following values in the three fields across the top of the window.

   Loan Amount: **1000**
   Annual Rate (in %): **9**
   Years: **5**

8. Click the **Calculate** button. Values appear in the Payment, Total Interest, and Total of Payments fields at the bottom of the window.

9. Click the **Exit** button.

10. Exit Visual Basic. Click **No** if you are asked to save any changes.

CRITICAL THINKING

ACTIVITY 1-1

1. Start Visual Basic.

2. Open the **LoanAnalysis** project.

3. View the properties of the **Calculate** button.

4. Move the form in the Form Layout window so that when the program runs, it will be in the upper-right corner.

5. Run the program.

6. Suppose you want to buy a new car for $20,000. The loan will be for a period of five years at an interest rate of 7 percent. What will the monthly payment be, how much interest will you have paid at the end of the five years, and how much will you actually end up paying for the car?

7. End the program.

8. Exit Visual Basic. Click **No** if you are asked to save any changes.

LESSON 2

FORMS, CONTROLS, AND PROPERTIES

OBJECTIVES

When you complete this lesson, you will be able to:

- Create a new Visual Basic project.
- Save a Visual Basic project.
- View and modify form properties.
- Create controls such as command buttons.
- Move, resize, and delete objects.
- Explain the concept of focus.
- Set additional properties (BackColor, Top, and Left).

Estimated Time: 2 hours

Creating a New Project

In Lesson 1, you started Visual Basic and ran an existing project. To create your own Visual Basic program, however, you must create a new project and begin building your program.

When you start Visual Basic, the New Project dialog box appears, as shown in Figure 2-1. Under the New tab in the New Project dialog box are your options for what kind of project to create. The options visible here may vary, depending on your version of the Visual Basic compiler.

For now, we are only interested in the Standard EXE project type. Selecting Standard EXE allows you to create a Windows program from scratch.

Note

The other options in the New Project dialog box allow you to more easily create a variety of specialized programs. For example, the *Application Wizard* helps you create a complete program with standard Windows features already included. On some versions of Visual Basic, other options allow you to create components such as *ActiveX* controls for Web pages.

FIGURE 2-1
The New Project dialog box allows you to choose what kind of project you want to build.

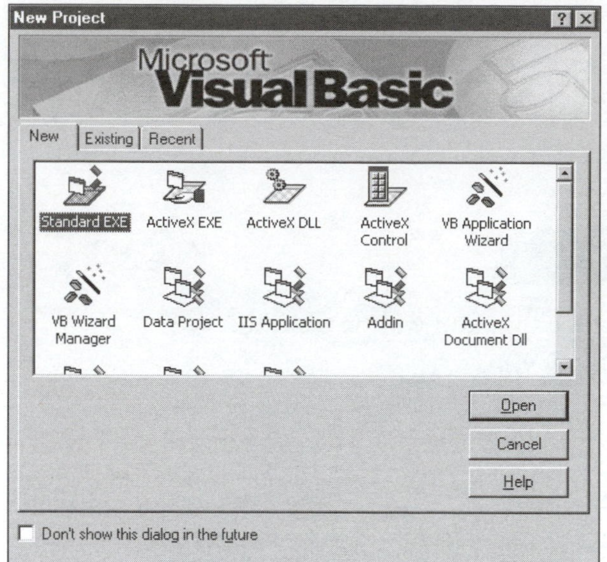

STEP-BY-STEP 2.1

1. Start **Visual Basic** from the **Microsoft Visual Basic 6.0** menu. After Visual Basic starts, the New Project dialog box will appear.

2. Click **Standard EXE** to select it, then click the **Open** button (or click the OK button if you opened the New Project dialog box from the File menu). A new project named **Project1** is created. The project includes one blank form by default, as shown in Figure 2-2.

3. Leave the project open for Step-by-Step 2.2.

Note

If the New Project dialog box does not automatically appear when you start Visual Basic, choose New Project from the File menu.

Note

If the Project Explorer, Properties, and Form Layout windows are not displayed, click the View menu and click the appropriate window names. If the Forms folder is not displayed in the Project Explorer, click the Toggle Folders button. If a form and a list of properties are not displayed, click the + sign next to the Forms folder in the Project Explorer, then double-click the form icon.

FIGURE 2-2
A standard new Visual Basic project includes one blank form.

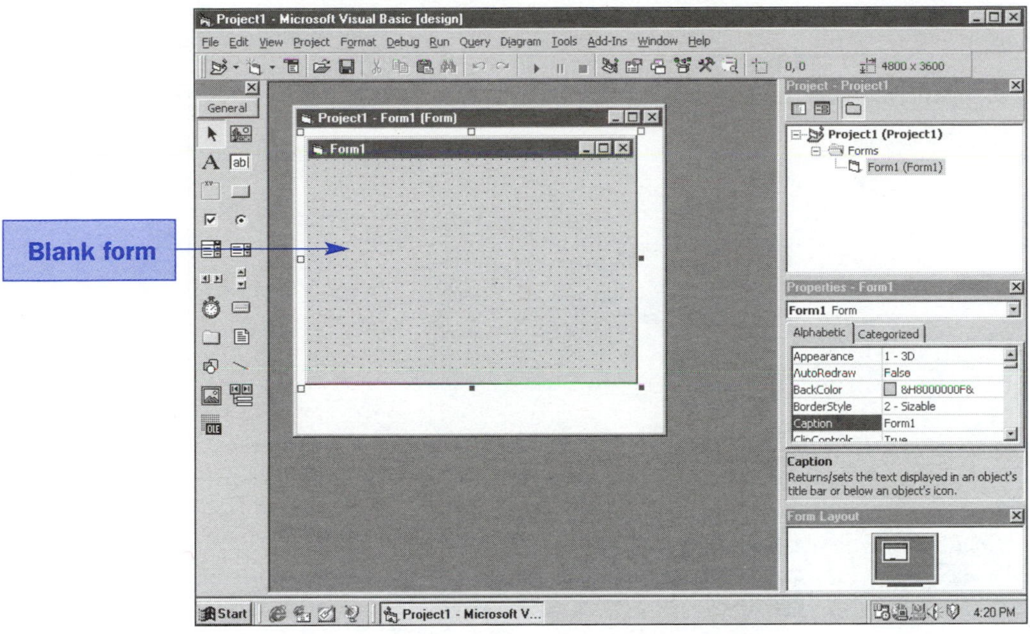

Forms

The project created by selecting the Standard EXE option consists of only one object: a blank form. Remember that objects are the pieces that make up a Visual Basic program. In Visual Basic, *forms* become the windows and dialog boxes when the program runs. Every program has at least one form because all other objects must be contained within forms. For example, a program cannot consist of a command button alone. The command button must be on a form.

There is no functionality in our program, except for the functions common to all forms. In the case of the default blank form, the window displayed when the program runs will have the ability to be moved, resized, maximized, minimized, and closed.

STEP-BY-STEP 2.2

1. Click the **Start** button from the standard toolbar. A blank window appears, as shown in Figure 2-3. This blank window is created as a result of the blank form in your project.

2. Click the **Maximize** button on the form. The form fills the screen, as shown in Figure 2-4.

3. Click the **Restore** button. The window returns to its original position on the screen.

4. Position the mouse pointer on the title bar and drag the window to the upper-left corner of the screen below the standard toolbar.

FIGURE 2-3
The form appears when the Start button is clicked.

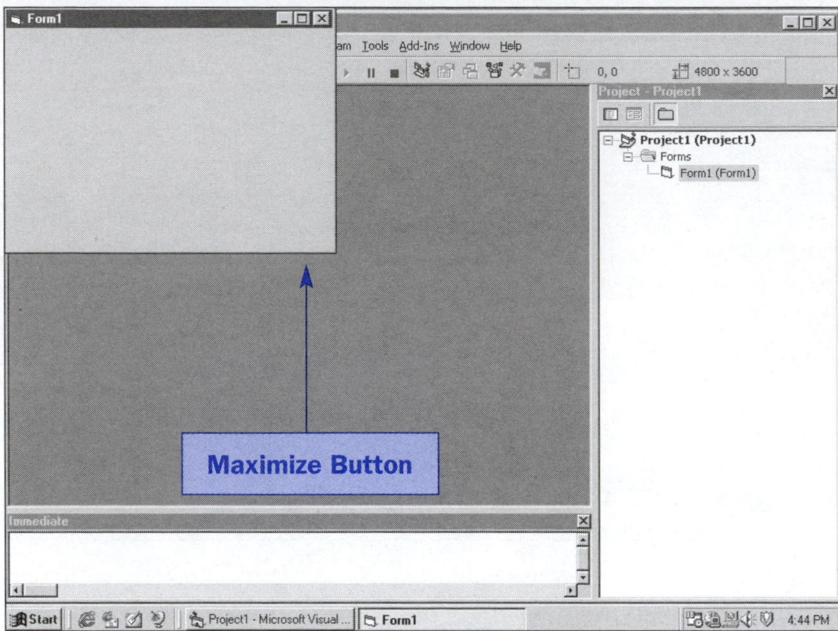

FIGURE 2-4
The window generated by your program can be maximized like most windows.

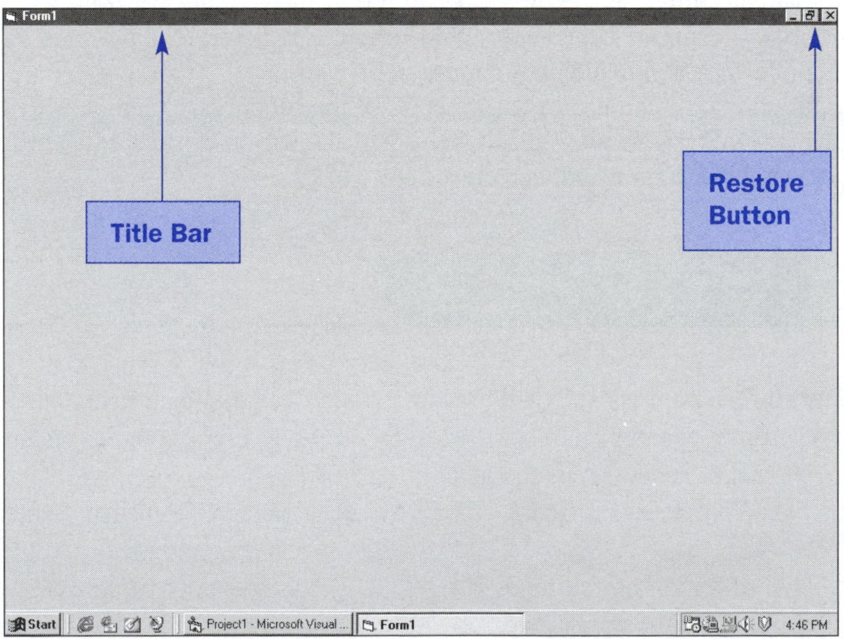

5. Position the mouse pointer in the lower-right corner of the window. The pointer becomes a double-headed arrow.

6. Drag the corner of the form until it is approximately 2 inches from the right edge of the screen and 2 inches from the bottom of the screen (exact sizing of the form is not important).

STEP-BY-STEP 2.2 CONTINUED

7. Click the **Close** button in the upper-right corner of the Form1 window. The form closes and the Visual Basic compiler with the default blank form is active again.

8. Leave the project open for Step-by-Step 2.3.

Saving the Project

When saving a project, you actually save the forms of the project and then the project itself. The most convenient way to accomplish this is to use the Save Project button on the toolbar. First, a dialog box will appear for saving the form. Once the form is saved, another dialog box will appear, allowing you to save the project.

STEP-BY-STEP 2.3

1. Click the **Save Project** button from the standard toolbar. The Save File As dialog box appears. You will first save the form.

2. Change the drive and folder to the location where your instructor would like you to save your files.

3. Click in the File name box and change the filename to **frmMyForm**, then click the **Save** button. The Save Project As dialog box appears. This time you will save the project information.

4. Click the File name box and change the filename to **MyVBProgram**.

5. Click the **Save** button.

6. Leave the project open for Step-by-Step 2.4.

Viewing and Modifying Properties

As you saw in Step-by-Step 2.2, a form has certain characteristics. One of the advantages of programming in Visual Basic is that so much functionality can be achieved without writing programming code. These characteristics of Visual Basic objects are called properties. Every object in Visual Basic has properties. You learned in Lesson 1 that the properties of objects can be viewed in the Properties window.

The Properties window allows you to easily alter the properties of objects. For example, you can alter the property that controls whether the window has Minimize and Maximize buttons.

Note

If you need to close Visual Basic at any point after this in the lesson, click the Save Project button on the standard toolbar to save your work, then exit Visual Basic. To reopen the project, click the Existing tab in the New Project dialog box, change drives and folders until you locate *MyVBProgram*, then double-click it. If necessary, click the + sign next to the Forms folder in the Project Explorer and double-click the form icon.

STEP-BY-STEP 2.4

1. Click on **Form1** to select it, if it is not already selected. Handles will appear around the border of the form when it is selected and the title bar will be darkened, as shown in Figure 2-5. (Do not be concerned if you see fewer than eight handles. You could resize the form to see more handles but it is not necessary now.)

> **Note**
>
> If the Properties box is empty, click the + sign next to the Forms folder in the Project Explorer, then double-click the Form1 icon.

FIGURE 2-5

An object must be selected in order to alter the object's properties.

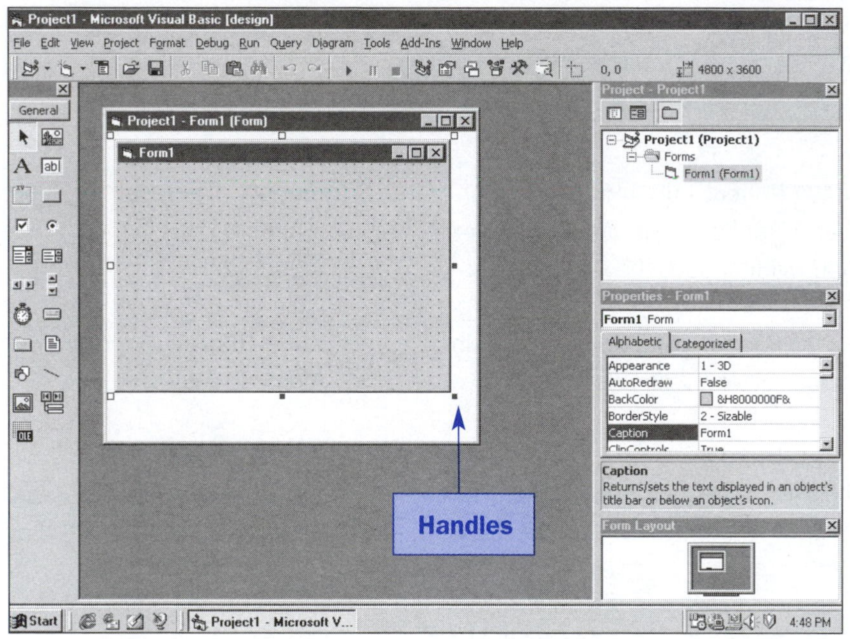

2. Click the down scroll bar arrow in the Properties window until you see the MaxButton property. Click the **MaxButton** property. A down arrow appears at the right edge of the MaxButton property field. An arrow at the right edge of a field indicates that there are predefined options from which to choose.

3. Click the **down arrow** at the right edge of the MaxButton property field and select **False** from the drop down menu. Notice that the Maximize button on the form becomes inactive (dimmed).

4. Click the **MinButton** property from the Properties window and set its value to **False**. Notice that the Maximize and Minimize buttons on the form disappear.

5. Click the **Moveable** property and set it to **False**.

6. Click the **Start** button from the standard toolbar to run the program.

7. Position the mouse pointer on the title bar of the window and attempt to drag it to the lower-right corner of the screen. The form remains in its original position because the Moveable property is set to False.

STEP-BY-STEP 2.4 CONTINUED

8. Click the **End** button from the standard toolbar.

9. Click the **Save Project** button (no dialog box will appear since the project has already been named).

10. Leave the project open for Step-by-Step 2.5.

Two of the most important properties of a form are the Caption and Name properties. The Caption property allows you to specify the text that appears in the title bar of the form. The Name property has a less visible, but very important, purpose. Each object has a name. The name of the object becomes critical when you begin writing Visual Basic code to manipulate the objects.

When naming objects, you should use names that are meaningful and describe the object you are naming. Many programmers use names that specify the type of object, as well as describing the object. To identify the type of object, a prefix is added to the name of the object. Table 2-1 shows some of the common prefixes and sample names.

TABLE 2-1

OBJECT NAMING PREFIXES

PREFIX	TYPE OF OBJECT	EXAMPLE
cmd	Command button	cmdClose
frm	Form	frmPrintDialogBox
img	Image	imgLogo
lbl	Label	lblPrompt
txt	Text box	txtWidth

STEP-BY-STEP 2.5

1. Click on **Form1** to select it. Handles will appear around the border of the form when it is selected.

2. Scroll up in the Properties window and click the **Caption** property.

3. Key **My VB Program** as the new caption. The title bar of the form changes as each letter is keyed, as shown in Figure 2-6 (the caption shown in Figure 2-6 is not completely keyed).

4. Press the **Enter** key to exit from the Caption text box.

5. Click the **(Name)** property from the top of the Properties window.

Note

The Name property appears in parentheses to force it to appear at the top of the alphabetical list of properties.

6. Key **frmMyForm** as the new name, then press the **Enter** key to exit from the Name text box.

7. Save the changes but leave the project open for Step-by-Step 2.6.

FIGURE 2-6
The title bar of the form changes as the caption is keyed.

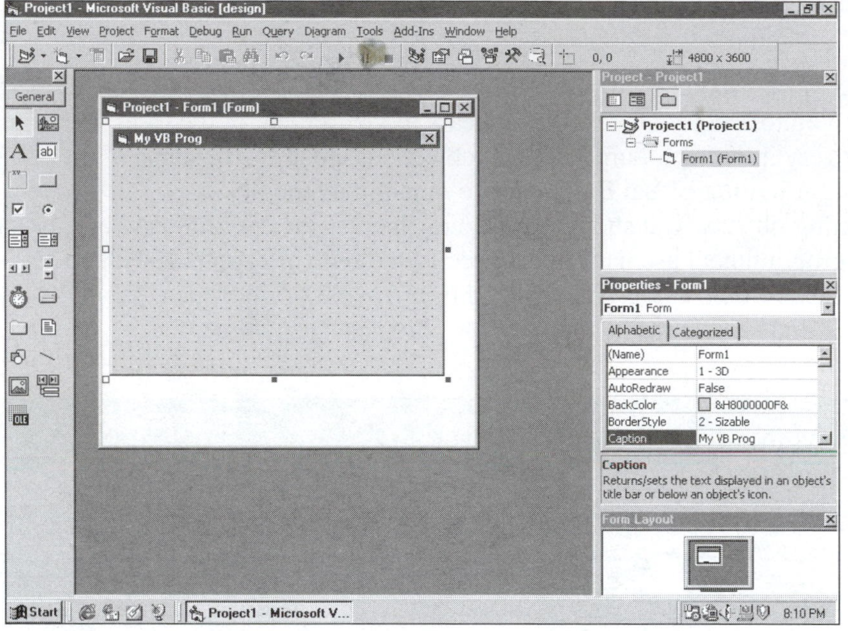

Creating Controls

FIGURE 2-7
The CommandButton tool is used to create command button controls.

General

CommandButton Tool

A blank form is not very exciting. To transform a blank form into a custom program, the first step is to add controls to the form. *Controls* are the command buttons, text boxes, scroll bars, and other objects that make up the user interface. Like forms, controls have properties that can be customized to suit your needs.

One of the most common controls is the command button. A *command button* is a standard pushbutton control. The OK and Cancel buttons that appear in many dialog boxes are examples of command buttons.

To create a command button, use the CommandButton tool on the toolbox (see Figure 2-7). You can double-click the tool to create a command button on the form or click the tool once and draw a command button on the form by dragging the mouse pointer in the area you want the command button to appear. The command button you create can be moved and resized if necessary.

STEP-BY-STEP 2.6

1. Double-click the **CommandButton** tool on the toolbox. A command button appears in the center of the form.

2. To create another command button, click the **CommandButton** tool on the toolbox one time to select it.

3. Position the mouse pointer in the lower-right corner of the form. Notice that the pointer changes from an arrow to a cross.

4. Drag the mouse pointer to create a second command button that is approximately the same size as the first command button, as shown in Figure 2-8.

5. Save the changes but leave the project open for Step-by-Step 2.7.

Note

Command buttons are named automatically as they are created. Generic names such as Command1 and Command2 will appear on newly created command buttons.

FIGURE 2-8
A control can be added to a form by double-clicking the control on the toolbox or by manually drawing the object to the desired size.

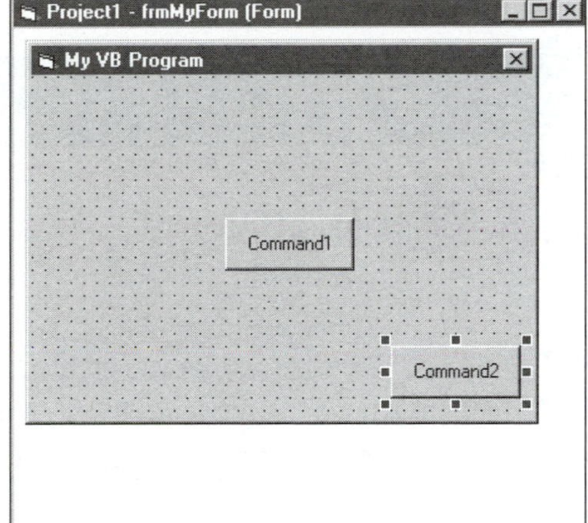

Setting Properties of the Command Buttons

Command buttons may seem simple at first. Like other objects, however, command buttons have many properties that can be set. The Name and Caption properties are among the most important. Be sure to name command buttons with meaningful names. The Caption property of a command button specifies the text that the user sees on the command button.

STEP-BY-STEP 2.7

1. Click the **Command1** button to select it (handles will surround it).

2. From the **Properties** window, click the **Caption** property and key **Show Image**, then press the **Enter** key.

3. Click the **(Name)** property and key **cmdShow**, then press the **Enter** key.

4. Click the **Command2** button.

STEP-BY-STEP 2.7 CONTINUED

5. Change the caption to **Exit** and change the name to **cmdExit**.

6. Save the changes but leave the project open for Step-by-Step 2.8.

Moving, Resizing, and Deleting Objects

Command buttons can be moved and resized easily. The objects in Visual Basic can be moved and resized using techniques that are common to most Windows programs. You can delete an object by selecting the object and pressing the Delete key.

Hot Tip

Visual Basic allows you to be imaginative with the size and position of objects. However, keep the Microsoft Windows standards in mind. Your programs will have a more professional appearance if the command buttons and other objects in your programs have a similar size and placement as those in other Windows programs.

STEP-BY-STEP 2.8

1. Drag the **Show Image** button towards the upper-right corner of the form.

2. Click the **Exit** button that you created. Handles appear around the border of the command button to indicate that it is selected.

3. Position the mouse pointer on the top middle handle bar and drag it up until it forms a box, as shown in Figure 2-9.

4. If it is not already selected (surrounded by handles), click the **Exit** button that you created.

5. Press the **Delete** key. The Exit button disappears.

6. Double-click the **CommandButton** tool from the toolbox.

7. Change the name of the button you just created to **cmdExit** and change the caption to **Exit**.

Note

If any of the eight handles are missing, you can drag to reposition the Show Image button again.

FIGURE 2-9
The handles are used to resize controls.

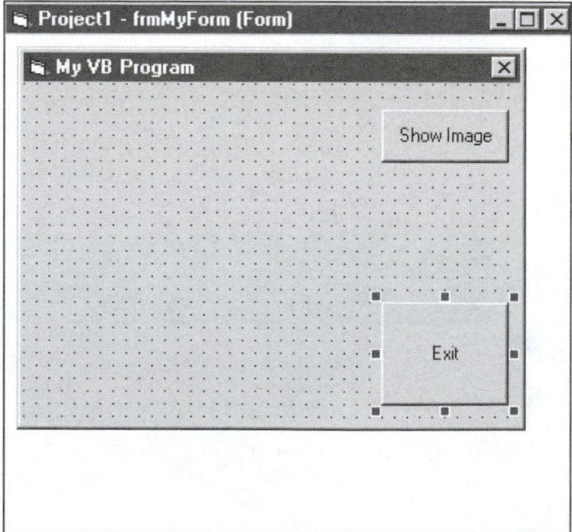

STEP-BY-STEP 2.8 CONTINUED

8. Drag the **Exit** button to the bottom-right corner of the form. Your form should appear similar to Figure 2-10.

9. Save the changes but leave the project open for Step-by-Step 2.9.

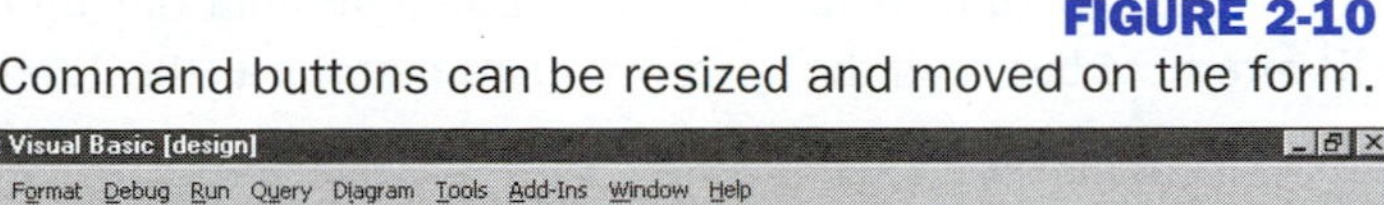

FIGURE 2-10
Command buttons can be resized and moved on the form.

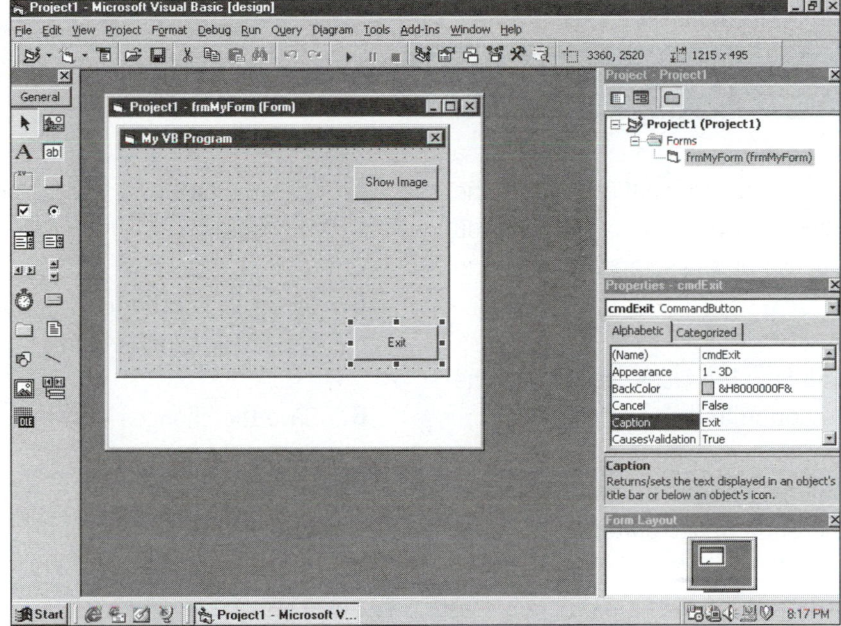

Understanding Focus

As you create programs that consist of controls (command buttons, scroll bars, and other objects) in windows, the concept of focus becomes an important one. As you have used programs, you have probably noticed that only one window at a time is active on the screen. You may have also noticed that within the window, only one control is active. For example, the cursor (blinking line) can only be in one text box. The object that is currently active is said to have the *focus*.

To see the focus move from one control to another, you can repeatedly press the Tab key while a dialog box is active. Each object in the window will get the focus in a sequence called the *tab order*.

STEP-BY-STEP 2.9

1. Choose the **Print** command from the **File** menu. The Print dialog box opens.

2. Press the **Tab** key. Notice how the focus moves from one control to another.

3. Press the **Tab** key repeatedly until the Cancel button is selected, and then press the **Enter** key. The Print dialog box disappears. Pressing the Enter key activated the command button with the focus.

STEP-BY-STEP 2.9 CONTINUED

4. Save the changes but leave the project open for Step-by-Step 2.10.

The project on which you are working has two command buttons on the form. When the program runs, the focus will alternate between the two command buttons as the Tab key is pressed.

STEP-BY-STEP 2.10

1. Click the **Start** button to run the program. The form, including the two command buttons you created, is active on the screen, as shown in Figure 2-11.

2. Press the **Tab** key. The focus moves from the Show Image button to the Exit button.

3. Click the **Show Image** button. The focus moves to the Show Image button.

4. Click the **Exit** button. The focus moves to the Exit button.

5. Click the **End** button from the standard toolbar. The program ends.

6. Save the changes but leave the project open for Step-by-Step 2.11.

FIGURE 2-11
When the program starts, the Show Image button has focus.

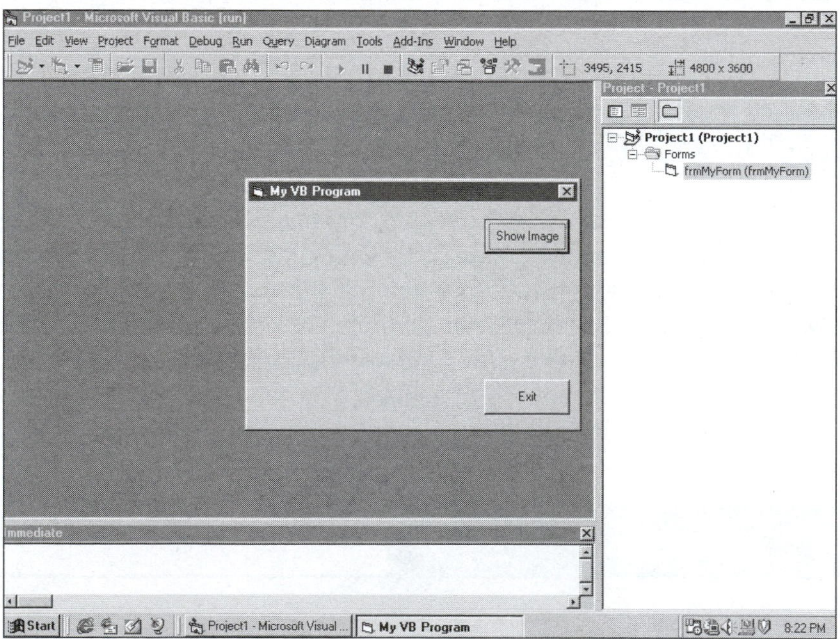

In Step-by-Step 2.10, you clicked the Show Image button and the Exit button. Activating those command buttons, however, produced no action. Creating a command button is only the first step. Giving a command button the caption Exit will not make the command button have the function of an Exit button. In the next lesson, you will learn how to write programming code to give these command buttons functionality.

Setting Additional Properties

Other properties that are commonly set when creating Visual Basic programs are the BackColor property and the properties that accurately set the position and size of objects.

Hot Tip

Color should be used sparingly in your programs. The more your programs have the color and appearance of standard Windows programs, the more professional your work will appear. Overusing colors can also make text in your programs harder to read.

Setting the BackColor Property

By default, forms have a gray background. The BackColor property can be changed to display a color other than gray. When setting the BackColor property, you can select from a palette of colors that is accessible from the Properties window.

STEP-BY-STEP 2.11

1. If **frmMyForm** is not already selected (surrounded by handles), click on it.

2. Click the **BackColor** property from the **Properties** window.

3. Click the **down arrow** at the right edge of the BackColor property field. A window of color options appears below the BackColor property, as shown in Figure 2-12.

4. Click the **Palette** tab. A selection of colors appears.

5. Click the white box located at the upper-left corner of the color palette. The form changes from gray to white.

FIGURE 2-12
The BackColor property can be easily altered from the Properties window.

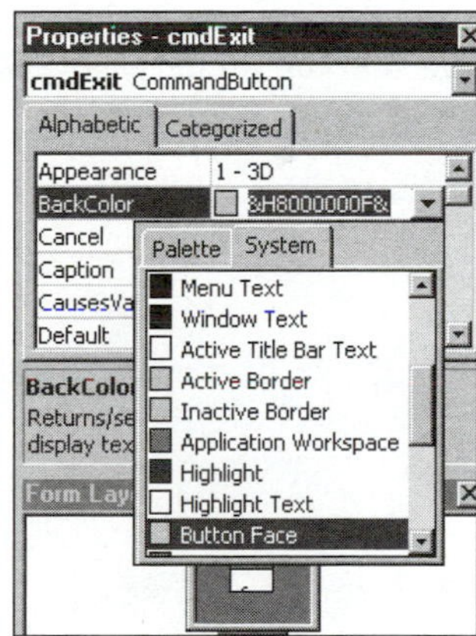

6. Save the changes but leave the project open for Step-by-Step 2.12.

Setting the Top and Left Properties

Note

There is no Right property. To specify how far a command button will appear from the right edge form, you must specify how far the command button is to appear from the left edge.

Often, you can use the mouse to size and position objects such as command buttons. However, if you want precise placement, you can use the Top and Left properties to specify the location of the command buttons. The Top property specifies the distance the top left corner of the command button will appear from the top edge of the form. The Left property specifies the distance the top left corner of the command button will appear from the left edge of the form. By default the unit of mea-sure for the Top and Left properties is *twips*. With twips, you can specify very precise measurements. There are 1440 twips in one inch.

STEP-BY-STEP 2.12

1. Click the **Exit** button to select it.
2. In the Properties window, scroll down, click the **Top** property and key **2500**, then press the **Enter** key.
3. Scroll up, click the **Left** property and key **3200**, then press the **Enter** key.
4. Click the **Show Image** button to select it.
5. Change the **Top** property to **250**, then press the **Enter** key.
6. Change the **Left** property to **3200**, then press the **Enter** key.
7. Save your changes, then choose **Exit** from the **File** menu to exit Visual Basic.

Note

If your button are no longer visible when you change the measurements in these steps, experiment with smaller measurements or drag to resize the form.

Summary

In this lesson, you learned:

- To create your own Visual Basic program, you must create a new project. The Standard EXE project type allows you to create a program from scratch.
- Projects created using the Standard EXE option begin with one blank form. Forms become the windows and dialog boxes when the program runs.
- Every program has at least one form. All other objects must be contained within forms.
- A window created from a Visual Basic form has certain functionality by default, such as the ability to be moved, resized, maximized, minimized, and closed.
- Properties are the characteristics of Visual Basic objects. Properties can be modified in the Properties window.
- The Caption and Name properties are two of the most important properties. The Caption controls what the user sees in the title bar of a form and other objects such as command buttons. When we add programming code later, the Name property allows us to refer to the object using a meaningful name. Programmers often use a naming standard when naming objects.
- Controls are the command buttons, text boxes, scroll bars, and other objects that make up the user interface.
- A command button is a standard pushbutton control that commonly appears in dialog boxes.
- Command buttons can be moved, resized, and deleted like other Windows objects.
- The term focus refers to the active status of one of the objects in a window. Only one object can have the focus.
- The BackColor property controls the background color of a form.
- The Top and Left properties can be used to accurately position objects. By default, the Top and Left properties use a measurement called twips. There are 1440 twips in one inch.
- When saving a Visual Basic project, the forms are saved first, followed by the project information.

LESSON 2 REVIEW QUESTIONS

TRUE/FALSE

Circle T if the statement is true or F if the statement is false.

T F 1. The ActiveX option helps you create a complete program with standard Windows features already included.

T F 2. Every program must have at least one form.

T F 3. Visual Basic programs have some functionality without writing any code.

T F 4. The btn prefix is commonly used when naming command buttons.

T F 5. The OK and Cancel buttons that appear in dialog boxes are examples of command buttons.

T F 6. A text box in a dialog box is an example of a control.

T F 7. An object can be deleted by selecting the object and pressing the Delete key.

T F 8. The inactive controls on a form are said to have focus.

T F 9. Selecting the Background property will allow you to change the background color of a form.

T F 10. When saving a project, you actually save the forms of the project and then the project itself.

WRITTEN QUESTIONS

Write a brief answer to the following questions.

1. What appears when the Standard EXE option is selected from the New Project dialog box?
2. A project created by the Standard EXE option consists of one object by default. What is that object?
3. What appears when an object is selected?
4. What term describes the characteristics of Visual Basic objects?
5. How do you specify the text that will appear in the title bar of a form?
6. What naming prefix is generally used when naming a form?
7. List three examples of controls.
8. What unit of measurement does Visual Basic use for the Top and Left properties?
9. What term describes the sequence in which the controls in a window become active as the Tab key is pressed?
10. What button on the standard toolbar is used to save a program?

LESSON 2 PROJECT

PROJECT 2-1

1. Start Visual Basic and create a new project.
2. Change the **(Name)** property of the form to **frmMyForm**.
3. Change the **Caption** property of the form to **Lesson 2 Project**.
4. Save the project with a form name of **frmMyForm2** and a project name of **MyVBProgram2**.

5. Add a command button to the form.
6. Change the **Caption** property of the command button to **Exit**.
7. Change the **(Name)** property of the command button to **cmdExit**.
8. Drag the **Exit** button to the lower-right corner of the form.
9. Draw a new command button on the form that is approximately the same size as the **Exit** button.
10. Change the **Caption** property of the new command button to **Go** and change the **(Name)** property of the command button to **cmdGo**.
11. Resize the **Go** button so it is approximately half as wide and twice as tall as the **Exit** button.
12. Click the **Start** button on the standard toolbar to run the program (the **Exit** button will have the focus).
13. Press the **Tab** key to switch the focus between the command buttons.
14. End the program.
15. Select and delete the **Go** button from the form.
16. Move the **Exit** button to the center of the form.
17. Click on the form and position the pointer on the lower-right corner. Resize the form so the **Exit** button appears in the lower-right corner.
18. Save the changes, then exit Visual Basic.

CRITICAL THINKING

ACTIVITY 2-1

1. Start Visual Basic and create a new project.
2. Give the form a caption and a descriptive name property.
3. Add an Install button and a Cancel button to the form, giving each a caption and a descriptive name property.
4. Move and resize each object so the form looks similar to Figure 2-13.
5. Save the project with an appropriate form name and project name, then exit Visual Basic.

FIGURE 2-13
Add an Install button and a Cancel button as shown here.

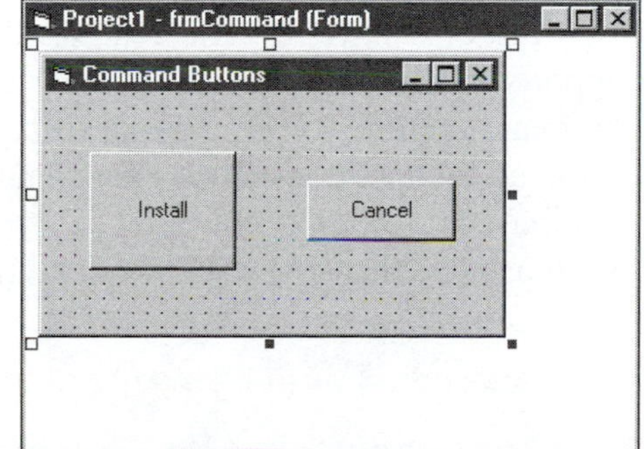

LESSON 3

EVENTS AND CODE

OBJECTIVES

When you complete this lesson, you will be able to:

- Describe events and how events are key to Windows programs.
- Access the Code window.
- Add code to a command button.
- Add an image to a form.
- Set image properties.
- Set properties from code.
- Set the Cancel and Default command button properties.
- Create a standalone Windows program.

Estimated Time: 2 hours

Events

Windows is an event-driven environment. In an *event-driven* system, the computer is constantly waiting for the user to take some action with the mouse, keyboard, or other device. That action triggers an *event*, and the software in the computer attempts to find something to do with that action.

Each object has a set of events that are supported by the object. When you create an object, such as a command button, it is up to you to write the code that will handle the events. That code is written in Visual Basic.

You only have to write code for the events you are interested in. For example, a command button supports events called Click, MouseDown, and MouseUp. The Click event occurs when the user clicks a command button. To be more specific, the MouseDown event occurs when the user presses the mouse button and holds it down over the command button. The MouseUp event occurs when the user releases the mouse button. Normally, you only need to write code for the Click event. The added control provided by MouseDown and MouseUp is not often needed.

The code you write to handle a specific event is called an *event procedure*. You write event procedures for events that you want to handle. For events you wish to ignore, you don't have to write anything.

In Lesson 2, you created two command buttons on a form and then ran the program. Recall that you clicked the command buttons, but nothing happened. When you clicked the Exit button that you created, a Click event was generated. Because your mouse pointer was over the Exit button, that command button was given the Click event to process. However, since you had not written any code for the command button, it did not know how to process the Click event and the event was ignored.

In this lesson, you will add code for handling the Click event to the command buttons you created in the previous lesson. As you progress through the lessons in this book, you will learn about additional events and how to write code for those events.

Accessing the Code Window

The first step in adding code to an object is to access the Code window. To add code to a command button, open the form that contains the command button and double-click the command button. The Code window will appear.

STEP-BY-STEP 3.1

1. Start Visual Basic and click the **Existing** tab (or choose **Open Project** from the **File** menu).
2. Change drives and folders as necessary, then double-click **MyVBProgram** that was created in Lesson 2 (not MyVBProgram2).
3. If necessary, use the View menu to open the Project Explorer, Properties, and Form Layout windows.
4. If necessary, click the + sign to open the Forms folder from the Project Explorer window. If the form is not already on your screen, double-click **frmMyForm**. The form appears in the middle of the screen.
5. Double-click the **Exit** button. The Code window appears. Your screen should appear similar to Figure 3-1.
6. Leave the project open for Step-by-Step 3.2.

Notice that the Code window already has some code written in it. A *subroutine* (a section of code to perform a specific task) has been set up for you. The name of the subroutine indicates that the routine is to handle the Click event of the cmdExit button. The code for the Exit button will be added at the location where the cursor is blinking.

FIGURE 3-1

The Code window allows you to enter code for an object or control.

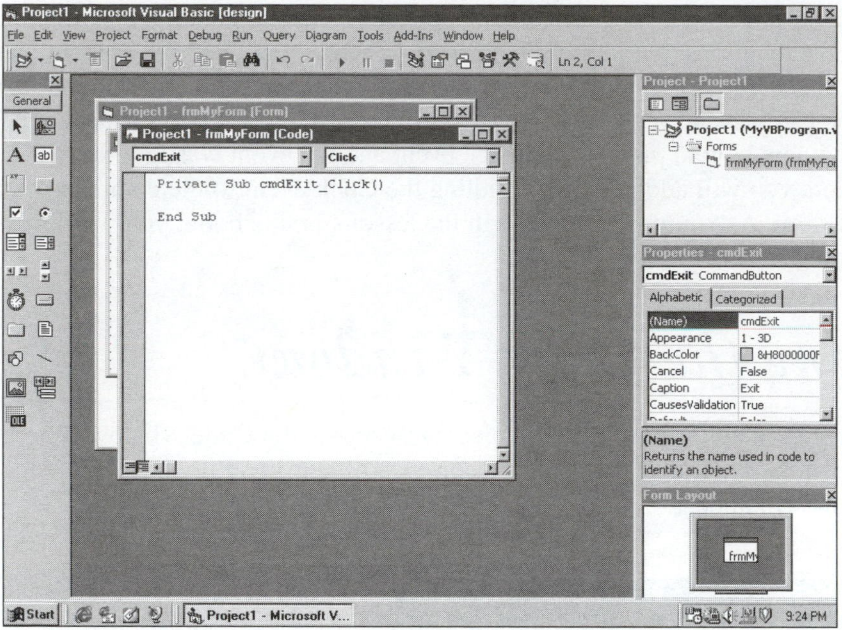

Adding Code to a Command Button

To add code to the Code window, you simply enter the code from the keyboard much like you would use a word processor. You can insert and delete text, and use cut, copy, and paste.

The Code window, however, has special features that automatically format your code and help you enter code more easily and more accurately. For example, using a technology called *Intellisense*[R], it will anticipate what you are about to key and complete your statements for you.

Visual Basic is not *case-sensitive*, meaning that capitalization of key words and other elements of the code is not critical. Keying a command in all caps, all lowercase, or a combination of case has no effect on the functionality. However, to keep things neat, the Code window editor will standardize the case of much of your code.

> **Note**
>
> The Code window does not automatically wrap text like a word processor. Each line of code should be complete on one line. Press the Enter key at the end of each line of code. Press the Backspace key to delete blank lines. You can resize the Code window to make seeing your code easier.

Let's begin by adding code for the Exit button. The Visual Basic command to end a program is the End statement.

STEP-BY-STEP 3.2

1. Press the **Tab** key to indent the line. It is common practice to use indention to improve the readability of programming code. The usefulness of indenting code will become more apparent in later lessons when the code is more complex.

2. Key **end** and press the **Enter** key. Notice that Visual Basic capitalizes the word *end* and changes the color to blue. Your Code window should appear similar to Figure 3-2.

Note

The color in which the key words in the Code window appear may vary.

FIGURE 3-2
Visual Basic automatically formats key words.

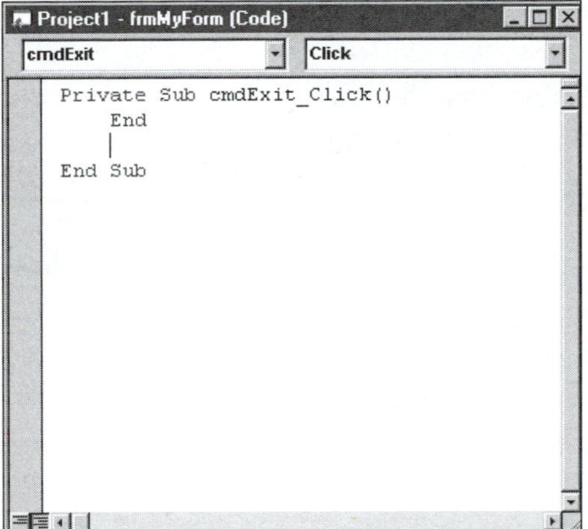

3. Press the **Backspace** key twice to remove the blank line below the code you just keyed.

4. Click the **Close** button on the Code window. The Code window closes and the form becomes active.

5. Click the **Start** button from the standard toolbar to run the program.

6. Click the **Exit** button. The event procedure you wrote is activated and the program ends.

7. Click the Save Project button on the standard toolbar to save the changes but leave the project open for Step-by-Step 3.3.

Adding an Image to a Form

Visual Basic allows you to easily add graphics to your programs. One of the easiest ways to add an image to a form is to use the Image tool (located towards the bottom of the toolbox). The Image tool creates an object called an *image control*. An image control provides a framework for displaying an image on a form.

Like the CommandButton tool, the Image tool can be double-clicked to place an object of a default size on the form. You can also click the Image tool once and then drag to draw an image control. The image control can be moved and resized like other controls.

Note

The Picture Box tool at the top of the toolbox creates a control similar to an image control. A picture box control is more flexible, but slightly less efficient than an image control.

STEP-BY-STEP 3.3

1. Double-click the **Image** button from the toolbox. An image control appears in the center of the form.

2. Position the mouse pointer in the center of the image control and drag it to the upper-left corner. Drag the lower-right corner of the image control to resize it. Your form should look similar to Figure 3-3.

3. While the image control is selected (surrounded by handles), click the **Picture** property from the **Properties** window. A button with three tiny dots, called an ellipsis, appears in the Properties field, as shown in Figure 3-4. The *ellipsis*, in this case, indicates that you can browse your hard drive for a file that will serve as the source of the image.

4. Click the ellipsis at the end of the Picture property field. The Load Picture dialog box appears on the screen, as shown in Figure 3-5.

FIGURE 3-3
The image control allows graphics to be shown in a program.

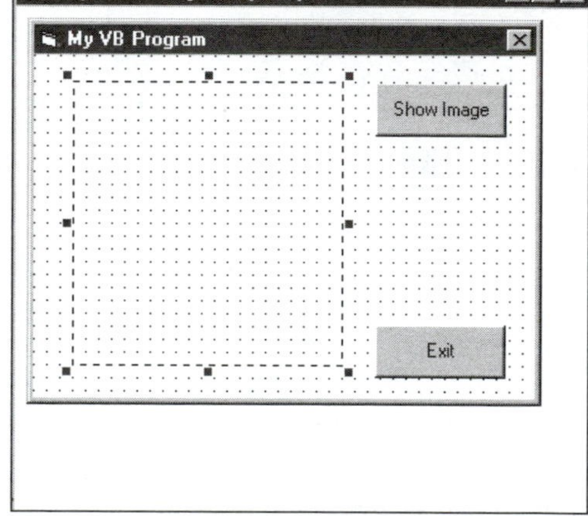

FIGURE 3-4
The ellipsis shown indicates that you can browse for a value.

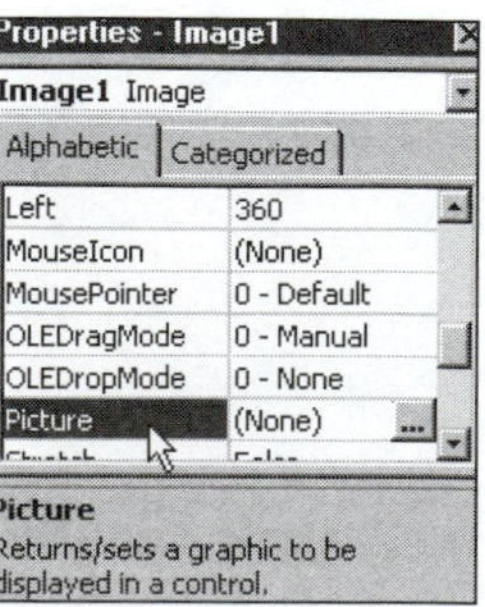

STEP-BY-STEP 3.6 CONTINUED

FIGURE 3-5
The Load Picture dialog box allows you to select a picture that will be the source of the image.

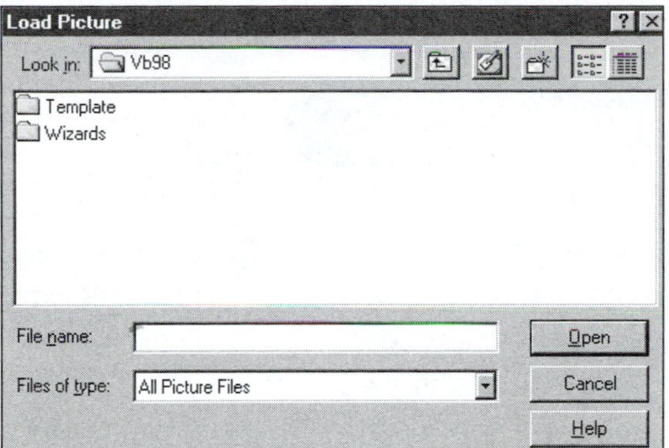

5. From the **Look in** box, select the drive and folder where your data files are located. A list of picture files appears in the Load Picture dialog box (depending on how your template files are organized on your system, there may be only one picture file listed for this lesson).

6. Click **VBasic** from the list of picture files and click the **Open** button. A picture of a textbook cover appears within the image control. Notice how the image control resizes itself to fit the size of the picture.

7. Save the changes but leave the project open for Step-by-Step 3.4.

Setting Image Properties

Like other objects, image controls have an extensive set of properties that can be changed. For our purposes, there are three properties that are of particular interest: the Name property, the Stretch property, and the Visible property.

The Name Property

Naming an image control is as important as naming other objects. The name you give the image control will be the name you use when you refer to the control in your Visual Basic code. The *img* prefix is often used when naming image controls.

STEP-BY-STEP 3.4

1. If necessary, click on the image control that you just created to select it.

2. Scroll up and click the **(Name)** property. Remember, the Name property appears in parentheses at the top of the Properties list.

3. Change the name of the image control to **imgMyImage** and press the **Enter** key.

4. Save the changes but leave the project open for Step-by-Step 3.5.

The Stretch Property

When you selected the image for the image control, the image control resized itself to fit the image. Often, however, the image you are placing on the form is not the size you would like displayed. The *Stretch property* allows the image to be resized to fit the size of the image control. By default, the Stretch property is set to False. Setting the Stretch property to True will allow the image to resize to fit the control.

STEP-BY-STEP 3.5

1. If necessary, click on the image control to select it. Resize the image control so it appears similar to Figure 3-6. Notice that the image control resizes, but the image itself remains the original size. The image does not resize because the Stretch property is set to False.

2. Change the **Stretch** property to **True** from the **Properties** window. The image stretches to fit inside the image control as shown in Figure 3-7.

3. Click the **Start** button on the standard toolbar to run the program. Notice the image appears in the window.

4. Click the **Exit** button to end the program.

5. Save the changes but leave the project open for Step-by-Step 3.6.

FIGURE 3-6
When the Stretch property is set to False, the image control can be resized, but the image will not stretch to fit the control.

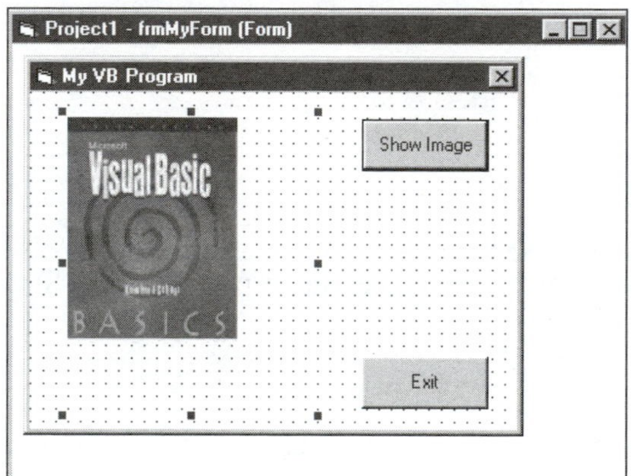

FIGURE 3-7
Changing the Stretch property to True causes the image to resize to fit the control.

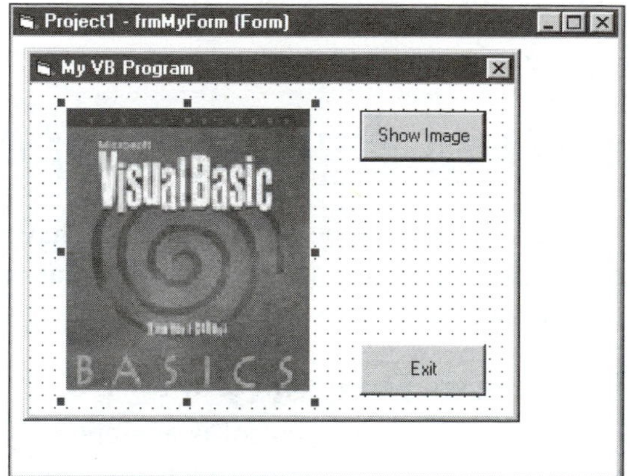

The Visible Property

The Visible property gives you control over when an image is visible to the user. Setting the Visible property to False makes the image invisible to the user. As you will see when you write the code for the Show Image button, the Visible property can be changed from code.

Note

In the Snake Game you played in Lesson 1, the large words "Snake Game" that appear when you first run the program are actually in an image control. The program uses the Visible property to make the words disappear when the game is started.

STEP-BY-STEP 3.6

1. Click on the image to select the image control.

2. Change the **Visible** property of **imgMyImage** to **False**.

3. Click the **Start** button on the standard toolbar. The program begins, but because the Visible property of the image control is set to False the image does not appear on the form. Your screen should appear similar to Figure 3-8.

4. Click the **Exit** button to end the program.

5. Save the changes but leave the project open for Step-by-Step 3.7.

FIGURE 3-8

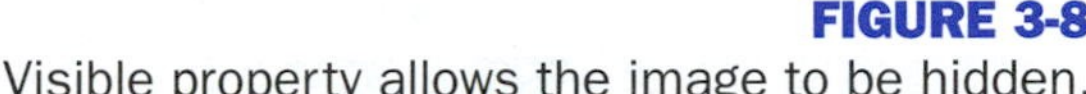

The Visible property allows the image to be hidden.

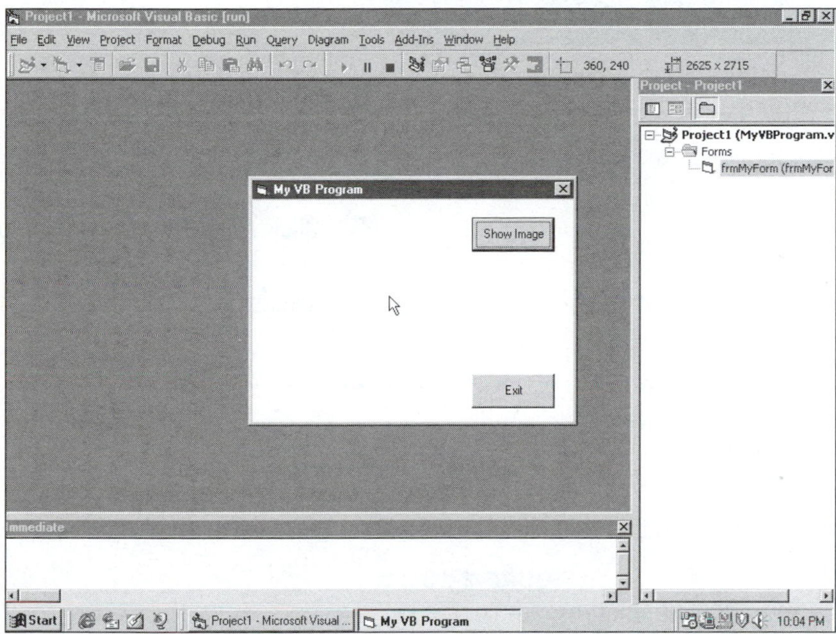

Setting Properties from Code

One of the most common tasks for Visual Basic code is setting properties of objects such as controls and forms. While it is true that the properties of objects can be set when the object is created, you will often want to manipulate those properties while the program runs.

Visual Basic allows you to change a property by specifying the name of the control, the property, and the value you want to give the property. Figure 3-9 shows a line of code that changes an image control's Visible property to False.

The period (usually referred to as a dot) separates the object from the property. The item to the right of the dot is called a *method*. The term method is common to object-oriented programming languages. In Figure 3-9, the word *Visible* is actually a method for changing the Visible property. There are other methods used in Visual Basic programming that do not relate to a property.

The image control object knows how to set its own Visible property, and it provides the Visible method for doing so. When you write the Visual Basic code, you are sending a message to the imgMyImage object, telling it to change its Visible property using the Visible method. *Message* is another object-oriented programming term. In object-oriented programming, you don't actually set the property—you ask the object to set its own property by sending it a message.

FIGURE 3-9
Properties can be changed from code.

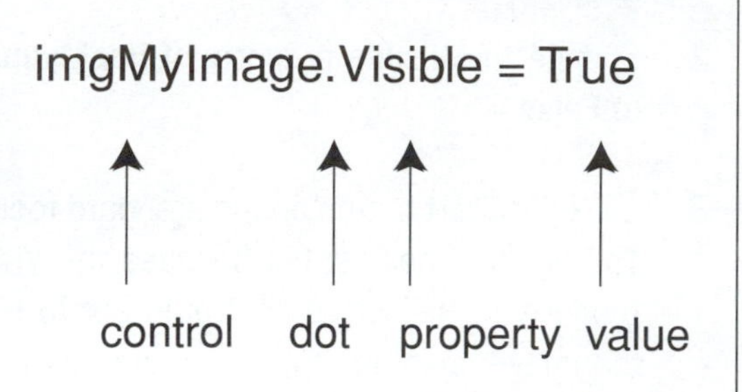

STEP-BY-STEP 3.7

1. Double-click the **Show Image** button. The Code window appears on the screen.
2. Press the **Tab** key.
3. Key **imgMyImage.Visible = True**, as shown in Figure 3-10 (ignore the drop down boxes that appear as you key).
4. Close the Code window.
5. Click the **Start** button from the standard toolbar. The program becomes active on the screen. Notice that the image is not visible.
6. Click the **Show Image** button on the form. The image appears on the screen. Your screen should appear similar to Figure 3-11.
7. Click the **Exit** button.
8. Save the changes but leave the project open for Step-by-Step 3.8.

FIGURE 3-10
The code in the Show Image button asks the image control to set its Visible property to True.

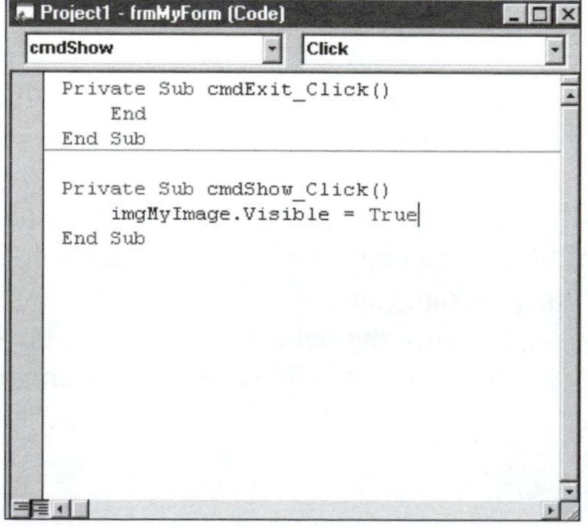

FIGURE 3-11
The image appears on the screen after the Show Image button is clicked.

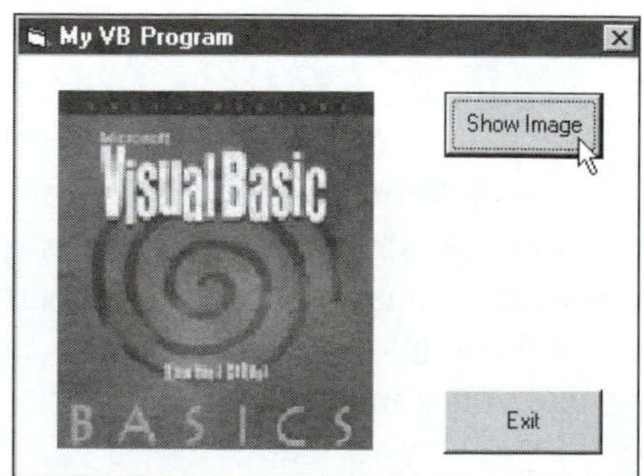

Setting the Cancel and Default Command Button Properties

As you have probably noticed in most windows that include command buttons, there is a command button that will be selected when you press the Enter key and a command button that will be selected when you press the Esc key. Often, the Enter key will select the OK button, and the Esc key will select the Cancel button.

There are two command button properties involved in adding this functionality to your programs: the Default property and the Cancel property. The command button with the *Default property* set to True will be activated when the user presses the Enter key. The command button with the *Cancel property* set to True will be activated when the user presses the Esc key.

Only one command button on a form can have the Cancel property set to True. The same is true for the Default property.

STEP-BY-STEP 3.8

1. Click the **Show Image** button and set the **Default** property to **True**.
2. Click the **Exit** button and set the **Cancel** property to **True**.
3. Click the **Start** button on the standard toolbar to run the program.
4. Press the **Enter** key. The Show Image button is activated and the image appears.
5. Press the **Esc** key. The Exit button is activated and the program ends.
6. Save the changes but leave the project open for Step-by-Step 3.9.

Creating a Standalone Program

Running programs from within the Visual Basic environment with the Start button from the standard toolbar is fine when you are developing a program. When you have a finished product, however, you will want to make a program file that can be run like other Windows programs, without Visual Basic being loaded.

Note

Some editions of Visual Basic may not have the feature for creating standalone programs.

By creating a *standalone program*, you can distribute a program you have written to anyone who is running Windows—whether they have Visual Basic or not.

To create a standalone program from your Visual Basic project, choose the Make command from the File menu. The Make command will show the name of your program in the menu, so it will vary depending on the project you have opened.

STEP-BY-STEP 3.9

1. Choose **Make MyVBProgram.exe** from the **File** menu. The Make Project dialog box appears, as shown in Figure 3-12.

2. Use the dialog box to locate the folder where you intend to save the standalone program. Your instructor may have special instructions for saving.

3. Change the filename within the Make Project dialog box to **VBStandalone** and click the **OK** button.

4. After the EXE file is created, exit Visual Basic. If necessary, save any changes that were made to your files.

5. Double-click the **My Computer** icon on your desktop (or click the Windows **Start** button, position the mouse pointer on **Programs**, and click **Windows Explorer**). Double-click drives and folders to locate the VBStandalone file.

6. Double-click the program named **VBStandalone**. The program starts.

7. Click the **Show Image** button on the form (or press the **Enter** key). The program runs exactly the same as it did within the Visual Basic compiler.

8. Click the **Exit** button (or press the **Esc** key). Close all the My Computer or Windows Explorer windows.

FIGURE 3-12
The Make Project dialog box allows you to select the location for your standalone program.

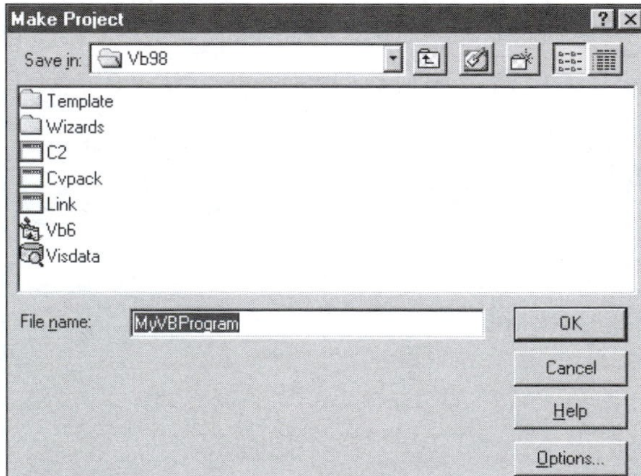

Summary

In this lesson, you learned:

- Windows is an event-driven environment. In an event-driven system, the user triggers events that control the work.
- To control what happens when an event occurs, you must write event procedures for each event that you want to handle.
- To access the Code window, double-click an object such as a command button.
- The code you write in Visual Basic is written in sections called subroutines.
- Adding code is much like working in a word processor. The basic text-editing features are available. In addition, Visual Basic has *Intellisense*R features to help format your program code.
- The End statement ends a program.
- The Image tool allows you to add an image control to a form.
- Using the Name property, you can give an image control a name. That name will be used when you refer to the control in code.
- The Stretch property set to True causes an image to resize to fit the dimensions of the image control.
- The Visible property controls whether an object is shown or hidden.
- Setting properties from code is one of the most common uses for Visual Basic code. Setting properties from code allows you to change properties while a program runs.
- To change an object's properties from code, you send a message to the object. The object uses a method to change the property.
- A command button with the Default property set to True will be activated when the user presses the Enter key.
- A command button with the Cancel property set to True will be activated when the user presses the Esc key.
- A standalone program is one that will run without any special programming language software being loaded. Visual Basic creates standalone Windows programs using the Make command from the File menu.

LESSON 3 REVIEW QUESTIONS

TRUE/FALSE

Circle T if the statement is true or F if the statement is false.

T F 1. Microsoft Windows is an event-driven environment.

T F 2. An event can be triggered only by the mouse.

T F 3. Double-clicking a command button control brings up the Code window.

T F 4. In Visual Basic, exact capitalization of all of the key words is critical.

T F 5. An image control provides a framework for an image.

T F 6. The Stretch property set to True allows an image to resize to fit the image control.

T F 7. When setting properties from code, every property of the object must be specified.

T F 8. The command button with the Default property set to False will be activated when the user presses Esc.

T F 9. Only one command button can have the Default property set to True.

T F 10. A standalone program can run on a computer that does not have Visual Basic installed.

WRITTEN QUESTIONS

Write a brief answer to the following questions.

1. What is the term for code that handles a specific event?

2. What is the term for the section of code that is set up for you when you access the Code window?

3. What is *Intellisense*R?

4. What does an ellipsis (…) at the edge of a Properties field indicate?

5. Why is it important to give a meaningful name to an image control?

6. What is the purpose of the Visible property?

7. When setting a property from code, what item immediately follows the dot in the line of code and what does it do?

8. Write a line of code that will cause the image held in an image control named imgLogo to be hidden.

9. What command button property causes the button to be activated when the Esc key is pressed?

10. Why would you want to create a standalone program?

LESSON 3 PROJECTS

PROJECT 3-1

In this project, you will use the Top property of an image control to move an image on the form while the program is running.

1. Start Visual Basic and create a new project.

2. Give the form the name **frmHighLow** and the caption **High Low**.

3. Use the **Properties** window to set the **Height** property of the form to **3750** and the **Width** property to **4500**.

Note

Height and Width properties are measured in twips, just like the Top and Left properties.

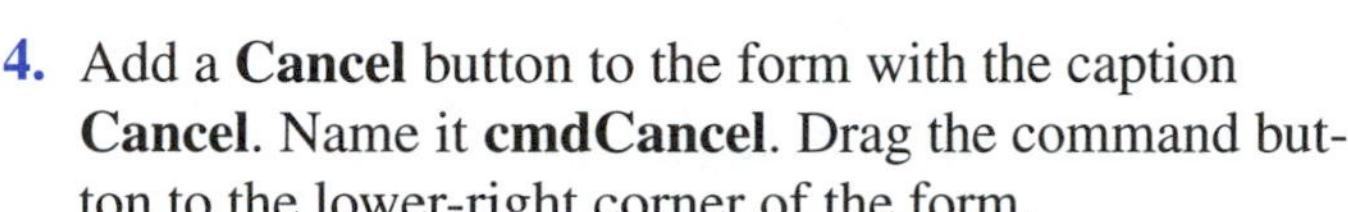

4. Add a **Cancel** button to the form with the caption **Cancel**. Name it **cmdCancel**. Drag the command button to the lower-right corner of the form.

5. Write an event procedure that will cause the program to end when the Cancel button is clicked.

6. Run the program to test it.

7. Add an image control to the form and drag it to the upper-left corner of the form.

8. Load the VBasic image into the image control and set the **Stretch** property to **True**. Name the image **imgVBasic**.

9. Set both the **Height** and **Width** properties of the image control to **1500**.

10. Set the **Top** property of the image control to **200**.

11. Set the **Left** property of the image control to **400**.

12. Add a command button with the caption **High** to the form. Name it **cmdHigh** and drag it to the upper-right corner of the form. (If it overlaps the image, click on the form and drag handles to resize it, then drag the command button again.)

13. Add a command button with the caption **Low** to the form. Name it **cmdLow** and place it below the High button.

14. Add the following code to the **High** command button Click event procedure.

```
imgVBasic.Top = 200
```

15. Add the following code to the **Low** command button Click event procedure.

```
imgVBasic.Top = 1500
```

16. Make the **Cancel** button the command button that will be activated when the Esc key is pressed.

17. Save the project with a form name of **frmHighLow** and a project name of **HighLow**.

18. Run the program and test the command buttons (remember to press the **Esc** key to test the Cancel button).

19. Exit Visual Basic.

PROJECT 3-2

A command button's Enabled property can be used to disable a command button so that it can no longer be clicked. This is commonly used to prevent a user from selecting an option that is not currently available. In this project, you will open the project you created in the lesson and disable the Show Image button after the image is visible.

1. Start Visual Basic, click the **Existing** tab, and open the **MyVBProgram** project (not MyVBProgram2).

2. If necessary, open the form.

3. Double-click the **Show Image** button to access its event procedure.

4. Press the **End** key to move to the end of the code that makes the image visible, then press the **Enter** key.

5. Add the following line of code.

   cmdShow.Enabled = False

6. Close the Code window.

7. Run the program to see the Show Image button become disabled after it is clicked. (When you run the program, the image is invisible. Then, when you click the Show Image button, the image appears and the button is disabled.)

8. Press the **Esc** key to end the program.

9. Make a standalone program named **VBStandalone2** that includes the new functionality, then exit Visual Basic (saving the changes).

10. Double-click the **My Computer** icon on the desktop, locate the new standalone file, and start the program.

11. Test the buttons, then close all the My Computer windows.

CRITICAL THINKING

ACTIVITY 3-1

Open the MyVBProgram project again (not the standalone program) and make the following modifications. (If you did not complete the steps in Project 3-2, perform those steps before making the modifications below.) Run the program to test the modifications, then exit Visual Basic, saving the changes.

1. Create a command button with the caption **Hide Image**. Give the command button an appropriate name and position it below the Show Image button.
2. From the Properties window, set the **Enabled** property of the Hide Image button to **False**.
3. Add code to the **Show Image** button event procedure that will enable the Hide Image button after the Show Image button is disabled.
4. Write an event procedure for the **Hide Image** button that hides the image, disables the Hide Image button, and enables the Show Image button.

LESSON 4

MATHEMATICAL OPERATORS

OBJECTIVES

When you complete this lesson, you will be able to:

- Describe the purpose of operators and how calculations are performed in Visual Basic.
- Create label controls.
- Use the addition and assignment operators.
- Use text boxes to get data from the user and use the Val function to extract a numeric value from a text box.
- Split code statements among lines in the Code window.
- Use the subtraction operator.
- Use unary minus.
- Use the multiplication and division operators with the Fix function to remove the fractional portion of numbers.
- Perform integer division and use the modulus operator.

Estimated Time: 2 hours

Performing Calculations in Visual Basic

It is no secret that computers are well-suited for math. In fact, most of the tasks a computer performs can be reduced to some mathematical function. Like other programming languages, Visual Basic allows you to use mathematical equations in your programs. In this lesson, you will learn how to perform the basic mathematical functions using the mathematical operators.

Operators are symbols that perform specific operations in Visual Basic statements. As you will learn in later lessons, there are operators that are not strictly mathematical. But for now, we will only be concerned with performing basic math operations using the common operators.

Since you began learning basic math, you have been using operators such as + and – to add and subtract values. To make Visual Basic statements as easy to read as possible, symbols were selected that are similar or identical to the symbols you are accustomed to using. Table 4-1 shows the mathematical operators you will use in this lesson.

TABLE 4-1

MATHEMATICAL OPERATORS

OPERATOR	DESCRIPTION
=	Assignment
+	Addition or unary plus
–	Subtraction or unary minus
*	Multiplication
/	Division
\	Integer division
Mod	Modulus

Creating Label Controls

Note

There may be a couple of operators in Table 4-1 that are new to you. Don't worry, in this lesson you will learn all about them and put each of them to work in a program.

The *label control* is used to place text on a form. Sometimes a label is used to identify a text box or to add a title or message to a form. The Caption property of a label specifies what text will appear on the label. The text that appears on the label cannot be directly changed by the user. Labels can also be used to provide output. To provide output, you write code for the desired calculation. The result of the calculation is then assigned to the Caption property of the label and the result also appears on the label on the form.

In Step-by-Step 4.1, you will open a Standard EXE project and create some labels.

STEP-BY-STEP 4.1

1. Start Visual Basic and open a new Standard EXE project. If necessary, open the Forms folder in the Project Explorer and double-click the Form icon.

2. In the **Properties** window, give the new form the name **frmAddition** and the caption **Addition**.

3. Double-click the **Label** tool, which is found in the toolbox. A label appears on the form. The caption of the label is Label1.

4. Click the **Caption** property from the **Properties** window.

STEP-BY-STEP 4.1 CONTINUED

5. Key your name as the caption for the label and press the **Enter** key. Notice that the caption changes on the label as you key the caption in the Properties window.

6. Click the **(Name)** property, key **lblMyName** and press the **Enter** key.

7. Position the mouse pointer in the center of the label and drag it to the upper-left corner of the form.

8. Save the project with the form named **frmAddition** and project named **Addition**. Leave Visual Basic open for Step-by-Step 4.2.

Hot Tip

Remember that another way to place controls such as labels on a form is to click the tool once, then drag to draw the control. You can then move, resize, or delete the control as needed.

Using the Addition and Assignment Operators

The addition operator (+) and *assignment operator* (=) perform just as you would expect. For example, in the statement below, the values 16 and 8 are added, and the result is placed in the caption of the label named lblAnswer. The assignment operator changes the value of the item on the left of the assignment operator to the value on the right of the assignment operator. After the statement is executed, the label will display the result of the addition (24).

```
lblAnswer.Caption = 16 + 8
```

The above statement is not very realistic, however. In most cases, rather than writing code that adds two hard-coded values, you will be adding values that may be entered by a user or other values that may change each time the program is run.

Note

The term *hard-coded* refers to information that is entered directly into the source code and cannot change while the program runs. Values that are keyed directly into source code are also called *literals*.

STEP-BY-STEP 4.2

1. Click the **Label** tool from the **Toolbox** to select it.

2. Draw a label in the center of the form that is about half the size of the other label.

3. Change the caption of the new label to the number zero (**0**) and press the **Enter** key.

4. Change the name of the new label to **lblAnswer**.

5. Click the **CommandButton** tool and create a command button near the bottom center of the form. Name the button **cmdCalculate** and change the button's caption to **Calculate**.

6. Double-click the **Calculate** button, press the **Tab** key, and add the code in CODE Step 6 in the Click event procedure.

7. Close the Code window. Click the **Start** button on the standard toolbar to run the program. The Answer label in the center of the form currently has a caption of 0.

8. Click the **Calculate** button. The caption for the Answer label changes to 24, the result of adding 16 and 8, as shown in Figure 4-1. Your screen should show your name in the top left corner of the form.

9. Click the **End** button on the standard toolbar to end the program.

10. Save the changes to your form.

11. Choose **Remove Project** from the **File** menu to close the project.

12. Leave Visual Basic open for Step-by-Step 4.3.

FIGURE 4-1
The Caption property of the label was changed by the code in the Calculate button.

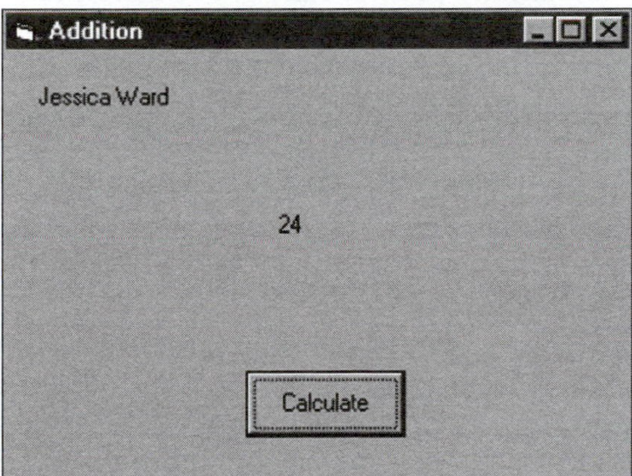

CODE STEP 6

```
lblAnswer.Caption = 16 + 8
```

Using Text Boxes and the Val Function

Text boxes are the fields placed on dialog boxes and in other windows that allow the user to enter a value. You have seen and used text boxes in the previous lessons. In this lesson, you will learn how to extract the value from a text box and use it in a mathematical operation. Figure 4-2 shows an example of a text box (the File name box). The Text property of a text box specifies what text will appear on the text box.

FIGURE 4-2
Text boxes are fields that get input from the user.

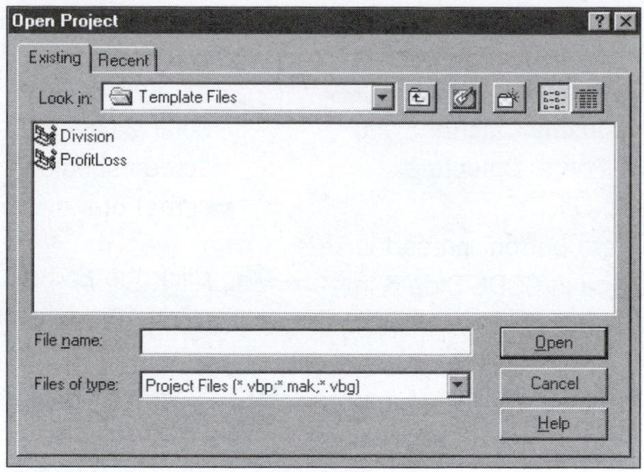

How Text Differs from Numeric Data

Text boxes accept data from the user. This data comes in the form of text. In a computer, text—which can include letters, symbols, and numbers—is treated differently from strictly numeric information. For example, if the user enters 234 in a text box, the computer treats that entry as three characters: a 2, a 3, and a 4. It does not automatically treat the entry as two hundred and thirty-four. Therefore, numbers in a text box must be converted to a true numeric value before they can be used in a calculation.

When a computer stores text, it uses a numeric value to represent each allowable character. For example, to your computer, the character "A" is represented by the value 65. The system of codes that the computer uses to represent characters is called the ASCII code. For now, just understand that the characters entered in text boxes need a conversion from numeric text to a numeric value before mathematical operations can be performed.

Using the Val Function

The conversion necessary to convert the numeric text characters in a text box to numeric values is done by the Val function. The *Val function* takes numbers that are in a text format and returns a numeric value that can be used in calculations. The statement below is an example of how the Val function is used. The items in parentheses are the text boxes.

```
lblTotal.Caption = Val(txtPrice.Text) + Val(txtSalesTax.Text)
```

In the statement above, notice that the text boxes (txtPrice and txtSalesTax) begin with the txt prefix. This makes it clear that the controls are text boxes. (Remember that controls are the objects you insert from the toolbox.) The *Text* following the period accesses the values entered by the user in the text boxes. The *Caption* following the period indicates that the answer of the calculation will be assigned to the Caption property of the label. The statement is instructing the computer to take the value in the txtPrice text box, add the value in the txtSalesTax text box to it, and assign the sum of the values to the Caption property of the label named lblTotal.

Splitting Code Statements among Lines

When you begin writing code that includes calculations, the lines of code often become long. Visual Basic provides a way to split a line of code among two or more lines. Within a line of code, you can key an underscore (_), known as the *line-continuation character*. The line-continuation character tells the compiler to skip to the next line and treat the text there as if it were a part of the same line. In Step-by-Step 4.3, you will use the line-continuation character to break a long line of code into two lines.

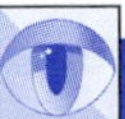

Important

Always key a space before the line-continuation character to avoid errors.

STEP-BY-STEP 4.3

1. Choose **Open Project** from the **File** menu.
2. Change to the drive and folder where your template files are located, then open the **ProfitLoss** project.
3. If the form is not displayed, open the **Forms** folder from the Project Explorer window and double-click the form **frmProfitLoss**. Your screen should appear similar to Figure 4-3.
4. Double-click the **Calculate** button. The Code window appears.
5. Add a blank line below the cmdCalculate_Click() line, then position the cursor on the blank line.
6. Press the **Tab** key to indent the line
7. Add the code in CODE Step 7 to total the expenses.

   This code will add the values in the Rent, Payroll, Utilities, Supplies, and Other text boxes and assign the sum of the values to the Caption property of the label named lblTotalExp. The Code window should appear similar to Figure 4-4.
8. Close the Code window and click the **Start** button on the standard toolbar to run the program.
9. Key the following data into the corresponding text boxes on the form.

Rent	**350**
Payroll	**600**
Utilities	**200**
Supplies	**100**
Other	**50**
10. Click the **Calculate** button. The expenses are totaled and the results are stored in the Total Expenses Field as shown in Figure 4-5.
11. Click the **Exit** button. The Profit & Loss program closes.
12. Save the changes but leave the project open for Step-by-Step 4.4.

CODE STEP 7

```
'Calculate Total Expenses
lblTotalExp.Caption = Val(txtRent.Text) + Val(txtPayroll.Text) + _
Val(txtUtil.Text) + Val(txtSupp.Text) + Val(txtOther.Text)
```

FIGURE 4-3
The Profit & Loss form appears on your screen.

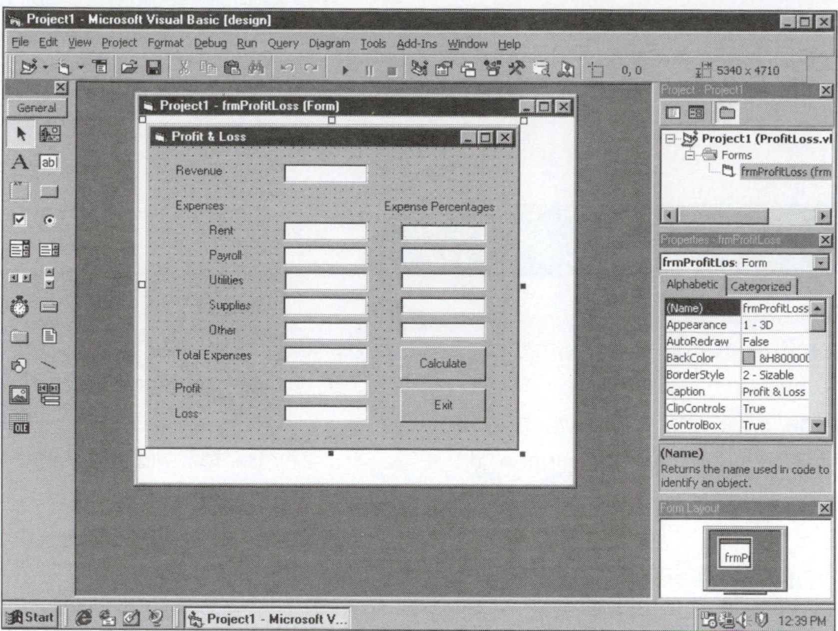

FIGURE 4-4
The underscore character allows a line of code to be broken into multiple lines.

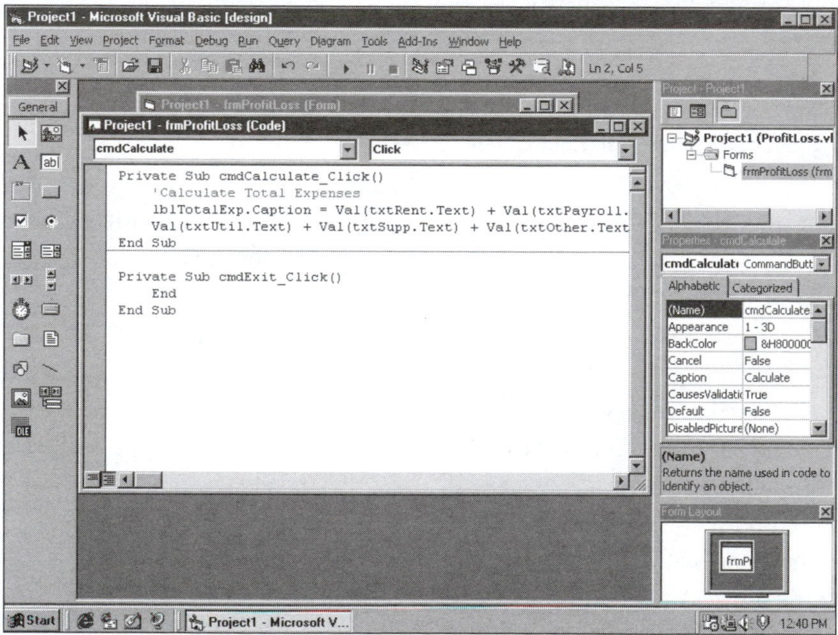

FIGURE 4-5
The Calculate button totals the data on the form.

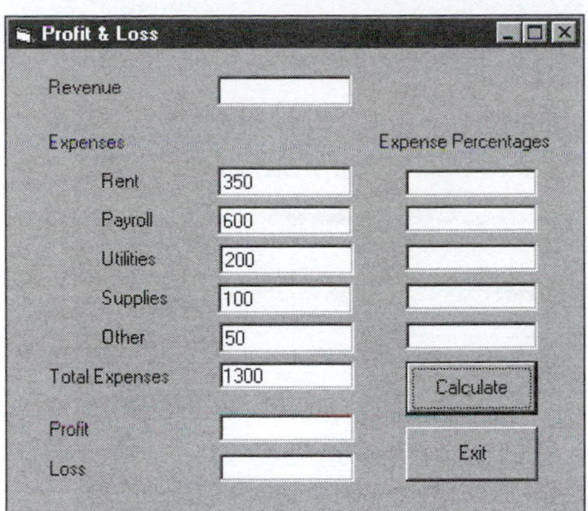

Hot Tip

When you use parentheses in code, count to be sure you have an equal number of left and right parentheses.

Using the Subtraction Operator

The subtraction operator subtracts the value to the right of the operator from the value to the left of the operator. In other words, it works just the way you learned in elementary school.

In Step-by-Step 4.4, notice that profit is calculated by subtracting the value in a label from the value in a text box. You extract the value from a label using the Caption property.

STEP-BY-STEP 4.4

1. Double-click the **Calculate** button.
2. Click at the end of the second line of code and press the **Enter** key twice to create a blank line.
3. Add code in CODE Step 3 to calculate the profit.

   This code will subtract the value in the label named lblTotalExp from the value in the text box named txtRev and assign the result to the Caption property of the label named lblProfit. Your screen should appear similar to Figure 4-6.
4. Close the Code window and run the program.
5. Key the same data for expenses that you keyed in Step-by-Step 4.3. Key **1200** in the Revenue field.
6. Click the **Calculate** button. Both the Profit field and the Total Expenses field store the results of the calculation as shown in Figure 4-7.
7. Click the **Exit** button to close the program.
8. Save the changes but leave the project open for Step-by-Step 4.5.

Note

In code step 3 for the profit calculation, the Val function is not necessary to extract the value from the lblTotalExp caption to a numeric value, we could assume that the caption is still a numeric value. However, using the Val function in cases like this is good practise.

CODE STEP 3

```
'Calculate Profit
lblProfit.Caption = Val(txtRev.Text) - Val(lblTotalExp.Caption)
```

FIGURE 4-6
The subtraction operator subtracts one value from another.

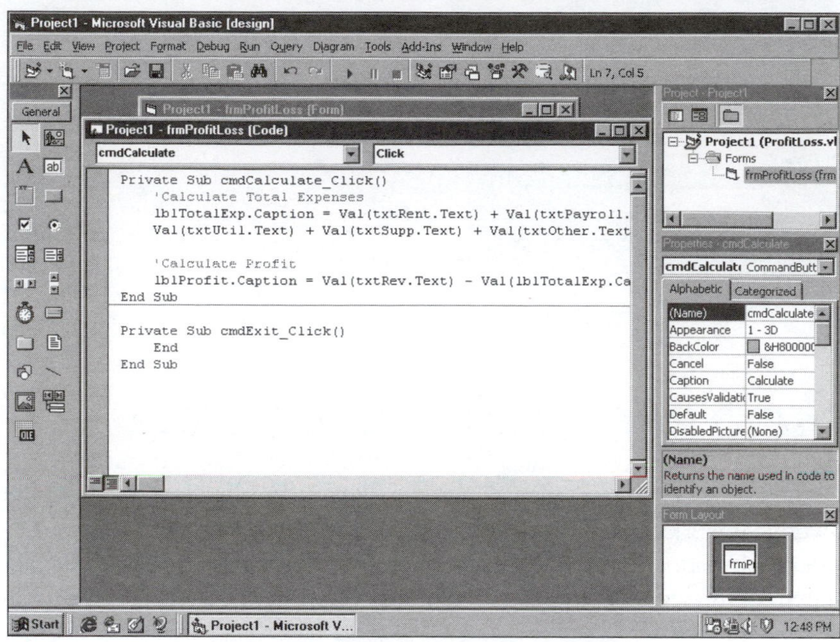

FIGURE 4-7
The Calculate button figures the profit.

Using Unary Minus

You can use the subtraction operator as *unary minus* to perform negation, which means making a positive value negative or making a negative value positive. For example, the statement below takes the value in the label named lblAnswer and changes the sign of the value. If lblAnswer is holding a negative number, the unary minus will make it positive. If the value in the label is already positive, the unary minus will make it negative.

```
lblNegatedAnswer.Caption = -Val(lblAnswer.Caption)
```

The addition operator can be used as a unary plus. The unary plus is rarely used, however, because it has little practical value. Values in Visual Basic are assumed to be positive unless they are specifically signed as negative.

STEP-BY-STEP 4.5

1. Double-click the **Calculate** button.
2. Add the code in CODE Step 2 beneath the code that calculates the profit.

   This code will convert the value in the label named lblProfit to a positive value and assign the result to the Caption property of the label named lblLoss.
3. Close the Code window and run the program.
4. Refer to Step-by-Step 4.3 – 4.4 for data to enter into the program for expenses and revenue.
5. Click the **Calculate** button. The loss is now calculated as well as the total expenses and profit, as shown in Figure 4-8.
6. Click the **Exit** button.
7. Save the changes but leave the project open for Step-by-Step 4.6.

CODE STEP 2

```
'Calculate Loss
lblLoss.Caption = -Val(lblProfit.Caption)
```

FIGURE 4-8
The negated profit represents the loss.

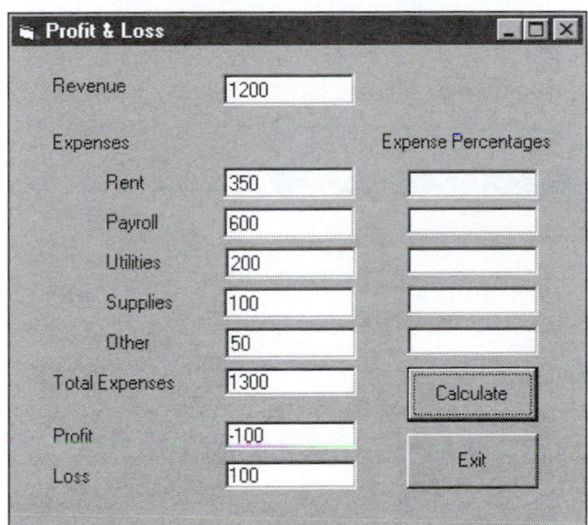

Using the Multiplication and Division Operators

Multiplication and division are represented by symbols that are slightly different from those used in standard mathematics. An asterisk (*) represents multiplication and a forward slash (/) represents division. These symbols are used for multiplication and division in most programming languages because they are available on a standard computer keyboard.

Using Fix

There are times when you are interested in only whole numbers after a calculation is performed. Most programming languages include a function that drops the fractional part of a number. In other words, the function removes everything to the right of the decimal point. This process is called *truncation*. In Visual Basic, the *Fix function* returns the truncated whole number.

In the program you have been creating in the step-by-steps of this lesson, we need to calculate the percentage of the total expenses that are allocated to each of the expense categories. For example, in the case of the Rent expense, the amount spent on rent must be divided by the total expenses and then multiplied by 100 to have a percentage. Using the multiplication and division operators, that calculation can be performed with the following code.

```
Val(txtRent.Text) / Val(lblTotalExp.Caption) * 100
```

The result of this calculation usually will have a fractional part. If all we are interested in is the whole number percentage, the Fix function can be used to truncate the result.

```
Fix(Val(txtRent.Text) / Val(lblTotalExp.Caption) * 100)
```

By placing the entire expression in parentheses, the Fix function is applied to the result of the entire expression.

STEP-BY-STEP 4.6

1. Double-click the **Calculate** button to open the Code window.
2. Add the code in CODE Step 2 beneath the code that calculates the loss.
3. Close the Code window and run the program.
4. Enter **1500** for Revenue, **350** for Rent, **700** for Payroll, **250** for Utilities, **100** for Supplies, and **60** for Other on the form.
5. Click the **Calculate** button. Each of the percentages is calculated, as well as the total expenses, profit, and loss, as shown in Figure 4-9.
6. Click the **Exit** button.
7. Save the changes to the project, then choose **Remove Project** from the **File** menu.
8. Leave Visual Basic open for Step-by-Step 4.7.

FIGURE 4-9
The program calculates the percentage of the total that each expense represents.

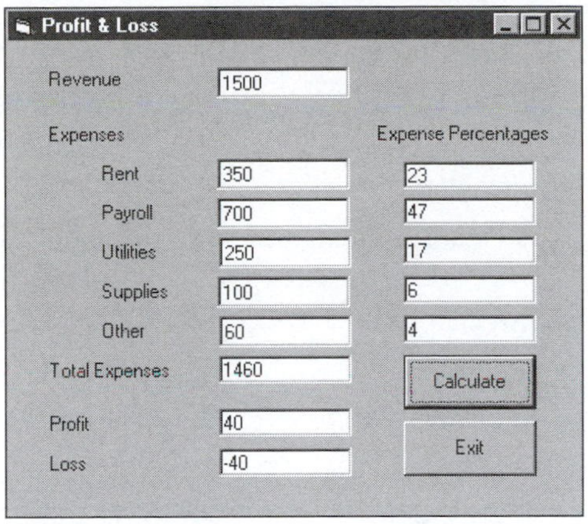

Profit & Loss			
Revenue	1500		
Expenses		Expense Percentages	
Rent	350	23	
Payroll	700	47	
Utilities	250	17	
Supplies	100	6	
Other	60	4	
Total Expenses	1460	Calculate	
Profit	40	Exit	
Loss	-40		

CODE STEP 2

```
'Calculate Expense Percentages
lblRentPerc.Caption = Fix(Val(txtRent.Text) / _
Val(lblTotalExp.Caption) * 100)
lblPayrollPerc.Caption = Fix(Val(txtPayroll.Text) / _
Val(lblTotalExp.Caption) * 100)
lblUtilPerc.Caption = Fix(Val(txtUtil.Text) / _
Val(lblTotalExp.Caption) * 100)
lblSuppPerc.Caption = Fix(Val(txtSupp.Text) / _
Val(lblTotalExp.Caption) * 100)
lblOtherPerc.Caption = Fix(Val(txtOther.Text) / _
Val(lblTotalExp.Caption) * 100)
```

Performing Integer Division and Using Modulus

In computer programming, there are times when you want to work exclusively with whole numbers, called *integers*. When performing division, however, the results are often fractional, even when you begin with whole numbers. For example, 5 and 3 are both integers, but when you divide 5 by 3, the result is fractional (1.666667).

For cases where you want to work strictly with integers, Visual Basic provides two special operations: integer division and modulus. *Integer division* returns only the whole number portion of the division of integers. *Modulus* returns the remainder of integer division.

Performing Integer Division

Integer division is performed using the backward slash (\), often called simply a back slash. This operation returns a whole number. For example, 5 \ 3 returns 1 as the result.

STEP-BY-STEP 4.7

1. Choose **Open Project** from the **File** menu. Open the **Division** project from your template files.

2. If necessary, open form **frmdivision**. Your screen should appear similar to Figure 4-10.

3. Double-click the **Calculate** button.

4. Add the code in CODE Step 4 to calculate the quotient. Be sure to use the back slash (\) for integer division when keying the code below.

5. Close the Code window and run the program.

6. Enter **6** in the field outside the division bar (the divisor) and **10** inside the division bar (the dividend).

7. Click the **Calculate** button. The quotient is calculated and the results are displayed to the left of the r as shown in Figure 4-11.

8. Click the **Exit** button. The program closes.

9. Save the changes but leave the project open for Step-by-Step 4.8.

FIGURE 4-10
The Division form appears on your screen.

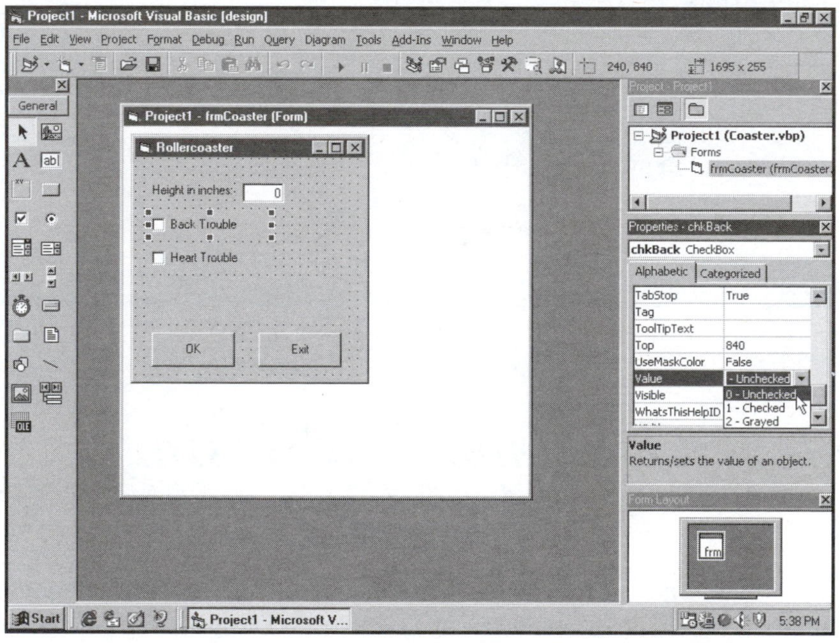

FIGURE 4-11
The Calculate button calculates the quotient.

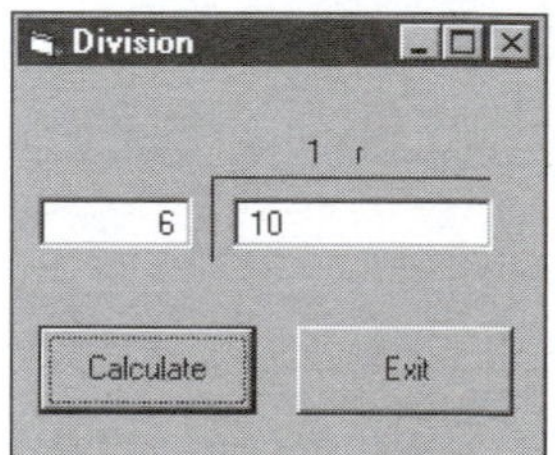

CODE STEP 4

```
'Calculate Quotient
lblQuotient.Caption = Val(txtDividend.Text) \ Val(txtDivisor.Text)
```

Using the Modulus Operator

The modulus operator (Mod) returns the remainder of integer division. For example, 5 Mod 3 returns the result 2 because 5 divided by 3 is 1 remainder 2.

Note

Unlike other operators, Mod is not a single character. Nevertheless, Mod functions as an operator.

STEP-BY-STEP 4.8

1. Double-click the **Calculate** button.
2. Add the code in CODE Step 2 to calculate the remainder.
3. Close the Code window.
4. Change the **Default** property of the **Calculate** button to **True**.
5. Change the **Cancel** property of the **Exit** button to **True**.
6. Run the program. Enter **5** in the field outside the division bar (the divisor) and **27** inside the division bar (the dividend).
7. Click the **Calculate** button. The quotient and remainder are calculated and the results are displayed above the division bar, as shown in Figure 4-12.
8. Click the **Exit** button. The program closes.
9. Save the changes to the project and form, then exit Visual Basic.

FIGURE 4-12
The Calculate button calculates the quotient and remainder.

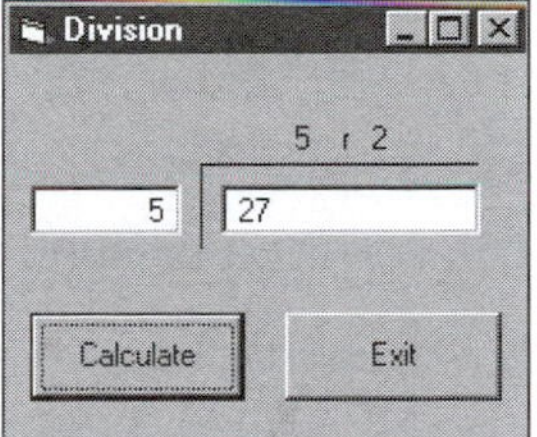

CODE STEP 2

```
'Calculate Remainder
lblRemainder.Caption = Val(txtDividend.Text) Mod Val(txtDivisor.Text)
```

Summary

In this lesson, you learned:

- Visual Basic allows you to use mathematical equations in your programs.
- Operators are symbols that perform specific operations in Visual Basic statements.
- The addition operator (+) adds values.
- The assignment operator (=) assigns the result of the expression on the right of the operator to the item to the left of the operator.
- Values keyed directly into Visual Basic code are called hard-coded values or literals.
- Text boxes are the fields placed on dialog boxes and in other windows that allow the user to enter a value.
- The numbers in a text box are considered to be text characters. To use the numbers as actual values in a calculation, the Val function must be used to convert the numeric text to a numeric value.
- When a line of code is long, you can split the code into two lines in the Code window by keying an underscore at the end of the line and continuing the statement on the next line. The underscore is called the line-continuation character.
- Placing an apostrophe in code allows you to enter text (called a comment) into the code. Everything from the apostrophe to the end of the line will be ignored.
- The subtraction operator (-) subtracts the value to the right of the operator from the value to the left of the operator.
- The subtraction operator can be used to perform negation. When used in this way, the subtraction operator is called the unary minus.
- Multiplication is represented by an asterisk (*).
- Division is represented by a forward slash (/).
- The Fix function removes the fractional portion of a number. The Fix function performs an operation called truncation.
- Integer division returns only the whole number portion of the division of integers.
- Integer division is represented by a backward slash (\).
- The modulus operator (Mod) returns the remainder of integer division.

LESSON 4 REVIEW QUESTIONS

TRUE/FALSE

Circle T if the statement is true or F if the statement is false.

T F 1. Operators are symbols that perform specific operations in Visual Basic statements.

T F 2. Values entered directly into Visual Basic code are called hard-coded or literals.

T F 3. Text boxes are fields on a form that allow the user to enter a value.

T F 4. Text boxes store user input in a numeric format.

T F 5. The subtraction operator and the unary minus operator are two different characters.

T F 6. The addition operator cannot be used as a unary plus.

T F 7. The back slash character is used for integer division.

T F 8. The result of integer division is the remainder of the division.

T F 9. The Val function truncates the fractional part of a number.

T F 10. In Visual Basic an expression cannot take up more than one line.

WRITTEN QUESTIONS

Write a brief answer to the following questions.

1. List the seven mathematical operators covered in this lesson.
2. What are the differences between the forward slash and the back slash?
3. Which operator returns the remainder of integer division?
4. Which character is used as the line-continuation character?
5. Which character is used to begin comment statements?
6. What is the purpose of the Fix function?
7. What prefix commonly begins text box names?
8. What must you do to use information stored in the Text property of a text box in numeric calculations?
9. Write the code for a command button that will calculate the result of multiplying values in two text boxes, *num1* and *num2*, and display the result in a label called *lblResult*.
10. The following code appears in the *cmd_Click* subroutine of a command button. What will happen when the button is clicked?

```
lblResult.Caption = 12 \ 7
```

LESSON 4 PROJECTS

PROJECT 4-1

Your local high school is having a bake sale to raise money for a local charity. You have been asked to write a program that will calculate the total sales and show the percentages of each item sold during the bake sale. The program's user interface should look similar to Figure 4-13. The form and each item on the form should be given a caption (use Figure 4-13 as your guide). Use the following names for the form and the items on the form: **frmBakeSale, lblSalesPercent, lblCookies, lblCakes, lblPies, lblMuffins, txtCookies, txtCakes, txtPies, txtMuffins, lblCookiesPerc, lblCakesPerc, lblPiesPerc, lblMuffinsPerc, lblTotalSalesLabel, lblTotalSales, cmdExit,** and **cmdCalculate**. For the four bake sale item text boxes, delete the text in the Text property box. For the four percent labels and the total sales label, delete the text in the Caption property and use the BackColor property and the Palette tab to change the labels to a white background and change the Border property to Fixed Single. You will need to align and resize items on the form by either dragging them or using the Top, Left, Height, and Width properties.

FIGURE 4-13
Create a program with a user interface like the one shown here.

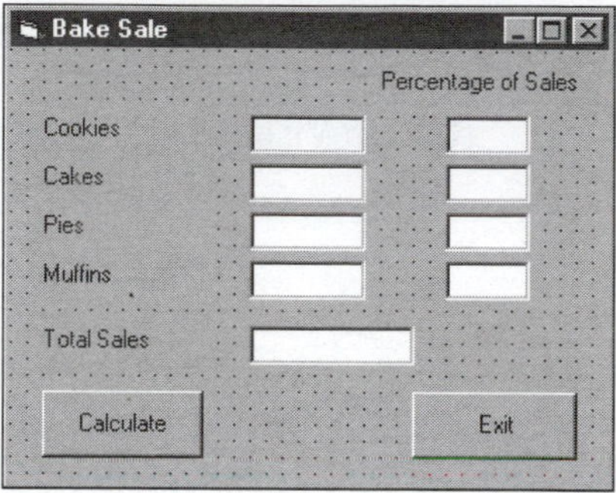

1. Start Visual Basic and open a new Standard EXE project.

2. Create the form on Figure 4-13 using the guidelines given above.

3. Save your program with an appropriate form and project name.

4. Add code so the **Exit** button will end the program.

5. Add code so the amounts in the four text boxes will be added and the result assigned to the Caption property of the label named lblTotalSales.

6. Add code so that the percent of total sales will be calculated for Cookies, Cakes, Pies, and Muffins. (Hint: Use the Fix function.)

7. Close the Code window, run the program, enter appropriate values, click the **Calculate** button to test the output labels, and then end the program.

8. Save the changes to your program and remove the project from the screen.

PROJECT 4-2

A local jewelry company has asked you to write a program that will calculate sales commission for their employees. The business gives their employees 4 percent of their total sales. Create the form similar to Figure 4-14.

1. Open a new project. Give your form an appropriate name and caption.
2. Create the labels for **Employee** and **Total Sales** with appropriate names and captions. Align the labels at the left.
3. Use the TextBox tool to create the text boxes to the right of Employee and Total Sales with appropriate names. Align them with the associated labels to the left. Delete the text for the Text property boxes for the two text boxes.
4. Create the label for **Commission Earned** and name it **lblCommissionLabel** (don't forget the caption). Create a label to the right of Commission Earned with the name **lblCommission** (delete the text in the Caption property box).
5. Create the **Calculate** and **Exit** command buttons with appropriate names and captions.
6. Add code to make the **Exit** button end the program.
7. Add code to calculate 4 percent of the amount entered in the Total Sales text box and assign the result to the caption of the label named lblCommission.
8. Close the Code window, run the program, enter appropriate values, click the **Calculate** button to test the Commission Earned box, then click the **Exit** button.
9. Save your program with an appropriate form and project name, then exit Visual Basic.

FIGURE 4-14
Create a program with a form similar to the one shown here.

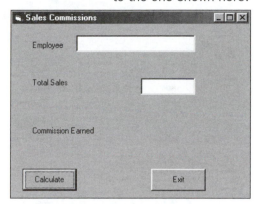

CRITICAL THINKING

Write a program to calculate the number of buses needed to transport a specified number of people to summer camp. Policy states that you can only order as many buses as you can completely fill. The remaining campers will ride in vans and cars. The program should prompt the user to input the number of people needing transportation and the number of people that can fit on a single bus. The program should calculate the number of buses that must be ordered and the number of people who will need to ride in vans and cars. (*Hint:* Use integer division and the modulus operator to calculate the outputs.)

LESSON 5

Exponentiation, Order of Operations, and Error Handling

OBJECTIVES

When you complete this lesson, you will be able to:

- Use the exponentiation operator to raise numbers to a power.
- Describe the order of operations.
- Use the Visible property to enhance output.
- Describe the purpose of comments in programs.
- Handle run-time errors using Debug and the On Error GoTo statement.
- Display messages using the MsgBox function.
- Control program flow using the Exit Sub statement.

Estimated Time: 2 hours

Exponentiation

In Lesson 4, you learned about the basic mathematical operators. There is one more operator required to complete the set of math operators: exponentiation. *Exponentiation* is the process of raising a number to a power.

The symbol that represents exponentiation is the caret (^). The operator raises the number to the left of the operator to the power that appears to the right of the operator. For example, to raise 2 to the 16th power, the Visual Basic code would appear thus by:

```
2^16
```

Order of Operations

From your math classes, you may recall the rules related to the order in which operations are performed. These rules are called the *order of operations*. Visual Basic uses the same set of rules for its calculations.

Ask yourself, what is the result of the calculation below?

```
1 + 2 * 3
```

Is it 9? Not if you follow the rules of the order of operations. The order of operations states that multiplication is performed before addition, so the calculation is performed as shown in Figure 5-1, resulting in the correct answer, which is 7.

The basic order of operations is as follows:

1. Exponentiation
2. Unary plus and minus
3. Multiplication, division, integer division, Mod
4. Addition and subtraction

Operations are performed from left to right. For example, if a formula includes three addition operators and two multiplication operators, the multiplication operators are applied from left to right, then the addition operators are applied from left to right.

Visual Basic allows you to use parentheses to override the order of operations. If you intend for 1 + 2 * 3 to result in 9, then you can use parentheses to force the addition to be performed first, as shown in Figure 5-2.

FIGURE 5-1
The order of operations causes multiplication to be performed before addition.

```
X = 1 + 2 * 3
X = 1 +   6
    X = 7
```

FIGURE 5-2
Parentheses can be used to override the order of operations.

```
X = (1 + 2) * 3
    X = 3   * 3
      X = 9
```

Note

Operations within parentheses are performed first. But within the parentheses, the order of operations still applies. You can, however, place parentheses inside of parentheses.

STEP-BY-STEP 5.1

1. Start Visual Basic.
2. Open the **Interest** project from your template files. The Interest project, when completed, will calculate the amount of money you will have in a savings account in the future if a specified amount of money is put into a savings account today.
3. If necessary, open the **Forms** folder from the Project Explorer window and double-click the form **frmInterest**. Your screen should appear similar to Figure 5-3.
4. Double-click the **Calculate** button.
5. Add the code in CODE Step 5 to calculate the total in the account at the end of the savings period and to show the number of years entered by the user in the output. Your screen should appear similar to Figure 5-4.

When calculating the future value, the Val function is used to extract the numeric values from the text boxes. The multiplication, addition, division, and exponentiation operators are used to perform the required calculation. The Fix function truncates the result to round it down to the nearest whole number. The truncated result is assigned to the Caption property of the label named lblTotal.

6. Close the Code window and run the program.

7. Enter the following data into the form.

Amount Deposited	**1500**
Interest Rate in %	**8**
Number of Years Saved	**15**

8. Click the **Calculate** button. The data is calculated and displayed on the form as shown in Figure 5-5.

9. Click the **Exit** button. The program closes.

10. Save the changes to the project but leave it open for Step-by-Step 5.2.

FIGURE 5-3
The Interest Calculation form appears on your screen.

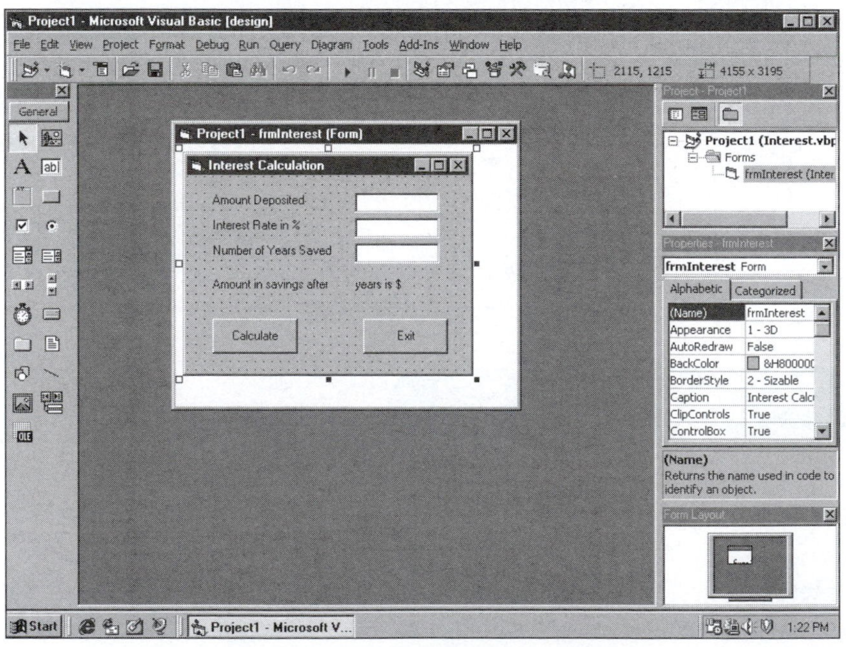

CODE STEP 5

```
'Calculate future value
lblTotal.Caption = Fix(Val(txtDeposit.Text) * _
(1 + (Val(txtInterest.Text) / 100)) ^ Val(txtYears.Text))

'Repeat the number of years saved in the output
lblYearsSaved.Caption = Val(txtYears.Text)
```

FIGURE 5-4
The formula that calculates the future value of the saved money uses exponentiation.

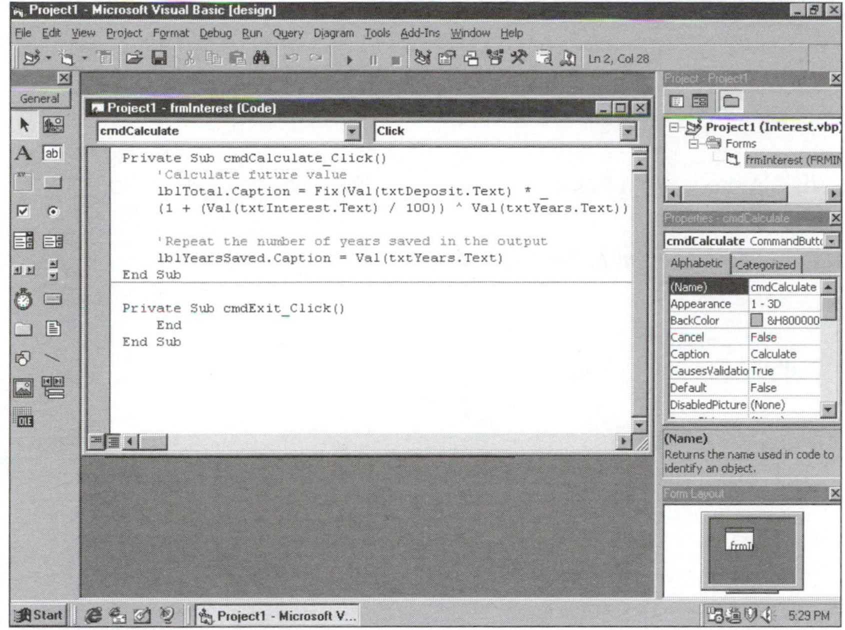

Using the Visible Property to Enhance Output

FIGURE 5-5
The Calculate button calculates the data and displays it on the form.

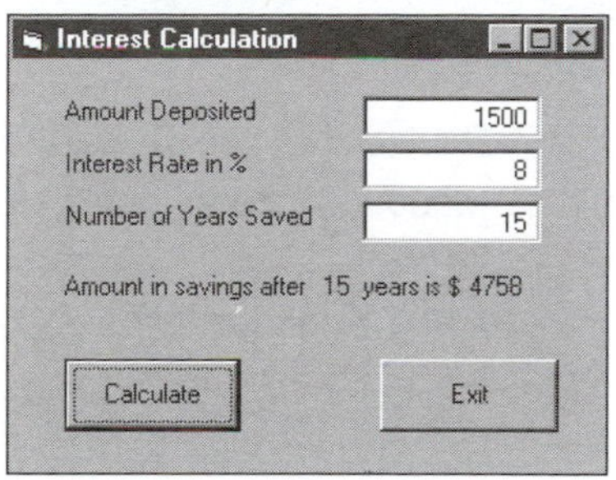

You have used the Visible property to make an image appear and disappear. There are many more uses for the Visible property. Another example of a useful application of the Visible property is preventing labels from appearing until you are ready for the user to see the label.

For example, in the Interest project, the user enters an amount of money deposited, the interest rate, and the number of years the money will be in the account. The program may have a better appearance if the line that displays the output is not visible until the output has been calculated.

By initially setting the Visible property of the output labels to False, the output will remain invisible until you make the labels visible in the code.

STEP-BY-STEP 5.2

1. Click the bottom-left label with the caption "Amount in savings after".

2. Change the **Visible** property to **False**.

3. Click the bottom-right label with the caption "years is $".

4. Change the **Visible** property to **False**.

5. Run the program to see that the labels do not appear, as shown in Figure 5-6.

6. Click the **Exit** button.

7. Save the changes to the project but leave it open for Step-by-Step 5.3.

FIGURE 5-6
The Visible property is used to hide the output labels.

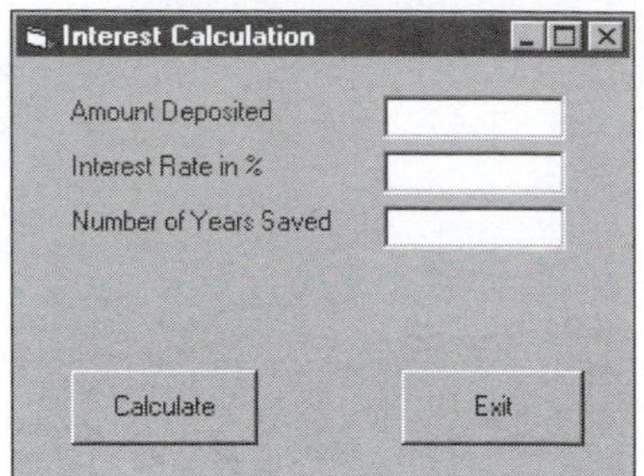

The code to make the labels visible can be placed in the Calculate button Click event procedure.

STEP-BY-STEP 5.3

1. Double-click the **Calculate** button. The Code window appears.

2. Add the code in CODE Step 2 at the bottom of the procedure to set the Visible property of the two hidden labels to True when the Calculate button is clicked.

3. Close the Code window and run the program.

4. Enter the following values in the input fields.

Amount Deposited	**2500**
Interest Rate in %	**7.5**
Number of Years Saved	**10**

5. Click the **Calculate** button. The output labels appear as shown in Figure 5-7.

6. Click the **Exit** button.

7. Save the changes to the project but leave it open for Step-by-Step 5.4.

FIGURE 5-7
The Calculate button sets the bottom two labels' Visible properties to True.

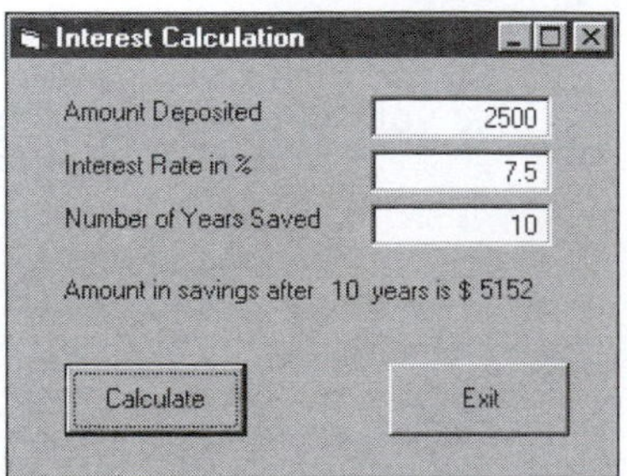

CODE STEP 2

```
'Make output visible
lblLabel1.Visible = True
lblLabel2.Visible = True
```

Using Comments

In the previous lesson, and in the Interest project you have been working on, you used the apostrophe to create comments in your code. Whenever you want to add a note or comment to a program, you can key an apostrophe, followed by any text you want to add to the line. The compiler will ignore everything from the apostrophe to the end of that line.

Comments can appear on their own line, like the comments you entered in the previous lesson. Comments can also be added to the end of a line of code. For example, the code below has a comment attached to the end of the statement.

```
lblAnswer.Visible = False   'Hide lblAnswer
```

When writing a program, you may think that you will remember what you did and why. Most programmers, however, eventually forget. But more importantly, others may need to make changes in a program you wrote. They probably will be unaware of what you did when you wrote the program. That is why comments are important.

You can use comments to:

- explain the purpose of a program
- keep notes regarding changes to the source code
- store the names of programmers for future reference
- explain the parts of your program

Comments added to programs are often called *internal documentation.*

Important

Remember, the compiler will ignore everything on the line that follows the apostrophe. Therefore, you can add a comment to the right of a code statement, but code added to the right of a comment will not execute.

Handling Run-Time Errors

The programs you have written up to this point have assumed that the user will always enter valid data and that nothing will go wrong with the calculations. In the real world, however, users will enter all kinds of unexpected data, or fail to enter required data. These error conditions are sometimes called *exceptions*. The term exception comes from the idea that normally things will go smoothly, with the *exception* of certain instances.

Exceptions are also called *run-time errors*. A run-time error is any error that occurs when the program is running. Run-time errors are not detectable at the time the program is compiled because the error is caused by conditions that do not exist until the program is running. A common run-time error is division by zero. Division by zero is not a legal mathematical operation. So if conditions are such that division by zero occurs while a program is running, a run-time error or exception occurs.

Let's take a look at an example of what happens when an error occurs in a Visual Basic program. The Interest project should still be open on your screen.

STEP-BY-STEP 5.4

1. Run the program.

2. Enter **999999** for Amount Deposited and for Number of Years Saved and enter **99** for Interest Rate.

3. Click the **Calculate** button. An error dialog box appears in the middle of the screen as shown in Figure 5-8.

4. Click the **Debug** button on the error dialog box. The Code window becomes active, and the line of code where the error occurred becomes highlighted. Your screen should appear similar to Figure 5-9.

5. Close the Code window and click the **End** button on the standard toolbar. The program ends and the form becomes active on the screen.

6. Save the changes to the project but leave the project open for Step-by-Step 5.5.

Hot Tip

Comments can help you debug programs (find and correct errors). If you are unsure whether a line of code should be removed from a program, add an apostrophe to the left of the code, rather than deleting the code. The line will be ignored the next time you run the program. If you change your mind about removing the line of code, just remove the apostrophe.

FIGURE 5-8
An error dialog box appears when the Calculate button is clicked and inaccurate data has been entered.

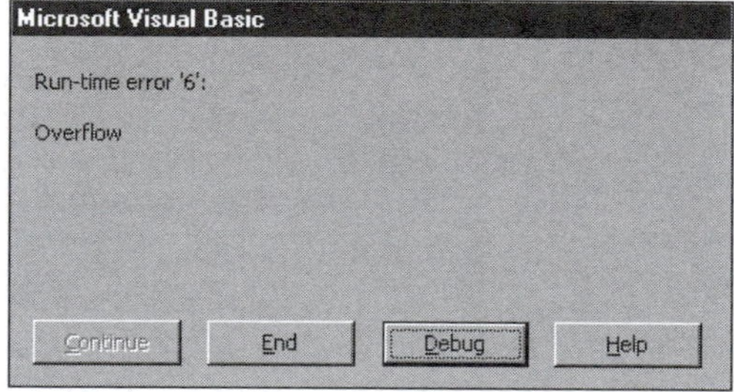

FIGURE 5-9
The Debug button highlights the failed code.

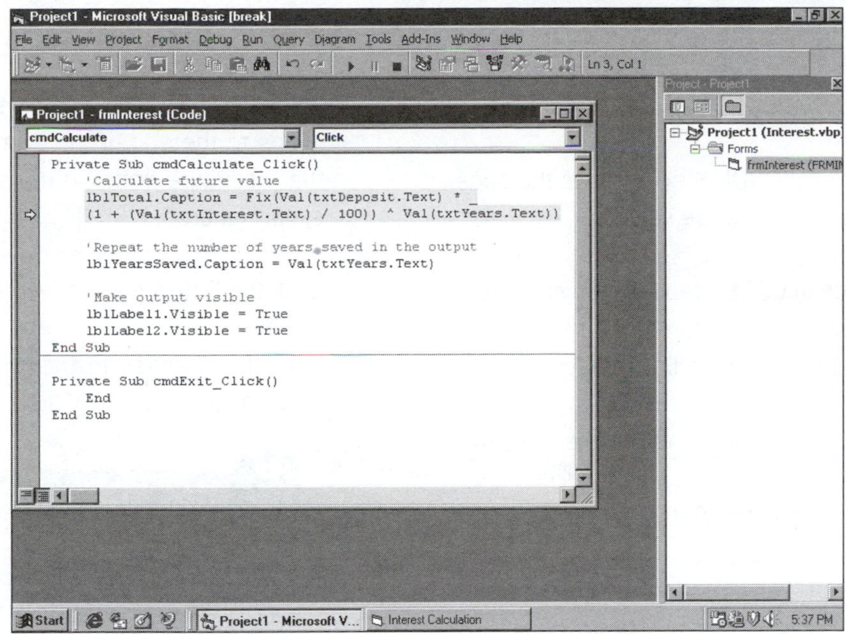

Trapping Run-Time Errors with the On Error GoTo Statement

When an error or exception occurs, you would rather your program handle the situation gracefully, rather than halt with some standard error message like the one in Step-by-Step 5.4.

Visual Basic allows you to write code that will be executed when a run-time error occurs. To specify what code will execute when an error occurs, you must turn on *error trapping*. Error trapping is the process of interrupting the normal chain of events that occurs when an error is encountered and replacing that chain of events with your own code.

To turn on error trapping, use the On Error GoTo statement above the code that might generate a run-time error. The On Error GoTo statement specifies the line of code that the program should jump to if an error occurs. The code that will be executed if an error occurs is often called an *error handler* or *error-handling routine*.

Using Code Labels

In order for the On Error GoTo statement to have a line to go to, you must use what is called a *code label* to create a spot to which the program can jump if an error occurs. A code label is just a name that appears in the code, followed by a colon. The code label marks the line in the code to which you want to jump if an error occurs.

The Code window will force code labels to appear against the left margin. If you indent a code label when you key it, the code label will jump back to the left margin when you press the Enter key.

Hot Tip

Code labels have uses other than in error trapping. There are ways to make an execution jump to a specific portion of a program, even when no error occurs. However, forcing execution to jump to other parts of the code should only be done in extreme circumstances, such as error condition.

STEP-BY-STEP 5.5

1. Double-click the **Calculate** button.

2. Add the code in CODE Step 2 above the code that calculates the future value.

3. Add the code in CODE Step 3 at the end of the event procedure, but before the End Sub. Your screen should appear similar to Figure 5-10.

4. Close the Code window and run the program.

5. Enter **99** for Interest Rate and **999999** for the other two values.

6. Click the **Calculate** button. Notice that this time the error dialog box does not appear. When an error occurs, the execution simply jumps to the end of the event procedure and the procedure ends. In essence, the error is simply ignored.

7. Click the **Exit** button.

8. Save the changes to the project but leave it open for Step-by-Step 5.6.

Hot Tip

The code label used for an error handler does not have to be named ErrorHandler. Any descriptive code label could be used.

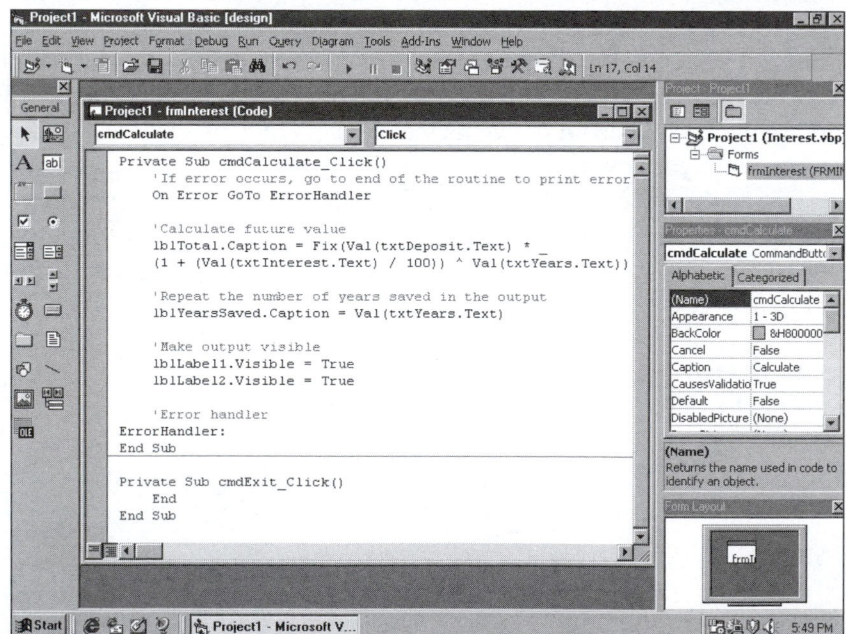

FIGURE 5-10
The On Error GoTo statement causes the execution to jump to the ErrorHandler code label if an error occurs.

CODE STEP 2

```
'If error occurs, go to end of the routine to print error message
On Error GoTo ErrorHandler
```

CODE STEP 3

```
'Error handler
ErrorHandler:
```

Using MsgBox

One of the easiest ways to display a message of your own, such as an error message, is to use the MsgBox function. The *MsgBox function* causes a dialog box to pop up, displaying a message that you specify. Besides being easy to use, the MsgBox function gives your programs a more professional look and feel.

The MsgBox function provides a convenient way to display an error message when you trap an error with the On Error GoTo statement. You can add the code for the MsgBox function after the ErrorHandler code label to cause a dialog box to appear, explaining the error to the user.

An example of how to use the MsgBox function appears below. In the parentheses that follow the MsgBox keyword, you can place a custom message that you want to appear in the dialog box. The message must appear in quotation marks.

```
MsgBox("Illegal entry. Please try again.")
```

STEP-BY-STEP 5.6

1. Double-click the **Calculate** button.
2. Add the code in CODE Step 2 just below the ErrorHandler code label to display a message box when an error occurs.
3. Close the Code window and run the program.
4. Enter **99** for Interest Rate and **999999** for the other two values.
5. Click the **Calculate** button. A message box appears explaining that incorrect values were entered, as shown in Figure 5-11.
6. Click the **OK** button to dismiss the message box.
7. Click the **Exit** button.
8. Save the changes to the project but leave it open for Step-by-Step 5.7.

CODE STEP 2

```
MsgBox ("The values you entered resulted in an error. Try Again.")
```

FIGURE 5-11
A message box appears when an error occurs.

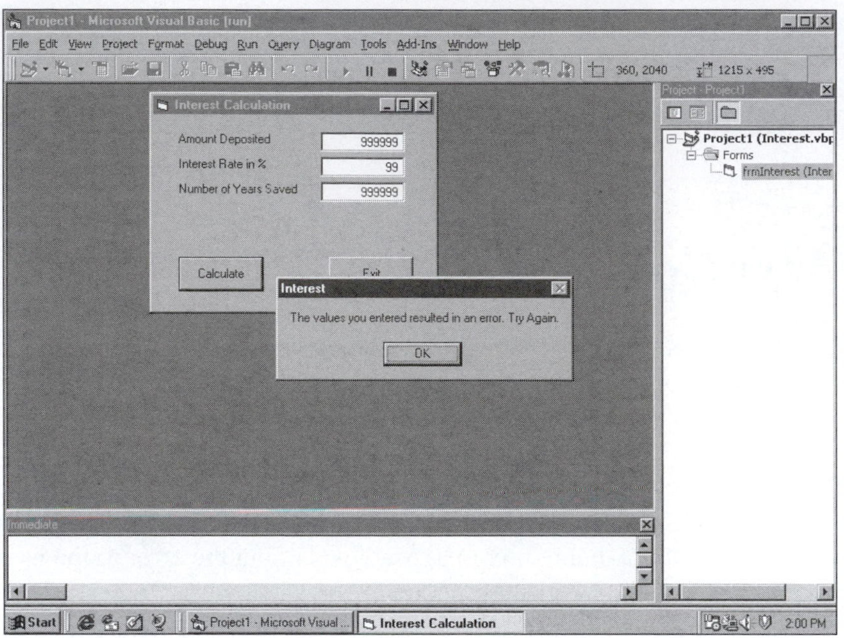

Controlling Program Flow around the Error Handler

The program appears to be trapping errors correctly. However, further use of the application will reveal that the program does not operate correctly. Even when no error occurs, the error message is displayed.

STEP-BY-STEP 5.7

1. Run the program again.
2. Enter **1500**, **8**, and **15** in the three fields, then click the **Calculate** button. The output is displayed correctly, and the error message still appears.
3. Click the **OK** button to dismiss the message box.
4. End the program.
5. Save the changes to the program but leave it open for Step-by-Step 5.8.

The reason the error message always appears is because the code for the error handler is at the bottom of the same event procedure that calculates the output. Therefore, when the code that generates the output is complete, execution continues right into the error handler. So even though the On Error GoTo statement did not force the flow of execution to the error handler, the flow of execution reached the error handler in its normal progress through the event procedure.

You can use the *Exit Sub statement* to prevent this from occurring. The Exit Sub statement forces the event procedure to end, regardless of whether there is more code in the procedure. By placing the Exit Sub statement *above* the error handler, you can cause the procedure to end before the error handler code is executed. The error trapping that you activated with the On Error GoTo statement will still be able to force the flow of execution to jump to the error handler. However, when no error occurs, the procedure will end when the flow of execution reaches the Exit Sub statement.

It is also a good idea to place an Exit Sub statement at the end of the error handler. Even though the procedure will terminate when the Exit Sub statement is reached, placing an Exit Sub at the end of the error handler will prevent problems in the future if an additional code label and code is placed below the error handler.

Figure 5-12 shows the revised event procedure code, with error handling and the Exit Sub statements in place.

FIGURE 5-12
The Exit Sub statements ensure proper program flow.

```
Private Sub cmdCalculate_Click()
    'If error occurs, go to end of the routine to print error message
    On Error GoTo ErrorHandler

    'Calculate future value
    lblTotal.Caption = Fix(Val(txtDeposit.Text) * _
    (1 + (Val(txtInterest.Text) / 100)) ^ Val(txtYears.Text))

    'Repeat the number of years saved in the output
    lblYearsSaved.Caption = Val(txtYears.Text)

    'Make output visible
    lblLabel1.Visible = True
    lblLabel2.Visible = True

    'End procedure
    Exit Sub

    'Error handler
ErrorHandler:
    MsgBox ("The values you entered resulted in an error. Try Again.")
    Exit Sub
End Sub
```

STEP-BY-STEP 5.8

1. Double-click the **Calculate** button.

2. Modify the code in the cmdCalculate_Click event procedure to match the code shown in Figure 5-12 (note that there are two places for the Exit Sub code).

3. Close the Code window.

4. Run the program, enter **99** for the Interest Rate and **999999** for the other two values and click the **Calculate** button to generate the error.

5. Click the **OK** button to dismiss the dialog box.

6. Enter **2500**, **7.5**, and **10** in the input fields and calculate again. When no error occurs, the message box is not displayed.

7. End the program.

8. Save the changes to the project and exit Visual Basic.

Summary

In this lesson, you learned:

- The exponential operator (^) raises a number to a power.
- The rules that dictate the order that math operators are applied in a formula are called the order of operations.
- Parentheses can be used to override the order of operations.
- The Visible property can be used to hide a label until you are ready for the user to see it.
- The apostrophe is used to add comments to Visual Basic code.
- Comments allow you to keep track of changes in code and explain the purpose of code.
- Comments are often called internal documentation.
- Errors that occur while a program is running are called run-time errors or exceptions.
- Visual Basic allows you to trap errors using On Error GoTo to direct program execution to code that you specify when an error occurs.
- A code label is a name that appears in code, followed by a colon. You can direct program execution to jump to the code label.
- The MsgBox function pops up a dialog box, delivering a message to the user.
- When you redirect the flow of execution using On Error GoTo, you must use the Exit Sub to end the event procedure before the error handler code is reached.

LESSON 5 REVIEW QUESTIONS

TRUE/FALSE

Circle T if the statement is true or F if the statement is false.

T F 1. Exponentiation is the process of raising a number to a power.

T F 2. Addition and subtraction are evaluated before multiplication and division.

T F 3. Exponentiation will be evaluated first since it appears first in the order of operations.

T F 4. Parentheses can appear within another set of parentheses.

T F 5. You cannot override the order of operations in Visual Basic.

T F 6. The Visible property can be used on labels as well as images.

T F 7. Visual Basic code will be executed if it appears to the right of comment statements.

T F 8. A program will not compile if it contains a run-time error.

T F 9. The Exit Sub statement can appear more than once in a subroutine.

T F 10. You can use the MsgBox function to display custom error messages.

WRITTEN QUESTIONS

Write a brief answer to the following questions.

1. Which symbol is used for the exponentiation operator?
2. Why is it important that programmers be aware of the order of operations?
3. Why might parentheses be used in an expression?
4. What symbol indicates a comment?
5. What is internal documentation?
6. What statement is used to trap exceptions?
7. Why are code labels important in error trapping?
8. What is an error-handling routine?
9. What happens when an Exit Sub statement is executed?
10. What is another name for run-time errors?

LESSON 5 PROJECTS

PROJECT 5-1

Evaluate the following expressions.

Expression	Result
2 * 3 + 1	____________
1 + 2 * 3	____________
4 / 2 + 6 * 2	____________
4 / (2 + 6) * 2	____________
4 * 4 + 2 – 1	____________

7 + 2 * 3 – 2 ______________

1 + 2 * 3 – 9 / 3 ______________

12 / 3 + 1 + 12 * 2 – 5 ______________

(5 + 7) / 3 + 7 * 2 – 5 ______________

5 + 8 / 2 – 16 / 2 + 3 * 6 ______________

PROJECT 5-2

Write a program that prompts the user for two values, as shown in Figure 5-13. The program should use the exponential operator to calculate the result of raising the first number to the second.

1. Start Visual Basic and open a new project.
2. Use the TextBox tool to insert two text boxes with one slightly above and to the right of the other, as shown in Figure 5-13. The lower text box should be named **txtBase** and the upper text box should be named **txtExponent**. Change the Text property for both text boxes to **0**.
3. Use the label tool to add the label for the equal sign. It should be named **lblEqual** and the caption should be the = sign. Change the **Font** property to **14 point**.
4. Use the Label tool to add a blank label to the right of the equal sign. It should be named **lblResult** and the caption should be deleted. The font should also be 14 point.
5. Add a **Calculate** command button.
6. Give your form an appropriate name and caption.
7. Add code to the **Calculate** button so the caption of the label named lblResult will contain the answer of the number entered for txtBase raised to the number entered for txtExponent.
8. Close the Code window, run the program, enter a value for the base (the lower text box) and a value for the exponent (the upper text box), and click the **Calculate** button.
9. End the program, save your form and project with an appropriate name, and remove the project from the screen.

FIGURE 5-13
Create a program with a form like the one shown below.

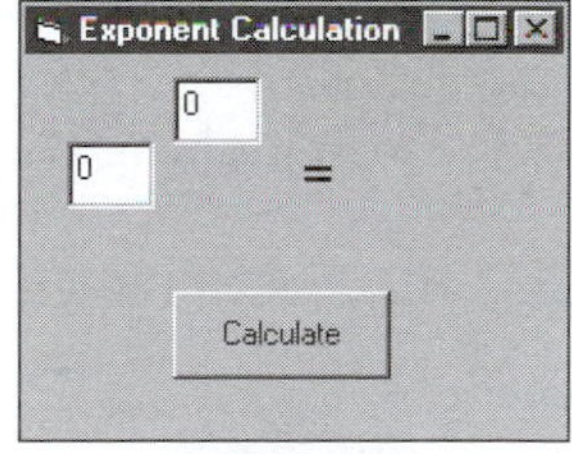

PROJECT 5-3

1. Open the **Division** project you worked with in Lesson 4.
2. Add code to the **Calculate** button for **On Error GoTo ErrorHandler** and **ErrorHandler:**, including comments for both lines.

3. Add code for a message of your choice.

4. Close the Code window and run the program with no values, then click the **OK** button to dismiss the error message.

5. Test again with valid entries (you should still get the error message). Click the **OK** button to dismiss the message, then end the program.

6. Add the **Exit Sub** statement to the code and test the program again with valid entries.

7. End the program, save the changes to your project, and remove the project from the screen.

PROJECT 5-4

1. Open the **Buses** project created from the Critical Thinking activity in Lesson 4.

2. Your project should have two labels at the top of the form with text boxes to their right. Below those four items your form should have two additional labels with blank labels to their right. Change the Visible property of the bottom four labels to False so they won't display when you first run the program.

3. Modify the code for the **Calculate** button so the four labels whose Visible property you changed to False will be displayed when you run the program with valid entries.

4. Run the program to verify that it works (the bottom four labels should be invisible until you enter numbers in the top two text boxes and click the Calculate button).

5. Save the changes to the project.

6. Exit Visual Basic.

CRITICAL THINKING

The National Weather Service at your local airport measures rainfall by taking readings from three rain gauges at different locations on the airport property. These three readings are averaged to determine the official rainfall total. Write a program that will accept the rainfall amounts from the three rain gauges and produce output that averages the three readings.

LESSON 6

DATA TYPES AND VARIABLES

OBJECTIVES

When you complete this lesson, you will be able to:

- Describe the purpose of data types and variables.
- Use the AutoSize property.
- Declare and use variables.
- Describe the scope of variables.
- Use the Variant data type and the Option Explicit statement.

Estimated Time: 2 hours

Data Types

Computers are all about data. Practically all useful programs are involved in collecting, processing, storing, and delivering data. There are many kinds of data. You might first think of numbers when you hear the word data. Of course, data also can be in the form of text, dates, sounds, and pictures.

> **Note**
>
> You already have some experience with data types. The Val function converts one type of data (text) to another (a numeric value).

All data in a computer is actually stored numerically. As you learned in an earlier lesson, even text is stored as numbers. When you program, however, it is often important to know what type of data you are working with and to specify types of data.

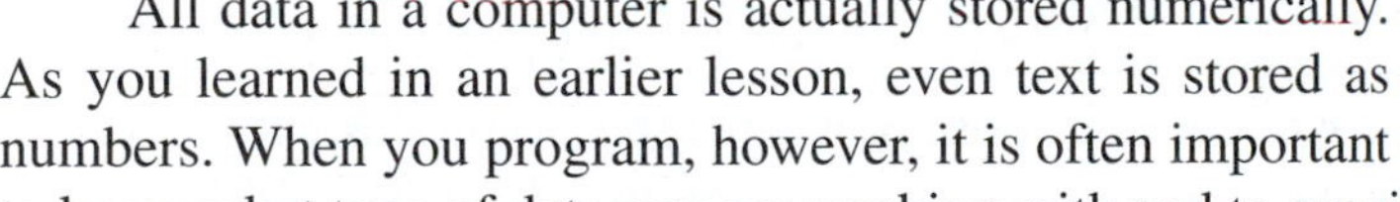

Visual Basic supports a certain set of data types. There are data types for whole numbers, floating-point numbers (decimals), text, dates, and more. Table 6-1 shows the ten most common Visual Basic data types.

The integer data types are used when you need to use whole numbers (numbers without a decimal point). There are three integer data types. The most common integer data type is the one named Integer. But if the values you intend to store might be outside the range of an Integer, use the Long data type instead.

The decimal types are Single, Double, and Currency. The Single data type can store data with up to seven digits of precision. If you need more precision than that, use the Double data type. For dollar amounts, use the Currency data type.

The other types of data are for storing text, dates, and True or False values. You will learn more about these data types in later lessons.

TABLE 6-1

DATA TYPES

DATA TYPE	RANGE
Integer Data Types	
Byte	0 to 255
Integer	-32,768 to 32,767
Long	-2,147,483,648 to 2,147,483,647
Decimal Types	
Single	-3.402823E+38 to 3.402823E+38
Double	-1.79769313486232E+308 to 1.79769313486232E+308
Currency	-922,337,203,685,477.5808 to 922,337,203,685,477.5807
Other Types	
String	1 to about 65,000 characters
Date	January 1, 100 to December 31, 9999
Boolean	True or False
Variant	Varies

You can choose to store data in memory locations called *variables*. Variables are a common feature of programming languages. Variables can be used to store and manipulate all kinds of data. For example, you can have a variable of the Integer data type that can store numbers from –32,768 to 32,767. Variables get their name from the fact that the value can vary as the program runs.

Using the AutoSize Property

The *AutoSize property* will adjust the size of a control to fit its contents. In the case of a label, the AutoSize property will shrink the label to fit the caption.

To learn about AutoSize and how variables can be used in a program, we are going to create a program that calculates your age in months.

STEP-BY-STEP 6.1

1. Start Visual Basic and create a new Standard EXE project.
2. Add five label controls to the form. Position them as shown in Figure 6-1.

STEP-BY-STEP 6.1 CONTINUED

3. Set the Name properties of the label controls to **lblAgeYears**, **lblMonths**, **lblYou**, **lblOutputMonths**, and **lblAgeMonths**.

4. Set the Name property of the form to **frmMonths** and the caption to **Month Converter**.

5. Save the form as **frmMonthConverter** and the project as **MonthConverter**.

6. Select all of the labels by positioning the pointer in the lower-right corner of the form and dragging up to the upper-left corner of the form.

7. From the **Properties** window, change the **AutoSize** property to **True**. The AutoSize of each of the selected labels is changed.

8. Set the captions of the five labels to **Age in years:**, **Months since last birthday:**, **You are**, **X**, and **months old.**, as shown in Figure 6-2. The size of each label changes as you key the captions.

9. Create two text boxes and one command button. Position and size the controls on the form as shown in Figure 6-2.

10. Set the name of the command button to **cmdMonths** and set the caption to **Calculate age in months**.

11. Change the names of the two text boxes to **txtYears** and **txtMonths** and delete the text in the Text property of the two text boxes. Your screen should appear similar to Figure 6-2.

12. Change the **Visible** properties of lblYou, lblOutputMonths, and lblAgeMonths to **False**. The output will not be visible when the program first runs.

13. Save the changes but leave the form open for Step-by-Step 6.2.

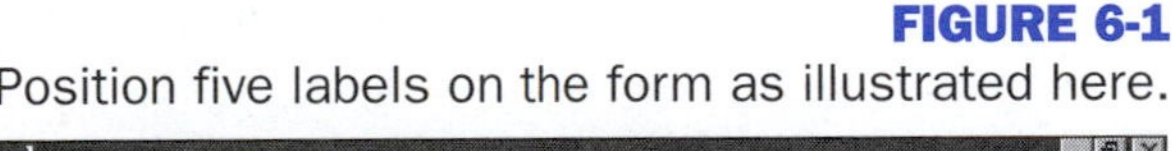

FIGURE 6-1
Position five labels on the form as illustrated here.

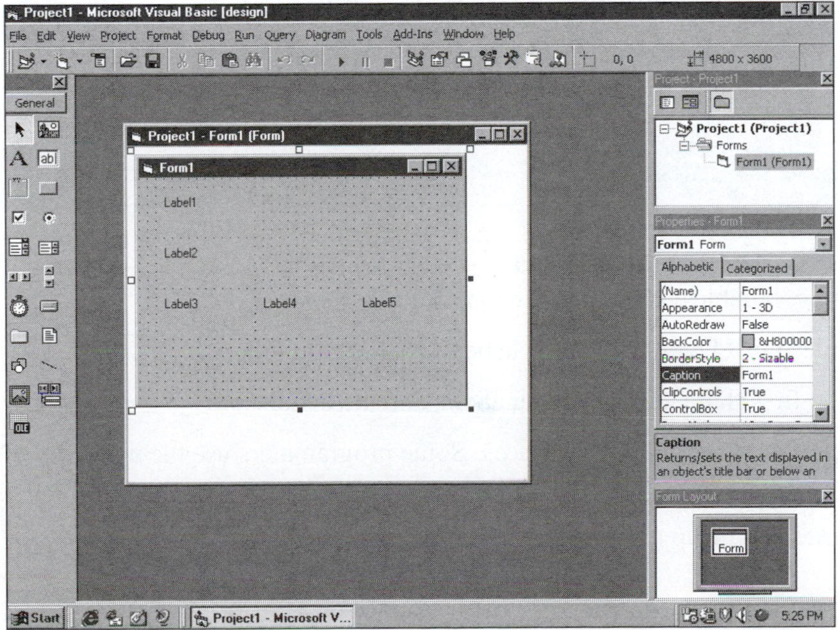

FIGURE 6-2
Change captions, and create text boxes and a command button like the ones shown here.

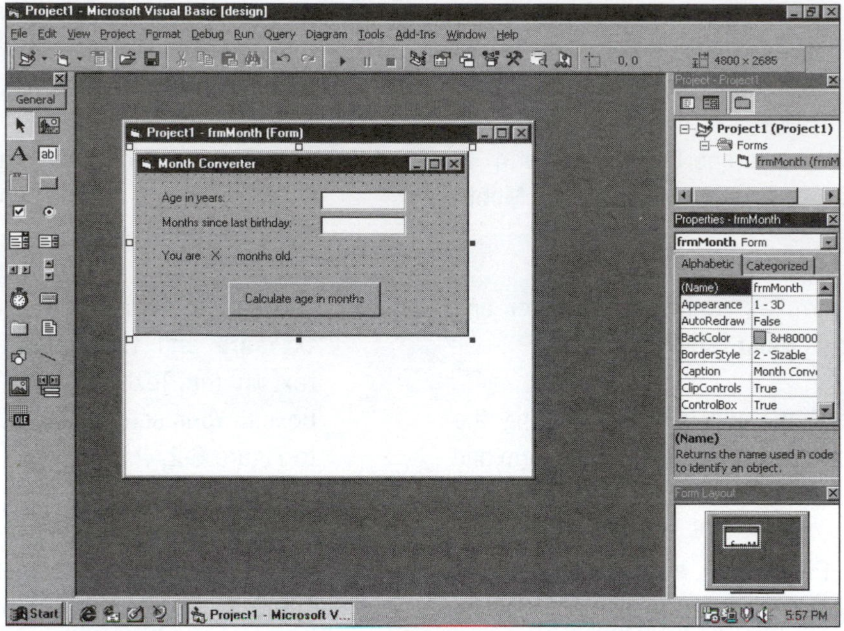

Declaring Variables

The first step to using a variable in your programs is to let the compiler know that you want to set up a memory location as a variable, what you want to call the variable, and what data type you want the variable to have. This process is called *declaring* a variable. To declare a variable, use the Dim statement as shown below.

```
Dim VariableName As DataType
```

For example, the following statement declares a variable named intAnswer with the Integer data type.

```
Dim intAnswer As Integer
```

Rules for Naming Variables

When naming variables, keep the following rules in mind.

1. Variable names must begin with an alphabetic character (a letter).
2. Following the first character, letters, numbers, and the underscore (_) are allowed.
3. Variable names cannot include any spaces. Some programmers use the underscore in places where you might want a space.
4. Variable names can be up to 255 characters long.

In the same way that a prefix can be used to identify a control's type, prefixes should be used to identify the data type of a variable. Table 6-2 shows the commonly used variable naming prefixes.

In Step-by-Step 6.2, you will declare a variable in a command button Click event procedure. Later in this lesson, you will learn that where you declare a variable affects the usage of the variable.

Note

Notice in the Dim statement example that the variable name is preceded by the int prefix. It is common to use naming prefixes with variables, as with controls.

TABLE 6-2

DATA TYPE PREFIXES

PREFIX	DATA TYPE	EXAMPLE
byt	Byte	bytCount
int	Integer	intPeople
lng	Long	lngInches
sng	Single	sngWeight
dbl	Double	dblMass
cur	Currency	curSalary
str	String	strName
dte	Date	dteAnniversary
bln	Boolean	blnSold
vnt	Variant	vntValue

STEP-BY-STEP 6.2

1. Double-click the **Calculate age in months** button. The Code window opens.

2. Key **Dim intMonths As Integer** at the top of the event procedure and press the **Enter** key twice.

   The intMonths variable will be used to store the user's age in months once that value is calculated.

3. Leave the Code window open for Step-by-Step 6.3.

Using Variables

Variables can be used in the same way you have been using labels and text boxes. Use the assignment operator to assign a value to a variable. For example, the code below assigns the value in the txtMonths text box to an Integer variable named intMonths.

```
intMonths = Val(txtMonths.Text)
```

You can also assign hard-coded values to a variable. For example, the code below assigns a value to a variable of type Double.

```
dblMass = 3.4568973
```

You can use the mathematical operators to perform calculations with numeric variables, as shown in the example below.

```
sngTotalWeight = sngProductWeight + sngPackagingWeight
```

To output or display the value in a variable, you can assign the value in a variable to a label, as shown in the example below.

```
lblTotalWeight.Caption = sngTotalWeight
```

Because variables have a specific data type, you do not have to use the Val function on a variable unless the variable is holding text (a string variable). Numeric variables cannot hold data that does not match the data type. Therefore, you can safely assume that the value in a numeric variable (such as sngTotalWeight) is a number.

STEP-BY-STEP 6.3

1. Below the variable declaration, add the code in CODE Step 1 to calculate the number of months.
2. Add the code in CODE Step 2 to display the results. Your screen should appear similar to Figure 6-3.
3. Close the Code window and run the program.
4. Enter **5** in the **Age in years** text box and enter **4** in the **Months since last birthday** text box.
5. Click the **Calculate age in months** button. The three labels become visible and display the results as shown in Figure 6-4.
6. Click the **Close** button on the Month Converter program's title bar. The program closes.
7. Save the changes to the project.
8. Leave the project open for Step-by-Step 6.4.

CODE STEP 1

```
'Calculate Months
intMonths = (Val(txtYears.Text) * 12) + Val(txtMonths.Text)
```

CODE STEP 2

```
'Display Number of Months Old
lblOutputMonths.Caption = intMonths
lblYou.Visible = True
lblOutputMonths.Visible = True
lblAgeMonths.Visible = True
```

FIGURE 6-3
The intMonths variable holds the results of the calculation.

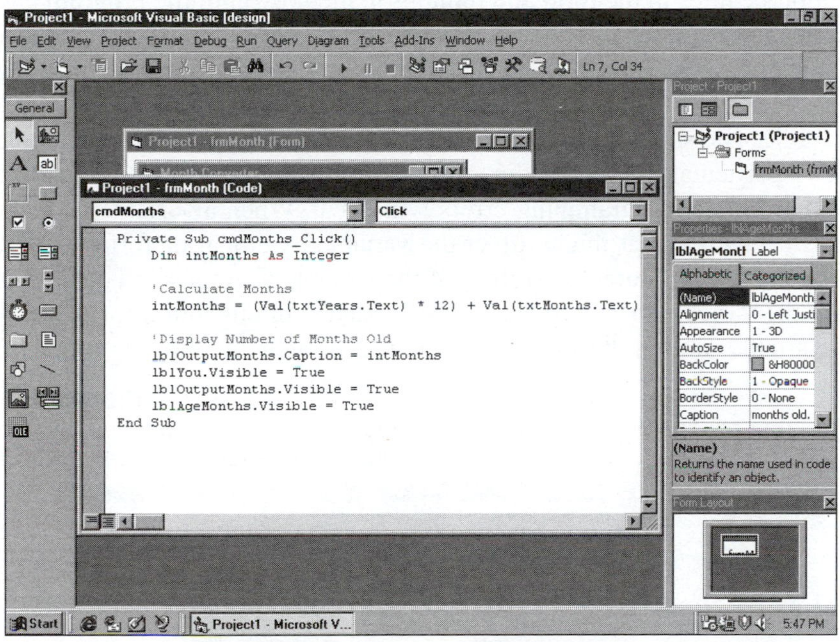

FIGURE 6-4
The Calculate age in months command button calculates the results and displays them on the form.

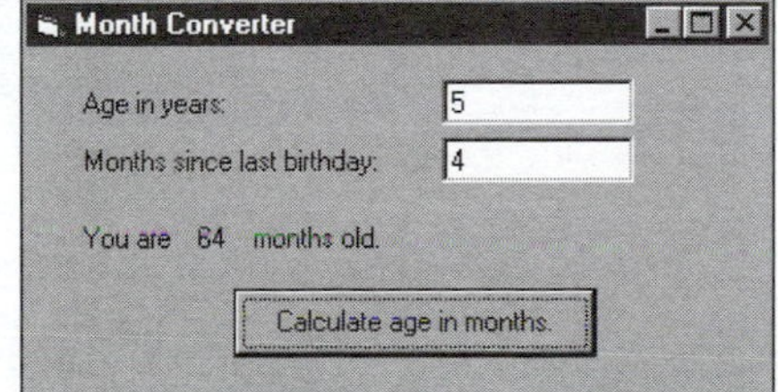

Scope

The term *scope* refers to the reach of a variable. In other words, a variable's scope indicates which procedures can use the variable. Where you declare a variable determines the variable's scope.

Three Levels of Scope

The scope of a variable in Visual Basic can be local, form-level, or global.

A *local variable* is declared within an event procedure, like the intMonths variable you declared in this lesson. The variable is only accessible to the code within that event procedure. In fact, the variable does not even exist outside of that procedure. The memory space is reserved for a local variable at the time the variable is declared in the event procedure. When the procedure ends, the variable is no longer kept in memory.

A *form-level variable* is declared in the General Declarations section of a form's Code window. You will learn how to access the General Declarations section later in this lesson. A form-level variable is accessible to all procedures in the form and remains in memory until the program ends.

A *global variable* is declared in a code module's General Declarations section. Global variables are primarily used in programs that involve multiple forms where data must be exchanged between the forms. You will not work with global variables in this textbook.

As a general rule, you should declare variables as locally as possible. For example, if a variable is needed only inside a particular event procedure, the variable should be declared locally. The more global a variable is, the more likely programming errors will occur. When a variable is declared locally, it is easier to trace all of the code that might affect the variable. A global or form-level variable could be affected by code in many procedures. Therefore, if the variable is not needed outside of the local event procedure, declare the variable locally. If a variable is needed throughout a form, declare it at the form level. Use global variables only if the variable is required throughout all of the forms of a program.

FIGURE 6-5
You can access the General Declarations section of the Code window by selecting (General) from the Object list.

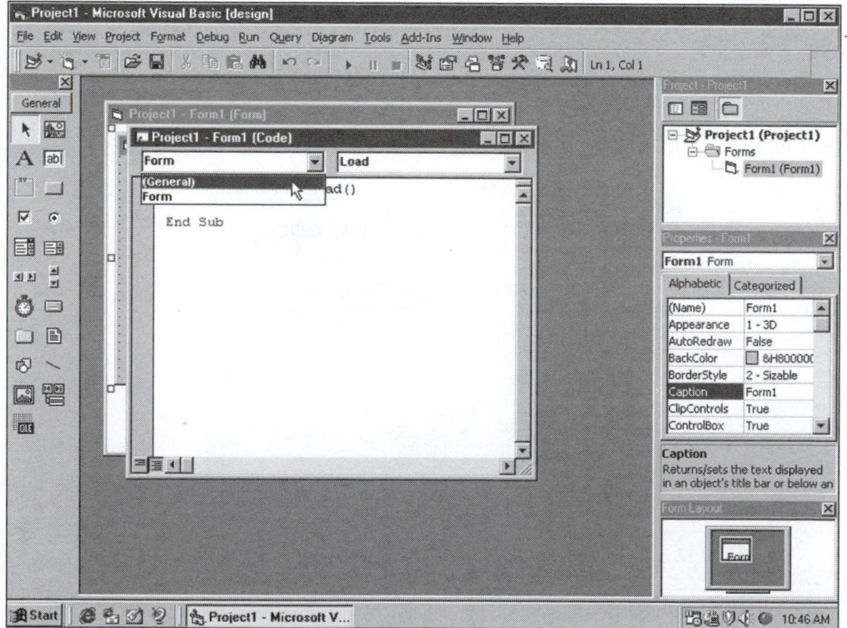

The General Declarations Section

You just learned that you can make a variable accessible to an entire form by declaring the variable in the General Declarations section of a form's Code window. To access the General Declarations section, select (General) from the Object list that appears at the top of the Code window, as shown in Figure 6-5.

In the next lesson, we are going to extend the month converter project to calculate the user's age in dog years, cow years, and mouse years. In order to calculate the dog years, cow years, and mouse years, we need the intMonths variable to be a form-level variable. As a form-level variable, we will be able to access intMonths from other event procedures on the form.

In Step-by-Step 6.4, you will move the intMonths variable declaration to the General Declarations section to give the variable form-level scope.

STEP-BY-STEP 6.4

1. Double-click the **Calculate age in months** button. The Code window opens.
2. Select **(General)** from the **Object** list at the top of the Code window (currently showing cmdMonth). The Code window should appear similar to Figure 6-6.
3. Key **Dim intMonths As Integer** and press the **Enter** key. A line appears below the General Declarations section.
4. Delete the intMonths declaration statement and the blank line below it from the Click event procedure.
5. Close the Code window.
6. Run the program and test with values to verify that the program still works.
7. Click the Close button on the corner of the Month Converter program.
8. Save the changes but leave the project open for Step-by-Step 6.5.

FIGURE 6-6
The General Declarations section is where you declare variables that need to be accessible to the whole form.

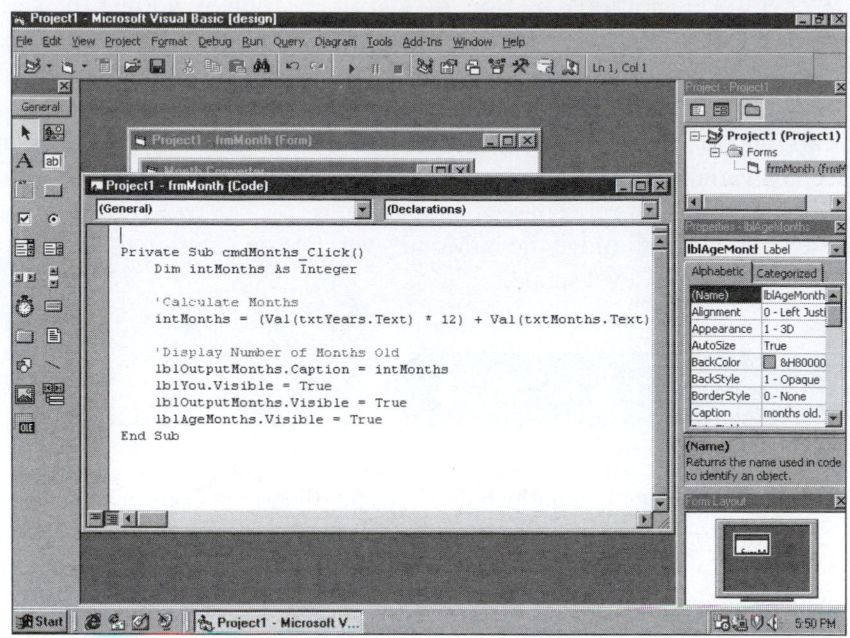

Using the Variant Data Type and Option Explicit

In Visual Basic, you should always declare your variables before you attempt to use them. However, if you fail to declare a variable before you use it, Visual Basic creates the variable for you and gives it the Variant data type. There is, however, a way to prevent variables from being used before they are declared.

The Variant Type

The *Variant* data type is very flexible. It can store many different types of data. It can store a number or text. A Variant is similar to a cell in a spreadsheet. When entering data in a spreadsheet, you don't have to declare a data type for each cell. If you key text in a spreadsheet cell, it will hold text. If you key an integer, it will hold an integer. If you key a dollar amount, it will hold that, too. The Variant type is not very efficient and should not be used unless you really need that flexibility. Whenever possible, you should select a specific data type for your variables.

There is a danger in Visual Basic's flexible way of working with variables. In most programming languages, if you try to use a variable that has not been declared, you will get an error message. In Visual Basic, the compiler just creates it for you. The danger is that you may declare a variable with one name and then attempt to use the variable with a different or misspelled name. For example, suppose you declared a variable named blnAllowed but when you use it, you accidentally key blnAlowed. Instead of giving an error, an additional variable named blnAlowed would be created, producing unpredictable results.

Option Explicit

Visual Basic has an option that prevents you from using variables that have not been declared. By entering the *Option Explicit* statement in the General Declarations section, you can cause Visual Basic to generate an error if you attempt to use a variable that has not been declared.

STEP-BY-STEP 6.5

1. Double-click the **Calculate age in months** button to access the Code window.
2. Move the cursor to the top line of the General Declarations section.
3. Press the **Enter** key to create a blank line above the intMonths declaration line.
4. Press the **up arrow** to move the cursor to the blank line you just created.
5. Key **Option Explicit** on the blank line. Your screen should appear similar to Figure 6-7.
6. Close the Code window and run the program to test it, then end the program.
7. Save your changes and exit Visual Basic.

FIGURE 6-7
The Option Explicit statement will prevent you from using undeclared variables.

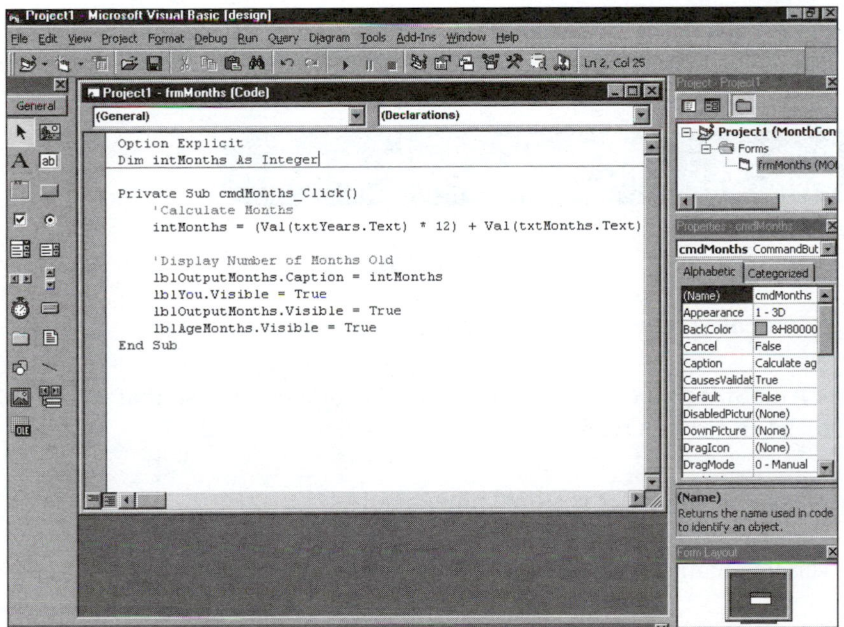

Summary

In this lesson, you learned:

- Data can be in the form of numbers, text, dates, pictures, and even sound.
- Visual Basic supports a set of data types. There are data types for whole numbers, floating-point numbers (decimals), text, dates, and more.
- You can choose to store data in memory locations called variables.
- The AutoSize property will adjust the size of a control to fit its contents.
- The first step to using a variable is to declare it using the Dim statement.
- When naming variables, keep the naming rules in mind. It is also a good idea to use naming prefixes to identify the data type of the variable.
- You can assign values to variables using the assignment operator. You can also use the other mathematical operators with numeric variables.
- A variable's scope indicates what procedures have access to a variable. A variable's scope can be local, form-level, or global.
- The General Declarations section of a form's Code window allows you to declare form-level variables.
- You should declare variables before you use them. Undeclared variables will have the Variant data type.
- The Variant data type can hold many different kinds of data, but it is less efficient than specific data types.
- The Option Explicit statement prevents variables from being used without first being declared.

LESSON 6 REVIEW QUESTIONS

TRUE/FALSE

Circle T if the statement is true or F if the statement is false.

T F 1. The AutoSize property will adjust the value of a number so that it will be in the range of a Visual Basic data type.

T F 2. All data in a computer is stored numerically.

T F 3. A variable name can begin with any alphanumeric character.

T F 4. In order to do calculations with variables, you must first convert them to hard-coded values.

T F 5. The position in which you declare a variable affects the usage of the variable.

T F 6. Variable scope refers to the range of the values a data type can hold.

T F 7. You can assign the value of a numeric variable to a label or text box without using the Val function.

T F 8. Visual Basic will always generate an error if you use a variable before it is declared.

T F 9. By declaring a variable in the General Declarations section of a form's Code window, you can make the variable accessible to an entire program.

T F 10. Using the Variant data type is much more efficient than using any of the other Visual Basic data types.

WRITTEN QUESTIONS

Write a brief answer to the following questions.

1. What are the three common integer data types?
2. What are the three common decimal data types?
3. What is the Dim statement used for?
4. Write Visual Basic code to declare an Integer variable called intNumber.
5. List three commonly used prefixes for naming variables.
6. Which operator assigns a value to a variable?
7. List the three levels of variable scope and give a brief description of each.
8. What type of data can be stored in a Variant variable?
9. What data type is given by default to undeclared variables?
10. What is the purpose of the Option Explicit statement?

LESSON 6 PROJECTS

PROJECT 6-1

1. Start Visual Basic and open the **Interest** program you worked with in Lesson 5.

2. Add the following code to the beginning of the Calculate button to declare three variables.

```
'Declare Variables
Dim intDeposit As Integer
Dim intInterest As Integer
Dim intYears As Integer
```

3. Just below the OnError GoTo statement, add code to set the values of the variables equal to the values in the corresponding text boxes. Example: **intDeposit = Val(txtDeposit.Text)**

4. Modify the code that calculates the future value so the three variables you added in step 2 are used in the calculation instead of the values in the text boxes. (Hint: Replace *txt* with *int* and delete the *.Text*. You can also delete the Val because the int variable always means numeric data. Do not delete the Fix. A left parenthesis follows Fix and precedes the number 1, and a right parenthesis follows 100 and intYears.)

5. Set the lblYearsSaved caption equal to the variable Years (intYears).

6. Run the program and verify that it works (do not use fractional interest rates such as 2.5).

7. Save the changes to the program.

8. Exit Visual Basic.

PROJECT 6-2

A railroad company has asked you to write a program to calculate the number of cars on a train and the total weight of the train when the cars are empty. The user interface of the program has already been created and saved as Train Template. The owner has given you the following data to use in each calculation.

Type of Car:	Weight of Car:
Box Car	65000
Caboose	48000
Refrigerated Car	59400
Tank Car	45200
Hopper Car	51300

1. Start Visual Basic and open **Train Template** from your data files.

2. Create two variables in the General Declarations section that stores the number of cars and the total weight of the train:
   a. Double-click any of the car command buttons and select **General** from the **Object** list box at the left.
   b. Key **Option Explicit** and press the **Enter** key.
   c. Key **Dim intTotalWeight As Long** and press the **Enter** key. (This variable will increment the caption for the lblWeight label each time you click a car command button when you run the program.)
   d. Key **Dim intCounter As Integer** and press the **Enter** key. (This variable will increment the caption for the lblNumber label each time you click a car command button when you run the program.)
   e. Close the Code window.

3. Add code (and comments) to each command button that adds the weight of the car named on the command button to the total weight of the train. Also add code to each button that adds 1 to the number of cars on the train. Display the results on the screen:
   a. Double-click the **Box Car** button.
   b. Key **'Add weight of car to total weight of train** and press the **Enter** key.
   c. Key **intTotalWeight = intTotalWeight + 65000**, then press the **Enter** key twice.
   d. Key **'Count total number of cars** and press the **Enter** key.
   e. Key **intCounter = intCounter + 1** and press the **Enter** key twice.
   f. Key **'Display Results** and press the **Enter** key.
   g. Key **lblNumber.Caption = intCounter** and press the **Enter** key.
   h. Key **lblWeight.Caption = intTotalWeight** and press the **Enter** key.
   i. Close the Code window, then repeat steps a-h for each of the cars' command buttons, using the appropriate weight. (Hint: You can copy the code from one car's event procedure to another, then change the weight.)

4. Add code to the **Exit** button to end the program.

5. Run the program and test it by clicking car command buttons at random. Each time you click a command button, the number of cars should increment by 1 and the total weight should increase by the weight of the car whose command button you clicked.

6. End the program and save your changes but leave the project open.

CRITICAL THINKING

The railroad company has asked you to modify the program you created in Project 6-2. The railroad would like the program to calculate the total length of the train as well as the total weight. Use the following values for the length of each car. Add labels for the total length on the form under the total weight, then add code for the length of each car. (Hint: Don't forget to add a line of code in the General Declarations section.)

Type of Car:	Length of Car in Feet:
Box Car	55
Caboose	36
Refrigerated Car	39
Tank Car	35
Hopper Car	46

STRINGS AND DECIMAL TYPES

LESSON 7

OBJECTIVES

When you complete this lesson, you will be able to:

- Declare string variables.
- Assign text to string variables.
- Concatenate strings.
- Use decimal data types.
- Use the Format function.
- Use the Enabled property.
- Use the SelStart and SelLength properties.

Declaring String Variables

In previous lessons, you have learned that Visual Basic has a special data type for working with text. Text is often called *alphanumeric* data because text can include letters or numbers. Text can also include other characters, such as periods, commas, and symbols.

In computer programming, data types that hold text are usually referred to as *strings*. The term string is used because text is a series of characters that have been strung together.

Visual Basic has a data type named String. When you declare a string using a statement like the one below, the resulting variable can hold a string of any practical length. The length of the string can also change as the program runs. The memory space required for the string is allocated as needed.

Note

Visual Basic does provide a way to create strings of fixed length. You will not use fixed-length strings in this unit. However, information about fixed-length strings can be found in the online help.

```
Dim strFirstName As String
```

Assigning Text to String Variables

When assigning text to a string variable, you must place the text in quotation marks, as shown in the code below.

```
strFirstName = "Kaley"
```

Hard-coded text, like the name *Kaley* in the example above, is called a *string literal*. You can also assign text from a text box to a string variable, as shown in the example below.

```
strFirstName = txtFirstName.Text
```

Often, you will assign the text from one string variable to another, as shown below.

```
strFirstName = strMyName
```

Actually, any expression that results in a string value can be assigned to a string variable. You will see other examples later.

Like a numeric variable, a string variable can only hold one string. Each time you assign a string to a string variable, the existing data in the variable is replaced.

STEP-BY-STEP 7.1

1. Start Visual Basic.
2. Open **StringCopy** from your data files and, if necessary, open the **frmCopy** form. Your screen should appear similar to Figure 7-1.
3. Double-click the **Copy Text** button. The Code window opens.
4. Select **General** from the **Object** list box (currently showing **cmdCopy**), then add the code in CODE Step 4 for the **General Declarations** section (press the **Enter** key after each line).
5. If necessary, select **cmdCopy** from the **Object** list box, then move the cursor just above the **End Sub** statement and press the **Tab** key.
6. Add the code in CODE Step 6 to copy the text in the first text box to a string variable and then copy the variable to the second text box.
7. Select **cmdReset** from the Object list box. A new section of code for the Reset Text Box 1 button appears in the Code window, as shown in Figure 7-2.
8. Add the code in CODE Step 8 to clear the text in the first text box and reset the strText variable.
9. Close the Code window and run the program.
10. Key **Visual Basic** in the first text box.
11. Click the **Copy Text** button. The words *Visual Basic* are copied to Text Box 2.
12. Click the **Reset Text Box 1** button. The first text is cleared.
13. Click the **Copy Text** button again. The contents of the strText variable (now blank) are copied to the second text box.

STEP-BY-STEP 7.1 CONTINUED

14. End the program and save the changes to the project.

15. Choose **Remove Project** from the **File** menu. The project closes.

16. Leave Visual Basic open for Step-by-Step 7.2.

FIGURE 7-1
This program will provide you with some practice declaring and using strings.

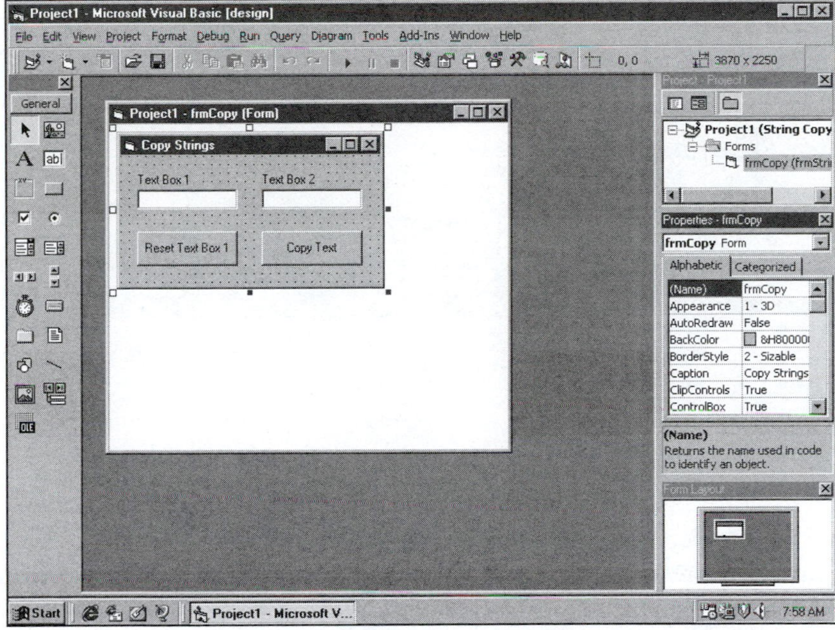

CODE STEP 4

```
Option Explicit
Dim strText As String
```

CODE STEP 6

```
'Copy txtText1 to txtText2
strText = txtText1.Text
txtText2.Text = strText
```

CODE STEP 8

```
'Reset the string variable and txtText1
strText = " "
txtText1.Text = strText
```

FIGURE 7-2
The Object list box generates the beginning code for an existing control.

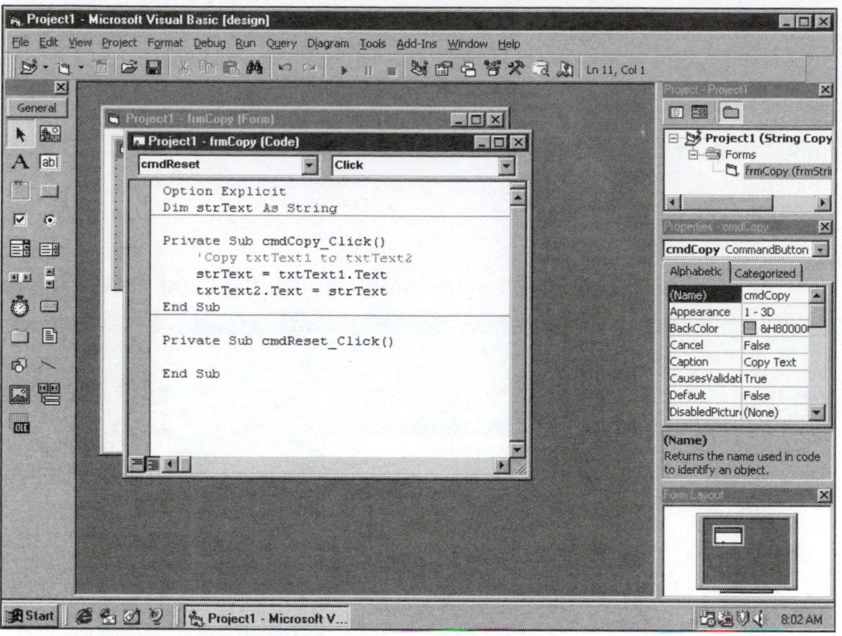

Concatenation

Just before Step-by-Step 7.1, you learned that each time you assign text to a string, the text already in the string is replaced. There are times, however, when you would like to add text to the existing string. In other words, you would like to "string" on more characters. Visual Basic allows you to do just that using an operation called *concatenation.*

Concatenation appends one string to the end of another. The ampersand (&) is used for concatenation. For example, the code below concatenates two string literals, resulting in a compound word, *bookkeeper.*

```
strCompoundWord = "book" & "keeper"
```

You can concatenate more than two strings in one expression. In addition, the strings can come from other variables or be string literals. In the example below, the first, middle, and last name are merged. String literals (in this case a pair of quotation marks with a blank space between them) are used to place a blank space between the names.

```
strFullName = strFirstName & " " & strMiddleName & " " & strLastName
```

The first, middle, and last names could just as easily come from text boxes.

```
strFullName = txtFirstName.Text & " " & txtMiddleName.Text & _
    " " & txtLastName.Text
```

STEP-BY-STEP 7.2

1. Open **Full Name** from your data files and, if necessary, open the **frmName** form. Your screen should appear similar to Figure 7-3.
2. Double-click the **OK** button.
3. Select **General** from the **Object** list box, then add the code in CODE Step 3 in the **General Declarations** section to create four String variables.
4. Select **cmdOk** from the **Object** list box.
5. Add the code in CODE Step 5 to set the variables equal to their corresponding text box.
6. Press the **Enter** key twice, then add the code in CODE Step 6 to concatenate the FirstName, MiddleName, and LastName variables into the FullName variable.
7. Press the **Enter** key twice, then add the code in CODE Step 7 to display the string on the form.
8. Close the Code window and run the program.
9. Key your first, middle, and last names into the appropriate text boxes.
10. Click the **OK** button. Your name appears at the bottom of the form as shown in Figure 7-4.
11. End the program and save the changes to the project.
12. Choose **Remove Project** from the **File** menu. The project closes.
13. Leave Visual Basic open for Step-by-Step 7.3.

CODE STEP 3

```
Option Explicit
Dim strFirstName As String
Dim strMiddleName As String
Dim strLastName As String
Dim strFullName As String
```

CODE STEP 5

```
'Initialize Variables
strFirstName = txtFirstName.Text
strMiddleName = txtMiddleName.Text
strLastName = txtLastName.Text
```

FIGURE 7-3
This program will use concatenation to create a string of your full name.

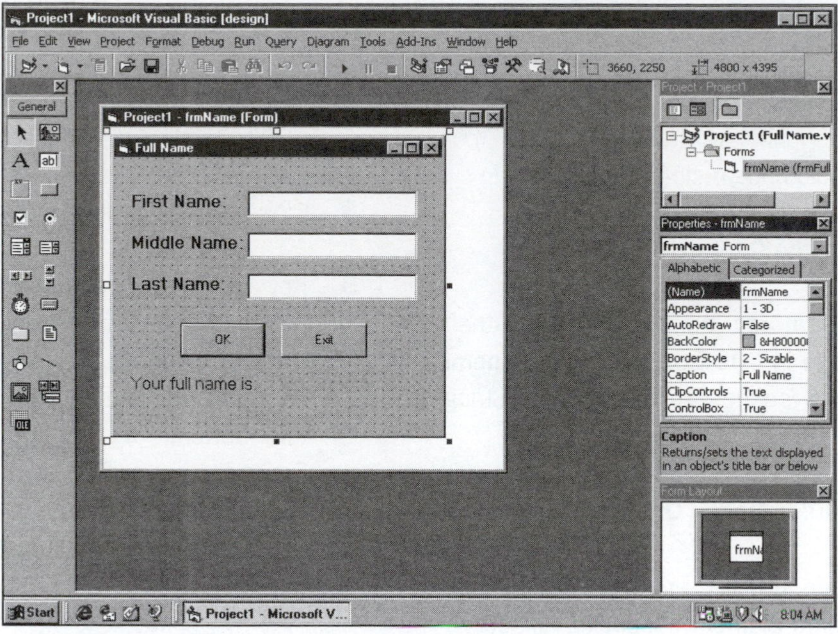

CODE STEP 6

```
strFullName = strFirstName & " " & strMiddleName & " " & strLastName
```

CODE STEP 7

```
lblFullName.Caption = strFullName
lblFullName.Visible = True
```

FIGURE 7-4
The concatenated string appears at the bottom of the form.

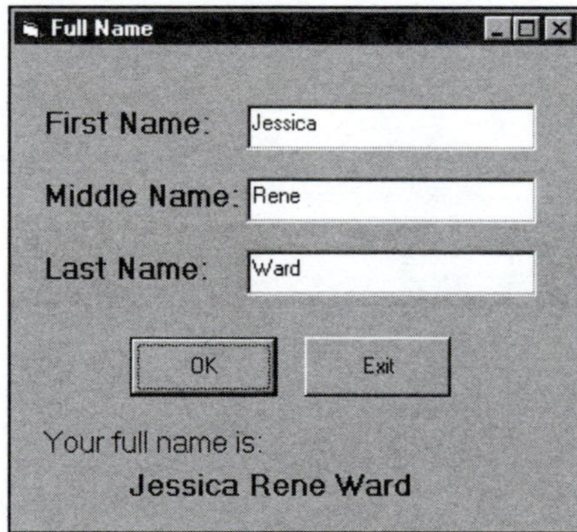

You can also use concatenation when creating the caption for a label. In Step-by-Step 7.3, you will use concatenation to create a single label to provide the user with the necessary output.

STEP-BY-STEP 7.3

1. Open the **Dog Years** program from your data files. The program is similar to the program you created earlier that calculates the number of months you have lived. By the end of this lesson, this program will convert your age into dog years. First, however, we will use concatenation to output your age in months.

2. If necessary, open the form **frmDogYears**. Your screen should appear similar to Figure 7-5.

3. Double-click the **Calculate age in months** button. The Code window appears.

4. Add blank lines below the intMonths code, then add the code in CODE Step 4 to create a string that will display the results.

5. Close the Code window and run the program.

6. Key **634** in the **Age in years** text box.

7. Click the **Calculate age in months** button. The answer is displayed above the command button. Your screen should appear similar to Figure 7-6.

8. End the program and save your changes but leave the project open for Step-by-Step 7.4.

CODE STEP 4

```
'Display Number of Months Old
lblOutputMonths.Caption = "You are " & intMonths & " months old."
lblOutputMonths.Visible = True
```

FIGURE 7-5
This program will convert your age into dog years.

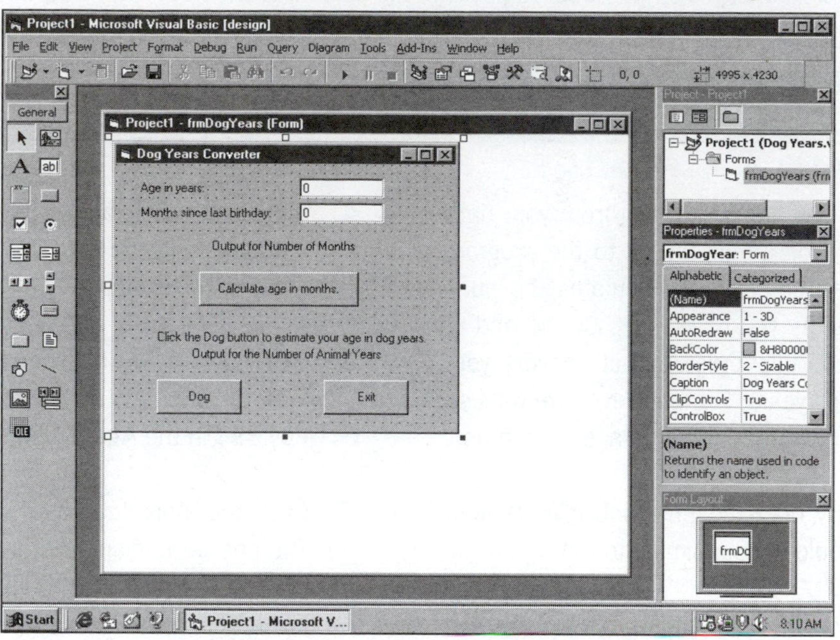

FIGURE 7-6
The label shows the concatenated string.

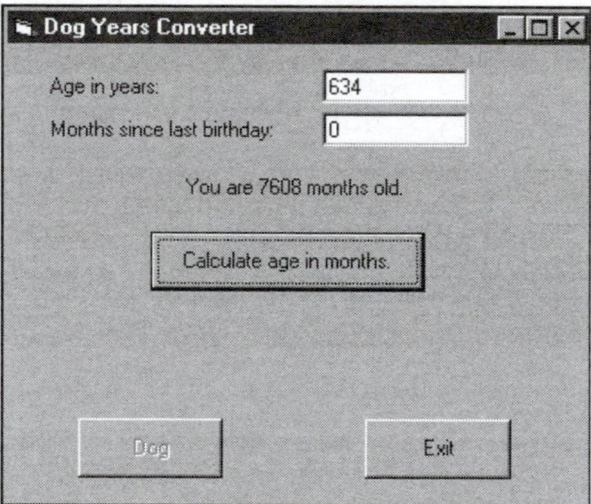

Using Decimal Types

The programs you have worked with up to this point have involved integer values. However, as you learned in Lesson 6, there are three data types for handling decimal data, also known as floating-point numbers.

The Single and Double data types are used for general decimal values. The *Single data type* is used for decimal values that will not exceed six or seven digits. The *Double data type* is used for decimal values with more than six or seven digits.

When you are working with dollars and cents, the *Currency data type* is ideal. It is specially designed to be precise in calculations involving money.

Hot Tip

The Double data type uses more memory than the Single type. Therefore, you should use the Single data type, except in cases where the extra capacity of the Double type is needed.

STEP-BY-STEP 7.4

1. Double-click the **Calculate age in months** button.
2. Add the code in CODE Step 2 to the end of **cmdMonths** (just above **End Sub**) to make the instructions for the program visible after the Calculate age in months button is clicked. (The instructions are the line that reads "Click the Dog button to estimate your age in dog years.")
3. Close the Code window and double-click the **Dog** button.
4. Key **Dim strYears as String** and **Dim sngYears As Single** at the beginning of the cmdDog event procedure to declare strYears and sngYears as String and Single variable data types.
5. Add the code in CODE Step 5 to calculate the number of dog years and set it equal to the variable years. Remember that the sng (Single) variable allows your answer to contain a value of up to six or seven decimal places.
6. Add the code in CODE Step 6 so that the instructions will be hidden after the Dog button has been clicked when you run the program.
7. Leave the Code window open for Step-by-Step 7.5.

CODE STEP 2

```
'Display Instructions
lblInstructions.Visible = True
```

CODE STEP 5

```
'Calculate Dog Years
sngYears = (7 * intMonths) / 12
```

CODE STEP 6

```
'Hide Instructions
lblInstructions.Visible = False
```

Using the Format Function

When you provide the result of a calculation as output, it is important for the data to appear in a format that is attractive and useful to the user. The *Format function* allows you to apply custom formatting to a number before displaying the value. The Format function can be used to format decimal values, phone numbers, and more.

You specify the format you want using special symbols. For example, the code below formats the value 1234.56 to appear as $1,234.56.

Note

The Format function can also be used to apply formatting to strings, dates, and times. The Visual Basic online help has additional information about how to format these data types.

```
strAmount = Format(1234.56, "$#,###.00")
```

The Format function can take a little getting used to. The first step is to learn the most common symbols used to apply formatting to numbers. Table 7-1 shows the symbols you will use when formatting numeric values. All of these are used in the code above except the % sign.

TABLE 7-1

FORMATTING SYMBOLS

SYMBOL	DESCRIPTION
0	The 0 symbol causes a digit to appear in the space. If the data has no value for that digit, a zero appears.
#	The # symbol is similar to the 0 symbol. The difference is that nothing appears in the space if the number being formatted does not require that digit to be used.
.	The period is used to specify where you want the decimal point to appear in the format.
,	By placing commas in the format in the usual places, commas will appear in the output.
%	The percent sign causes a number to be multiplied by 100 and a percent sign to be placed at the end of the number.

Use the symbols in Table 7-1 to create formats for your values. Let's take a look at some examples in Table 7-2.

TABLE 7-2

SAMPLE FORMATS	
CODE	**RESULT**
`Format(12345.67, "000000.000")`	`012345.670`
`Format(12345.67, "######.000")`	`12345.670`
`Format(12345.67, "######.###")`	`12345.67`
`Format(12345.67, "###,###.##")`	`12,345.67`
`Format(12345.67, "$###,###.##")`	`$12,345.67`
`Format(0.89, "##%")`	`89%`

STEP-BY-STEP 7.5

1. Add the code in CODE Step 1 to the end of the cmdDog Click event procedure to display the results and format the lblOutputAnimalYears label to display up to three digits followed by one required decimal place.

2. Close the Code window and run the program.

3. Enter **15** in the **Age in years** text box and enter **4** in the **Months since last birthday** text box.

4. Click the **Calculate age in months** button. Your age in months appears and the instructions for the Dog button appear.

5. Click the **Dog** button. The Visible property of lblOutputAnimalYears is set to True, the instructions disappear, and the results are displayed, as shown in Figure 7-7.

6. End the program.

7. Save the changes to your project but leave the project open for Step-by-Step 7.6.

FIGURE 7-7
The Dog button displays the results on the form.

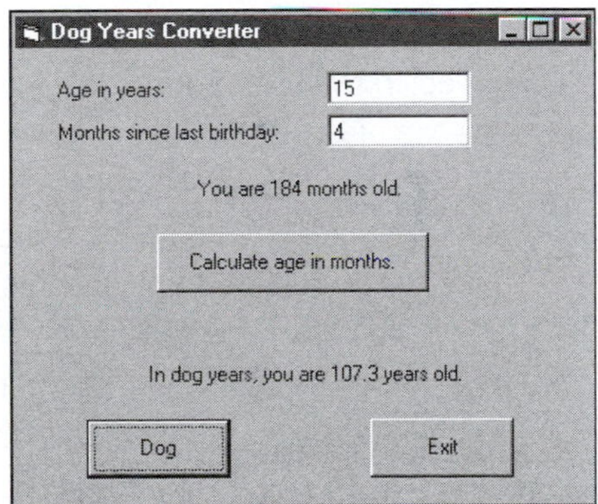

CODE STEP 1

```
'Display Results
strYears = Format(sngYears, "###.0")
lblOutputAnimalYears.Caption = "In dog years, you are " & _
    strYears & " years old."
lblOutputAnimalYears.Visible = True
```

Using the Enabled Property

You have used the Visible property to make command buttons and other controls appear and disappear from a form. The Enabled property performs a similar function. Using the *Enabled property*, you can make a control, such as a command button, take on a grayed appearance, making it inactive but still visible.

By default, objects are enabled. To disable an object, set the Enabled property to False using a statement like the one below.

```
cmdCalculate.Enabled = False
```

STEP-BY-STEP 7.6

1. Click the **Dog** button and change its **Enabled** property to **False**.
2. Double-click the **txtYears** text box. The Code window appears, showing an event procedure for the Change event.
3. Add the code in CODE Step 3 to disable the Dog button when the data in the text box is changed, hide the existing results on the form, and to enable the Calculate age in months button.
4. Select **txtMonths** from the **Object** list box at the top of the Code window.
5. Add the code in CODE Step 5 just above the End Sub statement to disable the Dog button when the data in the text box is changed, hide the existing results on the form, and to enable the Calculate age in months button.
6. Select **cmdMonths** from the **Object** list box.
7. Add the code in CODE Step 7 to enable the Dog button when the human months are calculated.
8. Close the Code window and run the program. Notice that the Dog button is disabled when the program starts.
9. Enter **21** in the **Age in years** text box and enter **1** in the **Months since last birthday** text box.
10. Click the **Calculate age in months** button. The Dog button becomes enabled and the instructions appear as well as the age in months.
11. Click the **Dog** button. The results for the number of dog years are displayed on the form.
12. Change the **Age in years** text box to **30**. The Dog button becomes disabled and the previous results for the number of dog years disappear, as shown in Figure 7-8.
13. Click the **Calculate age in months** button to recalculate the number of human months. The Dog button becomes enabled.
14. Click the **Dog** button. The recalculated results for the number of dog years appear on the form.
15. End the program.
16. Save the changes but leave the project open for Step-by-Step 7.7.

CODE STEP 3

```
'Enable Human Months Button
cmdMonths.Enabled = True
'Disable Dog Command Button
cmdDog.Enabled = False
  lblOutputAnimalYears.Visible = False
```

CODE STEP 5

```
'Enable Human Months Button
  cmdMonths.Enabled = True
'Disable Dog Command Button
  cmdDog.Enabled = False
lblOutputAnimalYears.Visible = False
```

CODE STEP 7

```
'Enable Dog Command Button
  cmdDog.Enabled = True
```

FIGURE 7-8
The Dog button becomes disabled when new data is entered.

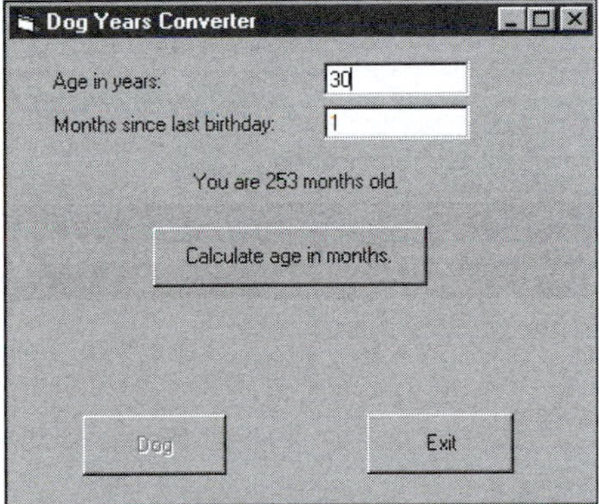

Using the SelStart and SelLength Properties

In the dialog boxes of various programs you have used, you may have noticed that when a text box gets focus, the text in the box is automatically highlighted. The advantage of this feature is that replacing the value in the text box with new characters requires only that you begin keying. You can add this functionality to your programs using the SelStart and SelLength properties.

The *SelStart property* specifies the location where the insertion point will be inserted when the text box gets the focus. The *SelLength property* specifies how many characters should be selected to the right of the cursor. Thus, to select the text in the text box, SelStart is set to zero to place the cursor at the far left of the text box. Then SelLength is set to the length of the text in the text box.

Because the length of the text in the text box will vary, we will use a new function. The *Len function* determines the length of the text in the text box. The code below shows how to select the text in a text box named txtFirstName.

```
txtFirstName.SelStart = 0
txtFirstName.SelLength = Len(txtFirstName.Text)
```

The first line of the above code positions the cursor before the first character in the txtFirstName text box. The second line of code uses the Len function to determine the length of the text in the text box. The value returned by the Len function is the number of characters currently in the text box. Setting the SelLength property to the length of the text in the text box causes all of the characters in the text box to be highlighted, as if you selected them with the mouse.

STEP-BY-STEP 7.7

1. Double-click the **txtYears** text box.
2. The list box on the top right of the Code window is the Procedure list box. Select **GotFocus** from the **Procedure** list box. An event procedure for the GotFocus event is added to the Code window.
3. Add the code in CODE Step 3 to highlight the text in the txtYears text box when it receives the focus.
4. Select **txtMonths** from the **Object** list box and select **GotFocus** from the **Procedure** list box.
5. Add the code in CODE Step 5 to highlight the text in the txtMonths text box when it receives the focus.
6. Close the Code window and run the program.
7. Enter **49** in the **Age in years** text box and enter **7** in the **Months since last birthday** text box.

Your screen should appear similar to Figure 7-9.

CODE STEP 3

```
'Select Text
txtYears.SelStart = 0
txtYears.SelLength = Len(txtYears.Text)
```

CODE STEP 5

```
'Select Text
txtMonths.SelStart = 0
txtMonths.SelLength = Len(txtMonths.Text)
```

STEP-BY-STEP 7.7 CONTINUED

8. Click the **Calculate age in months** button.

9. Click the **Dog** button. The results are displayed on the form.

10. Click the **Age in years** text box. Notice that the number 49 becomes highlighted, as shown in Figure 7-10.

11. Change the number to **24** and click the **Calculate age in months** button.

12. Click the **Dog** button. The results are again displayed on the form.

13. End the program. Save the changes to the project and exit Visual Basic.

FIGURE 7-9
The code in the GotFocus procedure will automatically select the text in the txtYears text box when the cursor is placed in the text box.

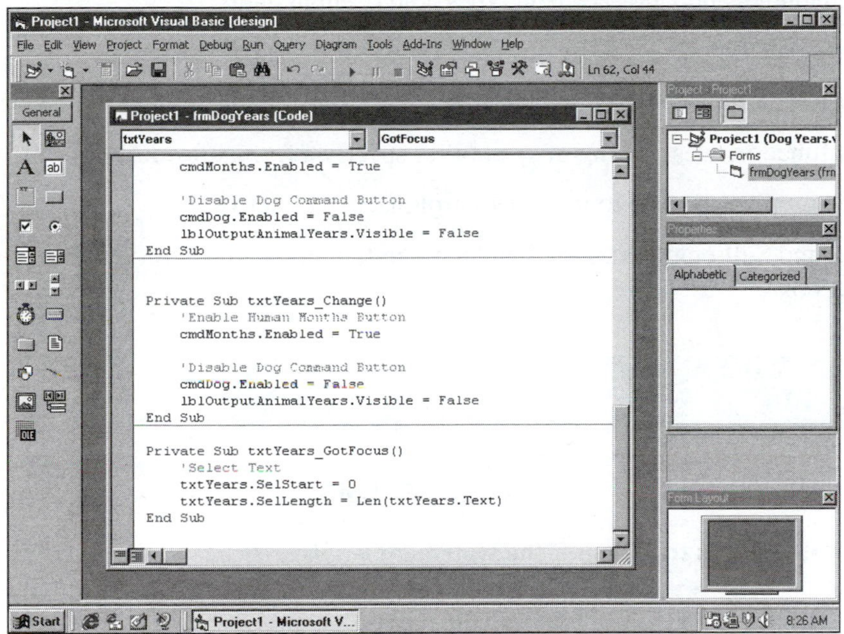

FIGURE 7-10
The contents in the Age in years text box become highlighted when you click in the text box.

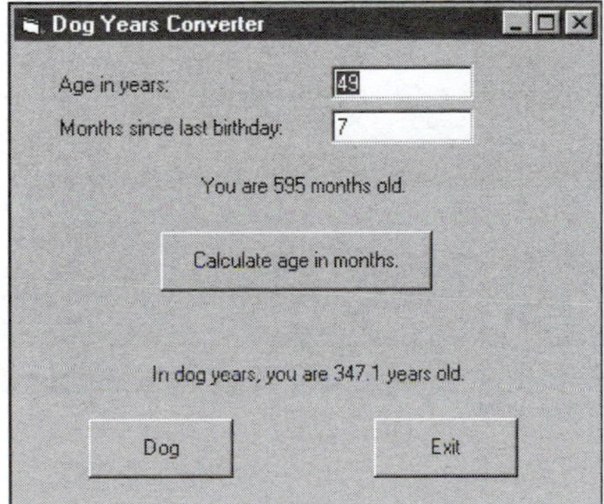

Summary

In this lesson, you learned:

- Strings hold text or alphanumeric data.
- Visual Basic has a data type for strings.
- Text assigned to a string variable must be placed in quotation marks.
- You can use the assignment operator to assign text from a text box to a string variable or from a string variable to another string variable.
- Concatenation is the process of appending one string to the end of another.
- The ampersand (&) is the symbol used for concatenation.
- The Single, Double, and Currency data types hold decimal data.
- The Currency data type is specially designed for handling dollars and cents.
- The Format function can be used to format decimal values, phone numbers, and more.
- The Format function uses a string of symbols to specify a format for data.
- The Enabled property is used to make a control inactive or active.
- The SelStart and SelLength properties and the Len function can be used together to highlight the text in a text box.

LESSON 7 REVIEW QUESTIONS

TRUE/FALSE

Circle T if the statement is true or F if the statement is false.

T F 1. Visual Basic contains a built-in data type for working with strings.

T F 2. The length of a string cannot change as a program runs.

T F 3. The assignment operator can be used to assign text to a string.

T F 4. You cannot assign text from one string variable to another.

T F 5. Concatenation appends one string to the end of another.

T F 6. You can concatenate more than two strings in one expression.

T F 7. The Single data type uses less memory than the Double data type.

T F 8. The Format function cannot be used on strings.

T F 9. The Enabled property behaves the same as the Visible property.

T F 10. The SelLength property alone can be used to select the text in a text box.

WRITTEN QUESTIONS

Write a brief answer to the following questions.

1. What term describes a series of characters that have been strung together?
2. Explain the difference between a string variable and a string literal.
3. What characters must enclose a string literal?
4. Which operator is used for concatenation?
5. What are the differences between the Single and Double data types?
6. Which floating-point data type allows you to do calculations with money?
7. What is the Format function used for?
8. What is the purpose of the # symbol when used with the Format function?
9. What property allows you to disable a control, making it inactive, but still visible?
10. Which two properties allow you to select text in a text box?

LESSON 7 PROJECTS

PROJECT 7-1

1. Start Visual Basic and open **Interest Calculation** from your data files. The program is similar to the Interest program you worked with in Lessons 5 and 6.
2. Add code for the **GotFocus** procedure for the three text boxes so the text will be highlighted when the text box is selected.
3. Close the Code window, then double-click the **Calculate** button.
4. Create a string variable named **strOutput** and a single variable named **sngTotal**.
5. Under the Calculate future value comment, delete lblTotal.Caption and change it to **sngTotal**.

6. Add the following code to store the output in the strOutput variable and display it on the form.

```
'Make output visible
strOutput = "Amount in savings after " & txtYears.Text & _
     " years is $" & Format(sngTotal, "###.00")
lblOutput.Caption = strOutput
lblOutput.Visible = True
```

7. Close the Code window and run the program.

8. Enter data into the text boxes to verify that everything works correctly (you can use interest rates that are not whole numbers).

9. End the program and save the changes to your project, but leave Visual Basic open.

PROJECT 7-2

Your school library has asked you to create a program that will calculate late fees students owe on overdue books. Your school charges $.05 per week for each book that is late.

1. Open **Library** from your data files.

2. Add code to each text box that will highlight the text when the text box is selected.

3. Double-click the **Calculate** button.

4. Create a string variable named **strFullName** and a single variable named **sngFine**.

5. Add the following code to set strFullName equal to the txtFirst and txtLast text boxes.

```
'Combine first and last name
strFullName = txtFirst.Text & " " & txtLast.Text
```

6. Add the following code to calculate the late fee.

```
'Calculate late fee
sngFine = Val(txtBooks.Text) * Val(txtWeeks.Text) * 0.05
```

7. Add the following code to display the results.

```
'Display Results
lblOutput.Caption = strFullName & " owes " & Format(sngFine, "$###.00")
lblOutput.Visible = True
```

8. Close the Code window and run the program.

9. Enter data into the text boxes to verify that the program works.

10. Change the data to verify that the text in the text boxes gets selected when you place the cursor in the text boxes.

11. End the program and save your changes, but leave Visual Basic open.

PROJECT 7-3

1. Open **Transportation Needs** from your data files.

2. Set the **Enabled** property of the **Calculate** button to **False**.

3. Add code to the **txtPeople** and **txtPeoplePerBus** Change event procedure that will enable the Calculate button.

4. Add code to each text box that will highlight the text when the text box is selected.

5. Add code to the **Calculate** button that will disable the command button when it is clicked.

6. Run the program and verify that it works.

7. End the program and save your changes, but leave Visual Basic open.

CRITICAL THINKING

Modify the Dog Years program you worked with in this lesson to include two new command buttons that convert human months to cow years and mouse years. (You may have to widen the form and reposition the controls. Don't forget to disable the new buttons.) Change the caption for the instructions so it applies to all three animals. The result of all calculations should be displayed in the label lblOutputAnimalYears. Use the following formulas to calculate the cow and mouse years.

Cow years = (5 * # of human months) / 12
Mouse years = (25 * # of human months) / 12

(Hint: Move the strYears and sngYears variables to the General Declarations section. You can then copy and paste from one section of code to another and change code as needed. Don't forget the code to enable and disable the buttons in the appropriate places.)

LESSON 8

IF STATEMENTS

OBJECTIVES

When you complete this lesson, you will be able to:

- Explain how decisions are made in a computer.
- Use the conditional operators.
- Use If statements to make decisions in programs.
- Create and read basic flowcharts.
- Use If...Else statements.
- Use check box controls.
- Use the logical operators.

Estimated Time: 2 hours

The Building Blocks of Decision Making

When you make a decision, your brain goes through a process of comparisons. For example, when you shop for clothes you compare the price with prices you have previously paid. You compare the quality to other clothes you have seen or owned. You probably compare the clothes to what other people are wearing or what is in style. You might even compare the purchase of clothes to other possible uses for your available money.

Although your brain's method of decision making is much more complex than that of a computer, decision making in computers is also based on comparing data.

Programs are limited without the ability to make decisions. Although some programs, like the ones you have been writing up to this point, progress through a fairly straightforward path, most programs require some decision making along the way. When two or more possible paths of execution are available, the program must have a means to make a decision.

Suppose you have a dialog box that asks the user the weight of a package that he or she wants to ship (see Figure 8-1). You cannot control what keys the user will press. You can, however, verify the validity of the entry. When the user clicks the OK button, you want to ensure that the value entered by the user is not less than zero. A package cannot weigh less than zero pounds.

FIGURE 8-1
When a program prompts the user for a value, you can't control what keys the user will press.

Decision making in a computer is generally done by a comparison that returns a True or False response. In the example above, the program asks "is the value entered by the user less than zero?" If the answer is Yes or True, the program can stop the operation and prompt the user again.

Using Conditional Operators

The first step to make a decision in a program is to make a comparison. Comparisons are made using the *conditional operators*. They are similar to the symbols you have used in math when working with equations and inequalities. The conditional operators are shown in Table 8-1.

TABLE 8-1

CONDITIONAL OPERATORS

OPERATOR	DESCRIPTION
=	Equal to
>	Greater than
<	Less than
>=	Greater than or equal to
<=	Less than or equal to
<>	Not equal to

The conditional operators are used to compare two values. The result of the comparison is either True or False. Recall from Lesson 6 that Visual Basic has a *Boolean data type* that can hold the values True or False. A *Boolean variable* can be used to store the results of an expression that includes conditional operators. The following are some examples of conditional operators in use.

```
blnTooBig = (Val(txtHeight.Text) > 72)
```

If the value keyed in the txtHeight text box is greater than 72, the variable blnTooBig is set to True.

```
lblOutput.Caption = (intLength >= 100)
```

If the value in intLength is greater than or equal to 100, the caption of the lblOutput label is set to True.

```
blnEqual = (sngA = sngB)
```

If the values in sngA and sngB are equal, the variable blnEqual is set to True.

Note

When a caption of a label is set to a Boolean result, the label is set to either the word *True* or the word *False*.

STEP-BY-STEP 8.1

1. Start Visual Basic and open **Compare** from your data files. If necessary, open the form in the Project Explorer.

2. Double-click the **Compare** button and add the code in CODE Step 2 to compare the values of each text box.

3. Close the Code window and run the program.

4. Key **10** in both text boxes and click the **Compare** command button. The word *True* appears as the label caption, as shown in Figure 8-2.

5. Change the value in the text box to the right of the equal sign to 15.

6. Click the **Compare** button. The word *False* appears as the label caption.

7. End the program and save the changes to the project.

8. Remove the project but leave Visual Basic open for Step-by-Step 8.2.

FIGURE 8-2
The label caption is set to the result of the expression.

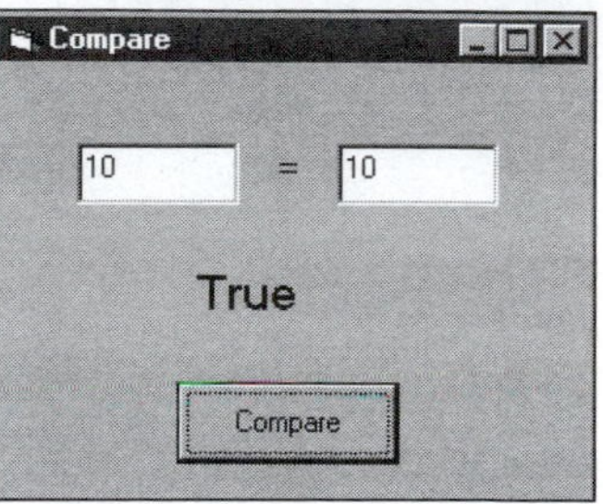

CODE STEP 2

```
lblOutput.Caption = (Val(txtLeft.Text) = Val(txtRight.Text))
```

Using If Statements

In Visual Basic, the If statement is the most common way to make a decision. An *If statement* allows you to execute specified code when the result of a conditional expression is true. For example, an If statement can be used to present the user with a message box *if* the user enters a value that is out of the normal range of values.

Suppose you have a program that asks the user to enter the weight in pounds of a package that is to be shipped. The shipping method requires that you enter the weight to the nearest pound with a one pound minimum. You can use an If statement like the one below to ensure that the user does not enter zero or a negative number for the weight.

```
intPackageWeight = Val(txtWeight.Text)

If (intPackageWeight < 1) Then
     MsgBox("Package weight must be one or more pounds.")
  End If
```

The code above converts the user's entry in the text box into an Integer variable. Then a conditional operator is used to test whether the value in the variable is less than one. The If statement is saying that *if* the result of the comparison is true, then present the message box. The End If statement marks the end of the If statement.

In many cases, there is more than one line of code between the If statement and the End If statement. All of the lines of code that appear between the If statement and End If statements are executed if the conditions specified in the If statement are true. Otherwise, the code between the If statement and the End If is skipped.

STEP-BY-STEP 8.2

1. Open the **Division** project you worked with in Lesson 5 and, if necessary, open the form.
2. Double-click the **Calculate** button and add the code in CODE Step 2 to the beginning of the code to display a warning message if the divisor equals 0.
3. Add code so the text in the two text boxes will be highlighted when you click in them. (Hint: Use the SelStart and SelLength properties.)
4. Close the Code window and run the program.
5. Enter **9** for the divisor and **17** for the dividend and click the **Calculate** button. The program displays the result (1 r 8).
6. Enter **0** for the divisor and **5** for the dividend and click the **Calculate** button. A message box appears warning you that the divisor cannot be zero, as shown in Figure 8-3.
7. Click the **OK** button in the message box. A second error message appears for the MsgBox code you added in Lesson 5.
8. Click the **OK** button to dismiss this message, then end the program.
9. Save the changes to the project and remove the project but leave Visual Basic open for Step-by-Step 8.3.

CODE STEP 2

```
'If divisor is 0 display message
If Val(txtDivisor.Text) = 0 Then
     MsgBox ("The divisor cannot be zero.")
End If
```

FIGURE 8-3
The message box displayed is a result of the If statement you added to the program.

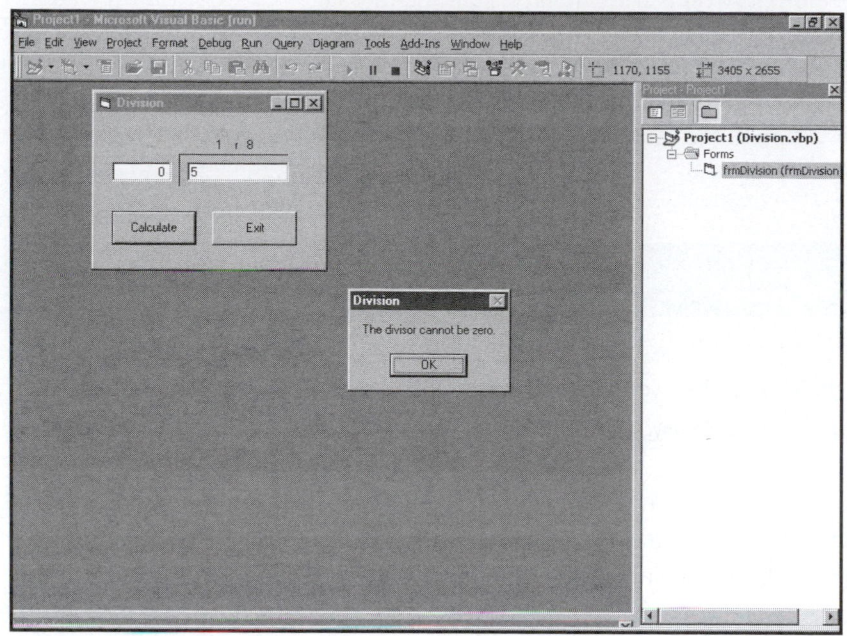

Creating and Reading Flowcharts

Now that you have used an If statement, you can see that programs often do more than just execute a list of instructions without variation. Input from a user, or other conditions, may require that a program's execution take a turn in a new direction or skip certain code. As the flow of execution in a program becomes more complex, it is often helpful to see in visual form the possible paths that a program might take.

For many years, programmers have been using *flowcharts* to plan and to document program code. A flowchart uses symbols and shapes connected by lines to illustrate the steps of a program. Figure 8-4 shows a flowchart of the If statement discussed earlier.

There are many symbols used to create flowcharts. For our purposes, we will only be concerned with the three most basic flowchart symbols, shown in Figure 8-5. The rectangle represents processing data or taking action. Use the diamond for making decisions, such as an If statement. Use the parallelogram to represent input and output.

FIGURE 8-4
A flowchart gives a visual representation of the flow of execution in a program.

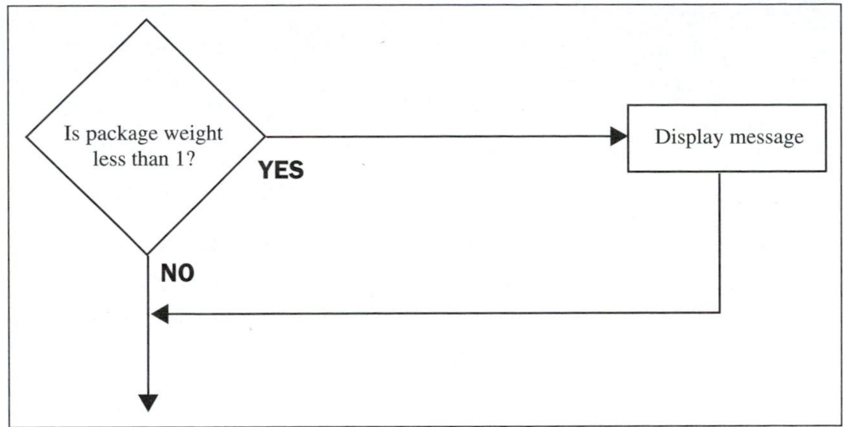

FIGURE 8-5
Each shape in a flowchart has a special meaning.

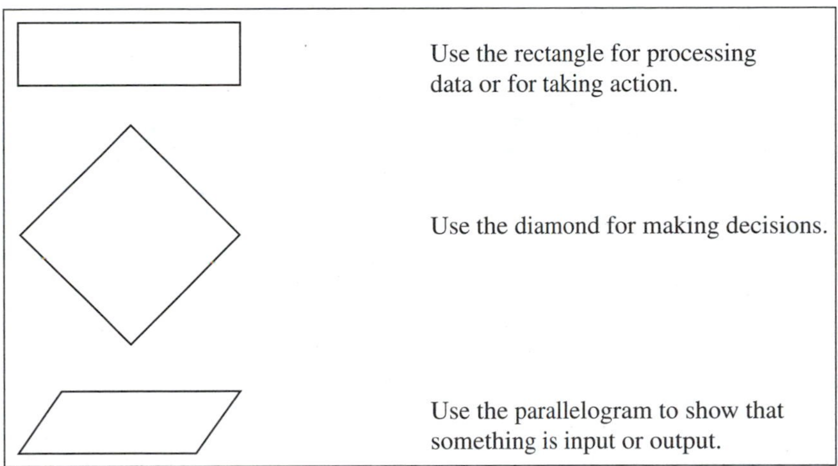

Using If...Else Statements

An If statement makes a decision to either perform some task or to do nothing. An If statement is called a one-way selection structure. A *one-way selection structure* is a program structure in which the decision is to go "one way" or just bypass the code in the If statement. But as you know from the everyday decisions you make, sometimes the decision involves more than Yes or No. Decisions are often a matter of choosing between two or more alternatives.

Note

Because Visual Basic is an event-driven environment, flowcharts are not generally used to chart an entire program. However, flowcharts can be very useful for organizing the flow of execution within an event procedure.

The If...Else statement allows you to choose between two paths. In an If...Else statement, one block of code is executed if the result of an expression is True and another block is executed if the result is False.

The code below displays one of two messages. If the value being tested is less than zero, a message is displayed announcing that the value is negative. If the value is not less than zero, a message is displayed saying that the value is either zero or positive.

```
If (intValue < 0) Then
     MsgBox("The value is negative.")
  Else
     MsgBox("The value is zero or positive.")
  End If
```

An If...Else statement is called a two-way selection structure. A *two-way selection structure* is a program structure in which one block of code is executed if the specified conditions are True or another block of code is executed if the specified conditions are False. The flowchart in Figure 8-6 charts the code shown above.

FIGURE 8-6
An If...Else statement is a two-way selection structure.

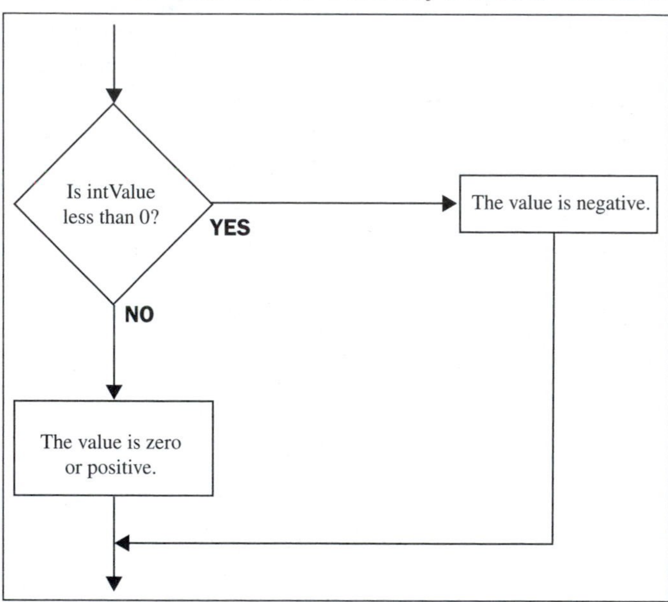

STEP-BY-STEP 8.3

1. Open **Numbers** from your data files and, if necessary, open the form.

2. Double-click the **OK** button and add the code in CODE Step 2 to display Positive if the number is greater than or equal to 0.

3. Add the code in CODE Step 3 to display Negative if the number is not greater than or equal to 0.

4. Close the Code window and run the program.

5. Key **38** in the text box and click the **OK** button. The output below the text box indicates that the number is positive, as shown in Figure 8-7.

6. Key **-7** in the text box and click the **OK** button. The output indicates that the number is negative.

STEP-BY-STEP 8.3 CONTINUED

7. End the program and save the changes to the project.

8. Remove the project but leave Visual Basic open for Step-by-Step 8.4.

FIGURE 8-7
The If...Else statement determined that the number is positive.

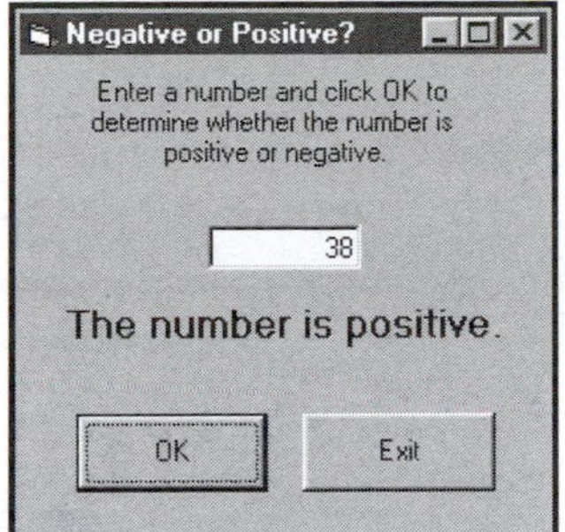

CODE STEP 2

```
'Determine if number is positive or negative
  If Val(txtNumber.Text) >= 0 Then
      lblResult.Caption = "The number is positive."
```

CODE STEP 3

```
Else
      lblResult.Caption = "The number is negative."
  End If
```

Using Check Boxes

Check boxes are an important part of the Windows interface. *Check boxes* allow the program to ask the user a Yes or No question or to turn an option on or off. For example, Figure 8-8 shows the Options dialog box from Visual Basic 6.0. The dialog box includes many options that are selected by clicking check boxes. The options with a check in the box are on and the options without a check in the box are off.

Each check box has a Value property that is set to 1 (one) if the box is checked and 0 (zero) if the box is not checked. The label that appears beside the check box is part of the check box control. Therefore, you do not have to create a label control next to the check box. The check box has a Caption property that specifies its label.

FIGURE 8-8
A check box allows the user to visually turn options on and off.

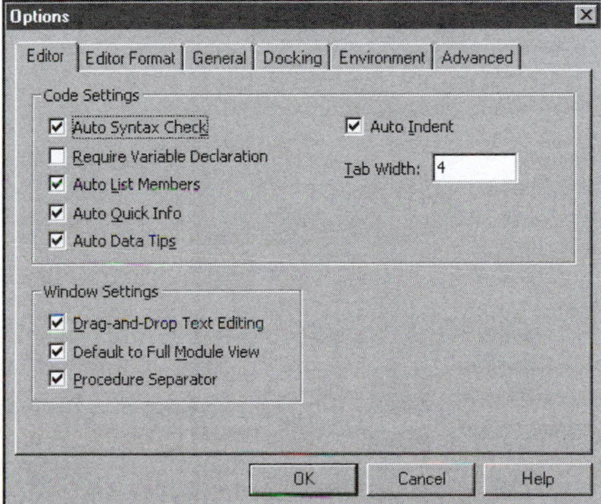

STEP-BY-STEP 8.4

1. Open **Coaster** from your data files and, if necessary, open the form.
2. Double-click the **CheckBox** tool from the toolbar. A check box control is added to the form.
3. Move the check box control below the **Height in inches** label.
4. Create another check box control.
5. Resize and position the two check box controls so your screen appears similar to Figure 8-9.
6. Change the **Name** property of the first check box control to **chkBack**.
7. Change the **Caption** property of chkBack to **Back Trouble.** If necessary, resize the control so that the entire caption is displayed on one line.
8. Change the **Name** property of the second check box control to **chkHeart**.
9. Change the **Caption** property of chkHeart to **Heart Trouble**. If necessary, resize the control so that the entire caption is displayed on one line.
10. Save the changes to the project but leave the project open for Step-by-Step 8.5.

FIGURE 8-9
Check box controls are created in a way similar to other controls.

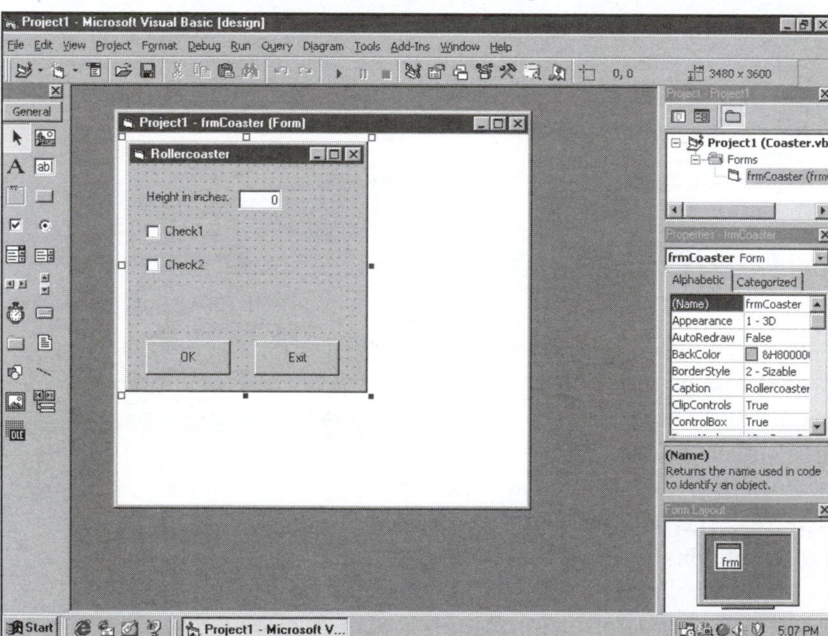

Check boxes can be set to be either checked or unchecked by default, as shown in Figure 8-10. The option to make the check box have a grayed appearance is used in cases where the check box represents a more detailed set of options, some of which are on and some of which are off.

FIGURE 8-10
Check boxes can default to a checked or unchecked state.

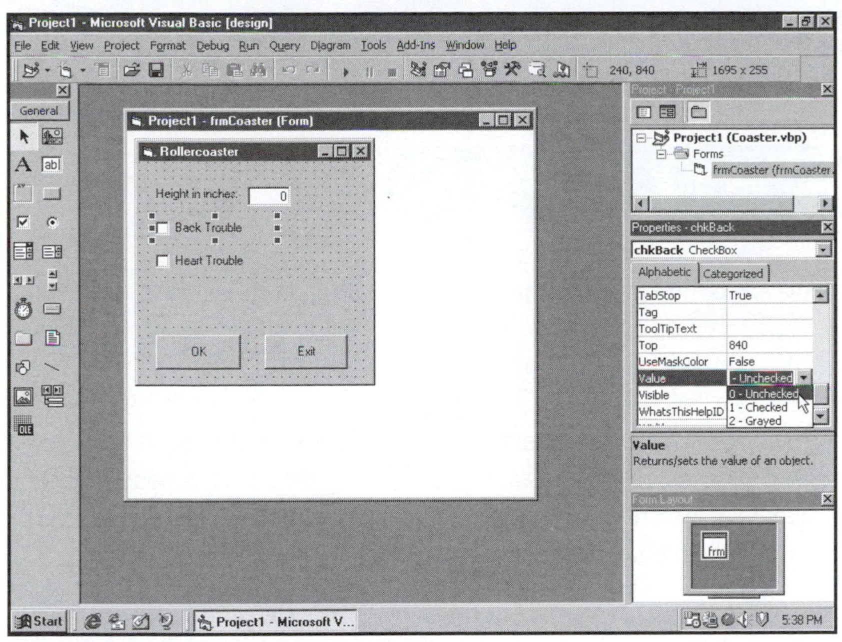

STEP-BY-STEP 8.5

1. Run the program. Notice that each check box is empty.
2. End the program.
3. Click the **Heart Trouble** check box to select it.
4. Change the **Value** property from **0 - Unchecked** to **1 - Checked**. Notice that a check mark appears in the check box on the form.
5. Run the program. The Heart Trouble check box is checked by default.
6. End the program.
7. Change the **Value** property of the Heart Trouble check box back to **0 - Unchecked**.
8. Leave the project open for Step-by-Step 8.6.

Note

In Visual Basic, the equal sign (=) is used for two operations. It is used to assign values and to compare values to determine if they are equal.

The Value property can be set and/or read from code. For example, the code below assigns the value one (1) to a check box, causing it to appear checked.

```
chkHeart.Value = 1
```

Similar code can be used to test whether the check box is checked, as shown on the next page.

```
If (chkHeart.Value = 1) Then
     MsgBox("The checkbox is checked")
  End If
```

STEP-BY-STEP 8.6

1. Double-click the **OK** button and add the code in CODE Step 1 to declare a variable named blnOKtoRide and set it equal to True. The blnOKtoRide variable will be used to track whether the rider passes the three tests for riding the roller coaster. The program will assume the rider is able to ride unless one of the pieces of information entered by the user disqualifies the rider.

2. Add the code in CODE Step 2 to determine if the rider is less than 45 inches tall. If the rider is less than 45 inches, the blnOKtoRide variable is set equal to False.

3. Add the code in CODE Step 3 to determine if the rider has back problems. If back problems are reported, the rider is not allowed to ride.

4. Add the code in CODE Step 4 to determine if the rider has heart problems. If heart problems are reported, the rider is not allowed to ride.

5. Add the code in CODE Step 5 to display whether the potential roller-coaster rider can ride depending on the value of blnOKtoRide. After all the code is entered, your screen should appear similar to Figure 8-11.

CODE STEP 1

```
Dim blnOKtoRide As Boolean
  blnOKtoRide = True
```

CODE STEP 2

```
'Check if rider is less than 45 inches tall
  If Val(txtHeight.Text) < 45 Then
   blnOKtoRide = False
  End If
```

CODE STEP 3

```
'Check for back problems
  If chkBack.Value = 1 Then
  blnOKtoRide = False
  End If
```

STEP-BY-STEP 8.6 CONTINUED

CODE STEP 4

```
'Check for heart problems
If chkHeart.Value = 1 Then
     blnOKtoRide = False
  End If
```

CODE STEP 5

```
'Display results
  If blnOKtoRide = True Then
     lblResult.Caption = "OK to Ride."
  Else
     lblResult.Caption = "Can't Ride!"
  End If
```

6. Close the Code window and run the program.
7. Key 30 in the text box and click the **OK** button. The label *Can't Ride!* appears on the form.
8. Key **46** in the text box, click the **Back Trouble** check box to add a check mark, and click the **OK** button. Again the label *Can't Ride!* appears on the form.
9. Remove the check mark from the **Back Trouble** check box, and click the **OK** button. The label *OK to Ride* appears on the form.
10. Check the **Heart Trouble** check box and click the **OK** button. The rider is refused.
11. End the program and save the changes to the program but leave the project open for Step-by-Step 8.7.

FIGURE 8-11
The code assumes the rider is allowed to ride unless one of the checks causes the Boolean variable blnOKtoRide to change to False.

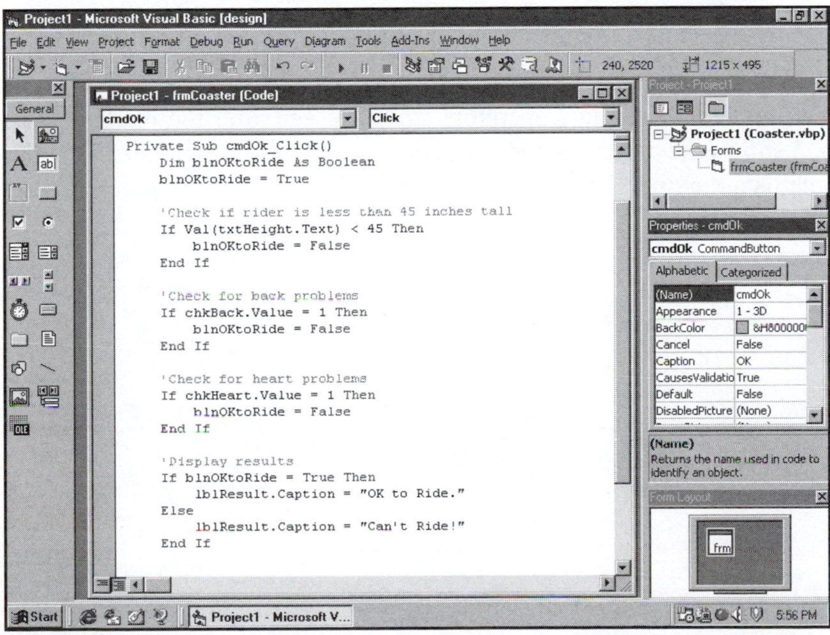

Using Logical Operators

There is another important set of operators: the logical operators. *Logical operators* can be used to combine several comparisons into one statement. Table 8-2 shows the three most common logical operators. Logical operators are used with True and False values. For example, the Not operator reverses the value. In other words, True becomes False and False becomes True.

TABLE 8-2

LOGICAL OPERATORS

OPERATOR	DESCRIPTION
Not	Reverses the value.
And	All expressions or values connected by the And operator must be True in order for the result to be True.
Or	Only one of the expressions or values connected by the Or operator must be True for the result to be True.

The And operator works like you might expect. The result of the And operator is True if both values connected by the And operator are True. For example, the code below sets the Boolean variable blnInRange to True if the variable intA is in the range of 0 to 100. It determines this by verifying that the value in intA is greater than or equal to 0 *and* less than or equal to 100.

```
blnInRange = (intA >= 0) And (intA <= 100)
```

The Or operator returns a True result if either of the values connected by the Or operator are True. For example, the code below sets the blnSellStock variable to True if the stock price moves higher than 92.5 per share *or* if the profits are less than one million.

```
blnSellStock = (sngStockPrice > 92.5) Or (curProfits < 1000000)
```

Order of Logical Operators

In the order of operations, logical operators are processed after the mathematical and conditional operators. Table 8-3 shows the order of operations, combining the mathematical, conditional, and logical operators. The table lists the operations from the first to the last. Items in parentheses are always evaluated first and will override the order here.

TABLE 8-3

ORDER OF OPERATIONS
Exponentiation
Unary plus and unary minus
Multiplication, division, integer division, and Mod
Addition and subtraction
The conditional operators
Not
And
Or

STEP-BY-STEP 8.7

1. Double-click the **OK** button.
2. Delete the three segments of code that check for height and for back and heart problems.
3. Add the code in CODE Step 3 to replace the lines you just deleted to combine the three If statements into one.
4. Close the Code window and run the program.
5. Key **25** in the text box and click the **OK** button. The label *Can't Ride!* appears on the form.
6. Key **73** in the text box, click the **Heart Trouble** check box to add a check mark, and click the **OK** button. Again the label *Can't Ride!* appears on the form.
7. Remove the **check mark** from the **Heart Trouble** check box, and click the **OK** button. The label *OK to Ride.* appears on the form.
8. Click the **Back Trouble** check box to add a check mark and click the **OK** button. The label *Can't Ride!* appears on the form.
9. End the program, save the changes to the project, and exit Visual Basic.

CODE STEP 3

```
'Check if rider is legal to ride
  If (Val(txtHeight.Text) < 45) Or (chkBack.Value = 1) Or _
      (chkHeart.Value = 1) Then
          blnOKtoRide = False
  End If
```

Summary

In this lesson, you learned:

- Decisions are reached by making comparisons.
- Comparisons in a computer generally return either a True or False value.
- The conditional operators compare two values and return either True or False, depending on whether the expression is True or False.
- A Boolean variable can be used to store the results of an expression that includes conditional operators.
- The If statement is the most common way to make a decision in a program. An If statement is a one-way selection structure.
- In an If statement, the code between the If and the End If is executed if the conditions in the If statement are met.
- Flowcharts allow programmers to plan and document program code using symbols connected by lines.
- An If...Else statement makes a decision between two paths. An If...Else statement is a two-way selection structure.
- Check boxes allow your program to ask the user Yes or No questions or to turn an option on or off.
- The Value property of a check box is set to 1 (one) when the check box is checked and 0 (zero) when the box is not checked.
- A check box can be set to be checked or unchecked by default.
- Logical operators can be used to combine several comparisons into one statement.
- Logical operators are used with True and False values.
- The Not operator reverses the value of a Boolean variable or expression.
- The And operator returns True if the values connected by the And operator are both True.
- The Or operator returns True if either value connected by the Or operator is True.
- The logical operators are last in the order of operations. Of the logical operators, Not comes first, then And, then Or.

LESSON 8 REVIEW QUESTIONS

TRUE/FALSE

Circle T if the statement is true or F if the statement is false.

T F 1. Decision making in computers is based on comparing data.

T F 2. Boolean variables can be used to store the result of a comparison.

T F 3. You cannot set the caption of a label to the result of a comparison.

T F 4. Flowcharts are generally used to chart an entire Visual Basic program.

T F 5. An If … Else statement is considered a one-way selection structure.

T F 6. An End If statement does not need to be used in conjunction with the If … Else statement.

T F 7. The check box control includes a label that can be set with the Caption property.

T F 8. Check boxes are always set to be unchecked by default.

T F 9. The same operator is used for assignment and equal comparison in Visual Basic.

T F 10. Logical operators can be used to combine several comparisons into one statement.

WRITTEN QUESTIONS

Write a brief answer to the following questions.

1. What type of operator is used to compare two values?
2. What is the result of a comparison in Visual Basic?
3. What operator is used to represent "Not equal to?"
4. List two types of statements used to make decisions in a Visual Basic program.
5. What statement marks the end of an If statement?
6. Why are flowcharts important to programming?
7. What two possible values can be stored in the Value property of a check box control?
8. List the three logical operators.
9. Where do the logical operators fall in the order of operations?
10. What is the Not operator used for?

LESSON 8 PROJECTS

PROJECT 8-1

1. Start Visual Basic and open the **Buses** program you worked with in Lesson 5.

2. Add the following code to the **Calculate** button to display a warning message if the number of people equals 0. (Substitute the name of the top text box in your program for txtPeople.Text.)

```
'Check number of people
  If Val(txtPeople.Text) = 0 Then
         MsgBox ("The number of people cannot be zero.")
  End If
```

3. Add code so the text in the text boxes will be selected when you click in them.

4. Close the Code window and run the program.

5. Enter a **0** (zero) for number of people to verify that the changes made to the program work correctly.

6. Click the **OK** button to dismiss the message, and click **OK** again in response to the "Run-time error" dialog box, then end the program.

7. Save the changes to the project and remove the project but leave Visual Basic open.

PROJECT 8-2

Draw a flowchart of the roller-coaster ride program created in this lesson.

PROJECT 8-3

1. Open the **Numbers** program you worked with in this lesson.

2. Change the caption of the form to **Even or Odd?**.

3. Change the instructions at the top of the form to explain that the program will determine if the number is even or odd.

4. Edit the code for the **OK** button so it looks like the following code.

```
'Determine if number is even or odd
  If Val(txtNumber.Text Mod 2) = 0 Then
      lblResult.Caption = "The number is even."
  Else
      lblResult.Caption = "The number is odd."
  End If
```

5. Run the program to verify that it can determine whether a number is even or odd, then end the program.

6. Save the changes to the project and remove the project but leave Visual Basic open.

PROJECT 8-4

Your school is planning a trip for spring break. They have asked you to write a program that will calculate the total cost of the trip for each student. The basic price for the trip is $200.00. There are three additional options for the trip: rappelling, backpacking, and canoeing. Complete the steps below to finish the program.

FIGURE 8-12
Add three check boxes as shown here.

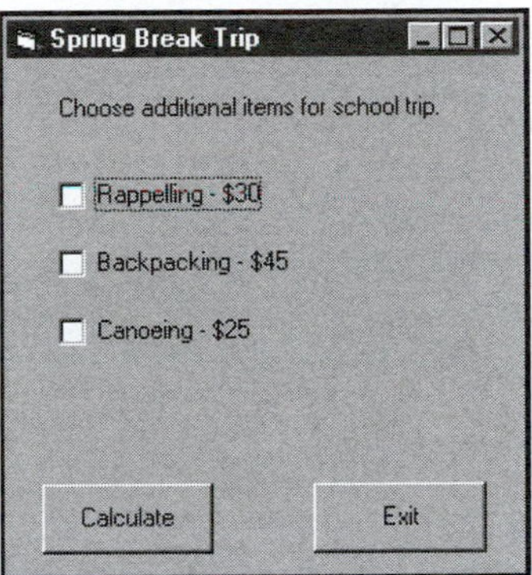

1. Open **Trip** from your template files.

2. Add three check boxes and change their captions so the form appears similar to Figure 8-12 (resize and reposition as necessary).

3. Change the name property of the check boxes to **chkRappel**, **chkBackpack**, and **chkCanoe**.

4. Add the following code to the **Calculate** button to declare three variables and initialize curTotal to 200.

```
Dim curTotal As Currency
  Dim strTotal As String
  Dim strOutput As String
  curTotal = 200
```

5. Add the following code to add $30 to curTotal if the rappelling check box is checked.

```
'Check if Rappelling
  If chkRappel.Value = 1 Then
       curTotal = curTotal + 30
  End If
```

6. Add the following code to add $45 to curTotal if the backpacking check box is checked.

```
'Check if Backpacking
  If chkBackpack = 1 Then
       curTotal = curTotal + 45
  End If
```

7. Add the following code to add $25 to curTotal if the canoeing check box is checked.

```
'Check if Canoeing
  If chkCanoe = 1 Then
       curTotal = curTotal + 25
  End If
```

8. Add the following code to display the results.

```
'Display Output
  strTotal = Format(curTotal, "$###.00")
  strOutput = "The total price of your trip will be " & strTotal & "."
  lblOutput.Caption = strOutput
```

9. Close the Code window and run the program to verify that all three check boxes work correctly (you can check more than one check box at a time).

10. End the program, save the changes to the project and exit Visual Basic.

CRITICAL THINKING

Extend the Coaster program to do additional verification. The program should ask for the age of the rider. Regardless of height, if the rider is under ten years old, the Child with Adult check box must be checked before the child can ride.

Make modifications to the user interface to match Figure 8-13 and add the required code to perform the checks. (Hint: Use And rather than Or in the code for the age requirement.)

FIGURE 8-13
Modify the Rollercoaster form to include a new label, text box, and check box as shown here.

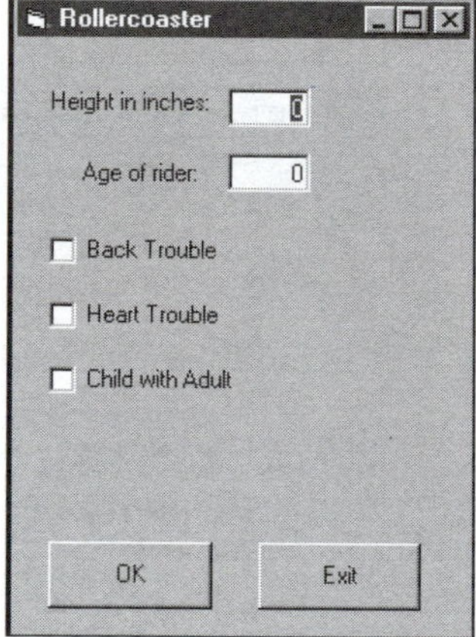

LESSON 9

NESTED IF STATEMENTS AND OPTION BUTTONS

OBJECTIVES

When you complete this lesson, you will be able to:

- Use nested If statements.
- Use option buttons.
- Use the Form Load event.
- Use the Select Case statement.

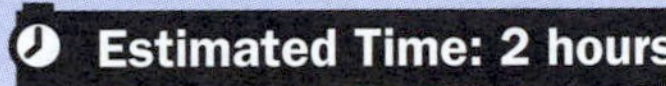

Using Nested If Statements

Decision making is sometimes more complicated than selecting one of two paths. Often, once on a path, there are more decisions to be made. For example, suppose a homeowner is deciding whether to paint her house this year or next year. If she decides to do the job this year, she will have to make additional decisions such as which color to use. She won't have to decide the color unless she makes the decision to go ahead and paint.

In programming, you regularly have decision making similar to the example above. Recall that you can place multiple lines of code between an If statement and its End If statement. The lines of code within an If statement can be practically any kind of Visual Basic code, including more If statements.

When you place an If statement inside another If statement, the If statement inside is called a *nested If statement*. The code below reports the status of an automobile's fuel level to the driver. The first If statement checks to see if the fuel level is less than one-quarter of a tank. If more than a quarter of a tank exists, the Else clause reports that the Fuel level is fine. If less than a quarter of a tank exists, an additional If statement checks the distance to the next gas station. Based on the distance to the next possible fill-up, the driver is either alerted to get fuel now or warned that fuel will be needed soon.

```
If sngFuelLevel < 0.25 Then
   If sngDistanceToNextGas > 30 Then
      MsgBox("Get fuel now.")
   Else
      MsgBox("Will need fuel soon.")
   End If
Else
   MsgBox("Fuel level OK.")
End If
```

When using nested If statements, it is important that you properly indent the code. As you can see, the code above is a little confusing at first. Just imagine how confusing it would be if there was no indentation to group the statements logically.

Other than careful attention to indentation, there is no new or special syntax to learn in order to use nested If statements. However, you will get errors if you fail to include the End If for every If statement.

In the exercise that follows, you will use nested If statements to recommend a type of checking account to a new bank customer. Banks normally have two or more types of checking accounts that are tailored for customers with different amounts of money to keep in the account. Often, banks have a low-cost account for people who plan to keep low balances and a free-checking account for those who will maintain a slightly higher balance. They may also have an account that pays the customer interest if the customer will maintain a certain minimum balance.

The code in Figure 9-1 will recommend an account to the user. First, an If statement determines if the amount being deposited is less than $1000. If the deposit is less than $1000, further comparisons must be made. If the deposit is $1000 or greater, the Else clause recommends the interest-bearing account.

FIGURE 9-1
Nested If statements allow multilevel decisions.

```
'Determine checking account
  If curDeposit < 1000 Then
    If curDeposit < 100 Then
     lblOutput.Caption = "Consider the EconoCheck account."
    Else
     lblOutput.Caption = "Consider the FreeCheck account."
    End If
  Else
    lblOutput.Caption = "Consider an interest-bearing account."
  End If
```

The nested If statement is only executed if the deposit is less than $1000. Its job is to choose between the two accounts that do not pay interest. If the deposit is less than $100, the EconoCheck account is recommended, otherwise (or else) the FreeCheck account is recommended.

STEP-BY-STEP 9.1

1. Start Visual Basic and open **Check** from your data files. If necessary, open **frmMain** from the **Forms** folder.

2. Double-click the **OK** button and add the code in CODE Step 2 to declare curDeposit as a Currency variable.

3. Add code in CODE Step 3 to set curDeposit equal to the value in the text box.

4. Add the code from Figure 9-1 into the event procedure. Your screen should appear similar to Figure 9-2.

5. Close the Code window and run the program.

6. Key **700** into the text box and click the **OK** button. The output "Consider the FreeCheck account." appears on the form.

7. Key **50** into the text box and click the **OK** button. The output "Consider the EconoCheck account." replaces the previous output.

8. Key **3500** into the text box and click the **OK** button. The output "Consider an interest-bearing account." appears on the form.

9. End the program and save the changes to the project.

10. Remove the project but leave Visual Basic open for Step-by-Step 9.2.

CODE STEP 2

```
Dim curDeposit As Currency
```

CODE STEP 3

```
curDeposit = Val(txtDeposit.Text)
```

FIGURE 9-2
Be sure to properly indent code that includes nested If statements.

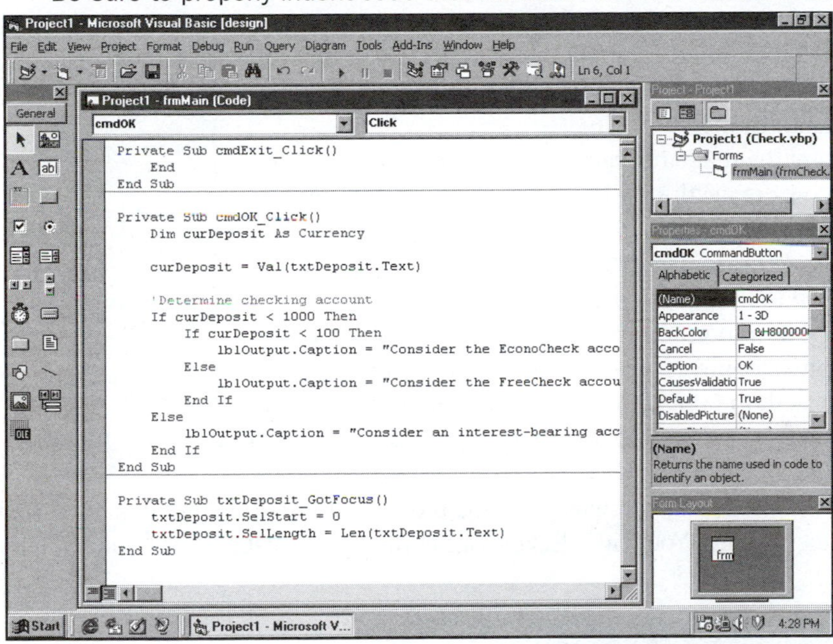

Using Option Buttons

Option buttons are similar to check boxes with one important difference. Option buttons always appear in groups and only one button in the group can be selected at a time. For example, the dialog box in Figure 9-3 is a typical Print Setup dialog box. When printing to most printers, you have the option of printing on the page across the top

Note

Option buttons are sometimes called *radio buttons*. They got the name from car radios. The buttons on a car radio that move the dial to a preset station are like option buttons. You can have only one station selected at a time.

(portrait orientation) or down the side (landscape orientation). You can only select one of the two options. Therefore, option buttons are ideal for selecting the page orientation in the Print Setup dialog box.

Using option buttons in your programs is more complex than working with any of the other controls you have included in your programs up to this point. To successfully use option buttons, there are three steps involved.

1. Create a frame to group the option buttons.
2. Create the option buttons in the frame.
3. Write code to use the option buttons.

FIGURE 9-3
Only one option button in a group can be selected.

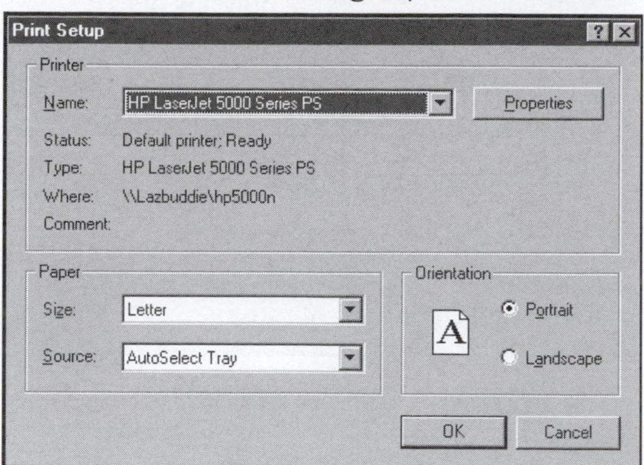

Creating a Frame Control

A *frame control* is a container for other controls. The controls that you place inside a frame are treated as one unit. If you move the frame, the controls in the frame move with it. If you delete the frame, the controls in the frame are deleted along with the frame. Figure 9-4 shows an example of a frame in a dialog box (the Choose a planet frame).

It is important to create the frame that will contain the option buttons before you create the option buttons themselves. When you draw the option buttons, you will draw them in the frame with which they are to be associated. Option buttons in a frame are sometimes referred to as an *option group*.

The two most important frame properties are Name and Caption. As in other controls, the Name property allows you to associate a name with the object in Visual Basic code. In a frame, the Caption property specifies the text that will appear at the top of the frame.

FIGURE 9-4
Frames are used to group controls into one unit.

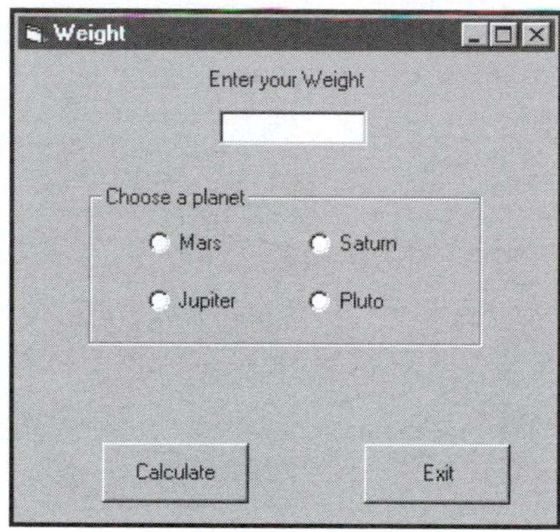

In Step-by-Step 9.2–9.8, you will create the program shown in Figure 9-4. The program will calculate your weight on other planets. You will select the planet for the calculation using option buttons.

STEP-BY-STEP 9.2

1. Open **Planets** from your data files and, if necessary, open **frmMain** from the **Forms** folder.
2. Double-click the **Frame** control from the toolbox. A frame appears in the center of the form.
3. Resize and move the frame so your screen appears similar to Figure 9-5.
4. Change the **Name** property of the frame to **fraPlanets** and change the **Caption** property to **Choose a planet**.
5. Save your changes but leave the project open for Step-by-Step 9.3.

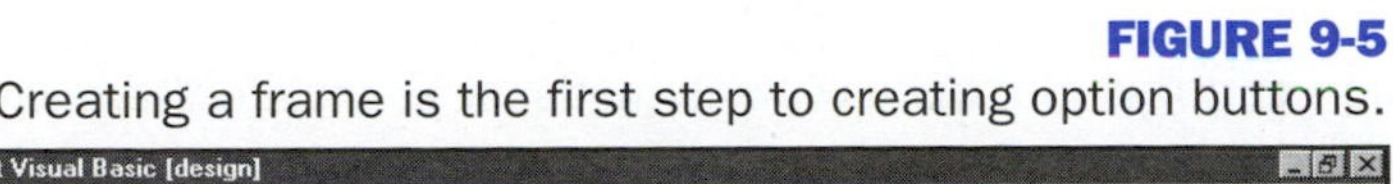

FIGURE 9-5
Creating a frame is the first step to creating option buttons.

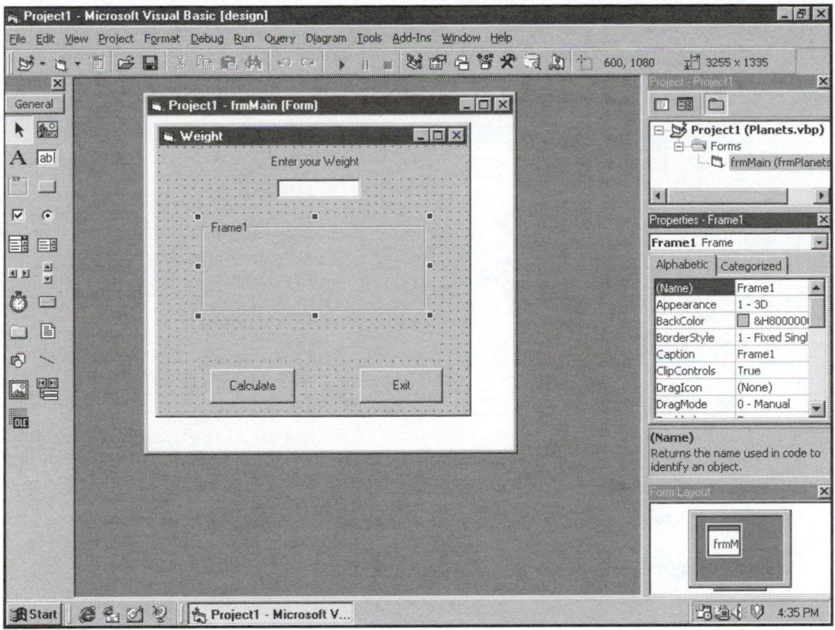

Creating Option Buttons in the Frame

Now that the frame is created, the next step is to add option buttons to the frame.

STEP-BY-STEP 9.3

1. Click the **OptionButton** control from the toolbox.
2. Position the mouse pointer inside the frame.
3. Drag to draw an option button inside the frame about ¼ inch tall and 1 ½ inches wide (1215 x 255).
4. Create three more identical option buttons inside the frame. Your screen should appear similar to Figure 9-6.
5. Save your changes but leave the project open for Step-by-Step 9.4.

Important

When you create option buttons, click the OptionButton tool from the toolbox and drag within the frame to create the option button. If you double-click the OptionButton tool, the option button that is created will not be associated with the frame, even if it appears to be in the frame.

FIGURE 9-6
Drawing option buttons in a frame will automatically associate them with the frame.

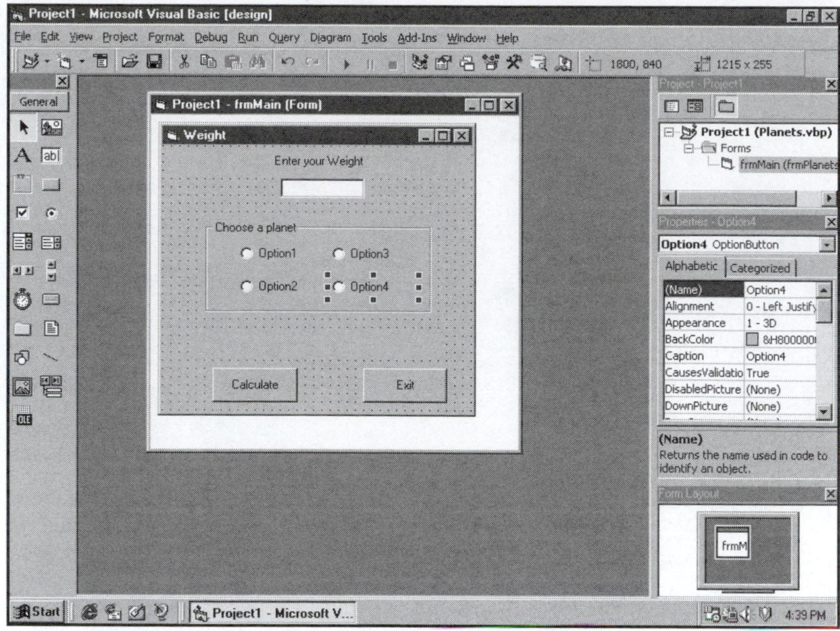

Like other controls, option buttons need to be named appropriately by using the Name property. The Caption property of an option button is similar to the Caption property of a check box. The Caption property specifies the text for the attached label.

STEP-BY-STEP 9.4

1. Select the first option button.
2. Change the Name property to **optMars** and change the Caption property to **Mars**.
3. Set the properties of the remaining option buttons as follows:

Name	Caption
optJupiter	Jupiter
optSaturn	Saturn
optPluto	Pluto

4. Run the program.
5. Click each of the option buttons to see that they are operating correctly.
6. End the program and save your changes but leave the project open for Step-by-Step 9.5.

Adding Code to the Option Buttons

Coding option buttons requires that you think in an event-driven way. Let's consider what happens when the user clicks an option button. The click on the option button generates a Click event. In addition, as you saw in the previous exercise, the option button is filled with the dot that indicates it is selected. It is in the Click event procedure that you have the opportunity to specify what you want to happen if that option is selected.

It is not that simple, however. The user may click several option buttons before finally settling on a choice. This means you must keep track of the most recently clicked option button in the group and yet be prepared for another option button to be clicked instead. Here is how you do it.

Use form-level variables as the scope to keep track of the option that has been selected. For example, in this program that will calculate your weight on other planets, the Click event of each option button will set two variables. The first variable will store the name of the planet the user selected. The second variable will store the conversion factor necessary to calculate the user's weight on that particular planet. The code for the Mars option button Click event appears below.

```
Private Sub optMars_Click()
    sngPlanetWeight = 0.38
    strPlanetName = "Mars"
End Sub
```

Each of the option buttons will have a Click event procedure similar to the one above. So no matter how many option buttons the user clicks, the variables will reflect the values of the most recently clicked option button. Then, when the user clicks the Calculate button, the values set in the option button's Click event procedure will be used in the calculation.

Note

Remember, the variables used in each of the option button event procedures must be declared at the form level.

STEP-BY-STEP 9.5

1. Double-click the **Calculate** button and select **General** from the Object list box.

2. Add the code in CODE Step 2 to create two form-level variables.

3. Select **optMars** from the Object list box and add the code in CODE Step 3 to assign the appropriate values to the two form-level variables when the Mars option button is clicked.

4. Select **optJupiter** from the Object list box and add the code in CODE Step 4 for the Jupiter Click event procedure.

CODE STEP 2

```
Option Explicit
Dim sngPlanetWeight As Single
Dim strPlanetName As String
```

CODE STEP 3

```
sngPlanetWeight = 0.38
strPlanetName = "Mars"
```

5. Select **optSaturn** from the Object list box and add the code in CODE Step 5 for the Saturn Click event procedure.

6. Select **optPluto** from the Object list box and add the code in CODE Step 6 to initialize the two form-level variables when the Pluto option button is selected. Your screen should appear similar to Figure 9-7.

7. Close the Code window and save your changes but leave the project open for Step-by-Step 9.6.

CODE STEP 4

```
sngPlanetWeight = 2.64
strPlanetName = "Jupiter"
```

CODE STEP 5

```
sngPlanetWeight = 1.15
strPlanetName = "Saturn"
```

CODE STEP 6

```
sngPlanetWeight = 0.04
strPlanetName = "Pluto"
```

FIGURE 9-7
Each option button must have a Click event procedure.

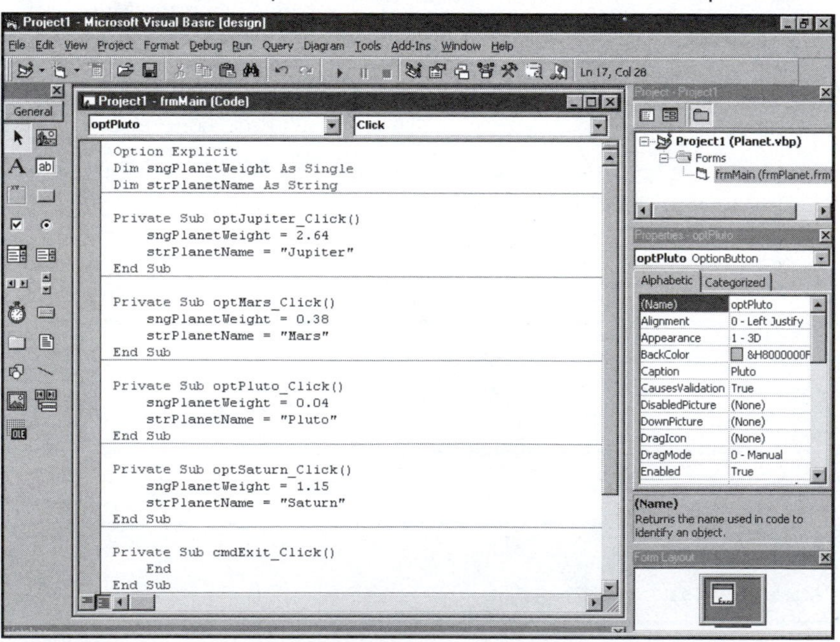

The final step is to calculate the result and create the output. To properly process the data, we will declare two variables in the Calculate command button's Click event procedure. We will use an integer to hold the result of the weight conversion and a string variable to hold the formatted result.

STEP-BY-STEP 9.6

1. Double-click the **Calculate** button and add the code in CODE Step 1 to declare the necessary local variables.
2. Add the code in CODE Step 2 to set intWeight equal to the value in the text box multiplied by the variable sngPlanetWeight.
3. Add the code in CODE Step 3 to display the results in the caption of the lblOutput label.
4. Close the Code window and run the program.
5. Enter **150** into the text box.
6. Click the **Jupiter** option button and click the **Calculate** button. The answer appears on the form.
7. Click each of the other option buttons and the **Calculate** button to test them. The answer should change each time.
8. End the program and save your changes but leave the project open for Step-by-Step 9.7.

CODE STEP 1

```
Dim intWeight As Integer
Dim strWeight As String
```

CODE STEP 2

```
'Calculate Weight
intWeight = Fix(sngPlanetWeight * Val(txtWeight.Text))
strWeight = Format(intWeight, "####")
```

CODE STEP 3

```
'Display Output
lblOutput.Caption = "Your weight on " & strPlanetName _
         & " would be " & strWeight & " pounds."
```

Using a Form Load Event Procedure

Although our program works, there is still a problem. When the program runs, none of the option buttons are yet selected. So if the user fails to click any of the option buttons and clicks the Calculate button, the program will give no weight and will have no planet name to display.

STEP-BY-STEP 9.7

1. Run the program.

2. Enter **150** into the text box and click the **Calculate** command button. The output displays "Your weight on would be pounds." with no weight or planet name because an option button was not selected.

3. End the program but leave the project open for Step-by-Step 9.8.

To correct this, we need to have one of the option buttons selected by default. Option buttons have a property that allows you to simulate a user's click from code. By setting the Value property of an option button to True, the option button is selected. In addition, the button's Click event is triggered. So the values are properly initialized as well. The code below, for example, will make the Mars option button the default button.

```
optMars.Value = True
```

But where can you place the code so that it is executed before the user has the opportunity to click the Calculate button? When a form is loaded and opened by the program, a special event called a *Load event* is triggered. Like other events, you can write an event procedure for the form's Load event.

STEP-BY-STEP 9.8

1. Double-click the form (but not the title bar or one of the controls) displayed on the screen. The Code window opens, displaying the form's Load event procedure.

2. Add the code in CODE Step 2 to set the Mars option button as the default when the program is run.

3. Close the Code window and run the program. Notice that the Mars option button is already selected.

4. Enter **123** into the text box and click the **Calculate** button. The program calculates the weight on Mars.

5. End the program and save the changes to the project.

6. Remove the project but leave Visual Basic open for Step-by-Step 9.9.

CODE STEP 2

```
optMars.Value = True
```

Using Select Case

If statements allow you to program one-way decisions and If...Else statements allow you to program two-way decisions. By nesting If statements, you have seen that you can actually make decisions that branch in more than two paths. Visual Basic, however, provides a statement especially for multi-way decisions: the Select Case statement.

In a *Select Case statement*, you specify a variable to test and then list a number of cases that you want to test for. For example, the code below uses a Select Case statement to recommend a type of vehicle that should be rented, based on the number of passengers.

```
'Select type of vehicle to rent
Select Case intPassengers
    Case 1 To 2
      lblOutput.Caption = "You should rent a compact car."
    Case 3 To 4
      lblOutput.Caption = "You should rent a full size car."
    Case 5 To 7
      lblOutput.Caption = "You should rent a minivan."
    Case 8 To 15
      lblOutput.Caption = "You should rent a 15 passenger van."
    Case Is > 15
      lblOutput.Caption = "You should rent a bus."
    Case Else
      lblOutput.Caption = "Incorrect data"
End Select
```

The first line in the Select Case statement specifies the piece of data that is involved in the decision; in this case, the number of passengers (intPassengers). The Select Case statement ends with an End Select statement. Between the Select Case and End Select statements are a series of Case statements. In this code, most of the Case statements specify a range of values. For example, if the value of intPassengers is 6, the third Case statement will apply because 6 is in the range of 5 to 7.

You can use conditional operators in a Case statement as well. To use a conditional operator requires that you include the Is keyword. The fifth Case statement is an example of the use of a conditional operator. If the value in intPassengers is greater than 15, the recommendation is to rent a bus.

Finally, as a default, the code under the *Case Else statement* will be applied if no other Case statement catches it first. In this case, the Case Else will be triggered if the value is zero or less.

STEP-BY-STEP 9.9

1. Open **Transportation** from your data files and, if necessary, open **frmMain** from the **Forms** folder.

2. Double-click the **OK** button and add the code in CODE Step 2 to declare an integer variable and set it equal to the value in the text box.

3. Add the Select Case statement in CODE Step 3.

4. Close the Code window and run the program.

5. Key **14** as the number of passengers and click the **OK** button. The output shown in Figure 9-8 appears.

6. Enter other values and click the **OK** button to verify that each case works correctly.

7. Change the number of passengers to **0** and click the **OK** button. The output states that you entered incorrect data.

8. End the program and save the changes to the project, then exit Visual Basic.

FIGURE 9-8
The Select Case statement selects the output to display.

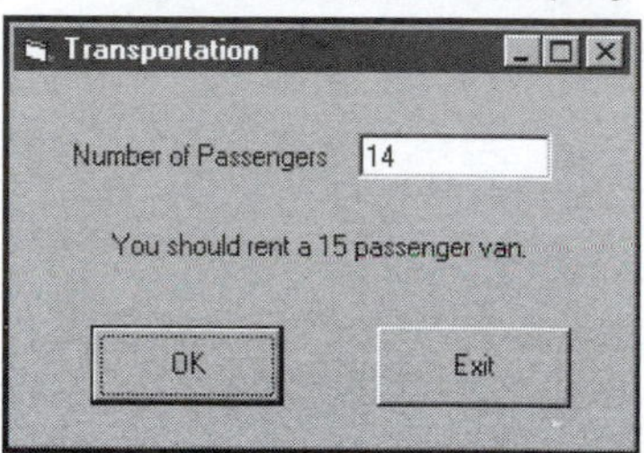

CODE STEP 2

```
Dim intPassengers As Integer
intPassengers = Val(txtPassengers.Text)
```

CODE STEP 3

```
'Select type of vehicle to rent
Select Case intPassengers
    Case 1 To 2
      lblOutput.Caption = "You should rent a compact car."
    Case 3 To 4
      lblOutput.Caption = "You should rent a full size car."
    Case 5 To 7
      lblOutput.Caption = "You should rent a minivan."
    Case 8 To 15
      lblOutput.Caption = "You should rent a 15 passenger van."
    Case Is > 15
      lblOutput.Caption = "You should rent a bus."
    Case Else
      lblOutput.Caption = "Incorrect data"
End Select
```

Summary

In this lesson, you learned:

- If statements can be nested to make additional decisions within the code of the If statement.
- It is important to indent the code in a nested If statement to make the code readable.
- Each If statement within a nested If statement must end with the End If statement.
- Option buttons appear in groups. Only one option button in the group can be selected at a time.
- Option buttons are sometimes called radio buttons.
- The first step in creating a group of option buttons is to create a frame control to contain the option buttons. The controls within a frame are treated as one unit.
- The Caption property of a frame control specifies the text that appears at the top of the frame.
- To associate an option button with a frame, you must click the OptionButton tool only once and draw the option button in the frame. If you double-click to create an option button, it will not associate itself with the frame.
- The Caption property of an option button specifies the text that appears on the label attached to the option button.
- Coding option buttons involves using form-level variables that carry values that reflect the selected option.
- A form's Load event procedure is executed each time a form is loaded and opened by the program.
- The Select Case statement allows you to make multi-way selections.
- The Case statements in a Select Case can test a range or use conditional operators.
- Conditional operators in a Case statement must include the Is keyword.
- As a default, the Case Else statement is applied if no other Case is true.

LESSON 9 REVIEW QUESTIONS

TRUE/FALSE

Circle T if the statement is true or F if the statement is false.

T F 1. It is possible to write nested If statements in Visual Basic.

T F 2. Only one option button in a group can be selected.

T F 3. The first option button you place on a form automatically creates a frame in which you can place other option buttons.

T F 4. The controls you place inside a frame are treated as one unit.

T F 5. Drawing option buttons in a frame will automatically associate them with that frame.

T F 6. The first option button you add to a form will be selected by default when you run the program.

T F 7. Double-clicking on a form will display the General Declarations section of the code for that form.

T F 8. To use a conditional operator in a Case statement, you must use the keyword Is.

T F 9. The Select Case statement ends with an End Select statement.

T F 10. Code under the Case Else statement is the default case in a Select Case statement.

WRITTEN QUESTIONS

Write a short answer to the following questions.

1. Why is it important to properly indent your code when using multi-way selection structures?
2. What is the main difference between option buttons and check boxes?
3. What is another name for option buttons?
4. What three steps are involved in creating a group of option buttons?
5. Which property specifies the text for the label attached to an option button?
6. What scope should the variables you use to keep track of a user's selection have?
7. How do you change the default selection in a group of option buttons?
8. What is a frame control?
9. What event procedure is triggered when a form is loaded?
10. Where is the piece of data involved in the decision located in a Select Case statement?

LESSON 9 PROJECTS

PROJECT 9-1

1. Start Visual Basic and open **Final** from your data files.

2. Create a Boolean form-level variable named **blnExempt**.

3. In the **OK** Click event procedure, set **blnExempt** equal to **False**.

4. Add the following code to determine if the student needs to take the final exam.

```
'Determine if final needs to be taken
If Val(txtAverage.Text) >= 90 Then
      If Val(txtAbsences.Text) <= 3 Then
          blnExempt = True
      End If
Else
      If Val(txtAverage.Text) >= 80 Then
          If Val(txtAbsences.Text) <= 1 Then
              blnExempt = True
          End If
      End If
End If
```

5. Add the following code to display the results.

```
'Display Results
If blnExempt = True Then
      lblResult.Caption = "You DO NOT need to take the final exam."
Else
      lblResult.Caption = "You DO need to take the final exam."
End If

lblResult.Visible = True
```

6. Close the Code window and run the program with various scores and number of absences to verify that it works correctly.

7. Save the changes to the project and remove the project but leave Visual Basic open.

PROJECT 9-2

1. Open **Animal Years9B** from your data files.

2. Add a frame with three option buttons to the form as shown in Figure 9-9.

3. Use Figure 9-9 to key the Caption properties of the frame and option buttons. Name the frame **fraAnimal** and name the option buttons **optDog**, **optCow**, and **optMouse**.

4. Add the following code in the General Declarations section to declare two new variables.

```
Dim strYears As String
Dim sngYears As Single
```

5. Add the following code into the Click event procedure of the Dog option button to calculate the number of Dog years.

```
'Calculate Dog Years
sngYears = (7 * intMonths) / 12
```

6. Add the following code into the Click event procedure of the Cow option button to calculate the number of Cow years.

```
'Calculate Cow Years
sngYears = (5 * intMonths) / 12
```

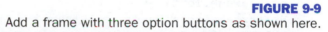

FIGURE 9-9
Add a frame with three option buttons as shown here.

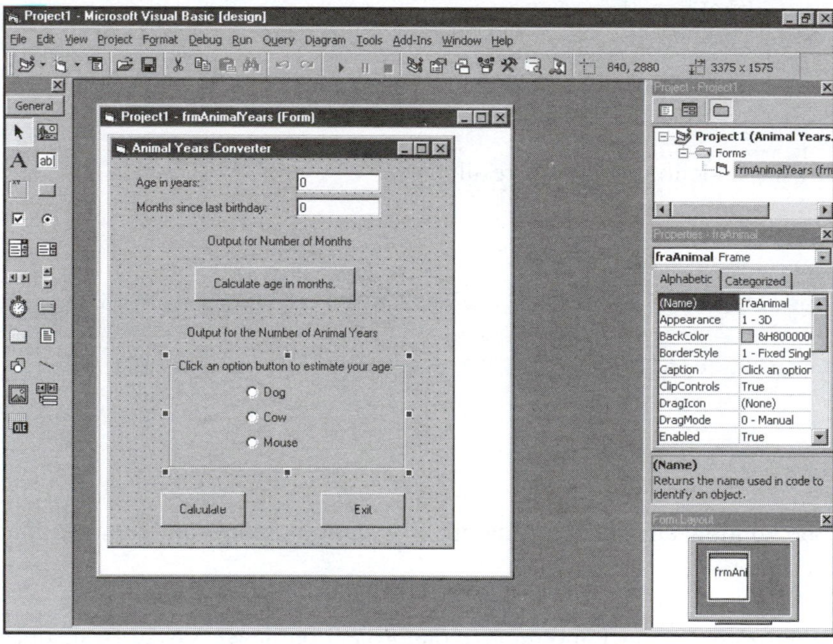

7. Add the following code into the Click event procedure of the Mouse option button to calculate the number of Mouse years.

```
'Calculate Mouse Years
sngYears = (25 * intMonths) / 12
```

8. Add the following code into the Click event procedure of the **Calculate** button to display the results.

```
'Display Results
strYears = Format(sngYears, "###.0")
lblOutputAnimalYears.Caption = "In animal years, you are " & _
        strYears & " years old."
lblOutputAnimalYears.Visible = True
```

9. Add the following code into the Click event procedure of the **Months** command button that will set the Dog option button to **True**.

```
'Set Dog option button as default
optDog.Value = True
```

10. Run the program and verify that everything works correctly.

11. Save the changes to the project and remove the project but leave Visual Basic open.

PROJECT 9-3

Write a program that will determine the price per copy based on the following information.

Number of Copies	Price Per Copy
1–200	0.10
201–500	0.08
501–1000	0.06
>1000	0.05

1. Open **Copies** from your data files.

2. Add the following code to the **OK** button to declare four different variables and set intNumber equal to the value in the text box.

```
Dim intNumber As Integer
Dim strNumber As String
Dim curTotal As Currency
Dim strTotal As String

intNumber = Fix(Val(txtCopies.Text))
```

3. Add the Case statement as follows to determine the total cost.

```
'Determine total cost
Select Case intNumber
      Case 1 To 200
          curTotal = intNumber * 0.1
      Case 201 To 500
          curTotal = intNumber * 0.08
      Case 501 To 1000
          curTotal = intNumber * 0.06
      Case Is > 1000
          curTotal = intNumber * 0.05
      Case Else
          lblOutput.Caption = "Incorrect data was entered."
End Select
```

4. Add the following code to display the results.

```
'Display results
If intNumber > 0 Then
          strNumber = intNumber
          strTotal = Format(curTotal, "$#,###.00")
          lblOutput.Caption = "The total cost for " & strNumber & _
              " copies is " & strTotal & "."
End If
```

5. Run the program and verify that everything works correctly with various numbers of copies, including entering a 0 (zero) to generate the incorrect data output.

6. End the program and save the changes to the project, then exit Visual Basic.

CRITICAL THINKING

Modify the Planets program you created in this lesson to calculate a person's weight on every planet in the solar system (resize your form and frame to include the new option buttons). Make Mercury the default option button. Use the following conversion factors for the new planets.

Planet:	Multiply by:
Mercury	0.37
Venus	0.88
Uranus	1.15
Neptune	1.12

LESSON 10

Do Loops

OBJECTIVES

When you complete this lesson, you will be able to:

- Explain what a loop is.
- Use the Do While and Do Until loops.
- Use the InputBox function.
- Use the DoEvents statement.
- Use nested loops.

Estimated Time: 2 hours

What Are Loops?

You have probably noticed that much of the work a computer does is repeated many times. For example, when a computer prints a personalized form letter for each person in a database, the same operation is repeated for each person in the database. When a program repeats a group of statements a number of times, the repetition is accomplished using a *loop*. The code required to create a loop is sometimes called an *iteration structure*.

In Visual Basic, there are three kinds of loops. In this lesson, you will learn about two of these: the Do While loop and Do Until loop. Both types of Do loops repeat a block of code statements a number of times. The *Do While loop* repeats the statements *while* a certain condition is True. The *Do Until loop* repeats the statements *until* a certain condition is True.

Using the Do Loops

Knowing which of the Do loops to use is just a matter of experience. Often, the same result can be achieved with either a Do While or a Do Until. It may come down to a decision of which loop is best in a specific case.

Both types of Do loops rely on a condition to be either True or False. A loop's condition is similar to the condition used in an If statement. The condition applies some test to determine either a True or False result. Consider the Do While loop in the code below.

```
intValue = 1
Do While intValue < 10
  intValue = intValue + 1
Loop
```

In the code above, the variable intValue is assigned the value 1. The Do While loop will repeat the indented statement until intValue is no longer less than 10. The Loop keyword at the end of the code indicates the end of the block of code statements that are included in the loop.

Note

A loop can contain more than one statement. All of the statements between the Do While and the Loop keywords will be repeated.

Using Do While

A Do While loop is used when you want a block of code to repeat as long as a condition remains True. For example, suppose you want to write a program that calculates the number of times that a given number can be divided by two before the result of the division is less than 1. A Do While loop can be used in this case. The code below shows a Do While loop that will repeatedly divide a number in half as long as the result of the division is greater than or equal to 1.

```
Do While dblX >= 1
   dblX = dblX / 2
Loop
```

Suppose we want to write a program that counts the number of times the division must occur before the result is no longer greater than or equal to 1. The code below adds a counter to the loop to count the number of times the code in the loop is executed.

```
intCounter = 0
'Divide number
Do While dblX >= 1
   dblX = dblX / 2
   intCounter = intCounter + 1
Loop
```

STEP-BY-STEP 10.1

1. Start Visual Basic and open **DoLoop** from your data files. If necessary, open the form.
2. Double-click the **Count** button and add the code in CODE Step 2 to count the number of times a number can be divided by two before the result is less than 1.
3. Close the Code window and run the program.

STEP-BY-STEP 10.2 CONTINUED

4. Key **8** and click the **Count** button. The program shows that the number 8 must be divided by 2 four times to obtain a result less than 1, as shown in Figure 10-1.

5. End the program and save your changes but leave the project open for Step-by-Step 10.2.

FIGURE 10-1
The program reports the value of intCounter.

CODE STEP 2

```
Dim dblX As Double
Dim intCounter As Integer

'Initialize variables
dblX = Val(txtStart.Text)
intCounter = 0

'Divide number
Do While dblX >= 1
   dblX = dblX / 2
   intCounter = intCounter + 1
Loop

'Display Results
lblCounter.Caption = intCounter
lblCounter.Visible = True
```

Using Do Until

A Do Until loop is used when you want a block of code to repeat until a condition becomes true. For example, the program from the previous exercise could easily be rewritten to use a Do Until loop instead of a Do While. Consider the following code.

```
intCounter = 0
Do
  dblX = dblX / 2
  intCounter = intCounter + 1
Loop Until dblX < 1
```

In the code above, the loop uses reversed logic. Instead of repeating as long as the number being divided is greater than or equal to 1, the code repeats until the number being divided becomes less than 1.

STEP-BY-STEP 10.2

1. Double-click the **Count** button and replace the loop under the comment **Divide number** with the code in CODE Step 1. Your screen should appear similar to Figure 10-2.

2. Close the Code window and run the program.

3. Key **156** and click the **Count** button. The number 156 can be divided eight times before the result is less than 1.

4. End the program. Do *not* save your changes but leave the project open for Step-by-Step 10.3.

CODE STEP 1

```
Do
   dblX = dblX / 2
   intCounter = intCounter + 1
Loop Until dblX < 1
```

FIGURE 10-2
The Do While loop is replaced with a Do Until loop.

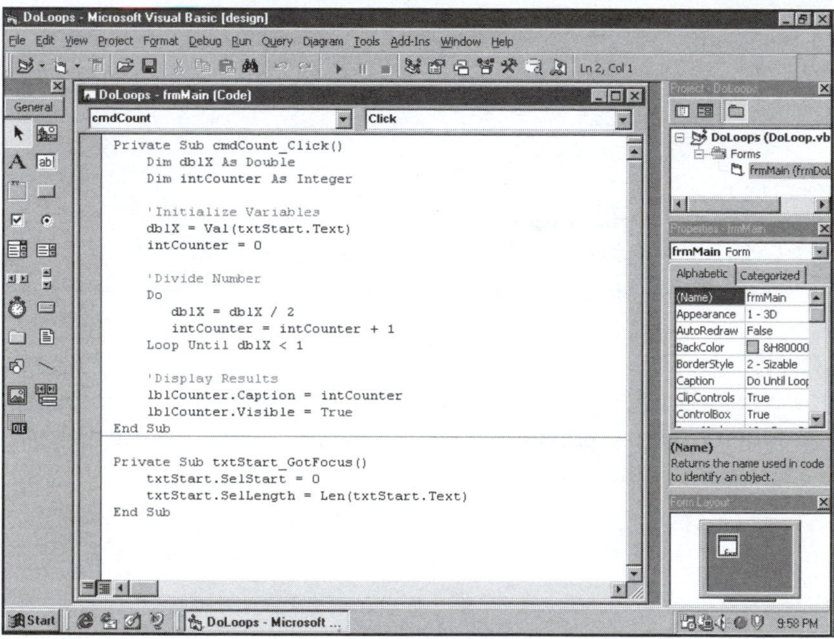

One of the primary differences between the two kinds of Do loops is where the condition is tested. A Do While loop tests the condition at the top of the loop. If the condition is False, the code inside the loop is never executed. The Do Until loop tests the condition at the bottom of the loop. Therefore, in a Do Until loop, the code in the loop is executed at least once.

The difference between the Do While and Do Until loops is important. For example, the program in Step-by-Step 10.2 actually provides an inaccurate answer in some cases because of the behavior of the Do Until loop. Let's run the Do Until loop again and identify the problem.

STEP-BY-STEP 10.3

1. Run the program.

2. Key **.75** and click the **Count** button. Notice that the program reports that the division occurred one time, as shown in Figure 10-3. Because the condition is tested at the end of the loop, the instructions in the loop are performed at least once, even though they did not need to be performed. The result is that the program produced an incorrect result.

3. End the program and remove the project. Do *not* save your changes but leave Visual Basic open for Step-by-Step 10.4.

FIGURE 10-3
In this case, the Do Until loop did not generate the correct answer.

The program that uses the Do Until can be fixed by adding an If statement that causes the loop to be skipped if the value in dblX is already less than 1, as shown.

```
intCounter = 0
If dblX >= 1 Then
  Do
    dblX = dblX / 2
    intCounter = intCounter + 1
  Loop Until dblX < 1
End If
```

Rather than add the If statement to the code, however, most programmers would probably choose to use the Do While loop.

Using the InputBox Function

The InputBox function is the opposite of the MsgBox function. Recall that the MsgBox function creates a window to display output. The *InputBox function* displays a window asking the user for input. Figure 10-4 shows an example of an input box created with the InputBox function.

To use the InputBox function, you must supply two strings: the text that will prompt the user and the title for the window's title bar. It is optional to supply a third string: the text that you want to appear in the text box by default. The InputBox function will return a string value. For example, the code below will create the input box shown in Figure 10-4.

```
strName = InputBox("What is your name?", "Enter Name", _
                   "John Q. Public")
```

In the code above, strName is the String variable that will hold the text entered by the user. Inside the parentheses that follow the InputBox keyword, separated by commas, you supply the prompt that kthe user will see, the title bar text, and the optional default entry.

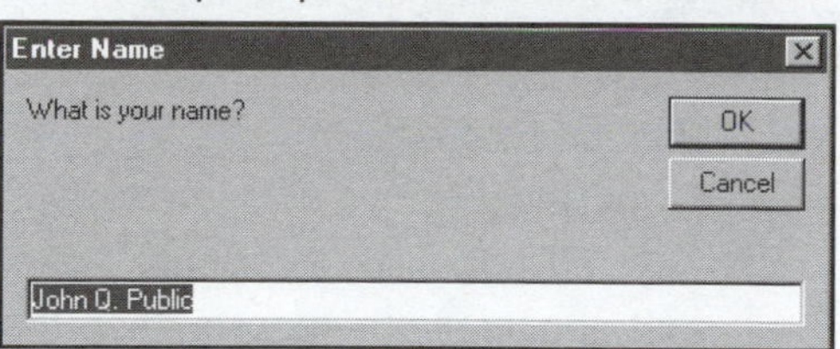

FIGURE 10-4
The InputBox function displays a window to prompt the user for information.

STEP-BY-STEP 10.4

1. Open **InputBox** from your data files and, if necessary, open the form.
2. Double-click the **Enter Name** button and add the code in CODE Step 2 to create an input box and display the text entered into it.
3. Close the Code window and run the program.
4. Click the **Enter Name** button. An input box appears on your screen, as shown in Figure 10-5.
5. Key your name and click the **OK** button. Your name appears on the form.
6. End the program, save your changes, and remove the project. Leave Visual Basic open for Step-by-Step 10.5.

CODE STEP 2

```
Dim strName As String

'Input name
strName = InputBox("What is your name?", "Enter Name", _
                   "John Q. Public")

'Display name
lblName.Caption = strName
```

FIGURE 10-5
The input box appears when the Enter Name button is clicked.

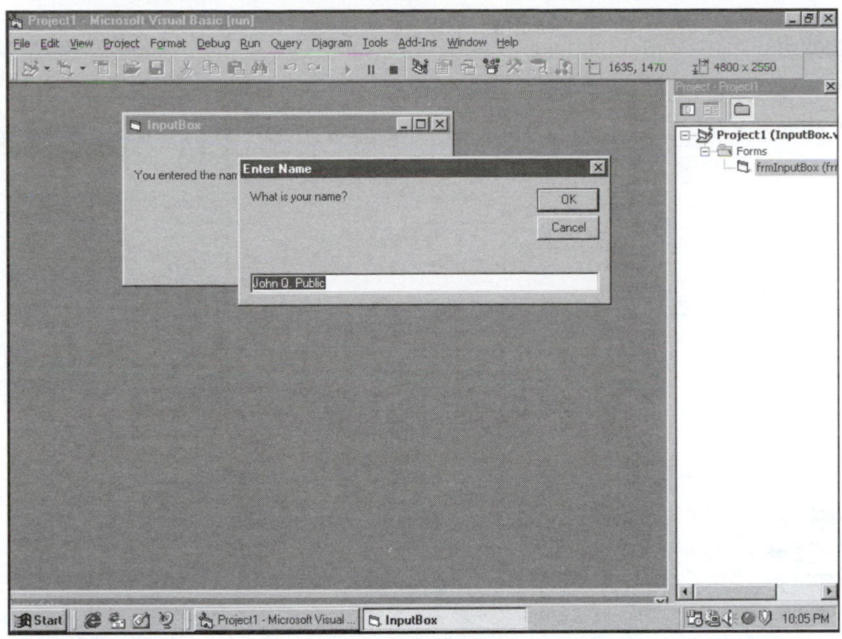

The InputBox function can be used inside a Do Until loop to repeatedly ask the user for data until a specified condition is met. For example, suppose you want to prompt the user for a list of numbers to be averaged. You do not know how many numbers the user will enter. All you know is that when the user enters a zero (0), the program should stop accepting numbers and calculate the average. This can be accomplished by placing a call to the InputBox function inside a Do Until loop.

STEP-BY-STEP 10.5

1. Open **Numbers10** from your data files and, if necessary, open the form.
2. Double-click the **Input Numbers** button and add the code in CODE Step 2 to declare and initialize the variables in the program.
3. Add the code in CODE Step 3 to input the numbers entered, perform the calculations, and display the results.
4. Close the Code window and run the program.
5. Click the **Input Numbers** button. An input box appears.
6. Key **10** and click the **OK** button. The input box reappears because a zero was not entered.
7. Key **20** and click the **OK** button.
8. Key **30** and click the **OK** button.
9. Key **0** and click the **OK** button. Because a zero was entered, the loop stops and the program displays the results on the form, as shown in Figure 10-6.

STEP-BY-STEP 10.5 CONTINUED

10. End the program, save your changes, and remove the project. Leave Visual Basic open for Step-by-Step 10.6.

FIGURE 10-6
Keying a zero stops the Do Until loop.

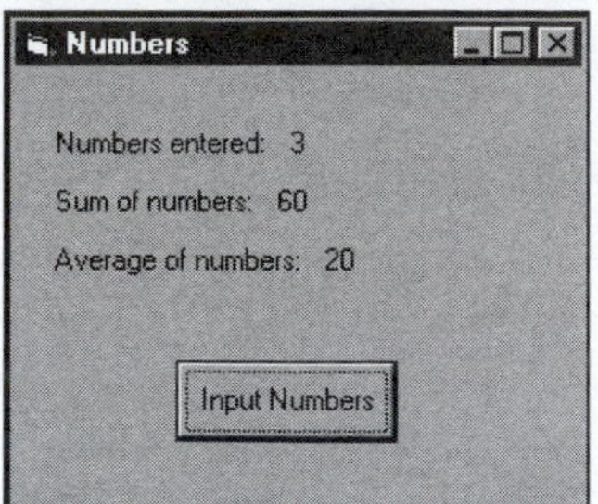

CODE STEP 2

```
Dim intNumber As Integer
Dim intAverage As Integer
Dim strAverage As String
Dim lngSum As Long
Dim strSum As String
Dim intCounter As Integer
Dim strCounter As String
Dim strDisplayTotal As String
Dim strDisplayAverage As String
Dim strDisplaySum As String

intCounter = 0
lngSum = 0
```

CODE STEP 3

```
'Input Numbers
Do
  intNumber = Val(InputBox("Enter an Integer (0 to Quit):", _
              "Input Number"))
  If (intNumber > 0) Then
     lngSum = lngSum + intNumber
     intCounter = intCounter + 1
  End If

Loop Until (intNumber = 0)

intAverage = lngSum / intCounter

'Store Results
strAverage = Format(intAverage, "###")
strCounter = Format(intCounter, "#####")
strSum = Format(lngSum, "#####")

strDisplayTotal = "Numbers entered:    " & strCounter
strDisplaySum = "Sum of numbers:    " & strSum
strDisplayAverage = "Average of numbers:    " & strAverage
```

CODE STEP 3 (CONTINUED)

```
'Display Results
lblTotal.Caption = strDisplayTotal
lblSum.Caption = strDisplaySum
lblAverage.Caption = strDisplayAverage
lblTotal.Visible = True
lblSum.Visible = True
lblAverage.Visible = True
```

Using the DoEvents Statement

As you already know, when an event is triggered, an event procedure is executed to handle the event. The event procedures you have created up to this point have been relatively short. The computer executes the code in the event procedure so quickly that you may not notice that it takes any time at all. When you begin using loops, however, an event procedure may occupy several seconds of the computer's time. There is also the potential that an endless loop may occur. Let's look at both of those possibilities.

Long Event Procedures

Suppose you have written a program that includes a loop that processes thousands of instructions. While the program is busy executing the loop, the program is unresponsive to other events because it is busy handling the current event.

STEP-BY-STEP 10.6

1. Open **LongLoop** from your data files and if necessary open the form.
2. Double-click the **Go** button and add the code in CODE Step 2 to create a loop that will count to five million.
3. Close the Code window and run the program.
4. Click the **Go** button. Notice that the program is unresponsive for a few seconds before the "Loop Ended" message appears.
5. Click the **Clear Label** button. The label becomes blank.
6. Click the **Go** button again. Again the program becomes unresponsive.
7. End the program and save your changes but leave the project open.

CODE STEP 2

```
Dim lngCounter As Long

lngCounter = 1
Do While lngCounter < 5000000
    lngCounter = lngCounter + 1
Loop
lblStatus.Caption = "Loop Ended"
```

Endless Loops

In an *endless loop*, the condition that is supposed to stop the loop from repeating never becomes True. This is usually a programming error. Inside every loop there should be code that causes a change that will eventually lead to the end of the looping. If no such code exists inside the loop, the loop may repeat endlessly.

Note

Depending on the speed of your computer, you may want to adjust the value in the Do While loop's condition expression to more or less than five million.

STEP-BY-STEP 10.7

1. Double-click the **Go** button.

2. Change the code inside the loop from lngCounter = lngCounter + 1 to **lngCounter = lngCounter + 0**.

Your screen should appear similar to Figure 10-7. This will create an endless loop because the counter will never reach five million.

3. Close the Code window and run the program.

4. Click the **Go** button. Notice that the computer seems to freeze.

5. Allow a short time to confirm that the computer is not responding, then press **Ctrl + Break** to pause the program. The Code window opens and highlights the code where the program stopped.

6. Click the **End** button to end the program.

7. Change the code in the loop back to lngCounter + 1.

8. Close the Code window and save your changes but leave the project open.

FIGURE 10-7

Changing the code in the loop as shown will produce an endless loop.

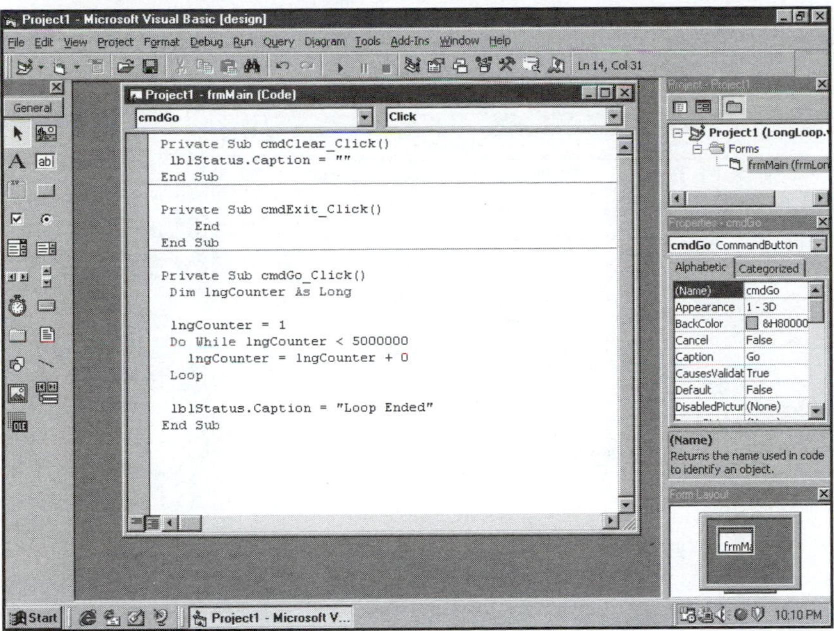

The DoEvents Statement

The *DoEvents statement* allows the computer to process other events, even though the current event procedure is not yet complete. By adding the DoEvents statement inside the loop that may occupy a lot of the computer's time, you make it possible to handle other events while the loop is finishing its work. Let's look at the difference the DoEvents statement makes.

Note

Pressing Ctrl + Break while a program is in an endless loop does not end the program. It suspends the execution so that you can see the line of code being executed. It also gives you the opportunity to end the program with the End button.

STEP-BY-STEP 10.8

1. Double-click the **Go** button and add **DoEvents** as the first instruction of the loop as shown in Figure 10-8.
2. Close the Code window and run the program.
3. Click the **Go** button. The long loop starts again; however, by using DoEvents the computer allows other events to take place. The DoEvents statement actually slows down the loop, making it take a long time to reach five million.
4. Click the **Exit** button. The loop ends and the program closes.
5. Change the value in the loop condition to 100000 and run the program again. The event procedure now completes in a shorter amount of time.
6. End the program and save your changes but leave the project open.

FIGURE 10-8
Adding the DoEvents code allows the computer to process other events while a loop is still taking place.

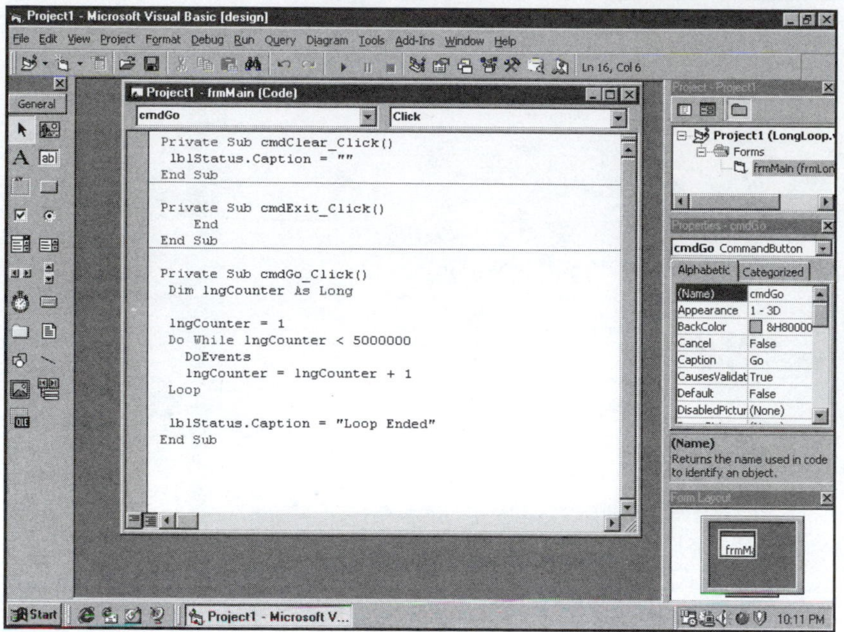

There is one more thing you should understand about using DoEvents. When the DoEvents statement is executed, the computer can process whatever other events are waiting to be processed, including the event that is not yet complete. For example, suppose you click a button to begin processing data. If the button's Click event procedure includes the DoEvents statement, you could actually click the same button again, starting the same process to begin again. This can have unpredictable and possibly disastrous results.

Note

The time required to complete the loop will vary between machines.

How do you prevent this from happening? It is a good idea to disable the button at the beginning of the event procedure to prevent the user from clicking the button again until the event is completely processed. Of course, you will want to enable the button again at the end of the procedure. Remember, the purpose of the DoEvents statement is to allow other events to be processed, not to allow the same event to be processed simultaneously.

STEP-BY-STEP 10.9

1. Double-click the **Go** button and above the loop add the code in CODE Step 1 to disable the Go button.
2. Below the loop add the code in CODE Step 2 to enable the Go button.
3. Close the Code window and run the program.

STEP-BY-STEP 10.9 CONTINUED

4. Click the **Go** button. Notice that the Go button becomes disabled until the loop finishes counting, as shown in Figure 10-9.

5. When the Go button is enabled again, click the **Exit** button.

6. Save your changes and remove the project but leave Visual Basic open.

FIGURE 10-9
Disabling the Go button prevents the same event procedure from being restarted before it is complete.

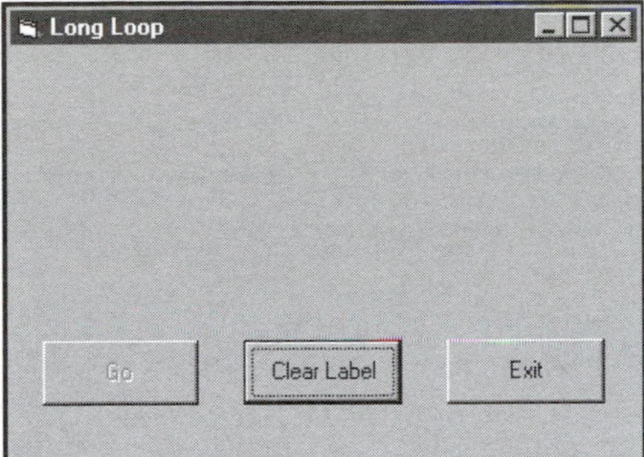

CODE STEP 1

```
cmdGo.Enabled = False
```

CODE STEP 2

```
cmdGo.Enabled = True
```

Using Nested Loops

Like If statements, loops may be nested. It is not uncommon to need a loop within a loop. For example, suppose you have a program that counts from 1 to 1000 on the screen. The program is executing so fast that the first value that appears is 1000. Inside the loop that is doing the counting, you can place another loop that simply slows the computer down.

STEP-BY-STEP 10.10

1. Open **Counter** from your data files and if necessary open the form.

2. Run the program and click the **Go** button. Notice that the program counts to 1000 too quickly to see that it is counting.

3. End the program.

4. Add the code in CODE Step 4 between the line intDelay = 1 and the line Loop 'End of outer loop.

5. Run the program again. You will be able to watch the numbers increase toward 1000. The Go button is disabled while the event is handled. After the count reaches 1000, the Go button is enabled again.

6. End the program, save your changes, and exit Visual Basic.

CODE STEP 4

```
'Begin nested loop
Do While intDelay <= 100
  DoEvents
  intDelay = intDelay + 1
Loop 'End of nested loop
```

Summary

In this lesson, you learned:

- Much of the work a computer does is repeated many times.
- Repetition in programs is accomplished using loops.
- A Do While loop repeats a group of statements while a certain condition is True.
- A Do Until loop repeats a group of statements until a certain condition becomes True.
- A Do loop condition applies a test to determine either a True or False result.
- A Do While loop tests the condition at the top of the loop.
- A Do Until loop tests the condition at the bottom of the loop. The code in a Do Until loop is always executed at least once.
- The InputBox function creates a window that prompts the user for input.
- To use the InputBox function, you supply the text for the prompt, the title for the window's title bar, and the optional default text for the text box.
- Sometimes, long event procedures can make a program unresponsive to other events.
- An endless loop is a loop in which the condition which stops the loop is never met.
- Pressing Ctrl + Break will pause a program with an endless loop and will highlight the code where the program stopped.
- The DoEvents statement allows the program to process other events while an event procedure is executing.
- Loops can be nested in the same way that If statements are nested.

LESSON 10 REVIEW QUESTIONS

TRUE/FALSE

Circle T if the statement is true or F if the statement is false.

T F 1. A loop will repeat a specified block of code a number of times.

T F 2. Both types of Do loops rely on a condition to be either True or False.

T F 3. A Do While loop tests the condition at the bottom of the loop.

T F 4. In a Do Until loop, the code in the loop is executed at least once.

T F 5. The MsgBox function displays a window to ask the user for input.

T F 6. In an endless loop, the condition that will stop the loop from repeating never becomes true.

T F 7. Unlike If statements, loops cannot be nested.

T F 8. Using a DoEvents statement prevents the computer from running multiple programs.

T F 9. You can use Ctrl + Break to pause a program that has entered an endless loop.

T F 10. A loop can contain only one statement.

WRITTEN QUESTIONS

Write a short answer to the following questions.

1. What is another name for the code required to create a loop?
2. What is the main difference between a Do While loop and a Do Until loop?
3. What keyword marks the end of the block of code contained within a loop?
4. Where is the condition of a Do Until loop tested?
5. What three parameters must you supply to the InputBox function?
6. What is the purpose of using the DoEvents statement?
7. How can you prevent the DoEvents statement from allowing a routine to be executed a second time before it is completely finished?
8. How many times will the following loop be executed?

```
intCount = 0
Do While intCount <= 5
     intCount = intCount + 1
Loop
```

9. How many times will the following loop be executed?

```
intCount = 7
Do While Count < 5
     intCount = intCount - 1
Loop
```

10. How many times will the following loop be executed?

```
intCount = 9
Do
     intCount = intCount - 1
Loop Until intCount <= 5
```

LESSON 10 PROJECTS

PROJECT 10-1

1. Start Visual Basic and open **Multiply** from your data files. If necessary, open the form.

2. Add the following code to the **Enter Number** button to create two input boxes.

```
Dim intNumber As Integer
Dim intTimes As Integer
Dim intCounter As Integer
Dim lngTimeWaster As Long

intCounter = 1

intNumber = Val(InputBox("Enter a number:", "Enter Number"))
intTimes = Val(InputBox("Multiply number by 2 how many times?", _
                      "Multiply"))
```

3. Add the following code to create a loop that will multiply intNumber by 2 intTimes number of times.

```
Do While intCounter < intTimes
    DoEvents
    intNumber = intNumber * 2
    lblAnswer.Caption = intNumber
    lngTimeWaster = 0
    'Slow program
    Do While lngTimeWaster < 500000
        lngTimeWaster = lngTimeWaster + 1
    Loop
    intCounter = intCounter + 1
Loop
```

4. Close the Code window and run the program to verify that it works correctly. (Remember that the maximum integer value is 32,767.)

5. Save your changes and remove the project but leave Visual Basic open.

PROJECT 10-2

1. Open **Ball** from your data files and if necessary open the form.

2. Add the following code to the **Go** button to create an input box that will determine the number of times the ball will bounce.

```
Dim intBounces As Integer
Dim intCounter As Integer

intCounter = 0

'Input bounces
intBounces = Val(InputBox _
    ("How many times should the ball bounce back and forth?", _
    "Input Bounces"))
```

3. Add the following code below the code for the input box to move the ball on the form.

```
'Bounce ball
Do
    DoEvents

    'Move ball right
    Do While shpBall.Left < 4200
        DoEvents
        shpBall.Left = shpBall.Left + 10
    Loop

    'Move ball left
    Do While shpBall.Left > 0
        DoEvents
        shpBall.Left = shpBall.Left - 10
    Loop

    intCounter = intCounter + 1

Loop Until intCounter = intBounces
```

4. Close the Code window and run the program.

5. Click the **Go** button and enter data into the input box to verify that the ball will bounce back and forth across the screen.

6. End the program and save your changes but leave the project open.

PROJECT 10-3

1. If necessary, open the **Ball** program you worked with in Project 10-2 and open the form.

2. Double-click the **Go** button and create an Integer variable named intTimeWaster.

3. Add the following code within each loop that moves the ball to slow down the speed of the ball.

```
'Slow the speed of the ball
intTimeWaster = 0
Do While intTimeWaster < 100
    DoEvents
    intTimeWaster = intTimeWaster + 1
Loop
```

4. Run the program and verify that the speed of the ball has decreased.

5. End the program and save your changes, then exit Visual Basic.

CRITICAL THINKING

Extend the **Numbers10** program you worked with in Step-by-Step 10.5 to do additional calculations. The program should also find the largest and smallest numbers entered by the user. (Hint: Set the largest number variable equal to the smallest possible integer and set the smallest number variable equal to the largest possible integer.)

LESSON 11

FOR NEXT LOOPS AND MULTIPLE FORMS

OBJECTIVES

When you complete this lesson, you will be able to:

- Use the Print statement to print text into a window.
- Use For Next loops.
- Nest For Next loops.
- Change label font settings.
- Use multiple forms in a project to add splash screens and About boxes.

Estimated Time: 2 hours

Using the Print Statement

Visual Basic includes a statement for printing to the screen that is a holdover from the original BASIC language. The Print statement will print text into the current window. There does not have to be a label control in the form. The Print statement prints directly into the window. For example, the statement below will print "Visual Basic" in the current window.

```
Print "Visual Basic"
```

The text produced by the Print statement is cleared using the Cls statement, which is short for *clear screen*. This is also a statement inherited from the original BASIC language.

Let's create a simple program that uses the Print and Cls statements.

STEP-BY-STEP 11.1

1. Start Visual Basic and open a new Standard EXE project.

2. Create one command button near the bottom of the form. Name the button **cmdDisplay** and change the caption to **Display**.

3. Add the code in CODE Step 3 to the Click event procedure of the Display button.

4. Close the Code window and run the program.

5. Click the **Display** button. The text appears in the window as shown in Figure 11-1.

6. Click the **Display** button again. The text prints again, below the original text.

7. Click the **Display** button several more times. The text extends below the bottom of the window.

8. End the program.

9. Add the code in CODE Step 9 to the top of the **Display** button Click event procedure.

10. Close the Code window and run the program again. Click the **Display** button several times to verify that the Cls statement is clearing the window each time the button is clicked.

11. End the program.

12. Save the form as **frmPrintCls** and save the project as **PrintCls**.

13. Remove the project but leave Visual Basic open for Step-by-Step 11.2.

FIGURE 11-1
The Print statement prints text in the active window.

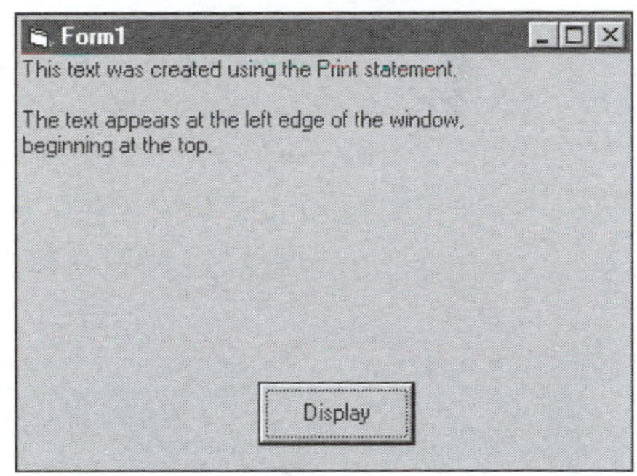

CODE STEP 3

```
Print "This text was created using the Print statement."
Print " "  'This statement inserts a blank line.
Print "The text appears at the left edge of the window,"
Print "beginning at the top."
```

CODE STEP 9

```
Cls 'Clear the window of any existing text
```

Using For Next Loops

The Do loops that you used in Lesson 10 repeat while a certain condition is True or until a certain condition is True. Sometimes, however, you simply want to repeat a block of code a specific number of times. For example, you might have some code that you would like to repeat ten times. You can do this with a Do While loop, using code like the following.

```
intCounter = 1
Do While intCounter <= 10
   'code that you want to repeat ten times would go here
   intCounter = intCounter + 1
Loop
```

There is nothing wrong with using a Do While loop like the one above. However, Visual Basic provides another kind of loop, the *For Next loop*, that is designed for repeating a block of code a specific number of times. Using a For Next loop, the same task provided by the Do While loop above can be achieved with code that is simpler and easier to read, like the example below.

```
For intCounter = 1 To 10
    'code that you want to repeat ten times would go here
Next
```

A For Next loop always begins with a For statement and ends with a Next statement. The statements between the For and Next statements are repeated the number of times specified in the For Next loop.

For Next loops always involve a Counter variable. This variable is usually an integer. If your loop will be counting in a range exceeding about 32,000, use a variable of type Long. While the loop is repeating, the Counter variable changes with each iteration of the loop.

STEP-BY-STEP 11.2

1. Open **ForNext** from your template files and if necessary open the form.
2. Add the code in CODE Step 2 to the **Count by One** button Click event procedure.
3. Close the Code window and run the program.
4. Click the **Count by One** button. The For Next loop prints the numbers 1 through 10 in the window, as shown in Figure 11-2.
5. End the program and save your changes but leave the project open for Step-by-Step 11.3.

FIGURE 11-2
The For Next loop causes the numbers 1 to 10 to appear in the window.

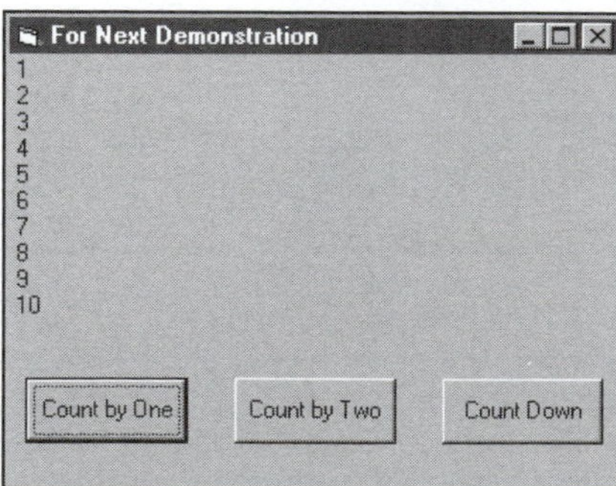

CODE STEP 2

```
Dim intCounter As Integer
Cls
For intCounter = 1 To 10
   Print intCounter
Next
```

Using the Step Keyword

Another useful feature of the For Next loop is the ability to specify the way the For Next loop counts. The Step keyword is used to cause the loop counter to count by an increment other than one. For example, the For Next loop below will count from 2 to 10 by twos.

```
For intCounter = 2 To 10 Step 2
   Print intCounter
Next
```

STEP-BY-STEP 11.3

1. Add the code in CODE Step 1 to the **Count by Two** button Click event procedure.
2. Close the Code window and run the program.
3. Click the **Count by Two** button. The counter counts by two, as shown in Figure 11-3.
4. End the program and save your changes but leave the project open for Step-by-Step 11.4.

FIGURE 11-3
The Step keyword can be used to cause the loop to count by two.

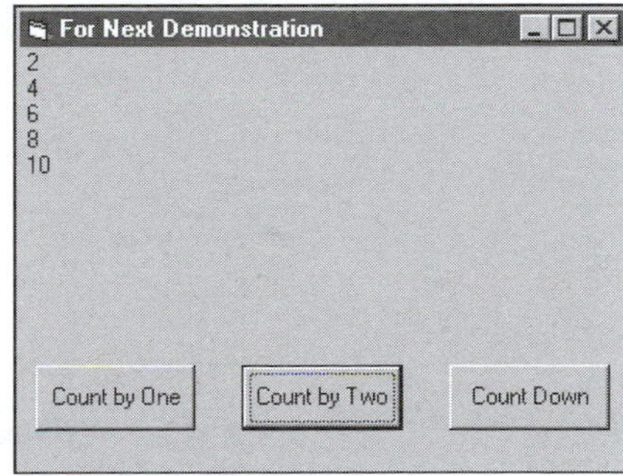

CODE STEP 1

```
Dim intCounter As Integer
Cls
For intCounter = 2 To 10 Step 2
   Print intCounter
Next
```

Would you like to count backwards? The Step keyword will allow you to do that, too. Just use a negative value after the Step keyword. If you use a negative Step value, make sure that the value on the left of the To keyword is greater than the value to the right of the To keyword. For example, in the code below, the For Next loop counts from 10 to 0.

```
For intCounter = 10 To 0 Step -1
  Print intCounter
Next
```

STEP-BY-STEP 11.4

1. Add the code in CODE Step 1 to the **Count Down** button Click event procedure.

2. Close the Code window and run the program.

3. Click the **Count Down** button. The counter counts backwards, as shown in Figure 11-4.

4. End the program and save your changes. Remove the project but leave Visual Basic open for Step-by-Step 11.5.

FIGURE 11-4
The Step keyword can be used to cause the loop to count backwards.

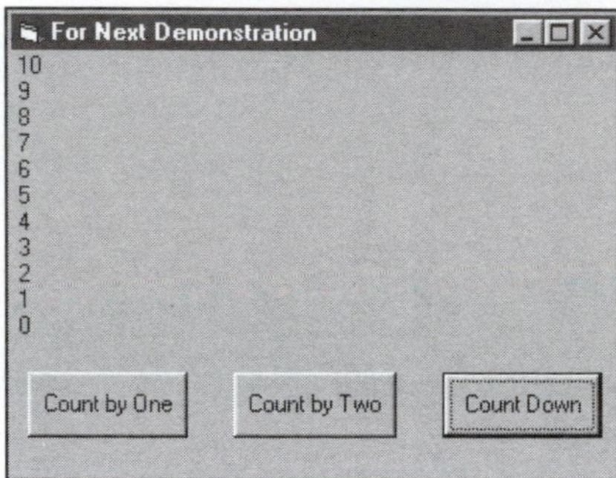

CODE STEP 1

```
Dim intCounter As Integer
Cls
For intCounter = 10 To 0 Step -1
   Print intCounter
Next
```

Nesting For Next Loops

For Next loops can be nested within other For Next loops or within Do loops. When you nest For Next loops, each nested loop must be completely contained within the outer loop. For example, in the code below, two For Next loops are nested within an outer For Next loop.

```
For intOuter = 1 To 10
  For intInner1 = 1 To 2
    'Code goes here
  Next
  For intInner2 = 1 To 4
    'Code goes here
  Next
Next
```

The indentation of the code helps you to identify which Next statement is paired with each For statement. However, there is an optional feature that can be used to make code for nested loops clearer. Following the Next keyword, you can specify which loop the Next keyword is ending by including the counter variable name. For example, the nested loops shown above could be coded as shown below to increase readability.

```
For intOuter = 1 To 10
  For intInner1 = 1 To 2
    'Code goes here
  Next intInner1
  For intInner2 = 1 To 4
    'Code goes here
  Next intInner2
Next intOuter
```

In Step-by-Step 11.5, you will create a set of nested loops that will generate a pattern of the letters A, B, and C in a window. You may have noticed in your use of the Print statement that each time the Print statement is used, the cursor automatically moves to the next line, as if the Enter key were pressed. This automatic advance of the cursor to the next line is called a *carriage return*. In the code in Step-by-Step 11.5, you will use the semicolon (;) to cause the Print statement to leave the cursor on the current line. In other words, the semicolon prevents the automatic hard carriage return.

Note

The term carriage return originated with the typewriter. The carriage was part of a mechanical typewriter. Even though there is no carriage involved in the electronic representation of text on your screen, the term is still used.

STEP-BY-STEP 11.5

1. Open **NestedFor** from your template files and if necessary open the form. The Clear Window and Exit buttons have already been coded for you.
2. Add the code in CODE Step 2 to create the Click event procedure for the **Begin Loop** button. Don't forget to place the semicolons after the Print statements that appear in the loops.
3. Try to predict the pattern that will be created by the nested loops. Write your prediction on paper.
4. Close the Code window and run the program.
5. Click the **Begin Loop** button. The pattern appears at the top of the window. Was your prediction correct? (ABCCBCCBCC four times)

STEP-BY-STEP 11.5 CONTINUED

6. Click the **Begin Loop** button again. The pattern is repeated below the first pattern.

7. Click the **Clear Window** button. The window clears, as shown in Figure 11-5.

8. End the program and save your changes. Remove the project but leave Visual Basic open for Step-by-Step 11.6.

FIGURE 11-5
The Clear Window button uses the Cls statement to clear the window.

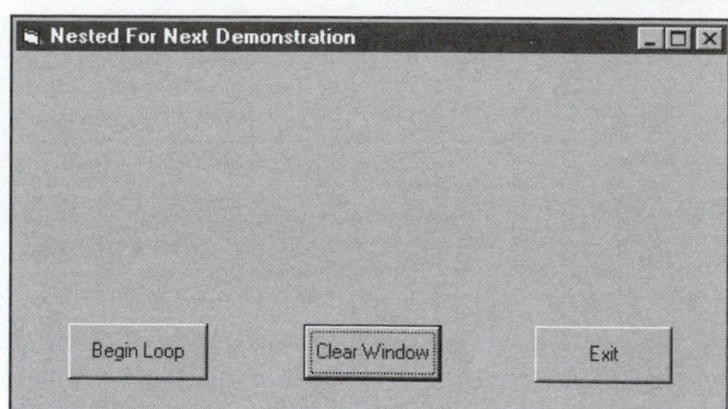

CODE STEP 2

```
Private Sub cmdLoop_Click()
  'Declare loop counters
  Dim intA As Integer
  Dim intB As Integer
  Dim intC As Integer
  'Create a blank line in the window
  Print ""
  'Print the character pattern
  For intA = 1 To 4
    Print "A";
    For intB = 1 To 3
      Print "B";
      For intC = 1 To 2
        Print "C";
      Next intC
    Next intB
  Next intA
  Print " End" 'Print "End" to end the pattern
End Sub
```

Changing Label Font Settings

When you create label controls on forms, you can control the font, style, and size using the Font property of the label control. You can make labels appear in any font installed on your computer.

To set the Font property of a label, select the label and click the ellipsis (...) in the Font property field in the Properties list. The Font dialog box appears, as shown in Figure 11-6.

FIGURE 11-6
The Font dialog box allows you to set the font, style, and size of a label.

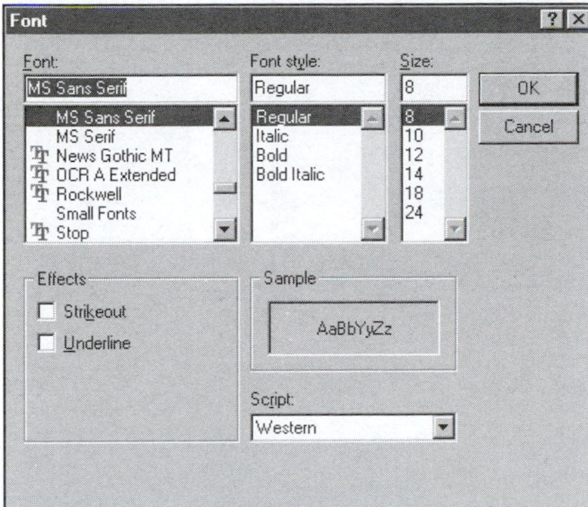

STEP-BY-STEP 11.6

1. Choose **New Project** from the **File** menu to open a new Standard EXE project.

2. Create a new label control on the form.

3. Name the label **lblLarge** and set the caption to **Large Label**.

4. With the label control selected, click the **Font** property field in the Properties list. Then click the ellipsis that appears at the end of the field. The Font dialog box appears.

5. Select **Arial** as the font, **Bold Italic** as the style, and **18** for the size. If your computer does not have Arial installed, select another font.

6. Click the **OK** button. The label's text appears in the larger font. However, the label control needs to be expanded to make all of the text visible.

7. Set the label control **AutoSize** property to True. The label is resized, as shown in Figure 11-7.

8. Save the form as **frmLabelFont**. Save the project as **LabelFont**, then exit Visual Basic.

FIGURE 11-7
The label appears in the new font.

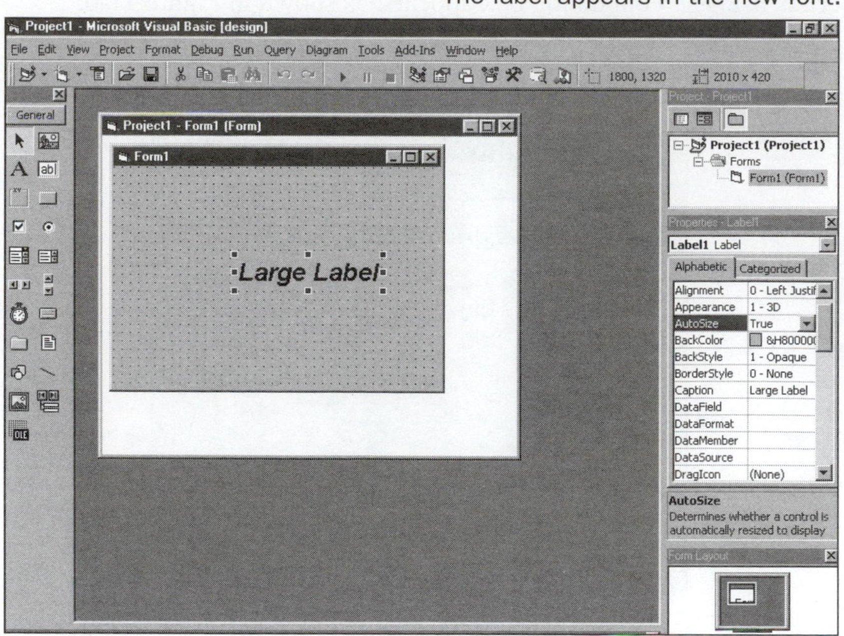

Using Multiple Forms

The programs you have been working with up to this point have involved only one form. Visual Basic, however, allows you to work with multiple forms. Common uses for additional forms include dialog boxes, splash screens, and About boxes.

You've seen examples of dialog boxes. Dialog boxes appear often in Windows programs. A *splash screen* is a window that appears briefly when a program is started. Programs like Microsoft Word have a splash screen that appears briefly while the program makes itself ready for use. An *About box* is a window that provides information about the program. An About box might include information like a registration number, version number, copyright, and information about the developer of the software.

STEP-BY-STEP 11.7

1. Start Visual Basic. Watch closely to see the splash screen that appears as Visual Basic loads, as shown in Figure 11-8.

2. The New Project dialog box that appears when you start Visual Basic is a good example of a dialog box. Click the **Cancel** button to remove the dialog box.

3. Choose **About Microsoft Visual Basic** from the **Help** menu. An About box opens, as shown in Figure 11-9.

4. Click the **OK** button. The About box closes.

5. Leave Visual Basic open for Step-by-Step 11.8.

FIGURE 11-8
A splash screen is a window that appears briefly as a program loads.

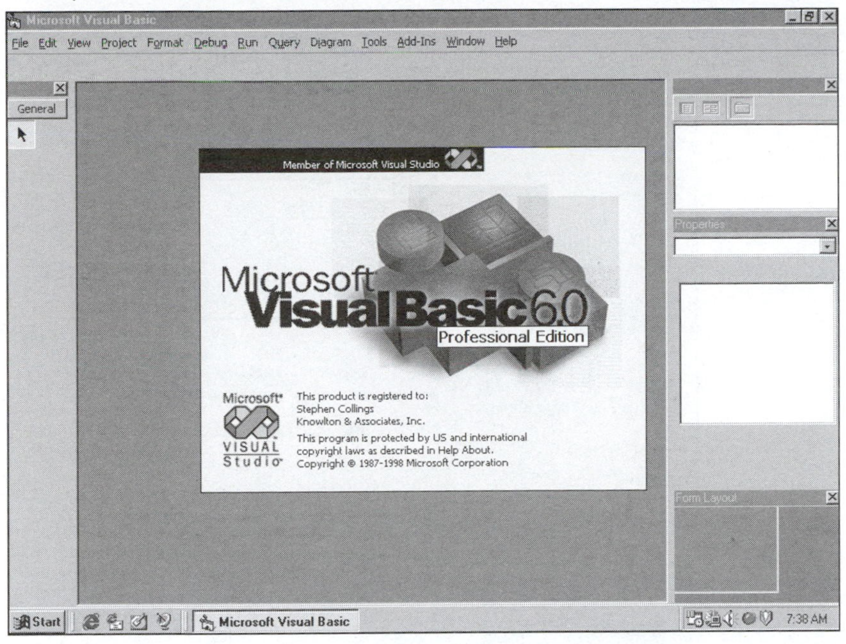

FIGURE 11-9
An About box tells you something about the program itself.

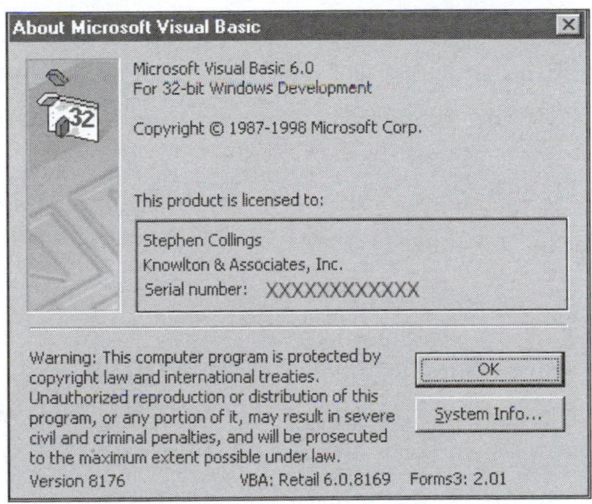

Visual Basic makes it easy to add additional forms to your programs. While there are many things that can be done with multiple forms, we are going to focus on two uses for multiple forms: splash screens and About boxes.

Setting Project Properties

Visual Basic will do most of the work of creating a splash screen and an About box for you. The splash screen and About box forms will automatically include the name and version number of your program. Visual Basic allows you to set these properties in the Make section of the Project Properties dialog box, as shown in Figure 11-10 (your dialog box may vary depending on which version of Visual Basic you are using).

FIGURE 11-10
The Project Properties dialog box allows you to set many options regarding the way your program is compiled and run.

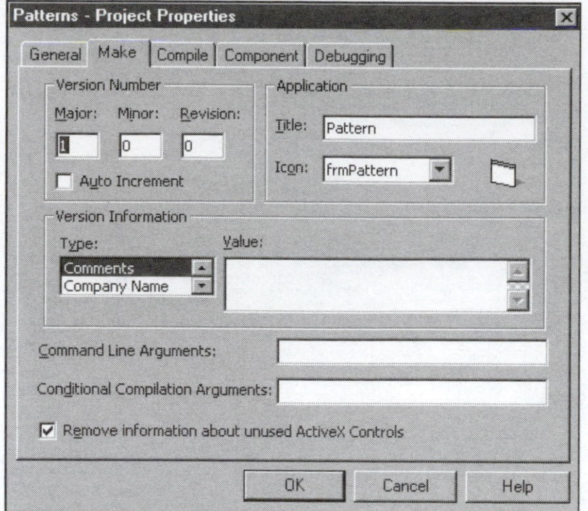

STEP-BY-STEP 11.8

1. Open **Patterns** from your template files and if necessary open the form. This program will create a pattern in the window, based on three nested loops, like the nested loop program you ran earlier in this lesson. This program allows you to specify the number of times each loop will repeat.

2. Run the program using various values in the three text fields and clicking the **Create Pattern** button. (Hint: The program runs best with values of 6 or less in the text boxes.) If the Create Pattern button becomes disabled, click the Clear Window button.

3. End the program.

4. Choose **Patterns Properties** (or choose Project 1 Properties) from the **Project** menu. The Project Properties dialog box appears.

5. Click the **Make** tab. The section of the dialog box that includes the application name and version number appears.

6. In the Version Number frame, change the zero (0) in the Minor text box to one (**1**). The version number is now 1.1.0.

7. In the application frame, change the Title to **Pattern Demonstrator**.

8. Click the **OK** button to close the dialog box.

9. Save your changes but leave the project open for Step-by-Step 11.9.

Adding a Splash Screen

When you want to give your programs a professional look, a splash screen is a good place to start. Like many other features, Visual Basic makes the process easy.

First, open the project to which you want to add the splash screen. Then choose Add Form from the Project menu. A dialog box will appear, allowing you to choose the kind of form you want to add, as shown in Figure 11-11 (options shown may vary).

FIGURE 11-11
There are several kinds of forms that can be added to a Visual Basic project.

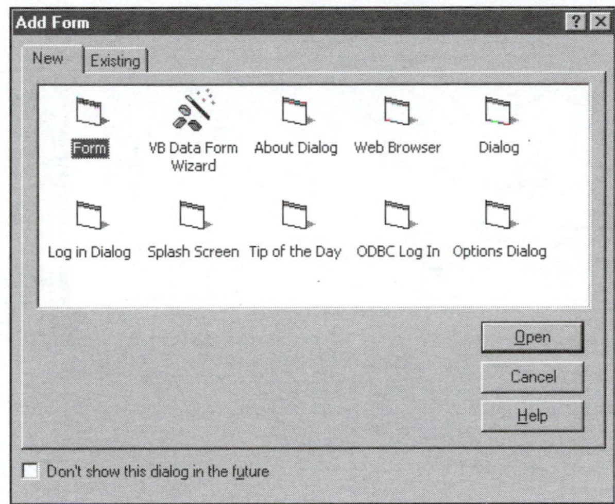

When you choose to add a splash screen, the form that appears already has a suggested layout. However, you can place any images and labels on the form that you like. The form also has labels that will be used to display the program name and version that you entered in the Project Properties dialog box. The code to insert the name and version number is generated automatically when the splash screen is created.

STEP-BY-STEP 11.9

1. Choose **Add Form** from the **Project** menu. The Add Form dialog box shown in Figure 11-11 appears.

2. Select the **Splash Screen** icon from the dialog box and click the **Open** button. A splash screen form appears, as shown in Figure 11-12 (options shown may vary).

3. There are several labels on the form to help create a suggested layout. For now, let's keep ours simple. Leave the image in place, but delete all of the labels except for the Product label and the Version label.

4. Change the font size of the Product label to **18** point. The splash screen form should appear similar to Figure 11-13.

5. Run the program. The splash screen does not appear. Why not?

6. End the program.

7. Save your changes (accept the proposed name for the splash screen file) but leave the project open for Step-by-Step 11.10.

FIGURE 11-12
The splash screen form has a suggested layout for a splash screen already created.

FIGURE 11-13
The splash screen form is now ready.

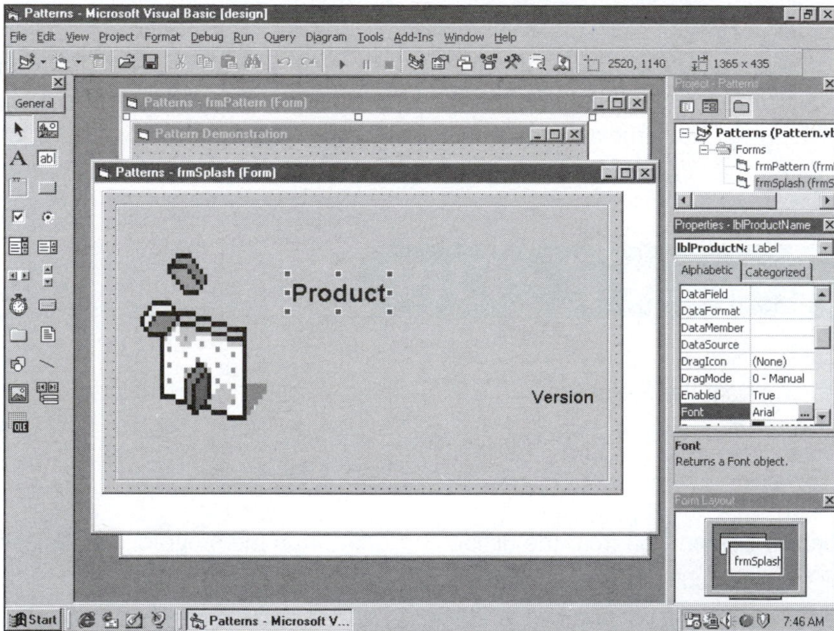

To get the splash screen you created to appear, you have to tell the project that you want to start with the splash screen form. But that's not all. You also have to code the splash screen to ensure that the correct form opens when the splash screen closes.

STEP-BY-STEP 11.10

1. Choose **Patterns Properties** (or choose Project 1 Properties) from the **Project** menu. The Project Properties dialog box appears, as shown in Figure 11-14 (your dialog box may vary).

2. In the General section of the dialog box, choose **frmSplash** as the Startup Object.

3. Click the **OK** button. The Project Properties dialog box closes.

4. If necessary, double-click the splash screen form in the Project Explorer window to open the splash screen.

5. Double-click the center of the splash screen form. The frmSplash Code window appears.

6. Locate the event procedure named Form_KeyPress. After the Unload Me statement, add the statement **frmPattern.Show**. The procedure should appear similar to the code in CODE Step 6. This procedure is executed when the user presses any key while the splash screen is on the screen. The Unload Me statement closes the splash screen and the frmPattern.Show statement opens the program's main form.

CODE STEP 6

```
Private Sub Form_KeyPress(KeyAscii As Integer)
    Unload Me
    frmPattern.Show
End Sub
```

FIGURE 11-14
The Project Properties dialog box allows you to choose the form which appears on startup.

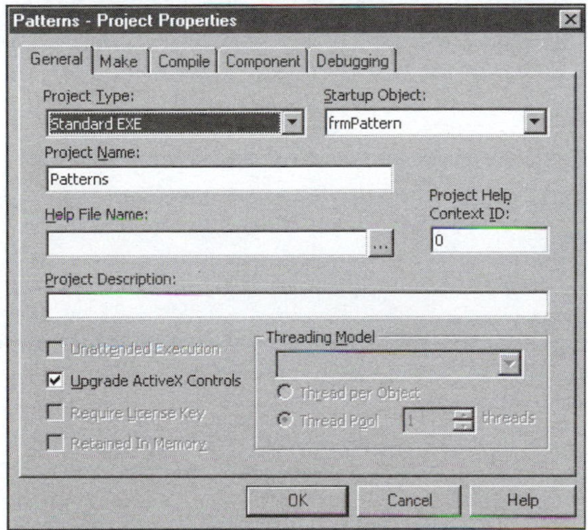

7. We also want the splash screen to close when the splash screen is clicked. Locate the event procedure named Frame1_Click. Modify the procedure to appear as shown in CODE Step 7.

8. Close the Code window and run the program. The splash screen appears. Notice that the program name and version number that you entered in the Project Properties dialog box appears in the splash screen, as shown in Figure 11-15.

9. Press any key to activate the Form_KeyPress event procedure, which closes the splash screen and opens the program's main form.

10. End the program.

11. Run the program again. This time, click the splash screen to test the Frame1_Click event procedure.

12. End the program and save your changes but leave the project open for Step-by-Step 11.11.

FIGURE 11-15
The splash screen you created appears each time the program is run.

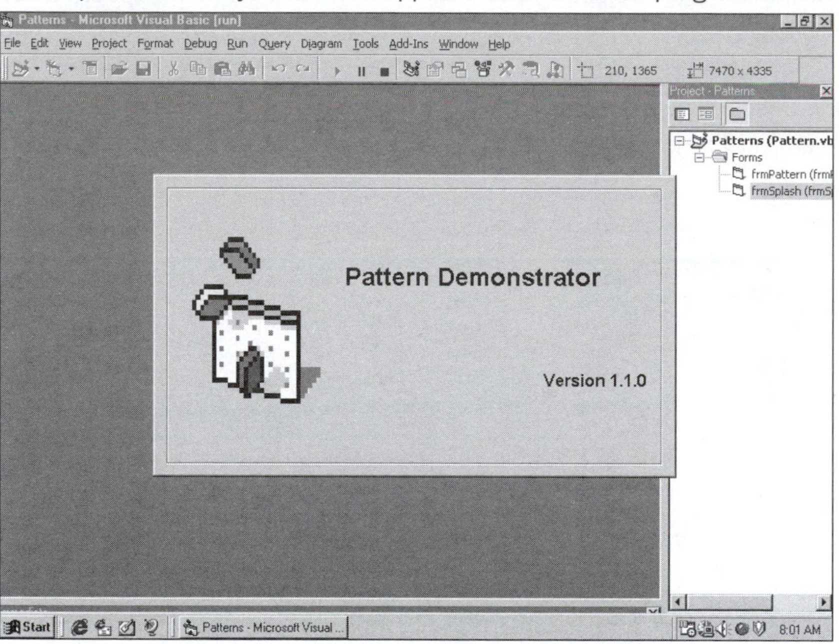

CODE STEP 7

```
Private Sub Frame1_Click()
Unload Me
    frmPattern.Show
End Sub
```

Adding an About Box

Adding an About Box is similar to adding a splash screen. Visual Basic will create a suggested About box for you. Rather than have the program start by displaying the About box, the About box is usually accessed by a command button or menu.

STEP-BY-STEP 11.11

1. Choose **Add Form** from the **Project** menu. The Add Form dialog box appears.

2. Select the **About Dialog** icon from the dialog box and click **Open**. An About box form appears, as shown in Figure 11-16.

3. Delete the label that has the caption that begins with *Warning*.

4. Change the caption of **lblDescription** (the one that has the caption of App Description) to the sentence below.

```
This program demonstrates how For
Next loops can be used to create
patterns of letters.
```

5. Close frmAbout. Make sure the main form (frmPattern) is open.

6. Double-click the **About** button. Add the code in CODE Step 6 to the button's Click event procedure.

7. Close the Code window and run the program. The splash screen should appear.

8. Click the splash screen to remove it from the screen.

9. Click the **About** button to display the About box. Notice the program's name and version number appear in the About box.

10. Click the **OK** button to close the About box.

11. End the program.

12. Save your changes (accept the proposed name for the About file) and exit Visual Basic.

CODE STEP 6

```
frmAbout.Show
```

FIGURE 11-16
Visual Basic creates a suggested About box automatically.

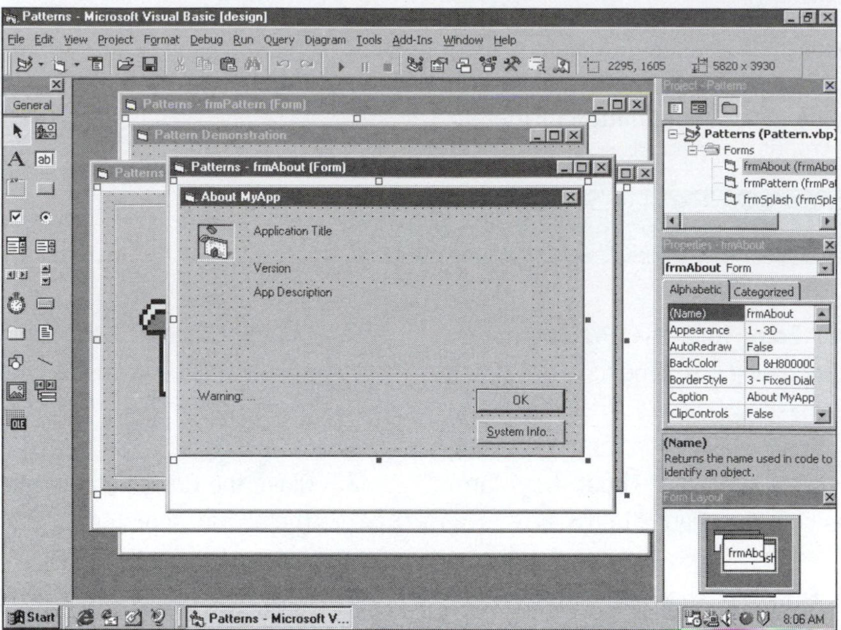

Summary

In this lesson, you learned:

- Visual Basic includes the Print statement for printing text in the current window.
- The Cls statement will clear the text from a window.
- A For Next loop is designed for repeating a block of code a specific number of times.
- A For Next loop always begins with a For statement and ends with a Next statement. The statements between the For and Next statements are repeated the number of times specified in the For Next loop.
- For Next loops always involve a Counter variable.
- If you want a For Next loop to count by an increment other than one, you can use the Step keyword. The Step keyword can also be used to make a For Next loop count backwards.
- For Next loops can be nested.
- Indenting your code can help make nested For Next loops easier to read. You can also use Next statements that specify the Counter variable of the loop.
- Using a semicolon in a Print statement will prevent the automatic carriage return at the end of the Print statement.
- You can use the Font property to change the font, style, and size of a label.
- Visual Basic programs can include multiple forms. Splash screens and About boxes are two common uses for additional forms in a program.

LESSON 11 REVIEW QUESTIONS

TRUE/FALSE

Circle T if the statement is true or F if the statement is false.

T F 1. The Print statement will print text into the current window.

T F 2. A Do While loop cannot be used to repeat a block of code a specific number of times.

T F 3. A For Next loop always begins with a For statement and ends with a Next statement.

T F 4. A For Next loop always involves a Counter variable.

T F 5. You cannot count backwards with a For Next loop.

T F 6. When For Next loops are nested, each nested loop must be completely contained within the outer loop.

T F 7. The term carriage return is no longer used since computers, unlike typewriters, do not have a carriage.

T F 8. A label's Font property can be used to control its appearance on a form.

T F 9. An About box is a window that appears briefly when a program is started.

T F 10. When you choose to add a splash screen to your program, Visual Basic already has a default layout for the form that you cannot change.

WRITTEN QUESTIONS

Write a short answer to the following questions.

1. The Print statement originated in which programming lanuguage?
2. Where does text appear on a form when displayed using the Print statement?
3. What statement clears text produced by the Print statement?
4. For what purpose is the For Next loop specifically designed?
5. What keyword allows you to count by an increment other than one when used with a For Next loop?
6. Why might you include a Counter variable name after the Next statement of a For Next loop?
7. Which character allows you to leave the cursor on the current line when using the Print statement?
8. Name three uses of multiple forms in a project.
9. What is a splash screen?
10. How do you choose which form will appear first when your program runs?

LESSON 11 PROJECTS

PROJECT 11-1

1. Start Visual Basic and open **Name** from your data files. If necessary, open the form.
2. Add the following code to the **OK** button so a Print statement will display on the form using the name that is entered in the textbox.

```
Cls
Print "Hello " & txtName.Text; "!"
Print ""
Print "How are you today?"
```

3. Close the Code window and run the program.

4. Key your first name and click the **OK** button to verify that the program works.

5. End the program and save the changes. Remove the project but leave Visual Basic open.

PROJECT 11-2

1. Open **ForNextLoops** from your data files and if necessary open the form.

2. Add the following code to the **Count by Three** button.

```
Dim intCounter As Integer
Cls
For intCounter = 3 To 21 Step 3
   Print intCounter
Next
```

3. Add the following code to the **Count Down by Four** button.

```
Dim intCounter As Integer
Cls
For intCounter = 24 To 0 Step -4
   Print intCounter
Next
```

4. Close the Code window and run the program.

5. Before clicking each button, try to determine what the output is going to be.

6. Click both buttons to verify if you were correct.

7. End the program and save your changes. Remove the project but leave Visual Basic open.

PROJECT 11-3

1. Open the **InputBox** program you worked with in Lesson 10.

2. Change the font size of the **lblName** label to **12** and change the font style to **Bold**.

3. Run the program.

4. Enter data into the input box and notice how the name on the form has changed when you click the **OK** button.

5. End the program and save your changes. Remove the project but leave Visual Basic open.

PROJECT 11-4

1. Open **ABC Pattern** from your data files and if necessary open the form.

2. Add the following code for the Begin Loop button to create a pattern using the letters A, B, and C.

```
'Declare loop counters
Dim intA As Integer
Dim intB As Integer
Dim intC As Integer
'Create a blank line in the window
Print ""
'Print the character pattern
For intA = 1 To 3
    Print "A";
    For intB = 1 To 4 Step 2
        Print "B";
    Next intB
    For intC = 3 To 9 Step 3
        Print "C";
    Next intC
Next intA
Print "    --- End ---"
```

3. Close the Code window and run the program.

4. Try to determine what the output is going to be, then click the Begin Loop button to verify if you are correct. (ABBCCC three times)

5. End the program, save your changes, and exit Visual Basic.

Create a splash screen and an About box for the NestedFor project you worked with in

CRITICAL THINKING

Step-by-Step 11.5. You can decide whether you want to modify all the label control captions on the splash screen form or delete the labels that you don't need. Keep in mind the following items when completing this activity:

1. You will need to change the version number of the program.

2. You will need to create an About button on the form.

3. You will need to type a description of the program in the lblDescription label of the About form.

Visual Basic Review

UNIT REVIEW

REVIEW QUESTIONS

TRUE/FALSE

Circle T if the statement is true or F if the statement is false.

T F 1. Command buttons, text boxes, and labels are all Visual Basic objects called controls.

T F 2. The label control's Text property can be used to display output information or the result of a calculation.

T F 3. A variable can be made visible to an entire form by declaring the variable in the Global Declarations section of the form's code window.

T F 4. The Value property of a check box control will contain a value of 1 if the check box is checked.

T F 5. When using the InputBox function, you must pass three string parameters to the function.

FILL-IN-THE-BLANK

1. An image contained in a form can be hidden from view by setting the ______________ property to False.

2. A(n) ______________ label is a statement in a Visual Basic program that is terminated by a colon.

3. The ______________ property specifies the location where the cursor will be placed when a text box gets the focus.

4. An object that is used as a container for other objects is the ______________ control.

5. The ______________ keyword can be used with the For Next loop to count by some increment other than one.

PROJECTS

PROJECT 2-1

In this project, you will use the Left property of an image control to move an image on the form while the program is running.

1. If necessary, start Visual Basic and create a new project.
2. Use the **Properties** window and give the form the name **frmLeftRight** and the caption **LeftRight**.
3. Use the **Properties** window to set the **Height** property of the form to **3400**, then press the **Enter** key.
4. Use the **Properties** window to set the **Width** property of the form to **4700**, then press the **Enter** key.
5. Add an **Exit** button (with an appropriate caption and name) to the bottom-right corner of the form. Add code to make the program end when the button is active.
6. Add the VBasic image to the form with the name **imgVBasic** and set the **Stretch** property to **True**.
7. Set both the **Height** and **Width** properties of the image control to **1500**.
8. Set the **Top** property of the image control to **200**.
9. Set the **Left** property of the image control to **400**.
10. Add a **Left** button to the lower-left corner of the form and give it an appropriate caption and name.
11. Add a **Right** button between the Left and Exit buttons and give it an appropriate caption and name.
12. Add code to the **Left** button that will position the image as close as possible to the left side of the form.
13. Add code to the **Right** button that will position the image as close as possible to the right edge of the form.
14. Make the **Exit** button the button that will be activated when the **Esc** key is pressed.
15. Save the form as **frmLeftRight** and save the project as **LeftRight**.
16. Run the program and test all of the buttons.
17. End the program, then exit Visual Basic.

If your Left and Right buttons did not place the image correctly when you ran the program, double-click the command buttons, change the measurements in the Code window, then run the program again.

PROJECT 2-2

In this project you will use text boxes to receive information and calculate a value based on the information received. The result of the calculation will be displayed in a label control.

1. If necessary, start Visual Basic and create a new Standard.exe project.

2. In the **Properties** window, change the form name to **frmAmps**, and Caption property to **Calculate Amps**.

3. Create a **label** control on the left side of the form. Change the label Name property to **lblVolts**, and the Caption property to **Amount of Voltage**. Add a **text box** control to the right of the **lblVolts** control, and change the property name to **txtVolts**, and change the default Text property to **0**.

4. Create another **label** control on the left side of the form. Change the label Name property to **lblOhms**, and the Caption property to **Resistance in Ohms**. Add a **text box** control to the right of the **lblOhms** control, and change the property name to **txtOhms**, and change the default Text property to **0**.

5. Add another **label** control below the **lblOhms** and **txtOhms** control. Name the new control **lblAmps**. Delete the default text in the Caption property, and leave the caption **blank**. Set the Visible property for the control to **False**.

6. Add two **buttons** to the bottom of the form. Place one of the buttons on the left side of the form, and change its Name property to **cmdCalculate**, and its Caption property to **Calculate**. Place the other button on the right side of the form, and change its Name property to **cmdExit**, and its Caption property to **Exit**.

7. Add code for the **cmdCalculate** button to calculate the number of amps for the given voltage and ohms, using the formula **amps = voltage / ohm**. Declare a variable of type **Single** named **sngAmps** to hold the result of the calculation. Use the **Val** function to convert the values in the text boxes to numeric values.

8. Set the **lblAmps** Caption property to display the message, "**The amount of Current in Amps is**", and concatenate the value in **sngAmps** to the string. Use the **Fix** function to convert the variable to a string format. Change the visible property of the program to **True**.

9. Add code to the **cmdExit** button to end the program when it is pressed.

10. Close the Code window and run the program. Enter values into the text boxes and click the **Calculate** button. If the program does not work correctly, fix any errors and run it again.

11. End the project and save it. Save the form as **frmAmps**, and Project as **CalcAmps**. Exit Visual Basic.

PROJECT 2-3

In this project you will modify an existing project to add additional functionality and features.

1. If necessary, start Visual Basic and create a new Standard.exe project.
2. Open the **CalcAmps** project created in **Project 2-2**. Change the name of the form to **frmAmps2**. Save the form using that name, and save the project as **CalcAmps2**.
3. Select the form, and change the Height property to **4200**, change the Width property to **5400**.
4. Add a **label** control below the command buttons, nearly as wide as the form itself. Change the Name property to **lblWarning**, and **delete the text** in the Caption property. Set the BackColor property to **white**, and change the BorderStyle property to **1 - single**. Set the Visible property to **False**. Set the Font property size to **12**, and the font style to **Bold**.
5. **Double-click** the cmdCalculate button to open the Code window. Below the existing code for this button, add If...Else statements to do the following. If **sngAmps** is greater than 5 but less than 10, set the **lblWarning** caption to: "**Caution: Current is greater than 5 amps**." Set the visible property to **True**, and set the font color to **blue**. (To do this, use the statement: **lblWarning.ForeColor = vbBlue**). If **sngAmps** is **greater than 10**, change the caption to: "**Warning, Current is greater than 10 amps**." Set the forecolor to **vbRed**, and make the label visible. If the current is **less than or equal to 5**, **clear** the Caption property and set the Visible property to **False**.
6. Add a new **command button** between cmdCalculate and cmdExit. Set the name of the new button to **cmdReset**, and set its caption to **Reset**. **Double-click** the button to add code to reset the form to accept new values. Clear the **lblWarning** Caption property and the **lblAmps** Caption property. Set the Visible properties for those two labels to **False**.
7. Open the Code window if necessary and modify the **GotFocus** procedure to select the current text for both the **txtVolts**, and the **txtOhms** text boxes when they receive the focus.
8. Add code to the beginning of the cmdCalculate **Click** event procedure to **disable** the **cmdCalculate** button, and to **enable** the **cmdReset** button. Add code to the beginning of the cmdReset **click** event procedure to **disable** the **cmdReset** button, and to **enable** the **cmdCalculate** button.
9. Add code to the form **Load** procedure to **disable** the **cmdReset** button.
10. Run the program and try several combinations to be sure all buttons and code are working properly. Save the project and exit Visual Basic.

PROJECT 2-4

The factorial of a number is the product of all the positive whole numbers from 1 to n. The symbol for factorial is !. In the following steps you will add code to a program so it will calculate the factorial of a number entered by the user.

1. Start a new Visual Basic standard.exe project. Change the form Name property to **frmFact**, and the Caption property to **Calculate Factorial**. Save the form as **frmFact** and the project as **Factorial**.

2. Add a **label** control about the width of the form. Change the Name property to **lblHeading**, and set the Caption property to: "**This program will calculate the factorial value of a given number**".

3. Add another **label** control, change the Name property to **lblPrompt**, and the Caption property to: "**Enter an integer value**".

4. Add a **text box** control, change its Name property to **txtValue**, and set the Text property to **zero**.

5. Add a **command button** to the bottom of the form. Change the Name property of the button to **cmdCalculate**, and set the Caption property to **Calculate**.

6. Add the following code to the **Calculate** event procedure.

```
Dim strMessage As String
Dim dblNumber As Double
Dim dblResult As Double

dblNumber = Val(txtValue.Text)

If dblNumber > 17 Then
      MsgBox "The value is too big. Please enter another number."
Else
            Dim I As Integer
            dblResult = dblNumber
            For I = (dblNumber - 1) To 1 Step -1
                  dblResult = dblResult * I
      Next I
      strMessage = dblNumber & "! = " & dblResult
      MsgBox strMessage
End If
```

7. Add another **command button** to the bottom of the form. Change the Name property to **cmdExit**, and the Caption property to **Exit**. Add code to end the program when clicked.

8. Add code for the **text box** that will highlight the text when the text box is clicked.

9. Test the program by running it, then entering a value and clicking the **Calculate** button.

10. Stop the program by clicking the **Exit** button.

11. Add a **splash screen** to the program. The splash screen should contain at least the name of the program. Save this form as **frmSplash.frm**.

12. Add code to the project, and make the necessary changes to the project settings so that the splash screen is displayed when the program is run. Also add any required code to make the splash screen close and display the main form when the splash screen is **clicked**.

13. Run the program and test your changes. When everything is working correctly, save your changes, remove the project, and exit Visual Basic.

SIMULATION

SIMULATION 2-1

Create a new Visual Basic project to calculate the length of a movie in hours. The program will ask the user to input the length of a movie in minutes, and display the result in hours and remaining minutes if any. For example, if a movie lasts 125 minutes, the time displayed by the program would indicate that it runs 2 hours and 5 minutes. You can use variables of type Integer if calculating only in whole numbers, or you can use Single if you choose to allow fractional minutes. Create the program with your own user interface design and save the project with an appropriate form and project name.

SIMULATION 2-2

It is common for a computer to be connected to a device called an uninterruptible power supply (UPS). A UPS is a battery backup that immediately begins supplying power to the computer when a power outage or other power problem occurs. UPSs come in many sizes, which are measured in volt-amps. When you purchase a UPS, you must decide how large a UPS is necessary for your system. For example, if you just need time to save your documents and shut down the computer in the event of an outage, you may only need five or ten minutes of power to be provided by the UPS. Some computers, such as network servers, need much more time. In fact, you hope that the power will be restored to normal before the battery backup is exhausted.

In this project, you will design a program that recommends a UPS to a user based on the number of minutes of backup time required. The program should prompt the user for a number of minutes and use the Select Case statement below to decide which model UPS to recommend.

```
Select Case intMinutes Case 1 To 9
      strModel = "Power 300" Case 10 To 15
      strModel = "Power 450" Case 16 To 30
      strModel = "Power 650" Case 31 To 40
      strModel = "Power 750" Case 41 To 60
      strModel = "Power 1000" Case Is > 60
      strModel = "See sales representative" Case Else
      strModel = "Invalid or incomplete data"
End Select
```

Create the program using your own user interface design and save the project with an appropriate form and project name.

SIMULATION 2-3

Find an image that represents your school. The image can be found in a yearbook or magazine, or school publication. Scan the image to your computer. If you don't have access to a scanner, find any appropriate image on the Internet. Add the image to a form and create check boxes or option buttons to perform the following tasks:

- Double or halve the size of the image.
- Show and hide the image.
- Change the position of the image.
- Change the BackColor of the form.

Save the form and project using an appropriate name and exit Visual Basic.

GLOSSARY

A

About box A window that provides information about the program.

ActiveX A type of control for Web pages that can be added to your programs.

alphanumeric Text that can include letters or numbers.

Application Wizard A feature of Visual Basic that allows you to create a complete program with standard Windows features already included.

assignment operator (=) Assigns the value to the right of the operator to the item to the left of the operator.

AutoRedraw property Allows you to choose whether you want to draw temporary graphics or persistent graphics.

AutoSize property Adjusts the size of a control to fit its contents.

B

Boolean data type A data type that can hold the values True or False.

Boolean variable A variable that can store the results of an expression that includes conditional operators.

C

Cancel property The property that when set to True activates a certain command button when the Esc key is pressed.

carriage return Automatic advance of the cursor to the next line.

Case Else statement The default code applied if the code for no other Case statement is executed.

case-sensitive A system where an uppercase letter is distinguished from its lowercase counterpart.

checkboxes Allow a program to ask the user a Yes or No question or to turn an option on or off.

clear screen (Cls) A statement for clearing the text produced by a Print statement.

code label A name that appears in code.

command button A standard pushbutton control.

comments Notes in the code that will be ignored by the compiler.

concatenation Appending one string to the end of another.

conditional operators Symbols used in making comparisons.

controls The command buttons, text boxes, scroll bars, and other objects that make up the user interface.

currency Data type used for dollars and cents calculations.

D

declaring The process of letting the compiler know that you want to set up a memory location as a variable, what you want to call the variable, and what data type you want the variable to have.

Default property The property that when set to True activates a certain command button when the Enter key is pressed.

Do Until loop Repeats statements *until* a certain condition is True.

Do While loop Repeats statements *while* a certain condition is True.

DoEvents statement Allows the computer to process other events, even though the current event procedure is not yet complete.

double Data type used for general decimal types exceeding six or seven digits.

E

ellipsis Three small dots appearing in a row, representing the opportunity to browse the hard drive.

Enabled property Can make a control take on a grayed appearance, making it inactive but still visible.

endless loop A loop in which the condition that is supposed to stop the loop from repeating never becomes True.

error handler (error-handling routine) The code that will be executed if an error occurs.

error trapping The process of interrupting the normal chain of events that occurs when an error is encountered and replacing that chain of events with your own code.

event procedure The code written to handle a specific event.

event An action taken by the user or generated by some process that causes an event-driven program to respond.

event-driven A system where user-triggered events direct the operation of the program.

exception An unexpected error condition.

Exit Sub statement Forces the event procedure to end, regardless of whether there is more code in the procedure.

exponentiation The process of raising a number to a power.

F

factorial The product of all the positive whole numbers from 1 to n.

Fix function Returns a truncated whole number after a calculation is performed.

flowcharts Charts used to plan and to document program code.

focus The object that is currently active.

For Next loop A loop specifically designed for repeating a block of code a specific number of times.

Form Layout window The window that shows the position the form will take when the program is run.

Format function Allows you to apply custom formatting to a number before displaying the value.

form-level variable Declared in the General Declarations section of a form's Code window and is accessible to all objects on the form.

forms Objects that become the windows and dialog boxes when the application runs.

frame control A container for other controls.

G

global variable Declared in a code module's General Declarations section and is accessible to all forms in the program.

H

hard-coded Refers to information that is entered directly into the source code and cannot change while the program runs.

I

If statement Allows you to execute specified code when the result of a conditional expression is True.

image control An object that provides a framework for displaying an image on a form.

InputBox function Displays a window to ask the user for input.

integer division Returns only the whole number portion of division of integers.

integers Whole numbers.

Intellisense® The technology used in Visual Basic that will anticipate what you are about to key and will complete your statements for you.

internal documentation Comments added to programs.

iteration structure The code required to create a loop.

L

label control Used to place text on a form.

Len function Determines the length of the text in a textbox.

Line method A method for drawing lines and boxes on a form from code.

line-continuation character Tells the compiler to skip to the next line and treat the text there as if it were a part of the same line.

literals Values that are keyed directly into source code.

Load event The event that is triggered when a form is loaded and opened.

local variable Declared within an event procedure and is accessible only within that procedure.

logical operators Operators that can be used to combine several comparisons into one statement.

loop A method to repeat a group of statements a number of times.

M

Menu Editor A feature that allows you to create menu items and set the properties of the menu controls.

message The order sent to an object to trigger a method to be performed.

method A command that directs an object to make a change to its state.

modulus Returns the remainder of integer division.

MsgBox function Causes a dialog box to pop up, displaying a message that you specify.

N

nested If statement An If statement inside another If statement.

O

objects The items that make up a Visual Basic program.

one-way selection structure A program structure in which the decision is whether to go "one way" or just bypass the code in the If statement.

operators Symbols that perform specific operations in Visual Basic statements.

option buttons A group of buttons that can only be selected one at a time.

Option Explicit A statement that causes Visual Basic to generate an error message if you attempt to use a variable that has not been declared.

option group Option buttons in a frame.

order of operations The rules related to the order in which operations are performed in mathematical calculations.

P

persistent graphic A graphic that will automatically redraw itself and be redisplayed after being hidden by another window or object.

Point method Retrieves the Visual Basic color constant of the specified pixel.

Printer object A collection of programming code that allows you to communicate with the printer.

PrintForm command A command that sends the contents of the form to the printer.

project A group of files comprising a program.

Project Explorer The window that allows you to see the forms and files that make up your program.

Properties window The window that allows you to see and change characteristics of a selected object.

properties The characteristics of an object.

PSet method A feature that allows you to change the color of individual pixels on a form.

R

radio buttons Option buttons.

run-time error Any error that occurs when the program is running.

S

ScaleMode property Allows you to adjust the coordinate system on a form to be measured in points, pixels, or twips.

scope The reach of a variable.

Select Case statement A statement in which you specify a variable to test and then list a number of cases that you want to test for.

SelLength property Specifies how many characters should be selected to the right of the cursor.

SelStart property Specifies the location where the cursor will be inserted when the textbox gets the focus.

separator lines Lines used to group items on a menu.

single data type Used for general decimal types not exceeding six or seven digits.

software development tool A tool that allows you to create computer programs.

splash screen A window that appears briefly when a program is started.

standalone program A program that will run in a Windows environment whether or not the system has Visual Basic installed.

standard toolbar The toolbar that appears by default.

Stretch property The property that allows the image to be resized to fit the size of the image control.

string literal Coded text.

strings Data types that hold text.

submenus (cascading menus) Used to further organize options in a menu.

subroutine A section of code set up for you when you open the Code window. The subroutine performs a specific task.

T

tab order The sequence in which the objects in a window get focus as the Tab key is pressed.

temporary graphic A graphic that is not redrawn once another window or object hides the graphic.

text boxes The fields placed on dialog boxes and in other windows that allow the user to enter a value.

tool tip A name that appears when you position the mouse pointer on a toolbar button.

toolbox The collection of tools that allows you to add objects to the forms you create in Visual Basic.

truncation The process of removing everything to the right of the decimal point.

twips A unit of measurement used to position objects on forms. There are 1440 twips in one inch.

two-way selection structure A program structure in which one block of code is executed if the specified conditions are True or another block of code is executed if the specified conditions are False.

U

unary minus Using the subtraction operator to perform negation (making a positive value negative or making a negative value positive).

V

Val function Takes numbers that are in a text format and returns a numeric value that can be used in calculations.

variables Memory locations where temporary data is stored.

variant A data type that can hold data of any type.

INTRODUCTION TO C++

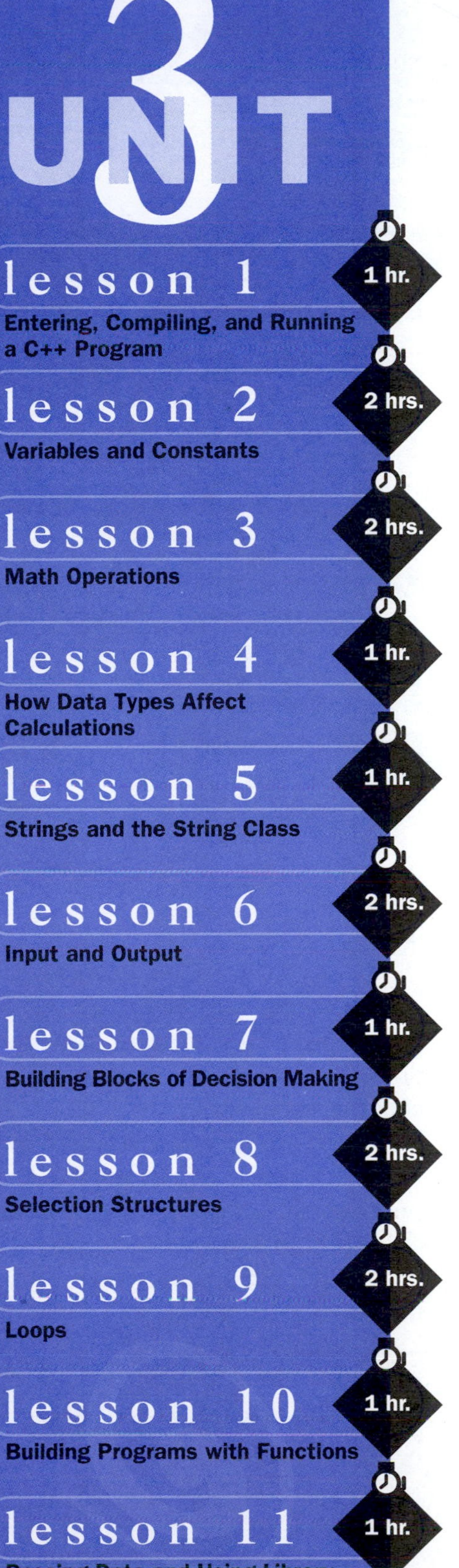

LESSON 1

ENTERING, COMPILING, AND RUNNING A C++ PROGRAM

OBJECTIVES

Upon completion of this lesson, you should be able to:

- Describe the process required to enter, compile, link, and run a C++ program.
- Explain the structure of a C++ program.
- Access the text editor and enter C++ source code.
- Compile, link, and run C++ programs.
- Modify source code.
- Create a standalone program.
- Load, compile, and run an existing source code file.

Estimated Time: 1 hour

Using a C++ Compiler

You have learned that C++ is a compiled language. Compiling a C++ program, however, is just one step in the process of writing and running a C++ program. C++ source code has to be entered into a text editor, translated by a compiler, and made into an executable program by a linker.

Your task in this lesson will be to create an actual C++ program on your system. You will first examine the structure of a C++ program. Then you will enter a simple program into the text editor and compile, link, and run the executable file that is created.

Various brands of C++ compilers are available. It is important that you learn to use your particular compiler while you are in this lesson. At the appropriate point in this lesson, you will be directed to seek information specific to your compiler.

Did You Know?

The C++ language evolved from a language called C. The language C got its name because it is a descendent of a language called B. Both languages were developed at Bell Laboratories. There was no A language. The language B probably got its name because it was based on a language named BCPL.

C++ Program Structure

C++ programs have the basic structure illustrated in Figure 1-1. They are:

1. **Comments**. Comments are remarks that are ignored by the compiler.
2. **Compiler directives**. Compiler directives are commands for the compiler that are needed to compile and run your program.
3. **Main function**. The main function is where every C++ program begins.
4. **Braces**. Braces are special characters used to mark the beginning and ending of blocks of code.
5. **Statements**. A statement is a line of C++ code. Statements end with a semicolon.

FIGURE 1-1
A C++ program has several parts.

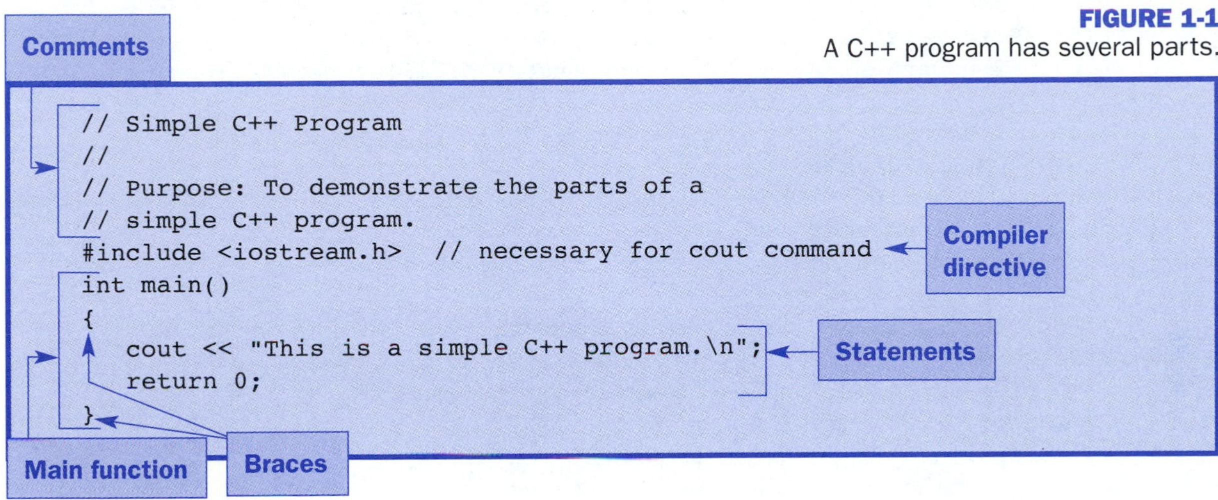

Comments
// Simple C++ Program
//
// Purpose: To demonstrate the parts of a
// simple C++ program.
#include <iostream.h> // necessary for cout command
int main()
{
cout << "This is a simple C++ program.\n";
return 0;
}
Compiler directive
Statements
Main function
Braces

Let us examine each part of a C++ program in more detail.

Comments

As you will learn later in this unit, a C++ program can have other functions in addition to the main function.

When writing a program, you may think that you will always remember what you did and why. Most programmers, however, eventually forget. But more importantly, others may need to make changes in a program you wrote. They probably will be unaware of what you did when you wrote the program. That is why comments are important.

Use comments to:

- explain the purpose of a program.
- keep notes regarding changes to the source code.
- store the names of programmers for future reference.
- explain the parts of your program.

Code List 1-1 is an example of a program that is well-documented with comments. The comments at the top of the program assign the program a name, identify its programmer as Jonathan Kleid, and indicate that the purpose of the program is to calculate miles per gallon and price per mile. Within the program, comments help the reader identify what the lines in the program do.

CODE LIST 1-1

```
// Travel Efficiency
// Programmer: Jonathan Kleid
//
// Purpose: Calculates miles per gallon and price per mile when
// given miles traveled, number of gallons used, and gas price.
#include <iostream.h> // necessary for cin and cout commands
int main()
{
  // Variable declarations
  float MilesTraveled;      // stores number of miles
  float GallonsUsed;        // stores number of total gallons used
  float PricePerGallon;     // stores price per gallon
  float PricePerMile;       // stores price per mile
  float MilesPerGallon;     // stores number of miles per gallon
  // Ask user for input values.
  cout << "How many miles did you travel? ";
  cin  >> MilesTraveled;
  cout << "How many gallons of gas did you use? ";
  cin  >> GallonsUsed;
  cout << "How much did one gallon of gas cost? $";
  cin  >> PricePerGallon;
  // Divide the number of miles by the number of gallons to get MPG.
  MilesPerGallon = MilesTraveled / GallonsUsed;
  // Divide price per gallon by miles per gallon
  // to get price per mile.
  PricePerMile = PricePerGallon / MilesPerGallon;
  // Output miles per gallon and price per mile.
  cout << "You got " << MilesPerGallon << " miles per gallon,\n";
  cout << "and each mile cost $" << PricePerMile << "\n";

  return 0;
}
```

Comments, which are ignored by the compiler, begin with a double slash (//) and may appear anywhere in the program. The comment can take up an entire line or can appear to the right of program statements, as shown in Code List 1-2. Everything to the right of the // is ignored. Therefore, do not include any program statements to the right of a comment. Be sure to use the forward-leaning slash (/) rather than the back slash (\), or the compiler will try to translate your comments and an error message will result.

CODE LIST 1-2

```
float MilesTraveled;      // stores number of miles
float GallonsUsed;        // stores number of total gallons used
float PricePerGallon;     // stores price per gallon
float PricePerMile;       // stores price per mile
float MilesPerGallon;     // stores number of miles per gallon
```

Compiler Directives

Directives are instructions to the compiler rather than part of the C++ language. The most common compiler directive is the #include directive, which instructs the compiler to treat the text file that is enclosed in brackets as if it were keyed into the source code. See Figure 1-2.

#include is pronounced simply as "include." Ignore the # sign when you pronounce the word.

FIGURE 1-2
The #include compiler directive inserts other code into your program as if it were actually keyed into your program.

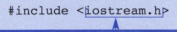

```
#include <iostream.h>
```

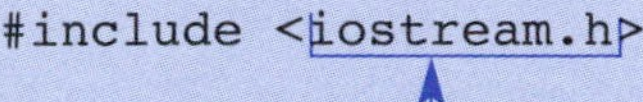

Name of file to be included

So why do you need other code included in your source code? The code you are including makes additional commands available to you. For example, the #include <iostream.h> directive that you have seen in programs in this lesson makes a set of input and output commands available. These commands make it easy to get input from the user and print it to the screen.

Did You Know?

Files such as iostream.h are called header files. They may be identified by their file extension .h. A header file serves as a link between your program code and standard C++ code that is needed to make your program run.

The main Function

Every C++ program has a main function (see Figure 1-1). A **function** is a block of code that carries out a specific task. Although simple programs can be written entirely within the main function, C++ programs are typically divided into multiple functions, which are accessed through the main function. No matter how many functions you have, the main function runs first.

Suppose, for example, that your program needs to calculate the area of a circle. A function could be written to calculate that area. The function could be used (or "called") wherever the calculation is needed in the program. You will see examples of this sort in a later lesson when you learn to use and create functions.

You may have noticed that the word **int** appears before the word **main** in Figure 1-1. The main function returns an integer value (a whole number) to the operating system when the program ends. Functions written in C++ often return a value of some kind to the function that called it. The main function is "called" by the computer's operating system. The int keyword allows the main function to return an integer to the operating system. When you learn to work with multiple functions, this will make more sense. For now, it is best to get in the habit of putting the int before the word main when you write your main function.

The parentheses that follow the word main are required. They tell the compiler that main is a function. All functions have parentheses, although many of them have information inside the parentheses. You will learn more about using functions in a later lesson.

The program ends with a return 0; statement. The return statement is what actually returns the value to the operating system or calling function. In this case, it returns a value of 0 to the operating system.

Braces

Braces are used to mark the beginning and end of blocks of code. Every opening brace must have a closing brace. Notice in Code List 1-3 that the main function is enclosed in a set of braces. Providing comments after each closing brace helps to associate it with the appropriate opening brace. Also, aligning the indention of opening and closing braces is a good idea.

CODE LIST 1-3

```
// comments.cpp
// This program prints the common uses for comments
// to the screen.
// Program written by Greg Buxkemper
#include <iostream.h>  // necessary for output statements
int main()
{
   cout << "Use comments to:\n";
   cout << " – explain the purpose of a program.\n";
   cout << " – keep notes regarding changes to the program.\n";
   cout << " - store the names of programmers.\n";
   cout << " - explain the parts of a program.\n";
   return 0;
} // end of main function
```

Statements

Functions contain statements that consist of instructions or commands, which make the program work. Each statement in C++ ends with a semicolon.

Semicolons

You must have a semicolon after every statement. The semicolon terminates the statement. In other words, it tells the compiler that the statement is complete. Notice, however, that directives such as `#include` and function declarations such as `int main()` are exempt from being punctuated by semicolons.

C++ and Blank Space

C++ allows for great flexibility in the spacing and layout of code. Use this feature to make it easier to read the code by indenting and grouping statements as shown in the sample program in Code List 1-1.

Uppercase or Lowercase

In the computer, A and a are different characters. The capital letters are referred to as uppercase, and small letters are called lowercase.

C++ is known as **case-sensitive** because it interprets uppercase and lowercase letters differently. For example, to a C++ compiler, the word *cow* is different from the word *Cow*. Be careful to use the same combination of lettering (either uppercase or lowercase) when you enter source code. Whatever capitalization was used when the command was originally named must be used throughout the program. In most cases, you will use lowercase letters in C++ programs. If you key a command in uppercase that is supposed to be lowercase, you will get an error message.

From Source Code to Finished Product

The exact process required to enter source code and compile, link, and run will vary depending on the compiler you are using. There are several compilers available for you to use. Additional information about compilers is provided in Appendix G.

Hot Tip

You can also check http://www.programcpp.com/basics on the Internet or refer to the documentation that came with your compiler.

Entering Source Code

The first step is to enter your C++ source code into a text file. Most C++ compilers have an integrated programming environment that contains a text editor you can use. An integrated programming environment allows you to enter your source code, compile, link, and run the program while your text editor is on the screen.

STEP-BY-STEP 1.1

1. Start your text editor with a new, blank file.
2. Enter the C++ source code exactly as it is shown below.

```
// myprog.cpp
// My first C++ program
#include <iostream.h>
int main()
{
cout << "My first C++ program.\n";
  return 0;
}
```

3. Save the file as myprog.cpp and leave the program on your screen for the next Step-by-Step exercise.

Computer Concepts

The "\n" causes the compiler to move the cursor to the beginning of the next line after printing the output to the screen.

Compiling, Linking, and Running the Program

Most compilers allow you to compile, link, and run with a single command from the integrated environment.

STEP-BY-STEP 1.2

1. Compile, link, and run the program you entered in Step-by-Step 1.1. If your compiler allows all of these operations to be performed with a single command, use that command. If your program fails to compile or link, check to see whether you entered the code exactly as shown in Step-by-Step 1.1 and try again.

2. If your program runs successfully, you should see the text *My first C++ program* on the screen. Otherwise, ask your instructor for help.

3. Leave the source file open for the next exercise.

Making Changes and Compiling Again

You can add, change, or delete lines from a program's source code and compile it again. The next time the program is run, the changes will be in effect.

STEP-BY-STEP 1.3

1. Add the statement below to the main function, substituting your name in place of Allison Brackeen.

```
cout << "By Allison Brackeen\n";
```

Your program should now appear like the one below, except your name should be on the new line.

```
// myprog.cpp
// My first C++ program
#include <iostream.h>
int main()
{
cout << "My first C++ program.\n";
cout << "By Allison Brackeen\n";
  return 0;
}
```

2. Compile, link, and run the program again to see the change.

3. Save the source code file and leave it open for the next exercise.

Creating a Standalone Program

Compiling, linking, and running the program probably created a standalone program on the disk. The executable file is typically located in the same directory as the source code. A standalone program becomes important if you want to pass the program you have created on to another user. By passing on the standalone program, you make it possible for the recipient of your program to run the program even if he or she does not have a C++ compiler. By distributing a standalone program, you also do not have to share your program's source code.

Computer Concepts

When you purchase a computer program in a store, you are purchasing a standalone program.

STEP-BY-STEP 1.4

1 If a standalone program was generated as a result of completing Step-by-Step 1.3, quit the integrated programming environment and run the standalone program from the operating system. Otherwise, complete steps 2 through 4 below.

2. Select the option that allows you to compile and link to disk so that a standalone executable file is created.

3. Quit the integrated programming environment.

4. Run the executable program from the operating system.

Hot Tip

When you run the standalone program, the program is likely to disappear from your screen as soon as the output is printed to the screen. In a later lesson, you will learn how to write code that will cause the program to pause until you are ready for the program to end.

Loading and Compiling an Existing Source File

Often you will load an existing source code file and compile it. Most integrated programming environments have an Open command that can be used to open source files.

STEP-BY-STEP 1.5

1. Start your integrated programming environment.

2. Open the source file travel.cpp. Your instructor will either provide you with a work disk or give you instructions for accessing the file from the hard disk or network.

3. Compile, link, and run the program.

4. When the program prompts you for data, enter values that seem realistic to you and see what output the program gives.

5. Run the program several times with different values.

6. Close the source file and quit.

Congratulations

Congratulations. You now know the basics of creating and running C++ programs. From here, you will simply add to your knowledge to enable you to write more useful programs. If you feel you need more experience with compiling and running C++ programs, repeat this lesson or ask your instructor for additional help. Future exercises require that you know how to compile, link, and run.

Summary

In this lesson, you learned:

- A C++ program has several parts.
- Comments are remarks that are ignored by the compiler. They allow you to include notes and other information in the program's source code.
- Directives are commands for the compiler, rather than part of the C++ language.
- All C++ programs have a main function. The main function is where the program begins running.
- Braces mark the beginning and end of blocks of code.
- Statements are the lines of code the computer executes. Each statement ends with a semicolon.
- C++ allows you to indent and insert space in any way that you want. You should take advantage of this flexibility to format source code in a way that makes programs more readable.
- C++ is case sensitive, which means that using the wrong capitalization will result in errors.
- Most C++ compilers have an integrated programming environment that contains a text editor for entering source code. The programming environment allows you to enter source code, compile, link, and run while your text editor is on the screen.

LESSON 1 REVIEW QUESTIONS

TRUE/FALSE

Circle T if the statement is true or F if the statement is false.

T F 1. Comments begin with \\.

T F 2. Comments may appear on the same line with program statements.

T F 3. Compiler directives are not part of the C++ language.

T F 4. The .hfl extension indicates that the file is a header file.

T F 5. The parentheses after the word main indicate to the compiler that it is a function.

T F 6. The int keyword that appears before the word main indicates that the function is an internal function.

T F 7. Every opening brace must have a closing brace.

T F 8. It is a good idea to align the opening and closing braces in source code to improve readability.

T F 9. Every C++ statement ends with a colon.

T F 10. Capital letters are called uppercase letters.

WRITTEN QUESTIONS

Write a brief answer to the following questions.

1. List four uses for comments.
2. What compiler directive inserts source code from another file into your program?
3. What is a function?
4. What purpose do braces serve?
5. What does the term "case sensitive" mean?
6. What company developed the compiler you are using?
7. What is the name of the compiler you are using and its version number?
8. What command or commands are used to run a program with your compiler?
9. What command opens a source code file from a disk?
10. What command saves a source code file?

LESSON 1 PROJECTS

PROJECT 1-1

Enter the program shown below but substitute your name and the appropriate information for your compiler. Compile, link, and run. Save the source code as compinfo.cpp.

```
// compinfo.cpp
// By Jeremy Wilson
#include <iostream.h>
int main()
{
  cout << "This program was compiled using\n";
  cout << "Colossal C++ version 2.5.\n";
  return 0;
}
```

PROJECT 1-2

Enter the program shown in Code List 1-3, compile it, link, and run. After you have run the program, close the source file.

PROJECT 1-3

Open the source file braces.cpp. Look at the program and observe how the pairs of braces match up. Compile, link, and run the program. After you have run the program, close the source file and quit.

CRITICAL THINKING

Write a program that prints the message of your choice to the screen. Make the message at least four lines long. Save the source code file as my_msg.cpp.

VARIABLES AND CONSTANTS

LESSON 2

OBJECTIVES

When you complete this lesson, you will be able to:

- Explain the terms data structure, variable, and constant.
- Explain the different integer variable types used in C++.
- Declare, name, and initialize variables.
- Use character variables.
- Explain the different floating-point types and use variables of those types.
- Describe Boolean variables.
- Use constants.

Estimated Time: 2 hours

Understanding Variables and Constants

Computer programs process data to provide information. The job of the programmer is to properly organize data for storage and use. Computers store data in many complex arrangements called data structures.

Any organized way of storing data in a computer is a data structure. The simplest type of data storage takes place in data structures known as primitive data structures, or simply primitives. These primitive data structures come in two varieties: variables and constants.

A **variable** holds data that can change while the program is running. A **constant** is used to store data that remains the same throughout the program's execution.

C++ has more than a dozen types of variables to store numbers and characters. Some variables are for storing **integers** (whole numbers); other variables are for **floating-point numbers** (real numbers).

You may recall from math courses that an integer is a positive or negative whole number, such as –2, 4, or 5133. Real numbers can be whole numbers or decimals and can be either positive or negative, such as 1.99, –2.5, 3.14159, or 4.

When programming in C++, you must select a type of variable, called a **data type**, that best fits the nature of the data itself. In this lesson, you will first learn about the data types used to store variables and how to use them in your programs. Then you will learn how to use data types for characters and floating-point numbers. Finally, you will learn how to work with constants in your programs.

Integer Data Types

Computer Concepts

In general, new C++ compilers use 4 bytes for the int type. Older compilers or compilers for older operating systems are more likely to use only 2 bytes for the int type.

When you are working with either positive or negative whole numbers, you should use integer data types for your variables. Several integer data types are available in C++ (integer data types can vary by compiler). Selecting which integer data type to use is the next step.

Table 2-1 lists some of the most common integer data types. The table also shows the range of values each type typically holds and the number of bytes of memory required to store a variable of that type. However, these ranges and the number of bytes occupied may vary among compilers, especially in regard to the int type.

TABLE 2-1
Common integer data types

DATA TYPE	MINIMUM RANGE OF VALUES	MINIMUM NUMBER OF BYTES OCCUPIED
char	-128 to 127	1
unsigned char	0 to 255	1
short	-32,768 to 32,767	2
unsigned short	0 to 65,535	2
int	-2,147,483,648 to 2,147,483,647	4
unsigned int	0 to 4,294,967,295	4
long	-2,147,483,648 to 2,147,483,647	4
unsigned long	0 to 4,294,967,295	4

STEP-BY-STEP 2.1

1. Locate the reference manual or online documentation for your compiler.

2. Search for the sizes of the integer data types used in your compiler. Figure 2-1 shows the information found in the Microsoft online documentation.

3. Record the information specific to your compiler or print the information from your online documentation.

FIGURE 2-1

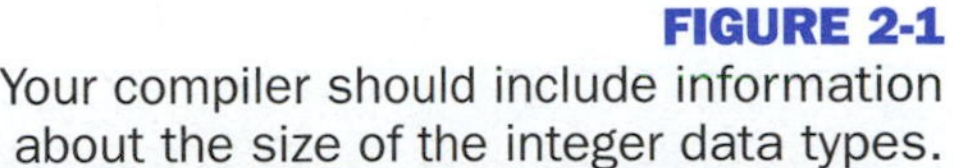

Your compiler should include information about the size of the integer data types.

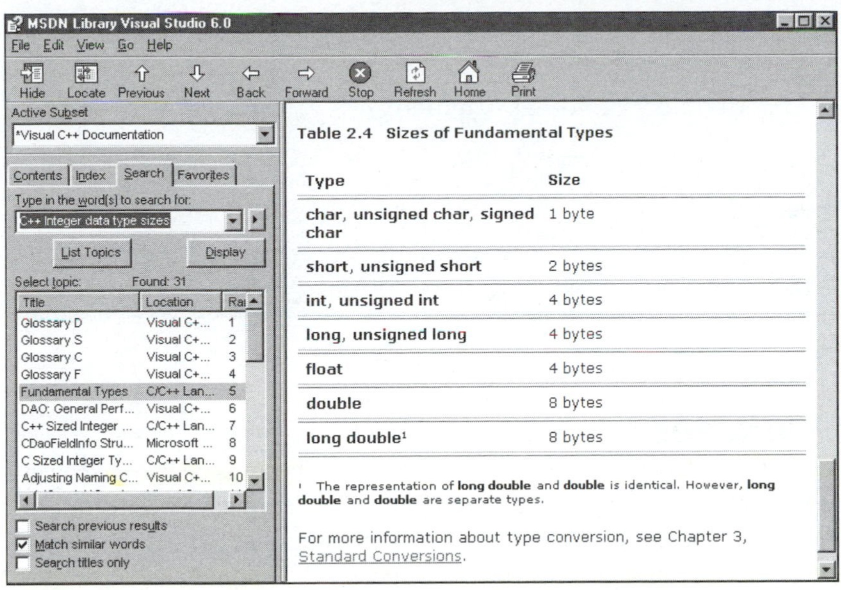

Table 2.4 Sizes of Fundamental Types

Type	Size
char, unsigned char, signed char	1 byte
short, unsigned short	2 bytes
int, unsigned int	4 bytes
long, unsigned long	4 bytes
float	4 bytes
double	8 bytes
long double[1]	8 bytes

[1] The representation of **long double** and **double** is identical. However, **long double** and **double** are separate types.

For more information about type conversion, see Chapter 3, Standard Conversions.

Take a moment to notice the range of values that each type can hold (Table 2-1). For example, any value from –32,768 to 32,767 can be stored in a variable if the short data type is chosen. If you need to store a value outside of that range, you must choose a different data type such as int or long.

An unsigned variable can store only positive numbers. For example, if you were to store the weights of trucks in variables, an unsigned data type might be a good choice. A truck can't weigh less than zero. If you are sure that the integers you are storing cannot be less than zero and will not exceed 65,535, then an unsigned short may be a good choice.

Why would you want to use the short type when the long type has a bigger range? The answer is that you can use the int or long types when a short would do, but there is more to consider. Notice the third column of Table 2-1. The variables with the larger ranges require more of the computer's memory. Saving memory used to be much more important than it is today. Computers now have vast amounts of memory. However, conserving space may become more important when lots of data are involved.

In addition, it often takes the computer longer to access data types that require more memory. Also, it is more common now for data to be transferred over networks such as the Internet. The smaller the space occupied by data, the faster the data can be delivered. Having all of these data types gives the programmer the ability to use only what is necessary for each variable, to decrease memory usage, and to increase speed.

Declaring and Naming Variables

Indicating to the compiler what type of variable you want and what you want to name it is called **declaring** the variable.

Declaring Variables

You must declare a variable before you can use it. The C++ statement declaring a variable must include the data type followed by the name you wish to call the variable and a semicolon. An integer variable named i is declared in Code List 2-1.

CODE LIST 2-1

```
#include <iostream.h>  // necessary for cout command

int main()
{
  int i;    // declare i as an integer

  i = 2; // initialize i to 2
  cout << i  << '\n';
  return 0;
}
```

Initializing Variables

The compiler assigns a location in memory to a variable when it is declared. However, a value already exists in the space reserved for your variable. A random value could have been stored when the computer was turned on, or the location could retain data from a program that ran earlier. Regardless, the memory location now belongs to your program and you must specify the initial value to be stored in the location. This process is known as initializing.

To **initialize** a variable, you simply assign it a value. In C++, the equal sign (=) is used to assign a value to a variable. In Code List 2-1, the variable `i` is initialized to the value of 2.

STEP-BY-STEP 2.2

1. Enter the program shown in Code List 2-1 into a blank editor screen.

2. Save the source code file as ideclare.cpp.

3. Compile and run the program. The program should print the number 2 on your screen. If no errors are encountered, leave the program on your screen. If errors are found, check the source code for keyboarding errors and compile again.

4. Change the initialization statement to initialize the value of i to –40 and run again. The number –40 is shown on your screen. Save the source code again and close the program. You may have to close a project or workspace to completely close the current program.

Table 2-2 shows that declaring variables for other data types is just as easy as the example in Code List 2-1. You can also see in Table 2-2 that variable names can be more interesting than just `i`.

TABLE 2-2
Variables for other data types

DATA TYPE	EXAMPLE C++ DECLARATION STATEMENT
short	short temperature;
unsigned short	unsigned short k;
int	int DaysInMonth;
unsigned int	unsigned int Age_in_dog_years;
long	long PopulationChange;
unsigned long	unsigned long j;

Naming Variables

The names of variables in C++ are typically referred to as **identifiers**. When naming variables, use descriptive names and consider how they might help the programmer recall the variable's purpose. For example, a variable that holds a bank balance could be called balance, or the circumference of a circle could be stored in a variable named circumference. The following are rules for creating identifiers.

Did You Know?

C++ will allow you to declare a variable anywhere in the program as long as the variable is declared before you use it. However, you should get into the habit of declaring all variables at the top of the function. Declaring variables at the top of the function makes for better-organized code, enables the variables to be more easily located, and helps you plan for the variables you will need.

- Identifiers must start with a letter or an underscore (_). You should avoid, however, using identifiers that begin with underscores because the language's internal identifiers often begin with underscores. By avoiding the use of underscores as the first character, you will ensure that your identifier does not conflict with C++ internal identifiers.
- As long as the first character is a letter, you can use letters, numerals, or underscores in the rest of the identifier.
- Use a name that makes the purpose of the variable clear, but avoid making it unnecessarily long. Most C++ compilers will recognize only the first 31 or 32 characters.
- There can be no spaces in identifiers. A good way to create a multi-word identifier is to use an underscore between the words: for example, last_name.
- The following words, called **keywords**, must NOT be used as identifiers because they are part of the C++ language. Your compiler may have additional keywords not listed here.

Note

Recall from the previous lesson that C++ is case-sensitive. The capitalization you use when the variable is declared must be used each time the variable is accessed. For example, *total* is not the same identifier as *Total*.

asm	catch	continue
auto	char	default
break	class	delete
case	const	do
double	new	switch
else	operator	template
enum	private	this
extern	protected	throw
float	public	try
for	register	typedef
friend	return	union
goto	short	unsigned
if	signed	virtual
inline	sizeof	void
int	static	volatile
long	struct	while

Table 2-3 gives some examples of illegal identifiers.

TABLE 2-3
Illegal identifiers

IMPROPER C++ VARIABLE NAMES	WHY ILLEGAL
Miles per gallon	Spaces are not allowed
register	register is a keyword
4Sale	Identifiers cannot begin with numerals

STEP-BY-STEP 2.3

1. Open the source code file named ideclare.cpp that you saved in Step-by-Step 2.2.
2. Save the source code as intdecl.cpp.
3. Change the name of the variable i to MyInteger. Be sure to change the name in every line of code where it appears.
4. Compile and run the program. The output of the program should be unaffected by the change in the variable name.
5. Close the current program.

Declaring Multiple Variables in a Statement

You can declare more than one variable in a single statement as long as all the variables are of the same type. For example, if your program requires three variables of type int, all three variables could be declared by placing commas between the variables like this:

```
int x, y, z;
```

Characters and the Char Data Type

As you probably know, all data in a computer is represented by numbers, including letters and symbols. Letters and symbols, called **characters**, are assigned a number that the computer uses to represent them. Most computers assign numbers to characters according to the American Standard Code for Information Interchange (ASCII). Table 2-4 shows some of the ASCII (pronounced "ask-e") codes. For a complete ASCII table, see Appendix A.

The basic ASCII code is based on 7 bits, which gives 128 characters. About 95 of these are upper and lowercase letters, numbers, and symbols. Some of the characters are used as codes for controlling communication hardware and other devices. Others are invisible characters such as Tab and Return. Most computers extend the ASCII code to 8 bits (a whole byte) to represent 256 characters. The additional 128 characters are used for graphical characters and characters used with foreign languages.

When a computer stores a character, software keeps track of whether the number stored is to be treated as an integer or interpreted as a character. To make it easy, C++ includes a char data type especially for storing characters. The char data type, however, is just an integer. If you use the char data type, the integer you store will be interpreted as a character when you print the character to the screen.

TABLE 2-4
ASCII codes

Character	Equivalent Decimal Value
$	36
*	42
A	65
B	66
C	67
D	68
a	97
b	98
c	99
d	100

For example, the program shown in Code List 2-2 declares a variable of type char, initializes it, and outputs the character to the screen.

CODE LIST 2-2

```
#include <iostream.h>  // necessary for cout command

int main()
{
  char MyChar;   // declare MyChar as a char

  MyChar = 'A';   // initialize MyChar to 'A'
  cout << MyChar  << '\n';
  return 0;
}
```

STEP-BY-STEP 2.4

1. Enter the program shown in Code List 2-2 into a blank editor screen.

2. Save the source code file as chardecl.cpp.

3. Compile and run the program. The program should print the letter A on your screen. If no errors are encountered, leave the program on your screen. If errors are found, check the source code for keyboarding errors and compile again.

4. Change the initialization statement to initialize the value of `MyChar` to `B` and run again. The letter B is shown on your screen. Save the source code again and close the program.

Each variable of the char data type can hold only one character. In order to store words or sentences, you must string characters together. A group of characters put together to make a word or phrase is called a **string**. You will learn more about characters and strings in a later lesson.

Did You Know?

Fonts used on modern operating systems such as Microsoft Windows and the Macintosh OS also use the ASCII codes. Have you ever changed a font and noticed that some special characters changed to unrecognizable characters or squares? That happens when the font you selected does not have a character for that particular ASCII value or uses an ASCII value for a different character. All the standard characters—letters, numerals, and basic punctuation—are consistent among fonts.

Floating-Point Data Types

Integer variables are inappropriate for certain types of data. For example, tasks as common as working with money call for using floating-point numbers. Just as there is more than one integer data type, there is more than one data type for floating-point variables.

Table 2-5 lists the three floating-point data types and their range of values. The ranges of floating-point data types are more complicated than the range of integers. Selecting an appropriate floating-point type is based on both the range of values and the required decimal precision.

TABLE 2-5
Floating-point data types

DATA TYPE	APPROXIMATE RANGE OF VALUES	DIGITS OF PRECISION	NUMBER OF BYTES OCCUPIED
float	3.4×10^{-38} to 3.4×10^{38}	7	4
double	1.7×10^{-308} to 1.7×10^{308}	15	8
long double	3.4×10^{-4932} to 1.1×10^{4932}	19	10

When you are choosing a floating-point data type, first look to see how many digits of precision are necessary for the value you need to store. For example, to store π as 3.1415926535897 requires 14 digits of precision. Therefore you should use the double type. You should also verify that your value will fit within the range of values the type supports. But unless you are dealing with very large or very small numbers, the range is not usually as important an issue as the precision.

Note

The information in Table 2-5 may vary among compilers. Check your compiler's manual for exact data type ranges and bytes occupied for both integers and floating-point numbers.

Let's look at some examples of values and what data types would be appropriate for the values:

- Dollar amounts in the range \$–99,999.99 to \$99,999.99 can be handled with a variable of type float. A variable of type double can store dollar amounts in the range \$–9,999,999,999,999.99 to \$9,999,999,999,999.99.
- The number 5.98×10^{24} kg, which happens to be the mass of the Earth, can be stored in a variable of type float because the number is within the range of values and requires only three digits of precision.

Assigning a floating-point value to a variable works the way you probably expect, except when you need to use exponential notation. You may have used exponential notation and called it scientific notation. In exponential notation, very large or very small numbers are represented with a fractional part (called the mantissa) and an exponent. Use an e to signify exponential notation. Just place an e in the number to separate the mantissa from the exponent. Below are some examples of statements that initialize floating-point variables.

```
x = 2.5;
ElectronGFactor = 1.0011596567;
Radius_of_Earth = 6.378164e6;    // radius of Earth at equator
Mass_of_Electron = 9.109e-31;    // 9.109 x 10-31 kilograms
```

Code List 2-3 shows a program that declares and initializes three floating-point variables.

CODE LIST 2-3

```
// floatdec.cpp
// Example of floating-point variable declaration.

#include <iostream.h>

int main()
{
  float x;
  double Radius_of_Earth, Mass_of_Electron;
```

CODE LIST 2-3 (CONTINUED)

```
    x = 2.5;
    Radius_of_Earth = 6.378164e6;
    Mass_of_Electron = 9.109e-31;

    cout << x << '\n';
    cout << Radius_of_Earth << '\n';
    cout << Mass_of_Electron << '\n';
    return 0;
}
```

STEP-BY-STEP 2.5

1. Enter the program shown in Code List 2-3.

2. Save the source code as floatdec.cpp.

3. Compile and run the program. The three values should appear, as shown in Figure 2-2.

4. When the program runs successfully, save and close the program.

Note

The format in which the floating-point values appear on your screen may differ from Figure 2-2, depending on the compiler you are using.

FIGURE 2-2
The program prints three floating-point values to the screen.

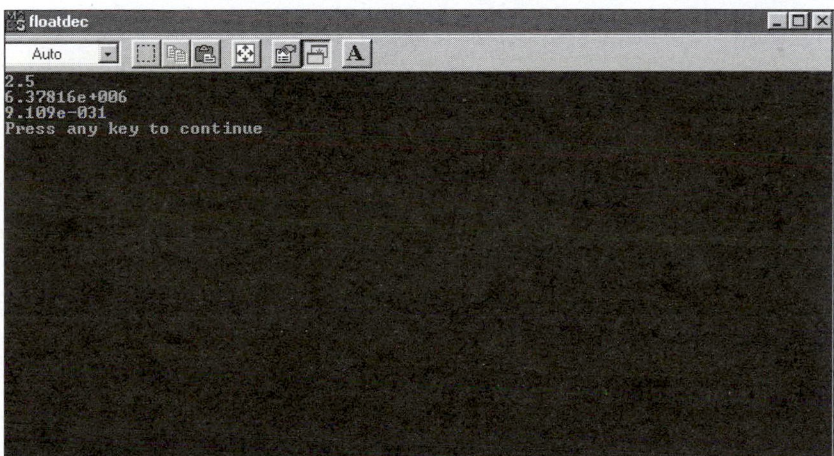

Boolean Variables

Did You Know?

Boolean variables are named in honor of George Boole, an English mathematician who lived in the 1800s. Boole created a system called Boolean algebra, which is a study of operations that take place using variables with the values true and false.

A **Boolean variable** is a variable that can have only two possible values. One of the values represents true (or some other form of the affirmative), and the other value represents false (or some other form of the negative). Boolean variables are very useful in programming to store information such as whether an answer is yes or no, whether a report has been printed or not, or whether a device is currently on or off.

Some C++ compilers do not support a Boolean variable. Others have a data type bool, which can be used to declare Boolean variables. If your compiler does not support the bool data type, you can use the `bool.h` header file on your work disk to make the feature available in your programs. Your instructor can help you access this header file. Later in this unit, you will use the bool data type and examine the header file that makes it work.

Constants

In C++, a constant holds data that remains the same as the program runs. Constants allow you to give a name to a value that is called several times in a program so that the value can be more easily used. For example, if you use the value of π (3.14159) several times in your program, you can assign the value 3.14159 to the name PI. Then, each time you need the value 3.14159, you need only use the name PI.

Constants are defined in a similar manner to the way you define a variable. You still must select a data type and give the constant a name. But you also tell the compiler that the data is a constant using the const keyword and assign a value in the same statement.

The statement below declares `PI` as a constant.

```
const double PI = 3.14159;
```

Any valid identifier name can be used to name a constant. The same rules apply as with variables. Traditionally, uppercase letters have been used when naming constants. Lowercase letters are generally used with variable names. In this way, uppercase letters help distinguish constants from variables. Some C++ programmers, however, think lowercase letters should be used for constants as well as variables. In this book, we will use uppercase letters for constants because it will help you quickly identify constants in programs. Just be aware that you may see programs elsewhere that use lowercase letters for constants.

Code List 2-4 shows a complete program that uses a constant for `PI`. Notice that the identifier `PI` is used in the line that calculates the circumference of the circle. Because `PI` is a constant, you do not have to be concerned about the value of `PI` changing while the program runs. The double data type is used for two reasons. By using the larger data type, the floating-point values have more digits of accuracy. In addition, some compilers will give a warning if you use a constant of type float because of concern about losing digits of accuracy.

CODE LIST 2-4

```
// circle.cpp
// Example of using a constant.

#include <iostream.h>

int main()
{
  const double PI = 3.14159;     // declare PI as a constant
  double circumference, radius;

  // Ask user for the radius of a circle
  cout << "What is the radius of the circle? ";
  cin  >> radius;

  circumference = 2 * PI * radius;  // calculate circumference

  // Output the circle's circumference
  cout << "The circle's circumference is ";
  cout << circumference << '\n';
  return 0;
}
```

STEP-BY-STEP 2.6

1. Enter the program shown in Code List 2-4. Save the source code as circle.cpp.

2. Compile and run the program. Enter 4 as the radius of the circle. The program will return 25.1327 as the circumference. The number of digits displayed after the decimal point may vary.

3. An error message is generated if you add the following line at the end of the program because you cannot change the value of a constant while the program is running. Add the line before the return line at the end of the program.

```
PI = 2.5;
```

4. Compile the program again to see the error generated.

5. Delete the line causing the error and compile the program again.

6. Save and close the program.

Computer Concepts

C++ error messages are often not very helpful to beginning programmers. For example, when you attempted to reassign a value to the constant `PI`, you may have received an error such as "l-value specifies const object," which may not tell you much. If you get an error message that does not make sense and you cannot detect your error, try using the help system or your compiler's documentation to get a clearer explanation of the error.

The compiler prohibits the assignment of another value to a constant after the declaration statement. If you fail to initialize the constant in the declaration statement, however, whatever value is in the memory location remains assigned to the constant throughout the execution of the program.

A good reason to use constants in a large program is that they give you the ability to easily change the value of the constant in more than one place in the program. For example, suppose you have a program that needs the sales tax rate in several places. If you declare a constant named `TAX_RATE`, when the tax rate changes you have to change the constant only where it is declared. Every place in the program that uses the `TAX_RATE` constant will use the new value.

Summary

In this lesson, you learned:

- Computers store data in many complex arrangements called data structures.
- Most data is stored in either variables or constants. Variables hold data that can change while the program is running. Constants are used to store data that remains the same throughout the program's execution.
- Integer data types are selected based on the range of values you need to store. Some integer data types are unsigned, meaning they can store only positive numbers.
- Variables must be declared before they are used. Variables should also be initialized to clear any random values that may be in the memory location. When a variable is declared, it must be given a legal name called an identifier.
- Characters are stored in the computer as numbers. The char data type can store one character of data.
- Floating-point data types are selected based on the range of values and the required precision.
- Boolean variables are variables that can have only two possible values: true or false.
- Constants are declared in a way similar to variables. The const keyword tells the compiler that the data is a constant. The constant must be assigned a value in the declaration statement.

LESSON 2 REVIEW QUESTIONS

TRUE/FALSE

Circle T if the statement is true or F if the statement is false.

T F 1. An integer is a number with digits after the decimal point.

T F 2. The unsigned char data type has a range of values of 0 to 255.

T F 3. Each char variable can store one character.

T F 4. Variables must be declared before they are used.

T F 5. Identifiers must start with a letter or a numeral.

T F 6. Underscores are not allowed to be a part of an identifier.

T F 7. Variables must be initialized because they have an indeterminant value when declared.

T F 8. A constant is data that remains the same as the program runs.

T F 9. Constants do not have data types.

T F 10. Constants must be named with uppercase characters.

WRITTEN QUESTIONS

Write a short answer to the following questions.

1. Why is it important to use data types that store your data efficiently?
2. What floating-point data type provides the most digits of precision?
3. What is a string?
4. What are words called that cannot be used as identifiers because they are part of the C++ language?
5. Why can't "first name" be used as an identifier?
6. What character is used to assign a value to a variable?
7. What is a constant?
8. What keyword is used to declare a constant in C++?
9. When is it appropriate to use constants?
10. When must the value of a constant be assigned?

LESSON 2 PROJECTS

PROJECT 2-1

Write code statements for each of the following.

1. Write a statement to declare an integer named age as an unsigned short.
2. Write a statement that declares four int data type variables i, j, k, and l in a single statement.
3. Write a constant declaration statement to create a constant for the number of feet in a mile (5,280).
4. Write a statement that declares a variable of type double named MyDouble.
5. Write a statement that assigns the value 9.999 to the variable MyDouble.

PROJECT 2-2

1. Enter, compile, and run the following program. Save the source code file as datatype.cpp.

```
// datatype.cpp
// Examples of variable declaration and
// initialization.

#include <iostream.h>

int main()
{
  // declare a constant for the square root of two
  const double SQUARE_ROOT_OF_TWO = 1.414214;

  int i;                  // declare i as an integer
  long j;                 // j as a long integer
  unsigned long k;        // k as an unsigned long integer
  float n;                // n as a floating-point number

  i = 3;                  // initialize i to 3
  j = -2048111;           // j to -2,048,111
  k = 4000000001;         // k to 4,000,000,001
  n = 1.887;              // n to 1.887

  // output constant and variables to screen
  cout << SQUARE_ROOT_OF_TWO << '\n';
  cout << i << '\n';
  cout << j << '\n';
  cout << k << '\n';
  cout << n << '\n';
  return 0;
}
```

2. Add declarations using appropriate identifiers for the values below. Declare *e*, the speed of light, and the speed of sound as constants. Initialize the variables. Use any identifier you want for those values that give you no indication as to their purpose.

100	*e* (2.7182818)
–100	Speed of light (3.00 × 108 m/s)
–40,000	Speed of sound (340.292 m/s)
40,000	

3. Print the new values to the screen.

4. Save, compile, and run. Correct any errors you have made.

5. Close the program.

CRITICAL THINKING

1. Write a program that declares two constants (A and B).
2. Initialize A = 1 and B = 2.2.
3. Declare an int named C and a float named D.
4. Initialize C = A and D = B.
5. Write statements to print C and D to the screen.
6. Save the source code as abcddec.cpp.
7. Compile and run. Correct any errors you have made.
8. Close the program.

MATH OPERATIONS

LESSON 3

OBJECTIVES

Upon completion of this lesson, you should be able to:

- Use the assignment operator.
- Use the arithmetic operators.
- Use operators in output statements.
- Explain the problem with division by zero.
- Increment and decrement variables.
- Explain the order of operations.

Estimated Time: 2 hours

Assignment Operator

You have used the assignment operator (=) to initialize variables, so you already know most of what there is to know about the assignment operator. The **assignment operator** changes the value of the variable to the left of the operator. Consider the statement below:

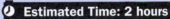

```
i = 25;
```

The statement `i = 25;` changes the value of variable `i` to 25, regardless of what it was before the statement.

Note

When the instructions in this book direct you to close a program, close the entire project or workspace to prepare the compiler to work with another source code file.

STEP-BY-STEP 3.1

1. Turn on your computer and access the C++ compiler's text editor. Enter the program in Code List 3-1 and save your source code file as iassign.cpp.

2. Compile and run the program. Notice the difference between the value of i when it is displayed after the first output statement and after the second.

3. Close the program.

CODE LIST 3-1

```
#include <iostream.h> // necessary for cout command

int main()
{
  int i;          // declare i as an integer
  i = 10000;      // assign the value 10000 to i
  cout << i << '\n';
  i = 25;         // assign the value 25 to i
  cout << i << '\n';
  return 0;
}
```

Recall from Lesson 2 that you can declare more than one variable in a single statement. For example, instead of:

```
int i;
int j;
int k;
```

you can use:

```
int i,j,k;
```

You can use a similar shortcut when initializing multiple variables. If you have more than one variable that you want to initialize to the same value, you can use a statement such as

```
i = j = k = 25;
```

STEP-BY-STEP 3.2

1. Enter the program in Code List 3-2 and save your source code file as multinit.cpp.

2. Compile and run the program. The program's output is:

```
10
10
10
```

3. Close the program.

Hot Tip

You may want to create a source code file that consists of the `#include` statement, `int main()`, and the opening and closing braces and use it as a starting point every time you need to create a new source code file. Just open the template file and save it under a new name before compiling.

CODE LIST 3-2

```
#include <iostream.h> // necessary for cout command

int main()
{
  int i,j,k;          // declare i, j, and k as integers

  i = j = k = 10;     // initialize all of the variables to 10
  cout << i << '\n';
  cout << j << '\n';
  cout << k << '\n';
  return 0;
}
```

Variables may also be declared and initialized in a single statement. For example, both of the following are valid C++ statements.

```
int i = 2;
float n = 4.5;
```

Arithmetic Operators

A specific set of **arithmetic operators** is used to perform calculations in C++. These arithmetic operators, shown in Table 3-1, may be somewhat familiar to you. Addition and subtraction are performed with the familiar + and – operators. Multiplication uses an asterisk (*), and division uses a forward slash (/). C++ also uses what is known as a modulus operator (%) to determine the integer remainder of division. A more detailed discussion of the modulus operator is presented later in this lesson.

TABLE 3-1
Arithmetic operators

SYMBOL	OPERATION	EXAMPLE	READ AS...
+	Addition	3 + 8	three plus eight
–	Subtraction	7 – 2	seven minus two
*	Multiplication	4 * 9	four times nine
/	Division	6 / 2	six divided by two
%	Modulus	7 % 3	seven modulo three

Using Arithmetic Operators

The arithmetic operators are used with two operands, as in the examples in Table 3-1. The exception to this is the minus symbol (–), which can be used to change the sign of an operand. Arithmetic operators are most often used on the right side of an assignment operator, as shown in the examples in Table 3-2. The portion of the statement on the right side of the assignment operator is called an expression.

TABLE 3-2
Examples of expressions

STATEMENT	RESULT
cost = price + tax;	cost is assigned the value of price plus tax.
owed = total – discount;	owed is assigned the value of total minus discount.
area = l * w;	area is assigned the value of l times w.
one_eighth = 1 / 8;	one_eighth is assigned the value of 1 divided by 8.
r = 5 % 2;	r is assigned the integer remainder of 5 divided by 2 by using the modulus operator.
x = -y;	x is assigned the value of -y.

The assignment operator (=) functions differently in C++ from the way the equal sign functions in algebra. Consider the following statement:

```
x = x + 10;
```

This statement is invalid in algebra because the equal sign is the symbol around which both sides of an equation are balanced. The left side equals the right side. But your C++ compiler looks at the statement differently. The expression on the right side of the equal sign is evaluated, and the result is stored in the variable to the left of the equal sign. In the statement `x = x + 10;`, the value of x is increased by 10.

STEP-BY-STEP 3.3

1. Retrieve the file named assign.cpp. The program shown in Code List 3-3 appears.

2. Look at the source code and try to predict the program's output.

3. Run the program and see whether you were correct in your prediction.

4. Close the program.

Did You Know?

Did you know that C++ compilers ignore blank spaces in math operations? Both of the statements shown below are valid and produce the same result.

```
x=y+z;
x = y + z;
```

CODE LIST 3-3

```
// assign.cpp

#include <iostream.h>

int main()
{
 int i = 2;
 int j = 3;
 int k = 4;
 int l;
 float a = 0.5;
 float b = 3.0;
 float c;

 l = i + 2;
 cout << l << '\n';

 l = l - j;
 cout << l << '\n';

 l = i * j * k;
 cout << l << '\n';

 l = k / i;
 cout << l << '\n';
```

CODE LIST 3-3 (CONTINUED)

```
  c = b * a;
  cout << c << '\n';

  c = b / a;
  cout << c << '\n';

  return 0;
}
```

More About Modulus

The **modulus operator**, which may be used only for integer division, returns the remainder rather than the result of the division. As shown in Figure 3-1, integer division is similar to the way you divide manually.

FIGURE 3-1
The division operator and the modulus operator return the quotient and the remainder.

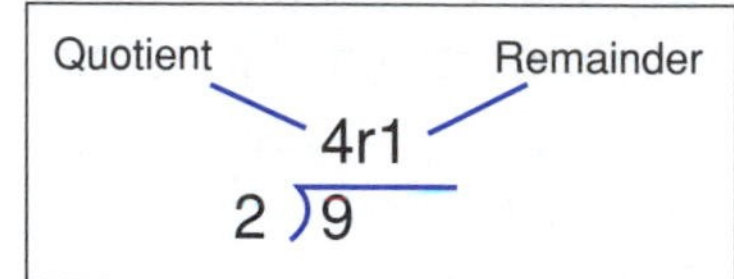

When integer division is performed, any fractional part that may be in the answer is lost when the result is stored into the integer variable. The modulus operator allows you to obtain the fractional part of the result as an integer remainder.

Consider the program in Code List 3-4. The user is prompted for two integers. Notice the program calculates the quotient using the division operator (/) and the remainder using the modulus operator (%).

CODE LIST 3-4

```
// remain.cpp

#include <iostream.h> // necessary for cin and cout commands

int main()
{
  int dividend, divisor, quotient, remainder;

  // Get the dividend and divisor from the user
  cout << "Enter the dividend ";
  cin >> dividend;
  cout << "Enter the divisor ";
  cin >> divisor;

  // Calculate the quotient and remainder
  quotient = dividend / divisor;
  remainder = dividend % divisor;

  // Output the quotient and remainder
  cout << "The quotient is " << quotient;
  cout << " with a remainder of " << remainder << '\n';
  return 0;
}
```

STEP-BY-STEP 3.4

1. Enter the program from Code List 3-4. Save the source file as remain.cpp.
2. Run the program several times using values that will produce different remainders. On paper, record the inputs you used and the quotients and remainders produced.
3. Leave the source code file open for the next Step-by-Step exercise.

Using Operators in Output Statements

The program in Code List 3-4 required four variables and nine program statements. The program in Code List 3-5 accomplishes the same output with only two variables and seven statements. Notice in Code List 3-5 that the calculations are performed in the output statements. Rather than storing the results of the expressions in variables, the program sends the results to the screen as part of the output.

CODE LIST 3-5

```
// remain2.cpp

#include <iostream.h> // necessary for cin and cout commands

int main()
{
  int dividend, divisor;

  // Get the dividend and divisor from the user.
  cout << "Enter the dividend ";
  cin >> dividend;
  cout << "Enter the divisor ";
  cin >> divisor;

  // Output the quotient and remainder
  cout << "The quotient is " << dividend/divisor;
  cout << " with a remainder of " << dividend % divisor << '\n';
  return 0;
}
```

Avoid including the calculations in the output statements if you need to store the quotient or remainder and use them again in the program. In situations like this, it is perfectly fine to use operators in the output statement.

STEP-BY-STEP 3.5

1. Modify the program on your screen to match Code List 3-5. Verify that you have changed each line that needs modification and removed the lines that are no longer necessary. Save the source file as remain2.cpp. Compile it and run it.

2. Test the program using the data you recorded on paper in Step-by-Step 3.4 to make sure you are still getting the same results.

3. Leave the source code file open for the next Step-by-Step exercise.

Dividing by Zero

In mathematics, division by zero is without a practical purpose. The same is true with computers. In fact, division by zero always generates some type of error.

STEP-BY-STEP 3.6

1. Run the program on your screen again. Enter 0 for the divisor and see what error message is generated.

2. Close the program.

Most programs that have the potential of creating or allowing a division by zero include code that checks for this condition before the division occurs.

Incrementing and Decrementing

Adding or subtracting 1 from a variable is very common in programs. Adding 1 to a variable is called **incrementing**, and subtracting 1 from a variable is called **decrementing**. For example, you increment or decrement a variable when a program must execute a section of code a specified number of times or when you need to count the number of times a process has been repeated.

The ++ and – – Operators

C++ provides operators for incrementing and decrementing. In C++, you can increment an integer variable using the ++ operator, and decrement using the -- operator, as shown in Table 3-3.

Did You Know?

The ++ operator is also part of the C programming language, which was the language from which C++ evolved. Can you guess where the name C++ came from? The ++ operator was made part of the new language's name to suggest that the C language had been incremented.

TABLE 3-3
Incrementing and decrementing

STATEMENT	EQUIVALENT TO...
counter++;	counter = counter + 1;
counter- -;	counter = counter – 1;

Earlier in this lesson you learned that spacing does not matter in math operations. The only time you must be careful with spacing is when you use the minus sign to change the sign of a variable or number. For example, `x = y – -z;` is perfectly fine. The sign of the value in the variable `z` is changed and then it is subtracted from `y`. If you failed to include the space before the `--z`, you would have created a problem because two minus signs together (--) are interpreted as the decrement operator.

STEP-BY-STEP 3.7

1. Retrieve the file inc_dec.cpp. The program shown in Code List 3-6 appears.
2. Compile and run the program.
3. Examine the output and leave the source code file open for the next Step-by-Step exercise.

CODE LIST 3-6

```
// inc_dec.cpp

#include <iostream.h>

int main()
{
  int j;    // declare j as int

  j = 1;    // initialize j to 1
  cout << "j = " << j << '\n';
  j++;      // increment j
  cout << "j = " << j << '\n';
  j--;      // decrement j
  cout << "j = " << j << '\n';

  return 0;
}
```

Variations of Increment and Decrement

At first glance, the ++ and -- operators seem very simple. But there are two ways that each of these operators can be used. The operators can be placed either before or after the variable. The location of the operators affects the way they work.

Note

The ++ and -- operators can be used with any arithmetic data type, including all the integer and floating-point types.

Used in a statement by themselves, the ++ and -- operators can be placed before or after the variable. For example, both of the statements shown below increment whatever value is in `j`.

```
j++;
++j;
```

The difference in where you place the operator becomes important if you use the ++ or - - operator in a more complex expression, or if you use the operators in an output statement. First, look at how the placement of the operators affects the following statement. Assume that `j` holds a value of 10.

```
k = j++;
```

In the case of this statement, `k` is assigned the value of the variable `j` before `j` is incremented. Therefore, the value of 10 is assigned to `k` rather than the new value of `j`, which is 11. If the placement of the ++ operator is changed to precede the variable `j` (`k = ++j;`), then `k` is assigned the value of `j` after `j` is incremented to 11.

STEP-BY-STEP 3.8

1. Add a statement to the file named inc_dec.cpp that declares k as a variable of type int.

2. Add the following lines to the program on your screen before the return 0; command line.

```
k = j++;
cout << "k = " << k << '\n';
cout << "j = " << j << '\n';
k = ++j;
cout << "k = " << k << '\n';
cout << "j = " << j << '\n';
```

3. Save the new source code file as inc_dec2.cpp.

4. Compile and run the program to see the new output. Remember, you may have to close the current project or workspace to compile and run inc_dec2.cpp.

5. Close the program.

Order of Operations

You may recall from your math classes the rules related to the order in which operations are performed. These rules are called the order of operations. The C++ compiler uses a similar set of rules for its calculations. Calculations are processed in the following order:

1. Minus sign used to change sign (–)
2. Multiplication and division (* / %)
3. Addition and subtraction (+ –)

FIGURE 3-2
Parentheses can be used to change the order of operations.

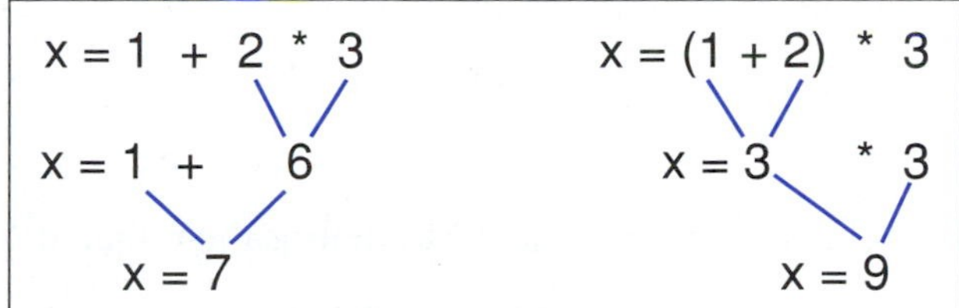

C++ lets you use parentheses to change the order of operations. For example, consider the two statements in Figure 3-2. For a complete table of the order of operations, see Appendix D.

STEP-BY-STEP 3.9

1. Retrieve the file named order.cpp. The program in Code List 3-7 appears.
2. Look at the source code and try to predict the program's output.
3. Run the program and see whether your prediction is correct.
4. Close the program.

CODE LIST 3-7

```
// order.cpp

#include <iostream.h>

int main()
{
 int answer;

 answer = 1 + 2 * 2 + 3;
 cout << answer << '\n';

 answer = (1 + 2) * (2 + 3);
 cout << answer << '\n';

 answer = 1 + 2 * (2 + 3);
 cout << answer << '\n';

 answer = (1 + 2) * 2 + 3;
 cout << answer << '\n';

 return 0;
}
```

Summary

In this lesson, you learned:

- The assignment operator (=) changes the value of the variable to the left of the operator to the result of the expression to the right of the operator.
- You can initialize multiple variables to the same value in a single statement.
- The arithmetic operators are used to create expressions.
- The modulus operator (%) returns the remainder of integer division.
- Expressions can be placed in output statements.
- Dividing by zero generates an error in C++.
- Spaces can be placed around all operators but are not required in most cases.
- The ++ and - - operators increment and decrement arithmetic variables, respectively.
- The placement of the ++ and - - operators becomes important when the operators are used as part of a larger expression or in an output statement.
- C++ calculations follow an order of operations.

LESSON 3 REVIEW QUESTIONS

TRUE/FALSE

Circle T if the statement is true or F if the statement is false.

T F 1. Variables can be declared and initialized in the same statement.

T F 2. You can initialize multiple variables to the same value in the same statement.

T F 3. The * operator performs multiplication.

T F 4. The modulus operator is the @ sign.

T F 5. C++ allows you to divide by zero.

T F 6. Subtracting 1 from a variable is called incrementing.

T F 7. You can increment and decrement variables without the ++ and - - operators.

T F 8. The ++ and - - operators do not work on floating-point numbers.

T F 9. The ++ operator can appear before or after a variable.

T F 10. Addition and subtraction are performed before multiplication and division.

WRITTEN QUESTIONS

Write short answers to the following questions.

1. What is the assignment operator?
2. When using the assignment operator, on which side of the operator must you place the variable getting the new value?
3. What symbol is used to represent the division operation?
4. What symbol is used to represent the subtraction operation?
5. What does the modulus operator do?
6. When is it not a good idea to perform calculations in output statements?
7. Using the addition operator, write a statement that is equivalent to

```
x = x++;
```

8. If the value of i is 10 before the following statement is executed, what is the value of j after the statement?

```
j = i++;
```

9. If the value of i is 4 before the following statement is executed, what is the value of j after the statement?

```
j = --i;
```

10. What can be used to override the order of operations?

LESSON 3 PROJECTS

PROJECT 3-1

1. Write a program that declares an integer named up_down and that initializes it to 3.
2. Have the program print the value of up_down to the screen.
3. Have the program increment the variable and print the value to the screen.
4. Add statements to the program to decrement the variable and print the value to the screen again.
5. Save the source code as updown.cpp, compile it, and run it.
6. Close the program.

PROJECT 3-2

1. Retrieve the file named salestax.cpp. The file is a complete program with the exception of one line of code.

2. Under the comment line that reads "Calculate sales tax due," enter a line of code that will calculate the amount of tax due. To calculate the tax due, you must divide the tax rate by 100 and then multiply that value by the cost of the item.

3. Save the modified source code and run the program.

4. Test the program several times before closing it.

PROJECT 3-3

Write a program that evaluates the following expressions and prints the different values that result from the varied placement of the parentheses. Store the result in a float variable to allow for fractional values. Save the source code file as paren.cpp.

2 + 6 / 3 + 1 * 6 – 7

(2 + 6) / (3 + 1) * 6 – 7

(2 + 6) / (3 + 1) * (6 – 7)

PROJECT 3-4

The volume of a box is calculated using the formula V = abc, where a, b, and c are the lengths of the box's sides. Write a program that calculates the volume of a box based on the input of the length of three sides by the user. Use the code from salestax.cpp as an example of using cin to get the input. Save the source code file as volbox.cpp. Compile, run, and test the program.

CRITICAL THINKING

Suppose you have a group of people who need to be transported on buses and vans. You can charter a bus only if you can fill it. Each bus holds 50 people. You must provide vans for the 49 or fewer people who will be left over after you charter the buses. Write a program that accepts a number of people and determines how many buses must be chartered and reports the number of people left over who must be placed on vans. *Hint*: Use the modulus operator to determine the number of people left over.

HOW DATA TYPES AFFECT CALCULATIONS

LESSON 4

OBJECTIVES

Upon completion of this lesson, you will be able to:

- Properly mix data types in calculations.
- Avoid overflow in calculations.
- Avoid underflow in calculations.
- Explain floating-point rounding errors.

Mixing Data Types

C++ allows you to mix data types in calculations (for example, dividing a float value of 125.25 by an integer such as 5). Many programming languages do not allow the mixing of data types because it can lead to errors if you do not understand the proper way to deal with mixed data types and the consequences of mixing them.

You learned in Lesson 2 that each data type is able to hold a specific range of values. When you perform calculations, the capacity of your variables must be kept in mind. It is possible for the result of an expression to be too large or too small for a given data type.

C++ can automatically handle the mixing of data types (called promotion), or you can direct the compiler on how to handle the data (called typecasting).

Promotion

Consider the program in Code List 4-1. The variable `number_of_people` is an integer. The other variables involved in the calculation are floating-point numbers. Before you mix data types, you should understand the way the compiler is going to process the variables.

CODE LIST 4-1

```
// share.cpp

#include <iostream.h>

int main()
{
  int number_of_people;   // declare number_of_people as an integer
  float money;            // declare money as a float
  float share;            // declare share as a float

  cout << "How many people need a share of the money? ";
  cin >> number_of_people;
  cout << "How much money is available to share among the people? ";
  cin >> money;

  share = money / number_of_people;

  cout << "Give each person $" << share << '\n';

  return 0;
}
```

In cases of mixed data types, the compiler makes adjustments to produce the most accurate answer. In the program in Code List 4-1, for example, the integer value (number_of_people) is temporarily converted to a float so that the fractional part of the variable money can be used in the calculation. This is called **promotion**. The variable called number_of_people is not actually changed. Internally, the computer treats the data as if it were stored in a float. But after the calculation, the variable is still an integer.

The reason that data types must match when a calculation is performed has to do with the way the microprocessor handles calculations. The values involved in the calculation must be of the same number of bytes and same format to ensure correct results. Converting all values in the calculation to the data type with the most precision before performing the calculation guarantees the most accurate results.

STEP-BY-STEP 4.1

1. Retrieve the file named share.cpp. The program from Code List 4-1 appears in your editor.

2. Compile and run the program and observe how the mixed data types function.

3. Close the program.

Promotion of the data type can occur only while an expression is being evaluated. Consider the program in Code List 4-2.

CODE LIST 4-2

```
// losedata.cpp

#include <iostream.h>

int main()
{
  int answer, i;
  float x;

  i = 3;
  x = 0.5;
  answer = x * i;

  cout << answer << '\n';
  return 0;
}
```

The variable i is promoted to a float when the expression is calculated, which gives the result 1.5. But then the result is stored in the integer variable answer. You are unable to store a floating-point number in space reserved for an integer variable. The floating-point number is truncated, which means the digits after the decimal point are dropped. The number in answer is 1, which is not correct.

Computer Concepts

Truncation is the equivalent of chopping off everything to the right of the decimal point. When a number is truncated, 1.00001 becomes 1 and 1.999999 also becomes 1.

STEP-BY-STEP 4.2

1. Retrieve the file losedata.cpp. The program in Code List 4-2 appears.
2. Compile the program. You may get a warning that a loss of data will occur when the program is run.
3. Run the program and verify that the result is truncated.
4. Close the program.

Typecasting

Even though C++ handles the mixing of data types fairly well, unexpected results can occur. To give the programmer more control over the results when data types are mixed, C++ allows you to explicitly change one data type to another using operators called *typecast operators*. Using a typecast operator is usually referred to as *typecasting*.

Consider the program you ran in Step-by-Step 4.1 (share.cpp), shown again in Code List 4-3. The calculated value in the variable `share` is of type float. If you are interested only in round dollar amounts, you can force the compiler to interpret the variable `money` as an integer data type by typecasting.

CODE LIST 4-3

```
// share.cpp

#include <iostream.h>

int main()
{
  int number_of_people;   // declare number_of_people as an integer
  float money;            // declare money as a float
  float share;            // declare share as a float

  cout << "How many people need a share of the money? ";
  cin >> number_of_people;
  cout << "How much money is available to share among the people? ";
  cin >> money;

  share = money / number_of_people;

  cout << "Give each person $" << share << '\n;

  return 0;
}
```

To typecast a variable, simply supply the name of the data type you want to use to interpret the variable, followed by the variable placed in parentheses. The statement below, for example, typecasts the variable diameter to a float.

```
C = PI * float(diameter);
```

In cases where the data type to which you want to typecast is more than one word (for example, long double), place both the data type and the variable in parentheses, as shown in the following example.

```
C = PI * (long double)(diameter);
```

STEP-BY-STEP 4.3

1. Retrieve the file share.cpp again.
2. Change the type of share to int.
3. Change the calculation statement to read as shown in Code List 4-4.
4. Compile and run the program again.
5. Save the source code file and close it.

CODE LIST 4-4

```
share = int (money) / number_of_people;
```

There are a number of ways to accomplish what was done in Step-by-Step 4.3. The purpose of the exercise is to show you how to use the typecast operator in case you ever need it.

Overflow

Overflow is the condition where a value becomes too large for its data type. The program in Code List 4-5 shows a simple example of overflow. The expression j = i + 2000; results in a value of 34000, which is too large for the short data type.

CODE LIST 4-5

```
// overflow.cpp

#include <iostream.h>

int main()
{
  short i,j;

  i = 32000;
  j = i + 2000; // The result (34000) overflows the short int type
  cout << j << '\n';
  return 0;
}
```

STEP-BY-STEP 4.4

1. Retrieve the file overflow.cpp. The program shown in Code List 4-5 appears.
2. Compile and run to see the result of the overflow.
3. Change the data type from short to long. Compile and run again. This time the result should not overflow.
4. Save and close the program.

Underflow

Underflow is similar to overflow. Underflow occurs with floating-point numbers when a number is too small for the data type. For example, the number 1.5×10^{-144} is too small to fit in a standard float variable. It is such a small number that the float data type considers it to be zero.

STEP-BY-STEP 4.5

1. Enter the program shown in Code List 4-6. Save the source code as unflow.cpp.

2. Compile and run the program to see that the small value underflows the variable, giving an incorrect output. You may get a compiler warning because of the potential for underflow.

3. Change the data type of x to double and run again. The value can now be successfully stored in the variable.

4. Change the data type of x back to float and run again. The value again underflows.

5. Save and close the program.

CODE LIST 4-6

```
// unflow.cpp

#include <iostream.h>

int main()
{
  float x;

  x = 1.5e-144;

  cout << x << '\n';
  return 0;
}
```

Floating-Point Rounding Errors

Using floating-point numbers can produce incorrect results if you fail to take the precision of floating-point data types into account.

In Lesson 2, you assigned floating-point values to variables using statements such as the one below.

```
Mass_of_Electron = 9.109e-31;    // 9.109 x 10-31 kilograms
```

The form of exponential notation used in the statement above is called "E" notation. "E" notation makes it possible to represent very large and very small floating-point numbers. For example, the number 3.5×10^{20} can be represented as 3.5e20 in your program.

You must keep the precision of your data type in mind when working with numbers in "E" notation. Look at the program in Code List 4-7.

CODE LIST 4-7

```
// floaterr.cpp

#include <iostream.h>  // necessary for cout command

int main()
{
 float x,y;

 x = 3.9e10 + 500.0;
 y = x - 3.9e10;

 cout << y << '\n';
 return 0;
}
```

At first glance, the two calculation statements appear simple enough. The first statement adds 3.9×10^{10} and 500. The second one subtracts the 3.9×10^{10}, which should leave the 500. The result assigned to y, however, is not 500. Actual values vary depending on the compiler, but the result is incorrect whatever the case.

The reason is that the float type is not precise enough for the addition of the number 500 to be included in its digits of precision. If you converted 3.9×10^{10} to standard notation, the value would be represented as 39,000,000,000. Adding 500 to that number would result in 39,000,000,500. In exponential notation, that is $3.90000005 \times 10^{10}$.

In science you may have worked with the concept of significant digits. This concept states that the accuracy of the result of a calculation is only as good as the accuracy of your least accurate value. The accuracy of floating-point values in a computer must be treated in a similar way. Because the float type is precise to only about seven digits, the 5 gets lost after the string of zeros and is too insignificant to have ever been properly added to such a large number.

However, the double data type is accurate to about 15 digits, which is more than enough to properly include the addition of the 500 to the 39 billion.

STEP-BY-STEP 4.6

1. Enter, compile, and run the program in Code List 4-7. See that the result in the variable y is not 500.

2. Change the data type of x and y to double and run again. The increased precision of the double data type should result in the correct value in y.

3. Save the source code file as floaterr.cpp and close the source code file.

Summary

In this lesson, you learned:

- C++ allows data types to be mixed in calculations.
- When C++ is allowed to handle mixed data types automatically, variables are promoted to other types.
- You can explicitly change data types using typecasting.
- When the digits after the decimal point are dropped from a value, it is said to have been truncated.
- Overflow is a condition in which an integer becomes too large for its data type.
- Underflow occurs when a floating-point number is so small that a data type interprets it as zero.
- Floating-point rounding errors can occur if you are not aware of the data types used in calculations.

LESSON 4 REVIEW QUESTIONS

TRUE/FALSE

Circle T if the statement is true or F if the statement is false.

T F 1. Many programming languages do not allow the mixing of data types in calculations.

T F 2. Promotion permanently changes the data type of a variable.

T F 3. The way C++ automatically converts data types is called typecasting.

T F 4. Assigning an integer value to a floating-point variable can result in truncation.

T F 5. Overflow can occur only with floating-point variables.

T F 6. Sometimes an overflow can be connected by changing data types.

T F 7. Underflow occurs when a number is too small for a variable.

T F 8. Floating-point precision can affect calculations.

T F 9. "E" notation prevents variable overflow and underflow.

T F 10. The float and double data types have the same amount of precision.

WRITTEN QUESTIONS

Write a brief answer to the following questions.

1. When a variable of type int is multiplied by a variable of type float, which variable is promoted?

2. After a calculation in which a variable of type float is promoted to another type, what data type does the variable retain?

3. If a calculation results in the value 4.9, and that value is assigned to a variable of type short, what value will the variable of type short contain after the assignment is complete?

4. What is the term that means the numbers to the right of the decimal point are removed?

5. What operator is used to explicitly change one data type to another?

6. Write a statement that changes the contents of a variable named radius to type float, multiplies it by 2.5, and assigns the result to a variable named A.

7. Define overflow.

8. What floating-point data type is the most likely to have difficulty with underflow?

9. How would you write 6.9 x 10^8 in "E" notation?

10. How would you write –3.1 x 10^{-6} in "E" notation?

LESSON 4 PROJECTS

PROJECT 4-1

1. Enter and compile the program that appears below. Save the source code as datatest.cpp.

```
// datatest.cpp

#include <iostream.h>

int main()
{
  short x;

  cout << "Enter a value: ";
  cin >> x;

  cout << "The value you entered is: ";
  cout << x << '\n';
  return 0;
}
```

2. Run the program repeatedly. Enter increasing large values until you create an overflow. Try the following values: 290, 1000, 30000, 35000, 70000.

3. Refer to the documentation you gathered about your compiler in Step-by-Step 2.1 in Lesson 2. Test the limits of the short data type to see if the overflow occurs where expected.

4. Leave the program open for the next project.

PROJECT 4-2

1. Change the data type of x in datatest.cpp to int.

2. Using the information you have about the range of a variable of type int, run the program several times to test the limits of the int data type. Test the range of the positive and negative ends.

3. Change the data type of x to unsigned int.

4. Test the range of the x by running the program several times. Test the largest positive value and verify that the data type will not hold negative values.

5. Leave the program open for the next project.

PROJECT 4-3

1. Change the data type of x in datatest.cpp to float.

2. Run the program repeatedly. Use the following values for input and record the output on paper. Note: The format of the output will vary among compilers.

   3.14159
   2.9e38
   2.9e39
   5.1e-38
   5.1e-39
   0.0000000005

3. Close the program.

CRITICAL THINKING

Write a program similar to the datatest.cpp program you wrote in Projects 4-1, 4-2, and 4-3. Name the source code file floattst.cpp. The program should declare a variable of each floating-point data type (x, y, and z). Have the program prompt the user for three values and output the values back to the screen. Run the program repeatedly. Each time you run the program, use the same value in all three variables and compare the three outputs.

Some values to try are:

3.4e38
3.4e100
1.7e308
1.7e309
4.6e1000
1.1e4932
1.1e4933

LESSON 5

STRINGS AND THE STRING CLASS

OBJECTIVES

Upon completion of this lesson, you should be able to:

- Define strings and literals.
- Explain classes and objects.
- Use the string class to store strings in your programs.
- Perform basic string operations.

Estimated Time: 1 hour

Introduction to Strings and Literals

In Lesson 2, you learned about the character data type and that a group of characters put together to create text is called a **string**. Strings are one of the most useful kinds of data in a program. Strings help programs communicate with the user and allow computers to process data other than numbers. For example, when you prompt the user with a statement such as "Enter the cow's weight:" you are using a string. Or when you ask the user to enter the cow's name, the name the user enters is a string.

C++ does not have a data type specifically for strings. Many C++ programmers work with strings by manually manipulating groups of characters, called **character arrays**. Working with character arrays requires a thorough understanding of how the C++ language deals with strings. Character arrays provide programmers with considerable flexibility. However, as you will learn in this lesson, C++ also allows you to hide the details of the character array by using a special set of code and data called a **string class**. In this lesson, you will learn a little about strings, and then use a string class for your own programs.

Recall that when you have worked with numeric values, some of the values are keyed directly into the source code and some values are calculated or are entered by the user. Values that are keyed directly into the source code are often called hard-coded values. Values or strings that are hard-coded into the source code are called **literals**. A hard-coded numeric value is called a **numeric literal**. A string of text that is hard-coded is called a **string literal**.

A single character can also be hard-coded. A **character literal** appears in single quotation marks. A string literal appears in double quotation marks. Code List 5-1 shows examples of literals.

CODE LIST 5-1

```
x = 6.3;          // 6.3 is a numeric literal
cout << "Hello"; // "Hello" is a string literal
MyChar = 'A';     // 'A' is a character literal
```

Obviously, literals do not change when the program runs. However, when a literal is used to initialize a variable, the value in the variable can change.

Just as you have used numeric literals when working with numeric data types and variables, you will use string literals and character literals when working with strings and characters.

Introduction to Classes and Objects

You may have heard that C++ is an object-oriented programming language. **Object-oriented programming (OOP)** is a way of programming that treats parts of a computer program as objects that are similar to real-world objects. The best way to understand object-oriented programming is to consider an example.

In the lessons you have completed in this book, you have used floating-point data types such as double to store data. You have also used the addition operator to add values together. The double data type and the addition operator are part of the C++ language. You don't have to know how they work. All you have to know is how to use them. When a line of code like the one below is executed, the addition takes place and the result is stored. You do not have to know exactly how the addition is achieved or exactly how the data is stored; those details have been taken care of for you.

```
x = x + 4.2;
```

As you learned earlier in this unit, the purpose of a high-level language is to hide the details and make programming a more rapid and dependable process. You saw how a simple statement like the one preceding is translated into many machine-language instructions.

Object-oriented programming takes the concept of a high-level language to a new level by allowing programmers to create their own operations and even data types, while hiding the details in a way similar to the built-in features of the language. For example, you learned earlier in this lesson that C++ has no built-in string data type. The object-oriented features of C++, however, allow you (or better yet, someone else) to create a string data type for you to use. And like the double data type, you will not have to know how the string data type works. You will just have to know how to use it.

When working with OOP, it is important to understand some basic object-oriented programming terms. To learn these terms, let us stick with the example of the object-oriented string data type. An object-oriented string data type is referred to as a string class. A string class is actually a definition used to create a string object.

The distinction between a class and an object is important. Think of a class as a generic definition from which an object is created. In the real world, dog would be an example of a class, while Rover would be an object based on the dog class. An object is said to be an **instance** of a class. Therefore, Rover is an instance of the dog class, or, in programming terms, a string object is an instance of a string class. In order to store an actual string, a programmer creates a string object using a string class.

This will make more sense once you have used a class yourself. In the Step-by-Step exercises to follow, you will use a string class that is provided with this textbook to store strings.

Using the String Class

Using the string class is a little more complicated than using the built-in data types. However, once you have mastered a few simple tasks, you will see how easy using the string class really is.

Preparing to Use the String Class

To use the string class, you must include a header file in your source code, in this case oostring.h. The string class used in this book consists of two files: oostring.h and oostring.cpp. Your compiler must also be set up properly to compile a program that uses the string class. For general tips on compilers and how to get more information on your specific compiler, see Appendix G.

To give the string class a try with your compiler, let us compile and run a program that uses the string class.

Hot Tip

If your compiler does not have the bool data type, you will receive an error message when you compile oostring.cpp.

STEP-BY-STEP 5.1

1. Open oostring.cpp and stringex.cpp into a project in your compiler. The file oostring.h must also be available to your compiler.
2. Compile and run the program. The program creates a string object, assigns the string "Hello World!" to the string object, and prints the string to the screen.
3. Leave the project open for the next exercise.

Declaring a String Object

Now that you have successfully compiled and run a program that uses the string class, we can look at the features offered by the string class.

When you declare a string object, you can create an empty string object or you can initialize the object with a string. As the code in Code List 5-2 shows, the process of declaring a string object is similar to declaring other data.

CODE LIST 5-2

```
oostring MyString1;           // declare an empty string object
oostring MyString2("ABCDEF"); // initializing while declaring
```

Assigning Strings to String Objects

You can assign strings to string objects in one of three ways:

1. You can assign the contents of one string object to another string object.
2. You can assign a string literal to a string object.
3. You can assign a character literal to a string object.

Code List 5-3 shows an example of each of the three ways to assign a string to a string object.

Did You Know?

The string class uses an array of characters that can adjust its length as the program runs. Therefore, when you declare a string object, declaring a size is not necessary. When you assign a string to the object, the length is adjusted to properly contain the string. There is no official limitation on the length of a string in a string object. A string object can easily hold thousands of characters.

CODE LIST 5-3

```
MyString1 = MyString2;
MyString1 = "string literal";
MyString1 = 'A';
```

Printing the Contents of a String Object to the Screen

You can use cout to display the contents of a string object. The statement below shows a typical line of code that outputs the contents of a string class.

```
cout << MyString1 << '\n';
```

STEP-BY-STEP 5.2

1. Modify the source code of stringex.cpp to match the program in Code List 5-4.
2. Save the source code. Compile and run the program. The program stores two strings using separate objects.
3. Leave the program open for the next exercise.

CODE LIST 5-4

```
// stringex.cpp

#include <iostream.h>
#include "oostring.h"

int main()
{
  oostring MyString1;
  oostring MyString2("ABCDEFGHIJKLMNOPQRSTUVWXYZ");

  MyString1 = "Hello World!";

  cout << MyString1 << '\n';
  cout << MyString2 << '\n';

  return 0;
}
```

Step-by-Step 5.2 is an example of how more than one object can be created from the same class. A program can include as many string objects as necessary. The name of the object is used to distinguish among them.

Computer Concepts

The #include statements you have been using have placed angle brackets (<>) around the filename being included. These statements are precompiled libraries that are stored in a special directory when the compiler is installed. When you include oostring.h, you place it in double quotation marks to tell the compiler that it is not precompiled and to look for it in the current directory.

String Operations

Programs that use strings often need to perform a variety of operations on the strings it has stored. For example, to properly center a string, you may need to know the number of characters in the string. You may also need to add strings together.

One of the reasons that objects are especially useful is that they do more than hold data. Objects also perform operations on the data they hold. A string object is no exception. In fact, as you will see, a string object is a great example of an object that holds data and performs operations on that data.

String objects should be used to store numbers such as ZIP codes, Social Security numbers, and phone numbers. These kinds of numbers often include parentheses or hyphens, which are not allowed in numeric data types. In a string, however, characters other than numerals are allowed.

Messages

One of the important concepts behind the use of objects is the idea of **containment** (or encapsulation). These terms refer to the way an object hides the details of how data is stored and how operations work. The data, and the code required to work with that data, is contained or encapsulated within the object itself. To make the object do what we want it to do, we send the object a **message**.

For example, when you want to know the length of the string stored in a string object, you send the object a message that asks the object to report the string's length. How it calculates the length of the string does not matter. We just want an accurate answer. It is the object's job to provide that answer.

Did You Know?

Objects got their name because they have characteristics similar to real-world objects.

Obtaining the Length of a String

The message used to obtain the length of a string is simply *length*. The following statement shows an example of the code required to send the length message to a string object.

```
l = MyString2.length();
```

Let us look at the statement piece by piece. First, `l` is an integer variable that will store the length that the object reports. The assignment operator (=) assigns the value returned by the string object to the variable `l`. `MyString2` is the name of the string object to which we want to send the message. The period that follows the name of the object is called the **dot operator** (or class-member operator). The dot operator separates the name of the object from the message, in this case `length`.

The code inside the object that performs the length operation is called a **method**. Therefore, when you are sending the length message you could say that you are using the length method of the string class.

STEP-BY-STEP 5.3

1. Modify the source code of stringex.cpp to match the program in Code List 5-5. See whether you can predict the output of the program.
2. Save the source code. Compile and run the program to see if your prediction was correct.
3. Leave the program open for the next exercise.

CODE LIST 5-5

```
// stringex.cpp

#include <iostream.h>
#include "oostring.h"

int main()
{
  int len1, len2;
  oostring MyString1;
  oostring MyString2("ABCDEFGHIJKLMNOPQRSTUVWXYZ");

  MyString1 = "Hello World!";

  len1 = MyString1.length();
  len2 = MyString2.length();
```

CODE LIST 5-5 (CONTINUED)

```
    cout << MyString1 << '\n';
    cout << "Length = " << len1 << '\n';
    cout << MyString2 << '\n';
    cout << "Length = " << len2 << '\n';

    return 0;
}
```

String Concatenation

Concatenation is a big word that describes the operation of adding one string onto the end of another string. Suppose, for example, that you have one string object holding a first name and another string object holding a last name. To get both strings together in one string object, you need to concatenate the last name onto the first name. Actually, you would first concatenate a space onto the end of the first name to insert a space between the first and last names.

The string class includes the ability to perform concatenation. To make the concatenation process the most flexible, the string class makes use of an operator called a compound operator. The operator is +=. The += operator is specifically intended to provide a shorthand method for adding a value to an existing variable or object. For example, x += 1 is equivalent to x = x + 1. Table 5-1 gives some more examples.

To concatenate strings using the compound operator, use statements like the examples in Table 5-2.

TABLE 5-1
Concatenation examples

SHORTHAND METHOD	LONG METHOD
j += 7;	j = j + 7;
k += n;	k = k + n;

TABLE 5-2
Concatenation statements

STATEMENT	DESCRIPTION
`MyString1 += MyString2;`	Add MyString2 to the end of MyString1.
`MyString1 += "string literal";`	Add a string literal to the end of MyString1.
`MyString1 += Ch;`	Add a character to the end of MyString1.
`MyString1 += 'A';`	Add a character literal to the end of MyString1.

Consider the statements in Code List 5-6. The statements build a new string in MyString1 by performing three concatenations.

CODE LIST 5-6

```
MyString1 = "Tracy";
MyString2 = "Stewart";

MyString1 += ' ';            // add a space after the first name
MyString1 += MyString2;      // add the last name to MyString1
MyString1 += " was here."; // add a string literal to MyString1

cout << MyString1 << '\n';
```

STEP-BY-STEP 5.4

1. Add the code in Code List 5-6 to the end of the program on your screen (before the return 0;). Can you predict the output of the concatenated string?

2. Compile and run the program to see the result of the concatenation.

3. Close the program.

Summary

In this lesson, you learned:

- Strings allow computers to process text as well as numbers.
- Hard-coded numeric values are called numeric literals. Hard-coded text is called a string literal.
- Object-oriented programming is a way of programming that treats parts of a computer program as objects that are similar to real-world objects.
- A class is a definition used to create an object. An object is said to be an instance of a class.
- Compiling a program that uses classes requires special setup.
- When declaring a string object, you can declare an empty object or initialize the object with a string.
- You can assign one string to another, a string literal to a string object, or a character literal to a string object.
- You can use cout to display the contents of a string object.
- Objects hold data and the operations you can perform on that data.
- To make an object perform an operation on itself, you send the object a message.
- The length method is used to determine the length of a string stored in a string object.
- Concatenation is the operation of adding one string onto the end of another string.

LESSON 5 REVIEW QUESTIONS

TRUE/FALSE

Circle T if the statement is true or F if the statement is false.

T F 1. C++ has a built-in data type specifically for strings.

T F 2. A hard-coded string of text is called a string literal.

T F 3. A class is said to be an instance of an object.

T F 4. A string class must be initialized when it is declared.

T F 5. You can assign a character literal to a string object.

T F 6. A string object adjusts its length as necessary as the program runs.

T F 7. Each program can declare only one string object at a time.

T F 8. To make an object do what we want it to do, we send it a message.

T F 9. The dot operator separates the name of the object from the assignment operator.

T F 10. Concatenation refers to the process of disposing of a string object when you are done with it.

WRITTEN QUESTIONS

Write a brief answer to the following questions.

1. What kind of literal appears in single quotes?
2. Explain the distinction between a class and an object.
3. What are the names of the two files that make up the string class?
4. Write a statement that declares a string object named FirstName and initializes the string object with your first name.
5. Write a statement that assigns the contents of a string object named NewName to a string object named MyName.
6. Write a statement that displays the contents of the string object named MyName to the screen.
7. Explain the concept of encapsulation.
8. What is the method used to determine the length of a string in a string object?
9. Write a statement that assigns the length of the string named MyName to an integer variable named len.
10. What is the compound operator used to concatenate strings?

LESSON 5 PROJECTS

PROJECT 5-1

1. Write a program that declares two string objects named FavoriteColor and FavoritePlace. Initialize FavoriteColor with the name of your favorite color at the time the object is declared. Leave FavoritePlace empty.
2. Use the assignment operator to assign the name of your favorite place to visit to the FavoritePlace object.
3. Write statements to produce output similar to the following lines. The statements should use the contents of your string objects to fill in the blanks.

My favorite color is ______________.

My favorite place to visit is ______________.

4. Save the source code as favorite.cpp, compile, and run the program.

5. Close the program.

PROJECT 5-2

1. Write a program that declares a string object named MyString. Leave the object empty.
2. Use the assignment operator to assign the character 'A' to the string object.
3. Print the contents of the string to the screen.
4. Concatenate the character 'B' to the end of the string.
5. Print the contents of the string to the screen.
6. Print the length of the string to the screen using a statement like the one below.

```
cout << MyString.length() << '\n';
```

7. Concatenate the string "CDEFG" to the end of the string.
8. Print the contents of the string to the screen.
9. Print the length of the string to the screen again.
10. Save the source code as abc.cpp, compile, and run the program.
11. Close the program.

CRITICAL THINKING

1. Write a program that declares a string object named spacer and initializes the object to hold nine blank spaces.

2. Declare a string object named ruler.

3. Use concatenation to build a string that matches the string shown below. The first character in the string should be a zero (0) and the last character should be a three (3). There should be nine spaces between each numeral. Hint: You can use multiple concatenation statements.

   0   1   2   3

4. Print the concatenated string to the screen.

5. Report the length of the concatenated string to the screen.

6. Name the source code file spacer.cpp.

LESSON 6

INPUT AND OUTPUT

OBJECTIVES

Upon completion of this lesson, you should be able to:

- Use cin and cout.
- Use special characters.
- Use the cout format options.
- Use the I/O manipulators.
- Accept characters as input.
- Accept strings as input.

Using cin and cout

We have treated cin and cout (pronounced "see-in" and "see-out") as commands up to this point. You may be surprised, however, to learn that the << and >> symbols actually represent the action. Consider the following simple statements.

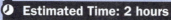

```
cout << j;
cin >> i;
```

The << and >> symbols are operators, as + and * are operators. The << symbol is the output operator, and >> is the input operator. As you know, the variable to the right of the << or >> operator is what is being input or output. So what are cout and cin? They are actually objects. The cout object is the destination of the output, and the cin object is the source of the input.

The >> operator is also referred to as the **extraction operator** because it extracts data from the stream. The << operator is also referred to as the **insertion operator** because it inserts data into the stream.

The #include <iostream.h> directive is required to use streams.

Streams

The cin and cout objects are known as streams. When you think of a stream, you probably think of water flowing from one place to another. In C++, a **stream** is data flowing from one place to another. You should think of C++ streams as channels that exist to provide an easy way to get data to and from devices. The stream that brings data from your keyboard is cin, and the stream that takes data to your screen is cout.

Some beginning programmers find it difficult to remember when to use << and when to use >>. There is a method you can use to help you remember: the symbols in the input and output operators point in the direction that the data is flowing. For example, in the statement `cout << j;`, the data is flowing from the variable `j` to the destination of the output (`cout`). When you use the input operator (as in `cin >> i;`), the data flows from the source of the input (`cin`) to the variable `i`.

For example, your monitor (screen) is a device. You do not have to understand exactly how output gets to the screen. You just have to know that the cout object is the stream that leads to your screen. When you use the output operator to place something in the cout stream, your screen is the destination.

The cin and cout objects may represent devices other than the keyboard and screen. The cin stream reads from what is called the **standard input device**, and the cout stream leads to the **standard output device**. By default, the standard input device is the keyboard and the standard output device is the screen. But they can be changed to other devices. There are other streams that you will learn about in later lessons.

Using Console I/O

The term *console I/O* refers to using the screen and keyboard for input and output (I/O is an abbreviation of input/output). In other words, the standard use of cin and cout is console I/O. Let us look at some examples of console I/O to make sure you understand the role of each part of the statements.

Figure 6-1 illustrates the general form of the << operator. The << operator indicates to the compiler that the statement is producing output. The destination of the output is the standard output device (the screen). The output can be any valid C++ expression.

FIGURE 6-1
The << operator is used for output.

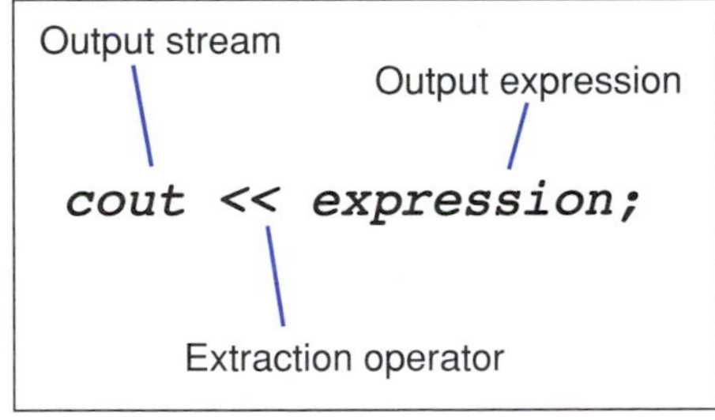

Note

Remember, << is an operator. Therefore, you can use it many times in the same output expression, just as you can use a mathematical operator multiple times in the same expression. For example, the statement n = 2 + 4 + 5 uses the addition operator twice. In the same way, the output operator can appear more than once in a statement.

The examples in Code List 6-1 show how the output can be a string literal, a variable, or a mathematical expression. The figure also shows that more than one item can be output in a single statement by using multiple output operators.

CODE LIST 6-1

```
cout << "This string literal will appear on the screen. \n";
cout << distance;
cout << length_of_room * width_of_room;
cout << "The room is " << area << " square feet.\n";
```

Figure 6-2 illustrates the general form of the >> operator. The >> operator tells the compiler that the statement is requesting input. The source of the input is the standard input device (the keyboard). The destination of the input must be a variable or variables.

FIGURE 6-2
The >> operator is used for input.

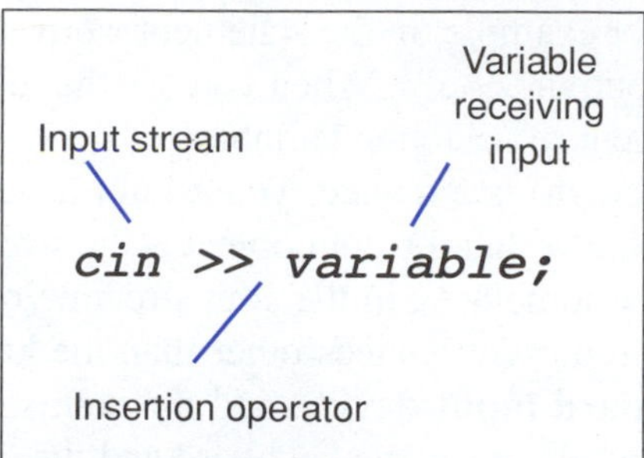

STEP-BY-STEP 6.1

1. Load, compile, and run basicio.cpp to review the basic use of input and output operators.
2. Close the program.

New Line and Other Special Characters

You have been including `'\n'` in output statements without a good explanation of what `'\n'` does. It is an important part of formatting output because it causes the cursor to return to the next line of the screen. The `\n` character is one of the special characters available in C++.

What Is \n?

The `\n` character is called the **new line character** or the **end-of-line character**. Use it in any output statement that completes a line. The new line character has the same effect in an output statement as pressing the Return or Enter key in a word processor.

The `\n` character must appear in double quotation marks if it is used in conjunction with other characters or may be used with single quotation marks if it appears alone. See the examples in Code List 6-2.

CODE LIST 6-2

```
cout << i << '\n';  // single quotes because it is a single character
cout << "String\n"; // double quotes because it is part of a string
```

Special Characters

The end-of-line character is called a **special character**. Although `\n` appears as two characters in the source code, the compiler interprets it as one character. The backslash (\) tells the compiler that a special character is being formed. The reason for this system is because there is no single keyboard character available to represent the end-of-line character.

Hot Tip

The `\n` character can be enclosed in double quotation marks, even when it appears alone. The compiler will treat the character as a string because it is in double quotes. The statement will, however, produce the same result.

Table 6-1 shows other special characters available for use in output statements. The first one generates a tab character. The others are used to print characters to the screen that would otherwise be unprintable because they have other meanings to the compiler. For example, because the backslash is used by the compiler to signify a special character, you must use a special character to print a backslash. There are also special characters for printing single and double quotation marks.

TABLE 6-1
Special characters used in output statements

CHARACTER SEQUENCE	RESULT
`\t`	Generates a tab character to move the cursor to the next tab stop.
`\\`	Prints a backslash (\).
`\'`	Prints a single quotation mark (').
`\"`	Prints a double quotation mark (").

Using endl

There is an alternative to \n that you may find easier to enter and more readable. You can enter endl in the place of '\n'. For example, the two statements in Code List 6-3 are functionally identical.

CODE LIST 6-3

```
cout << i << '\n';
cout << i << endl;
```

You can use endl in place of the character '\n', but do not use endl as part of a larger string. Think of endl as a constant that holds the value '\n'. If used in a statement such as `cout << "String endl";`, the endl will be considered as part of the string, and no end-of-line character will be included. To use endl with string literals, use a statement similar to the following one.

```
cout << "How now brown cow." << endl;
```

FIGURE 6-3
The special characters allow you to print characters to the screen that otherwise would not be able to display.

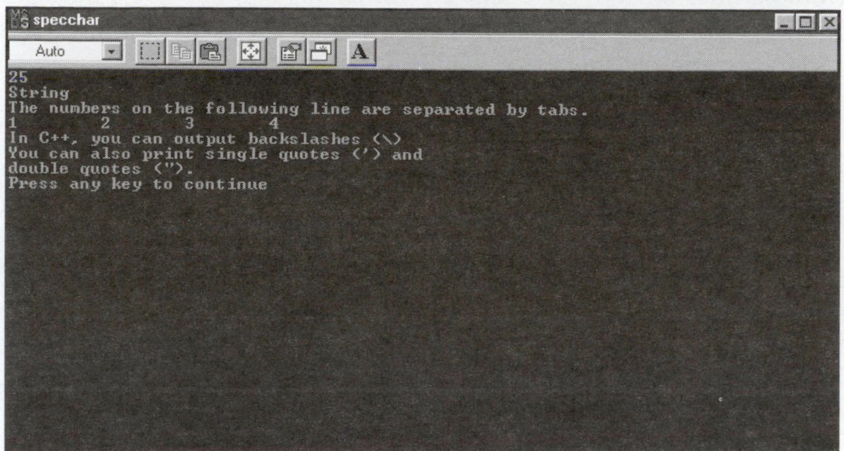

STEP-BY-STEP 6.2

1. Enter the program shown in Code List 6-4. Save the source code as specchar.cpp.

2. Compile and run the program. The output window should appear similar to Figure 6-3.

3. Compare the output on your screen to the statements in the source code to see that you understand the way the output was achieved.

4. Add the numbers 5 and 6 to the line of tab-separated numerals. Be sure to include the tab character in between the numbers.

5. Run the program again to verify that your modifications worked.

6. Add a statement before the first cout statement that prints your name to the screen in double quotation marks. For example, "Dale Lee".

7. Run the program again.

8. When you have the program producing the correct output, close the program.

CODE LIST 6-4

```
// specchar.cpp
// Example of new line and special characters

#include <iostream.h>

int main()
{
  int i;

  i = 25;
  cout << i << '\n';  // single quotes because it is a single character
  cout << "String\n"; // double quotes because it is part of a string

  cout << "The numbers on the following line are separated by tabs.\n";
  cout << "1 \t 2 \t 3 \t 4 \n";

  // The following lines use endl
  cout << "In C++, you can output backslashes (\\)" << endl;
  cout << "You can also print single quotes (\') and" << endl;
  cout << "double quotes (\")." << endl;

  return 0;
}
```

Using setf and unsetf

The exact result of the format options may vary slightly among compilers.

The cout object has format options that can be changed. To change these options, you send a message to the object using setf and unsetf. Table 6-2 lists the options that can be used.

Now, examine how the format option *right* (indicating that the output is to be right-justified) is used in the expanded format statement below.

```
cout.setf(ios::right);
```

You will learn more about how to use statements like the preceding one later. What is important now is that you understand that the word *right* is the format option and the setf method is what changes the option in the cout object.

You can remove the options by replacing setf with unsetf, as in the following example.

```
cout.unsetf(ios::scientific);
```

TABLE 6-2
cout format options

OPTION	DESCRIPTION
left	Left-justifies the output
right	Right-justifies the output
showpoint	Displays decimal point and trailing zeros for all floating-point numbers, even if the decimal places are not needed
uppercase	Displays the "e" in E-notation as "E" rather than "e"
showpos	Displays a leading plus sign before positive values
scientific	Displays floating-point numbers in scientific ("E") notation
fixed	Displays floating-point numbers in normal notation

STEP-BY-STEP 6.3

1. Enter the program in Code List 6-5 and save the source code file as coutsetf.cpp.

2. Run the program to see how the format options change the output. Your compiler's results may vary slightly from the predictions made in the program's comments.

3. Close the program.

CODE LIST 6-5

```
// coutsetf.cpp

#include <iostream.h>

int main()
{
  float x = 24.0;

  cout << x << endl;            // displays 24

  cout.setf(ios::showpoint);
  cout << x << endl;            // displays 24.0000

  cout.setf(ios::showpos);
  cout << x << endl;            // displays +24.0000

  cout.setf(ios::scientific);
  cout << x << endl;            // displays +2.400000e+001
```

CODE LIST 6-5 (CONTINUED)

```
    cout.setf(ios::uppercase);
    cout << x << endl;            // displays +2.400000E+001

    cout.unsetf(ios::showpoint);
    cout << x << endl;            // displays +2.400000E+001

    cout.unsetf(ios::showpos);
    cout << x << endl;            // displays 2.400000E+001

    cout.unsetf(ios::uppercase);
    cout << x << endl;            // displays 2.400000e+001

    cout.unsetf(ios::scientific);
    cout << x << endl;            // displays 24

    return 0;
}
```

Using the I/O Manipulators

Another set of format options is available in C++: the **I/O manipulators**. The most common of these are setprecision and setw. They may be placed directly in the output statement.

Did You Know?

If neither the scientific nor fixed option is set, most compilers decide the method to display floating-point numbers based on whether the number can be displayed more efficiently in scientific or fixed notation.

Using setprecision

When used in conjunction with the fixed format option, the setprecision I/O manipulator sets the number of digits that are to appear to the right of the decimal point. This is very convenient when printing amounts of a specific number of digits is important—for example, when printing dollars and cents.

Look at the example in Code List 6-6. First the fixed format option is set. Then, in the output statement, the desired precision is set. The setprecision manipulator sets the number of digits displayed to the number provided in the parentheses. The setprecision manipulator affects all floating-point numbers that follow it in the statement. It also affects any floating-point numbers output to the cout stream until setprecision is called again to set another precision.

If you do not set the fixed option before using setprecision, the results will vary, depending on your compiler. Some compilers will set the number of digits to the right of the decimal point anyway. Others will set the overall number of digits on both sides of the decimal point. To be safe, you should set the fixed option.

Hot Tip

In order to use I/O manipulators, you must use the directive `#include <iomanip.h>` to include the necessary code to make the manipulators available.

CODE LIST 6-6

```
cout.setf(ios::fixed);
cout << setprecision(2) << price << '\n';
```

STEP-BY-STEP 6.4

1. Retrieve the source code file named iomanip.cpp. The program shown in Code List 6-7 appears. Notice that the program uses two new line characters in a row to cause the output to skip a line.

2. Compile and run the program to see the difference that the formatting makes.

3. Change the line that includes the setprecision I/O manipulator to match Code List 6-8. The new line includes text to print a dollar sign as part of the output. Notice that the dollar sign appears in single quotation marks because it is a single character.

4. Run the program again to see the dollar sign display.

5. Leave the program open for the next exercise.

CODE LIST 6-7

```
// iomanip.cpp

#include <iostream.h>
#include <iomanip.h>

int main()
{
  double cost = 34.99;
  double total;

  total = cost + (cost * 0.07875);  // add tax to cost to get total

  // Display total without formatting
  cout << "Total with no formatting:\n";
  cout << total << "\n\n"; // use two new line characters to skip line

  // Display total with fixed precision
  cout << "Total with formatting:\n";
  cout.setf(ios::fixed);
  cout << setprecision(2) << total << "\n\n";

  return 0;
}
```

CODE LIST 6-8

```
cout << setprecision(2) << '$' << total << "\n\n";
```

Using setw

The setw manipulator can be used to change the number of spaces the compiler uses when it displays a number. The amount of space used to display a number is called the *field width*. You can use setw to set a minimum field width or use it to format numbers.

For example, if i = 254, j = 44, and k = 6, the statement `cout << i << j << k << '\n';` produces the output 254446 because only the space necessary to output the numbers is used. The statement below, however, adds spaces to the left of each number to give formatted output.

```
cout << setw(10) << i << setw(10) << j << setw(10) << k << endl;
```

The output of the statement above appears as shown below.

```
254       44        6
```

The best way to see the difference is to try it yourself in the next Step-by-Step exercise.

STEP-BY-STEP 6.5

1. Add the declarations in Code List 6-9 to the top of the program on your screen.
2. Add the code in Code List 6-10 before the `return` statement at the end of the program.
3. Compile and run to see how the setw manipulators affect the output of the integers.
4. Save and close the program.

CODE LIST 6-9

```
int i = 1499;
int j = 618;
int k = 2;
```

CODE LIST 6-10

```
// Output with no field widths
cout << "Output of i, j, and k with no field widths specified:\n";
cout << i << j << k << "\n\n";

// Output with field widths set
cout << "Output of i, j, and k with field widths specified:\n";
cout << setw(10) << i << setw(10) << j << setw(10) << k << "\n\n";
```

Inputting Characters

The >> operator can be used to input characters. If the user enters more than one character, only the first character will be stored in the variable.

STEP-BY-STEP 6.6

1. Retrieve the source code file named inchar.cpp. The program shown in Code List 6-11 appears.
2. Run the program to see how inputting a character works. Run the program several times. Try entering a variety of characters and more than one character at a time.
3. Close the program.

CODE LIST 6-11

```
// inchar.cpp

#include <iostream.h>

int main()
{
  char c;

  cout << "Enter a single character: ";
  cin >> c;
  cout << "You entered " << c << '\n';
  return 0;
}
```

Inputting Strings

In Lesson 5, you assigned strings to string objects at the time of declaration and later, using the assignment operator. You may have been thinking, "How do I enter a string provided by the user into a string object?" As you might have guessed, the string object has a method for doing just that. It is called getline.

Consider the statement below. The getline method is used somewhat differently from the other object methods you have used. When using getline, the parentheses are used to specify the input stream object and the string object you want to input the string into.

Did You Know?

When you enter a number such as 4 into a character variable, the character '4' is stored rather than the integer 4. Therefore, you perform mathematical operations on numbers when they are stored as characters.

```
getline(cin, MyString);
```

When you use getline, you can use it just like the preceding statement. Just change MyString to the name of your string object.

STEP-BY-STEP 6.7

1. Retrieve the source code file named instring.cpp. The program shown in Code List 6-12 appears.

2. Compile and run the program. As an object is supposed to do, the string object hides the details of the operation, making getline easy to use.

3. Close the program.

CODE LIST 6-12

```
// instring.cpp

#include <iostream.h>
#include "oostring.h"

int main()
{
  oostring FirstName;
  oostring LastName;

  cout << "Enter your first name: ";
  getline(cin, FirstName);

  cout << "Enter your last name: ";
  getline(cin, LastName);

  cout << "Your name is " << FirstName << " " << LastName << ".\n";

  return 0;
}
```

Flushing the Input Stream

The cin object is often referred to as the **input stream**. Think of the input stream as a line at a checkout stand. Characters are lined up in the input stream as keys are pressed on the keyboard. Each character, however, must wait its turn to be processed. Therefore, if a prompt for input does not use every character in the input stream, the remaining characters wait in the input stream for the next prompt.

Using statements such as `cin >> x;` for inputting numbers and getline for inputting strings works well—until you try to use them together. The problem arises because after you have input a number using a statement like the preceding one, the new line character that is generated when you press Enter stays in the input stream. That character stays in the stream until the program requests something else from the stream. In other words, statements such as `cin >> x;` do not clean up after themselves very well.

This is not a problem if the next input from the user is another number, because C++ will ignore the new line character that is still waiting in the stream and wait for a number to come down the stream. When the next input is a string, however, you have a problem. The problem arises because the getline method is looking for any sequence of characters ending in a new line character. If a new line character, or any other character for that matter, is waiting in the input stream, that is what you get in your string.

Let's see the problem firsthand.

STEP-BY-STEP 6.8

1. Retrieve the source code file named flush.cpp. The program asks for a numeric value and then asks for a string.

2. Compile and run the program. Enter 12 for the quantity and press Enter. Notice that the program rushes to the end without stopping to ask for the description. The new line character left over from the input of the integer was accepted as input by the getline method.

3. Leave the program open for the next Step-by-Step exercise.

To remedy this problem, you must remove the extra characters from the input stream before the getline method is executed. This operation is called flushing the input stream. To flush the input stream, insert the line below after the statement where the number was input.

```
cin.ignore(80, '\n');
```

The `80` tells the program to ignore the next 80 characters in the stream. The `'\n'` tells the function to stop ignoring characters when it gets to a new line character. You could use a number smaller than 80 in most cases. The function will usually stop ignoring after only a few characters because it will find a new line character. Most programmers use 80 to play it safe.

Code List 6-13 shows the flush.cpp program with the addition of the flush statement.

It is a good idea to flush the input stream after all numeric input statements in programs where strings are also used.

CODE LIST 6-13

```
// flush.cpp

#include <iostream.h>
#include "oostring.h"

int main()
{
  int quantity;
  oostring desc;

  cout << "Enter the quantity desired: ";
  cin >> quantity;
  cin.ignore(80, '\n'); // Flush the input stream
```

CODE LIST 6-13 (CONTINUED)

```
    cout << "Enter the description of the item: ";
    getline(cin, desc);

    cout << "You requested " << quantity << " of item described as \n";
    cout << desc << ".\n";

    return 0;
}
```

STEP-BY-STEP 6.9

1. Add the line required to flush the input stream. Use Code List 6-13 as a reference.
2. Compile and run the program again. The prompt for description now works properly.
3. Close the program.

Using Descriptive Prompts

When writing programs that interact with the user, be sure to output prompts that clearly explain the input the program is requesting. For example, if prompting the user for his or her name, use a descriptive prompt like the one below.

```
Please enter your last name:
```

If prompting for a telephone number or some other formatted data, you may want to use the prompt to give an example.

```
Please enter your phone number using the format (555) 555-5555:
```

The more descriptive and clear your prompts are, the more likely the user is to enter the information in the form your program is expecting.

Clearing the Screen and Printing a Hard Copy

Now that you have learned more about screen I/O, you may be interested in learning how to clear the screen or print to a printer. The techniques required to clear the screen and print to a printer vary, depending on the compiler and operating system you are using. Your compiler may have a function available for clearing the screen, or you may have to use another technique. Modern operating systems sometimes require special programming in order to send output to a printer. You may want to send output to a text file on disk and then use a text editor to print the contents of the file.

Summary

In this lesson, you learned:

- The << and >> symbols are actually operators. The cin and cout keywords are actually objects.
- The cin and cout objects are streams. A stream is data flowing from one place to another.
- The cin object brings data from the standard input device. The cout object takes data to the standard output device.
- Console I/O refers to using the screen and keyboard for input and output.
- The \n character is a special character called the new line character or end-of-line character.
- There are special characters for printing characters such as tab, the backslash, and quotation marks.
- You can use endl in place of the character '\n'.
- The cout object has format options that can be changed with the setf and unsetf methods.
- The setprecision I/O manipulator is used to set the number of digits that will appear to the right of the decimal point.
- The setw I/O manipulator is used to set a field width for numbers that are output to the screen.
- The >> operator can be used to input characters.
- To input strings, use the getline method of the string class.
- When a program includes numeric and string input, it is necessary to flush the input stream after each numeric entry to remove characters left in the input stream.
- Programs should use prompts that clearly explain the input that the program is requesting.
- The process for clearing the screen and printing a hard copy varies among compilers and operating systems.

LESSON 6 REVIEW QUESTIONS

TRUE/FALSE

Circle T if the statement is true or F if the statement is false.

T F 1. The << and >> symbols are actually objects.

T F 2. A stream is data flowing from one place to another.

T F 3. The cin stream reads from the standard output device.

T F 4. The new line character is represented as `\l`.

T F 5. The special character for generating a tab character is `\t`.

T F 6. The forcepoint format option displays decimal point and trailing zeros for all floating-point numbers, even if the decimal places are not needed.

T F 7. The setprecision I/O manipulator sets the field width for output.

T F 8. The >> operator can be used to input characters.

T F 9. The getline method is part of the string object.

T F 10. Flushing the input stream removes all characters from the stream.

WRITTEN QUESTIONS

Write a brief answer to the following questions.

1. What is the name of the standard output stream object?
2. What is another name for the input operator (>>)?
3. What is another name for the output operator (<<)?
4. What is the special character used to print a backslash?
5. What is the alternative to entering \n to generate a new line character?
6. What format option displays floating-point numbers in E-notation?
7. What I/O manipulator sets the number of digits to be displayed after the decimal point?
8. What two pieces of information must be provided when using getline?
9. Write the statement used to flush the input stream.
10. Why is it important to use descriptive prompts when prompting for data?

LESSON 6 PROJECTS

PROJECT 6-1

Write a program that asks the user for three floating-point numbers. Print the numbers back to the screen with a precision of one decimal point. Use a field width for the output that places the three numbers across the screen as in the following example. Save the source code as float3.cpp.

```
123.4       33.2        1.9
```

PROJECT 6-2

Write a program that asks the user for a name, address, city, state, ZIP code, and phone number and stores each in appropriate string objects. Use descriptive prompts for each input. After the strings are stored, print the information back to the screen in the following format. Save the source code as address.cpp.

Name
Address
City, State ZIP Code
Phone Number

PROJECT 6-3

Write a program that prompts the user for the names of three colors and stores the responses in three string objects. Use descriptive prompts for each input. After the strings are stored, print the information back to the screen on one line, separated by tabs. Save the source code as tabs.cpp.

CRITICAL THINKING

ACTIVITY 6-1

Write a program that uses the special characters to print the following line of code to the screen. The code should appear on the screen exactly as shown below, including backslashes, single quotation marks, and double quotation marks. Save the source code as special.cpp.

```
cout << "The answer is: " << Answer << '\n';
```

ACTIVITY 6-2

Write a program that asks the user for two floating-point numbers. The program should multiply the numbers together and print the product to the screen. Next, have the program ask the user how many digits to display to the right of the decimal point and print the product again with the new precision. Save the source code as setprec.cpp.

LESSON 7

BUILDING BLOCKS OF DECISION MAKING

OBJECTIVES

Upon completion of this lesson, you should be able to:

- Describe how decisions are made in programs.
- Describe how true and false are represented in C++.
- Use relational operators.
- Use logical operators.
- Describe short-circuit evaluation.

Estimated Time: 1 hour

Decision Making in Programs

When you make a decision, your brain goes through a process of comparisons. For example, when you shop for clothes you compare the prices with those you previously paid. You compare the quality with other clothes you have seen or owned. You probably compare the clothes to what other people are wearing or what is in style. You might even compare the purchase of clothes to other possible uses for your available money.

Although your brain's method of decision making is much more complex than what a computer is capable of, decision making in computers is also based on comparing data. In this section, you will learn to use the basic tools of computer decision making.

Almost every program that is useful or user-friendly involves decision making. Although some algorithms progress sequentially from the first to the last instruction, most algorithms branch out into more than one path. At the point at which the branching takes place, a decision must be made as to which path to take.

Did You Know?

Each shape used in a flowchart has a special meaning. The shapes are connected with arrows that show the direction of the flow of the program. Rectangles represent processing or action. Diamonds represent a decision. Parallelograms like those in Figure 7-1 represent input or output.

It often helps to illustrate the flow of a program with a special drawing called a *flowchart*. A flowchart maps the decisions a program is to make and the path down which each decision leads. The flowchart in Figure 7-1 is part of an algorithm in which the program is preparing to output a document to the printer. The user enters the number of copies he or she wants to print. To make sure the number is valid, the program verifies that the number of copies is not less than zero. If the user enters a negative number, a message is printed and the user is asked to reenter the value. If the user's input passes the test, the program simply goes on to the next step.

FIGURE 7-1
The decision-making part of this flowchart prevents the program from proceeding with invalid data.

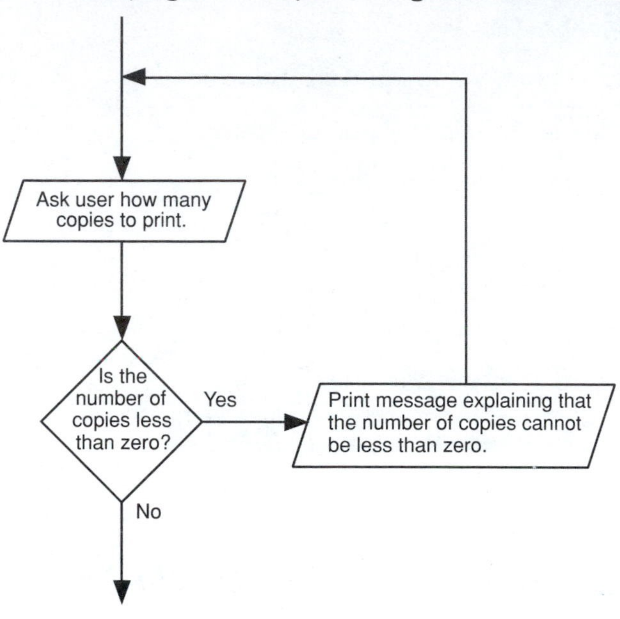

FIGURE 7-2
The path a program takes may be dictated by the user.

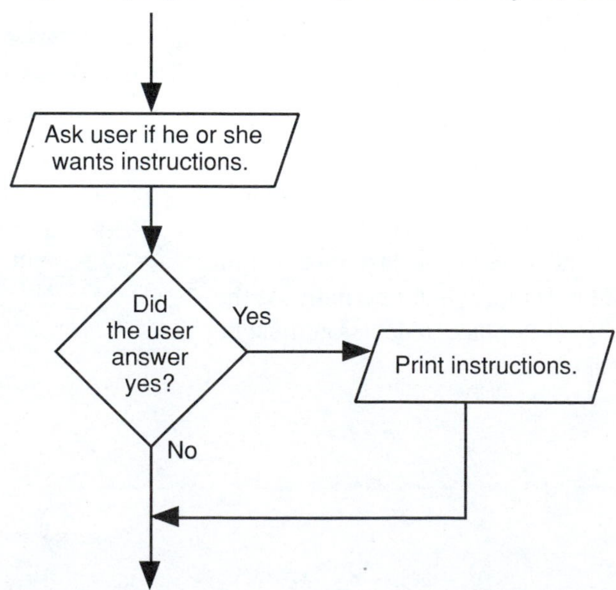

Decisions may also have to be based on the wishes of the user. The flowchart in Figure 7-2 shows how the response to a question changes the path the program takes. If the user wants instructions printed on the screen, the program displays the instructions. Otherwise, that part of the program is bypassed.

The examples in Figures 7-1 and 7-2 show two common needs for decisions in programs. There are many other instances in which decisions must be made. As you do more and more programming, you will use decision making in countless situations.

Representing True and False in C++

The way computers make decisions is very primitive. Even though computers make decisions similar to the way the human brain does, computers do not have intuition or "gut" feelings. Decision making in a computer is based on performing simple comparisons. The microprocessor compares two values and "decides" whether they are equivalent. Clever programming and the fact that computers can do millions of comparisons per second sometimes make computers appear to be "smart."

Fuzzy logic is a system that allows more than simply true or false; it allows for some gray area. For example, instead of having a 0 for false and a 1 for true, fuzzy logic might allow a 0.9 as a way of saying "it's probably true."

In Lesson 2 you learned about the Boolean data type, which provides a convenient way to store true and false values. Internally, however, true and false are represented as numbers. When the computer makes a comparison, the comparison results in a value of either 0 or 1. If the resulting value is 0, it means the comparison proved false. If the result is 1, the comparison proved true. So in C++, the Boolean value of false is represented by the integer 0 and true is represented by the integer 1.

Relational Operators

To make comparisons, C++ provides a set of *relational operators*, shown in Table 7-1. They are similar to the symbols you have used in math when working with equations and inequalities.

TABLE 7-1
Relational operators

OPERATOR	MEANING	EXAMPLE
==	equal to	i == 1
>	greater than	i > 2
<	less than	i < 0
>=	greater than or equal to	i >=6
<=	less than or equal to	i <= 10
!=	not equal to	i != 12

Relational operators are used to create expressions like the examples in Table 7-1. The result of the expression is 1 (true) if the data meets the requirements of the comparison. Otherwise, the result of the expression is 0 (false). For example, the result of 2 > 1 is 1 (true), and the result of 2 < 1 is 0 (false).

The program in Code List 7-1 demonstrates how expressions are made from relational operators. The result of the expressions is to be displayed as either a 1 or 0.

Important

Do not confuse the relational operator (==) with the assignment operator (=). Use == for comparisons and = for assignments.

CODE LIST 7-1

```
// relate.cpp

#include <iostream.h>

int main()
{
  int i = 2;
  int j = 3;
  bool true_false;

  cout << (i == 2) << endl; // displays a 1 (true)
  cout << (i == 1) << endl; // displays a 0 (false)
  cout << (j > i) << endl;
  cout << (j < i) << endl;  // Can you predict
  cout << (j <= 3) << endl; // the output of
  cout << (j >= i) << endl; // these statements?
  cout << (j != i) << endl;

  true_false = (j < 4); // The result can be stored
                        // to a Boolean variable.
  cout << true_false << endl;
  return 0;
}
```

STEP-BY-STEP 7.1

1. Enter the program from Code List 7-1 into a blank editor screen. Save the source code file as relate.cpp. Can you predict its output?
2. Compile, link, and run the program.
3. After you have analyzed the output, close the program.

Logical Operators

Sometimes it takes more than two comparisons to obtain the desired result. For example, if you want to test to see whether an integer is in the range 1 to 10, you must do two comparisons. In order for the integer to fall within the range, it must be greater than 0 and less than 11.

C++ provides three *logical operators*. Table 7-2 shows the three logical operators and their meaning.

Note

The key used to enter the two vertical lines of the or operator (||) is usually located near the Enter or Return key. It is usually on the same key with the backslash (\).

TABLE 7-2
Logical operators

OPERATOR	MEANING	EXAMPLE
&&	and	(j == 1 && k == 2)
||	or	(j == 1 || k == 2)
!	not	result = !(j == 1 && k == 2)

Figure 7-3 shows three diagrams called *truth tables*. They will help you understand the result of comparisons with the logical operators and, or, and not.

FIGURE 7-3
Truth tables illustrate the results of logical operators.

AND			OR			NOT	
A	B	A && B	A	B	A || B	A	!A
false (0)	false (0)	false (0)	false (0)	false (0)	false (0)	false (0)	true (1)
false (0)	true (1)	false (0)	false (0)	true (1)	true (1)	true (1)	false (0)
true (1)	false (0)	false (0)	true (1)	false (0)	true (1)		
true (1)	true (1)	true (1)	true (1)	true (1)	true (1)		

Consider the following C++ statement.

```
in_range = (i > 0 && i < 11);
```

The variable in_range is assigned the value 1 if the value of i falls into the defined range, and 0 if the value of i does not fall into the defined range.

The not operator (!) turns true to false and false to true. For example, suppose you have a program that catalogs old movies. Your program uses an integer variable named InColor that has the value 0 if the movie was filmed in black and white and the value 1 if the movie was filmed in color. In the statement below, the variable Black_and_White is set to 1 (true) if the movie is not in color. Therefore, if the movie is in color, Black_and_White is set to 0 (false).

```
Black_and_White = !InColor;
```

STEP-BY-STEP 7.2

1. Retrieve the source code file named logical.cpp. The program shown in Code List 7-2 appears. Look closely at the statements that include the logical operators.

2. Compile and run the program to see the output.

3. After you have analyzed the output, close the source code file.

CODE LIST 7-2

```
// logical.cpp

#include <iostream.h>

int main()
{
  int i = 2;
  int j = 3;
  bool true_false;

  true_false = (i < 3 && j > 3);
  cout << "The result of (i < 3 && j > 3) is "
          << true_false << '\n';

  true_false = (i < 3 && j >= 3);
  cout << "The result of (i < 3 && j >= 3) is "
          << true_false << '\n';

  cout << "The result of (i == 1 || i == 2) is "
        << (i == 1 || i == 2) << '\n';

  true_false = (j < 4);
  cout << "The result of (j < 4) is "
        << true_false << '\n';

  true_false = !true_false;
  cout << "The result of !true_false is "
        << !true_false << '\n';

  return 0;
}
```

Combining More Than Two Comparisons

You can use logical operators to combine more than two comparisons. Consider the following statement, which decides whether it is okay for a person to ride a roller coaster.

```
ok_to_ride = (height_in_inches > 45 && !back_trouble
             && !heart_trouble);
```

In the preceding statement, `back_trouble` and `heart_trouble` hold the value 0 or 1 depending on whether the person being considered has the problem. For example, if the person has back trouble, the value of `back_trouble` is set to 1. The not operator (!) is used because it is okay to ride if the person does not have back trouble and does not have heart trouble. The entire statement says that it is okay to ride if the person's height is greater than 45 inches and the person has no back trouble and no heart trouble.

Order of Logical Operations

You can mix logical operators in statements as long as you understand the order in which the logical operators will be applied. The not operator (!) is applied first, then the and operator (&&), and finally the or operator (||). Consider the following statement.

```
dog_acceptable = (white || black && friendly);
```

This example illustrates why it is important to know the order in which logical operators are applied. At first glance it may appear that the statement would consider a dog to be acceptable if the dog is either white or black and also friendly. But in reality, the statement above considers a white dog that wants to chew your leg off to be an acceptable dog. Why? Because the and operator is evaluated first and then the result of the and operation is used for the or operation. The statement can be corrected with some additional parentheses, as shown below.

```
dog_acceptable = ((white || black) && friendly);
```

C++ evaluates operations in parentheses first just as in arithmetic statements. The program in Code List 7-3 demonstrates the difference that the parentheses make. Also notice that the Boolean variables `white` and `black` are initialized using the `true` and `false` keywords. These keywords provide a more readable way to assign one and zero to the Boolean variables.

CODE LIST 7-3

```
// logical2.cpp

#include <iostream.h>

int main()
{
 bool white, black, friendly, acceptable;

 white = true;        // dog is white
 black = false;       // dog is not black
 friendly = false;    // dog is not friendly
```

CODE LIST 7-3 (CONTINUED)

```
    // The following statement produces incorrect results due to the
    // order of operations.
    acceptable = (white || black && friendly);
    cout << acceptable << endl;
    // The parentheses in the following statement override the
    // order of operations and the statement produces the correct result.
    acceptable = ((white || black) && friendly);
    cout << acceptable << endl;

    return 0;
}
```

STEP-BY-STEP 7.3

1. Open logical2.cpp. The program shown in Code List 7-3 appears.
2. Compile, link, and run the program to see the effect of the parentheses.
3. Close the source code file.

Short-Circuit Evaluation

Suppose you decided you want to go to a particular concert. You can only go, however, if two conditions are met: You must get tickets and you must get off work the night of the concert. Before you check whether you can get off work, you find out that the concert is sold out and you cannot get a ticket. There is no longer a need to check whether you can get off work because you do not have a ticket anyway.

C++ has a feature called *short-circuit evaluation* that allows the same kind of determinations in your program. For example, in an expression such as `in_range = (i > 0 && i < 11);`, the program first checks to see whether `i` is greater than 0. If it is not, there is no need to check any further because regardless of whether `i` is less than 11, `in_range` will be false. So the program sets `in_range` to false and goes to the next statement without evaluating the right side of the &&.

Short-circuiting also occurs with the or (||) operator. In the case of the or operator, the expression is short-circuited if the left side of the || is true, because the expression will be true, regardless of the right side of the ||.

Compilers often have an option to disable short-circuit evaluation.

Summary

In this lesson, you learned:

- Computers make decisions by comparing data.
- A flowchart is an illustration that helps show the flow of a program.
- In C++, true is represented by 1 and false is represented by 0.
- Relational operators are used to create expressions that result in a value of 1 or 0.
- Logical operators can combine relational expressions.
- Parentheses can be used to control the order in which logical expressions are evaluated.
- Short-circuit evaluation allows the evaluation of a logical expression to be stopped early if the ultimate result of the expression is already determined.

LESSON 7 REVIEW QUESTIONS

TRUE/FALSE

Circle T if the statement is true or F if the statement is false.

T F 1. Decision making in computers is based on comparing data.

T F 2. A flowchart is a special drawing used to illustrate the flow of a program.

T F 3. Internally, true and false are represented by characters.

T F 4. The result of an expression that includes relational operators is either true or false.

T F 5. The equal to relational operator is represented by =.

T F 6. There are four different logical operators available.

T F 7. The not operator turns a result to false regardless of its previous value.

T F 8. Parentheses can be used to change the order of logical operations.

T F 9. The and operator is applied before the or operator.

T F 10. Compilers often have an option to disable short-circuit evaluation.

WRITTEN QUESTIONS

Write a brief answer to the following questions.

1. What flowchart symbol represents processing or action?
2. What flowchart symbol represents a decision?
3. What is the value that represents the Boolean condition false?
4. What is fuzzy logic?
5. What is the relational operator that performs the "not equal to" operation?
6. What do you call the tables that show the combination of results of logical operators?
7. What logical operator performs the or operation?
8. Why is the order of logical operations important?
9. In the order of logical operations, what operator is applied first?
10. What is short-circuit evaluation?

LESSON 7 PROJECTS

PROJECT 7-1

In the blanks beside the statements in the program below, write a T or F to indicate the result of the expression. Fill in the answers beginning with the first statement and follow the program in the order the statements would be executed in a running program.

```
int main()
{
 int i = 4;
 int j = 3;
 bool true_false;

true_false = (j < 4);                              ______
true_false = (j < 3);                              ______
true_false = (j < i);                              ______
true_false = (i < 4);                              ______
true_false = (j <= 4);                             ______
true_false = (4 > 4);                              ______
true_false = (i != j);                             ______
true_false = (i == j || i < 100);                  ______
true_false = (i == j && i < 100);                  ______
true_false = (i < j || true_false && j >= 3);      ______
```

```
true_false = (!(i > 2 && j == 4));      _______
true_false = !1;                         _______
 return 0;
}
```

PROJECT 7-2

1. Retrieve the file named truth.cpp.
2. Compile, link, and run the program. The program displays a truth table for the AND operation.
3. Duplicate the code that displays the AND truth table and modify it to display an OR truth table.
4. Save and close the program.

CRITICAL THINKING

Modify the truth.cpp program from Project 7-2 to also display a truth table for the NOT operation. Use Figure 7-3 as a reference.

LESSON 8

SELECTION STRUCTURES

OBJECTIVES

Upon completion of this lesson, you should be able to:

- Describe selection structures.
- Use the if structure.
- Use the if/else structure.
- Use nested if structures.
- Use the switch structure.

Estimated Time: 2 hours

Introduction to Selection Structures

Programs consist of statements that solve a problem or perform a task. Up to this point, you have been creating programs with sequence structures. *Sequence structures* execute statements one after another without changing the flow of the program. Other structures, such as the ones that make decisions, do change the flow of the program. The structures that make decisions in C++ programs are called *selection structures*. When a decision is made in a program, a selection structure controls the flow of the program based on the decision. In this lesson, you will learn how to use selection structures to make decisions in your programs. The three selection structures available in C++ are the if structure, the if/else structure, and the switch structure.

Computer Concepts

When only one statement appears between the braces in an if structure, the braces are not actually necessary. It is, however, a good idea to always use braces in case other statements are added later.

Using if

Many programming languages include an *if structure*. Although the syntax varies among programming languages, the if keyword is usually part of every language. If you have used if in other programming languages, you should have little difficulty using if in C++. The if structure is one of the easiest and most useful parts of C++.

The expression that makes the decision is called the *control expression*. Look at the code segment in Code List 8-1. First the control expression `(i == 3)` is evaluated. If the result is true, the code in the braces that follow the if statement is executed. If the result is false, the code in the braces is skipped.

You can place more than one line between the braces, as shown in Code List 8-2.

Figure 8-1 shows the flowchart for an if structure. The if structure is sometimes called a *one-way selection structure* because the decision is whether to go "one way" or just bypass the code in the if structure.

CODE LIST 8-1

```
if (i == 3)
  {
    cout << "The value of i is 3\n";
  }
```

CODE LIST 8-2

```
if (YesNo == 'Y')
  {
    cout << "Enter the title: ";
    getline(cin, title);
  }
```

FIGURE 8-1
The if structure is sometimes called a one-way selection structure.

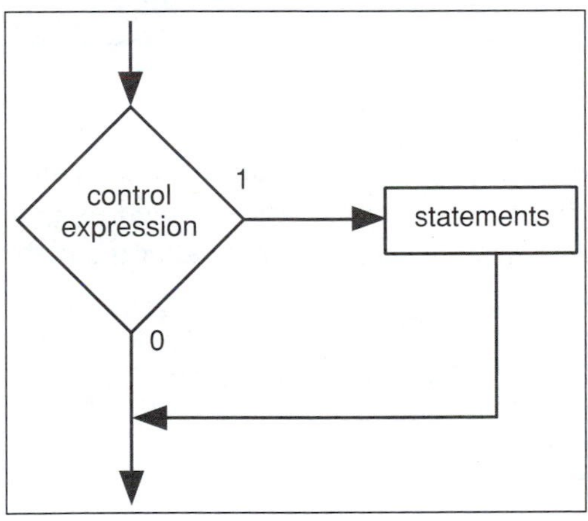

Important

Remember to be careful not to confuse the == operator with the = (assignment) operator. Entering if (i = 3) will cause i to be assigned the value 3, and the code in the braces that follow will be executed regardless of what the value of i was before the if structure.

Analyze the program in Code List 8-3. The program declares a string object and an unsigned long integer. The user is asked for the name of his or her city or town and for the population of the city or town. The if structure compares the population to a value that would indicate whether the city is among the 100 largest U.S. cities. If the city is one of the 100 largest U.S. cities, the program prints a message saying so.

CODE LIST 8-3

```
// city.cpp

#include <iostream.h>
#include "oostring.h"

int main()
{
 oostring city_name;
 unsigned long population;

 cout << "What is the name of your city or town? ";
 getline(cin, city_name);

 cout << "What is the population of the city or town? ";
 cin >> population;
 cin.ignore(80,'\n');

 if (population >= 185086)
 {
   cout << "According to estimated population figures, "
        << city_name << endl
        << "is one of the 100 largest U.S. cities.\n";
 }

 return 0;
}
```

Accidentally putting a semicolon at the end of the control expression will end the if structure, causing unexpected results. For example, in the code below, the semicolon at the end of the control expression ends the if structure. Therefore, the statement that follows in braces is executed regardless of the value of i. The compiler thinks the statement in braces is just the next statement after the if structure.

```
if (i == 3);          // don't do this!!
  { cout << "The value of i is 3\n"; }
```

STEP-BY-STEP 8.1

1. Open city.cpp. The program from Code List 8-3 appears without the if structure.

2. Add the if structure shown in Code List 8-3 to the program. Enter the code carefully.

3. Compile, link, and run the program. Enter your city or town to test the program.

4. If your city or town is not one of the 100 largest cities, or if you do not know your city or town's population, enter Albuquerque, a city in New Mexico with a population of about 420,000. Warning: Do not enter the comma when entering populations.

5. Leave the source code file open for the next exercise.

Using if/else

The *if/else structure* is sometimes called a *two-way selection structure*. Using if/else, one block of code is executed if the control expression is true and another block is executed if the control expression is false. Consider the code fragment in Code List 8-4.

The else portion of the structure is executed if the control expression is false. Figure 8-2 shows a flowchart for a two-way selection structure.

Computer Concepts

Notice how the braces in Code List 8-4 are on the same line as the code they enclose. Some programmers prefer this more compact way of entering code.

CODE LIST 8-4

```
if (i < 0)
  {cout << "The number is negative.\n";}
else
  {cout << "The number is zero or positive.\n";}
```

FIGURE 8-2
The if/else structure is a two-way selection structure.

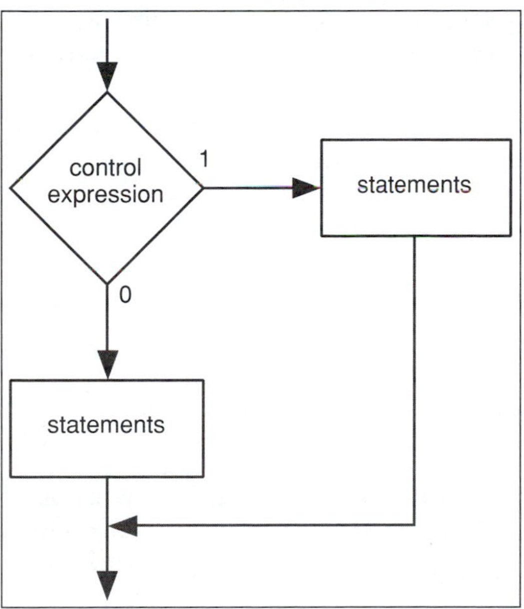

The code shown in Code List 8-5 adds an else clause to the if structure in the program in Step-by-Step 8.1. Output is improved by providing information on whether the city's population qualifies it as one of the 100 largest U.S. cities. If the population is 185,086 or more, the first output statement is executed; otherwise, the second output statement is executed. In every case, one or the other output statement is executed.

Computer Concepts

Many programmers make the mistake of using > or < when they really need >= or <=. In the code segment in Code List 8-5, using > rather than >= would cause Glendale, California, the 100th largest city, to be excluded because its population is 185086, not greater than 185086.

CODE LIST 8-5

```
if (population >= 185086)
 {
   cout << "According to estimated population figures, "
        << city_name << endl
        << "is one of the 100 largest U.S. cities.\n";
 }
else
 {
   cout << "According to estimated population figures, "
        << city_name << endl
        << "is not one of the 100 largest U.S. cities.\n";
 }
```

STEP-BY-STEP 8.2

1. Add the else clause shown in Code List 8-5 to the if structure in the program on your screen. Save the new program as cityelse.cpp.

2. Compile, link, and run the program.

3. Enter the city of Gary, Indiana (population 108,469). The program reports that Gary is not one of the 100 largest cities in the United States.

4. Run the program again using Lubbock, Texas (population 190,974). Lubbock is among the 100 largest U.S. cities.

5. Close the program.

Nested if Structures

You can place if structures within other if structures. When an if or if/else structure is placed within another if or if/else structure, the structures are said to be *nested*. The flowchart in Figure 8-3 decides whether a student is exempt from a final exam based on grade average and days absent.

FIGURE 8-3
This flowchart can be programmed using nested if structures.

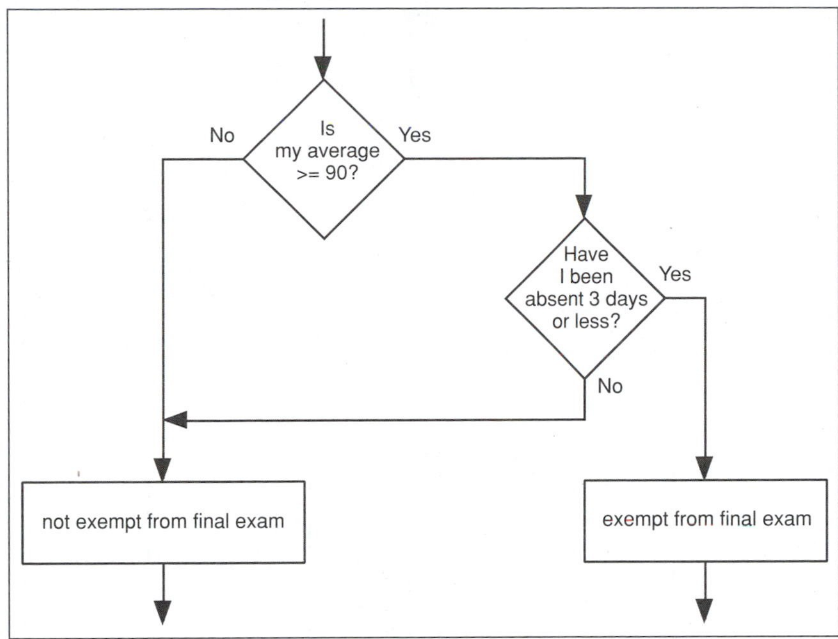

To be exempt from the final, a student must have a 90 average or better and cannot have missed more than three days of class. The algorithm first determines if the student's average is greater than or equal to 90. If the result is false, the student must take the final exam. If the result is true, the number of days absent is checked to determine if the other exemption requirement is met. Code List 8-6 shows the algorithm as a C++ code segment.

The code in Code List 8-6 is written to initially assume that the student is not exempt from the final exam. If the requirements are met, as determined by the nested if structures, the exemption will be granted.

CODE LIST 8-6

```
exempt_from_final = false;

if (my_average >= 90)
  {                                    // If your average is 90 or better
   if (my_days_absent <= 3)            // and you have missed three days
   { exempt_from_final = true; }       // or less, you are exempt.
  }
```

Algorithms involving nested if structures can get more complicated than the one in Code List 8-6. Figure 8-4 shows the flowchart from Figure 8-3 expanded to include another way to be exempted from the final exam. In this expanded algorithm, students can also be exempted if they have an 80 or higher average, as long as they have been present every day or missed only one day.

As you can probably imagine, programming the algorithm in Figure 8-4 will require careful construction and nesting of if and if/else structures. Code List 8-7 shows you how it is done.

Computer Concepts

Earlier you learned that it is a good idea to always use braces with if structures. Code List 8-7 illustrates another reason you should do so. Without the braces, the compiler may assume that the else clause goes with the nested if structure rather than the first if.

FIGURE 8-4

This algorithm provides two paths to exemption from the final exam.

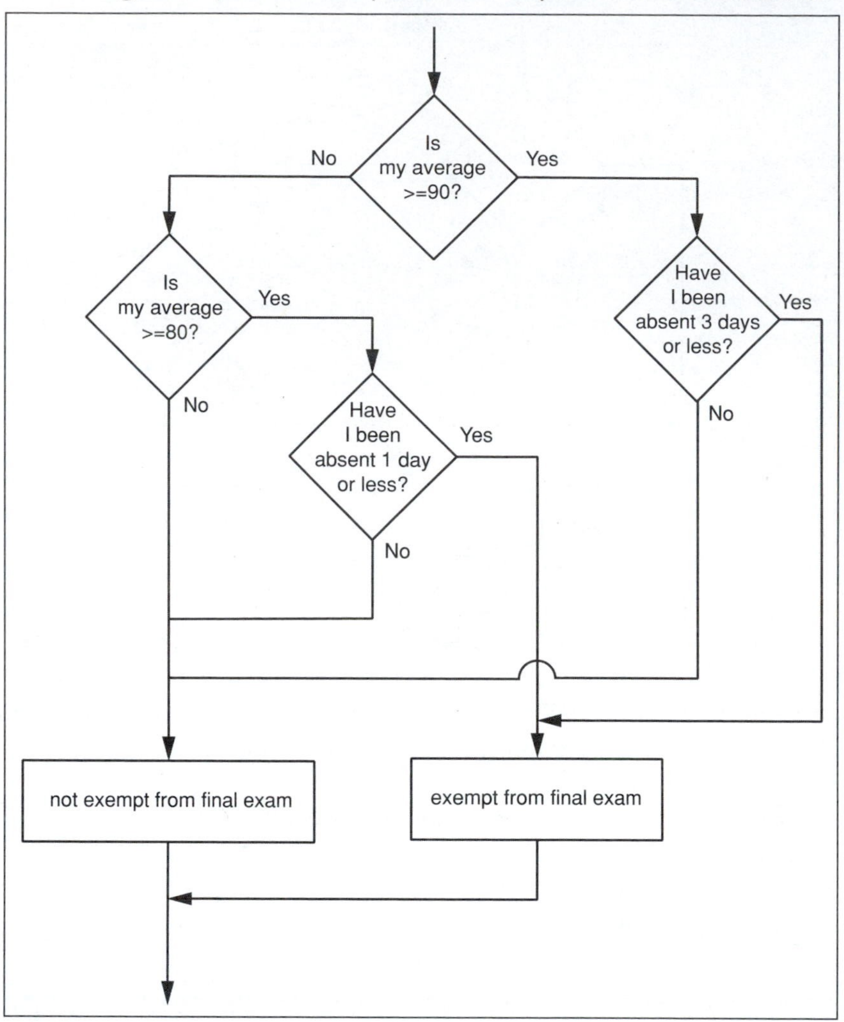

CODE LIST 8-7

```
exempt_from_final = false;

if (my_average >= 90)
  {                                  // If your average is 90 or better
   if (my_days_absent <= 3)          // and you have missed three days
   { exempt_from_final = true; }     // or less, you are exempt.
  }
else  // If you don't have a 90+ average, you still have a chance.
  { if (my_average >= 80)
    {                                  // If your average is 80 or better
     if (my_days_absent <= 1)          // and you have missed one day or
       { exempt_from_final = true; } // less, you are exempt.
    }
  }
```

STEP-BY-STEP 8.3

1. Open final.cpp.
2. Compile, link, and run the program.
3. Enter 90 as your grade average and 3 as your days absent. The program reports that you are exempt from the final exam.
4. Run the program again. Enter 88 as your grade average and 1 as your days absent. You are still exempt.
5. Run the program again. Enter 89 as your grade average and 2 as your days absent. The program reports that you must take the final.
6. Run the program again using values of your choice.
7. Close the program.

Code List 8-8 shows a simple program that includes a nested if structure. The program asks the user to input the amount of money he or she wants to deposit in order to open a new checking account. Based on the value provided by the user, the program recommends a type of account.

CODE LIST 8-8

```
// deposit.cpp

#include <iostream.h>

int main()
{
  float amount_to_deposit;

  cout << "How much do you want to deposit to open the account? ";
  cin  >> amount_to_deposit;

  if(amount_to_deposit < 1000.00 )
   {
    if(amount_to_deposit < 100.00 )
     { cout << "You should consider the EconoCheck account.\n"; }
    else
     { cout << "You should consider the FreeCheck account.\n"; }
   }
  else
   { cout << "You should consider an interest-bearing account.\n"; }
  return 0;
}
```

STEP-BY-STEP 8.4

1. Open deposit.cpp. The program in Code List 8-8 appears.

2. Compile, link, and run the program. Run the program several times, using values that are less than $100, between $100 and $1000, and greater than $1000.

3. Close the program.

The switch Structure

You have studied one-way (if) and two-way (if/else) selection structures. C++ has another method of handling multiple options known as the *switch structure*. The switch structure has many uses but is most often used with menus. A *menu* is a set of options presented to the user of a program. Code List 8-9 displays a menu of choices and asks the user to enter a number that corresponds to one of the choices. Then a case statement is used to handle each of the options.

CODE LIST 8-9

```
cout << "How do you want the order shipped?\n";
cout << "1 – Ground\n";
cout << "2 - 2-day air\n";
cout << "3 - Overnight air\n";
cout << "Enter the number of the shipping method you want: ";
cin >> shipping_method;

switch(shipping_method)
 {
   case 1:
     shipping_cost = 5.00;
     break;
   case 2:
     shipping_cost = 7.50;
     break;
   case 3:
     shipping_cost = 10.00;
     break;
   default:
     shipping_cost = 0.00;
     break;
 }
```

Let's analyze the switch structure in Code List 8-9. It begins with the keyword `switch`, followed by the control expression (the variable `shipping_method`) to be compared in the structure. Within the braces of the structure are a series of `case` keywords. Each one provides the code that is to be executed in the event that `shipping_method` matches the value that follows `case`. The `default` keyword tells the compiler that if nothing else matches, execute the statements that follow.

The break keyword, which appears at the end of each case segment, causes the flow of logic to jump to the first executable statement after the switch structure.

Note

In C++, only integer or character types may be used as control expressions in switch statements.

STEP-BY-STEP 8.5

1. Open shipping.cpp. The program includes the segment from Code List 8-9.
2. Compile, link, and run the program. Choose shipping method 2. The cost of shipping by second-day air appears.
3. Add a fourth shipping option called Carrier Pigeon to the menu.
4. Add the code below to the switch structure, before the default keyword.

```
case 4:
  shipping_cost = 99.99;
  break;
```

5. Compile, link, and run to test your addition to the options.
6. Save the source code and close.

Nested if/else structures could be used in place of the switch structure. But the switch structure is easier to use and a programmer is less prone to making errors that are related to braces and indentations. Remember, however, that an integer or character data type is required in the control expression of a switch structure. Nested ifs must be used if you are comparing floating-point values.

When using character types in a switch structure, enclose the characters in single quotation marks as in any other character literal. The code segment in Code List 8-10 is an example of using character literals in a switch structure.

CODE LIST 8-10

```
switch(character_entered)
 {
   case 'A':
     cout << "The character entered was A, as in albatross.\n";
     break;
   case 'B':
     cout << "The character entered was B, as in butterfly.\n";
     break;
   default:
     cout << "Illegal entry\n";
     break;
 }
```

STEP-BY-STEP 8.6

1. Open chswitch.cpp. The program includes the segment from Code List 8-10.

2. Compile, link, and run the program. Enter A as input. The appropriate output is generated.

3. Run the program again. Enter B as input. The second case is executed.

4. Run the program again. Enter C as input. The input is reported to be illegal.

5. Close the program.

Computer Concepts

C++ allows you to place your case statements in any order. You can, however, increase the speed of your program by placing the more common choices at the top of the switch structure and less common ones toward the bottom. The reason is that the computer makes the comparisons in the order they appear in the switch structure. The sooner a match is found, the sooner the computer can move on to other processing.

Summary

In this lesson, you learned:

- Selection structures are how C++ programs make decisions.
- The if structure is a one-way selection structure. When a control expression in an if statement is evaluated to be true, the statements associated with the structure are executed.
- The if/else structure is a two-way selection structure. If the control expression in the if statement evaluates to true, one block of statements is executed; otherwise, another block is executed.
- It is possible to nest if structures and if/else structures.
- The switch structure is a multi-way selection structure that executes one of many sets of statements, depending on the value of the control expression. The control expression must evaluate to an integer or character value.

LESSON 8 REVIEW QUESTIONS

TRUE/FALSE

Circle T if the statement is true or F if the statement is false.

T F 1. Selection structures execute statements one after another without changing the flow of the program.

T F 2. The expression that makes the decision in an if structure is called a control expression.

T F 3. The if keyword is unique to C++.

T F 4. If the condition in an if structure is true, the code in the braces that follow the if statement is executed.

T F 5. The = operator and the == operator are interchangeable.

T F 6. The if/else structure is a two-way selection structure.

T F 7. Placing if structures within if structures is called stacking if structures.

T F 8. The operation of a switch structure can be replaced by if/else structures.

T F 9. The switch structure includes an else keyword.

T F 10. The control expression of a switch structure works only with integers and characters.

WRITTEN QUESTIONS

Write a brief answer to the following questions.

1. What are the three selection structures available in C++?
2. What are sequence structures?
3. When are the braces in an if structure not necessary?
4. When is the else portion of an if/else structure executed?
5. Write an if structure that prints the word *complete* to the screen if the variable named `percent_complete` is equal to 100.
6. Write an if structure that assigns the value 100 to the variable named `percent_complete` if the character in the variable named `Done` equals *Y*.
7. Write an if/else structure that prints the word *complete* to the screen if the variable named `percent_complete` is equal to 100, and prints the phrase *not complete* to the screen otherwise.
8. What structure is often used when working with menus?
9. What keyword in a switch structure tells the compiler which statements to execute if none of the options match?
10. What does the `break` keyword in a switch structure do?

LESSON 8 PROJECTS

PROJECT 8-1

Write a program that uses the if/else structure in Code List 8-4 to report whether an integer entered by the user is positive or negative. Save the source code file as sign.cpp.

PROJECT 8-2

Rewrite final.cpp so that it begins with the assumption that the student is exempt and makes comparisons to see whether the student must take the test. Save the revised source code as final2.cpp.

PROJECT 8-3

1. Open lengths.cpp and analyze the source code.
2. Compile and link the program. Note: The program requires the string class.
3. Run the program several times and try different conversions and values.
4. Add a conversion for miles to the program. Use 0.00018939 for the conversion factor.
5. Test the program to ensure that your addition is working properly.

PROJECT 8-4

1. Obtain the exchange rates for at least three foreign currencies. Currency exchange rates can be found in most newspapers or on the Internet at the Web sites of major banks and financial services companies. You can also call a local bank to obtain the information you need.
2. Write a program similar to lengths.cpp that asks the user for an amount of money in dollars, and then prompts the user to select the currency into which the dollars are to be converted.
3. Save the program as currency.cpp.

CRITICAL THINKING

Write a program that asks for an integer and reports whether the number is even or odd. *Hint*: Use if/else and the modulus operator. Save the source code file as evenodd.cpp.

LESSON 9

LOOPS

OBJECTIVES

Upon completion of this lesson, you should be able to:

- Describe the purpose of loops.
- Use for loops.
- Use while loops.
- Use do while loops.
- Use the break and continue statements.
- Nest loops.

Estimated Time: 2 hours

Introduction to Loops

We all know that much of the work a computer does is repeated many times. When a program repeats a group of statements a given number of times, the repetition is accomplished using a *loop*.

In Lesson 8, you learned about sequence structures and selection structures. In this lesson, you will learn about another category of structures: *iteration structures*. Loops are iteration structures. Each loop or pass through a group of statements is called an *iteration*. A condition specified in the program controls the number of iterations performed. For example, a loop may iterate until a specific variable reaches the value 100.

The for Loop

The *for loop* repeats one or more statements a specified number of times. A for loop is difficult to read the first time you see one. Like an if statement, the for loop uses parentheses. In the parentheses are three items called *parameters*, which are needed to make a for loop work. Each parameter in a for loop is an expression. Figure 9-1 shows the format of a for loop.

FIGURE 9-1
A for loop repeats one or more statements a specified number of times.

```
for (initializing expression; control expression; step expression)
  { statements to execute }
```

Look at the program in Code List 9-1. The variable i is used as a counter. The counter variable is used in all three of the for loop's expressions. The first parameter, called the *initializing expression*, initializes the counter variable. The second parameter is the expression that will end the loop, called the *control expression*. As long as the control expression is true, the loop continues to iterate. The third parameter is the *step expression*. It changes the counter variable, usually by adding to it.

Computer Concepts

As with if structures, you are not required to use braces in for loops when there is only one statement in the loop.

CODE LIST 9-1

```
// forloop.cpp

#include <iostream.h>

int main()
{
 int i; // counter variable
 for(i = 1; i <= 3; i++)
    { cout << i << endl; }
 return 0;
}
```

In Code List 9-1, the statements in the for loop will repeat three times. The variable i is declared as an integer. In the for statement, i is initialized to 1. The control expression tests to see if the value of i is still less than or equal to 3. When i exceeds 3, the loop will end. The step expression increments i by 1 each time the loop iterates.

Important

Placing a semicolon after the closing parenthesis of a for loop will prevent any lines from being iterated.

STEP-BY-STEP 9.1

1. Key the program from Code List 9-1 into a blank editor screen.
2. Save the source code file as forloop.cpp.
3. Compile and run the program. The program counts to 3.
4. Close the source file.

Counting Backward and Other Tricks

A counter variable can also count backward by having the step expression decrement the value rather than increment it. The program in Code List 9-2 counts backward from 10 to 1. The counter is initialized to 10. With each iteration, the decrement operator subtracts 1 from the counter.

CODE LIST 9-2

```
// backward.cpp

#include <iostream.h>

int main()
{
  int i; // counter variable
  for(i = 10; i >= 0; i--)
    { cout << i << endl; }
  cout << "End of loop.\n";
  return 0;
}
```

STEP-BY-STEP 9.2

1. Enter the program in Code List 9-2 into a blank editor screen.

2. Save the source file as backward.cpp.

3. Compile and run the program. Figure 9-2 shows the output you should see.

4. Close the source code file.

FIGURE 9-2
A for loop can decrement the counter variable.

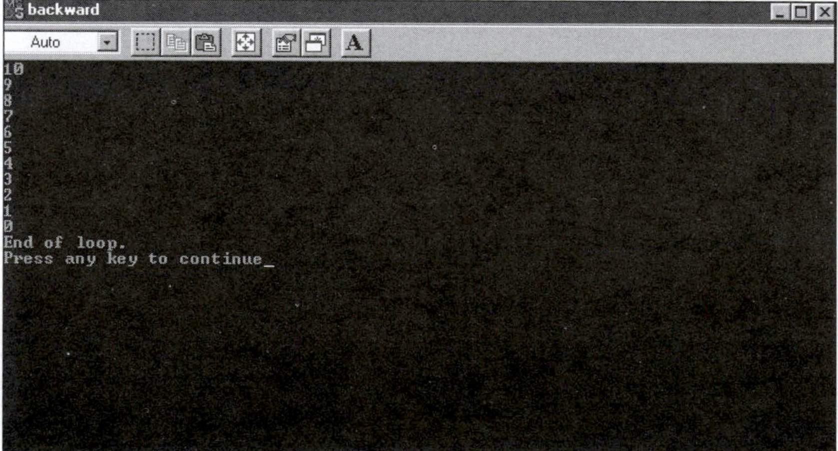

The output prints numbers from 10 to 0 because i is being decremented in the step expression. The phrase "End of loop." is printed only once because the loop ends with the semicolon that follows the first cout statement.

The counter variable can do more than step by 1. In the program in Code List 9-3, the counter variable is doubled each time the loop iterates.

CODE LIST 9-3

```
// dblstep.cpp

#include <iostream.h>

int main()
{
 int i;    // counter variable
 for(i = 1; i <= 100; i = i + i)
   { cout << i << endl; }
 return 0;
}
```

STEP-BY-STEP 9.3

1. Enter the program from Code List 9-3 into a blank editor screen.
2. Save the source file as dblstep.cpp. Can you predict the program's output?
3. Compile and run the program to see whether your prediction was right.
4. Close the program.

The for statement gives you a lot of flexibility. As you have already seen, the step expression can increment, decrement, or count in other ways. Some more examples of for statements are shown in Table 9-1.

TABLE 9-1
Examples of for statements

FOR STATEMENT	COUNT PROGRESSION
for (i = 2; i <= 10; i = i + 2)	2, 4, 6, 8, 10
for (i = 1; i < 10; i = i + 2)	1, 3, 5, 7, 9
for (i = 10; i <= 50; i = i + 10)	10, 20, 30, 40, 50

Using a Statement Block in a for Loop

If you need to include more than one statement in the loop, place all the statements that are to be part of the loop inside braces. The statements in the braces will be repeated each time the loop iterates. The statements that follow the braces are not part of the loop.

In Code List 9-4, an output statement has been added inside the loop of the **backward.cpp** program. The phrase *Inside Loop* will appear with each iteration of the loop.

CODE LIST 9-4

```
// backward.cpp

#include <iostream.h>

int main()
{
  int i; // counter variable
  for(i = 10; i >= 0; i--)
  {
       cout << i << endl;
       cout << "Inside Loop\n";
  }
  cout << "End of loop.\n";
  return 0;
}
```

STEP-BY-STEP 9.4

1. Open backward.cpp and edit the source code to match the Code List 9-4.

2. Compile and run the program to see that the phrase Inside Loop prints on every line. The second cout statement is now part of the loop because it is within the braces.

3. Close the source file without saving changes.

while Loops

A ***while loop*** is similar to a for loop. Actually, while loops are sometimes easier to use than for loops and are better suited for many loops. With a for loop, the parameters in the parentheses control the number of times the loop iterates, and the statements in the loop structure are just along for the ride. In a while loop, something inside the loop triggers the loop to stop.

For example, a while loop may be written to ask a user to input a series of numbers until the number 0 is entered. The loop would repeat until the number 0 is entered.

There are two kinds of while loops: the standard while loop and the do while loop. The difference between the two is where the control expression is tested. Let's begin with the standard while loop.

The while Loop

The while loop repeats a statement or group of statements as long as a control expression is true. Unlike a for loop, a while loop does not use a counter variable. The control expression in a while loop can be any valid expression. The program in Code List 9-5 uses a while loop to repeatedly divide a number by 2 until the number is less than or equal to 1.

CODE LIST 9-5

```
// while1.cpp

#include <iostream.h>

int main()
{
 float num;

 cout << "Please enter the number to divide: ";
 cin >> num;
 while (num > 1.0)
  {
   cout << num << endl;
   num = num / 2;
  }
 return 0;
}
```

In a while loop, the control expression is tested before the statements in the loop begin. Figure 9-3 shows a flowchart of the program in Code List 9-5. If the number provided by the user is less than or equal to 1, the statements in the loop are never executed.

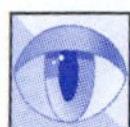

Important

As with the for loop, placing a semicolon after the closing parenthesis of a while loop will prevent any lines from being iterated.

FIGURE 9-3

A while loop tests the control expression before the loop begins.

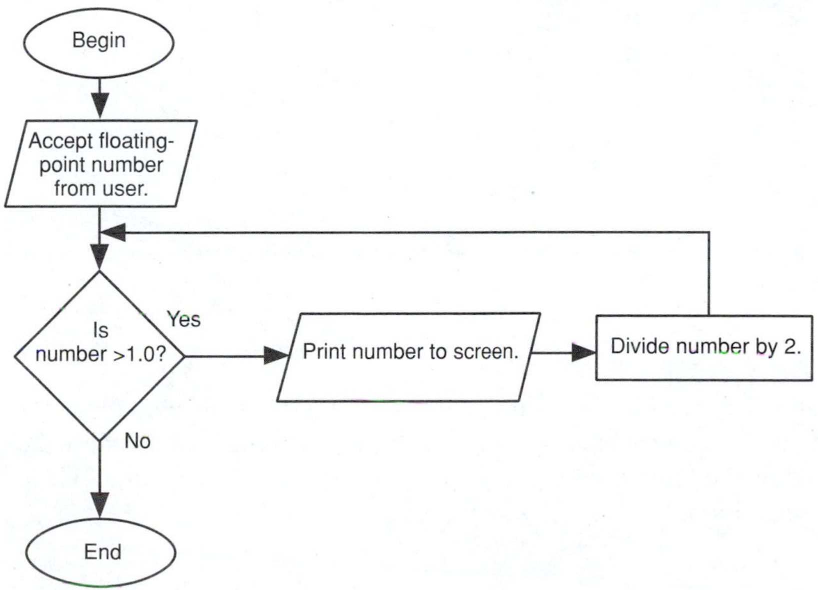

STEP-BY-STEP 9.5

1. Enter the program shown in Code List 9-5 into a blank editor screen.

2. Save the source file as while1.cpp.

3. Compile and run the program. Run the program several times. Try the following numbers as input: 8, 21, 8650, 1, 2.1, 0.5.

4. Close the program.

In order for a while loop to come to an end, the statements in the loop must change a variable used in the control expression. The result of the control expression must be false for a loop to stop. Otherwise, iterations continue indefinitely in what is called an *infinite loop*. In the program you compiled in Step-by-Step 9.5, the statement `num = num / 2;` divides the number by 2 each time the loop repeats. Even if the user enters a large value, the loop will eventually end when the number becomes less than 1.

A while loop can be used to replace any for loop. So why have a for loop in the language? Because sometimes a for loop offers a better solution. Figure 9-4 shows two programs that produce the same output. The program using the for loop is better in this case because the counter variable is initialized, tested, and incremented in the same statement. In a while loop, a counter variable must be initialized and incremented in separate statements.

FIGURE 9-4
Although both of these programs produce the same output, the for loop gives a more efficient solution.

```
#include <iostream.h>

int main()
{
  int j;
  for(j = 1; j <= 3; j++)
    { cout << j << endl; }
  return 0;
}
```

```
#include \iostream.h>

int main()
{
  int j;
  j = 1;
  while(j <= 3)
    {
      cout << j << endl;
      j++;
    }
  return 0;
}
```

The do while Loop

The last iteration structure in C++ is the *do while loop*. A do while loop repeats a statement or group of statements as long as a control expression is true at the end of the loop. Because the control expression is tested at the end of the loop, a do while loop is executed at least one time. Code List 9-6 shows an example of a do while loop.

CODE LIST 9-6

```
// dowhile.cpp

#include <iostream.h>

int main()
{
 double num, squared;
 do
  {
   cout << "Enter a number (Enter 0 to quit): ";
   cin >> num;
   squared = num * num;
   cout << num << " squared is " << squared << endl;
  }
 while (num != 0);
 return 0;
}
```

To help illustrate the difference between a while and a do while loop, compare the two flowcharts in Figure 9-5. Use a while loop when you need to test the control expression before the loop is executed the first time. Use a do while loop when the statements in the loop need to be executed at least once.

FIGURE 9-5
The difference between a while loop and a do while loop is where the control expression is tested.

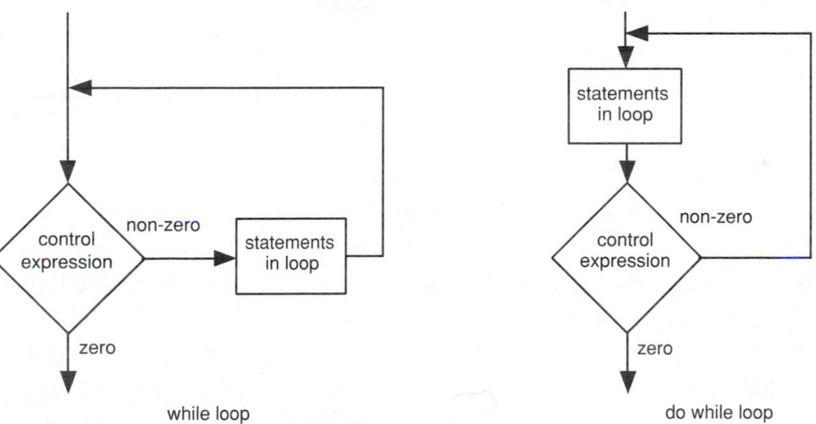

STEP-BY-STEP 9.6

1. Enter the program from Code List 9-6 into a blank editor screen.
2. Save the source file as dowhile.cpp.
3. Compile and run the program. Enter several numbers greater than 0 to cause the loop to repeat. Enter 0 to end the program.
4. Leave the program open for the next exercise.

Stopping in the Middle of a Loop

The keyword `break`, also used with switch statements, can be used to end a loop before the conditions of the control expression are met. Once a break terminates a loop, the execution begins with the first statement following the loop. In the program you ran in Step-by-Step 9.6, entering 0 caused the program to end. But the program squares 0 before it ends, even though the step is unnecessary. The program in Code List 9-7 uses a break statement to correct the problem.

CODE LIST 9-7

```
// dowhile.cpp

#include <iostream.h>

int main()
{
 double num, squared;
 do
  {
   cout << "Enter a number (Enter 0 to quit): ";
   cin >> num;
   if (num == 0.0) // Break out of loop if
   { break; }      // number entered is zero.
   squared = num * num;
   cout << num << " squared is " << squared << endl;
  }
 while (1); // Create an infinite loop and allow the
            // break statement to end the loop.
 return 0;
}
```

In the program in Code List 9-7, the value entered by the user is tested immediately with an if statement. If the value is 0, the break statement is executed to end the loop. If the value is any number other than 0, the loop continues.

The while loop's control expression can remain num `!= 0` without affecting the function of the program. In this case, however, the break statement will stop the loop before the control expression is reached. Therefore, the control expression can be changed to 1 to create an infinite loop. The 1 creates an infinite loop because the loop continues to iterate as long as the control expression is true, which is represented by the value 1. The loop will repeat until the break statement is executed.

STEP-BY-STEP 9.7

1. Modify the program on your screen to match Code List 9-7.

2. Save the source file.

3. Compile and run the program. Enter several numbers greater than 0 to cause the loop to repeat. Enter 0 to end the program. Notice that the program now ends without squaring the zero.

Computer Concepts

You should allow the control expression to end an iteration structure whenever practical. Whenever you are tempted to use a break statement to exit a loop, make sure that using the break statement is the best way to end the loop.

4. Close the program.

The continue statement is another way to stop a loop from completing each statement. But instead of continuing with the first statement after the loop, the continue statement skips the remainder of a loop and starts the next iteration of the loop. Code List 9-8 shows an example of how the continue statement can be used to cause a for loop to skip an iteration.

CODE LIST 9-8

```
// continue.cpp

#include <iostream.h>

int main()
{
 int i;
 for(i = 1; i <= 10; i++)
  {
   if (i == 5)
   { continue; }
   cout << i << endl;
  }
 return 0;
}
```

The continue statement in Code List 9-8 causes the statements in the for loop to be skipped when the counter variable is 5. The continue statement also can be used in while and do while statements.

STEP-BY-STEP 9.8

1. Open continue.cpp. The program shown in Code List 9-8 appears.

2. Compile and run the program. Notice that the number 5 does not appear in the output because of the continue statement.

3. Close the program.

Nesting Loops

You have already learned how to nest if structures. Loops can also be nested. In fact, loops within loops are very common. You must, however, trace the steps of the program carefully to understand how nested loops behave. The program in Code List 9-9 provides output that will give you insight into the behavior of nested loops.

CODE LIST 9-9

```
// nestloop.cpp

#include <iostream.h>

int main()
{
 int i,j;
 cout << "BEGIN\n";
 for(i = 1; i <= 3; i++)
  {
   cout << " Outer loop: i = " << i << endl;
   for(j = 1; j <= 4; j++)
    { cout << "      Inner loop: j = " << j << endl;}
  }
 cout << "END\n";
 return 0;
}
```

The important thing to realize is that the inner for loop (the one that uses `j`) will complete its count from 1 to 4 every time the outer for loop (the one that uses `i`) iterates. That is why in the output, for every loop the outer loop makes, the inner loop starts over.

STEP-BY-STEP 9.9

1. Open nestloop.cpp.
2. Compile and run the program.
3. Close the source file.

Hot Tip

If you know how to use your compiler's debugger, step through the program to trace the flow of logic.

Summary

In this lesson, you learned:

- A loop is used to cause a program to repeat a group of statements a given number of times.
- Loops are iteration structures.
- Each loop through a group of statements is called an iteration.
- A for loop repeats one or more statements a specified number of times.
- A for loop uses three parameters to control the loop.
- A for loop can count backward by having the step expression decrement the value rather than increment it. The step expression can also count by values other than 1.
- Braces group the statements in a loop.
- A while loop repeats a statement or group of statements as long as a control expression is true. The control expression is tested at the top of the loop.
- A do while loop repeats a statement or group of statements as long as a control expression is true at the end of the loop.
- The `break` keyword ends a loop before the conditions in the control expression are met.
- The `continue` keyword skips the remainder of the statements in the loop and continues with the next iteration of the loop.
- Loops may be nested to have loops inside loops.

LESSON 9 REVIEW QUESTIONS

TRUE/FALSE

Circle T if the statement is true or F if the statement is false.

T F 1. A loop is a sequence structure.

T F 2. A for loop repeats a group of statements a specified number of times.

T F 3. The items in the parentheses of a for loop are called parameters.

T F 4. Counting backward in a for loop is accomplished by the initializing expression.

T F 5. In a while loop, the control expression is tested at the end of the loop.

T F 6. In order for a while loop to come to a natural end, the statements in the loop must change a variable used in the control expression.

T F 7. The statements in a while loop are always executed at least once.

T F 8. A do while loop allows the program to do other things while the statements in the loop repeat.

T F 9. The break keyword ends a loop before the conditions of the control expression are met.

T F 10. Only for loops may be nested in programs.

WRITTEN QUESTIONS

Write a brief answer to the following questions.

1. What is each "loop" or pass through a group of statements in a loop called?

2. What are the three expressions in the parentheses of a for loop?

3. Describe the purpose of the counter variable in a for loop.

4. What is the count progression of the following for loop?
```
for (j = 5; j <= 40; j = j + 5)
```

5. What is wrong with the following while loop?
```
while (num > 1.0);
  {
   cout << num << endl;
   num = num – 2.0;
  }
```

6. What term describes a loop that loops indefinitely?

7. Explain the difference between a while loop and a do while loop.

8. What is the result of using a control expression of 1 in a do while loop?

9. What effect does the continue statement have on a loop?

10. In the code below, what message will be printed to the screen the most times, "Red" or "Blue"?
```
for(j = 1; j <= 3; j++)
  {
    cout << "Red\n";
    for(k = 1; k <= 3; k++)
     { cout << "Blue\n"; }
  }
```

LESSON 9 PROJECTS

PROJECT 9-1

Write a program that uses a for loop to print the odd numbers from 1 to 21. Save the source code file as oddloop.cpp.

PROJECT 9-2

Write a program that implements the flowchart in Figure 9-6. Save the source code file as sumitup.cpp.

FIGURE 9-6

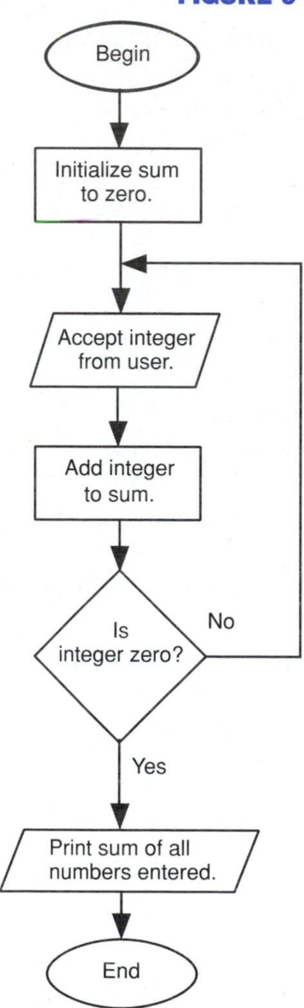

PROJECT 9-3

Write a program that prints the numbers 1 to 20, but skips the numbers 3, 11, and 16. Save the source code file as skipthem.cpp.

CRITICAL THINKING

ACTIVITY 9-1

Write a program that uses nested loops to produce the following output. Save the source code file as abbb.cpp.

A1B1B2B3A2B1B2B3

ACTIVITY 9-2

Write a program that asks the user for a series of integers one at a time. When the user enters the integer 0, the program displays the following information:

- the number of integers in the series (not including zero)
- the average of the integers
- the largest integer in the series
- the smallest integer in the series
- the difference between the largest and smallest integer in the series

Save the source file as ints.cpp.

LESSON 10

BUILDING PROGRAMS WITH FUNCTIONS

OBJECTIVES

Upon completion of this lesson, you should be able to:

- Build structured programs that are divided into functions.
- Describe the flow of execution in a program with multiple functions.
- Describe what is meant by the phrase "scope of variable."

Estimated Time: 1 hour

How to Build Programs with Functions

Examine the source code in Code List 10-1. The program consists of one function, `main()`. You may have difficulty, however, quickly determining what the program accomplishes.

CODE LIST 10-1

```
// series.cpp

#include <iostream.h>

int main()
{
 int choice;  // variable for user input

 int i;       // variable for loops and output


 do  // loop until a valid choice is entered
  {
   cout << "Which series do you wish to display?\n";
   cout << "1 - Odd numbers from 1 to 30\n";
   cout << "2 - Even numbers from 1 to 30\n";
   cout << "3 - All numbers from 1 to 30\n";
   cin >> choice;  // get choice from user
```

CODE LIST 10-1 (continued)

```
if ((choice < 1) || (choice > 3))  // if invalid entry, give message
   {
    cout << "Choice must be 1, 2, or 3\n";
    }
  } while ((choice < 1) || (choice > 3));

  switch (choice)
    {
     case 1:
       for (i = 1; i <= 30; i = i + 2)
       cout << i << ' ';
       cout << endl;
       break;
     case 2:
       for (i = 2; i <= 30; i = i + 2)
       cout << i << ' ;';
       cout << endl;
       break;
     case 3:
       for (i = 1; i <= 30; i++)
       cout << i << ' ';
       cout << endl;
       break;
    }
  return 0;
}
```

When the program is run, the user is prompted from a menu to choose to view a series of numbers. Depending on the user's choice, the program displays a series of odd numbers, even numbers, or all integers from 1 to 30.

Let us run the program to see its output.

STEP-BY-STEP 10.1

1. Retrieve the source file series.cpp.
2. Compile and run the program to see the program's output.
3. Close the source code file.

The program you just executed could have been better built using more than one function. The diagram in Figure 10-1, known as a Visual Table of Contents (VTOC), illustrates the point. The lines represent connections between functions. Each function can be accessed by the function above it as long as a line connects them.

FIGURE 10-1
A diagram that shows the functions of a program is sometimes called a Visual Table of Contents.

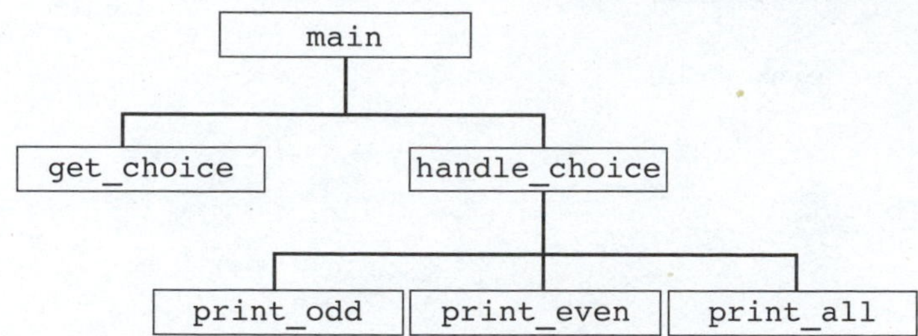

In this case, the `main` function "calls" the `get_choice` function to ask the user to choose the series to display. Next, the `handle_choice` function is called to direct the program flow to one of the three functions under it—one for each series. The source code for Figure 10-1 is presented in the next lesson.

Guidelines for Building a Program with Functions

Using functions helps the programmer develop programs that can be easily coded, debugged, and maintained. Keep the following guidelines in mind when building programs of more than one function.

1. **Organization**. A large program is easier to read and modify if it is logically organized into functions. It is easier to work with a program in parts, rather than one large chunk. A well-organized program, consisting of multiple functions, is easier to read and debug. Once a single function is tested and performs properly, you can set it aside and concentrate on problem areas.
2. **Autonomy**. Programs should be designed so that they consist mainly of standalone functions or modules. Each function is autonomous, meaning the function does not depend on data or code outside the function any more than necessary.
3. **Encapsulation**. The term encapsulation refers to enclosing the details of a function within the function itself, so that those details do not have to be known in order to use the function.
4. **Reusability**. Because functions typically perform a single and well-defined task, they may be reused in the same program or even in other programs.

Functions may be written for any purpose. For example, you could create a function that converts Fahrenheit temperatures to Celsius or a function that gets input from the user. A function can also be a go-between for other parts of the program, as illustrated in the `handle_choice` function of Figure 10-1.

There are two popular methods of designing programs. The first method, called *top-down design*, begins with the functions at the top of the VTOC and works toward the functions at the bottom of the VTOC. In other words, the general organization and flow of the program is decided before the details are coded.

Bottom-up design involves beginning with the bottom of the VTOC and working your way up. Some programmers prefer to work out the details of how the program will perform specific tasks and then bring the details together to create the overall organization and flow.

Whether you use top-down or bottom-up design, it is important to take an organized approach to writing a multifunction program.

The Syntax of Functions

With each program you have written, you have created a main function. You can use a similar syntax to create other functions. But before we look at other functions, let us take another look at the `main` function. The `main` function in the programs shown in this book have looked like the one in Code List 10-2.

CODE LIST 10-2

```
int main()
{
 // body of program
 return 0;
}
```

When the program reaches the `return 0;` statement, the value 0 is returned to the operating system. This value tells the operating system that the program ended normally. The value returned is a standard integer because we specified an `int` data type when the `main` function was declared.

There are times when a function has no reason to return a value. To prevent a value from being returned, the `void` keyword is used in place of a data type. You may have seen programs with a `main` function like the one in Code List 10-3.

CODE LIST 10-3

```
void main()
{
 // body of program
}
```

In a void function, no value is returned; therefore, no `return` statement is included. Newer operating systems are more likely to take advantage of the value returned by the `main` function. Therefore, you should get into the habit of creating `main` functions that return a zero when they terminate normally. The void `main` functions are used less frequently now than in the past.

As mentioned earlier, creating other functions in C++ programs is similar to creating the `main` function. Code List 10-4 shows a simple function that prints a message to the screen.

CODE LIST 10-4

```
void print_title()
 {
  cout << "Soccer Tournament Scheduler Program\n";
  cout << "By Ben and Conrad McCue\n";
 }
```

The name of the function is `print_title`. The `void` keyword indicates that no value is returned. The parentheses after the name let the compiler know that `print_title` is a function. The statements between the braces are executed when the function `print_title` is "called." The `main` function in Code List 10-5 includes an example of a call to the `print_title` function.

CODE LIST 10-5

```
int main()
 {
  print_title(); // call to print_title

  // insert the rest of the program here

  return 0;
 }
```

Function Prototypes

There is one more thing you have to do to make your own functions work. At the top of your program, you must tell the compiler that your function exists. You do this by creating a *prototype*. Basically, a prototype defines the function for the compiler. Code List 10-6 shows the functions from Code Lists 10-4 and 10-5 assembled into a working program, including the required function prototype.

CODE LIST 10-6

```
// 1stfunct.cpp

#include <iostream.h>

void print_title();  // prototype for print_title function

int main()
{
  print_title(); // call to print_title

  // insert the rest of the program here

  return 0;
} // end of main function

   // function to print program title to the screen
   void print_title()
   {
     cout << "Soccer Tournament Scheduler Program\n";
     cout << "By Ben and Conrad McCue\n";
   } // end of print_title
```

The function prototype is identical to the first line of the function itself. There is, however, a semicolon at the end of the prototype.

To understand why a function prototype is necessary, consider the way a compiler works. A program is compiled one line at a time. As the compiler works its way down the program, it interprets the source code it reads and compiles that source code into machine code. The function prototypes at the top of the program inform the compiler that later in the source code it will find references to a custom-made function.

For example, in Code List 10-6, the function prototype for `print_title` tells the compiler to be expecting a call to a function named `print_title`. It also tells the compiler important information such as the fact that `print_title` is a void function. With this information, the compiler will know whether `print_title` is being called correctly. The compiler is content to wait for the bottom of the program before learning what the `print_title` function actually does.

Computer Concepts

The compiler itself does not care whether it finds an actual function to match the prototype at the top of the program. It is the linker's job to link all the pieces together and find the functions referred to in a prototype. Often, a function prototype exists in C++ source code and the actual function is in another file or in a precompiled library. For example, when you include iostream.h in your programs, you are basically including function prototypes for the iostream features. The linker takes care of linking your program to those actual functions.

STEP-BY-STEP 10.2

1. Carefully enter the program in Code List 10-6 into a blank editor screen. Save the program as 1stfunct.cpp.
2. Compile, link, and run the program. The main function calls the `print_title` function and prints the message to the screen.
3. Leave the program open for the next Step-by-Step exercise.

Functions and Program Flow

In Step-by-Step 10.1, the `main` function began executing when the program was run. The first statement in the `main` function called the `print_title` function. The call caused execution to jump to the `print_title` function. When a function is called, the computer executes the statements in the function beginning with the first statement. When the end of the function is reached, program execution resumes with the statement that follows the call to the function.

Suppose you are washing a car and you hear the phone ring. You leave the car for a moment and answer the phone. When you complete the phone call, you return to the car and begin washing where you left off. That is basically how the flow of a program works. Programs execute one statement at a time. Functions are just another way of controlling the flow of a program to make the program more efficient and better organized.

Figure 10-2 shows the sequence of execution in a simple three-function example.

FIGURE 10-2
The numbers next to the statements show the order of execution.

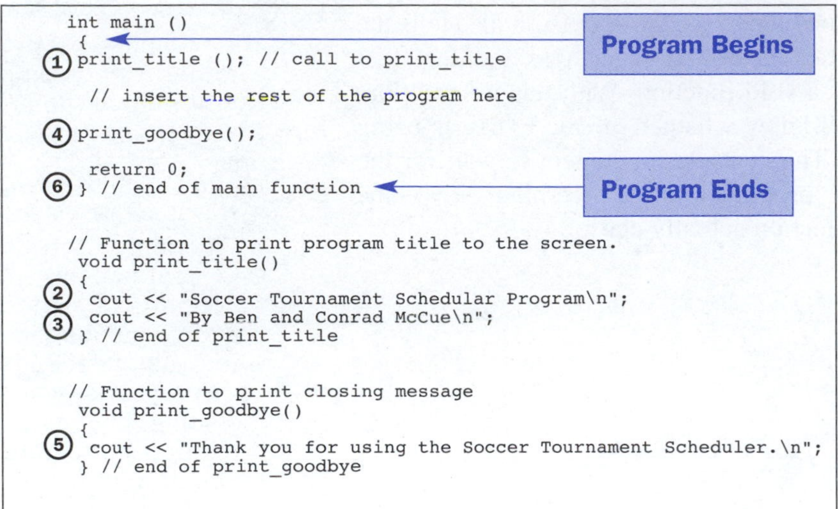

int main ()
{
1 print_title (); // call to print_title
// insert the rest of the program here
4 print_goodbye();
return 0;
6 } // end of main function
Program Begins
Program Ends
// Function to print program title to the screen.
void print_title()
{
2 cout << "Soccer Tournament Schedular Program\n";
3 cout << "By Ben and Conrad McCue\n";
} // end of print_title
// Function to print closing message
void print_goodbye()
{
5 cout << "Thank you for using the Soccer Tournament Scheduler.\n";
} // end of print_goodbye

The program begins with the first statement of the `main` function (1), which is a call to the `print_title` function. The flow of logic goes to the `print_title` function, which includes two statements (2 and 3), and they are executed next. When the last statement (3) in the `print_title` function is executed, the flow of logic returns to the statement (4) that follows the previous function call in `main()`. The statement in the `print_goodbye` function (5) is then executed. The flow of logic then returns to `main()`, where the program ends (6).

Hot Tip

Notice that a function's prototype is just like the first line of the function, except for the semicolon. An error will result if you forget to include the semicolon at the end of a prototype.

CODE LIST 10-7

```
// 1stfunct.cpp

#include <iostream.h>

void print_title();   // prototype for print_title function
void print_goodbye(); // prototype for print_goodbye function

 int main()
 {
  print_title(); // call to print_title

  // insert the rest of the program here

  print_goodbye();

  return 0;
 } // end of main function


// function to print program title to the screen
 void print_title()
 {
   cout << "Soccer Tournament Scheduler Program\n";
   cout << "By Ben and Conrad McCue\n";
 } // end of print_title


// function to print closing message
 void print_goodbye()
 {
   cout << "Thank you for using the Soccer Tournament Scheduler.\n";
 } // end of print_goodbye
```

STEP-BY-STEP 10.3

1. Modify 1stfunct.cpp to match the program shown in Code List 10-7. Don't forget to add the new function prototype.

2. Compile, link, and run the program.

3. When you have run the program successfully, close the program.

Scope of Variables

When building a program that consists of functions, you must be concerned with how data is made available to the functions. In this section, you will learn about the accessibility of variables in functions and how to get data to and from functions.

As programs get larger, it is important to keep tight control over variables to prevent errors in your programs. One way to do this is to make the data in variables accessible only in the areas where that data is needed. When data is needed in another part of the program, it is better to send that data and that data only to the part of the program that needs it.

You have been working primarily with programs that have only one function: `main()`. Within `main()`, you declared variables. These variables, however, would be inaccessible outside of `main()`. The "availability" of a variable is known as its *scope*. While this may sound difficult, in C++ the scope of variables is easy to understand.

Note

Local variables are sometimes called *automatic variables*, and global variables are sometimes called *external variables*.

Variables in C++ can either be local or global. A *local variable* is declared within a function and is accessible only within that function. A *global variable* is declared before the `main` function. Global variables are accessible by any function.

Consider the program in Code List 10-8. One variable (`i`) is declared before the `main` function, making it a global variable. Because `j` and `k` are declared in the `main` function, they are local to the `main` function. Therefore, `j` and `k` cannot be used outside of the `main` function. Within the function named `myfunction`, the variable `l` is declared. It too is local and accessible only within `myfunction`. After the last statement in `myfunction` is executed, the variable `l` is gone from memory.

CODE LIST 10-8

```
// scope.cpp

#include <iostream.h>

int i = 3;     // global variable

void myfunction();

int main()
 {
  int j,k; // variables local to the main function
           // j and k are not accessible outside of the main function
  j = 2;

  k = i + j;
  cout << "j = " << j << " and k = " << k << '\n';
  cout << "i = " << i << " before the call to myfunction.\n";
  myfunction(); // call to myfunction
  cout << "i = " << i << " after the call to myfunction.\n";
  return 0;
 }

void myfunction()
```

CODE LIST 10-8 (continued)

```
{
 int l;    // local variable
 l = ++i; // the variable i is accessible because i is global
          // the variable i is changed globally
 cout << "l = " << l << '\n';
 cout << "The variable l is lost as soon as myfunction exits.\n";
}
```

Because the variable `i` is accessible from the entire program, changes made to `i` while in `myfunction` will be made to the global variable. Therefore, those changes will still be in effect when the program returns to the `main` function.

If a statement were added to `myfunction` that attempted to access the variable `k`, located in `main`, an error would result. The variable `k` is accessible only from within the `main` function. In a similar manner, the variable `l` is inaccessible outside of `myfunction` because it is local to `myfunction`.

STEP-BY-STEP 10.4

1. Open scope.cpp. The program from Code List 10-8 appears on your screen.

2. Compile and run the program as it appears. Study the source code to get clear in your mind where each variable is available.

3. Enter the following statement at the end of myfunction.

```
k = i + j;
```

4. Compile the program to see the errors the new statement generates. Your compiler will probably generate an error telling you that the variables j and k are not defined. The error is generated because j and k are available only in the main function.

5. Delete the erring statement and close the program.

Why have local variables if they are inaccessible to other parts of the program? One reason is that they exist only while the function is executing and memory is released when the function terminates. If a variable is needed only within a particular function, you save memory by creating and disposing of the variable within the function.

Using local variables could limit the number of errors that occur in a program. If all variables were global, an error made in a variable and used by various functions could cause multiple errors. However, if you use local variables, any errors are limited to the function in which the variable is declared.

Use local variables whenever possible. Even a large program should have very few global variables. Using local variables keeps a tighter control over your program's data, resulting in fewer bugs and programs that are easier to maintain.

You may be wondering how data can get to other functions if everything is local. As you will learn in the next lesson, when a function is created, you can choose what data you want to send to the function.

Summary

In this lesson, you learned:

- Designing a program that consists of functions results in code that is better organized, reusable, and easier to debug.
- The syntax of functions you create is very similar to that of the main function. The parentheses after the function name tell the compiler that you are defining a function.
- You must create a prototype for your function to let the compiler know your function exists. Prototypes are placed at the top of the program.
- A local variable is created within a function and is accessible only from within that function. A global variable is declared outside of all functions and is accessible from any function.

LESSON 10 REVIEW QUESTIONS

TRUE/FALSE

Circle T if the statement is true or F if the statement is false.

T F 1. When a program jumps from one function to another, we say that the first function called the second.

T F 2. Dividing a program into functions can improve the organization of a program.

T F 3. A drawback to dividing a program into functions is that it makes it more difficult to debug.

T F 4. Encapsulation refers to protecting programs from being copied.

T F 5. In a top-down design, the main function is written first.

T F 6. When the end of a function is reached, the next statement to be executed is the first statement of the main function.

T F 7. A prototype of a function tells the compiler that your function exists.

T F 8. The scope of a variable refers to the way the variable is passed to another function.

T F 9. A local variable is sometimes called an automatic variable.

T F 10. A variable that is available anywhere in your program is called a global variable.

WRITTEN QUESTIONS

Write a brief answer to the following questions.

1. What is one advantage of dividing a program into multiple functions?
2. What is the name of the diagram that shows the functions that make up a program?
3. What are two guidelines to help you build programs of more than one function?
4. Briefly describe top-down and bottom-up design.
5. Why is a `return` statement unnecessary in a void function?
6. Suppose a program includes a function with the prototype shown below. What is the line of code necessary to call the function?

```
void print_message();
```

7. What is meant by the scope of a variable?
8. What is one advantage of using local variables?
9. Where must a variable be declared in order for it to be local?
10. Where must a variable be declared in order for it to be global?

LESSON 10 PROJECTS

PROJECT 10-1

1. Open gascheck.cpp. An incomplete program appears. To complete the program, you will add two functions and an if structure that calls the new functions.
2. Add a void function called `print_warning` that warns the user that the program has calculated the user will run out of gas before the next available gas station. Do not forget to add the necessary function prototype.
3. Add a void function called `print_okay` that tells the user he or she will make it to the next gas station. Do not forget to add the necessary function prototype.
4. Add an if/else structure to the `main` function that calls `print_warning` if `fuel_miles` is less than `miles_remaining`. Otherwise, `print_okay` should be called.
5. Save and run the program.
6. Close the program.

PROJECT 10-2

Write a program that asks the user for an integer. The program should call one of three functions, based on the value entered. If the value is negative, call a function that prints a message indicating the value is negative. Create similar functions to call when the value is 0 and positive. Save the source code as valtest.cpp.

PROJECT 10-3

Write a program source code template that you can use as a starting point for programs you create in the future. Include comments at the top that give your name and provide places for you to fill in the date and description of the program. Set aside a place for `#include` directives, prototypes, constants, and global variables. Create an empty `main` function. Save the source code file as newprog.cpp and close the file.

CRITICAL THINKING

Write a program that meets the following requirements. Save the program as scopex.cpp. The program should:

1. Declare a global integer variable named `x` and initialize it to zero.
2. Declare a local integer variable within `main` named `y`.
3. From within `main`, prompt the user for a value for `y`.
4. Include a loop that calls a function named `incx` `y` number of times.
5. Include the function `incx` to increment the value of `x` by 1.
6. Print the value of `x` after each iteration of the loop.

PASSING DATA AND USING LIBRARY FUNCTIONS

OBJECTIVES

Upon completion of this lesson, you should be able to:

- Pass data to functions.
- Get values from functions using return.
- Describe and use library functions.
- Use common math functions.
- Use character manipulation functions.

Estimated Time: 1 hour

Getting Data to and from Functions

You have learned that the parentheses following a function's name let the compiler know that it is a function. The parentheses can serve another purpose as well. That is, parentheses can be used to *pass* data to a function and in some cases to return data from a function.

When a function is called, the data in the parentheses (called the *argument*) is passed into the receiving function. There are two ways to pass data to functions: *passing by value* and *passing by reference*.

Computer Concepts

Getting data to and from functions is called *passing data*. Programmers talk about passing data to a function and the function passing a value back.

Passing by Value

When you pass a variable to a function by value, a copy of the value in the variable is given to the function for it to use. If the variable is changed within the function, the original copy of the variable in the calling function remains the same. Code List 11-1 is an example of a function that accepts data using the passing by value technique.

CODE LIST 11-1

```
void print_true_or_false(bool True_False)
 {
  if True_False          // If True_False is true,
   {                     // display the word TRUE.
    cout << "TRUE\n";
   }
  else                   // If True_False is false,
   {                     // display the word FALSE.
    cout << "FALSE\n";
   }
 }
```

A value comes into the function through the parentheses, and the copy of the value will be placed in the variable `True_False`. The variable `True_False` is called a *parameter*.

When you write a call to a function, you can put any variable or literal in the parentheses to be passed to the function as long as the data types do not conflict. For example, the statements in Code List 11-2 are all legal calls to the `print_true_or_false` function.

In Code List 11-2, as long as the variable named `complete` is a Boolean variable, the first line is legal. The second line is legal because `true` is actually a Boolean literal. The third line is legal because the expression in the parentheses evaluates to a Boolean value.

Did You Know?

Many people use the terms *argument* and *parameter* interchangeably, but there is a difference. An argument is a value or expression passed to a function through the parentheses when a function is called. A parameter is the variable that receives the value or any other identifier in the parentheses of the function declaration. In other words, an argument is passed to a function, but once in the function, the argument is a parameter.

CODE LIST 11-2

```
print_true_or_false(complete);            // passes a variable
print_true_or_false(true);                // passes a literal
print_true_or_false(j == 3 && k == 2);    // passes the result
                                          // of an expression
```

The program in Code List 11-3 illustrates how a value passed to the function named `print_value` does not pass back to the `main` function. Notice that the `print_value` function uses a variable named j, even though the `main` function passes a variable named i. The data types must match, but the names are often different.

CODE LIST 11-3

```
// passval.cpp

#include <iostream.h>

void print_value(int j);   // function prototype

int main()
 {
  int i = 2;
  cout << "The value before the function is " << i << endl;
  print_value(i);
  cout << "The value after the function exits is " << i << endl;
  return 0;
 }

void print_value(int j)
 {
  cout << "The value passed to the function is " << j << endl;
  j = j * 2; // the value in the variable i is doubled
  cout << "The value at the end of the function is " << j << endl;
 }
```

STEP-BY-STEP 11.1

1. Enter the program shown in Code List 11-3. Save the source code as passval.cpp.
2. Compile and run the program to see that the value passed to the print_value function is not passed back to the main function.
3. Leave the source code file open for the next Step-by-Step exercise.

Passing by Reference

Functions that pass variables by reference will pass any changes you make to the variables back to the calling function. For example, suppose you need a function that gets input from the user. The function in Code List 11-4 uses passing by reference to get two values from the user and pass them back through parentheses.

CODE LIST 11-4

```
void get_values(float &income, float &expense)
 {
  cout << "Enter this month's income amount: $";
  cin >> income;
  cout << "Enter this month's expense amount: $";
  cin >> expense;
 }
```

To pass a variable by reference, simply precede the variable name with an ampersand (&) in the function definition. But even though it is easy to pass by reference, you should do so sparingly. You should write functions that pass variables by value whenever possible because passing variables by value is safer. When you pass a variable by value, you know it cannot be changed by the function you call. When you pass a variable by reference, a programming error in the function could cause a problem throughout the program.

As a general rule, you should use passing by reference only when data needs to be passed back to the calling function. In the preceding example, the data entered by the user must be passed back to the calling function.

The program you ran in Step-by-Step 11.1 passed a variable by value. Let us modify the program to make it pass the variable by reference.

STEP-BY-STEP 11.2

1. Add an ampersand (&) before the identifier j in both the prototype and the function declaration. Save the source code as passref.cpp.
2. Compile and run the program again to see the difference passing by reference makes.
3. Close the source code file.

Returning Values Using `return`

As you learned earlier in this lesson, unless a function is declared with the keyword `void`, the function will return a value. In the case of the `main` function, it returns a value to the operating system. Other functions, however, return a value to the calling function. The value to be returned is specified using the `return` statement.

The function in Code List 11-5 is an example of a function that returns a value of type double. The temperature in Celsius is passed into the function by value and the temperature in Fahrenheit is returned using the `return` statement.

CODE LIST 11-5

```
double celsius_to_fahrenheit(double celsius)
 {
  double fahr;  // local variable for calculation
  fahr = celsius * (9.0/5.0) + 32.0;
  return(fahr);
 }
```

Any function that is not declared as void should include a return statement. The value or expression in the return statement is returned to the calling function. In the celsius_to_fahrenheit function, the value stored in fahr is returned to the calling function.

The program in Code List 11-6 shows how you can use this function. The statement `fahrenheit = celsius_to_fahrenheit(celsius);` calls the `celsius_to_fahrenheit` function and passes the value in the variable `celsius` to the function. The function returns the temperature in Fahrenheit degrees, and the calling statement assigns the Fahrenheit temperature to the variable `fahrenheit`.

CODE LIST 11-6

```
// ctof.cpp

#include <iostream.h>

int main()
 {
  double fahrenheit;
  double celsius = 22.5;

  fahrenheit = celsius_to_fahrenheit(celsius);

  cout << celsius << " C = " << fahrenheit << " F\n";
  return 0;
 }
```

The `celsius_to_fahrenheit` function could be rewritten as shown in Code List 11-7 to include only one statement and return the same result. Any valid expression can appear in the parentheses of the return statement. In this case, performing the calculation in the `return` statement eliminates the local variable `fahr`.

Computer Concepts

You can use any data type when declaring a function.

CODE LIST 11-7

```
double celsius_to_fahrenheit(double celsius)
 {
  return(celsius * (9.0/5.0) + 32.0);
 }
```

When using the `return` statement, keep the following important points in mind.

1. The `return` statement does not require that the value being returned be placed in parentheses. You may, however, want to get into the habit of placing variables and expressions in parentheses to make the code more readable.
2. A function can return only one value using `return`. Use passing by reference to return multiple values from a function.
3. When a `return` statement is encountered, the function will exit and return the value specified, even if other program lines exist below the `return`.
4. A function can have more than one `return` statement to help simplify an algorithm. For example, a `return` statement could be in an if structure allowing a function to return early if a certain condition is met.
5. The calling function is not required to use or even to capture the value returned from a function it calls.

STEP-BY-STEP 11.3

1. Open ctof.cpp. The complete Celsius to Fahrenheit program appears.

2. Compile, link, and run the program.

3. Leave the program open for the next Step-by-Step exercise.

One additional important note: When the last line of a function is reached, or when a `return()` statement is executed, the function ends and the program returns to the calling function and begins executing statements from where it left off. Do not end functions with a call back to the original function or the function will not terminate properly. Continually calling functions without returning from them will eventually cause the program to crash.

If you call the `main` function at the end of a function you wrote, the `main` function will begin with the first statement, rather than beginning with the statement following the call to your function.

More About Function Prototypes

A function prototype consists of the function's return type, name, and argument list. In this lesson, the function prototypes specified the parameter names in the argument list. However, this is not necessary as long as the type is specified. For example, the prototype for the `celsius_to_fahrenheit` function could be written as:

```
double celsius_to_fahrenheit(double);
```

The prototype for the `get_values` function could be written as:

```
void get_values(float &, float &);
```

STEP-BY-STEP 11.4

1. Change the function prototype in ctof.cpp to specify the data type only, as shown in the examples above.

2. Compile, link, and run the program. The program still functions normally. After you have seen it work, close the program.

Dividing the Series Program into Functions

Now that you have practiced creating functions and moving data to and from them, let us take another look at the program from Step-by-Step 11.1. In Lesson 10, you studied a VTOC of the program divided into functions. That VTOC appears again in Figure 11-1.

FIGURE 11-1
This Visual Table of Contents shows the series program divided into functions.

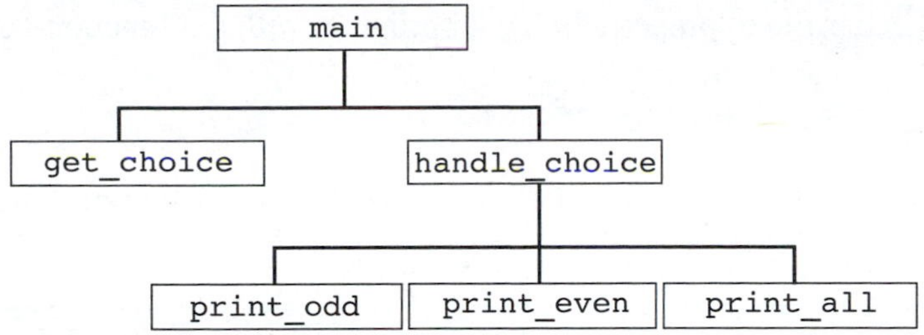

STEP-BY-STEP 11.5

1. Retrieve the source code file series2.cpp. Analyze the source code to see that the program is divided into functions.

2. Compile and run the program to see that it has the same result as the single-function version you ran in Step-by-Step 11.1.

3. Close the program.

Using Library Functions

C++ compilers include prewritten, ready-to-use functions to make programming easier. The number and type of functions available to you will vary depending on your compiler. The functions that come with your compiler are called *library functions*. This section shows you how to use some of the more common library functions.

Library functions are just like functions you create and may be used in the same way. The difference is that the source code for library functions does not appear in your program. The prototypes for library functions are provided to your program using the `#include` compiler directive.

Let us examine a common C++ library function, `pow()`, which is used to raise a value (`x`) by a designated power (`y`). The `pow()` function prototype is shown below.

```
double pow(double x, double y);
```

The function `pow` receives two values or expressions of type double and returns the result as a double. Below is an example of a call to the `pow` function.

```
z = pow(x, y); // z equals x raised to the y power
```

In order to use the pow function, you must include the math.h header file using the compiler directive below. A *header file* is a text file that provides the prototypes of a group of library functions. The linker uses the information in the header file to properly link your program with the function you want to use.

```
#include <math.h>
```

The program in Code List 11-8 is a simple example of the use of the pow function.

CODE LIST 11-8

```
// power.cpp

#include <iostream.h>
#include <math.h>

int main()
  {
    double base;
    double exponent;
    double answer;

    cout << "Enter the base: ";      // prompt user for base
    cin >> base;
    cout << "Enter the exponent: "; // prompt user for exponent
    cin >> exponent;

    answer = pow(base, exponent);    // calculate answer

    cout << "The answer is " << answer << endl;

    return 0;
  }
```

STEP-BY-STEP 11.6

1. Enter the program in Code List 11-8 into a blank editor screen. Save the program as power.cpp.
2. Compile, run, and test your program.
3. Close the program.

Popular Math Functions

Many C++ compilers provide basic math functions, such as the one you used to calculate xy. Table 11-1 describes some basic math functions and shows their prototypes and their purpose.

Note

All the functions in Table 11-1 require that math.h be included in the calling program.

TABLE 11-1
Basic math functions

FUNCTION	PROTOTYPE	DESCRIPTION
`abs`	`int abs(int x);`	Returns the absolute value of an integer
`labs`	`long int labs(long int x);`	Returns the absolute value of a long integer
`fabs`	`double fabs(double x);`	Returns the absolute value of a floating-point number
`ceil`	`double ceil(double x);`	Rounds up to a whole number
`floor`	`double floor(double x);`	Rounds down to a whole number
`hypot`	`double hypot(double a, double b);`	Calculates the hypotenuse (c) of a right triangle, where $c^2 = a^2 + b^2$
`pow`	`double pow(double x, double y);`	Calculates x to the power of y
`pow10`	`double pow10(int x);`	Calculates 10 to the power of x
`sqrt`	`double sqrt(double x);`	Calculates the positive square root of x

STEP-BY-STEP 11.7

1. Open math.cpp and analyze the source code to see the usage of the ceil and floor functions.
2. Compile and run the program. Be sure to enter a value with a fractional part, such as 2.4.
3. Add the line shown in Code List 11-9 to the program, below the other output statements.
4. Save, compile, and run the program again. Run the program several times, entering both positive and negative numbers.
5. Close the program.

CODE LIST 11-9

```
cout << "The absolute value of " << x >> "is " << fabs(x) << endl;
```

Functions for Working with Characters

C++ compilers also include many functions for analyzing and changing characters. The header file ctype.h must be included for a calling program to use the functions listed in Table 11-2. The conditional functions in the table return a nonzero integer if the condition is true and zero if the condition is false.

TABLE 11-2
Character functions

FUNCTION	PROTOTYPE	DESCRIPTION
isupper	int isupper(int c);	Determines if a character is uppercase
islower	int islower(int c);	Determines if a character is lowercase
isalpha	int isalpha(int c);	Determines if a character is a letter (a–z, A–Z)
isdigit	int isdigit(int c);	Determines if a character is a digit (0–9)
toupper	int toupper(int c);	Converts a character to uppercase
tolower	int tolower(int c);	Converts a character to lowercase

The program in Code List 11-10 demonstrates the use of the `isalpha`, `isupper`, and `isdigit` functions. The program asks for a character and then reports to the user whether the character is uppercase or lowercase. If the user enters a numeral, the program detects and reports that as well. Finally, the program detects and reports if the character is neither a letter nor a number.

CODE LIST 11-10

```
// charfun.cpp

#include <iostream.h>
#include <ctype.h>

int main()
{
  char c;

  cout <<"Enter a character\n";
  cin >> c;

  if(isalpha(c))
   {
    if(isupper(c))
       { cout << c <<" is an uppercase letter\n";}
    else
       { cout << c <<" is a lowercase letter\n";}
   }

  if(isdigit(c))
   { cout << c <<" is a number\n";}

  if(!(isdigit(c)||isalpha(c)))
   {cout << c <<" is neither a letter nor a number\n";}

  return 0;
}
```

STEP-BY-STEP 11.8

1. Open charfun.cpp. The program in Code List 11-10 appears, without the three if structures.

2. Enter the missing if structures using Code List 11-10 as a reference.

3. Save, compile, and run the program. Run it several times, trying uppercase and lowercase letters, numbers, and symbols.

4. Close the program.

Summary

In this lesson, you learned:

- Getting data to and from functions is called passing data.
- Data can be passed to functions by value or by reference.
- When possible, you should pass by value. Passing by value passes a copy of the data, and the original data cannot be changed from within the function.
- Data passed by reference brings back changes made to it within a function.
- A value can be passed to the calling function using return.
- A void function does not return a value.
- In a function prototype, you are only required to provide the data types of the parameters.
- Library functions are functions that come with the compiler.
- A header file provides the prototypes for library functions.
- C++ includes common math functions and functions for working with characters.

LESSON 11 REVIEW QUESTIONS

TRUE/FALSE

Circle T if the statement is true or F if the statement is false.

T F 1. Passing by value gives the function a copy of the passed variable.

T F 2. An @ symbol signifies a variable is to be passed by reference.

T F 3. The data in parentheses when a function is called is the argument.

T F 4. Use passing by value to return two values from a function.

T F 5. You should pass data by reference whenever possible.

T F 6. Any function that is not void should include a return statement.

T F 7. Any valid expression can appear in the parentheses of a return statement.

T F 8. A function can have only one return statement.

T F 9. The source code for a library function appears in your program.

T F 10. The ceil function rounds a floating-point number up to the next whole number.

WRITTEN QUESTIONS

Write a brief answer to the following questions.

1. What is the difference between an argument and a parameter?
2. What happens when a variable is passed by value?
3. What happens when a variable is passed by reference?
4. What data types can be used when declaring a function?
5. What happens when a return statement is encountered?
6. What happens in a void function after the last line in a function is executed?
7. What do you call the functions that come with the compiler?
8. What header file is required to use the pow function?
9. What function returns the absolute value of a floating-point number?
10. What function determines whether a character is uppercase?

LESSON 11 PROJECTS

PROJECT 11-1

1. Open the version of ctof.cpp that you saved in Step-by-Step 11.4.
2. Add the following function to the program.

```
double get_celsius()
 {
  double celsius_in;

  cout << "Enter the temperature in Celsius: ";
  cin >> celsius_in;
  return celsius_in;
 }
```

3. Add the appropriate function prototype for the new function.
4. Add the following line to the main function, immediately following the variable declarations.

```
celsius = get_celsius();
```

5. Change the declaration of the variable celsius to remove the initialization.

6. Save, compile, and run the program.

PROJECT 11-2

Write a program that uses the `sqrt` function to calculate the circumference of a circle, given its area. Use the formula $2\sqrt{\pi * \text{area}}$. Save the program as circ.cpp and close the source code when you have completed the exercise.

SCANS

PROJECT 11-3

Write a program that prompts the user for a single character that must be either an uppercase or lowercase letter. The program should use a do while loop to repeat the prompt if the character entered is not a letter. Once the user has entered a letter, the program should change the case of the letter. If the letter was entered as uppercase, the program should change the character to lowercase, and vice versa. The changed letter should be output, along with the original character entered by the user. (*Hint:* The syntax for converting a character's case is shown in the example below.)

```
c = tolower(c);
```

Save the source code as `charchng.cpp`.

PROJECT 11-4

Modify `series2.cpp` so that the call to `get_choice` and `handle_choice` are in a do while loop. Add an item to the menu numbered 0 (zero) that exits the program. Have the loop continually redisplay the menu until zero is chosen. Note: Make sure you change the do while loop in the `get_choice` function so that zero is a valid input. Save the source code as series3.cpp.

CRITICAL THINKING

Modify the get_celsius function in the program you saved in Project 11-1 to use passing by reference to return the temperature to the main function.

C++ Review

UNIT REVIEW

TRUE/FALSE

Circle T if the statement is true or F if the statement is false.

T F 1. Although it is a good idea to keep variable names fairly short, they can be up to 64 characters long.

T F 2. An attempt to store a value in a variable that is too large for the variable's declared data type results in a condition called leakage.

T F 3. The \n newline character can be enclosed in single or in double quotes, and will produce the same result either way.

T F 4. When you are using a char data type as the control expression for a switch structure, the characters coded on each case statement must be contained in single quotes.

T F 5. If the C++ compiler processes a function prototype statement when compiling a program, it will generate an error if the function itself is not found within the program.

FILL-IN-THE-BLANK

1. In the C++ programming language, the % symbol represents the __________ operator.
2. A C++ __________ is a generic definition from which an object is created.
3. A Boolean data type variable containing a value of 1 (one) represents a(n) __________ condition.
4. A(n) __________ loop tests the control expression at the beginning of the loop.
5. When a variable is passed by __________ to a function, the called function is given a copy of the variable for its use and the original variable remains unchanged.

PROJECTS

PROJECT 3-1

In this project, you will use the input and output streams to prompt the user for information, and input the values from the user. You will declare variables and perform a calculation.

1. Start your C++ compiler or IDE application. Create a new C++ source code file and save it to your student folder as **ellipse.cpp**.

2. Add **comments** to the beginning of the file to indicate its name and purpose.

3. Add an **include** statement for the **iostream** header file.

4. Create a **constant** for the value of **Pi**, using the value **3.14159**. Be sure to use an appropriate data type.

5. Create a **main** function and **declare** variables named **length**, **width**, and **area**, using the **double** data type.

6. Use the **output stream** to prompt the user to enter a value for the **width** of an ellipse, and input the value into the **width** variable.

7. Prompt the user to enter a value for the **length** of the ellipse, and input the value into the **length** variable.

8. Add statements to **calculate the area** of the ellipse using the formula **area = length times width times Pi**. Store the result in the **area** variable, and use the output stream to show the value to the user.

9. End the program and exit your compiler. Be sure to save your latest changes to the source file.

PROJECT 3-2

In this project, you will create a program that declares and manipulates string variables. This project requires the oostring.h and oostring.cpp files to be copied from the data file folder to your student project folder, if they are not already there from a previous project.

1. Start your C++ compiler or IDE application. Create a new C++ source code file and save it to your student folder as **tststrng.cpp**.

2. Add **comments** to the beginning of the file to indicate its name and purpose.

3. Add an **include** statement for the **iostream** header file and for the **oostring** header file.

4. Create a **main** function and declare a **string** variable named **city**, and an **integer** variable named **length**.

5. Initialize the **city** string variable to contain the value "**MyTown**" and display the variable's current value using the output stream.

6. Change the contents of the **city** variable to "**Grand Rapids**", display the new value using the output stream, and use the string class **length()** function to get and display the length of the string.

7. **Concatenate ", Michigan"** to the end of the **city** string variable, display the new value, and get and display the **length** of the new value.

8. Use the output and input streams to prompt the user to enter a new city and state value, and use the **getline()** function to obtain the new value and assign it to the **city** variable. Display the new value of the **city** variable, and obtain and display its **length**.

9. End the program and exit your compiler. Be sure to save your latest changes to the source file.

PROJECT 3-3

In this project, you will create a program that creates and tests Boolean expressions, and uses the selection and loop structures to obtain and process input values.

1. Start your C++ compiler or IDE application. Create a new C++ source code file and save it to your student folder as **tststruc.cpp**.

2. Add **comments** to the beginning of the file to indicate its name and purpose.

3. Add an **include** statement for the **iostream** header file.

4. Create a **main** function and declare a **Boolean** variable named **t_f**, two **integer** variables named **x** and **y**, and one **char** variable named **int_state**.

5. Prompt the user to enter an **integer** value for **x**, and input the value to the **x** variable. Prompt the user to enter an **integer** value for **y**, and input the value to the **y** variable.

6. Use an **if/else** structure to **compare x** to **y** and print one message if **x is less than or equal** to y, and a different message if **x is greater than** y.

7. Add a statement to set the **t_f** variable equal to the result of the expression **(x == 4)**, and display the result value to the user.

8. Create a **while** loop that will examine values input by the user and determine if they are in the range **1 through 5**, or the range **6 through 10**, and display a message indicating which range applies to that value. If a value was entered **outside of the range 1 through 10**, and it is **not zero**, **display an error message** indicating an invalid value was supplied. If the value **zero** was supplied, **terminate** the loop. (*Hint*: prompt for input and obtain the first value before entering the loop, and prompt for input and obtain a value again at the end of the loop.)

9. Set the **t_f** variable to a value of **true**. Create a **do while** loop that loops as long as **t_f remains true**. The loop will prompt for and input an integer value. If a **zero** is entered, set **t_f to false**. If a value other than zero is entered, determine if the value entered was **negative**, a positive **even** number, or a positive **odd** number. Set the **int_state** variable to a value of **N**, **E**, or **O**, depending on the integer input value. Create a **switch** structure using **int_state** as the control value, and print a message indicating if the input value was negative, even, or odd. The **default** case should indicate the user wants to exit the loop.

10. End the program and exit your compiler. Be sure to save your latest changes to the source file.

PROJECT 3-4

In this project, you will create a program that calls several functions provided with the C++ compiler.

1. Start your C++ compiler or IDE application. Create a new C++ source code file and save it to your student folder as **tstfuncs.cpp**.

2. Add **comments** to the beginning of the file to indicate its name and purpose.

3. Add **include** statements for the **iostream**, **math**, and **ctype** header files.

4. Define function **prototype** statements for the **floor()**, **pow()**, **abs()**, **toupper()**, and **islower()** library functions.

5. Create a **main** function, and define **double** variables named **x**, **y**, and **z**. Define two **char** variables named **a** and **c**. Define an **integer** variable named **b**.

6. Prompt the user to enter a value for x, input the value, pass it to the **floor()** function, and display the result.

7. Set **x** equal to **4**, and call the **pow()** function to raise **x** to the **power of 7**. Display the result.

8. Prompt the user to enter a positive or negative integer. Input the value to **b**, pass it to the **abs()** function, and display the result.

9. Prompt the user to enter a lowercase value, input it to **c**, pass the value to the **toupper()** function, and display the result.

10. Prompt the user to enter an uppercase or a lowercase character, input the value to **c**, pass the value to **islower(),** test the result using an **if** statement, and print a message indicating if the value is uppercase or lowercase.

11. End the program. Save your changes, compile and run the program. Exit the compiler.

SIMULATION

SIMULATION 3-1

Create a new C++ program to analyze the daily gain or loss for a user's stock holding. The program should prompt the user for the name of a stock, the opening price of the stock, the closing price of the stock, and the number of shares held. It should then calculate and display the opening value for that number of shares, the closing value for that number of shares, and the net loss or gain in value for the day. The program should incorporate some sort of loop structure to enable it to process multiple stocks and include some mechanism for the user to terminate the loop when done. Save the program as **stocks.cpp**. Compile and run the program and test it with a variety of values.

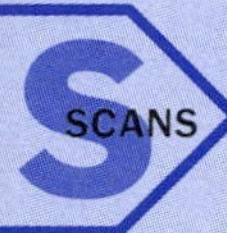

SIMULATION 3-2

Create a program to calculate a person's weight on different planets. The program should prompt the user for his or her weight, and then display a menu with the planet names shown below. Use a switch structure to calculate the person's weight based on the planet they choose. Use the conversion values given for each planet to calculate the weight. Use a loop structure to allow users to select another planet or to exit when they are done. Save the program as **planets.cpp**.

Planet	**Multiply By**	**Planet**	**Multiply By**
Mercury	0.37	Saturn	1.15
Venus	0.88	Uranus	1.15
Mars	0.38	Neptune	1.12
Jupiter	2.64	Pluto	0.04

SIMULATION 3-3

The owner of the We-R-Lunch Deli needs a program to help her process lunch orders. She has a lunchtime special on sandwiches. The customer can order roast beef, ham, or turkey as the meat for their sandwich, and can choose from lettuce, tomatoes, pickles, and mayonnaise to be included on their sandwich. Additionally, they can choose either American or Swiss cheese as an extra cost option. Only one meat can be selected per sandwich. If the customer wants cheese on the sandwich, only one cheese can be selected. They can choose as many of the other items (lettuce, etc.) as they wish. The program should calculate and display the total cost of the sandwich when the customer has selected all options. Would you use C++ or Visual Basic to construct this program? Explain why you would choose one or the other, and explain what features of that language you would likely use for this application.

GLOSSARY

++ operator A C++ operator that increments an integer.

-- operator A C++ operator that decrements an integer.

A

algorithm A set of sequential instructions that are followed to solve a problem.

American Standard Code for Information Interchange (ASCII) A code most computers use to assign a number to each character. The numbers are used to represent the character internally.

appending The process of adding data to the end of an existing file.

argument Data passed to a function.

arithmetic operators Operators that perform math operations such as addition, subtraction, multiplication, and division.

array A group of variables of the same data type that appear together in the computer's memory.

assembly language A programming language that uses letters and numbers to represent machine-language instructions.

assignment operator An operator (=) that changes the value of the variable to the left of the operator.

automatic variables *See* Local variable.

B

Boolean variable A variable that can have only two possible variables: true or false.

bottom-up design A program design method that involves beginning at the bottom of the VTOC (Visual Table of Contents) and working up.

braces Special characters used to mark the beginning and ending of blocks of code.

C

case sensitive A characteristic of the C++ language that provides for the interpretation of uppercase and lowercase letters differently.

characters The letters and symbols available for use by a computer.

close The final step of using a data file.

comments Remarks in a program that are ignored by the compiler.

compiler A program that translates a high-level language into machine language, then saves the machine language so that the instructions do not have to be translated each time the program is run.

compiler directive Commands for the compiler, which are needed to effectively compile your program.

concatenation Adding one string onto the end of another string.

console I/O Using the screen and keyboard for input and output (I/O is an abbreviation of input/output).

constant Stores data that remains the same throughout a program's execution.

constructors Tell the compiler how to create an object in memory and what the initial values of its data will be.

containment The term used to describe a has-a relationship among classes.

control expression An expression that provides for a decision to be made in an if statement or to end a loop.

D

data type A specification that defines the type of data that can be stored in a variable or constant.

declaring Indicating to the compiler what type of variable you want and its name or identifier.

decrementing Subtracting 1 from a variable.

dot operator The operator used to access the members of a structure.

do while loop An iteration structure that repeats a statement or group of statements as long as a control expression is true at the end of the loop.

E

"E" notation Exponential notation.

elements Variables in an array.

end-of-line character *See* New line character.

executable file The output of a linker that can be executed without the need for an interpreter.

exponential notation A method of representing very large and very small numbers (also called scientific notation).

expression A math statement made up of terms, operators, and functions.

external variables *See* Global variable.

extraction operator The operator that outputs data to a stream.

F

field width The width of a formatting field when using the I/O manipulators.

file streams Objects that provide a data path to a file.

floating-point number A number that includes a decimal point.

flowchart A diagram made up of symbols used to illustrate an algorithm.

for loop An iteration structure that repeats one or more statements a specified number of times.

function A block of code that carries out a specific task.

fuzzy logic A logic system that allows for true, false, and variations in between.

G

global variable A variable declared before the main function and accessible by any function.

graphical user interface (GUI) A system for interacting with the computer user through pictures or icons.

H

Has-a relationship The relationship between classes where one class contains another class.

header file A file that serves as a link between your program code and standard C++ code that is needed to make your program run.

high-level language A programming language in which instructions do not necessarily correspond with the instruction set of the microprocessor.

I

identifiers Names given to variables and constants.

if structure A programming structure that executes code if certain conditions are met.

if/else structure A programming structure that executes one block of code if certain conditions are met and another block of code if the same conditions are not met.

incrementing Adding 1 to a variable.

infinite loop An iteration structure in which iterations continue indefinitely.

information hiding Data protection that is an important benefit of encapsulation.

inheritance The ability of one object to inherit the properties of another object.

initialize To assign a value to a variable.

input stream A stream used to receive input.

insertion operator The operator that gets data from a stream and puts it into a variable.

instance The data for one object that has been created in memory and has the behaviors defined by the class.

integer A whole number.

interpreter A program that translates the source code of a high-level language into machine language.

I/O manipulators A set of format options available in C++ that may be placed directly in the output statement.

Is-a relationship The relationship in which one object inherits characteristics from another class.

iteration A single loop or pass through a group of statements.

iteration structures Programming structures that repeat a group of statements one or more times (loops).

K

keyword Words that cannot be used as identifiers because they are part of the C++ language.

L

library functions Functions that come with your compiler.

linker A program that links object files created by a compiler into an executable program.

literals Hard-coded values.

local variable A variable declared within a function that is accessible only within the function.

logical operators Operators that allow *and*, *or*, and *not* to be implemented as part of logical expressions.

loop A programming structure that repeats a group of statements one or more times.

lowercase The noncapital (small) letters of the alphabet.

low-level language A programming language in which each instruction corresponds to one or only a few microprocessor instructions.

M

machine language The programming language (made up of ones and zeros) that a microprocessor understands.

main function The function by which every C++ program begins.

member functions Allow programmers using an object to send information to an object and receive information from an object.

members The functions and variables in a class definition.

menu A set of options presented to the user of a program.

message In object-oriented programming, the method used to transfer data.

method Code inside an object that is necessary to perform the operations on the object.

modulus operator The operator that provides integer division.

N

new line character The end-of-line character.

O

object code The machine-language code produced by a compiler.

object file The file produced by a compiler that contains machine-language code.

object-oriented paradigm A way of programming in which data and operations are seen as existing together in objects that are similar to objects in the real world.

object-oriented programming Building programs using the object-oriented paradigm.

one-way selection structure A selection structure in which the decision is whether to go "one way" or just bypass the code in the if structure.

open The operation that associates a physical disk file with a file pointer so that data in the file may be accessed.

operating system The program in charge of the fundamental system operations.

order of operations The rules related to the order in which operations (such as math operations) are performed.

overflow The condition where an integer becomes too large for its data type.

P

paradigm A model or set of rules that defines a way of programming.

parameter The variable that receives the value or any other identifier in the parentheses of the function declaration.

pass To send an argument to a function.

passing by reference A method of passing variables in which any changes you make to the variables are passed back to the calling function.

passing by value A method of passing variables in which a copy of the value in the variable is given to the function for it to use.

procedural paradigm A way of programming that focuses on the idea that all algorithms in a program are performed with functions and data that a programmer can see, understand, and change.

programming language A language that provides a way to program computers using instructions that can be understood by computers and people.

promotion The condition in which the data type of one variable is temporarily converted to match the data type of another variable so that a math operation can be performed using the mixed data type.

prototype A statement that defines the function for the compiler.

Q

quotient Quantity that results when one number is divided by another.

R

random-access file A data file that allows you to move directly to any data in the file.

relational operators Operators used to make comparisons.

remainder Quantity remaining when a number does not divide evenly into another.

reusability Using an object again after it has been coded and tested.

S

scope The availability of a variable to functions.

scope-resolution operator The operator that separates the class name and the function name in a member function.

selection structures Structures that allow for logical decisions in C++ programs.

sequence structures Execute statements one after another without changing the flow of a program.

sequential-access file A file with which you must start at the beginning and search each record to find the one you want.

short-circuit evaluation A feature of C++ that allows the program to stop evaluating an expression as soon as the outcome of the expression is known.

source code A program in the form of a high-level language.

special character A character that extends the normal alphanumeric characters.

standard input device The default input device, usually the keyboard.

standard output device The default output device, usually the screen.

statement Line of C++ code; statements end with a semicolon.

stream Data flowing from one place to another.

stream operation modes A mode that specifies the way you want to access the file.

string A group of characters put together to make one or more words.

string class An object-oriented class that allows strings to be included in programs.

string object An object for storing and processing strings.

subscript An index value that accesses an element of an array.

switch structure A selection structure capable of handling multiple options.

T

template class A class that can be used with any data type.

top-down design A program design method in which the general organization and flow of the program are decided before the details are coded.

truncate To drop the digits to the right of the decimal point, without rounding the value.

truth tables Diagrams that show the result of logical operations.

two-way selection structure A selection structure in which one block of code is executed if the control expression is true and another block is executed if the control expression is false.

typecast operator An operator that forces the data type of a variable to change.

typecasting Changing the data type of a variable using a typecast operator.

U

underflow When a value becomes too small for a variable to hold accurately.

uppercase The capital letters of the alphabet.

V

variable Holds data that can change while the program is running.

vector A one-dimensional array of any data type.

W

while loop An iteration structure that repeats a statement or group of statements as long as a control expression is true.

INTRODUCTION TO WEB PROGRAMMING WITH HTML AND JAVASCRIPT

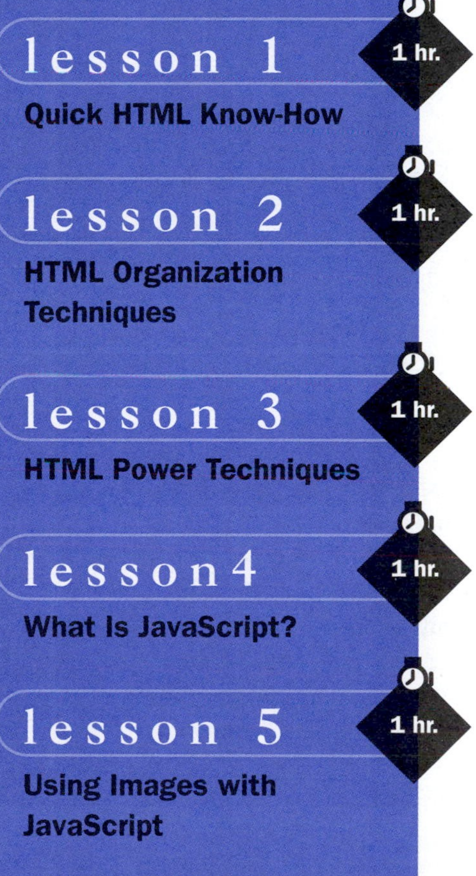

Estimated Time for Unit 4: 5 hours

LESSON 1

Quick HTML Know-How

OBJECTIVES

Upon completion of this lesson, you should be able to:

- Discover HTML tags.
- Enter your starting tags.
- Learn to save correctly.
- Integrate levels of headings into Web pages.
- Create unordered, ordered, and embedded lists.

Communicating on the Web

HTML, or Hypertext Markup Language, allows you to create Web pages. HTML organizes documents and tells Web browsers how Web pages should look on your computer screen. The colors, pictures, and backgrounds on Web pages are determined by HTML tags.

HTML tags work with any Web browser. If you create an HTML page, and do it correctly, your Web browser can read it. In fact, HTML is the official language of the World Wide Web. While there are many other languages spoken in cyberspace (like Java, VRML, and JavaScript), HTML is the most widely used.

HTML tags work everywhere on the Web. HTML tags display HTML pages on Macintosh or Windows computers. They work on Unix and Sun computers. They even work on Web television sets and on portable phones.

HTML tags are so simple that anyone can learn a few of the essential tags quickly. They usually appear in pairs enclosed in angle brackets. These brackets can be found on the comma and period keys on your keyboard. Press the Shift key to create them.

To more clearly understand how tags work, analyze this example. If you want to center the title of this lesson on a Web page, you can write:

```
<CENTER>Quick HTML Know-How</CENTER>
```

Notice that there is a starting tag, <CENTER>, and a closing tag, </CENTER>. The only difference between the two tags is a slash / following the first angle bracket in the closing tag. The tags, <CENTER> </CENTER>, form a pair of tags. And if you haven't guessed already, these tags are called "center" tags. Anything between these tags will be centered on the page. Anything outside of the tags will not be affected by the command. It can't get any simpler than that!

Uncover the Page Beneath the Page

The Web is full of Web pages. Some are very interesting and exciting, some are too busy, and some are dull and boring. It doesn't matter if a page is interesting or dull; all Web pages have some very similar characteristics. Let's see what we mean. Look at Figure 1-1A.

Net Fun

If you want to visit the best listing of super Web pages on the Web, you don't have to look any further than Yahoo! Yahoo! catalogs all the great Web pages in categories like Entertainment, Business, Education, and our two favorite categories, HTML and JavaScript. Visit Yahoo! at www.yahoo.com.

FIGURE 1-1A
This is a sample Web page.

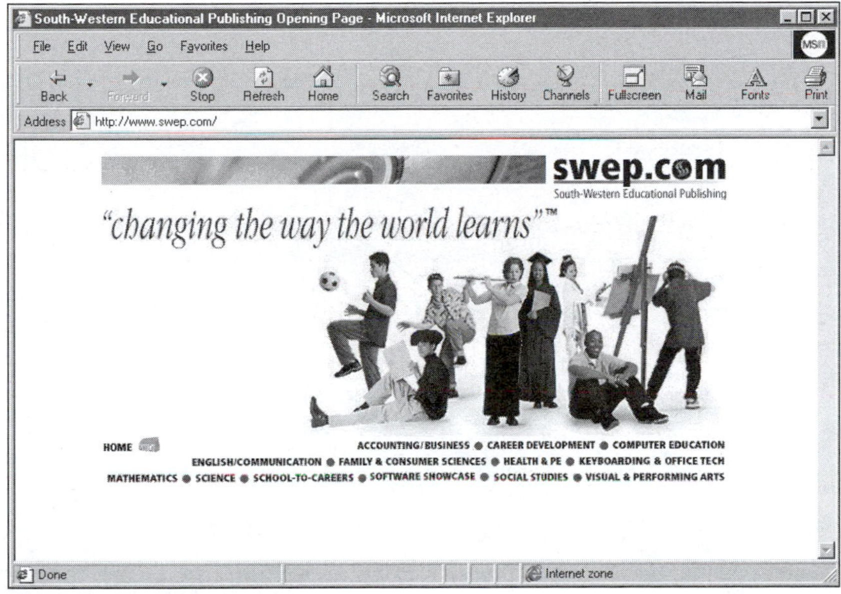

All of the words, pictures, and colors that you see in Figure 1-1A are organized and created by the HTML tags you see in the next figure, Figure 1-1B. Figures 1-1A and 1-1B are actually the same page viewed in different ways.

FIGURE 1-1B

These are the HTML tags for the Web page shown in Figure 1-1A.

```
swep.html - Notepad
File  Edit  Search  Help
<html>

<head>
<title>South-Western Educational Publishing Opening Page</title>
</head>
<script LANGUAGE="JavaScript">
<!-- hide script

function preloadImages() {
    if (document.images) {
    if (typeof document.WM == 'undefined'){
      document.WM = new Object();
    }
    document.WM.loadedImages = new Array();
    var argLength = preloadImages.arguments.length;
    for(arg=0;arg<argLength;arg++) {
      document.WM.loadedImages[arg] = new Image();
      document.WM.loadedImages[arg].src = preloadImages.arguments[arg];
    }
  }
}

function pickgif(x,iname)
{
        var docname = "window.document." + iname;
        var fulliname = "images/"+iname;
        var maininame = "images/";

        if (x) {
           fulliname=fulliname+"roll.gif";
           maininame=maininame+iname+"rollmain.gif";}
        else {
           fulliname=fulliname+".gif";
           maininame=maininame+"shoes.jpg";}
```

INTERNET MILESTONE

The World Wide Web (WWW) was created in the late 1980s in Europe. It was used mostly in academic circles for the next five years. However, it didn't capture the public's imagination until 1994, when a Web browser called Mosaic came on the scene. Mosaic was created at the University of Illinois. It was the first Web browser that allowed pictures and sound to accompany Web pages.

In just a few short years, the World Wide Web became the advertising and commercial medium that we see today. Billions of dollars were invested by companies hoping to cash in on this new information-sharing system. Suddenly, thousands of corporate Webmasters began to learn HTML so they could put their business Web pages online.

Figure 1-1B isn't very pretty. It shows the HTML tags that create the more exciting page shown in Figure 1-1A. Figure 1-1B shows exactly what the page behind the colorful page really looks like. The Web browser interprets the tags and creates the Web page the average Web surfer sees.

There are lots of tags and lots of ways to use them. But this hint should help you from getting confused: Remember that HTML tags are just instructions to the Web browser. They tell the browser how to display information. Many times you can look at the final Web page and guess what tags created the effect. If you remember this hint, learning HTML will be much easier.

Now it's your turn. Follow these steps to open a Web page you like. Viewing the page behind the page is as easy as selecting Source or some similar command from the View menu in your browser, as you can see in Figures 1-2A and 1-2B.

STEP-BY-STEP 1.1

1. Open your Web browser by double-clicking on its icon, as shown in Figures 1-2A and 1-2B.

2. When a page appears, use your mouse to move the pointer over the View menu, as shown in Figures 1-3A and 1-3B.

3. Select View followed by Source in the Internet Explorer (IE) browser or View followed by either Source, Page Source, or Document Source in your version of the Netscape Navigator browser. (Note: Different browsers may use different words for this command. Look around; the option will be there.)

4. Examine the tags that appear on the page beneath the colorful page most people see. The tags will look something like the tags you saw in Figure 1-1B at the start of this lesson.

5. Jump around to three or four other Web pages and view the source code. List seven tags that you keep running into, and try to guess what they do.

FIGURE 1-2A
Double-click the Netscape Communicator icon.

FIGURE 1-2B
Double-click the Internet Explorer icon.

FIGURE 1-3A
Select the View, Page Source command in Netscape.

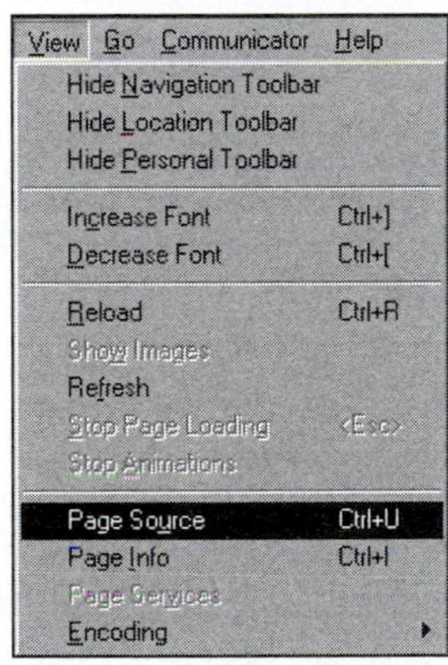

FIGURE 1-3B
Select the View, Source command in Internet Explorer.

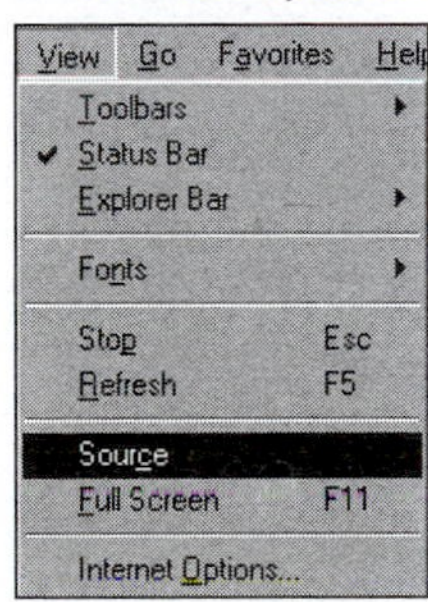

Thinking About Technology

The World Wide Web is a large Web of computer networks that share HTML files. How many millions or billions of Web pages are there out in cyberspace? You could visit a new Web page every minute of every day for the rest of your life and never come close to reading a fraction of the available Web pages. While HTML has allowed people to share Web pages easily, has HTML also contributed to information overload?

Web Page, Home Page, Welcome Page, HTML Page . . . What's the Difference?

There are many terms used to describe HTML pages or documents. The truth is, these names are used so interchangeably that most people are totally unaware that there are slight distinctions in the meaning for the following terms:

- **Web page:** A Web page, or Web document, is any page created in HTML that can be placed on the World Wide Web.
- **Home page:** A home page is the main or primary Web page for a corporation, organization, or individual. Your home page is the first page you see as you start up your Web browser. When you click on the Home icon in your browser, you will go directly to your starting home page.
- **Welcome page:** A welcome page is designed especially for new visitors to a Web site.
- **HTML page:** An HTML page, or HTML document, is any document created in HTML that can be displayed on the World Wide Web.
- **Web site:** A Web site can include a collection of many interconnected Web pages organized by a specific company, organization, college or university, government agency, or individual. Web sites are stored on Web servers. There may be many Web sites on each service and thousands of HTML pages on each Web site.

Don't let these subtle distinctions get in the way of your understanding of how the Web works. Underneath it all, you will still find HTML tags doing their job.

Enter Your Mystery Tags the Old-Fashioned Way

There are many ways to create HTML Tags. You can use specialized software, such as FrontPage by Microsoft or Dreamweaver from Macromedia, to create super Web pages. With these programs, you can organize your HTML page, enter text, move things around, and create superior Web page effects without ever entering an HTML tag. You can do the same with many of the newer versions of word processing programs, such as Microsoft Word, WordPerfect, or WordPro. These word processors have HTML tags built right in.

You will want to use one of these programs for most of your Web pages. They are easy to use and give you lots of powerful HTML tools with which to work. However, for this activity, you are going to enter HTML tags the old-fashioned way. And there are good reasons for doing this:

- By entering a few tags, you will develop a deeper understanding of how HTML really works.
- You will be able to troubleshoot Web pages when picky little errors occur.
- You will be able to view other pages and learn how they achieved certain effects.

- You will better understand the file and folder structures found on Web computers.
- Most importantly, you will understand how HTML and JavaScript work together.

Learning to enter a few HTML tags in the old-fashioned way will give you a big advantage as you start to learn JavaScript later in this unit. So, let's quickly cover the basics.

What to Use

Almost any word processing program or text editor will work for creating both HTML and JavaScript. This is one of the reasons HTML and JavaScript are so popular. You don't need specialized software tools to create exciting Web pages like you need for Java, Shockwave, or some of the other software-intensive options. Our recommendation is to use the simplest, most basic tools available:

- In Windows, you can use Notepad from the Accessories menu.
- On a Macintosh, you can use SimpleText.

These programs are easy to use and available on nearly every computer on the planet. You can also use your favorite word processing program, such as Microsoft Word, WordPerfect, WordPro, ClarisWorks, or even Microsoft Works. However, you will need to experiment a bit with each word processing program to learn its little idiosyncrasies. Instructions for Word and ClarisWorks are provided as examples. Most other word processors have similar features. Check the software's help system if you have any difficulties, or revert to Notepad or SimpleText to complete the activities.

Net Tip

Uppercase or Lowercase
HTML is not case-sensitive. You can use uppercase <TAGS>, or you can use lowercase <tags>. It really doesn't matter. However, each Web page designer has a preference. When asked, most HTML taggers will tell you that uppercase <TAGS> are easier to see. So, if you are emphasizing the tags, use uppercase <TAGS>. But, if you would rather emphasize the words in the document, use lowercase <tags>. You can even mix uppercase <TAGS> and lowercase <tags> together, like this <Tag>, or like this <TAG> </tag>. However, mixing cases is not considered good form. Do it if you like, but it's best to use all uppercase or all lowercase.

Other more sophisticated programs, like FrontPage and Dreamweaver, really get the job done. Both provide options that allow you to see the tags. If you are using one of these two programs, click the HTML Source option so you can enter the tags directly.

In this step-by-step activity, you will learn how to enter tags. In the next activity, you will learn to save your tags correctly. You will want to complete these activities together. Otherwise, you may have to enter everything twice!

STEP-BY-STEP 1.2

1. Open Notepad, SimpleText, or your favorite word processing software.
2. Start a new document if necessary.
3. Enter the tags shown in Figure 1-4 in the exact order. Don't leave out an angle bracket < or a slash /. Everything is important.

FIGURE 1-4
Enter these tags exactly as shown here.

```
<HTML>
<TITLE></TITLE>
<BODY>
<CENTER></CENTER>
<P></P>
<P></P>
<P></P>
<P></P>
<P></P>
</BODY>
</HTML>
```

4. The tags you just entered are called the basic tags. They include a standard set of tags that appear in most Web pages. But your page will look very sad without some text. Enter the text between the tags, as shown in Figure 1-5. Notice that the new text to be entered is shown in bold.

5. Go on to Step-by-Step 1.3 now and learn how to save HTML pages so you won't have to enter all of this data again!

FIGURE 1-5
Enter the text between the tags exactly as shown here.

```
<HTML>
<TITLE>HTML and JavaScript</TITLE>
<BODY>
<CENTER>Creating HTML and JavaScript</CENTER>
<P>Learning to create HTML tags can help you in many ways:</P>
<P>You will develop a deeper understanding of how HTML really works.</P>
<P>You will be able to troubleshoot Web pages when errors occur.</P>
<P>You will be able to view other pages and learn how certain effects are
   created.</P>
<P>You will understand how HTML and JavaScript work together.</P>
</BODY>
</HTML>
```

Save and View Your HTML Page

HTML documents are text files. This means that they are saved in the simplest way possible. For the most part, text files only save the letters you see on your keyboard. All of the sophisticated word processing commands are erased, leaving just the letters.

Saving as text allows HTML to move quickly over the Web. However, the problem with text files is that most people don't know how to save them. Before you save, there are a few things you need to know.

File Types and File Extensions

To tell one kind of file from another, computers often add file extensions to filenames. Sometimes you can see these extensions on your computer and sometimes you can't. Depending on your computer's settings, the extensions may or may not be visible, but the software on your computer knows the kinds of file types it can open.

Extensions are used a lot. For example, in Windows, text files are saved with a .txt ending or extension. If you use a word processor much, you may have seen these popular extensions:

.doc	Microsoft Word documents
.rtf	Microsoft's Rich Text Format
.wpd	Corel WordPerfect documents
.txt	text files
.html	HTML files
.htm	HTML files on some computer systems

HTML files are text files with an .html or an .htm extension. While the format you need for HTML is called text, the ending or extension must be .html (or .htm if you are using some older Windows-based software programs). The .html extension signals to the Web browser that this is an HTML text file. The .html extension is like putting up a sign saying, "Hey browser, read me. I'm an HTML document."

Follow along. We are going to show you how to save with different software programs. Pick the software that most closely resembles the software on your computer system. They are:

- Notepad
- Microsoft Word
- SimpleText
- ClarisWorks for Macintosh

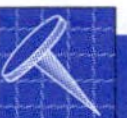

Net Tip

Create a folder in which to keep your files. Creating folders is easy. On a Macintosh, select **New Folder** from the **File** menu. Name the folder with a name you will remember. On a newer Windows computer, it's the same process. Select **File**, **New**, and then **Folder**. Or, click the **Create New Folder** box in the **Save As** dialog box. Name the folder.
On an older Windows 3.1 computer, open File Manager, select **File**, and then select **Create Directory**.
The term *directory* was used long before the word *folders*. Folders inside other folders were called subdirectories. Remember the terms *directory* and *subdirectory*. They are still commonly used in cyberspace.

STEP-BY-STEP 1.3

1. Select Save As from the File menu. (Word users beware! DO NOT select Save As HTML from the File menu if that option appears! Use the regular Save As command.)
2. From the Save As dialog box, create a New Folder in which to save your HTML and JavaScript work.

3. For both Notepad in Windows and SimpleText for Macintosh, the steps are very similar. (Note: Word processing users should skip to step 4.)
   a. Select the folder into which you wish to save your files.
   b. Name your file as One.html, as shown in Figure 1-6. (Note: Older Windows systems will only accept an .htm extension.) Check with your insructor to make sure you saved your file properly. If everything saved okay, skip to step 5.

4. In your word processing software, there are a few additional steps. While Notepad and SimpleText automatically save as text only, word processors save in their own unique format. You must select the proper text format from your saving options. Instructions for Word and ClarisWorks are provided to help you learn this important step. Other word processors also have text saving options. Check with your instructor to make sure you are following the steps properly for your software.

MICROSOFT WORD FOR WINDOWS 95, 98, OR NT

   a. Locate the folder in which you want to place your file.
   b. Select Text Only as the Save as type, as shown in Figure 1-7.
   c. Name your file One.html. (Note: In older Windows programs, the name will be truncated or shortened to One.htm.)
   d. Click Save.

FIGURE 1-6
Name the text file with an .html extension.

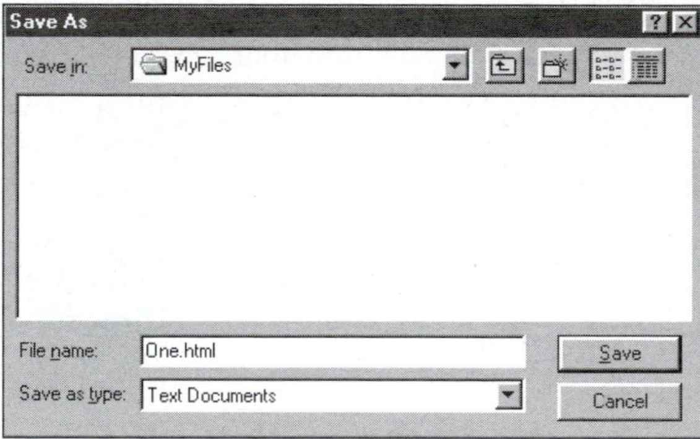

FIGURE 1-7
This saves text files in Microsoft Word.

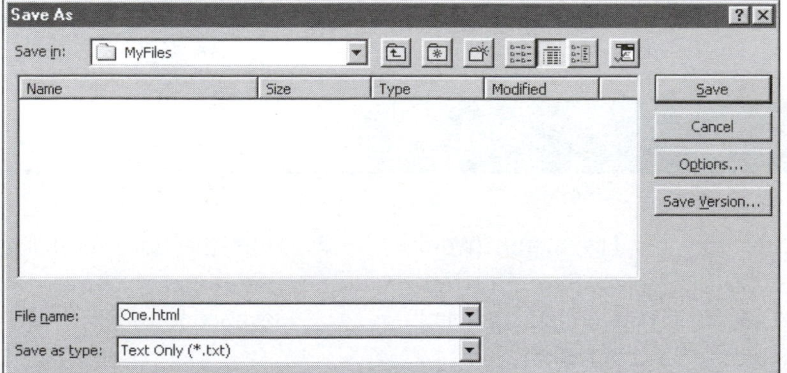

CLARISWORKS FOR MACINTOSH

Macintosh computers make saving text files very easy.

a. Locate the folder into which you want to place your file.

b. Select Text as the Save As option.

c. Name your file One.html, as shown in Figure 1-8.

d. Click Save.

5. Viewing your HTML page in your Web browser is easy. There are a few minor browser variations, however, so we will give you several examples to look at. We will show you how to do this in Windows and with Macintosh browsers.

INTERNET EXPLORER 4.0 IN WINDOWS 95, 98, NT, OR HIGHER

a. Open your Web browser.

b. Click File, and then click Open.

c. Click on the Browse button to locate the folder in which you saved your file.

d. Select your HTML file, and click Open.

e. Click OK, as shown in Figure 1-9.

FIGURE 1-8
This saves text files in ClarisWorks.

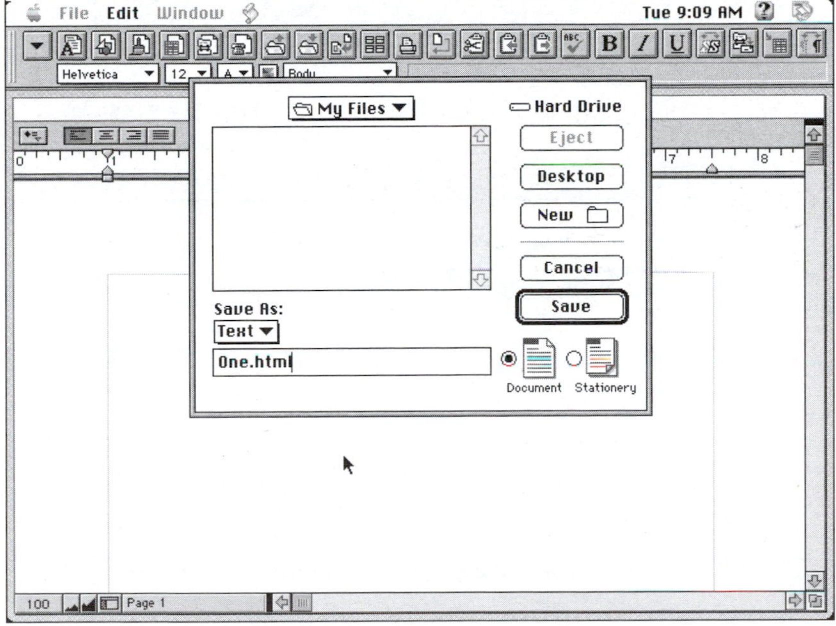

FIGURE 1-9
Find your file.

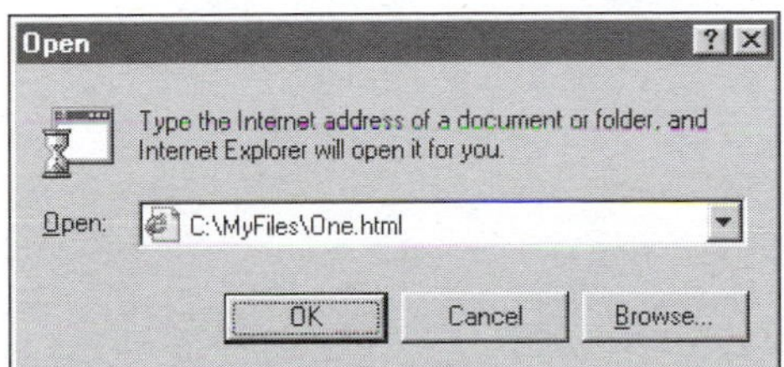

STEP-BY-STEP 1.3 CONTINUED

NETSCAPE 4.0 IN WINDOWS 95, 98, NT, OR HIGHER

a. Open your Web browser.

b. Click File, and then click Open Page.

c. Click on the Choose File button to locate the folder in which you saved your file.

d. Select your HTML file, and click Open.

e. Click Open, as shown in Figure 1-10.

INTERNET EXPLORER FOR MACINTOSH

a. Open your Web browser.

b. Click File, and then click Open.

c. Browse to the folder where you saved your file.

d. Select your HTML file, and click Open.

e. Click Open, as shown in Figure 1-11.

FIGURE 1-10
Search for your file.

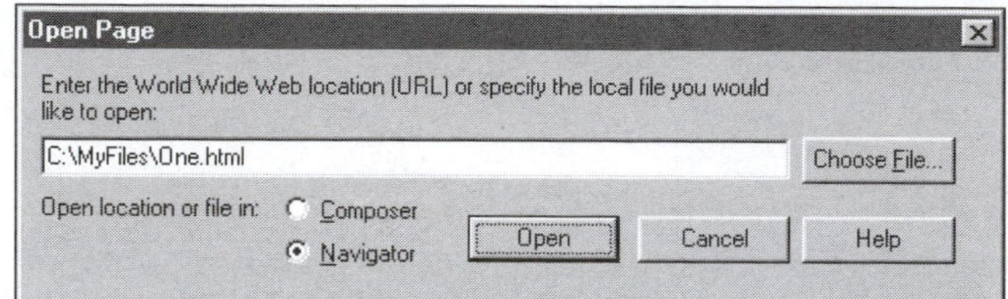

FIGURE 1-11
Find your file.

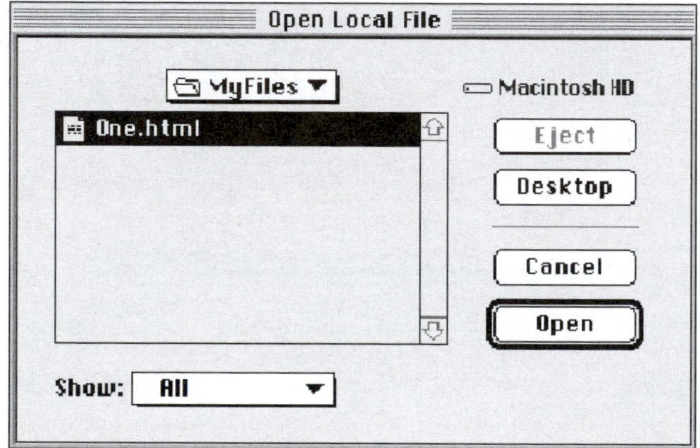

NETSCAPE FOR MACINTOSH

a. Open your Web browser.
b. Click File, and then click Open File.
c. Browse to the folder where you saved your file.
d. Select your HTML file, and click Open.
e. Click Open, as shown in Figure 1-12.

6. View your file. It should look like Figure 1-13.

7. How does your Web page look? If you need to make corrections, make the corrections in the HTML file, save again, then return to your browser and look again at the changes you have made.

FIGURE 1-12
Find your file.

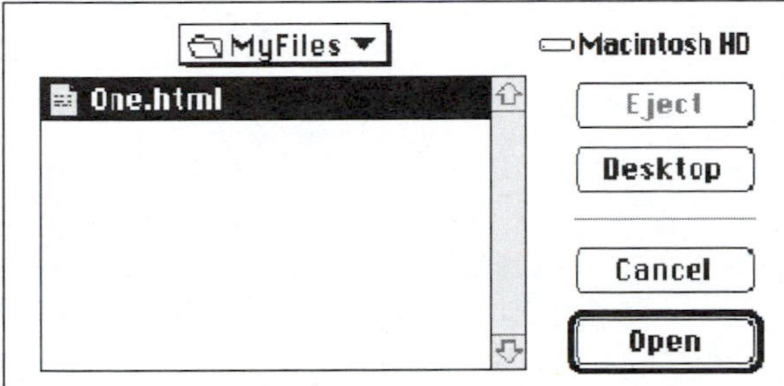

FIGURE 1-13
Congratulations! Your Web page probably looks like this sample.

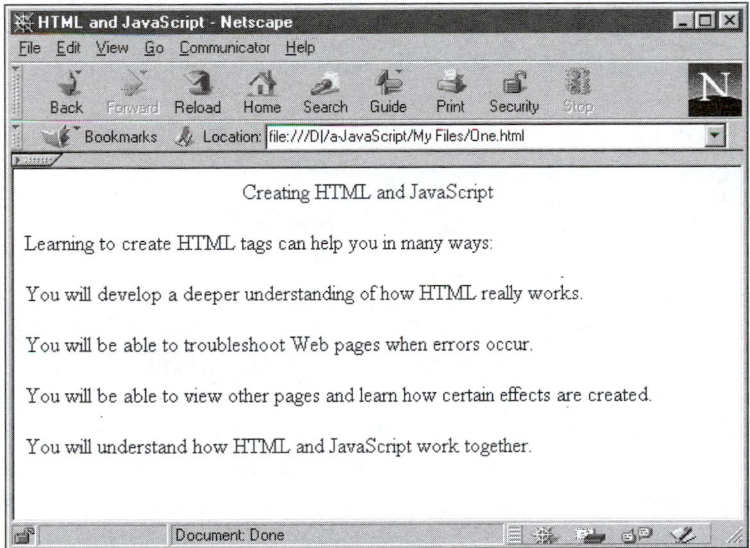

Using Headings

Most printed documents use headings to help the reader find important portions of text. Think of a report you have written for school. The main heading usually appears at the top and in the center of the page. Subheadings or secondary headings usually appear at the side of the paper. They are often shown in bold.

HTML gives you six standard headings or title sizes to choose from. In later activities, you will learn more sophisticated ways to manipulate the size and appearance of text. Nevertheless, the heading tags give you an easy way to control the size of selected text, making it stand out so your reader can view the headings clearly.

The heading tags are easy to remember. They use a letter H with a number from 1 to 6 to indicate the level of the heading. Heading numbers indicate the level of importance for marked headings, with 1 being the most prominent and 6 being the least prominent. Look for:

```
<H1></H1>
<H2></H2>
<H3></H3>
<H4></H4>
<H5></H5>
<H6></H6>
```

Anything inside the heading tags will be made larger or smaller, depending on the number. For example:

```
<H1>VERY BIG</H1>
<H3>In the Middle</H3>
<H6>Very Small</H6>
```

INTERNET MILESTONE

In the last few years, Netscape's Navigator and Microsoft's Internet Explorer browsers have been fighting it out for supremacy in the Web browser world. This wasn't the first browser battle. In 1994, the dominant browser was called Mosaic. At the time Netscape came on the scene, Mosaic was adding 600,000 new users a month. But things changed in a hurry. In the first three months of 1995, Netscape's Navigator browser gained a reputation for being a faster browser. By the end of the year it commanded a whopping 80 percent of the browser market.

Netscape's dominance was quickly challenged by rival Microsoft, which came out with its Internet Explorer browser. Microsoft gave away copies of its browser in hopes of cutting into Netscape's lead. Microsoft also had an advantage in that its Windows operating system ran on over 90 percent of personal computers. By making Windows and Internet Explorer work together, Microsoft created a more user-friendly Web system.

Microsoft's advantage, however, led to many legal battles. Several antitrust lawsuits argued that Microsoft was using its dominance in Windows to crush Netscape and to eliminate competition unfairly. Microsoft claimed it was simply adding more value for its customers by making its Internet Explorer browser easier to access.

In this step-by-step activity, you will open the HTML file you have been working on and add the heading or title tags.

STEP-BY-STEP 1.4

1. Open your word processing software.

2. Reopen your One.html or One.htm file.

IMPORTANT NOTE to Notepad users: Select All Files under the Files of type option, as shown in Figure 1-14A. Otherwise, you will not be able to view your .html or .htm file!

IMPORTANT NOTE to Microsoft Word users: When you open an .html file, Word may display your Web page as it would appear in a Web browser. In order to view the HTML tags, select HTML Source from the View menu, as shown in Figure 1-14B, and you can continue to work on your tags.

FIGURE 1-14A
Notepad users must select **All Files** in order to view their tags.

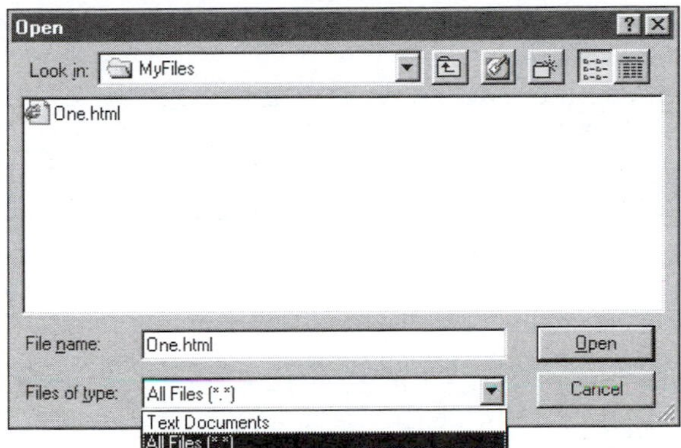

FIGURE 1-14B
Microsoft Word users must select **HTML Source** in order to view their tags.

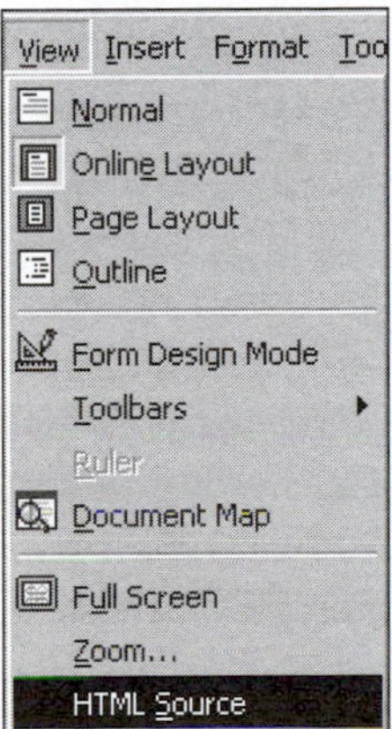

STEP-BY-STEP 1.4 CONTINUED

3. Enter the heading tags shown in Figure 1-15.

4. Save your new HTML page as Two.html or Two.htm.

5. Open your Web browser, open the Two.html file, and view it. It should look like Figure 1-16.

FIGURE 1-15
Add these heading tags.

```
<HTML>
<TITLE> HTML and JavaScript</TITLE>
<BODY>
<CENTER><H1>Creating HTML and JavaScript</H1></CENTER>
<P><H2>Learning to create HTML tags can help you in many ways:</H2></P>
<P><H3>You will develop a deeper understanding of how HTML really
  works.</H3></P>
<P><H4>You will be able to troubleshoot Web pages when errors
  occur.</H4></P>
<P><H5>You will be able to view other pages and learn how certain effects
  are created.</H5></P>
<P><H6>You will understand how HTML and JavaScript work together.</H6></P>
</BODY>
</HTML>
```

FIGURE 1-16
Headings appear in a Web page.

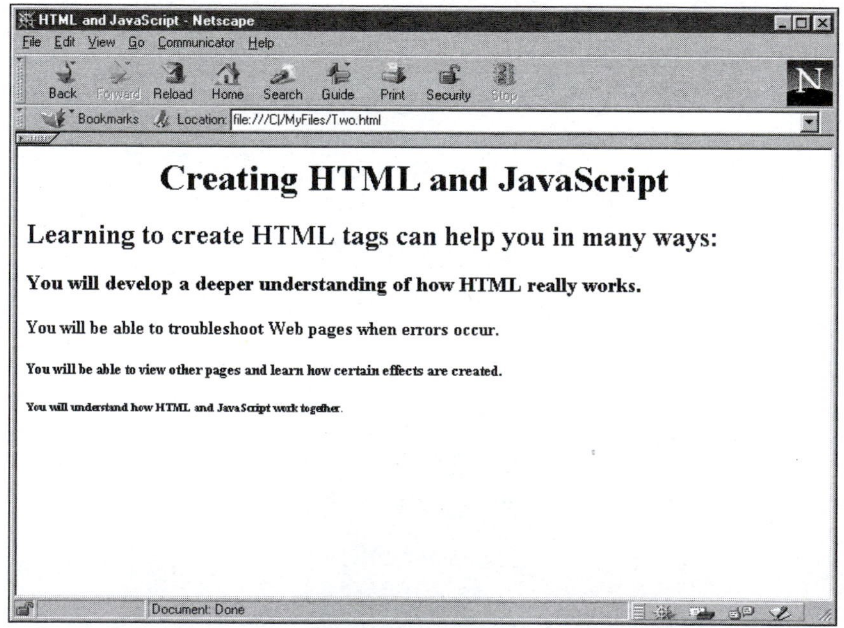

Thinking About Technology

Heading tags really change the look of a page. In our example in Figure 1-16, however, the heading tags are misused. At best, there are only three levels of the document information:

<H1> The title at the top

<H2> The introductory line followed by a colon (:)

<H3> The list of four reasons to learn HTML tags

Return to your document and reorganize the heading tags. Use no more than three <H></H> tags. Think about it for a second, then make your document comfortable to read, emphasizing the three levels this document dictates. Then save as Two.html.

IMPORTANT NOTE to Notepad users: Remember to select All Files under the Files As Type option, as shown in Figure 1-14A. Otherwise, you will not be able to view your .html or .htm file!

IMPORTANT NOTE to Microsoft Word users: Remember that when you open an .html file, Word may display your Web page as it would appear in a Web browser. To view the HTML tags, select HTML Source from the View menu, as shown in Figure 1-14B, and you can continue to work on your tags.

Numbered and Bulleted Lists

Net Fun

Do you want to visit an exciting place? Try Excite at www.excite.com. Excite is one of the most popular Web searching systems. With Excite, you can look up anything on everything. Try entering the search words HTML or JavaScript in the search window and see what you get.

In the last section, you were asked to reorganize your Two.html file and use the <H> tags in a more consistent manner. In this activity, we are going to whip things into shape even further.

One of the most powerful ways to organize information on a Web page is by the use of lists. There are several kinds of lists, including the following:

Unordered (usually bulleted) lists <UL></UL>

Ordered or numbered lists <OL></OL>

The unordered list tags <UL></UL> will create a bulleted list. Start your list with the opening <UL> unordered list tag, mark the items to be listed with the list <LI></LI> tag, and place a </UL> tag at the end of your list. Try it!

Creating an Unordered List

Unordered lists are used whenever the items in the list can appear in any order. This step-by-step activity shows you how to create an unordered list in HTML.

STEP-BY-STEP 1.5

IMPORTANT NOTE to Notepad users: Remember to select All Files under the Files As Type option, as shown in Figure 1-14A. Otherwise, you will not be able to view your .html or .htm file!

NOTE to Microsoft Word users: Remember that when you open an .html file, Word may display your Web page as it would appear in a Web browser. In order to view the HTML tags, select HTML Source from the View menu, as shown in Figure 1-14B, and you can continue to work on your tags.

1. Open your Two.html file.
2. Enter the <UL></UL> tags at the start and at the end of the list, as shown in Figure 1-17.
3. Add the <LI></LI> tags for each sentence in the list, as shown in Figure 1-17.
4. Save your file as Three.html.
5. View your page to see how it looks. It should be similar to Figure 1-18.

FIGURE 1-17
Enter the Unordered list tags.

```
<HTML>
<TITLE> HTML and JavaScript</TITLE>
<BODY>
<CENTER><H1>Creating HTML and JavaScript</H1></CENTER>
<P><H2>Learning to create HTML tags can help you in many ways:</H2></P>

<UL>
<LI><P><H3>You will develop a deeper understanding of how HTML really
  works.</H3></P></LI>
<LI><P><H3>You will be able to troubleshoot Web pages when errors
  occur.</H3></P></LI>
<LI><P><H3>You will be able to view other pages and learn how certain
  effects are created.</H3></P></LI>
<LI><P><H3>You will understand how HTML and JavaScript work
  together.</H3></P></LI>
</UL>

</BODY>
</HTML>
```

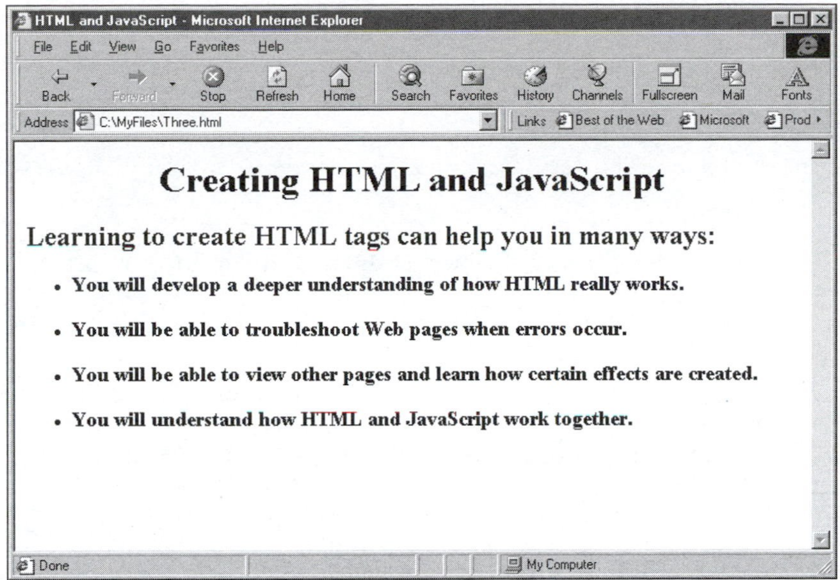

HTML and JavaScript - Microsoft Internet Explorer
File Edit View Go Favorites Help
Back Forward Stop Refresh Home Search Favorites History Channels Fullscreen Mail Fonts
Address C:\MyFiles\Three.html
Links Best of the Web Microsoft Prod
Creating HTML and JavaScript
Learning to create HTML tags can help you in many ways:
You will develop a deeper understanding of how HTML really works.
You will be able to troubleshoot Web pages when errors occur.
You will be able to view other pages and learn how certain effects are created.
You will understand how HTML and JavaScript work together.
Done
My Computer

FIGURE 1-18
An unordered list appears.

Creating an Ordered List

Ordered lists are used whenever the items should appear in a specific order or if you are counting items in a list. This list gives four reasons to learn HTML tags. Let's quickly convert it to an ordered or numbered list:

6. Open your Three.html file.

7. Change the pair of <UL></UL> tags to <OL></OL> tags, as shown in Figure 1-19. No other changes are necessary. (Note: Don't use a zero; use the letter O for *ordered.*)

IMPORTANT NOTE to Notepad users: Remember to select All Files under the Files As Type option, as shown in Figure 1-14A. Otherwise, you will not be able to view your .html or .htm file!

NOTE to Microsoft Word users: Remember that when you open an .html file, Word may display your Web page as it would appear in a Web browser. In order to view the HTML tags, select HTML Source from the View menu, as shown in Figure 1-14B, and you can continue to work on your tags.

STEP-BY-STEP 1.5 CONTINUED

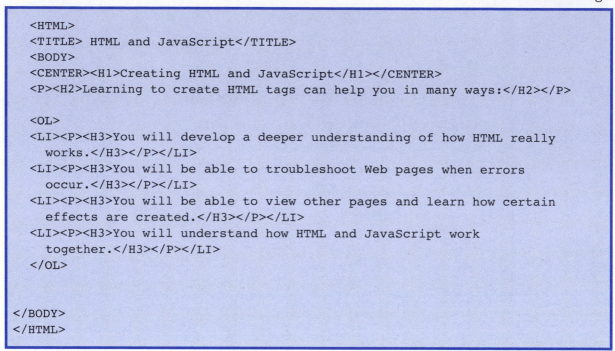

FIGURE 1-19
Enter the ordered list tags.

```
<HTML>
<TITLE> HTML and JavaScript</TITLE>
<BODY>
<CENTER><H1>Creating HTML and JavaScript</H1></CENTER>
<P><H2>Learning to create HTML tags can help you in many ways:</H2></P>

<OL>
<LI><P><H3>You will develop a deeper understanding of how HTML really
  works.</H3></P></LI>
<LI><P><H3>You will be able to troubleshoot Web pages when errors
  occur.</H3></P></LI>
<LI><P><H3>You will be able to view other pages and learn how certain
  effects are created.</H3></P></LI>
<LI><P><H3>You will understand how HTML and JavaScript work
  together.</H3></P></LI>
</OL>


</BODY>
</HTML>
```

8. Save your file as Four.html.

9. View your page to see how it looks. It should look similar to Figure 1-20.

FIGURE 1-20
An ordered or numbered list appears.

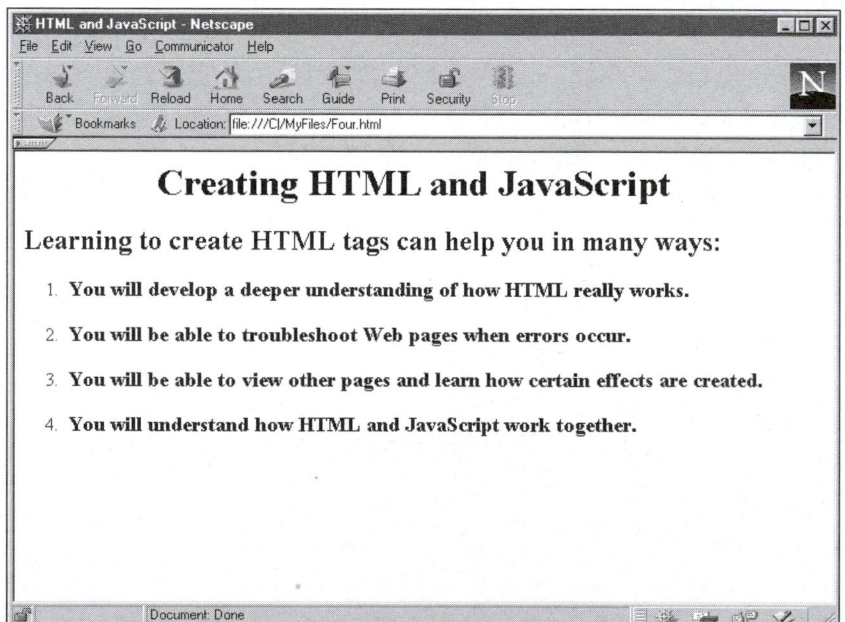

STEP-BY-STEP 1.5 CONTINUED

Embedding and Indenting Lists

Sometimes you may want to have a list inside a list, as you would in an outline. In this set of steps, you will indent and create unordered lists inside the numbered list.

10. Open your Four.html file.

11. Add two pairs of <UL></UL> tags in the middle of the list, as shown in Figure 1-21.

FIGURE 1-21
Enter the unordered list tags.

```
<HTML>
<TITLE> HTML and JavaScript</TITLE>
<BODY>
<CENTER><H1>Creating HTML and JavaScript</H1></CENTER>
<P><H2>Learning to create HTML tags can help you in many ways:</H2></P>

<OL>
<LI><P><H3>You will develop a deeper understanding of how HTML really
  works.</H3></P></LI>

<UL>
<LI><P><H3>You will be able to troubleshoot Web pages when errors
  occur.</H3></P></LI>
<UL>

<LI><P><H3>You will be able to view other pages and learn how certain
  effects are created.</H3></P></LI>
</UL>
</UL>

<LI><P><H3>You will understand how HTML and JavaScript work
  together.</H3></P></LI>
</OL>
</BODY>
</HTML>
```

STEP-BY-STEP 1.5 CONTINUED

12. Save your file as Five.html.

13. View your page to see how it looks. It should look similar to Figure 1-22.

FIGURE 1-22
Embedded and indented lists are shown.

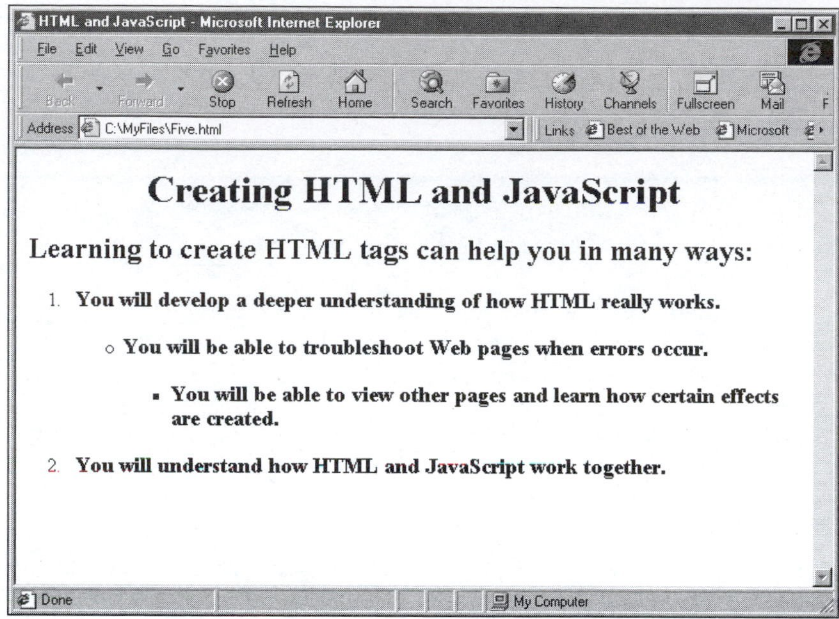

HTML and JavaScript - Microsoft Internet Explorer
File Edit View Go Favorites Help
Back Forward Stop Refresh Home Search Favorites History Channels Fullscreen Mail
Address C:\MyFiles\Five.html
Links Best of the Web Microsoft
Creating HTML and JavaScript
Learning to create HTML tags can help you in many ways:
1. You will develop a deeper understanding of how HTML really works.
You will be able to troubleshoot Web pages when errors occur.
You will be able to view other pages and learn how certain effects are created.
2. You will understand how HTML and JavaScript work together.
Done
My Computer

Thinking About Technology

How can you create a sophisticated outline in HTML? You know, the kind you had to do for your last research paper? Can you see yourself doing your next research paper online in HTML? Find the error in the following list:

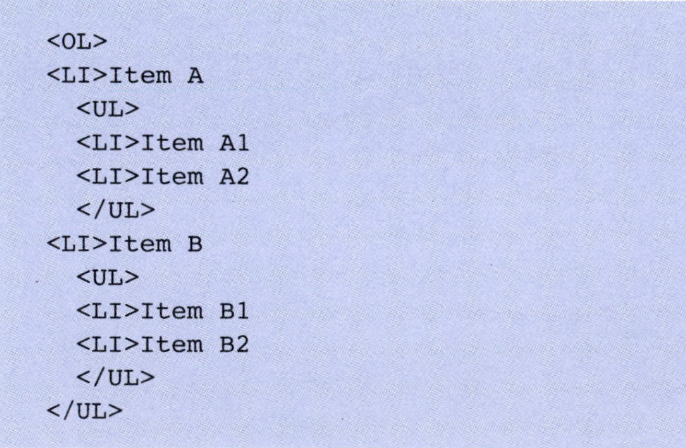

```
<OL>
<LI>Item A
  <UL>
  <LI>Item A1
  <LI>Item A2
  </UL>
<LI>Item B
  <UL>
  <LI>Item B1
  <LI>Item B2
  </UL>
</UL>
```

Net Careers

A Webmaster is the person assigned to maintain Web pages for a Web site. Not only do Webmasters need to know how to create Web pages, they also need to know how to write clearly, use artwork effectively, and create links from one page to another. They also must help others post their documents on the Web in an attractive and readable way. Webmasters often work long hours, updating pages late into the night when other people are home watching reruns. Some of the best ways to prepare for a Webmaster job would be to take every Computer Education, Language Arts, and Art class that your school offers.

LESSON 1 REVIEW QUESTIONS

Write a brief answer to the following questions.

1. Think of a way to explain how HTML tags work to people who have never before created a Web page. How would you explain HTML to a novice?

2. Explain the process of viewing the HTML source code for an HTML Web page.

3. Explain how to save HTML text pages.

4. What are file name extensions? Give examples.

5. What are Mosaic, Netscape Navigator, and Internet Explorer? What has each contributed to the growth of the Web?

LESSON 1 PROJECTS

PROJECT 1-1

You have just been hired as the Webmaster for Great Applications, Inc., but your HTML skills are limited. You need to find some good HTML information fast! What do you do?

The answer is obvious. Hit the Web. Pick a search engine, such as Yahoo!, Excite, Lycos, or some other search tool, and enter these search words:

- Hypertext Markup Language
- HTML
- HTML Guides
- Learning HTML

Record the title and URL or Web address, and write a brief summary of the helpful HTML Web pages you find.

PROJECT 1-2

Great Applications, Inc. is looking for design ideas for their new Web site welcome page. In a team of three or four, create a list of your favorite Web pages. Find seven great Web pages and discuss what makes them so cool. Vote to rank the seven welcome pages from Number 1 to Number 7.

SCANS

PROJECT 1-3

Web sites are important for many companies, groups, and individuals. We all know that many businesses would fail without a quality Web site. But just how important is a great-looking Web site for noncommercial organizations and government agencies? List reasons why these organizations need Web sites.

Government agencies:

Nonprofit organizations:

Universities:

LESSON 2

HTML Organization Techniques

OBJECTIVES

Upon completion of this lesson, you should be able to:

- Organize page information with single and double spacing.
- Organize page information with lines.
- Implement attributes and values.
- Change Web page color defaults by altering attributes and values.
- Alter the text colors.
- Create links to another spot within your own document.
- Create links to a URL or Web page anywhere on the WWW.
- Create links to another Web page on your own computer.

Estimated Time: 1 hour

Creating Better Web Pages

The World Wide Web is the creation of hundreds of thousands of people who are constantly creating, improving, and posting Web pages. The Web is a place to be totally creative. All you need to know to join in the fun is a little knowledge of HTML and JavaScript. With these tools, you will be limited only by your imagination.

As you have surfed the Web, you have seen wonderfully exciting Web pages, and you have seen other pages that fall flat. The main difference between a great page and a dull page comes down to the little things—the choice of fonts, colors, pictures, and the selection of elements that help with the overall organization of your pages.

There are many HTML techniques you can use to make your pages perfectly presentable. There are single- and double-spacing techniques, line techniques, and other specialized organizing tags that can make any Web page easy to read. For example, Web pages can be made more appealing by adding white space between paragraphs or by placing lines between different sections of a Web page. Changing the colors of your text and page background can also make an HTML document more appealing. Color choices are extremely important. There is nothing uglier in cyberspace than a Web page that mixes all the wrong colors. Use the right colors, and your page will be fabulous.

Fonts, or the style of letters, can be altered. Every font has a style all its own. Here are some samples of the most common fonts.

- This is Times New Roman.
- This is Arial.
- `This is Courier.`

Hypertext links help to make Web pages interesting and easy to navigate. Hyperlinks allow users to click and zoom off to another place in cyberspace, to another page on the Web site, or to a spot within the current document. If you have lots of information on a single page, creating an index can help your reader hyper-jump to the exact information for which they are looking.

As you learn the new HTML elements taught in this lesson, new ideas on how to organize your Web pages will come to you.

Net Fun

Want to drive someone crazy? Use the blink tag. Put the tags <BLINK></BLINK> around any group of words and they will blink on and off like the neon lights on a third-rate casino in Atlantic City. The blink tag will drive your Web page viewers to distraction.

Single and Double Spacing

Most early Web pages, before 1995, are best described as long collections of words. Early versions of HTML supplied only the simplest ways to break up text into readable sections. That has changed. There is no longer any reason to create a boring, hard-to-read Web page. In this step-by-step activity, you will see firsthand how to improve the readability and organization of your page.

STEP-BY-STEP 2.1

1. Open your word processing software.

2. Enter the following Web page information exactly as you see it in Figure 2-1.

Note for Notepad users: Select the Word Wrap option from the Edit menu before you enter the text.

FIGURE 2-1
Enter these tags and words exactly as shown.

```
<HTML>
<TITLE>HTML and JavaScript</TITLE>

<BODY>
<CENTER><H1>Organizing Tags</H1></CENTER>
```

FIGURE 2-1 (continued)

```
There are many ways to organize a Web page. This Web page will organize
text, hypertext links, colors, and fonts. It will also demonstrate
single spacing, double spacing, and the use of line breaks.

This Web page will display how to organize Web pages in a number of ways
using:
Powerful Lines
Hyperlinks to HTML and JavaScript Sources
Hyperlinks to Previously Created Web Pages
Fancy Fonts
Perfect Pictures
Orderly Tables
Extraordinary Extras

</BODY>
</HTML>
```

3. Save the file as you learned in Step-by-Step 1.3 with the name Six.html or Six.htm.

4. Open your Web browser and view your page. It should look messy, as seen in Figure 2-2. (Refer back to Step-by-Step 1.3 if you need a reminder on how to view an .html file in your Web browser.)

FIGURE 2-2
This is an unorganized Web page.

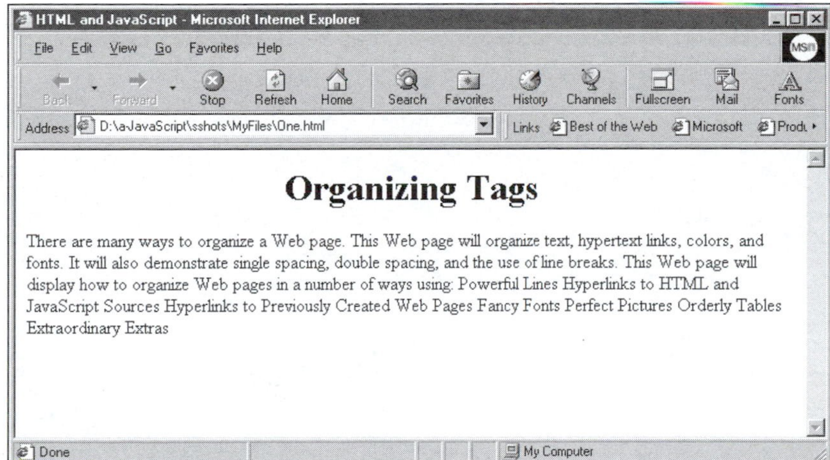

STEP-BY-STEP 2.1 CONTINUED

Notice that while the page may have looked organized when you entered it in HTML, the organization of the page "fell apart" on the Web without a few organizing tags. As you will see, the use of a few selected tags can really clean up a page. The two easiest tags to use to organize a page are the <P></P> or paragraph tags, and the <BR> or break tag.

- The <P></P> tags create a double space around the text.
- The <BR> tag creates a single-spaced break.

5. Reopen your Six.html file in your word processor.

Note for Notepad users: Select the Word Wrap option from the Edit menu when you open the file so that you can see all of the text on your screen.

6. Add the <P></P> and <BR> tags, as marked in bold in Figure 2-3.

7. Use the Save As option to save your reorganized file as Seven.html or Seven.htm.

8. Review your work. It should look much better this time, as shown in Figure 2-4.

FIGURE 2-3
Enter the <P></P> and <BR> tags.

```
<HTML>
<TITLE>HTML and JavaScript</TITLE>

<BODY>
<CENTER><H1>Organizing Tags</H1></CENTER>

<P>There are many ways to organize a Web page. This Web page will orga-
nize text, hypertext links, colors, and fonts. It will also demonstrate
single spacing, double spacing, and the use of line breaks. </P>

<P>This Web page will display how to organize Web pages in a number of
ways using: </P>

<BR>Powerful Lines
<BR>Hyperlinks to HTML and JavaScript Sources
<BR>Hyperlinks to Previously Created Web Pages
<BR>Fancy Fonts
<BR>Perfect Pictures
<BR>Orderly Tables
<BR>Extraordinary Extras

</BODY>
</HTML>
```

FIGURE 2-4
The <P></P> and <BR> tags clean up a Web page.

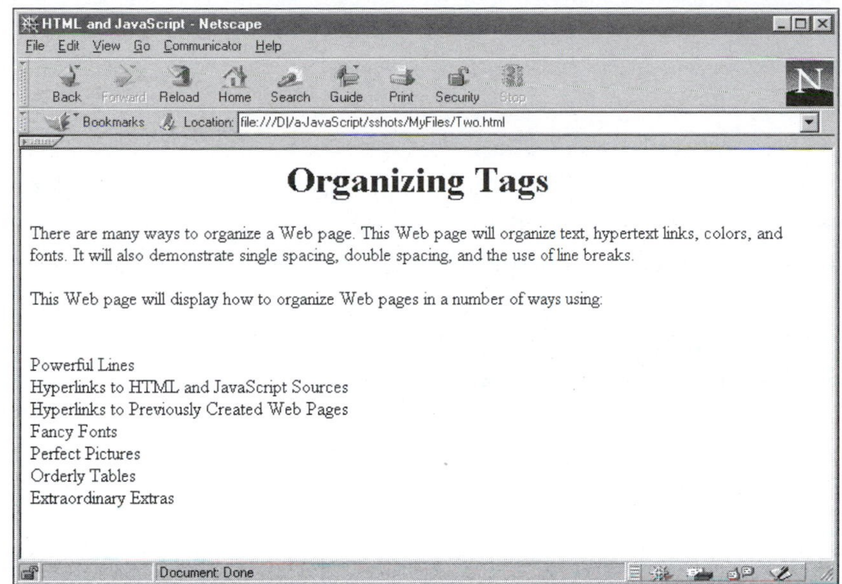

HTML and JavaScript - Netscape
File Edit View Go Communicator Help
Back Forward Reload Home Search Guide Print Security Stop
Bookmarks Location: file:///D|/a-JavaScript/sshots/MyFiles/Two.html
Organizing Tags
There are many ways to organize a Web page. This Web page will organize text, hypertext links, colors, and fonts. It will also demonstrate single spacing, double spacing, and the use of line breaks.
This Web page will display how to organize Web pages in a number of ways using:
Powerful Lines
Hyperlinks to HTML and JavaScript Sources
Hyperlinks to Previously Created Web Pages
Fancy Fonts
Perfect Pictures
Orderly Tables
Extraordinary Extras
Document: Done

Thinking About Technology

White space is important for the readers of a document. White space is a term used to describe the area around text that allows the user's eye to rest and find important parts of a document. White space helps open up a document to the human eye. Compare Figures 2-2 and 2-4 to see what we mean by the lack of white space. Figure 2-2 looks terrible. There is no white space breaking up the words in the text. In Figure 2-4, the problem has been corrected. The document is much easier to read. How does white space make a document easier to read?

Net Tip

Some tags, like the <BR> or line break tag, don't always need to be entered as pairs. For example, the <HR> or horizontal rule tag can create a line all by itself. The paragraph tag can also appear without a closing </P> tag. The <P> tag can do the job all by itself in most cases. Keep your eye out. Are there any other tags that don't need a pair?

Lines and Background Colors

Attributes and Values

HTML tags can be enhanced by giving them attributes and values. Take the <BODY> tag. You can add elements to the body tag that will dramatically change the look of your Web page. For example, to change the background color of your Web page, you can add the background attribute command and give the tag a color value, as shown in Figure 2-5.

Computers speak only in numbers. Values are expressed as numbers that the computer understands. Color values can be carefully controlled and changed to match virtually every color in the rainbow by using the hexadecimal values for certain colors.

Hexadecimal digits operate on a base-16 number system rather than the base-10 number system we humans normally use. Hexadecimal numbers use the letters A, B, C, D, E, and F along with the numbers 0 to 9 to create their 16 different digits.

For example, look at the following color values expressed as numbers:

White	=	#FFFFFF	Green	=	#00FF00
Black	=	#000000	Blue	=	#0000FF
Red	=	#FF0000	Yellow	=	#FFFF00

Shades of these colors are created by changing the numbers. For example, a really great sky blue can be created on your HTML page with the number 00CCFF. Do you want a nice light purple? Try FF95FF. An ugly slime green can be created with AAFF00.

STEP-BY-STEP 2.2

1. Open your Seven.html file.

Reminder for Notepad users: Don't forget to select the Word Wrap option from the Edit menu when you open the file.

2. Enter BGCOLOR=YELLOW inside the <BODY> tag near the top of your Web page, as shown in bold in Figure 2-5.
3. Save your work as Eight.html.
4. View these changes in your Web browser. Your page should turn yellow.
5. Experiment. Change the attribute to BLUE, GREEN, RED, WHITE, or another color of your choice.

FIGURE 2-5
Add code to change background colors.

```
<BODY BGCOLOR=YELLOW>
```

Attributes and values are powerful tools to help you organize your Web pages. One of the most widely used tags is the <HR>, or horizontal rule. With your Eight.html file open, add the set of tags shown in Figure 2-6. The first <HR> tag marked in Figure 2-6 doesn't use attributes or values. The tag simply creates a horizontal line across the page. The other three <HR> tags use attributes and values to change the shape and size of the lines.

6. Reopen your Eight.html file. Enter the various <HR> tags, attributes, and values as marked in bold near the end of Figure 2-6 before the </BODY> tag.

FIGURE 2-6
You can add background colors and lines.

```
<HTML>
<TITLE>HTML and JavaScript</TITLE>

<BODY BGCOLOR=YELLOW>

<CENTER><H1>Organizing Tags</H1></CENTER>
```

FIGURE 2-6 (continued)

```
<P>There are many ways to organize a Web page. This Web page will orga-
nize text, hypertext links, colors, and fonts. It will also demonstrate
single spacing, double spacing, and the use of line breaks. </P>

<P>This Web page will display how to organize Web pages in a number of
ways using: </P>

<BR>Powerful Lines
<BR>Hyperlinks to HTML and JavaScript Sources
<BR>Hyperlinks to Previously Created Web Pages
<BR>Fancy Fonts
<BR>Perfect Pictures
<BR>Orderly Tables
<BR>Extraordinary Extras

<HR>
<P><H2>Powerful Lines</H2></P>

A Horizontal Rule tag 50% wide and 10 increments high.
<HR WIDTH="50%" SIZE=10>

A Horizontal Rule tag 25% wide and 20 increments high.
<HR WIDTH="25%" SIZE=20>

A Horizontal Rule tag 10% wide and 30 increments high.
<HR WIDTH="10%" SIZE=30>

A Horizontal Rule tag without attributes and values.
<HR>

</BODY>
</HTML>
```

7. Save your file as Nine.html.

8. View the horizontal lines in your Web browser. The page should look like Figure 2-7.

Bad Color Choices

It is considered impolite to display a Web page that is hard to read. However, some Web page builders select backgrounds and colors that make their Web pages hard to read. Before you post your Web page to the WWW, test your pages and make sure all of the text appears clearly on the page and that your color choices don't detract from what you are trying to say.

Also, it is a good idea to think about the visually impaired and those who may suffer from color blindness when making your color selections. Mixing red and green color shades in an incorrect way can cause color-blind people to struggle with the text. Making your font sizes too small can cause trouble for those who have a hard time seeing. Having a dark background and dark letters can make a page difficult for anyone to read.

FIGURE 2-7
Powerful lines can be inserted in a Web page.

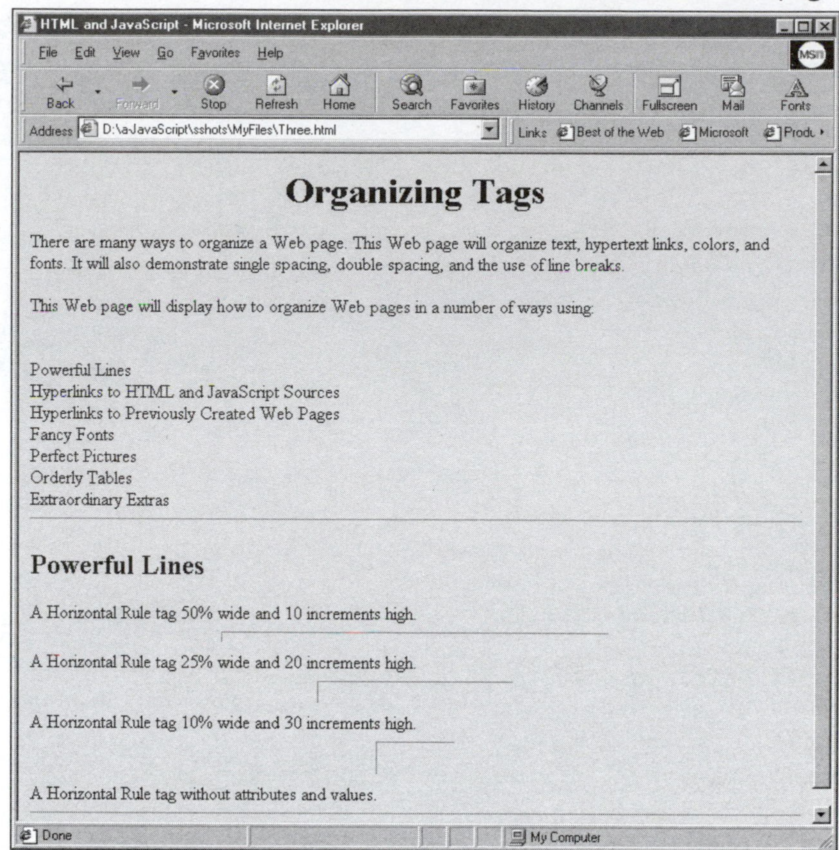

Thinking about Technology

How can you use lines and colors to jazz up your pages? When is it appropriate to use a full 100 percent line? When is it better to use a half or 50 perent line or even a smaller 25 percent line? How wide can you make lines appear?

Hyperlinks Inside Your Document

Web pages became popular because they could link easily to other pages, or to various sections inside a document at the speed of an electron. Hyperlinks are easy to use, but a little difficult to understand at first.

To use a hyperlink, you just click on the link. Links may be pictures or words that are underlined and appear in a different color, as shown in Figure 2-8.

Hyperlinks are created with special tags called anchor tags. The tag has several parts. The opening and closing tags are called the anchor or link tags and look like this:

```
<A HREF="insert location of file"></A>
```

Link or anchor tags are fairly useless unless you define a place to which you are linking. There are several ways to use link tags. You can:

- Link to another spot within your own document.
- Link to a URL or Web page anywhere on the WWW.
- Link to another Web page on your own computer.

FIGURE 2-8
A hypertext link is often underlined and in a different color.

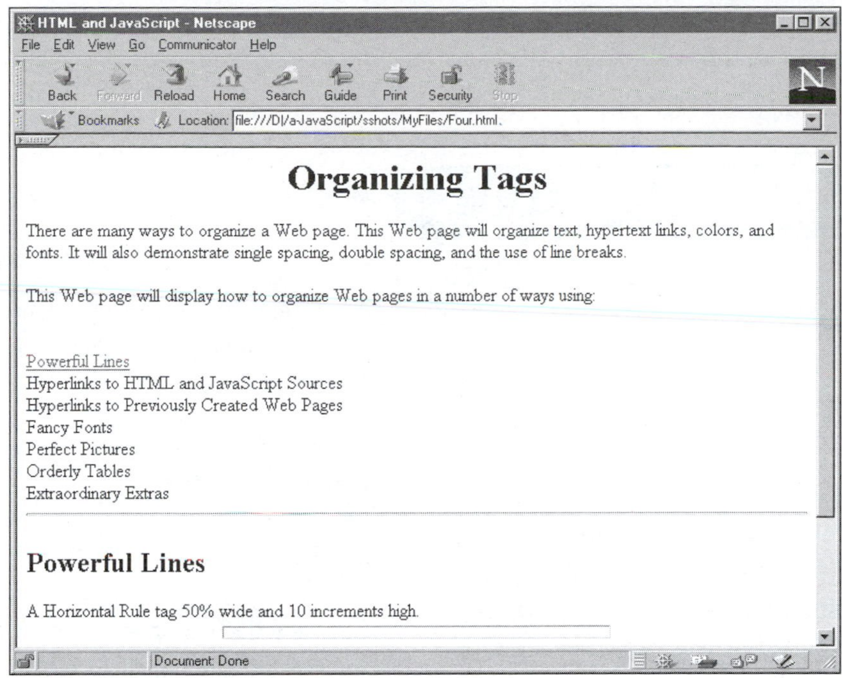

In Step-by-Step 2.4 you will link to the WWW, and in Step-by-Step 2.5 you will create hyperlinks to all the Web pages you have created so far. In this activity, we will start linking within your HTML page. These internal hyperlinks help users navigate between important parts of your Web page.

NET ETHICS

What you write in a Web page should not be offensive to others. You are responsible for what you create and post on the WWW. RESPECT the Web. When creating your Web pages, consider these guidelines:

R = Responsibility: Assume personal responsibility, and create only ethical and appropriate pages.
E = Everybody: Try to create Web pages that everybody will enjoy, appreciate, and consider of value.
S = Simplicity: Make your Web pages easy to navigate. Make information simple to find.
P = Purpose: Have a clear purpose for every Web page you put on the Web. Don't post unnecessary pages.
E = Ethical: Make sure all the content of every Web page you post corresponds to your values and has a beneficial purpose.
C = Correct: Make sure all the words on your page are spelled correctly, all the sentences are written correctly, and that all the hyperlinks work.
T = Totally worth visiting: Try to create pages that others will think are totally worth someone's time to visit.

The first <A> tag you insert will create a hypertext link to a location within your document. You will create the tag in Step 2. The attribute is HREF= and the value is "#POWERFUL." The quotation marks are necessary, as is the # or pound sign.

The second anchor tag will identify the exact location in your Web page to which you want to link. In Step 4, you will create a tag with the attribute NAME= and a value called "POWERFUL."

STEP-BY-STEP 2.3

1. Open your Nine.html file.

2. Change the background color back to white by changing the BGCOLOR attribute from YELLOW to WHITE.

3. Add the following anchor <A></A> tags before and after the first Powerful Lines list item, as shown here and in Figure 2-9. (Note: The pound sign # can be created by holding the Shift key down and pressing the number 3. The double quote marks " are created by holding down the Shift key and pressing the single quote ' character.)

```
<BR> <A HREF="#POWERFUL">Powerful
Lines</A>
```

4. Insert the following anchor <A></A> tags around the second Powerful Lines list item, as shown here and marked in bold in Figure 2-9.

```
<P><H2><A NAME= "POWERFUL">Powerful
Lines</A></H2></P>
```

5. Save your new file as Ten.html.

6. View the changes in your Web browser. Your link should look like the sample in Figure 2-8. When you click the link, you should jump down the page to the Powerful Lines heading in your document.

FIGURE 2-9
Insert these internal linking tags.

```
<HTML>
<TITLE>HTML and JavaScript</TITLE>

<BODY BGCOLOR=WHITE>
<CENTER><H1>Organizing Tags</H1></CENTER>

<P>There are many ways to organize a Web page. This Web page will orga-
nize text, hypertext links, colors, and fonts. It will also demonstrate
single spacing, double spacing, and the use of line breaks.</P>

<P>This Web page will display how to organize Web pages in a number of
ways using: </P>

<BR><A HREF="#POWERFUL">Powerful Lines</A>
<BR>Hyperlinks to HTML and JavaScript Sources
<BR>Hyperlinks to Previously Created Web Pages
<BR>Fancy Fonts
<BR>Perfect Pictures
```

FIGURE 2-9 (continued)

```
<BR>Orderly Tables
<BR>Extraordinary Extras

<HR>
<P><H2><A NAME="POWERFUL">Powerful Lines</A></H2></P>

A Horizontal Rule tag 50% wide and 10 increments high.
<HR WIDTH="50%" SIZE=10>

A Horizontal Rule tag 25% wide and 20 increments high.
<HR WIDTH="25%" SIZE=20>

A Horizontal Rule tag 10% wide and 30 increments high.
<HR WIDTH="10%" SIZE=30>

A Horizontal Rule tag without attributes and values.
<HR>

</BODY>
</HTML>
```

Thinking About Technology

Can you figure out how to create an internal hypertext link that will allow you to move from the bottom of your document to the very top? Use the same steps you learned in this activity to create a link just before the </BODY> tag that will take you to the top of the page. Your link should look like this: Top of Page. Resave your extra-effort work as TenToTop.html.

Why do you think a link back to the top of a page would be valuable?

Creating Hypertext Links to the Web

The thing that first made the WWW popular was the ability to jump from one page to another anywhere in the world. Before you can do this, however, you must know all about URLs. URLs are Uniform Resource Locators. URLs allow a Web browser to pinpoint an exact file on the Web. The concept is really quite simple.

Have you ever seen a URL similar to this sample?

http://www.company.com/webpagefolder/anotherfolder/afileyouwant.html

When you enter a URL (Uniform Resource Locator) into your HTML Web page, you are identifying a path to a specific HTML file located somewhere in cyberspace. This file may be on your local computer or somewhere on the Web.

You often can see the name of a file at the end of a URL. Look at the end of our sample URL. The filename *afileyouwant.html* is the name of an HTML file (*afileyouwant*). The *.html* extension identifies the file as an HTML document that your Web browser can display.

However, before you can get to *afileyouwant.html*, you need to know the path or the way to this filename. The key in finding the filename's path is in the URL or Web address. Let's see what this means by breaking down the sample URL into its various parts.

In some URLs, you may see the letters *http* followed by a colon and a couple of slashes. The *http://* tells your network how to transfer or move the file you are requesting. The *http* stands for *Hypertext Transfer Protocol*. A *protocol* is a communications system that is used to transfer data over networks. It is like a digital language that Web servers use to communicate with Web browsers.

The second part of the address (*www.company.com*) is the actual name of the server that hosts the Web page for which you are looking. The *www* stands for the World Wide Web. The *www* tells you that this server uses Web technology. The *.company* part is the name of the company that maintains the Web server. The *.com* says this is a commercial or business site. You may see other addresses that are marked as *.edu* for education, or *.gov* for government Web sites.

The slashes and names in the rest of the URL (*/webpagefolder/anotherfolder/*) represent folders on the Web computer. These are also called subdirectories. You have subdirectories on your computer also. Figure 2-10 shows how folders are organized on a Windows computer. All computers use some sort of folder system to organize files. If you want to find a file on a computer, you need to know the path through the many possible folders in which the file is hidden. Knowing the path is the key to finding the Web page you want.

Before you can find a Web site's welcome page, you need to know the URL. In this step-by-step activity, you will enter URLs for some of the most important companies in the race to create a better, more exciting Web. Many of these sites have information on HTML, JavaScript, and other important Web tools. They include:

http://www.microsoft.com
http://home.netscape.com
http://www.sun.com
http://www.oracle.com

FIGURE 2-10
A Windows folder or subdirectory organization is shown here.

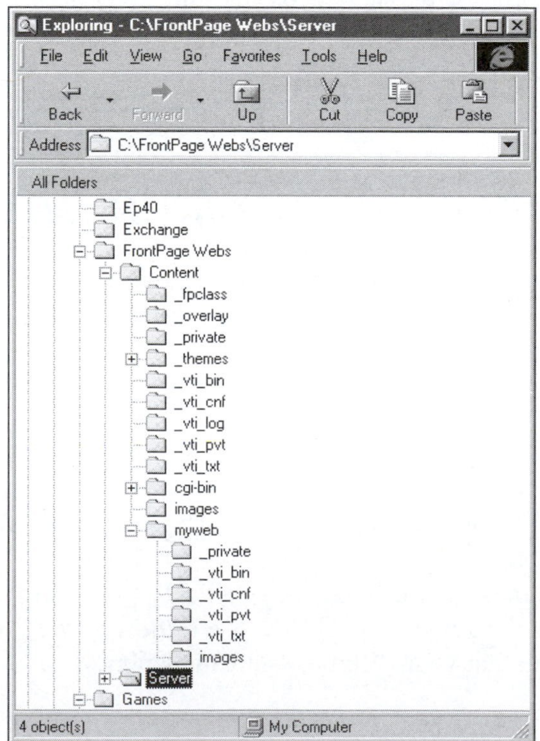

STEP-BY-STEP 2.4

1. Open your Ten.html file.

2. Create a hypertext link (as shown here and in bold in Figure 2-11) from the list near the top of the page and the new section you are creating.

```
<BR><A HREF="#HYPERLINKS">
Hyperlinks to HTML and JavaScript
Sources</A>
```

3. Add a new level 2 heading with the words Hyperlinks to HTML and JavaScript Sources just below the last <HR> tag of your Web page and just before the </BODY> tag, as shown in Figure 2-11. Include the <A NAME> tag so you can create an internal hypertext link from the link you created in step 2.

```
<P><H2><A NAME= "HYPERLINKS">
Hyperlinks to HTML and JavaScript
Sources</A></H2></P>
```

4. Below your new heading and before the </BODY> tag, create the following hypertext links exactly as shown here and in bold in Figure 2-11.

```
<BR><A HREF="http://www.microsoft.
com">Microsoft</A>
<BR><A HREF="http://home.netscape.
com">Netscape</A>
<BR><A HREF="http://www.sun.com">
Sun Microsystems</A>
<BR><A HREF="http://www.oracle.com
">Oracle</A>
```

FIGURE 2-11
Insert these hypertext linking tags to sample Web resources.

```
<HTML>
<TITLE>HTML and JavaScript</TITLE>

<BODY BGCOLOR=WHITE>
<CENTER><H1>Organizing Tags</H1></CENTER>

<P>There are many ways to organize a Web page. This Web page will orga-
nize text, hypertext links, colors, and fonts. It will also demonstrate
single spacing, double spacing, and the use of line breaks.</P>

<P>This Web page will display how to organize Web pages in a number of
ways using: </P>

<BR><A HREF="#POWERFUL">Powerful Lines</A>
<BR><A HREF="#HYPERLINKS">Hyperlinks to HTML and JavaScript Sources</A>
<BR>Hyperlinks to Previously Created Web Pages
<BR>Fancy Fonts
<BR>Perfect Pictures
<BR>Orderly Tables
<BR>Extraordinary Extras
```

FIGURE 2-11 (continued)

```
<HR>
<P><H2><A NAME="POWERFUL">Powerful Lines</A></H2></P>

A Horizontal Rule tag 50% wide and 10 increments high.
<HR WIDTH="50%" SIZE=10>

A Horizontal Rule tag 25% wide and 20 increments high.
<HR WIDTH="25%" SIZE=20>

A Horizontal Rule tag 10% wide and 30 increments high.
<HR WIDTH="10%" SIZE=30>

A Horizontal Rule tag without attributes and values.
<HR>

<P><H2><A NAME="HYPERLINKS"> Hyperlinks to HTML and JavaScript Sources
</A></H2></P>

<BR><A HREF="http://www.microsoft.com">Microsoft</A>
<BR><A HREF="http://home.netscape.com">Netscape</A>
<BR><A HREF="http://www.sun.com">Sun Microsystems</A>
<BR><A HREF="http://www.oracle.com">Oracle</A>

</BODY>
</HTML>
```

5. Your entire page of tags should now appear as those in Figure 2-11. Save your work as Eleven.html.

6. View your work in your Web browser. Your new links should look like Figure 2-12.

7. If you have a live connection to the Web, try your links and see if they work! (Note: If your links don't work properly, carefully review your tags and make any necessary corrections. Resave your work. Then, reload or refresh your page in your Web browser and try again. Remember that your browser won't look for your newly corrected Web page unless you tell it to. You can do this in a couple of ways. You can open the page again, or you can click on the Reload or Refresh buttons to load an updated copy of your Web page into your browser.)

Thinking About Technology

What are the ten most important Web sites? What makes them important to you? Create a new HTML page that indexes and lists your most important personal Web pages. Call the page My Web Resources. Keep adding to your Web resources page as you work through this text.

FIGURE 2-12
Hyperlinks in your Web browser appear.

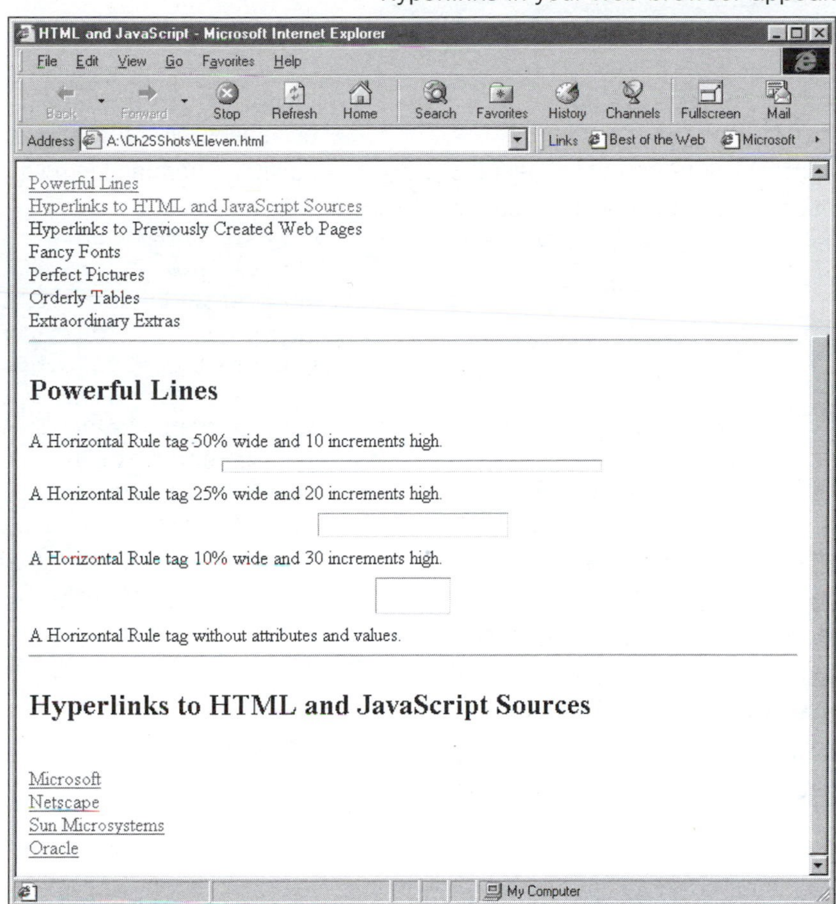

Linking to Pages You've Already Created

In this step-by-step activity, you will link to the first 11 HTML pages you have already created in this unit. Keeping track of all of your pages in this way will help you quickly review the progress you have made.

Net Tip

YOU HAVE PROBABLY BEEN TOLD THAT USING ALL CAPITAL LETTERS IN AN E-MAIL MESSAGE IS CONSIDERED SHOUTING. ON A WEB PAGE, ENTERING TEXT IN CAPITAL LETTERS IS NOT CONSIDERED SHOUTING. INSTEAD, CAPITAL LETTERS ALLOW YOU TO EMPHASIZE TEXT.
HOWEVER, CAPITAL LETTERS OFTEN MAKE TEXT HARD TO READ. THE USE OF CAPITAL LETTERS SHOULD BE RESERVED FOR HEADINGS OR FOR IMPORTANT WORDS YOU WANT READERS TO NOTICE. PARAGRAPHS THAT APPEAR IN ALL CAPITAL LETTERS ARE HARD TO READ! SO, USE CAPITAL LETTERS SPARINGLY.

STEP-BY-STEP 2.5

1. Open your Eleven.html file.

2. Create a hypertext link from your list near the top of the page and the new section you are creating. The text to be entered is shown here and in bold in Figure 2-13.

```
<BR><A HREF="#PREVIOUS">
Hyperlinks to Previously Created
Web Pages</A>
```

3. Create a new <HR> tag, as shown in Figure 2-13, following your list of Web links you created in Step-by-Step 2.4.

4. As shown in Figure 2-13, add a new level 2 heading called Hyperlinks to Previously Created Web Pages just below the new HR tag you just created, and just before the </BODY> tag. Include the <A NAME> tag so you can link to this exact spot from the tag you created in step 3.

```
<HR>
<P><H2><A NAME= "PREVIOUS">
Hyperlinks to Previously Created
Web Pages</A></H2></P>
```

5. Below the new heading near the end of your document, create the hypertext links exactly as shown here and in bold in Figure 2-13.

```
<BR><A HREF="One.html">One</A>
<BR><A HREF="Two.html">Two</A>
<BR><A HREF="Three.html">Three</A>
<BR><A HREF="Four.html">Four</A>
<BR><A HREF="Five.html">Five</A>
<BR><A HREF="Six.html">Six</A>
<BR><A HREF="Seven.html">Seven</A>
<BR><A HREF="Eight.html">Eight</A>
<BR><A HREF="Nine.html">Nine</A>
<BR><A HREF="Ten.html">Ten</A>
<BR><A HREF="Eleven.html">Eleven
</A>
```

6. Your entire page of tags should now appear like those in Figure 2-13. Save your work as Twelve.html.

FIGURE 2-13
Creating links to your own Web pages is easy.

```
<HTML>
<TITLE>HTML and JavaScript</TITLE>

<BODY BGCOLOR=WHITE>
<CENTER><H1>Organizing Tags</H1></CENTER>

<P>There are many ways to organize a Web page. This Web page will orga-
nize text, hypertext links, colors, and fonts.
It will also demonstrate single spacing, double spacing, and the use of
line breaks.</P>

<P>This Web page will display how to organize Web pages in a number of
ways using: </P>

<BR><A HREF="#POWERFUL">Powerful Lines</A>
<BR><A HREF="#HYPERLINKS">Hyperlinks to HTML and JavaScript Sources</A>
```

FIGURE 2-13 (continued)

```
<BR> <A HREF="#PREVIOUS">Hyperlinks to Previously Created Web Pages</A>
<BR>Fancy Fonts
<BR>Perfect Pictures
<BR>Orderly Tables
<BR>Extraordinary Extras

<HR>
<P><H2><A NAME= "POWERFUL">Powerful Lines</A></H2></P>

A Horizontal Rule tag 50% wide and 10 increments high.
<HR WIDTH="50%" SIZE=10>

A Horizontal Rule tag 25% wide and 20 increments high.
<HR WIDTH="25%" SIZE=20>

A Horizontal Rule tag 10% wide and 30 increments high.
<HR WIDTH="10%" SIZE=30>

A Horizontal Rule tag without attributes and values.
<HR>

<P><H2><A NAME= "HYPERLINKS">Hyperlinks to HTML and JavaScript Sources
</A></H2></P>

<BR><A HREF="http://www.microsoft.com">Microsoft</A>
<BR><A HREF="http://home.netscape.com">Netscape</A>
<BR><A HREF="http://www.sun.com">Sun Microsystems</A>
<BR><A HREF="http://www.oracle.com">Oracle</A>

<HR>
<P><H2><A NAME= "PREVIOUS"> Hyperlinks to Previously Created Web
Pages</A></H2></P>

<BR><A HREF="One.html">One</A>
<BR><A HREF="Two.html">Two</A>
<BR><A HREF="Three.html">Three</A>
<BR><A HREF="Four.html">Four</A>
<BR><A HREF="Five.html">Five</A>
<BR><A HREF="Six.html">Six</A>
<BR><A HREF="Seven.html">Seven</A>
<BR><A HREF="Eight.html">Eight</A>
<BR><A HREF="Nine.html">Nine</A>
<BR><A HREF="Ten.html">Ten</A>
<BR><A HREF="Eleven.html">Eleven</A>

</BODY>
</HTML>
```

STEP-BY-STEP 2.5 CONTINUED

7. View your work in your Web browser. Your new links should look like Figure 2-14. Test each link and make sure they all work. Make any corrections that are necessary. (Note: Once again, if your links don't work properly, review your tags, make any necessary corrections, and resave your work. Then, reload or refresh the page in your Web browser.)

FIGURE 2-14
This shows links to previously created Web pages.

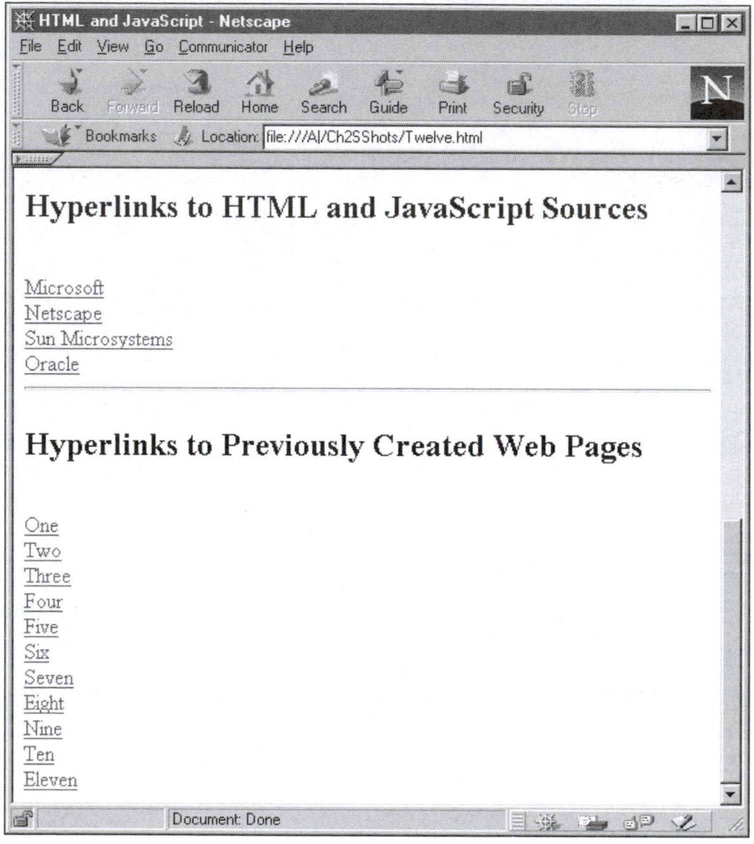

HTML Standards

HTML is a powerful tool because it allows all kinds of computers to display Web pages. With HTML, it doesn't matter if you are running a Macintosh or a Windows machine. You can even be on a Unix workstation or some other type of computer.

The reason HTML Web pages are able to be seen by all types of computers is that HTML guardians maintain a certain set of standards that all Web browser makers voluntarily follow. New standards and new HTML tags and commands are being added all the time. Each new tag is submitted to a standards committee which reviews it. Every now and then, enough new commands are added to HTML that a new version of HTML appears. These versions are marked by numbers, HTML 1, HTML 2, HTML 3, HTML 4, and so on.

You can learn more about HTML standards and receive help expanding your HTML skills online. Go to your search engine and try these search words.

HTML Standards
HTML Standards Committee
HTML 1
HTML 2
HTML 3
HTML 4
HTML 5
HTML Learning
HTML Guides

Thinking About Technology

Now that you have created lists of hypertext links, how can you turn your lists into bulleted and numbered lists? Try using the <OL>, <UL>, and <LI> tags to turn your hyperlinks into bulleted and numbered lists.

Coloring Text

As you have surfed the Web, you may have noticed that the text colors often change from page to page. In Step-by-Step 2.2, you changed the background color of your Web page by inserting the YELLOW value into the BGCOLOR= attribute in the <BODY> tag. Then you changed the background to several other colors. Changing text color is just as easy.

There are three basic types of text color you can change:

Type of Text	Attribute
The text itself	TEXT=
The hypertext link color	LINK=
The visited link color (or the links you have already selected)	VLINK=

STEP-BY-STEP 2.6

1. Open your Twelve.html file.
2. In the body tag at the beginning of the Web page, leave the BGCOLOR as WHITE, but make the TEXT=BLUE, the LINK=RED, and the VLINK=GREEN, as shown in Figure 2-15.
3. Save your work as Thirteen.html.

FIGURE 2-15
You change text color in this way.

```
<HTML>
<TITLE>HTML and JavaScript</TITLE>

<BODY   BGCOLOR=WHITE   TEXT=BLUE   LINK=RED   VLINK=GREEN>
```

4. View your work in your Web browser. Your page should appear with blue text, red hyperlinks, and green visited links on a white background.

Thinking About Technology

Try experimenting by substituting the hexadecimal number values listed below for the names of colors in the <BODY> tag. Use the pound (#) sign before your number. Some of the most common hexadecimal number values are:

RED = #FF0000
GREEN = #00FF00
BLUE = #0000FF
WHITE = #FFFFFF
BLACK = #000000
YELLOW = #FFFF00

Net Fun

Another fun tag is the marquee tag. Anything you put between the marquee tags, <MARQUEE> </MARQUEE>, will scroll across the screen like a stock market ticker. The tag was designed for the Internet Explorer browser by Microsoft, and doesn't work on every browser. Experiment, and see what happens. In the right browser, it's cool.

Net Tip

Proofreading HTML tags can be difficult. Even the slightest error can drastically change the look and organization of a Web page. Here are some common things to look for.

- Make sure all your angle brackets < and > are facing in the proper direction.
- Often, Web page writers misuse the Shift key when making angle brackets or creating a slash. This results in a comma, a period, or a question mark where the angle brackets or slash should appear.
- If all the text appears centered, perhaps you forgot the close </CENTER> tag.
- If you want a double space instead of a single space, use a <P> tag instead of a <BR> tag.
- If bullets appear long after a list, perhaps you forgot the close unordered list tag, </UL>.
- Many times quotation marks are required to identify values. If a value doesn't work, check to see if "quotation" marks are needed.
- Make sure you save your file each time you make a correction to a Web page.
- Don't forget that Web pages must be reloaded or refreshed before changes can take effect.

LESSON 2 REVIEW QUESTIONS

WRITTEN QUESTIONS

Write a brief answer to the following questions:

1. What tag will make words flash on and off repeatedly?
2. What hexadecimal value will create the color yellow?
3. Which tags do you know that do not need a closing tag in order to work effectively?
4. What are three common HTML errors?
5. What do the letters in RESPECT stand for?
6. Why are there different versions of HTML?

LESSON 2 PROJECTS

PROJECT 2-1

In Project 1-2, you identified seven of the greatest Web pages you could find. In this project, Great Applications, Inc. wants you to identify the seven worst pages you can find. These pages are to be used in a training seminar to help new employees learn how to create high-quality Web pages. Your manager suggested that you surf the Web and find seven examples of hard-to-read, unorganized, or boring Web pages to show new interns exactly what `not` to do.

Surf the Web looking for awful Web page examples. Record the title and URL of each page and write a brief summary explaining why these pages are horrible!

PROJECT 2-2

Great Applications, Inc. is holding a design contest to see who can build the most informative and organized Web pages. Specifically, they are looking for a team that can create Web pages that introduce new products to customers over the Web.

The contest gives teams of three to five people two hours to create an informative Web page about a product of their choice. Form your team, and brainstorm a new product to introduce. It could be a new CD or a new computer game. It could be a new fashion or a new car. For the purpose of this contest, it doesn't really matter the product you pick, so don't take too much time deciding what product to use.

Create your team's Web page contest entry. Divide up the writing responsibilities. Have one person enter the basic tags and serve as Webmaster. Have each team member research and write a portion of the Web page. Collaborate by editing and revising each other's writing and HTML tags. Use the techniques you learned in this chapter to organize the information you wish to present.

PROJECT 2-3

We all know that teamwork is important. However, are there times when teamwork is harder than working alone? Answer the following questions about teams creating Web pages together.

1. As you worked together in a team in the previous activity, what problems did you encounter?
2. How did you organize your team? How did you divide up the work? Which team members were responsible for which activities?
3. Did teamwork create a better Web page? If so, how?
4. What advice would you give to other teams who are trying to create Web pages together?

HTML Power Techniques

LESSON 3

OBJECTIVES

Upon completion of this lesson, you should be able to:

- Control the size, style, and color of fonts.
- Download pictures from the Web.
- Insert pictures into your Web page.
- Change the size of graphics.
- Use tables to organize information.
- Turn pictures into hyperlinks.
- Insert a variety of data input options into a Web page.

Estimated Time: 1 hour

The Exciting Web

The Web is full of pictures, sounds, and movies that add interest to Web pages. Generally, there are two kinds of pictures (called *graphics* or *images*) on the WWW. They include *.gif* files (Graphics Interchange Format) and *.jpg* or *.jpeg* (Joint Photographic Expert Group) files. The extensions .gif and .jpg tell your browser that these files are pictures, not .html text files, and require special handling.

The more you learn about HTML, the more you can add exciting new effects and styles to your Web page. As we mentioned in Lesson 2, *fonts*, or the style of letters, can be changed. Every font has a style all its own.

By using the <FONT> tag's many attributes and values, you can manipulate fonts in millions of ways.

Tables allow a Web page to be divided up into parts, creating special spaces for each new element or piece of information you may want to include.

Tables, fonts, and pictures can add power to your pages. In this lesson, you will learn to manipulate these special HTML features. You will also learn about some extraordinary input tags that will allow visitors to your Web page to interact with your page.

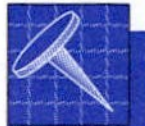

Net Tip

There are other ways to change the look of text. Try these tags around certain words and see what effect they create. Can you guess what they do?
<B></B>
<EM></EM>
<STRONG></STRONG>
<I></I>

Font Attributes and Values

When you change text colors in the <BODY> tag, as you did in Step-by-Step 2.6, you change the color of your words for the entire page. If you want to have more control (that is, if you want to change the size, color, or style of a single paragraph, a single sentence, or even a single word), use the <FONT> tag.

Use the <FONT> tag's attributes to control:

- The size of words with the SIZE attribute <FONT SIZE=#>
- The style of words with the FACE attribute <FONT FACE=#>
- The color of words with the COLOR attribute <FONT COLOR=#>

STEP-BY-STEP 3.1

1. Open your Thirteen.html file.

2. Create a hypertext link in the list near the top of the page that will hyperlink to the new section you will be creating in this activity. The text to be entered is shown in bold here and in Figure 3-1.

```
<BR><A HREF="#FONTS">Fancy
  Fonts</A>
```

3. Create a new <HR> tag, as shown in Figure 3-1, following the list of Web page links you created in Step-by-Step 2.5.

4. As shown in Figure 3-1, add a new level 2 heading called Fancy Fonts just below the new <HR> tag you just created, and just before the </BODY> tag. Include the <A NAME> tag to finish the internal hypertext link you started in step 2.

```
<HR>
<P><H2><A NAME="FONTS"> Fancy
  Fonts </A></H2></P>
```

5. Below the new heading, near the end of your document, enter the font tags, attributes, and values exactly as shown here and in bold in Figure 3-1.

```
<BR><FONT FACE=HELVETICA SIZE=4
  COLOR=RED>This is the Helvetica
   font at Size 4</FONT>
<BR><FONT FACE=TIMES SIZE=6
  COLOR=GREEN>This is the Times
  font at Size 6</FONT>
<BR><FONT FACE=ARIAL SIZE=8
  COLOR=ORANGE>This is the Arial
  font at Size 8</FONT>
<BR><FONT FACE=COURIER SIZE=2
  COLOR=BLACK>This is the Courier
   font at Size 2</FONT>
```

6. Your tags should now appear like those in Figure 3-1. Save your work as Fourteen.html.

7. View your work in your Web browser. Your changes should look like Figure 3-2. Make any corrections that appear necessary.

FIGURE 3-1
Apply these font styles, sizes, and colors.

```
<HTML>
<TITLE>HTML and JavaScript</TITLE>

<BODY BGCOLOR=WHITE TEXT=BLUE LINK=RED VLINK=GREEN>
<CENTER><H1>Organizing Tags</H1> </CENTER>

<P>There are many ways to organize a Web page. This Web page will
  organize text, hypertext links, colors, and fonts. It will also demon-
  strate single spacing, double spacing, and the use of line breaks.</P>

<P>This Web page will display how to organize Web pages in a number of
  ways using: </P>

<BR><A HREF="#POWERFUL">Powerful Lines</A>
<BR><A HREF="#HYPERLINKS">Hyperlinks to HTML and JavaScript sources</A>
<BR><A HREF="#PREVIOUS">Hyperlinks to previously created Web pages</A>
<BR><A HREF="#FONTS">Fancy Fonts</A>
<BR>Perfect Pictures
<BR>Orderly Tables
<BR>Extraordinary Extras

<HR>
<P><H2><A NAME= "POWERFUL">Powerful Lines</A></H2></P>

A Horizontal Rule tag 50% wide and 10 increments high.
<HR WIDTH="50%" SIZE=10>

A Horizontal Rule tag 25% wide and 20 increments high.
<HR WIDTH="25%" SIZE=20>

A Horizontal Rule tag 10% wide and 30 increments high.
<HR WIDTH="10%" SIZE=30>

A Horizontal Rule tag without attributes and values.
<HR>

<P><H2><A NAME="HYPERLINKS">Hyperlinks to HTML and JavaScript
  sources</A></H2></P>

<BR><A HREF="http://www.microsoft.com">Microsoft</A>
<BR><A HREF="http://home.netscape.com">Netscape</A>
<BR><A HREF="http://www.sun.com">Sun Microsystems</A>
<BR><A HREF="http://www.oracle.com">Oracle</A>

<HR>
<P><H2><A NAME= "PREVIOUS"> Hyperlinks to previously created Web
  pages</A></H2></P>

<BR><A HREF="One.html">One</A>
<BR><A HREF="Two.html">Two</A>
```

FIGURE 3-1 (continued)

```
<BR><A HREF="Three.html">Three</A>
<BR><A HREF="Four.html">Four</A>
<BR><A HREF="Five.html">Five</A>
<BR><A HREF="Six.html">Six</A>
<BR><A HREF="Seven.html">Seven</A>
<BR><A HREF="Eight.html">Eight</A>
<BR><A HREF="Nine.html">Nine</A>
<BR><A HREF="Ten.html">Ten</A>
<BR><A HREF="Eleven.html">Eleven</A>

<HR>
<P><H2><A NAME= "FONTS"> Fancy Fonts </A></H2></P>

<BR><FONT FACE=HELVETICA SIZE=4 COLOR=RED>This is the Helvetica font at
  Size 4</FONT>
<BR><FONT FACE=TIMES SIZE=6 COLOR=GREEN>This is the Times font at Size
  6</FONT>
<BR><FONT FACE=ARIAL SIZE=8 COLOR=ORANGE>This is the Arial font at Size
  8</FONT>
<BR><FONT FACE=COURIER SIZE=2 COLOR=BLACK>This is the Courier font at
  Size 2</FONT>

</BODY>
</HTML>
```

FIGURE 3-2
Various font styles, sizes, and colors are displayed.

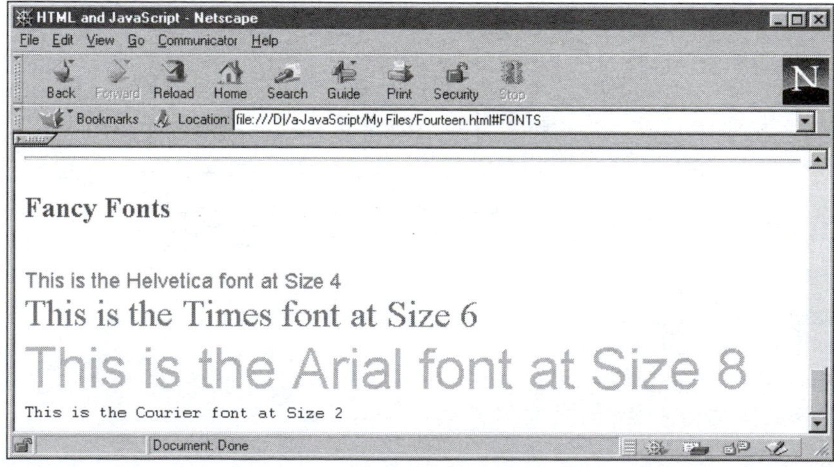

Thinking About Technology

You can make your pages nicer by changing font size, font colors, and font faces. What other font changes can you make? Try changing the font styles, colors, and sizes in the introductory paragraphs in your Fourteen.html Web page. Try several new font colors and font face combinations. Try various font sizes from 1 to 9. Save your new work as Fourteen-2.html.

Net Fun

It is easy to create a way for your readers to respond to your Web page in an e-mail message. Simply use the mailto tag that looks like this, <A HREF= "mailto:your_email@address"> Your Name</A>. When your users click the link, an e-mail form will appear. Not every Web browser is set up properly to handle the mailto tag, so experiment. You may need some help from your local Webmaster before you can actually send mail.

Downloading and Inserting Graphics

Pictures can be found in many places. You can find pictures in your clip art collection, scan pictures into your computer with a scanner, draw your own pictures, or copy them from the Web. However, before you can easily use pictures in your Web pages, you need to convert them into one of the acceptable Web formats. These commonly include:

- .gif
- .jpg or .jpeg

The first type of graphics or image format, .gif, was originally created by CompuServe to provide a compressed graphics format that could transfer easily over low-speed modems. The Graphics Interchange Format is usually abbreviated as GIF. There is some debate on how to say GIF. In some parts of the country, it is pronounced GIF as in Kathy Lee GIFford. In other parts of the country, it is pronounced GIF as in JIFfy Peanut Butter. Either pronunciation works. After all, the pronunciation doesn't change the file format in the least.

The second commonly used format is .jpg or .jpeg. It is pronounced J-Peg by Webmasters in the know. JPEG is short for Joint Photographic Expert Group. This format adheres to an international set of graphics standards. JPEG graphics, like GIF pictures, are compact enough for Internet use.

There are other graphic file formats emerging on the Web. But if you know how to work with these two formats, you will know how to work with any other picture format on the WWW.

Net Careers

Artists are in great demand among Web site development companies. There was a time when a Web page would be entirely made up of words or text. Today, pictures seem to dominate Web pages, attracting a greater number of visitors than ever before. If you are considering an artistic career, consider the Web. You may find that most of your artwork will end up on the Web. Big corporations with Web sites and Web site developers are always on the lookout for great artists. The best training for a Web artist would be to take as many art classes as you can. The graphics tools you need to convert your artwork are easily learned. The skills of an artist take much more time.

STEP-BY-STEP 3.2

1. Open your Web browser.

2. Enter the URL www.course.com/downloads/swep/htmljava/ in your Web browser.

3. Click on the Activity 3.2 link from the list you see. Scroll down until you see a dragon.

4. If you are on a Windows computer, click the right mouse key on the dragon's nose, as shown in Figure 3-3. If you are using a Macintosh, click and hold your mouse key on the dragon's nose.

5. Select the Save Image As or Save Picture As command from the list that appears, as shown in Figures 3-4A and 3-4B. (Note: The command on your browser may be worded differently. Keep trying the various commands that appear until you find the correct command.)

Net Tip

IMG SRC is short for IMaGe SouRCe. Many people misuse this tag by transposing the R and the C, and they enter IMG SCR. If you forget the tag, just spell out the words "ImaGe" and "SouRCe" to get the letters in the correct order.

FIGURE 3-4A
With Netscape, select Save Image As.

FIGURE 3-3
Click on the dragon's nose with the right mouse clicker in Windows, or hold your mouse clicker down on a Macintosh.

FIGURE 3-4B
With Internet Explorer, select Save Picture As.

STEP-BY-STEP 3.2 CONTINUED

6. Save your file (called Levy.gif) in the same folder in which you have been saving your Web pages.

7. Open your Fourteen.html Web page in your word processor or text editor.

8. Create a hypertext link in the list near the top of the page that will hyperlink to the new section you will be creating. The text to be entered is shown in bold here and in Figure 3-5.

```
<BR><A HREF="#PICTURES">Perfect
  Pictures</A>
```

9. Enter an <HR> tag, as shown in bold in Figure 3-5, after the Fancy Fonts section you created in the previous activity.

10. As shown in Figure 3-5, add a new level 2 heading called Perfect Pictures just below the <HR> tag you just created and just before the </BODY> tag. Include the <A NAME> tag so you can finish the internal hypertext link you started in step 8.

```
<HR>
<P><H2><A NAME= "PICTURES">
  Perfect Pictures </A></H2></P>
```

11. Below your new heading, near the end of your document, enter an Image Source <IMG SRC> tag, as shown here and in Figure 3-5. Notice that the name of the file you just downloaded appears between quotation marks.

```
<IMG SRC="levy.gif">
```

12. Your tags should now appear like those in Figure 3-5. If everything looks correct, save your work as Fifteen.html.

13. View your work in your Web browser. Your picture should look like Figure 3-6, but it may appear larger or smaller in your browser.

FIGURE 3-5
Insert a graphics or image file in this way.

```
<HTML>
<TITLE>HTML and JavaScript</TITLE>

<BODY BGCOLOR=WHITE TEXT=BLUE LINK=RED VLINK=GREEN>
<CENTER><H1>Organizing Tags</H1> </CENTER>

<P>There are many ways to organize a Web page. This Web page will orga-
  nize text, hypertext links, colors, and fonts. It will also demon-
  strate single spacing, double spacing, and the use of line breaks.</P>

<P>This Web page will display how to organize Web pages in a number of
  ways using: </P>

<BR><A HREF="#POWERFUL">Powerful Lines</A>
<BR><A HREF="#HYPERLINKS">Hyperlinks to HTML and JavaScript sources</A>
<BR><A HREF="#PREVIOUS">Hyperlinks to previously created Web pages</A>
<BR><A HREF="#FONTS">Fancy Fonts</A>
<BR><A HREF="#PICTURES">Perfect Pictures</A>
<BR>Orderly Tables
<BR>Extraordinary Extras
```

FIGURE 3-5 (continued)

```
<HR>
<P><H2><A NAME= "POWERFUL">Powerful Lines</A></H2></P>

A Horizontal Rule tag 50% wide and 10 increments high.
<HR WIDTH="50%" SIZE=10>

A Horizontal Rule tag 25% wide and 20 increments high.
<HR WIDTH="25%" SIZE=20>

A Horizontal Rule tag 10% wide and 30 increments high.
<HR WIDTH="10%" SIZE=30>

A Horizontal Rule tag without attributes and values.
<HR>

<P><H2><A NAME="HYPERLINKS">Hyperlinks to HTML and JavaScript
  sources</A></H2></P>

<BR><A HREF="http://www.microsoft.com">Microsoft</A>
<BR><A HREF="http://home.netscape.com">Netscape</A>
<BR><A HREF="http://www.sun.com">Sun Microsystems</A>
<BR><A HREF="http://www.oracle.com">Oracle</A>

<HR>
<P><H2><A NAME= "PREVIOUS"> Hyperlinks to previously created Web
  pages</A></H2></P>

<BR><A HREF="One.html">One</A>
<BR><A HREF="Two.html">Two</A>
<BR><A HREF="Three.html">Three</A>
<BR><A HREF="Four.html">Four</A>
<BR><A HREF="Five.html">Five</A>
<BR><A HREF="Six.html">Six</A>
<BR><A HREF="Seven.html">Seven</A>
<BR><A HREF="Eight.html">Eight</A>
<BR><A HREF="Nine.html">Nine</A>
<BR><A HREF="Ten.html">Ten</A>
<BR><A HREF="Eleven.html">Eleven</A>

<HR>
<P><H2><A NAME= "FONTS"> Fancy Fonts </A></H2></P>

<BR><FONT FACE=HELVETICA SIZE=4 COLOR=RED>This is the Helvetica font at
  Size 4</FONT>
<BR><FONT FACE=TIMES SIZE=6 COLOR=GREEN>This is the Times font at Size
  6</FONT>
<BR><FONT FACE=ARIAL SIZE=8 COLOR=ORANGE>This is the Arial font at Size
  8</FONT>
<BR><FONT FACE=COURIER SIZE=2 COLOR=BLACK>This is the Courier font at
  Size 2</FONT>
```

FIGURE 3-5 (continued)

```
<HR>
<P><H2><A NAME="PICTURES">Perfect Pictures</A></H2></P>

<IMG SRC="levy.gif">

</BODY>
</HTML>
```

FIGURE 3-6
Your GIF image can be seen in a browser.

Thinking About Technology

How do pictures add or detract from a Web site? Would you ever want to revisit a Web page that doesn't have pictures? Why or why not?

Download another picture and place it in your Web page. Follow steps 1 to 5 in Step-by-Step 3.2, but this time, download the picture of Dayna the Dragon Fighter found just below Levy the Dragon. Insert this picture into your Web page. Save your new work as Fifteen-2.html.

Net Fun

If you are interested in learning more about HTML, you can order HTML books right over the Web. A great place to visit is Amazon.com. Amazon.com is the largest bookstore on the World Wide Web. If you can't find the book you are looking for at Amazon.com, it probably doesn't exist.

Pictures of All Sizes

Pictures can be altered in a variety of ways by changing a tag's values. Pictures can be used as wallpaper that cover the entire background of a Web page. They can be aligned in the center, to the left side, or to the right side of a page. They can be made bigger or smaller, depending on your needs.

You can also change the size of the picture by using the HEIGHT and WIDTH attributes. Controlling the exact size of a picture can be very helpful in making a page look sharp and interesting.

Net Tip

To have a picture become your background, insert the BACKGROUND attribute in the <BODY> tag like this:
<BODY BACKGROUND="levy.gif">
Try another picture as your background. Make sure the filename appears between the quotation (" ") marks.

In the first part of this step-by-step activity, you will align your picture to the right of the page and make it small. In the second section, you will line three dragons of varying sizes across the page, and then you will place three dragons vertically down the Web page by manipulating a few tags.

STEP-BY-STEP 3.3

1. Open your Fifteen.html file.

2. Near the end of your document, add the following information to your <IMG SRC> tag, as shown in bold here and in Figure 3-7.

```
<P><IMG SRC="levy.gif"
  ALIGN=RIGHT HEIGHT=50
  WIDTH=50></P>
```

3. Save your changes as Sixteen.html.

4. View your changes in your Web browser.

5. Next, create three images that appear across the screen, with each graphic appearing as a different size. To do so, enter the following tags below your first IMG SRC tag, as shown here and in Figure 3-7.

```
<IMG SRC="levy.gif" HEIGHT=100
  WIDTH=100>
<IMG SRC="levy.gif" HEIGHT=150
  WIDTH=150>
<IMG SRC="levy.gif" HEIGHT=200
  WIDTH=200>
```

6. Resave your changes (using the same Sixteen.html filename) and view your additions in your Web browser. Your changes should appear similar to the three horizontal images in Figure 3-8. If your graphics don't appear, make any necessary corrections, resave, and view again.

7. Just below the three tags you entered in the previous step, add two more IMG SRC tags, using <P> tags to cause several graphics to appear vertically. Enter these tags exactly as shown here and in Figure 3-7.

```
<P><IMG SRC="levy.gif" HEIGHT=150
  WIDTH=150></P>
<P><IMG SRC="levy.gif" HEIGHT=200
  WIDTH=200></P>
```

8. Resave your changes as Sixteen.html, and view the result in your Web browser. Consult Figures 3-7 and 3-8 to evaluate how the tags and graphics should appear. Make corrections where necessary, and review any changes in your browser.

FIGURE 3-7
Place dragons everywhere.

```
<HTML>
<TITLE>HTML and JavaScript</TITLE>

<BODY BGCOLOR=WHITE TEXT=BLUE LINK=RED VLINK=GREEN>
<CENTER><H1>Organizing Tags</H1></CENTER>

<P>There are many ways to organize a Web page. This Web page will orga-
  nize text, hypertext links, colors, and fonts. It will also demon-
  strate single spacing, double spacing, and the use of line breaks.</P>

<P>This Web page will display how to organize Web pages in a number of
  ways using: </P>

<BR><A HREF="#POWERFUL">Powerful Lines</A> <BR><AHREF="#HYPERLINKS">
  Hyperlinks to HTML and JavaScript sources</A>
<BR><A HREF="#PREVIOUS">Hyperlinks to previously created Web pages</A>
<BR><A HREF="#FONTS">Fancy Fonts</A>
<BR><A HREF="#PICTURES">Perfect Pictures</A>
<BR>Orderly Tables
<BR>Extraordinary Extras

<HR>
<P><H2><A NAME="POWERFUL">Powerful Lines</A>
  </H2></P>

A Horizontal Rule tag 50% wide and 10 increments high.
<HR WIDTH="50%"SIZE=10>

A Horizontal Rule tag 25% wide and 20 increments high.
<HR WIDTH="25%"SIZE=20>

A Horizontal Rule tag 10% wide and 30 increments high.
<HR WIDTH="10%"SIZE=30>

A Horizontal Rule tag without attributes and values.
<HR>

<P><H2><A NAME= "HYPERLINKS">Hyperlinks to HTML and JavaScript
  sources</A></H2></P>

<BR><A HREF="http://www.microsoft.com">Microsoft</A>
<BR><A HREF="http://home.netscape.com">Netscape</A>
<BR><A HREF="http://www.sun.com">Sun Microsystems</A>
<BR><A HREF="http://www.oracle.com">Oracle</A>

<HR>
<P><H2><A NAME= "PREVIOUS">Hyperlinks to previously created Web
  pages</A></H2></P>

<BR><A HREF="One.html">One</A>
```

FIGURE 3-7 (continued)

```
<BR><A HREF="Two.html">Two</A>
<BR><A HREF="Three.html">Three</A>
<BR><A HREF="Four.html">Four</A>
<BR><A HREF="Five.html">Five</A>
<BR><A HREF="Six.html">Six</A>
<BR><A HREF="Seven.html">Seven</A>
<BR><A HREF="Eight.html">Eight</A>
<BR><A HREF="Nine.html">Nine</A>
<BR><A HREF="Ten.html">Ten</A>
<BR><A HREF="Eleven.html">Eleven</A>

<HR>
<P><H2><A NAME= "FONTS">Fancy Fonts </A></H2></P>

<BR><FONT FACE=HELVETICA SIZE=4 COLOR=RED>This is the Helvetica font at
  Size 4</FONT>
<BR><FONT FACE=TIMES SIZE=6 COLOR=GREEN>This is the Times font at Size 6
  </FONT>
<BR><FONT FACE=ARIAL SIZE=8 COLOR=ORANGE>This is the Arial font at Size 8
  </FONT>
<BR><FONT FACE=COURIER SIZE=2 COLOR=BLACK>This is the Courier font at
  Size 2</FONT>

<HR>
<P><H2><A NAME="PICTURES">Perfect Pictures </A></H2></P>

<P><IMG SRC="levy.gif" ALIGN=RIGHT HEIGHT=50 WIDTH=50></P>

<IMG SRC="levy.gif" HEIGHT=100 WIDTH=100>
<IMG SRC="levy.gif" HEIGHT=150 WIDTH=150>
<IMG SRC="levy.gif" HEIGHT=200 WIDTH=200>

<P><IMG SRC="levy.gif" HEIGHT=150 WIDTH=150></P>
<P><IMG SRC="levy.gif" HEIGHT=200 WIDTH=200></P>

</BODY>
</HTML>
```

FIGURE 3-8
Your GIF images reflect changing the attributes and values.

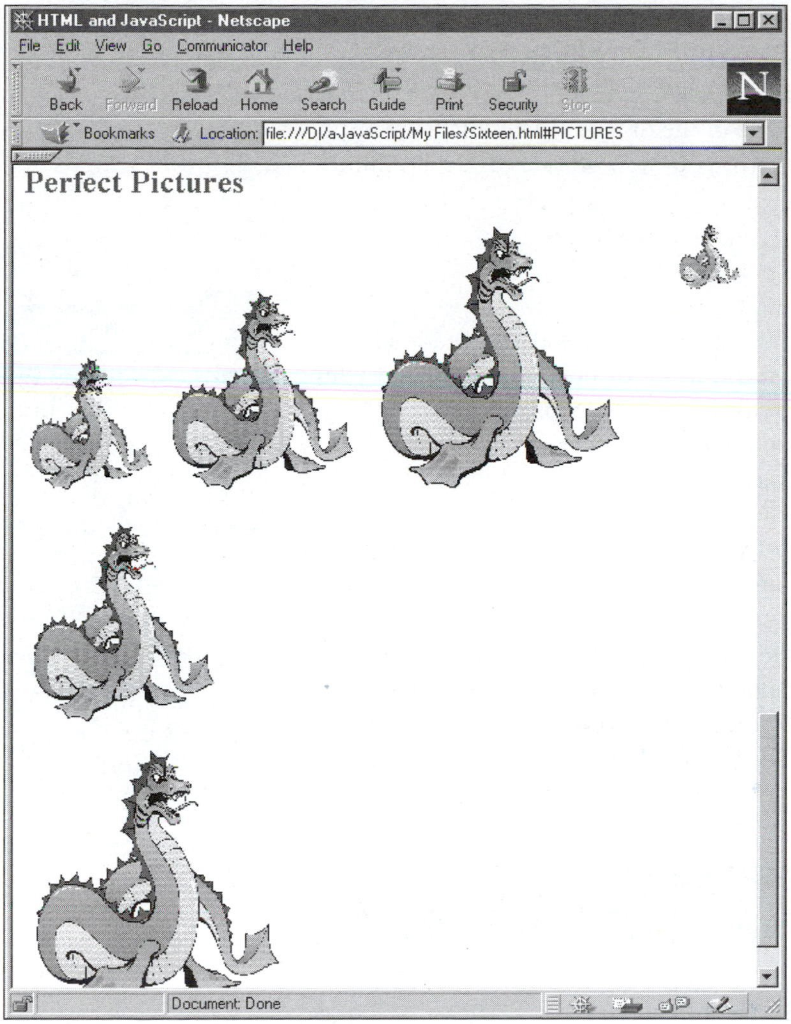

NET ETHICS

One of the big problems on the Web is picture piracy. Since it is so easy to pull pictures off the Web, many people do so without permission. Many pictures are copyrighted; that is, someone owns them. To use them, you need to obtain permission or pay a fee to the artist. Consider which pictures you download and use from the Web. Are they free for you to use? There are many places that allow the free download of images.

Thinking About Technology

How fast can you substitute another graphic for the levy.gif graphic? Think about another graphic you like. Find it on the Web and copy it to your Web page folder. (Be sure to check out the Net Ethics topic in this section first!) Change all the levy.gif filenames in your Sixteen.html file to match the name of the new graphic you want to display. For example, replacing levy.gif with dayna.gif will display the dragon slayer in place of the dragon. Manipulate the attributes and values to display your new graphic in a variety of sizes. Save your new work as Sixteen-2.hmtl.

Orderly Tables

When you think of a table, well set and ready for a big holiday dinner, you think of how organized everything is. All the place settings, plates, cups, and silverware are well organized and in just the right spot.

Electronic tables are just like that. Tables create little boxes in which you can place things to keep them organized. In this step-by-step activity, you will create a table and then insert many of the tags you have already learned into its little boxes called table cells.

Creating a table is easy with the <TABLE> tag. Cells can have a border by adding a BORDER attribute and a number value. You can also make cells appear larger around pictures and text with the CELLPADDING attribute. Within cells, you can align pictures and text to the center, left, or right.

Net Tip

How would you create a hyperlink when the link is a picture? It's easy. Use the same tag structure you used to create hypertext links, but use the IMG SRC tag to replace the words you would normally enter. Try it!

```
<P><A HREF="One.html">
<IMG SRC="levy.gif" HEIGHT=50
WIDTH=50></A>
```

This link will open the first page you created in this unit. Think about how much you have learned since then!

STEP-BY-STEP 3.4

1. Open your Sixteen.html file.

2. Create a hypertext link in your list near the top of the page that will hyperlink to the new section you are creating. The text to be entered is shown in bold here and in Figure 3-9.

```
<BR><A HREF="#TABLES">Orderly
  Tables</A>
```

3. Create a new <HR> tag following the graphics you inserted in Step-by-Steps 3.2 and 3.3.

4. As shown in Figure 3-9, add a new level 2 heading called Orderly Tables just below the <HR> tag you just created and just before the </BODY> tag. Include the <A NAME> tag so you can complete the internal hypertext link you started in step 2.

```
<HR>
<P><H2><A NAME= "TABLES"> Orderly
   Tables </A></H2></P>
```

STEP-BY-STEP 3.4 CONTINUED

5. Below the new heading, near the end of your document, enter the <TABLE> tags, attributes, and values, exactly as shown here and in bold in Figure 3-9.

```
<TABLE BORDER=5 CELLPADDING=10
  ALIGN=CENTER>
<TR>
  <TH>Dragons</TH>
  <TH>Colors</TH>
  <TH>Fonts</TH>
</TR>
<TR>
   <TD><IMG SRC="levy.gif"
   HEIGHT=50 WIDTH=50></TD>
   <TD BGCOLOR=RED
   ALIGN=CENTER>Red</TD>
   <TD ALIGN=CENTER><FONT
   FACE=TIMES SIZE=7
   COLOR=GREEN>Times</TD>
</TR>
<TR>
   <TD><IMG SRC="levy.gif"
      HEIGHT=75 WIDTH=50></TD>
   <TD BGCOLOR=GREEN
      ALIGN=CENTER>Green</TD>
   <TD ALIGN=CENTER><FONT
      FACE=COURIER SIZE=10>
Courier</TD>
</TR>
</TABLE>
```

6. Your tags should now appear like those in Figure 3-9. Save your work as Seventeen.html.

7. View your work in your Web browser. Your new links should look like Figure 3-10. Test each link and make sure they all work. Make any corrections that are necessary.

FIGURE 3-9
It's easy to create a table in HTML.

```
<HTML>
<TITLE>HTML and JavaScript</TITLE>

<BODY BGCOLOR=WHITE TEXT=BLUE LINK=RED VLINK=GREEN>
<CENTER><H1>Organizing Tags</H1></CENTER>

<P>There are many ways to organize a Web page. This Web page will orga-
  nize text, hypertext links, colors, and fonts. It will also demon-
  strate single spacing, double spacing, and the use of line breaks.</P>

<P>This Web page will display how to organize Web pages in a number of
  ways using: </P>

<BR><A HREF="#POWERFUL">Powerful Lines</A> <BR><AHREF="#HYPERLINKS">
  Hyperlinks to HTML and JavaScript sources</A>
<BR><A HREF="#PREVIOUS">Hyperlinks to previously created Web pages</A>
<BR><A HREF="#FONTS">Fancy Fonts</A>
<BR><A HREF="#PICTURES">Perfect Pictures</A>
<BR><A HREF="#TABLES">Orderly Tables</A>
<BR>Extraordinary Extras

<HR>
<P><H2><A NAME="POWERFUL">Powerful Lines</A></H2></P>
```

FIGURE 3-9 (continued)

```
A Horizontal Rule tag 50% wide and 10 increments high.
<HR WIDTH="50%"SIZE=10>

A Horizontal Rule tag 25% wide and 20 increments high.
<HR WIDTH="25%"SIZE=20>

A Horizontal Rule tag 10% wide and 30 increments high.
<HR WIDTH="10%"SIZE=30>

A Horizontal Rule tag without attributes and values.
<HR>

<P><H2><A NAME= "HYPERLINKS">Hyperlinks to HTML and JavaScript
  sources</A></H2></P>

<BR><A HREF="http://www.microsoft.com">Microsoft</A>
<BR><A HREF="http://home.netscape.com">Netscape</A>
<BR><A HREF="http://www.sun.com">Sun Microsystems</A>
<BR><A HREF="http://www.oracle.com">Oracle</A>

<HR>
<P><H2><A NAME= "PREVIOUS">Hyperlinks to previously created Web
  pages</A></H2></P>

<BR><A HREF="One.html">One</A>
<BR><A HREF="Two.html">Two</A>
<BR><A HREF="Three.html">Three</A>
<BR><A HREF="Four.html">Four</A>
<BR><A HREF="Five.html">Five</A>
<BR><A HREF="Six.html">Six</A>
<BR><A HREF="Seven.html">Seven</A>
<BR><A HREF="Eight.html">Eight</A>
<BR><A HREF="Nine.html">Nine</A>
<BR><A HREF="Ten.html">Ten</A>
<BR><A HREF="Eleven.html">Eleven</A>

<HR>
<P><H2><A NAME= "FONTS">Fancy Fonts </A></H2></P>

<BR><FONT FACE=HELVETICA SIZE=4 COLOR=RED>This is the Helvetica font at
  Size 4</FONT>
<BR><FONT FACE=TIMES SIZE=6 COLOR=GREEN>This is the Times font at Size
  6</FONT>
<BR><FONT FACE=ARIAL SIZE=8 COLOR=ORANGE>This is the Arial font at Size
  8</FONT>
<BR><FONT FACE=COURIER SIZE=2 COLOR=BLACK>This is the Courier font at
  Size 2</FONT>

<HR>
<P><H2><A NAME="PICTURES">Perfect Pictures </A></H2></P>
```

FIGURE 3-9 (continued)

```
<P><IMG SRC="levy.gif" ALIGN=RIGHT HEIGHT=50 Width=50></P>

<IMG SRC="levy.gif" HEIGHT=100 WIDTH=100>
<IMG SRC="levy.gif" HEIGHT=150 WIDTH=150>
<IMG SRC="levy.gif" HEIGHT=200 WIDTH=200>

<P><IMG SRC="levy.gif" HEIGHT=150 WIDTH=150></P>
<P><IMG SRC="levy.gif" HEIGHT=200 WIDTH=200></P>

<HR>
<P><H2><A NAME= "TABLES"> Orderly Tables </A></H2></P>

<TABLE BORDER=5 CELLPADDING=10 ALIGN=CENTER>
<TR>
      <TH>Dragons</TH>
      <TH>Colors</TH>
      <TH>Fonts</TH>
</TR>
<TR>
      <TD><IMG SRC="levy.gif" HEIGHT=50 WIDTH=50></TD>
      <TD BGCOLOR=RED ALIGN=CENTER>Red</TD>
      <TD ALIGN=CENTER><FONT FACE=TIMES SIZE=7 COLOR=GREEN>Times</TD>
</TR>
<TR>
      <TD><IMG SRC="levy.gif" HEIGHT=75 WIDTH=50></TD>
      <TD BGCOLOR=GREEN ALIGN=CENTER>Green</TD>
      <TD ALIGN=CENTER><FONT FACE=COURIER SIZE=10>Courier</TD>
</TR>
</TABLE>

</BODY>
</HTML>
```

FIGURE 3-10
An HTML table as seen in your browser.

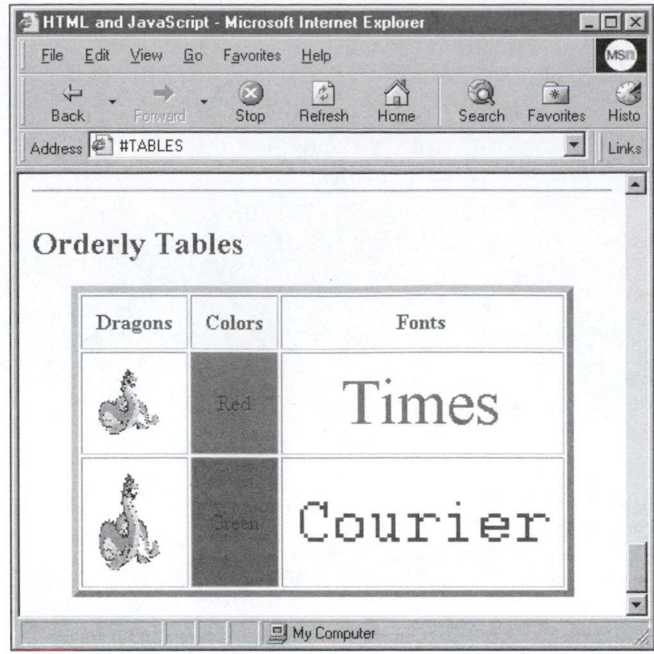

Thinking About Technology

How can tables be used to display information? What kinds of things can you create with the table tags? How could you create a monthly calendar using HTML table tags? Give it a try. Create a calendar for this month. Save your work as Calendar.html. You can use this file later in another activity.

Extraordinary Extras

In Step-by-Step 3.5, you will learn a few extra tags that add extraordinary power to your Web pages. These tags will allow those who visit your Web page to interact with the document.

Many data input, or <FORM> tag, options have been added to HTML. These options give you various ways to ask questions of visitors to your Web page. These tags not only give extra functionality to your Web page, they also make your page more exciting and extraordinary.

There are four basic input tags you will enter. They include:

- Text boxes
- Drop down lists
- Radio buttons
- Check boxes

Net Business

For many years, the Web was a tough place to make a living. The truth is, it took many years before the commercial potential of the Web was realized. Some of the first Web companies to start making a profit online were America Online, Yahoo!, and Amazon.com.
Some succeeded online by daring to go where no one else dared to go. For many years, Internet users said that the Web would soon replace printed books. The people of Amazon.com took exception to that theory and began selling books on the Web. They sold so many books that other book companies realized that they must go online or give away a big portion of their business to Amazon.com. Sony found that the Web was a great place to sell music CDs. Egghead found the Web a great place to sell software. Can you think of other things that might become big sellers online?

This is the last activity before you jump into JavaScript. So, this will be a test of sorts. We will not give you all the tags to refer to. Think about how you should integrate the new tags into your Web page. Don't worry; you will pass with flying font colors. If you have any questions, review the steps in previous activities. Figure 3-11 displays the new tags you will be adding to your Web page.

FIGURE 3-11
A variety of data input tags is shown.

```
<FORM>

Enter your first name: <INPUT TYPE="TEXT" SIZE="25">
<BR>
Enter your last name: <INPUT TYPE="TEXT" SIZE="25">
<P>

<SELECT>
<OPTION SELECTED>Pick your favorite team from this list:
<OPTION>Chicago Bulls
<OPTION>Utah Jazz
<OPTION>Los Angeles Lakers
<OPTION>Indiana Pacers
<OPTION>New Jersey Nets
<OPTION>Phoenix Suns
</SELECT>
<P>

The best place to eat is:
<BR>
<INPUT TYPE="RADIO" NAME="BEST">Wendy's<BR>
<INPUT TYPE="RADIO" NAME="BEST">McDonalds<BR>
<INPUT TYPE="RADIO" NAME="BEST">Taco Bell<BR>
<INPUT TYPE="RADIO" NAME="BEST">Burger King<BR>
<INPUT TYPE="RADIO" NAME="BEST">Kentucky Fried Chicken<BR>
<P>

I like to eat:
<BR>
<INPUT TYPE="CHECKBOX">Hamburgers<BR>
<INPUT TYPE="CHECKBOX">Tacos<BR>
<INPUT TYPE="CHECKBOX">Chicken Strips<BR>
<INPUT TYPE="CHECKBOX">Fries<BR>
<INPUT TYPE="CHECKBOX">Hot Dogs<BR>
<P>

</FORM>
```

STEP-BY-STEP 3.5

1. Open your Seventeen.html file.

2. Create a new section near the end of your Web page called Extraordinary Extras.

3. Create an internal hypertext link from the index list near the top of your Web page that will link to the new section you are creating. Call this link Extraordinary Extras.

4. Change the color, font size, and font face of the title of your new section in any way you see fit.

5. Enter the tags shown in Figure 3-11 in your new Extraordinary Extras section, just before the </BODY> tag at the bottom of the page.

6. Save your work as Eighteen.html.

7. Open your Web browser and try all the input options. They should appear like those found in Figure 3-12. Which ones work? Correct any errors you find, resave, and try them again.

8. Make your own form. Return to your Web page and change all the selection items.

9. Save your work as Eighteen-2.html and test your changes. How did they work?

FIGURE 3-12
Extraordinary Extras are created with forms.

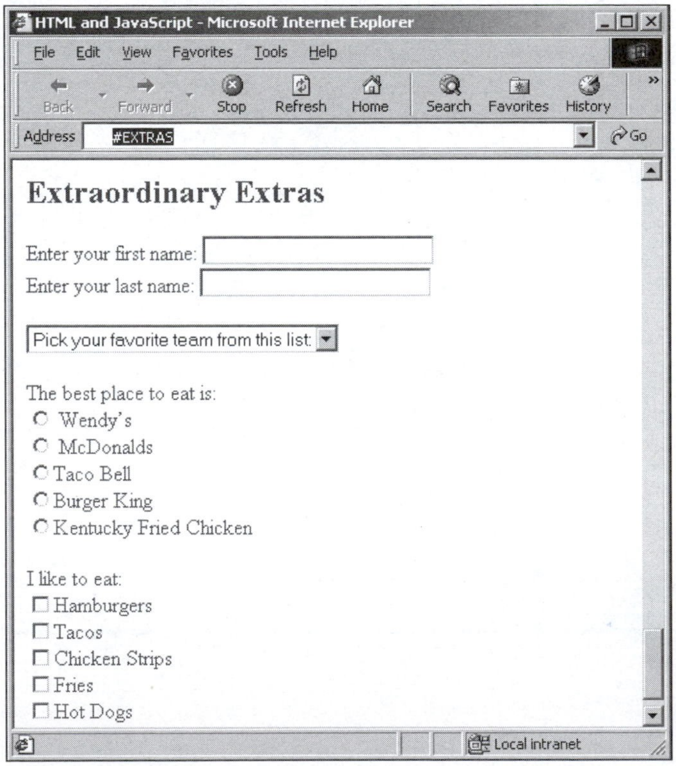

Thinking About Technology

Each of these extraordinary input boxes asks the user to supply a different kind of information. What kinds of responses would you expect from the following FORM attributes?

TEXT

OPTION

RADIO

CHECKBOX

NETIQUETTE

It is considered impolite to download pictures to your school or business network that you don't intend to use. Graphics take a great deal of space on a computer. Downloading hundreds of pictures and not using them is a waste of network server space. Consider deleting any pictures you aren't actually using.

LESSON 3 REVIEW QUESTIONS

WRITTEN QUESTIONS

Write a brief answer to the following questions.

1. Why are artists in such demand on the WWW?

2. When is it illegal to take pictures off the Web?

3. Why is it important not to download pictures to your school or workplace network if you do not plan to use them?

4. How and why would you use the following tags?

```
<B></B>
<EM></EM>
<STRONG></STRONG>
<I></I>
```

5. How and why would you use the BACKGROUND attribute?

6. What tags would you use to make a graphic a hyperlink?

LESSON 3 PROJECTS

PROJECT 3-1

Great Applications, Inc. wants to enter the online video game business. However, before it starts programming the next great online video game, it wants to survey potential customers to see what kinds of online games they want to play and buy.

Brainstorm ten questions that will help Great Applications learn what its customers want in a video game program. Use your <FORM> tag skills, and create an online survey to gather information from potential customers. Have your survey ask for the respondent's name and e-mail address. Ask questions that utilize drop down lists, radio selection items, and check boxes.

PROJECT 3-2

Great Applications, Inc. is asking your team to plan a world tour to demonstrate its new software video games to people in five major cities. You and your team have been asked to create a calendar of events for the tour using <TABLE> tags. The tour must be conducted during a single month and should involve five major cities.

When you create your calendar, create links to tourist information about the cities that you will be visiting on the tour. Use cell padding and cell borders to make the table interesting. You can even put pictures in the cells to illustrate the five cities you have selected for the software rollout.

To save some time, borrow the calendar you created in the Thinking About Technology section after Step-by-Step 3.4. Modify these tags to fit this exercise.

SCANS

PROJECT 3-3

Before you complete this section on HTML and move on to JavaScript, evaluate the impact and importance of HTML on worldwide communications and the economy.

How important is the WWW and HTML to the world's economy?

How does the Web benefit small businesses around the world?

Over 500 years ago, Gutenberg created the printing press and changed the history of the world. Five hundred years from now, how will people look back on the invention of HTML?

What extra features or tags would you like to see added to HTML? Are there any tags that you think should be added to give more power to HTML?

LESSON 4

WHAT IS JAVASCRIPT?

OBJECTIVES

Upon completion of this lesson, you should be able to:

- Understand the purpose of JavaScript.
- Use the <SCRIPT> and </SCRIPT> tags.
- Learn to use JavaScript objects.
- Learn to use JavaScript methods.
- Understand JavaScript syntax.

Estimated Time: 1 hour

The Exciting World of JavaScript

In the previous three lessons, you learned the fundamentals of creating Web pages with Hypertext Markup Language (HTML), but now it is time to move into a different realm of Internet development.

HTML is a powerful tool in many respects, and it is capable of doing a lot of interesting things on the Web. In fact, more than any other technology, HTML is responsible for the tremendous popularity of the Internet today. Nevertheless, HTML does have its limitations. There are a lot of Internet programming tasks that cannot be accomplished with HTML, so it did not take long for professional software developers to start demanding something more. As a result, there are now several different Internet technologies available that were developed by various companies. It is likely that you have heard of some of these products, such as CGI, PERL, CORBA, Java, and, of course, JavaScript. Each of these technologies was designed to address different programming needs, so professional programmers tend to choose different tools to solve different problems. But they all have one thing in common: they all rely on HTML to move around through cyberspace.

You could say that the Hypertext Transfer Protocol (HTTP) is the information superhighway, and HTML represents the various "vehicles" that travel on the superhighway. These vehicles come in numerous shapes and sizes, and they carry different types of payloads, but they all have a common bond.

HTML is the foundation of the Internet, and JavaScript was designed to enhance that foundation. At this point it probably won't surprise you to learn that Web page developers embed JavaScript code into their HTML documents by using two special tags:

```
<SCRIPT> </SCRIPT>
```

These tags inform the Web browser that the text that appears between these tags is to be interpreted as part of a JavaScript program, rather than as literal information to be displayed on the screen. This is where JavaScript begins to move you into the world of programming and away from the world of formatting. Unlike a true programming language, however, JavaScript does not require you to go out and purchase a specialized software package in order to convert it from its human-readable form (called source code) into a machine-readable form (called object code, binary code, executable code, or machine code). Traditional programming languages such as PASCAL, C++, or even Java perform the conversion by means of a compiler, and they usually come with a specialized editor, debugger, project manager, online help system, etc. These types of software packages are known as Integrated Development Environments (IDEs), and some of them are very expensive. But with JavaScript, you can create your source code in exactly the same way you create HTML code—with a simple text editor or word processor. When the HTML document, with its embedded JavaScript program, is loaded by a browser, the program is converted into machine code and executed. Its output is displayed as part of the resulting HTML document. JavaScript gives you many of the capabilities of a full-fledged programming language while maintaining the simplicity of HTML coding.

An Introduction to JavaScript

JavaScript is sometimes referred to as a programming language, but it is really more accurate to call it a scripting language. The difference between a programming language and a scripting language is fairly subtle but important to understand. Both types of languages must be converted from a human-readable form into a machine-readable form. For programming languages, this process is performed before the program runs, by a highly specialized piece of software called a *compiler*. The programmer is not only aware than this conversion must happen but also is in control of the operation. With a scripting language, however, there is no need to explicitly invoke the code conversion process. It happens automatically in the background when the source code is processed by the target program. To be more specific, an HTML document must be written by a human and then processed by a special type of program called a Web browser. And when that HTML document contains embedded JavaScript code, that code is interpreted by the Web browser and converted into a machine-readable format "on-the-fly." Interpretation is simply the term programmers use to describe this line-by-line conversion process that occurs automatically at run time.

Under normal conditions, the output of the JavaScript code will be nothing more than a string (or perhaps many strings) of text that are simply inserted into the HTML page. The resulting page is displayed by a Web browser just as it would be if that resulting text had been typed into the original HTML source document by a human. The real power of embedding JavaScript into HTML documents comes from the fact that the resulting text described above can change from one day to the next, or even from one minute to the next. It is entirely possible for one person to enter a particular URL into his Web browser and see a Web page that is completely different from that seen by another person who enters the exact same URL! These differences could be due to differences in time, differences in location, or even differences in Web browsers. JavaScript is capable of detecting various conditions in the current operating environment and reacting accordingly. This concept is explored in greater detail in Step-by-Step 4.3.

It is easy for a Web browser to detect whether or not a particular HTML page contains embedded JavaScript code. All that is required is for the person creating the document to use the <SCRIPT> tag to mark the beginning of a JavaScript section and then use the </SCRIPT> tag to indicate the end of that section. Everything between these two tags will be interpreted by the Web browser as JavaScript source code rather than standard HTML text. The browser will then convert the script (via the interpretation process) into its equivalent machine-readable form called binary code. This binary code will then be executed, and its output (if any) will be inserted into the HTML text stream and displayed as if it had been typed into the original HTML document by a human. Are you following?

It is also important to understand that the scripts you will be embedding between the <SCRIPT> and </SCRIPT> tags cannot be any old text you care to put in there. On the contrary, the text must conform to some fairly rigid rules, or the Web browser will display a nasty error message on the screen when you try to view your page. This is precisely why JavaScript is called a scripting language—because it must adhere to precise rules of grammar known as *program syntax*. In this lesson, you will learn about JavaScript objects and methods, as well as JavaScript keywords and operators. Once you have these basic programming elements under control, you will be able to start building sophisticated scripts in no time.

Many people who have only a casual knowledge of Internet technologies tend to think that Java programming language and JavaScript scripting language are the same thing. Actually, Java was created first by Sun Microsystems, Inc. Sun released its new cross-platform programming language to the general public in 1995, and it has continued to grow in popularity at an unprecedented rate ever since. Sun was not the only company looking for a way to enhance the capabilities of standard HTML. Netscape Communications Corporation also had been busy working on a way to embed programmable scripts into HTML Web pages, and they needed to incorporate a well-defined syntax into their design. When the Netscape developers saw how popular Java language was becoming, they decided to license the Java name from Sun and use the Java syntax in their own scripting language. The end result of Netscape's efforts was JavaScript, and the company has enjoyed considerable success with this technology as well.

Hello World Wide Web!

The primary purpose of JavaScript code is to generate text that will be inserted into the standard HTML text stream. JavaScript is essentially made up of a number of invisible entities, called objects, that contain a well-defined set of capabilities. In order for JavaScript programmers to make use of these capabilities, they must call upon the services of one or more specialized functions, known as *methods*, within those objects. The way in which a method is invoked is for the programmer to type in the name of the object, followed by a period (the . character), followed by the method name.

Method names are always followed by a parameter list, even though there are sometimes no items in the list. Perhaps the best way to understand method parameters is to visualize a list of ingredients for a recipe. The parameter list simply provides the method with the information it needs to perform its specific function correctly. The syntax of a parameter list consists of an opening parenthesis [( ], zero or more parameter items (separated by commas), and a closing parenthesis [ )]. For example, if you wanted to invoke the write() method of the JavaScript document object, you would do so like this:

```
document.write("A string of text")
```

Now that you've seen a simple example of JavaScript coding, let's give you a chance to incorporate this example into an actual HTML document that contains embedded JavaScript.

STEP-BY-STEP 4.1

1. Open your text editor or word processor, and type the HTML/JavaScript code exactly as it appears in Figure 4-1.

2. Save this file in the appropriate folder as js-one.html.

3. Open your Web browser.

4. View your js-one.html page. You should see an image that looks like Figure 4-2. (Refer to Step-by-Step 1.3 in this unit if you need a reminder on how to view an .html file in your Web browser.)

FIGURE 4-1
Key in this HTML and JavaScript code.

```
<HTML>
<HEAD>
<TITLE>JavaScript Activity #1</TITLE>
</HEAD>
<BODY>
<SCRIPT>
    document.write("Hello World Wide Web!");
</SCRIPT>
</BODY>
</HTML>
```

FIGURE 4-2
Your first page is created with JavaScript!

Hello World Wide Web!

At this point, you may be thinking that this Web page doesn't look all that impressive. But don't give up on JavaScript yet, because we are just getting started. By the time you have worked through a few more activities, you will start to see that JavaScript is capable of much more than this simplistic Web page demonstrates.

The main point is that you have now written one line of JavaScript code, and it actually worked!

Thinking About Technology

You will recognize that there is nothing special about the phrase, "Hello World Wide Web!" in this exercise. This phrase could be replaced with any other string of text, and the JavaScript code would still work just fine. The only thing you have to keep in mind is that the text you want displayed must appear between the opening and closing double quote characters (" "). Try changing the message in the write() method to make sure you understand what is happening here. Try typing in a very long string of text, and then see how the Web browser formats the text on the screen. Also, try inserting several document.write() statements and see how the browser handles them. You might be surprised!

Enhancing the Appearance of Your Web Page

As we mentioned earlier in this lesson, the JavaScript method called document.write() simply inserts a string of characters into the standard HTML text stream. Another way to think of it is that after the browser has finished processing the HTML document, the effective result is that the <SCRIPT> tag, the </SCRIPT> tag, and everything in between the two will be stripped out of the page and replaced by whatever string appears as the parameter of the write() method. This means that any HTML formatting tags we may put before or after the script will be processed just like they would be in a Web page without any embedded JavaScript code. To illustrate this point more clearly, let's modify the Web page we created in Step-by-Step 4.1. Let's add some HTML formatting codes so that our "Hello World Wide Web!" message looks a little more appealing on the screen. Let's also add a second message to the page to make sure you are understanding the interaction between HTML and JavaScript.

STEP-BY-STEP 4.2

1. Open your text editor or word processor and retrieve the js-one.html file you created in the previous activity.

2. Change the activity number to 2 in the title.

3. Next, you're going to make the text you just created with JavaScript an <H1> heading, and you'll create a new <H3> heading with more JavaScript. You'll also want to center both headings. To do all of this, inside the <BODY> and </BODY> tags, add the <CENTER></CENTER> tags, the <H1></H1> tags, the <H3></H3> tags, and a new line of JavaScript, as shown here and in Figure 4-3.

```
<BODY>
<CENTER>
<H1>
<SCRIPT>
   document.write("Hello World
  Wide Web!");
</SCRIPT>
</H1>
<H3>
<SCRIPT>
   document.write("Welcome to
  the exciting world of
  JavaScript.");
</SCRIPT>
</H3>
</CENTER>
```

FIGURE 4-3
The JavaScript Web page now contains HTML formatting tags.

```
<HTML>
<HEAD>
<TITLE>JavaScript Activity #2</TITLE>
</HEAD>
<BODY>
<CENTER>
<H1>
<SCRIPT>
    document.write("Hello World Wide Web!");
</SCRIPT>
</H1>
<H3>
<SCRIPT>
     document.write("Welcome to the exciting world of JavaScript.");
</SCRIPT>
</H3>
</CENTER>
</BODY>
</HTML>
```

4. Your new file should look like Figure 4-3.

5. Save your new file as js-two.html.

6. Open your Web browser and view your js-two.html file. Your page should look just like Figure 4-4.

FIGURE 4-4
A nicely formatted JavaScript Web page appears.

Hello World Wide Web!
Welcome to the exciting world of JavaScript.

If you clearly understood the HTML material presented in Lesson 1, you should be comfortable with the purpose of the center and heading tags we added to this document. You should also understand that the output string that comes from the first call to (or occurrence of) the document.write() method will be inserted into the HTML text stream between the <CENTER> and </CENTER> tags, as well as between the <H1></H1> tags. Likewise, the output string produced by the second call to (occurrence of) document.write() will also appear between the <CENTER></CENTER> tags, in addition to the <H3></H3> tags. In other words, the <H1></H1> tags will only affect the appearance of the first output string, and the <H3></H3> tags will only affect the second string. But the <CENTER></CENTER> tags will affect the position of both output strings. Got it?

WARNING: You may be tempted to place HTML formatting tags (such as <CENTER> or <H1>) around the document.write() statement, rather than outside of the <SCRIPT> and </SCRIPT> tags. Don't do it! You need to remember that everything you type between the script tags will be interpreted by the Web browser as JavaScript code, and misplaced HTML tags do not conform to the rules of JavaScript syntax. Even though it is possible to embed HTML tags in JavaScript output (as shown in the next activity), these tags cannot be placed around JavaScript statements. If you try it, the result will be an error message from your browser.

Thinking About Technology

It should be clear to you that you can use any HTML tags with JavaScript, not just the heading and center tags. Try inserting some of the other HTML tags described in the first three lessons into this step-by-step activity to see what effect they will have. Specifically, try using the tags that affect the foreground and background colors of the Web page. See if you can get your JavaScript Web page to appear as yellow text on a blue background, for example. Or try to make the <H1> text appear in a different color than the <H3> text. You can do that, right?

Net Tip

If you were to study the source code for JavaScript-enabled Web pages on the Internet, you would discover that many of them have semicolons (;) after each statement, while others do not. All of the source listings for the JavaScript activities in this lesson include semicolons, but they are not necessary. If you were to go through each activity and remove the terminating semicolons, all of the scripts would still function correctly. So you may be asking yourself, why are they there? The answer is that it is a matter of personal preference—at least in these examples. But if you were to move from JavaScript coding to some other programming languages (including Pascal, C++, and Java), you would find that the semicolons are no longer optional. Each of these languages will display an error message if you forget to put in a required semicolon, so we feel that it's a good idea to get used to them.

Conditional Statements in JavaScript

The astute student may look at the previous two activities and ask, "Why are we even using JavaScript to display text messages on the screen? Wouldn't it be easier to just type the text into the HTML document and eliminate the calls to the document.write() method?" Well, the honest answer is "Yes!" It would be easier to do it that way. In fact, the Web browser would even display the results slightly faster if we eliminated the script tags because it wouldn't have to invoke the JavaScript interpreter. However, don't forget that JavaScript is capable of performing a lot more functions than simply writing text to the screen. In this activity, you will use one of the most powerful features of the JavaScript language, the conditional statement. Every programming language possesses the ability to make decisions. Or, to put it in more technical terms, every language gives programmers the ability to evaluate a specific condition and then perform different actions depending on the results of that evaluation.

The syntax of the conditional statement in JavaScript is very important. The statement begins with the keyword *if*, and then a condition is specified within a pair of parentheses. A keyword is recognized as part of the language definition. It is reserved by the language and cannot be used as a variable. Some examples of keywords are *if*, *else*, and *return*.

The condition is followed by a *statement block* which consists of an opening brace ({), one or more JavaScript statements, and then a closing brace (}). The shell of a JavaScript conditional statement is shown in Figure 4-5.

FIGURE 4-5
The JavaScript conditional statement shell is shown.

```
if (<condition>)
{
   statement 1;
   statement 2;
   statement 3;
       .
       .
       .
   statement N;
}
```

INTERNET MILESTONE

When Netscape Communications Corporation introduced JavaScript in 1995, they were not the first company to provide Web content developers with a new technology to enhance the capabilities of HTML. However, they were the first to provide a full-featured scripting language, and it didn't take long for other companies to recognize the advantages of this technology. While scripting does not provide all of the features of a complete programming language, it does not require the use of complex or expensive compiler software. This makes it an ideal choice for novice programmers, educational institutions, or other organizations with limited financial resources.

So in 1996, Microsoft Corporation quickly joined the scripting bandwagon by offering both JScript and VBScript as alternatives to the industry-standard JavaScript.These scripting languages are roughly equivalent to JavaScript in terms of the capabilities they provide, but they also offer a few extra features to those users who run Microsoft's Internet Explorer on the Windows platform. Like JavaScript, JScript is based on the syntax of the Java programming language, while VBScript is based on the programming syntax of Visual Basic.

The scripting language of choice for professional developers depends upon their particular preferences and programming needs. But no matter which language they choose, they can thank JavaScript for getting the scripting movement started.

The JavaScript if statement also supports an optional else clause, which defines the action to take if the specified condition is not true. The else keyword appears immediately after the statement block of the if clause, and it contains a statement block of its own. An example of a JavaScript conditional statement that includes the optional else clause is shown in Figure 4-6.

FIGURE 4-6
This is the format for a JavaScript conditional statement shell with an else clause.

```
if (<condition>)
{
   statement i1;
   statement i2;
   statement i3;
      .
      .
      .
   statement iN;
}
else
{
   statement e1;
   statement e2;
   statement e3;
      .
      .
      .
   statement eN;
}
```

Now that you know the basic structure of JavaScript if and if/else statements, let's talk a little about the condition part of the syntax (shown as <condition> in Figures 4-5 and 4-6). A JavaScript condition will always consist of two tokens separated by a relational operator. A token can be either a variable name (such as *x* or *count*) or a literal constant (such as *10* or *Shane*). The relational operator may be any one of the following:

Operator	**Meaning**
==	is equal to
!=	is not equal to
<	is less than
>	is greater than
<=	is less than or equal to
>=	is greater than or equal to

NOTE: Make sure that you use two equal sign characters (= =) when testing for equality. If you forget and use only one equal sign, your Web browser will reprimand you with an error message!

Now that you have learned to create conditional statements in JavaScript, let's put that knowledge to work in an actual program. In this step-by-step activity, we will include a simple conditional statement, and teach you a useful programming technique in the process. It is fairly common for Web page developers to want to perform different tasks, depending on the type of browser a particular user has. The JavaScript program you are about to create will determine if the Web surfer is using Netscape Navigator or not, and then it will react accordingly.

STEP-BY-STEP 4.3

1. Open your text editor or word processor, and retrieve the js-two.html file.
2. Change the activity number to 3.
3. Just after the closing </H3> tag but before the closing </CENTER> tag, enter a new JavaScript statement, as shown in bold here and in Figure 4-7.

```
</H3>
<SCRIPT>
    if (navigator.appName ==
   "Netscape")
    {
      document.write("You are using N
      etscape Navigator.");
    }
    else
    {
      document.write("You are not
     using Netscape Navigator.<BR>"
     );
      document.write("I'll bet
      you're using Internet
      Explorer.");
    }
</SCRIPT>
</CENTER>
```

4. Your completed file should look like Figure 4-7.

FIGURE 4-7
HTML/JavaScript document with if/else conditional statement included.

```
<HTML>
<HEAD>
<TITLE>JavaScript Activity #3</TITLE>
</HEAD>
<BODY>
<CENTER>
<H1>
<SCRIPT>
    document.write("Hello World Wide Web!");
</SCRIPT>
</H1>
<H3>
<SCRIPT>
```

STEP-BY-STEP 4.3 CONTINUED

FIGURE 4-7 (continued)

```
    document.write("Welcome to the exciting world of JavaScript.");
</SCRIPT>
</H3>
<SCRIPT>
    if (navigator.appName == "Netscape")
    {
      document.write("You are using Netscape Navigator.");
    }
    else
    {
      document.write("You are not using Netscape Navigator.<BR>");
      document.write("I'll bet you're using Internet Explorer.");
    }
</SCRIPT>
</CENTER>
</BODY>
</HTML>
```

5. After you have completed your edits, save the resulting file with the name js-three.html.

6. Start your Web browser and load the js-three.html file, as you did in the previous two step-by-step activities. If you are using Netscape Navigator, your screen should now look like Figure 4-8A. But if you are not using Netscape Navigator, your screen should look like Figure 4-8B.

FIGURE 4-8A
This Web page results when using Netscape Navigator.

Hello World Wide Web!

Welcome to the exciting world of JavaScript.

You are using Netscape Navigator.

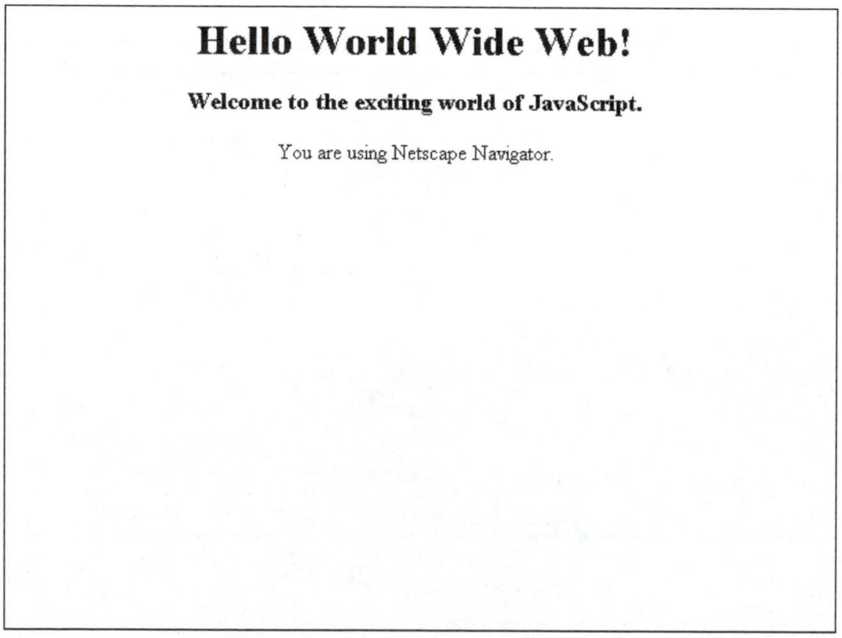

FIGURE 4-8B
This Web Page results when not using Netscape Navigator.

Hello World Wide Web!

Welcome to the exciting world of JavaScript.

You are not using Netscape Navigator.
I'll bet you're using Internet Explorer.

Even though we didn't add a whole lot of code to our JavaScript program, we did introduce several important concepts. Let's take a minute to review those concepts to make sure you have a solid understanding of what is happening here.

First of all, the condition being evaluated in this JavaScript program is:

```
(navigator.appName == "Netscape")
```

We mentioned earlier in this lesson that JavaScript objects contain special functions, called methods, that perform various tasks. Well, it just so happens that JavaScript objects also contain properties that programmers can access to obtain information about the object. In this case, we are utilizing the appName property of the navigator object in order to determine the application name of the current Web browser. (Please note that in this context, the word "navigator" can be used interchangeably with the word "browser.") If this name is "Netscape," then we know the user is running Netscape Navigator. Otherwise, we know the user is not running Netscape Navigator, so he or she probably is running Microsoft's Internet Explorer (although there is a small chance it could be some other browser).

The second important concept to learn here is that once the condition has been evaluated, either the if statement block will be executed or the else block will be executed—never both. If the result of the condition is true, the if block will run. If the condition is false, the else block will run. It's as simple as that.

There is a final point in this example you should recognize. Until now, we have repeatedly mentioned the concept of embedding JavaScript source code in HTML documents. Well, it turns out that it is also possible, not to mention useful, to embed HTML tags in JavaScript text strings! Look carefully at the first call to document.write() inside the *else* statement block. Notice that the HTML <BR> tag is embedded within the output text string. The reason this tag is present is because we wanted the second string of text to appear on a separate line, rather than on the same line as the first string. In order to accomplish this, we have to put a <BR> tag in the output text stream so that the browser will recognize the break command.

Thinking About Technology

Do you suppose that <BR> is the only HTML formatting tag that can be embedded in a JavaScript output string? Of course it isn't. You can use any formatting tags you wish in a document.write() parameter string. Try being creative for a moment, and see how many other tags you can put in the JavaScript code for this activity. What effect, if any, do they have on the resulting Web page? Is it better to place HTML tags outside of the script tags, or is it better to embed them in JavaScript text strings? Are there times when you might want to do both? Think about it!

Using the JavaScript Alert() Method

In the previous three step-by-step activities, we have made use of the document.write() method, which is probably the most common way for JavaScript programs to communicate with the user. However, there are other ways in which scripts can get the user's attention. One way is the JavaScript alert() method. The purpose of the alert() method is to allow the program to display a special dialog box that will alert the user that an expected event has occurred, or that some kind of user input is required. Unlike the write() method or the appName property, the alert() method is not part of an object. Instead, this method is part of the JavaScript interpreter itself, and it interacts directly with the underlying operating system. (A detailed description of what an operating system is and what functions it performs is beyond the scope of this book. However, the operating system is Microsoft Windows on most PCs, Mac OS on Macintosh computers, UNIX on some workstations, etc.) For this reason, it is not necessary to include an object name and a period (.) character when it is invoked.

STEP-BY-STEP 4.4

1. Open your text editor or word processor like before, and retrieve the js-three.html file.

2. Change the activity number located between the TITLE tags to 4.

3. Add an alert statement to the if block, as shown in bold below and in Figure 4-9.

```
{
   document.write("You are using
  Netscape Navigator.");
   alert("Netscape Navigator
 detected.");
}
```

4. Add a second alert statement to the else block, as shown in bold here and in Figure 4-9.

```
{
   document.write("You are not
 using Netscape
 Navigator.<BR>");
   document.write("I'll bet
 you're using Internet
 Explorer.");
   alert("Netscape Navigator
 required.");
}
```

FIGURE 4-9
This JavaScript source code calls to the alert() method.

```
<HTML>
<HEAD>
<TITLE>JavaScript Activity #4</TITLE>
</HEAD>
<BODY>
<CENTER>
<H1>
<SCRIPT>
    document.write("Hello World Wide Web!");
</SCRIPT>
</H1>
<H3>
<SCRIPT>
    document.write("Welcome to the exciting world of JavaScript.");
</SCRIPT>
</H3>
<SCRIPT>
    if (navigator.appName == "Netscape")
    {
      document.write("You are using Netscape Navigator.");
      alert("Netscape Navigator detected.");
    }
    else
    {
      document.write("You are not using Netscape Navigator.<BR>");
      document.write("I'll bet you're using Internet Explorer.");
      alert("Netscape Navigator required.");
    }
</SCRIPT>
</CENTER>
</BODY>
</HTML>
```

5. When you have made the necessary changes to the HTML document, save it with the new file name js-four.html.

6. Open your Web browser and view your js-four.html file. If you are running Netscape Navigator, your screen should look like Figure 4-10A. But if you are running Microsoft's Internet Explorer, your screen will look like Figure 4-10B.

FIGURE 4-10A
Your screen as shown in Netscape Navigator.

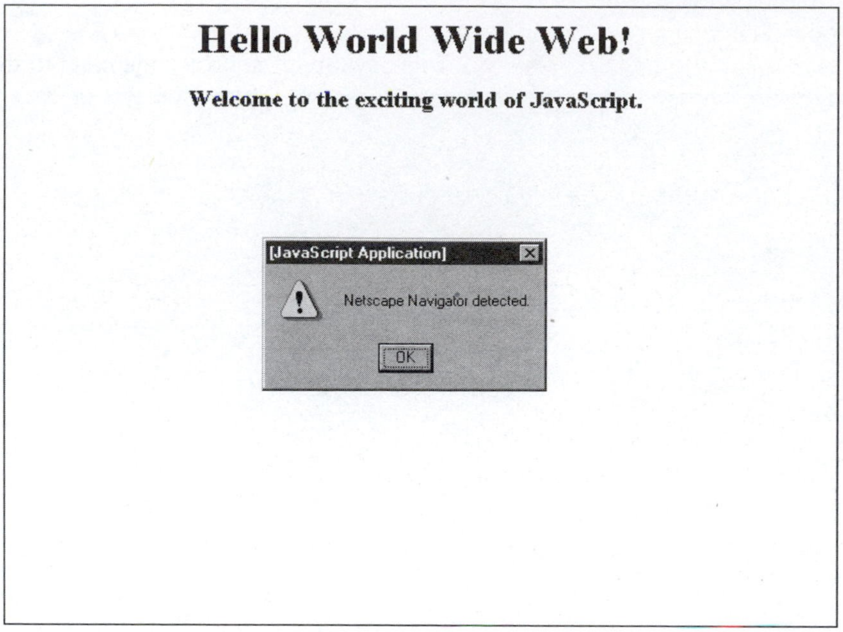

Hello World Wide Web!

Welcome to the exciting world of JavaScript.

[JavaScript Application]

Netscape Navigator detected.

OK

FIGURE 4-10B
Your screen as shown in Internet Explorer.

Hopefully, this activity has helped you to see how the alert() method could be useful in some situations. It normally is used in JavaScript programs when the user needs to be made aware that some unexpected error condition has occurred. It can also be used, however, if the program needs some kind of user acknowledgement before proceeding. In either case, the alert() method is an alternative way for JavaScript software to generate output.

Thinking About Technology

In this step-by-step activity, we have demonstrated how to define a conditional statement that evaluates the contents of the navigator.appName property to determine if it contains the value "Netscape." But if the appName property does not contain the value "Netscape," what value does it contain? How can you find out? Well, think about the document.write() method for a minute. Can it be used to display more than just a literal string (in double quotes)? Of course it can. It can also be used to display the contents of a JavaScript variable or an object property. Now you can write a JavaScript statement that displays the value of appName, can't you? Sure you can. Try it!

Using Curly Braces

One of the characteristics of the JavaScript language that novice programmers tend to struggle with is the use of "curly braces." The opening brace ({) indicates the beginning of a statement block, and the closing brace (}) marks the end of that block.

Although the rules of JavaScript syntax are somewhat flexible when it comes to the placement of these braces, we strongly recommend that you follow the style shown in this book. If you start getting sloppy or inconsistent with the way you place your braces, it is very easy to cause yourself some serious problems. When the number of opening braces does not correspond to the number of closing braces, your Web browser will report a syntax error. However, it is also possible for braces to be placed in such a way that no syntax error occurs, but the program still will not run correctly.

The bottom line is that you can save yourself a lot of headaches by following a few simple rules:

1. Always place the opening brace directly below the keyword to which it belongs.
2. Always indent the statements contained within the statement block.
3. Always place the closing brace so that it is vertically aligned with its corresponding open brace.

If you remember to follow these rules, it becomes very easy to see what statements are contained within a particular statement block and to what keyword the block belongs. Never forget that it is often necessary for someone else to read your code, and this becomes a difficult task when statement blocks are disorganized or carelessly defined. It is professional courtesy to write legible code that is formatted logically and indented consistently. So please be considerate!

Net Tip

If you look closely at the source code listing of Figure 4-7, you will see that there is a space between the if keyword and the opening parenthesis of the condition. You will also see that there is no space between the write method name and the opening parenthesis of its parameter list. Although this may seem inconsistent at first, it is the way that most professional programmers would do it.

As far as the JavaScript interpreter is concerned, the space is optional in both cases. You may put a space in or leave it out, and the script will still function correctly. However, there is a distinct syntactical difference between a JavaScript statement and a JavaScript method call. A JavaScript statement will always contain one or more keywords, and it is customary to place "white space" around keywords. On the other hand, every JavaScript method name must be accompanied by a parameter list, so it is preferable not to put a space between the name and its parameters.

Following these two programming style conventions will help make your JavaScript code much more readable by other programmers. You may have to think about it a little at first, but it will soon become second nature.

Accessing the Browser Status Line

You have probably noticed that when your Web browser is loading an HTML document that contains many objects, it displays various messages at the bottom of the window. This area of the screen is known as the status line, and it can be accessed from within a JavaScript program. In addition to the document.write() method and the alert() method, this is another way in which a JavaScript Web page can communicate information to the user.

How do you access the browser status line? Once again, the answer to this question is very simple. The message displayed in the status line is nothing more than a string value that is stored in the status property of the window object. This means you can change the message at any time within a JavaScript program by including a statement like this:

```
window.status = "A string of text";
```

Now that you understand how easy it can be, let's add two new lines of code to the JavaScript program you wrote in the previous step-by-step activity. This code will simply reinforce the messages that are displayed by the alert() method.

STEP-BY-STEP 4.5

1. Open your text editor or word processor like before, and retrieve the js-four.html file.

2. Change the activity number located between the title tags to 5.

3. Add a window status statement to the if block, as shown in bold here and in Figure 4-11.

```
{
    document.write("You are using
   Netscape Navigator.");
    window.status = "Netscape
  Navigator detected.";
    alert("Netscape Navigator
  detected.");
}
```

4. Add a second window status statement to the else block, as shown in bold here and in Figure 4-11.

```
{
    document.write("You are not
  using Netscape
  Navigator.<BR>");
    document.write("I'll bet
  you're using Internet
  Explorer.");
    window.status = "Netscape
  Navigator required.";
    alert("Netscape Navigator
  required.");
}
```

FIGURE 4-11
JavaScript source code can set the browser status line.

```
<HTML>
<HEAD>
<TITLE>JavaScript Activity #5</TITLE>
</HEAD>
<BODY>
<CENTER>
<H1>
<SCRIPT>
    document.write("Hello World Wide Web!");
</SCRIPT>
```

FIGURE 4-11 (continued)

```
</H1>
<H3>
<SCRIPT>
    document.write("Welcome to the exciting world of JavaScript.");
</SCRIPT>
</H3>
<SCRIPT>
    if (navigator.appName == "Netscape")
    {
      document.write("You are using Netscape Navigator.");
      window.status = "Netscape Navigator detected.";
      alert("Netscape Navigator detected.");
    }
    else
    {
      document.write("You are not using Netscape Navigator.<BR>");
      document.write("I'll bet you're using Internet Explorer.");
      window.status = "Netscape Navigator required.";
      alert("Netscape Navigator required.");
    }
</SCRIPT>
</CENTER>
</BODY>
</HTML>
```

5. When you have made the necessary changes to the HTML document, save your new file with the name js-five.html.

6. Open your Web browser and view your js-five.html file. If you are running Netscape Navigator, your screen should look like Figure 4-12A. But if you are running Microsoft's Internet Explorer, your screen will look like Figure 4-12B.

FIGURE 4-12A
Your screen shown in Netscape Navigator.

Hello World Wide Web!

Welcome to the exciting world of JavaScript.

[JavaScript Application]

Netscape Navigator detected.

OK

40%

Netscape Navigator detected.

FIGURE 4-12B
Your screen shown in Internet Explorer.

Welcome to the exciting world of JavaScript.

You are not using Netscape Navigator.
I'll bet you're using Internet Explorer.

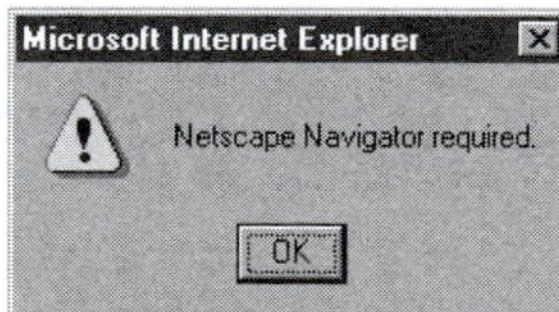

Netscape Navigator required.

As we mentioned in Step-by-Step 4.4, the most common way for JavaScript to interact with a Web surfer is by means of the document.write() method. But the browser status line also can be an effective way of communicating information to the user. In this case, we simply have used the status line to echo the message displayed in the alert dialog box. However, it is much more common to see JavaScript programs use the status line to let the user know what it is doing. Whenever your script is about to initiate a potentially lengthy process (such as download a large graphic image, for example), it is a good idea to display an appropriate message in the status line. This can go a long way toward making sure that the user knows his system hasn't crashed.

Thinking About Technology

One way in which some JavaScript programmers utilize the browser status line is to display instructions to the user. For example, in your current source code it might make sense to display a message that tells the user what to do when the alert dialog appears. That is, the status line could include a message that tells the user to click on the OK button to continue processing the script. Why don't you go ahead and make this change? Try to make the message as informative as possible without using a lot of words.

Net Fact

The next time you are in your local bookstore, take a few minutes to skim through the first few lessons of several different programming books. In many cases, you will see that the first programming example introduced demonstrates how to display the phrase "Hello, World!" in that particular language. Why do you suppose it is so common for authors to begin their books in this way?

In 1978, two employees of Bell Laboratories named Brian Kernighan and Dennis Ritchie published a book entitled *The C Programming Language*. This book proved to be one of the most enduring programming tutorials in the history of computer software. And as it turns out, the very first programming exercise in this book explains how to use the C function called printf to display the phrase "Hello, World." Though it is unlikely Kernighan and Ritchie intended to start an informal tradition among authors of programming books, that is exactly what they did! And although we took the liberty of modifying the phrase somewhat (to "Hello, World Wide Web!"), it is still based on this simple example from 20 years ago.

LESSON 4 REVIEW QUESTIONS

WRITTEN QUESTIONS

Write a brief answer to the following questions:

1. How does JavaScript enhance the capabilities of HTML?

2. What is a JavaScript object? What are object methods and object properties?

3. What JavaScript method is most commonly used to generate output?

4. What is the syntax of a conditional statement in JavaScript?

5. In what ways does the alert() method differ from the document.write() method?

LESSON 4 PROJECTS

PROJECT 4-1

Great Applications, Inc. is looking for a skilled Internet programmer who has a good understanding of HTML programming with JavaScript. In order to test the knowledge of potential employees, Great Applications is giving each candidate a simple HTML/JavaScript test. The test contains the 19-line source code listing found in Step-by-Step 4.2, and each applicant is given a simple task to perform. The instructions for completing the task are as follows:

- Remove the <H1> and </H1> tags from the HTML file, and reinsert them somewhere inside the first script section. After you have moved these two tags, the resulting HTML file must not cause the browser to generate an error message, but the Web page should look exactly the same on the screen as it did before.
- Do the same with the <H3> and </H3> tags. Move them to a new location within the second script so that the Web page continues to display correctly.

Can you do it? We're sure you can if you review Step-by-Step 4.3 carefully.

PROJECT 4-2

As a team of three or four, study the HTML/JavaScript file you created in Step-by-Step 4.5. Pretend that Great Applications, Inc. has just assigned your group the task of rewriting this program so that it is oriented toward Microsoft's Internet Explorer (IE) rather than toward Netscape's Navigator. This means that you will have to change the JavaScript conditional statement, as well as the wording of the text strings inside the if and the else statement blocks in your js-four.html file.

When you have completed your changes, view the new file with Netscape Navigator and with Microsoft's Internet Explorer to make sure that it operates correctly in both browsers.

Hint: The appName property will contain the value "Microsoft Internet Explorer" when Internet Explorer is running.

CRITICAL THINKING

SCANS

In the introduction to Step-by-Step 4.3., we mentioned that the conditional statement is one of JavaScript's most powerful features. This claim is merely an echo of a statement made more than 20 years ago by a great computer scientist by the name of Joseph Weizenbaum. In 1976, Mr. Weizenbaum published a book entitled *Computer Power and Human Reason,* in which he presented the idea that the real power of computer systems is their ability to make decisions. Think about this idea for a while, and then answer the following questions:

How useful would computers be if they could not make decisions?

Describe the general structure of the JavaScript decision-making statement.

What does it mean to "evaluate a condition"?

Why do you suppose the else clause of the if/else statement is optional?

LESSON 5

USING IMAGES WITH JAVASCRIPT

OBJECTIVES

Upon completion of this lesson, you should be able to:

- Understand the names and usage of JavaScript events.
- Understand the purpose and syntax of JavaScript functions.
- Create an image rollover.
- Create a hyperlink rollover.
- Create a cycling banner.
- Display random images.
- Create a JavaScript slide show.

Estimated Time: 1 hour

Making Graphic Images Come Alive

In Lesson 3 of this unit, we mentioned how important the effective use of graphic images can be to the overall success of a Web page. Well, that principle holds true whether the Web page is based on HTML or JavaScript technology. Standard HTML gives you the ability to do several interesting things with images, but JavaScript gives you some additional capabilities. In this lesson, we will focus on those features of JavaScript that are commonly used to make graphic images "come alive" on Web pages. Once you have learned these new techniques, you will quickly recognize their usage all over the World Wide Web. Then you will no longer wonder how the designers of these interesting pages were able to create such eye-catching effects.

Before you can accomplish anything spectacular with images, you need to acquire an understanding of JavaScript *events*. For our purposes, you can think of an event as a system-level response to the occurrence of some specific condition. Some of these conditions are generated by the Web browser software itself, but most of them are caused by the user performing some action. Such actions might include moving the mouse, clicking on a button object, or even selecting a block of text on the screen. But regardless of how a particular event is generated, JavaScript gives you the ability to create Web pages that react to it. And when these reactions are implemented skillfully, the user will definitely be impressed by your Web page.

Another important concept you need to master when working with images is the notion of JavaScript functions. A *function* is nothing more that a segment of JavaScript code that can be invoked (or called) just like the document.write() and alert() methods you used in Lesson 4. In fact, there is really no difference between a method and a function except that methods have already been defined as part of the JavaScript programming environment. Functions, on the other hand, are written by you and may contain any number of JavaScript statements, including calls to JavaScript methods or other functions.

It may not be obvious to you at this point how JavaScript events and functions relate to the use of graphic images in Web pages. But just be patient, and you will see the connection very soon. In fact, that is the very purpose of the activities in this lesson. We will be using events and functions with images to create some interesting effects that will improve the quality of your Web pages immensely.

Using JavaScript Events

All of the activities in this lesson make use of one or more JavaScript events. However, there are several JavaScript events available that are not discussed in this lesson. But that doesn't mean you can't do a little "independent study" and learn how to use them on your own. Here is an alphabetical list of the JavaScript events that are available, along with a brief description of the condition that will trigger the event.

Event Name	Event Trigger
onAbort	The user aborted the loading of a Web page.
onBlur	The user deactivated an object (the object lost focus).
onChange	The user changed an object in some way.
onClick	The user clicked the mouse on an object.
onError	The JavaScript interpreter encountered a script error.
onFocus	The user activated an object (the object received focus).
onLoad	The Web browser finished loading a page.
onMouseOver	The mouse pointer passed over an object.
onMouseOut	The mouse pointer moved off of an object.
onSelect	The user selected (highlighted) the contents of an object.
onSubmit	The user submitted an HTML form.
onUnload	The Web browser unloaded a page from memory.

Teaching an Image to Roll Over

In Lesson 3, you learned how to include a graphic image in your Web page, and you also learned how to turn an image into a hyperlink. Now we are going to show you how to use the power of JavaScript to make a graphical hyperlink respond to mouse movement. To be more specific, you are going to learn how to change the appearance of an image whenever the user moves the mouse pointer over it. This JavaScript programming technique is called an *image rollover*.

The first thing you need to know to implement a rollover is how to use the JavaScript events called onMouseOver and onMouseOut. The onMouseOver event is generated whenever the user moves the mouse over a particular object. Likewise, the onMouseOut event is generated when the user moves the mouse pointer off of the object. All you need to learn is how to use JavaScript to detect when these events occur, and then take some appropriate action. In this activity, we are going to display a blue arrow on the screen and then change that arrow to red when the mouse pointer rolls over it. We will then change the arrow color back to blue when the mouse pointer rolls off of the image.

STEP-BY-STEP 5.1

1. You will need to use some graphics in this activity, which you will download from the same site you accessed in Lesson 3. So, open your Web browser and enter the URL www.course.com/downloads/swep/htmljava/ in your Web browser.

2. Click on the Activity 5.1 link from the list you see.

3. Download the bluearrow.gif and redarrow.gif files to the exact same folder where you have been saving your Web pages.

4. Open your text editor or word processor, and type the HTML/JavaScript code exactly as it appears in Figure 5-1.

5. Save this file in the appropriate folder as js-six.html.

6. Open your Web browser if it is not already open.

7. View your js-six.html page.

FIGURE 5-1
Type this JavaScript code to create an image rollover.

```
<HTML>
<HEAD>
<TITLE>JavaScript Activity #6 </TITLE>
<SCRIPT>
    blueArrow = new Image;
    blueArrow.src = "bluearrow.gif";
    redArrow = new Image;
    redArrow.src = "redarrow.gif";
</SCRIPT>
</HEAD>
<BODY>
<CENTER>
<A HREF="webpage.html"
  onMouseOver="document.arrow.src = redArrow.src;"
  onMouseOut="document.arrow.src = blueArrow.src;">
<IMG SRC="bluearrow.gif"
    NAME="arrow"
    WIDTH=320
    HEIGHT=200>>
```

FIGURE 5-1 (continued)

```
</A>
</CENTER>
</BODY>
</HTML>
```

Even though the HTML/JavaScript source code in Figure 5-1 is not very large, it does introduce several new features that you have not seen before. Let's take a minute to make sure you understand all of these concepts, because you will be seeing them throughout this lesson.

First of all, you should be aware that the <SCRIPT> and </SCRIPT> tags appear in the header section of the HTML document rather than in the body section. This means that the Web browser will process the JavaScript code before it begins to display the contents of the document on the screen. This is an important point for this particular document because we want the browser to load both the blue and the red arrow images into memory before it displays the body of the Web page. If we fail to do this, the browser would not know what images to load when the onMouseOver and onMouseOut events occur, and the result would be a JavaScript error message.

Next, it is important to understand what the JavaScript code (lines 5 through 8 of Figure 5-1) actually does. The statement in line 5 (blueArrow = new Image;) tells the JavaScript interpreter to create a new Image object, and then to save a reference to that object in a variable that we have called blueArrow. (Remember that a JavaScript variable is nothing more than a name that is assigned to a literal value or to an object. Once this assignment has been made, the name can be used throughout the HTML document to refer to that particular value or object.)

The following statement, on line 6 (blueArrow.src = "bluearrow.gif";), tells JavaScript that the source (src) property of the blueArrow object will contain the graphic image stored in the file bluearrow.gif. This is the statement that actually causes the browser to load the blue arrow image into memory. Once this task is complete, the next two JavaScript statements perform essentially the same function as the first two statements.

The statement on line 7 (redArrow = new Image;) causes the interpreter to create a new Image object and assign it the name redArrow. The statement on line 8 (redArrow.src = "redarrow.gif";) sets the src property of the object to the image contained in the file redarrow.gif, so the browser will load this image into memory also. Any questions about this part of your Web page?

The next concept we need to discuss here is JavaScript event handling logic. This is an important feature of JavaScript because it demonstrates another way in which JavaScript code can interact with standard HTML tags. Until now, all of the JavaScript statements you have used were located between the <SCRIPT> and </SCRIPT> tags, right? But JavaScript event handling statements are actually placed within a standard HTML tag. In this case, the statements that handle the onMouseOver and onMouseOut events are located within the anchor (<A></A>) tags. When the onMouseOver event occurs, the source (src) property of the arrow object contained within the document object is set to the src property of the redArrow object. Likewise, when the onMouseOut event occurs, the src property of the document's arrow object is assigned the value of the blueArrow.src property. Thus, when the mouse pointer rolls over the arrow image, the onMouseOver event fires (occurs), and the image source is assigned the contents of the redarrow.gif file. In a similar fashion, moving the mouse pointer off of the arrow image causes the onMouseOut event to fire, and the image source is assigned the contents of the bluearrow.gif file. Is this making sense to you? Good!

The final point we would like to address concerns the origin of the document.arrow object. How does the browser know what object we are referring to when we use the name arrow? The answer, fortunately, is very simple. If you look closely at the <IMG> tag we used to define the original anchor image, you will see that we included a new attribute that you have not used before. This attribute is called NAME, and its purpose is to allow you to assign a variable name to the image object. In this example, we gave the image object the name arrow, and since this image is part of our HTML document, it can be referenced in JavaScript code as document.arrow.

Thinking About Technology

You may have noticed that if you click the mouse button when your mouse pointer is over the arrow image, your Web browser displays an error message. Why do you suppose this happens? Well, if you think about it for a minute, you should realize that the arrow image was defined as a hyperlink in this document, and the purpose of a hyperlink is to tell the browser to load a new HTML document when the user clicks on it. So look carefully at the HREF attribute of your <A> tag. What Web page file will the browser try to load if you click on this particular hyperlink? Obviously, the answer is the webpage.html file, since that is the filename assigned to the HREF attribute. But does this file really exist? Of course not. Someone will need to create it, right? We think that someone should be you! Go ahead and create a very simple HTML page, and then save it with the name webpage.html. Then view your js-six.html page again, and verify that your browser will really display your new page when you click on the arrow image. Don't forget that this new file must be saved in the same folder as the js-six.html file.

Teaching a Hyperlink to Roll Over

Now that you know how to make an image rollover, let's show you how to create a hyperlink rollover. As you might expect, a hyperlink rollover is very similar to an image rollover. The only difference is that a hyperlink rollover is triggered when the user moves the mouse over a hyperlink, rather than when the mouse rolls over an image.

So if you are expecting the JavaScript code required to make a hyperlink rollover to be similar to the code for an image rollover, you won't be disappointed. In fact, if we didn't tell you what changes to make, you would probably have to look at the new source code twice to determine what the differences are.

STEP-BY-STEP 5.2

1. Open your text editor or word processor and retrieve the js-six.html file you created in the previous step-by-step activity.

2. Change the activity number to 7.

3. Next, you're going to make a few changes to the opening anchor tag, <A>, that defines a hyperlink. Add the line, Next Page, as shown in bold here and in Figure 5-2.

```
<A HREF="webpage.html"
  onMouseOver="document.arrow.src
   = redArrow.src"
  onMouseOut="document.arrow.src
= blueArrow.src">
Next Page
```

4. Then you will move the arrow image outside of the closing anchor tag, </A>, so that it is no longer part of the hyperlink reference. You will also want to add a paragraph tag, as shown in bold here and in Figure 5-2.

```
Next Page
</A>
<P>
<IMG SRC="bluearrow.gif"
    NAME="arrow"
    WIDTH=320
    HEIGHT=200>
</CENTER>
```

5. When you're finished making these changes, your JavaScript source code should look just like Figure 5-2.

6. Save your new file as js-seven.html.

7. Open your Web browser and view your js-seven.html file.

FIGURE 5-2
This JavaScript code created a hyperlink rollover.

```
<HTML>
<HEAD>
<TITLE>JavaScript Activity #7</TITLE>
<SCRIPT>
    blueArrow = new Image;
    blueArrow.src = "bluearrow.gif";
    redArrow = new Image;
    redArrow.src = "redarrow.gif"
</SCRIPT>
</HEAD>
<BODY>
<CENTER>
<A HREF="webpage.html"
  onMouseOver="document.arrow.src = redArrow.src"
  onMouseOut="document.arrow.src = blueArrow.src">
Next Page
</A>
<P>
<IMG SRC="bluearrow.gif"
    NAME="arrow"
    WIDTH=320
    HEIGHT=200>
</CENTER>
</BODY>
</HTML>
```

If you are an astute observer, you will notice that the JavaScript statements in this HTML document (js-seven.html) are exactly the same as in the previous document (js-six.html). So let's make sure you have a solid understanding of what changes were made in the HTML tags, and how those changes relate to the JavaScript code.

First of all, the <A> and the </A> anchor tags no longer enclose the <IMG> tag, so the arrow image is no longer part of the hyperlink reference. Instead, the anchor tags now enclose the "Next Page" text you just added. This means that the onMouseOver and onMouseOut events will be fired when the mouse rolls over the new hypertext instead of when it rolls over the arrow image. However, the action performed by JavaScript code is the same as before, so the image changes color just like it did before.

You may be wondering why we inserted the paragraph tag between the hypertext and the arrow image. We did this because the paragraph tag forces the image down below the Next Page hyperlink. Otherwise, the image would appear to the right of the hypertext. (Feel free to remove the <P> tag and view the file again if you want to see what we mean.)

You may also be wondering why the arrow image was surrounded by a blue rectangle in the previous activity, but not in this one. The answer to this question is that in Step-by-Step 5.1, the image was defined as a hyperlink, and hyperlink images are normally displayed with a blue border by a Web browser. This is why the blue border is still visible when the arrow image is changed from blue to red. But in Step-by-Step 5.2, the image is not defined as a hyperlink, so the blue border is gone. Instead, the Next Page text is defined as the hyperlink, so it is displayed as blue and underlined, regardless of the color of the arrow image.

Thinking About Technology

In Step-by-Step 5.1, we showed you how to create a rollover that reacts when the mouse pointer passes over an image. In Step-by-Step 5.2, we showed you how to create a rollover that reacts when the mouse pointer passes over a hyperlink. But now we want to know if you can create a rollover that will react to *either* condition. That is, can you make a small modification to your js-seven.html file that will cause the arrow image to change color when the mouse passes over the hyperlink *or* the image. Can you do it? Of course you can! All you need to do is move one HTML tag from its current position to a new position. Can you figure out what tag needs to move and to where?

Net Tip

Whenever a graphic image is defined as a hyperlink in an HTML document, the Web browser will display that image with a rectangular border around it. But there are times when this border detracts from the overall appearance of the Web page. Fortunately, HTML provides Web page designers with the ability to adjust the size of the hyperlink border with the BORDER attribute. By including a BORDER= statement in the <IMG> (image) tag, the content developer can make the hyperlink border thicker or thinner or can make it disappear all together. To see how this attribute affects hyperlink images, try adding a BORDER=0 statement to the <IMG> tag in Step-by-Step 5.1. If you do this correctly, the blue hyperlink border should disappear. However, the image rollover should still function as it did before.

Creating a Cycling Banner

When you are out "surfin' the Web," it is probably quite common for you to encounter commercial Web sites containing advertisements that are constantly changing. As it turns out, these *cycling banners* (also known as ad banners) can be created in various ways using different Internet technologies. However, one of the easiest and most efficient ways to create these types of advertisements is by using JavaScript events and functions.

A cycling banner is really nothing more than a sequence of graphic images that are displayed one after another with a small pause between each image. After all of the images in the sequence have been displayed, then the browser will cycle back to the first image and start the sequence all over again. This is the reason why this particular Web page enhancement is called a "cycling" banner.

You may think that creating a cycling banner takes a lot of time and effort, but this is not the case with JavaScript! In this step-by-step activity, we will show you that it takes only a few minutes to integrate an effective ad display into your Web page. By utilizing a single JavaScript event, and by defining one simple JavaScript function, you will be well on your way to fame and fortune in the world of cycling banner design.

STEP-BY-STEP 5.3

1. Just as you did in Step-by-Step 5.1, you will need to use some graphics in this activity. So, open your Web browser and enter the URL www.course.com/downloads/swep/htmljava/.
2. Click on the Activity 5.3 link from the list you see.
3. Download the lions.gif, tigers.gif, bears.gif, and ohmy.gif files to the exact same folder where you have been saving your Web pages. (If you accidentally download the files to a different folder, your Web page will not function correctly.)
4. Open your text editor or word processor, and type the HTML/JavaScript code exactly as it appears in Figure 5-3.
5. Save this file in the appropriate folder as js-eight.html.
6. Open your Web browser if it is not already open.
7. View your js-eight.html page. Your Web page should initially look like Figure 5-4A. But after a two-second delay, the image should change to look like Figure 5-4B. After an additional two-second delay, it should change to look like Figure 5-4C, and then finally to Figure 5-4D.

FIGURE 5-3
Type this JavaScript code to create a cycling banner.

```
<HTML>
<HEAD>
<TITLE>JavaScript Activity #8</TITLE>
<SCRIPT>
    imgArray = new Array(4);
    imgArray[0] = new Image;
    imgArray[0].src = "lions.gif";
    imgArray[1] = new Image;
    imgArray[1].src = "tigers.gif";
    imgArray[2] = new Image
    imgArray[2].src = "bears.gif";
    imgArray[3] = new Image;
    imgArray[3].src = "ohmy.gif";
    index = 0;

    function cycle()
    {
        document.banner.src = imgArray[index].src;
        index++;
        if (index == 4)
        {
          index = 0;
```

FIGURE 5-3 (continued)

```
        }
        setTimeout("cycle()", 2000);
        return;
    }
</SCRIPT>
</HEAD>
<BODY onLoad="cycle();">
<CENTER>
<IMG SRC="lions.gif"
    NAME="banner"
    WIDTH=400
    HEIGHT=100>
</CENTER>
</BODY>
</HTML>
```

FIGURE 5-4A
The first image of your cycling banner appears!

LIONS

FIGURE 5-4B
The second image of your cycling banner is shown.

and TIGERS

FIGURE 5-4C
The third image of your cycling banner is displayed.

and BEARS

FIGURE 5-4D
The fourth image of your cycling banner appears.

Once again, we introduced several important JavaScript concepts within a relatively small amount of source code. Let's go through the source code listing in Figure 5-5 carefully to make sure you understand what's happening here.

First, take a look at line 5 (imgArray = new Array(4);). Here we are creating a new JavaScript object, one that you have not used before, called an array. An *array* is simply a collection of similar objects that can be accessed by means of a variable name and an index. Arrays are available in virtually every modern computer language, so it's important for you to become familiar with them. In this case, our array is defined to contain a maximum of four elements, and its variable name is called imgArray. In this case, the array will contain four Image objects, but arrays can contain any other type of JavaScript object as well.

Second, consider the JavaScript statements in lines 6 through 13. These statements should look somewhat familiar to you, since they are essentially the same as those in lines 5 through 8 of the previous step-by-step activity. Line 6 creates a new Image object and assigns it the name imgArray with an index of 0. Line 7 then sets the source (src) property of this new object to contain the contents of the file called lions.gif. Similarly, the JavaScript statements in lines 8, 10, and 12 also create new objects of type Image, and these new objects are assigned the name imgArray, with index values of 1, 2, and 3, respectively. The statements in lines 9, 11, and 13 set the src property of these three new objects to the contents of files tigers.gif, bears.gif, and ohmy.gif, respectively. Now these four graphic images can be displayed very quickly by other JavaScript statements, which we will describe shortly.

Third, the statement in line 14 (index = 0;) simply creates a JavaScript variable named index and assigns the value 0 to it. This variable will be used to access the various elements in the imgArray array.

Fourth, the JavaScript statements in lines 16 through 26 define a function called cycle(), and this function will cause the images in the cycling banner to appear one after the other. This is accomplished by setting the src property of the document.banner object to the src property of the current element of the imgArray array. Then we increment the value stored in the index variable (using the ++ operator) in order to access the next element of our image array. The term *increment* means adding 1 to a value. Since the only valid indices for this array are 0 to 3, we must test the value of index to see if it has exceeded the acceptable range. In other words, if index contains the value 4, we must set it back to 0 in order to make the banner images cycle back to the beginning of the sequence. Then our final task is to set a timer that will call the cycle( ) function again after 2000 milliseconds have elapsed. (2000 milliseconds is equal to 2 seconds.)

Finally, the last thing we need to explain is how the whole cycling banner process gets started. If you take a close look at the <BODY> tag of our HTML document (in line 29 of the source code listing), you will see that we have inserted a new JavaScript event. This event is called onLoad, and it is triggered when the Web browser has finished loading the body of the HTML Web page. In this example, the browser loads the image called lions.gif (which is assigned the variable name banner by the NAME attribute), and then fires the onLoad event, which in turn causes the cycle( ) function to be invoked. The cycle( ) function will then be called continuously every two seconds in response to the JavaScript setTimeout( ) method, which is called inside this same function.

Thinking About Technology

A timeout value of 2000 milliseconds works well for this particular example, but sometimes different values can be more effective. Try changing the delay value in the setTimeout( ) method call to see what effect different numbers will have. And if you are extremely clever, you may recognize the fact that there may be occasions when providing a different delay value for each image in the banner sequence could be desirable. If you are feeling up to the challenge, try creating a second four-element array in the header section of your HTML document called delay. Then assign different values to each element in this new array (like 1000, 4000, 2000, and 3000), and use these values in the setTimeout( ) method call. That is, replace the constant value 2000 with the variable name delay[index]. If you can complete this task correctly, then you are well on your way to understanding the fundamentals of JavaScript arrays.

Net Fact

Nearly every programming language supports the concept of arrays, but they don't all implement array indexing in the same way. If you define a ten-element array in BASIC, FORTRAN, or PASCAL, for example, you would use index values of 1, 2, 3, . . . 10 to access those ten elements. But some other languages (including C++, Java, and JavaScript) do not use this one-based indexing technique. Instead, they implement a zero-based technique that makes the valid array indices for a ten-element array 0, 1, 2, . . . 9. At first you might think that the one-based approach makes more sense because it is easier for novice programmers to understand. However, if you were to look at the low-level machine code generated by different language compilers, you would see that the one-based approach is less efficient for the computer hardware to process. This is one reason why professional programmers tend to use zero-based languages for their software development projects.

Displaying Random Images

In the previous activity, you learned how to display a sequence of graphic images in a specific order. But there are also times when Web page designers want their images to appear in a random order. This approach is normally used when a particular Web site contains a large collection of graphic images, and the site owner would like the system to randomly select an image for display.

At first, you might assume that displaying images in a fixed sequence is much easier than displaying them in a random order. But this is not the case when you are programming in JavaScript. In fact, it actually requires fewer lines of code to display random images than it does to create a cycling banner. This is primarily due to JavaScript's built-in support for random number generation.

Since much of the source code for this Step-by-Step activity is the same as for the previous activity, you will be able to use your previous file and make just a few changes. In fact, all you will need to do is replace the cycle() function with a similar function called select(). You don't even need to worry about downloading graphics files to the correct folder because we will use the same images as in the previous activity.

STEP-BY-STEP 5.4

1. Open your text editor or word processor and retrieve the js-eight.html file you created in the previous activity.

2. Change the activity number to 9.

3. Next, you're going to delete the cycle() function and replace it with a new function called select(), as shown in bold here and in Figure 5-5.

```
function select()
{
    index = Math.floor(Math.ran-
  dom() * 4);
    document.banner.src =
  imgArray[index].src;
    setTimeout("select()", 2000);
    return;
}
```

4. Then you will have to change the <BODY> tag so that the onLoad event calls the new select() function instead of the old cycle() function, as shown in bold here and in Figure 5-5.

```
<BODY onLoad="select();">
```

5. When you are finished, the resulting file should look just like the source code listing seen in Figure 5-5.

6. Save your new file as js-nine.html.

7. Open your Web browser and view your js-nine.html file. Your screen should initially look like Figure 5-4A, 5-4B, 5-4C, or 5-4D, and then it should change every two seconds. Unlike the previous activity, the images will not appear in any predictable order.

FIGURE 5-5
JavaScript code set to display random images.

```
<HTML>
<HEAD>
<TITLE>JavaScript Activity #9</TITLE>
<SCRIPT>
    imgArray = new Array(4);
    imgArray[0] = new Image;
    imgArray[0].src = "lions.gif";
    imgArray[1] = new Image;
    imgArray[1].src = "tigers.gif";
    imgArray[2] = new Image
    imgArray[2].src = "bears.gif";
    imgArray[3] = new Image;
    imgArray[3].src = "ohmy.gif";
    index = 0;

    function select()
    {
```

FIGURE 5-5 (continued)

```
        index = Math.floor(Math.random() * 4);
        document.banner.src = imgArray[index].src;
        setTimeout("select()", 2000);
        return;
    }
</SCRIPT>
</HEAD>
<BODY onLoad="select();">
<CENTER>
<IMG SRC="lions.gif"
    NAME="banner"
    WIDTH=400
    HEIGHT=100>
</CENTER>
</BODY>
</HTML>
```

Let's quickly review the JavaScript concepts that are introduced in this step-by-step activity.

First, we changed the function name from cycle() to select() because it more accurately reflects the purpose and behavior of the function. As a result of this name change, we also needed to modify the onLoad event statement in the HTML <BODY> tag so it would invoke the proper function name. If we had failed to make this change, the Web browser would have responded with an unpleasant error message.

Second, we needed to include the appropriate JavaScript code to generate a random number, and then convert that number into a valid array index in the range 0 to 3. The JavaScript method random() (which is part of the Math object) is guaranteed to return a real or floating-point number that is greater than or equal to 0.0 and less than 1.0. (A real number is a numerical value that includes a decimal portion.) Since numbers in this restricted range are not usable as array indices, we need to scale them to the proper range. In this case, we have four elements in our array, so we multiply (with the * operator) the random value by 4. Now we have a real number that is guaranteed to be greater than or equal to 0.0 and less than 4.0. The final step is to invoke the Math.floor() method, which will eliminate the decimal part of the resulting number. This means that the only possible values remaining are 0, 1, 2, and 3, and these are exactly the values we need to use as array indices.

Just to be sure you feel comfortable with this process, let's walk through an example. Let's suppose that the first three times the select() function is called, the Math.random() method generates random values of 0.137, 0.8312, and 0.54. When we multiply these numbers by 4, the resulting values are 0.548, 3.3248, and 2.16, respectively. Then, when we run these new real numbers through the Math.floor() method, the final numbers stored in the index variable will be 0, 3, and 2, respectively. Obviously, these are all valid array index values, so the images displayed will be the contents of the files lions.gif, followed by ohmy.gif, and finally bears.gif. In other words, you would see Figure 5-4a, followed by Figure 5-4d, and finally Figure 5-4c on your screen. Do you understand?

Thinking About Technology

Let's suppose for a moment that instead of just four graphic images, your collection has increased to eight. What changes would you need to make to your JavaScript program to make it work properly with eight images? To start with, you would need to change your array size from 4 to 8, right? Then you would need to instantiate the four new array elements just like we did for the first four. *Instantiation* is simply the process of creating a new object and assigning it a value. What do you suppose would be the valid index values for the four new array elements? If you guessed 4, 5, 6, and 7, you are absolutely right! After you have completed this step, though, you still need to modify one more line of code. Can you recognize which one it is? If you read through this activity carefully, we're sure you can!

Creating a JavaScript "Slide Show"

In the previous two step-by-step activities, we showed you how to create JavaScript programs that will automatically change the image on the screen every two seconds. But sometimes it is more desirable to let the user decide when to change the image. When you allow the user to change the image by clicking on some object with the mouse, the end result is something akin to an electronic slide show. In this step-by-step activity, you will create a JavaScript program that will provide the user with two hyperlinks labeled Back and Next. When the user clicks on one of these links, the image displayed will change appropriately.

In order to accomplish this task, you will need to modify the js-nine.html file you created in the previous activity. You will remove the select() function and insert two new functions named doBack() and doNext(). Then you will add some additional HTML tags to make the screen look good and to provide the user with the appropriate hyperlinks that will cause the slide show image to change.

NOTE: For the sake of simplicity, we will be using the same graphic image files that we used in the previous two activities.

Net Fact

In Lesson 1, you learned that HTML does not care if you type its tags in uppercase letters, lowercase letters, or a combination of the two. In other words, HTML is not case-sensitive. This means that you can type the HTML image tag as <IMG>, <img>, or even <iMg>, and the Web browser will process it just fine. Unfortunately, this is not true of many programming languages, including JavaScript. When you type the names of JavaScript objects, variables, or functions, you must make certain that you use the same case each time, since the JavaScript interpreter will treat index, Index, and INDEX as three different variables. As a consequence of JavaScript's case-sensitive nature, typing a variable name incorrectly will either result in an error message when your script runs, or you might simply see unexpected or inaccurate results. So do be careful!

STEP-BY-STEP 5.5

1. Open your text editor or word processor and retrieve the js-nine.html file you created in the previous step-by-step activity.
2. Change the activity number to 10.

STEP-BY-STEP 5.5 CONTINUED

3. Delete the select() function and replace it with two new functions called doBack() and doNext(), as shown in bold here and in Figure 5-6.

```
function doBack()
{
    if (index > 0)
    {
        index--;
        document.slideshow.src =
  imgArray[index].src;
    }
    return;
}

function doNext()
{
    if (index < 3)
    {
        index++;
        document.slideshow.src =
  imgArray[index].src;
    }
    return;
}
```

4. Change the <BODY> tag to delete the select() function.

5. Between the center tags, you will need to add additional HTML tags and text to make your slide show look good on the screen, as shown in bold here and in Figure 5-6.

```
<CENTER>
<H1>My JavaScript Slide Show</H1>
<P>
<IMG SRC="lions.gif"
    NAME="slideshow"
    WIDTH=400
    HEIGHT=200>
<P>
<H3>
<A
  HREF=javascript:doBack()>Back
  </A>
     
<A
  HREF=javascript:doNext()>Next
  </A>
</H3>
</CENTER>
```

6. When you are finished, the resulting file should look just like the source code listing shown in Figure 5-6.

7. Save your new file as js-ten.html.

8. Open your Web browser and view your js-ten.html file. Your screen should initially look like Figure 5-7A. But as you continually click the Next hyperlink, the image should change to look like Figures 5-7B, 5-7C, and 5-7D.

FIGURE 5-6
JavaScript code can also create a slide show.

```
<HTML>
<HEAD>
<TITLE>JavaScript Activity #10</TITLE>
<SCRIPT>
    imgArray = new Array(4);
    imgArray[0] = new Image;
    imgArray[0].src = "lions.gif";
    imgArray[1] = new Image;
    imgArray[1].src = "tigers.gif";
    imgArray[2] = new Image
    imgArray[2].src = "bears.gif";
    imgArray[3] = new Image;
```

FIGURE 5-6 (continued)

```
    imgArray[3].src = "ohmy.gif";
    index = 0;

    function doBack()
    {
        if (index > 0)
        {
            index--;
            document.slideshow.src = imgArray[index].src;
        }
        return;
    }
    function doNext()
    {
        if (index < 3)
        {
            index++;
            document.slideshow.src = imgArray[index].src;
        }
        return;
    }
</SCRIPT>
</HEAD>
<BODY>
<CENTER>
<H1>My JavaScript Slide Show</H1>
<P>
<IMG SRC="lions.gif"
    NAME="slideshow"
    WIDTH=400
    HEIGHT=200>
<P>
<H3>
<A HREF=javascript:doBack()>Back</A>
     
<A HREF=javascript:doNext()>Next</A>
</H3>
</CENTER>
</BODY>
</HTML>
```

FIGURE 5-7A
The first image of your slide show appears.

My JavaScript Slide Show

LIONS

Back Next

FIGURE 5-7B
The second image of your slide show is now shown.

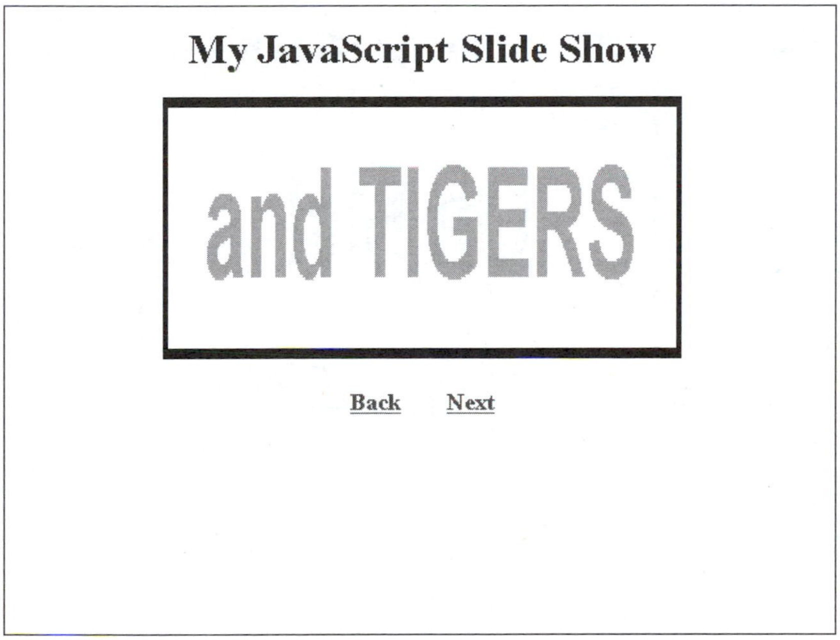

My JavaScript Slide Show

and TIGERS

Back Next

FIGURE 5-7C
The third image of your slide show is displayed.

My JavaScript Slide Show

and BEARS

Back Next

FIGURE 5-7D
The fourth image of your slide show comes up.

My JavaScript Slide Show

Oh My!

Back Next

Once again, we have introduced some new JavaScript concepts in this activity, so let's run through them to make sure nothing gets by you. The first several lines of JavaScript code (lines 5 through 14) are the same as in the previous two activities, so you should feel comfortable with them by now. But you may not be completely familiar with everything in the doBack() and doNext() functions. Let's walk through them, shall we?

The first thing we do in the doBack() function is to test the value of the index variable. If it is greater than 0, then we know we are not displaying the first image in the slide show, so we need to back up to the previous image in the sequence. This is done by decrementing the value stored in index (with the - - operator), and then loading a new image source into the slideshow object of our HTML document. As you might expect, the term *decrement* means to subtract 1 from the current value of a variable. But you should note that if the current value of index is 0, then the doBack() function performs no action.

The contents of the doNext() function is, of course, very similar to that of the doBack() function. We first check the value of index to see if its current value is less than 3. If it is, then we know we are not displaying the last image in our slide show sequence, so we need to change the image on the screen. This is done by incrementing the index variable, and then setting the src property of the slideshow object to the next image in the list. But if the value of index is 3, then the doNext() function performs no action.

If you have a firm understanding of the material in Lessons 1 to 3, then you should feel comfortable with most of the HTML code contained within the body tags of this Web page. However, there are a couple of things that you have not seen before, so let's explain them also.

You may have noticed that the HREF attribute of the Back hyperlink does not include a reference to another HTML document. Instead, it contains a reference to a JavaScript function named doBack(). Likewise, the HREF attribute of the Next hyperlink refers to the JavaScript function doNext(). This means that when the user clicks on one of these hyperlinks, the Web browser will perform the specified function rather than loading a new HTML page! Neat stuff, right?

The final item we would like to address in this activity concerns the three cryptic symbols   that occur on line 48 of the source code listing in Figure 5-8. Suffice it to say that these symbols are HTML commands that tell the Web browser to put a little extra space between the Back hyperlink and the Next hyperlink. They are not required for this JavaScript program to function correctly, but they improve the appearance of the page somewhat. Feel free to remove this line from the file if you wish.

Thinking About Technology

Sometimes Web designers like to create slide shows that function in a "circular" fashion rather than in a "linear" way. This means that whenever the user reaches either end of the image sequence, the program will allow him to jump to the opposite end and continue viewing the images. In other words, if the user is currently viewing the first image in the slide show sequence and he clicks on the Back hyperlink, the next image displayed will be the last image in the set. Similarly, when the user is viewing the last image in the sequence and then clicks on the Next hyperlink, he will immediately see the first slide show image. Do you think you can modify your js-ten.html file to operate in this way? If the answer isn't immediately obvious to you, go back and study the JavaScript cycle() function in Step-by-Step 5.3. It should tell you all you need to know!

NET ETHICS

We mentioned in Lesson 3 that it is unethical for Web page developers to download copyrighted images from commercial Web sites and then use those images for their own purposes. This obviously holds true whether the images are used in standard HTML pages or in JavaScript pages. But when you start developing JavaScript-enhanced Web pages, you should also be aware that script piracy is just as unethical as picture piracy. In fact, it is not just unethical, it is also illegal! Although downloading and studying scripts that were created by other people is sometimes a great way to learn JavaScript, you must keep in mind that the copyright laws still apply. You should feel free to use publicly accessible JavaScript code for educational purposes, but you should not simply copy scripts from someone else's Web site to use on your own Web page unless you get the owner's permission to do so.

LESSON 5 REVIEW QUESTIONS

Write a brief answer to the following questions:

1. What is a JavaScript event? How are events generated?

2. What is a JavaScript function? How does a function differ from a method?

3. How does an image rollover differ from a hyperlink rollover?

4. What is a cycling banner? Why is it called "cycling"?

5. What is the purpose of the Math object methods random() and floor()?

6. What is a JavaScript slide show?

LESSON 5 PROJECTS

PROJECT 5-1

Suppose that Great Applications, Inc. has just hired you to replace a JavaScript programmer who recently left the company. Your first assignment as a new employee is to prepare a report for your supervisor concerning one of the former employee's JavaScript programs. (The program in question is the cycling banner listing found in Figure 5-5.) He wants your report to contain a detailed description of what steps would be required to expand the content of the banner from four images to eight, and to make the delay value for each image variable. After reviewing the information presented in Step-by-Step 5.3 and 5.4, you should be able to create this report for your supervisor in practically no time.

SCANS

PROJECT 5-2

The management of Great Applications, Inc. has decided that they want to create an "Electronic Zoo," and they want to make it available to the public on their corporate Web site. Consequently, they have given your team the assignment of creating a JavaScript slide show that contains the images of many different kinds of animals. Each member of your team should spend some time searching the Web for suitable animal images, and then you must create a JavaScript slide show program to display them. Start with the source code listing in Figure 5-8, and then make the necessary modifications to get it to display the animal images you have collected. Some of the things you might want to change include:

- the Web page title
- the size of your image array
- the image filenames
- the size (dimensions) of your slide show window
- the "last" index value in the doNext( ) function

CRITICAL THINKING

In Step-by-Step 5.3, we showed you how to create a cycling banner, or ad banner, as it is sometimes called. We also mentioned that there are numerous commercial Web sites that include ad banners, usually at the top of their Web pages. But one thing we haven't explained is the reason there are so many sites like this in cyberspace. It basically boils down to a monetary issue. The owner of the host site will charge other companies a certain amount to include their advertisements in the host Web pages. In this way, many Web sites can provide free services to their users, but still cover their own operating costs. Otherwise, many Web site hosts would go out of business in a very short time. So consider the following questions:

What types of businesses might choose to pay various Web sites to host their ad banners?

What kinds of products and services are most likely to be advertised in this manner?

Why do you suppose most ad banners are defined as hyperlinks in the host HTML page?

What types of Web sites are most likely to host ad banners?

HTML and JavaScript Review

UNIT REVIEW

TRUE/FALSE

Circle T if the statement is true or F if the statement is false.

T F 1. The HTML tag used to create a numbered list is the <UL>...</UL> tag pair.

T F 2. The <P> tag can be used to create double spacing around text.

T F 3. A picture or image can be used as the background for a Web page by defining the image name and location within an <IMG> tag.

T F 4. JavaScript is just another name for the Java programming language.

T F 5. The JavaScript onRollOver event can be used to change the appearance of an object when the mouse is rolled over it by the user.

FILL-IN-THE-BLANK

1. Most HTML tags usually appear in pairs, and are enclosed in __________ brackets.

2. The use of __________ makes it easy to jump from one Web page to another, or to jump to a different section within the current page.

3. The two most commonly used graphics formats used in Web pages are __________ and .jpg, which is also called .jpeg.

4. JavaScript can use __________ statements, such as *if*, to customize processing within the JavaScript program.

5. A(n) __________ banner is a series of graphics images displayed one after the other with a short pause between images.

PROJECTS

PROJECT 4-1

In this project, you will expand a base HTML file to display a bulleted and a numeric list.

1. If necessary, start your text editor or Web page creation software.

2. Open the **HTML_Base.html** file from the Unit 4 Unit Review Data File folder. Save it to your student folder as **HTML_List.html**.

3. Add the statements required to **center** the text **"Test program for basic HTML tags"**. This text should also be displayed as an **H1** field.

4. Add the tag to create a **paragraph break**, and set the heading style to **H2**. Enter the following text, "**Some of my favorite things are:** ", and close the H2 style.

5. Create a **bulleted list** and include at least **four** list items. Include any four items that are your favorite things, such as good friends, good food, etc. Don't forget to end the list with the proper tag.

6. Add another **paragraph break**, set the heading style again to **H2**, and add the following text, "**The courses I'm taking this term are:** ", and then close the H2 heading style. Create a **numbered list** of the courses you are taking this term. End the list with the proper tag.

7. Save your latest changes and open the **HTML_List.html** file in your Web browser. Correct any errors and close your text editor.

PROJECT 4-2

In this project you will add several hyperlinks to the HTML file created in Project 4-1.

1. If necessary, start your text editor or Web page creation software.

2. Open the **HTML_List.html** file you created in Project 4-1. Change the **TITLE** line to reference **Project 4-2** instead of 4-1. Save the file as **HTML_Links.html** to your student folder.

3. Change the **BODY** tag to set a **background color** of **#00FFFF**. Set the **TEXT** to **BLACK**, the **LINK** to **RED**, and the **VLINK** to **BLUE**. Change the text in the centered line to read, "**Test program for HTML hyperlink tags**".

4. Below the numbered list created in Project 4-1, add a **paragraph break**, set the heading style to **H2**, and add the text, "**Some of my favorite links are:** ", then close the H2 heading style.

5. Create another **bulleted list**.

6. For the first list item, create a **hyperlink** to **http://www.nasa.gov**, and include the text "**Visit NASA to learn about space.**"

7. For the second list item, create a **hyperlink** to **http://www.yahoo.com**, and include the text "**Visit Yahoo to use a search engine.**"

8. For the third list item, create a **hyperlink** to **http://www.microsoft.com**, and include the text "**Visit Microsoft to learn about software.**"

9. For the fourth list item, create a **hyperlink** to **http://www.espn.com**, and include the text "**Visit ESPN to read about sports.**" End the bulleted list.

10. Save your latest changes to **HTML_Links.html**, and open the file in your Web browser. Correct any errors if necessary, and then test each of your hyperlinks.

11. Close your text editor or Web page creation software.

PROJECT 4-3

In this project you will add a calendar table to the file created in Project 4-2.

1. If necessary, start your text editor or Web page creation software.

2. Open the **HTML_Links.html** file you created in Project 4-2. Change the **TITLE** line to reference **Project 4-3** instead of 4-2. Save the file as **HTML_Table.html** to your student folder.

3. Change the text in the centered line to read, "**Test program for HTML Table tags**".

4. Add a **horizontal rule** between the bulleted list and the numbered list, between the numbered list and the hyperlink bulleted list, and another after the hyperlink list. Set the **WIDTH** to **100%**, and the **SIZE** to **10**.

5. Below the last horizontal rule you just added, create a **paragraph break**, set the heading style to **H2**, and add the text, "**My Monthly Calendar**", then close the H2 heading style.

6. Add the HTML tags to create a **table**, using **BORDER=5**, **CELLPADDING=10**, and **ALIGN=CENTER** parameters.

7. Add a table **row**, and include seven **table headers** for the row, using the text **Monday**, **Tuesday**, etc. as the text for each header. End the row.

8. Add another table **row**, and add **table data** items using the values **1 through 7**, then end the row.

9. Add another table **row**, and add **table data** items using the values **8 through 14**, then end the row.

10. Add another table **row**, and add **table data** items using the values **15 through 21**, then end the row.

11. Add another table **row**, and add **table data** items using the values **22 through 28**, then end the row.

12. Add another table **row**, and add **table data** items using the values **29 through 31.** Add three more **table data** items and insert a **period** as the character for the item, then end the row.

13. End the table. Save your latest changes, then open the page in your Web browser. Correct any errors if necessary. Exit your text editor or Web page creation software.

PROJECT 4-4

This project will use JavaScript to add some animation to a Web page.

1. If necessary, start your text editor or Web page creation software.

2. Create a new HTML file, and save it to your student folder as **JSCR_Ball.html**. Copy the seven .gif files named **basketball1.gif** through **basketball7.gif** from the Unit 4 Unit Review **Data File folder** to your student folder.

3. Add the opening **<HTML>** tag, the **<HEAD>** tag, and a **TITLE** tag with the text, "**HTML and JavaScript Project 4-4**", and then close the TITLE tag.

4. Add a **<SCRIPT>** tag, and define an array of **7** entries. Initialize each array entry to one of the .gif files copied in step one. Array **index zero** should contain **basketball1.gif**, **index one** should contain **basketball2.gif**, and so on, until all seven images have been assigned to an array cell.

5. Set an **index** variable to a value of **zero**.

6. Create a JavaScript **function** called **cycle** that will set the **document.banner.src** object to whatever image is currently pointed to by the **index** variable. **Increment** the **index** variable. **Test** the **index** variable, and if it has reached a value of **seven**, reset it to **zero**. Add a call to the **setTimout()** function, passing it the name of the **cycle** function, and a **time delay** of your choice. Try **500** as an initial time value.

7. Close the **SCRIPT** section, and the **HEAD** section tags.

8. Add a **BODY** tag that specifies the **cycle** function will be executed on **page load**.

9. Add a **CENTER** tag.

10. Add an **IMG** tag, specifying **basketball1.gif** as the **SRC** image. Specify the **NAME** tag as **banner**, set the **WIDTH** to **600**, and the **HEIGHT** to **375**.

11. Close the **CENTER** tag, close the **BODY** tag, and add the ending **HTML** tag.

12. Save your latest changes and open the page in your Web browser. Does the ball seem to bounce from the left side of the screen to the right side? If not, do you have a message about a JavaScript error in the browser's status line? If so, try typing **JAVASCRIPT:** into the browser's **Location** line and press enter. Some browsers will show you the program line causing the problem. If not, examine your code very carefully, or consult with another student whose animation is working correctly.

13. Close your text editor or Web page creation software.

SIMULATION

SIMULATION 4-1

You have been asked to provide a computerized interactive zoo program for a local school. The program should provide a list of animals, and by clicking on one of the animals a student can see a picture of the animal, a description of the animal, and information about its habitat. Would you use Visual Basic, or a combination of HTML and JavaScript to create this program? Give reasons for your answer.

SIMULATION 4-2

Create a Web page that includes a form to survey viewers of the page concerning their favorite TV shows, favorite movies, favorite foods, and favorite recreational activities. The form should include check boxes and radio buttons in some categories, and should also include text boxes to allow the user to enter items not explicitly listed in your form. Test the form to be sure that all fields work as expected. Include any graphics that may be appropriate to dress up the page, and feel free to experiment with color combinations to create a page that is appealing to look at and easy to read and follow.

SIMULATION 4-3

Open the JSCR_Ball.html file created in Project 4-4. This program currently creates a simulation of a basketball bouncing from the left side of a box to the right side of the box. It then jumps back to the left and starts again. Modify the program so that when the basketball reaches the right side of the box, the animation process is reversed and it follows the same path back to the left side. You need to define a new variable to indicate which direction the ball is currently going. You also need to modify the cycle function to check this direction variable, and either increment or decrement the index variable accordingly. You must also check for the boundary conditions, index = 7, or index = less than zero. Save the file as JSCR_Ball2.html. Open it in your Web browser to be sure it works correctly.

Glossary

A

ad banner See Cycling Banner.

angle brackets HTML tags appear in pairs and are enclosed in angle brackets. The brackets can be found on the comma and period keys on the keyboard.

array A collection of similar objects that are accessed by a variable name and an index. When you give several controls the same name, they are considered an array of objects. The array is required to have an index value that will always start with zero and increase for each element in the array.

attributes Attribute tags are used to enhance an HTML tag. The <BODY> tag is considered an attribute tag because many different types of values are used to change the appearance of the Web page's body or background.

B

binary code After JavaScript code has been translated by interpretation, it becomes binary code, or machine-readable code.

buttons Input controls that are defined with the TYPE attribute instead of the INPUT tag.

C

checkboxes An input control that allows the user to select any or all of the listed options from a set of options.

compiler A highly specialized piece of software that takes a programming language that humans can understand and converts it into language computers can understand.

components See Controls.

condition Made up of two tokens and a relational operator. A conditional statement tells the browser IF this condition is met, perform this function; if not (ELSE), perform a different function.

controls An interactive object within a JavaScript form. Controls or components must be given a name so they can be referenced within the JavaScript code.

cycling banner Several graphics that are displayed one after another with a pause between images. The graphics scroll in either a fixed or random order.

D

data validation The process of checking user input data to make sure it is complete and accurate.

decrement To subtract one number from a value.

E

event The operating system's response to the occurrence of a specific condition.

F

fonts Also known as the style of letters, fonts determine the appearance of text in Web documents. Fonts have three attributes that can be changed—size, style, and color of text.

function A piece of JavaScript code that can be called upon to perform certain tasks. Functions are written by the programmer and can contain any number of JavaScript statements, including calls to other functions or methods.

G

.gif An acronym for Graphics Interchange Format. Gif files are compact in size and are one of two popular graphic formats used in Web documents. The extension, .gif., helps to tell the Web browser that these files are pictures, not Web documents.

graphics Pictures that can be placed in Web documents.

Graphics Interchange Format Compact graphics, often called .gifs, that are small enough in size to use in Web documents.

H

hexadecimal Hexadecimal digits operate on a base-16 number system rather than the base-10 number system most people use. Hexadecimal numbers use the letters A, B, C, D, E, and F along with the numbers 0 to 9 to create their 16 different digits.

home page The main Web page for a corporation, individual or organization. A home page is often the first page you see when you start your Web browser.

HTML page An HTML page, or HTML document, is any document created in HTML that can be displayed on the World Wide Web.

hyperlink rollover The appearance of an image changes when the mouse pointer clicks on or moves over a hyperlink.

hyperlinks Allow users to click on a specific spot in a Web document and have it link to another page they've created, to another Web page on the World Wide Web, or to another spot within the current document.

hypertext links Used to make Web pages more interesting and easier to navigate.

Hypertext Markup Language (HTML) Tags created within a Web document that give instructions to a Web browser. These instructions determine the look and feel of a Web document on the Internet.

Hypertext Transfer Protocol (HTTP) A type of digital language that Web servers use to communicate with Web browsers. A protocol is a communication system that is used to transfer data over networks.

I

image Another term used to refer to a graphic in a Web document. The letters IMG of the word are part of the HTML tag used to determine attributes of an image on the World Wide Web.

image rollover The appearance of an image changes when the mouse pointer moves over the image.

increment To add one number to a value.

index A variable that usually has the value of zero assigned to it. The index variable is used to access information about the array.

instantiate The process of creating a new object and assigning it a value.

Internet Explorer One of two major Web browsers used to look at information on the World Wide Web. Internet Explorer was created by Microsoft Corporation and comes with every package of Windows 95, Windows 98, and Windows NT.

interpretation A term used by programmers to describe the line-by-line conversion process that occurs automatically at run time or when the Web browser launches the JavaScript commands that are embedded in the Web document.

J

Java A programming language that creates programs called applets. Applets can be added to Web documents using tags similar to HTML tags.

JavaScript More powerful than HTML, JavaScript allows novice Web page developers to add features to a Web document without having to know any programming language.

Joint Photographic Expert Group Compact graphics, often called .jpegs, that are small enough in size to use in Web documents.

.jpg or .jpeg An acronym for Joint Photographic Expert Group. .Jpg or .jpeg files are compact in size and are one of two popular graphic formats used in Web documents. The extensions, .jpg and .jpeg, tell the Web browser that these files are pictures, not Web documents.

K

keyword A word that is recognized by the programming language as part of its language. A keyword, like IF, ELSE, or RETURN, cannot be used as a variable.

M

methods Methods are specialized functions within the object, and they call upon the services of the object. A method is invoked after you type the name of the object, followed by a period.

Mosaic The first Web browser that allowed pictures and sound to accompany text on a Web page. Mosaic was created in 1994 at the University of Illinois.

N

Netscape Navigator One of two major Web browsers used on the Internet today. Navigator, created in 1995, added to the powerful features of Mosaic allowing additional features like animated graphics into a Web document.

O

objects Invisible entities that have a defined set of capabilities.

operators Placed between two tokens in a conditional statement.

P

parameter list A list of information that provides a programming method what it needs to perform a specific function correctly.

programming language A language that has to be converted from a human-readable format into machine-readable format. This process is accomplished by using a compiler to complete the operation.

R

radio buttons An input control that allows the user to select just one option from a set of options.

real number (floating-point number) A real number is a number that has a decimal portion.

return value Whenever a function is called, its name is replaced by the value it returns.

S

<SCRIPT> and </SCRIPT> tags The beginning and end tags that are necessary in a Web document for a JavaScript statement to be executed. All JavaScript code must be placed within the beginning and ending tag.

scripting language A language that does not have to be run through a compiler for it to be understood. Web browsers will take the human-readable format and convert it into machine-readable format "on the fly."

slide show A collection of images that change when the user clicks on the image.

syntax The rules of grammar for a scripting language.

T

table cell Boxes in which you can place things to keep your Web document organized. Each table box, or cell, can have different attributes applied to text, can have a different background color, or can contain a different graphic.

text fields An input control that allows someone to type a string value into a specific location on a Web page.

token Either a variable name or a literal constant, which is followed by a relational operator. A JavaScript condition will always consist of two tokens.

V

values Value tags can be used to change the background color of a Web document. The following value tag is an example of a color value BGCOLOR=RED. Value tags are often used in conjunction with attributes. In this example, the attribute would be the <BODY> tag.

variable A name that is assigned to a literal value or to an object. Once assigned, that name can be used throughout the HTML document to refer to that particular value or object.

VRML A language used on the World Wide Web that allows people to view and search three-dimensional landscapes and models. VRML stands for Virtual Reality Markup Language.

W

Web browser Often referred to as a Web client because it allows users to interface with different operating systems and view information on the World Wide Web. It allows Web page developers to have JavaScript compiled and interpreted "on the fly."

Web page A Web page, or Web document, is any page created in HTML that can be placed on the World Wide Web.

Web site A Web site can include a series of Web pages that can be linked to other Web sites on the Internet. Web sites are stored on Web servers.

Webmaster A person assigned to maintain Web pages for a Web site.

Welcome page An introduction page when you visit a Web site on the World Wide Web. Welcome pages often include the Web page owner's e-mail address and name.

INTRODUCTION TO JAVA

Estimated Time for Unit 5: 21 hours

LESSON 1

INTEGRATING APPLETS INTO WEB PAGES

OBJECTIVES

Upon completion of this lesson, you should be able to:

- Give the history of the Java language.
- Explain how Java applets are delivered over the Internet from Web servers to client computers.
- Discuss HTML and the common tags.
- Use the <APPLET> tag to embed Java applets into Web pages.
- Control Java applets by passing parameters.

Estimated Time: 2 hours

Overview

Java is a programming language with an interesting history. In this chapter, you will learn about the history of the development of the Java language and why it is so widely used on the World Wide Web. You will also learn how Java applets are integrated into Web pages and learn how to control the behavior of a Java applet.

More About Java

Java was not created with the World Wide Web in mind. The language was originally developed for consumer electronic devices. It wasn't until later that Java found its most comfortable home on the Internet. In this section, you will get a glimpse of the history of Java and learn how Java applets are delivered over the Internet and run on a Web browser.

Java History

In the early 1990s, a company called Sun Microsystems created a team of top software developers to study consumer electronic devices to see if they could be programmed in ways similar to general-purpose computers. The team, code-named Green, discussed and studied current technologies. They took apart different electronic devices, such as remote controls, cable boxes, gaming devices, TVs, and stereos. The team observed that the devices were not compatible with each other. To address this issue, the team began developing a new programming language called Oak.

Oak was based on the C++ programming lanugage, but it was stripped down to be more compatible with small electronic devices. However, Oak failed to generate excitement among electronics manufacturers, so it fell on hard times. The Green team pursued several different avenues to develop a niche for this language. Unfortunately, none of their attempts to establish the language in the electronics market met with success.

It also turned out that another company was using the name Oak for a different technology. So a new name had to be found. The story is that after a trip to a coffee shop, the team decided to change the name of the language to Java.

Just about the time the team was giving up on Java, the idea was born to use Java in conjunction with the World Wide Web. Java's ability to produce small yet functional programs was ideal for the Internet. Most World Wide Web users connect over a telephone line using a modem, which is much slower than the processing speed of the computer itself. Thus, short programs that transmit rapidly are very important. And Java programs by nature are very short and concise. Also working in Java's favor was the fact that Java programs do not compile for a specific type of computer. By enabling a Web browser to interpret the Java byte codes, any computer on the Internet can run the same Java programs. Web browsers written for Windows, OS/2, Unix, or the Mac OS can run the same Java byte codes.

Although Java has been mostly used as a way to add more interesting and dynamic content to WWW pages, it has evolved into a computing platform on which programmers can develop full-scale applications.

Serving Up Java

Let's take a closer look at how a Java applet is served up over the Internet. In Figure 1-1, a computer called a Web server stores a Java applet on its hard disk. A *Web server* is a computer that delivers Web pages to computers running Web browsers. The computers running the Web browsers are called *client computers*. The Web server typically has a full-time connection to the Internet so it can be available 24 hours a day.

FIGURE 1-1
Java applets are stored on a Web server, which delivers the applet to the Web browsers running on the client computers.

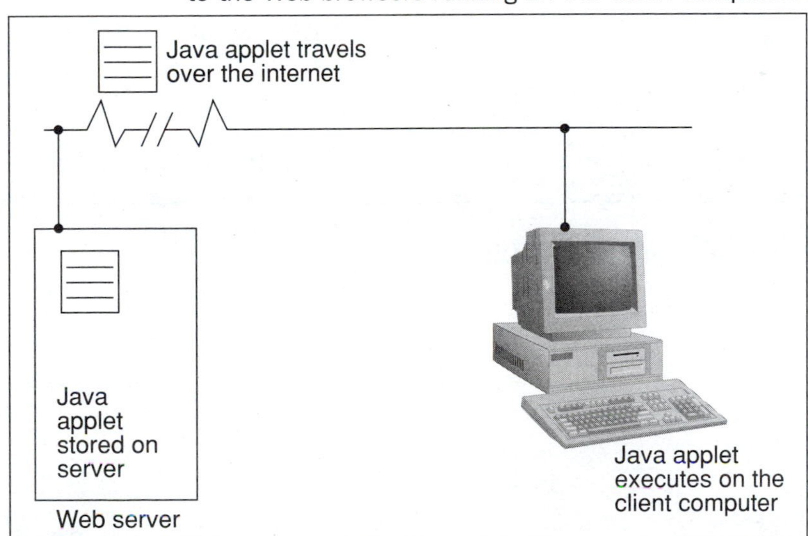

The Java applet on the Web server is sent to a client computer as part of a Web page. The program does not run on the server. Once the entire applet is delivered, the Web browser begins interpreting the byte codes. What you see on your screen is actually a program running on your computer.

Java applets can be run in a Web browser or from any other Java byte code interpreter. Java compilers typically include an interpreter to allow you to run Java programs from within your Java programming environment. In the next chapter, you will use your Java compiler's interpreter.

Note

Because the Java applet runs on the client computer, Java has built-in security to prevent the Java applet from doing harm to the client computer. For example, the built-in security prevents an applet from erasing files or implanting a virus on your computer.

Applets and Web Pages

You have probably used a World Wide Web browser to view an HTML document that contained a Java applet. You may be wondering how that Java applet got into that Web page. In this section, you will learn how to include Java applets in Web pages using the <APPLET> tag.

HTML and HTTP

HTML (Hypertext Markup Language) is the programming language used to create World Wide Web documents. HTML uses codes called tags to specify the structure of a document. Some tags specify titles and formatting for paragraphs. Other tags allow links to other HTML documents. *Hypertext Transfer Protocol (HTTP)* is the protocol that Web servers use to transfer HTML documents and other kinds of files to your Web browser.

Note

This section assumes you have some experience creating Web pages and are familiar with the basics of HTML. Only a quick review of HTML is provided in this section.

You may be wondering how HTML compares to what is actually being displayed on the screen. Figure 1-2 shows a World Wide Web page and Figure 1-3 shows the HTML that created that page.

FIGURE 1-2
A Web browser translates the HTML document into the image you see on the screen.

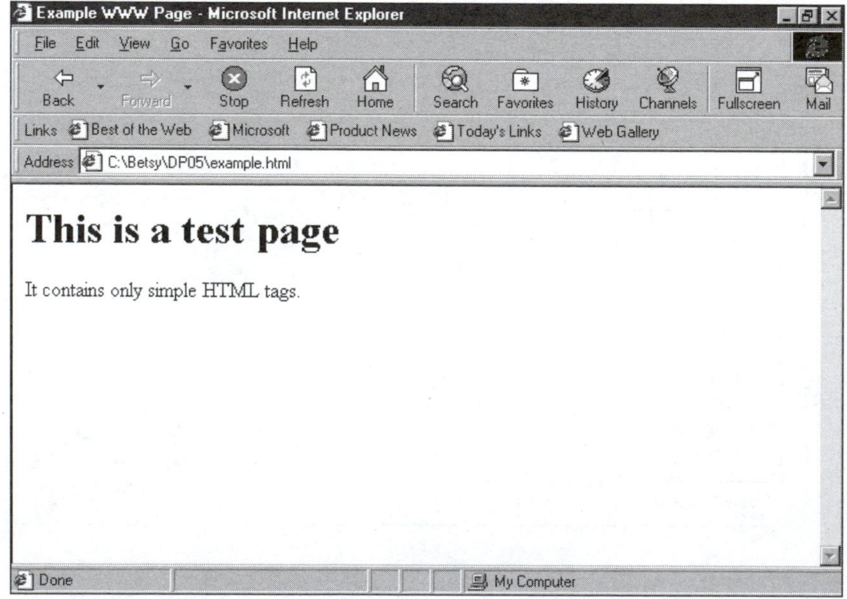

FIGURE 1-3
The HTML source for the page shown in Figure 1-2 is filled with special codes called tags.

```
<HTML>
<HEAD>
<TITLE>Example WWW Page</TITLE>
</HEAD>
<BODY>
</BODY>
<H1>This is a test page</H1>
<P>It contains only simple HTML tags.
</HTML>
```

Table 1-1 is a summary of the common HTML tags. If you are not familiar with all of the tags, take a moment to learn what tags are available.

TABLE 1-1
HTML Quick Reference

STRUCTURE TAGS	
<! ... >	creates a comment
<HTML> ... </HTML>	begins and ends an HTML document
<HEAD> ... </HEAD>	begins and ends the header
<BODY> ... </BODY>	begins and ends the body
TITLES	
<TITLE> ... </TITLE>	page title, must be in the header, appears at top of screen
HEADINGS	
<H1> ... </H1>	headings 1 through 6; 1 uses the largest font size, and
<H6> ... </H6>	6 uses the smallest font size
PARAGRAPHS	
<P> ... </P>	
CHARACTER FORMATTING	
<B> ... </B>	bold
<I> ... </I>	italic
<CODE> ... </CODE>	code sample (normally Courier font)

You can create a Web page by opening a simple text document in a program such as Notepad and keying in the HTML necessary to generate the page. This is acceptable for simple pages (although it is not very convenient). With more complex Web pages, generating the entire page from scratch by keying HTML is tedious. Fortunately, excellent software exists to help you create Web pages quickly.

Programs that help you create HTML documents are called *HTML editors*. There are many free and shareware HTML editors available that you may download over the Internet. More elaborate commercial software is also available. For example, programs like Microsoft FrontPage are complete Web site creation and management tools. They help you create Web pages and maintain them once they are created. The HTML creation programs allow you to work in an environment similar to a word processor or desktop publishing program, while saving your work in HTML. These programs are so easy that some people can create Web pages without knowing any HTML. However, most professional Web page designers who work with a tool like FrontPage know enough about HTML to allow them to tweak the pages and make the best use of technologies like Java.

STEP-BY-STEP 1.1

1. Open a text editor such as Notepad.
2. Enter the HTML code from Code List 1.1 into the document.
3. Save the document as mine.htm or mine.html to your student disk or folder. Depending on your operating system, you may use the html filename extension or the htm extension. In many cases, either one is acceptable.
4. Close the text editor.
5. Open your Web browser.

CODE LIST 1.1

```
<HTML>
<HEAD>
<TITLE>Example WWW Page</TITLE>
</HEAD>
<BODY>
</BODY>
<H1>This is a test page</H1>
<P>It contains only simple HTML tags.
</HTML>
```

6. In the address (or URL) field, enter `file://` followed by the path and filename of the document you just saved. For example, if you saved the file on a floppy disk in the A: drive of your computer, enter `file://a:\mine.htm`.
7. If you made any errors in the HTML, open the document with the text editor, make any necessary corrections, and view it again.
8. When the document displays correctly, close your Web browser.

The <APPLET> Tag

Note

The applet file is not Java source code. A Java compiler has already translated the Java source code into byte codes. The file with the .class extension is a file of byte codes.

Table 1-1 includes many popular HTML tags that are used to format Web pages. Java applets are put into Web pages using a special tag called the <APPLET> tag. The <APPLET> tag tells the Web browser that an applet is embedded in the page. In order to tell the applet where to appear and how to act, the <APPLET> tag includes information called attributes. Three of these attributes are required and others are optional.

Figure 1-4 shows the HTML source code for a simple page that includes an applet. The <APPLET> tag in the figure contains only the required attributes CODE, WIDTH, and HEIGHT. Note that, like many other tags, the <APPLET> tag is paired with a closing tag (</APPLET>).

The CODE attribute specifies what Java applet is to be executed. The name of the file is used to identify the applet. Java applets carry the .class extension.

FIGURE 1-4
An <APPLET> tag is included in the HTML source.

```
<HTML>
<HEAD>
<TITLE>A Simple Web Page with an Applet</TITLE>
</HEAD>
<BODY>
<H1>A WWW Page with a Java applet</H1>
<HR>
<APPLET CODE="HelloWorld.class" WIDTH=150 HEIGHT=25>
</APPLET>
</BODY>
</HTML>
```

The WIDTH and HEIGHT attributes tell the Web browser how much horizontal and vertical space, in pixels, to reserve in the page for the applet. Depending on the applet, these settings may not be necessary. However, in cases where the Java applet occupies a portion of the screen, these settings may be used to size the area devoted to the applet.

The <APPLET> tag can also contain several other attributes: ALIGN, HSPACE, VSPACE, and CODEBASE. Let's examine these one at a time.

ALIGN is used to align the applet with other elements of the page. Table 1-2 describes the possible values for the ALIGN attribute.

TABLE 1-2

LEFT	The applet is placed at the left margin.
RIGHT	The applet is placed at the right margin.
BASELINE	The bottom of the applet is aligned with the baseline of the text in the line in which the applet appears. The baseline of text is the line on which the text rests. Only descenders such as the bottom of a lowercase y extend below the baseline.
ABSMIDDLE	The middle of the applet is aligned with the middle of the largest item on the line on which the applet appears.
MIDDLE	The middle of the applet is aligned with the middle of the baseline of the text in the line in which the applet appears.
ABSBOTTOM	The bottom of the applet is aligned with the lowest item in the line.
BOTTOM	Same as BASELINE alignment.
TEXTTOP	The top of the applet is aligned with the top of the tallest text in the line.
TOP	The top of the applet is aligned with the tallest item in the line. The tallest item could be text or another applet or image.

The `HSPACE` and `VSPACE` attributes indicate the amount of horizontal and vertical space, in pixels, that a Web browser should put between the applet and any surrounding items. This is convenient if there is text or graphics near the space the applet will occupy. Using `HSPACE` and `VSPACE` ensures that the surrounding items do not crowd your applet.

The `CODEBASE` attribute is used when the executable applet is stored on the server in a directory different from the current Web page. You might use an applet in a variety of Web pages. Rather than store a copy of the applet in the directory of each Web page, you can specify the location of the applet.

Now that you have learned how the `<APPLET>` tag is used to embed an applet into a Web page, let's create a simple Web page with an applet embedded in it.

STEP-BY-STEP 1.2

1. Open a text editor such as Notepad.
2. Enter the HTML code from Code List 1.2 into the document.

CODE LIST 1.2

```
<HTML>
<HEAD>
<TITLE>A Simple Web Page with an Applet</TITLE>
</HEAD>
<BODY>
<H1>A WWW Page with a Java Applet</H1>
<HR>
<APPLET CODE="HelloWorld.class" WIDTH=150 HEIGHT=25>
```

STEP-BY-STEP 1.2 CONTINUED

CODE LIST 1.2 (continued)

```
</APPLET>
</BODY>
</HTML>
```

3. Save the document to your student disk or folder as hello.htm or hello.html. In future exercises and problems, HTML files will be assumed to have an .html extension. If your system can use only three-character extensions, use .htm instead.

4. Copy the applet named HelloWorld.class from the student data files that accompany this book to the same disk or directory where the HTML document is saved.

5. Use your Web browser to view hello.html and verify that the Java applet was properly included.

6. Experiment with some of the other <APPLET> attributes.

7. Close the Web browser.

Warning

You may find that changing the attributes in the HTML source file and then viewing the page again does not produce the changes you were expecting. In some cases, the Web browser will continue to run the applet with the same attributes as the first time it was run, even though the attributes have changed. The Refresh or Reload button may not be enough in some cases to make your changes take effect. You may have to exit the browser and restart it to cause the browser to apply your new attributes.

Passing Parameters to Applets

Many Java applets are programmed to allow themselves to be customized by the author of the Web page. This customization occurs by passing information called *parameters* to the applet. In this section, you will learn how to customize an applet by passing parameters.

An Example of a Customizable Applet

Many applets are customizable. Parameters can be used to set colors, modify the behavior of the applet, or provide an applet with information to be displayed. Only the programmer of the applet limits the possibilities. Let's look at an example of a customizable applet. In this case, the applet creates a scrolling marquee on the screen. Among other things, a parameter is used to specify the text to be displayed.

STEP-BY-STEP 1.3

1. Copy the ScrollText.class and the param.html files from the student data files to your student disk or folder. Open your Web browser. Rather than going to the World Wide Web for the document, open the param.html file from your student disk or folder. The document includes a Java applet that makes text scroll across the screen.

2. Leave the browser open for the next exercise.

Specifying Parameters

To specify parameters, use the <PARAM> tag as shown in Figure 1-5. An opening <APPLET> tag begins the applet section, and a closing </APPLET> tag closes the section. Between the opening and closing of the applet, parameters can be specified.

FIGURE 1-5
Parameters are specified with the <PARAM> tag.

```
<APPLET CODE="ScrollText.class"
        ALIGN="baseline" WIDTH="605" HEIGHT="30"
        NAME="ScrollText">
<PARAM NAME="ScrollingText"
       VALUE="Scrolling Message Goes Here">
<PARAM NAME="InitDir" VALUE="right">
<PARAM NAME="FinalDir" VALUE="left">
<PARAM NAME="TextColor" VALUE="blue">
<PARAM NAME="BgrdColor" VALUE="yellow">
<PARAM NAME="FontSize" VALUE="18">
<PARAM NAME="FontType" VALUE="Times New Roman">
<PARAM NAME="ScrollSpeed" VALUE="5">
<PARAM NAME="FadeSpeed" VALUE="6">
<PARAM NAME="xSize" VALUE="605">
<PARAM NAME="ySize" VALUE="z30">
</APPLET>
```

In order to customize an applet, you must know what customization the applet will accept. The parameter names and values are not necessarily standardized. The programmer of the applet can name the parameters anything he or she desires and can set the acceptable values. Before you pass a parameter to an applet, you have to know the name of the available parameters as well as the valid values.

The programmer of the applet should document the available parameters. If you do not have access to any documentation for the applet you are using, you can sometimes learn what parameters are available by looking at the HTML source of pages that customize the applet.

Note

In a <PARAM> tag, the parameter name is case-sensitive and the value must be placed in quotes. The term case-sensitive means that the capitalization of the characters in the <PARAM> tag must match the capitalization used by the Java programmer.

STEP-BY-STEP 1.4

1. View the source of the page from Step-by-Step 1.3 currently on your screen.
2. Locate the <PARAM> tags and see if you can determine what each parameter does. Which parameter is responsible for providing the message for the marquee?
3. Close the HTML source and the Web browser.

Notice that the <PARAM> tag has the syntax <PARAM NAME="name" VALUE="value">, where name is the parameter name and value is the value of that particular parameter. Parameter values are enclosed in double quotes.

STEP-BY-STEP 1.5

1. Open a text editor, and then open param.html.
2. Modify the ScrollingText parameter to display a message of your choice.
3. Modify the parameters that specify colors. The color values accepted by the applet are white, lightGray, darkGray, black, red, pink, orange, yellow, green, magenta, cyan, and blue.
4. Save the edited HTML source.
5. Open param.html with your Web browser and observe the effect of your parameters.
6. Close the Web browser.

Alternate HTML

Unfortunately, some Web browsers do not support Java applets. Web browsers without Java support can still view your page, but the applets will not display. To avoid leaving people who do not have Java-capable browsers completely in the dark, there is a special area where you can place HTML code that will display only on Web browsers that do not support Java. HTML code placed in this area is known as *alternate HTML*.

The code in Figure 1-6 is an example of HTML that includes alternate HTML for an applet.

FIGURE 1-6
Alternate HTML is used to display a message or alternate information when viewed on a Web browser not capable of interpreting Java.

```
<HTML>
<HEAD>
<TITLE>Java Sample</TITLE>
</HEAD>
<BODY>
<APPLET CODE="COOL.class" WIDTH=600 HEIGHT=450>
Your web browser does not support Java applets.<BR>
</APPLET>
</BODY>
</HTML>
```

Alternate HTML can be more complex than just a message. Any valid HTML code can appear in the alternate HTML area. For example, if your Java applet provides menu choices to the user, the alternate HTML could be used to provide those same choices to the user using a non-Java method.

The Four Main Parts of an <APPLET> Tag

To review, the <APPLET> tag has four main parts:

1. The opening <APPLET> tag, which includes the applet attributes.
2. The optional applet parameters.
3. The optional alternate HTML.
4. The closing </APPLET> tag.

Summary

In this lesson, you learned:

- Java was originally named Oak and was created for use with consumer electronic devices.
- Java became a popular language for use with the Internet because of the small size of Java programs and the fact that Java programs do not compile for any specific computer.
- Java applets are delivered over the Internet from a Web server to a client computer running a Web browser. The Web browser interprets the Java byte codes and the Java applet executes on the client computer.
- HTML (Hypertext Markup Language) is the programming language used to create World Wide Web documents. Within the HTML document are tags that specify the structure of the document.
- Web servers use the Hypertext Transfer Protocol (HTTP) to transfer HTML documents and other kinds of files to your Web browser.
- The `<APPLET>` tag is used to embed Java applets into HTML documents. A variety of attributes are available as part of the `<APPLET>` tag.
- Parameters may be passed to an applet to modify its behavior. The parameters are passed using the `<PARAM>` tag.
- For Web browsers that do not support Java, you can include alternate HTML. Alternate HTML is displayed only in cases where the Web browser is not Java-capable.

LESSON 1 REVIEW QUESTIONS

TRUE/FALSE

Circle T if the statement is true or F if the statement is false.

T F 1. Java was created especially for the World Wide Web.

T F 2. Java's original name was Oak.

T F 3. A Web server is a computer used to surf the Web with a Web browser.

T F 4. A Web browser interprets byte codes as they are transferred from the server.

T F 5. Java interpreters are found in places other than Web browsers.

T F 6. HTTP is the programming language used to create Web documents.

T F 7. Codes called tags are used to specify the structure of a Web document.

T F 8. Programs that help you create Web pages are called HTML editors.

T F 9. The `<APPLET>` tag tells the Web browser that an applet is embedded in the Web page.

T F 10. The CODEBASE attribute is used to place space around an applet.

T F 11. All Java applets are customizable.

T F 12. Java applets are customized by passing parameters to the applet.

T F 13. The programmer of the applet decides the names of parameters and acceptable values.

T F 14. The <OPTION> tag is used to pass parameters.

T F 15. Parameter names are case-sensitive.

WRITTEN QUESTIONS

Write a brief answer to the following questions.

1. Why did the original name for Java have to be changed?
2. What company created Java?
3. Identify two features of Java that make it ideal for use on the World Wide Web.
4. What is the function of a Web server?
5. What is a client computer?
6. What does the acronym HTML stand for?
7. What tags begin and end an HTML document?
8. What are the three required attributes of the <APPLET> tag?
9. What is the function of the CODE attribute?
10. What units of measurement do the WIDTH and HEIGHT attributes use?
11. Identify two common uses for applet parameters.
12. Which tag closes an applet section?
13. What is one way you might learn what parameters an applet accepts?
14. The value of a parameter must be enclosed in what kind of character?
15. Write a line of HTML code that passes a parameter named TextColor with the value green.

LESSON 1 PROJECTS

PROJECT 1-1

Explore the options available on your Web browser. Look for an option that prevents the Web browser from running Java applets. Set the option to disable Java and view one of the pages you created that includes alternate HTML. Finally, re-enable Java in your browser.

CRITICAL THINKING

ACTIVITY 1-1

Search the Internet for information about Java and the history of Java. Use a search engine or investigate the www.studio-jplus.com site for links. Write a short report based on what you find.

ACTIVITY 1-2

Search the Internet for galleries of sample Java applets. Search for interesting uses for Java, such as chat rooms that use Java applets. After seeing some uses for Java, write a brief report about how Java is being used and how it might be used in the future.

ACTIVITY 1-3

Write an HTML source file that will display your name at the top of the page. Below your name, embed the Java applet named JAVAMouseOver.class from the student data files. Use a width of 200 pixels and a height of 150 pixels. Load your page into a Web browser to test it. Save the HTML file as Problem1-3.html.

ACTIVITY 1-4

Modify the page you created above to place the applet on the same line with your name and align the middle of the Java applet with the middle of the baseline of the text. Save the HTML file as Problem1-4.html.

ACTIVITY 1-5

Open the file param.html from the student data files. Modify the file to occupy a WIDTH of 400 and a HEIGHT of 60. Set the FontSize parameter to 36, the xSize to 400, and the ySize to 60. Save the modified source as param2.html to your student disk or folder. Then, load the page into your Web browser to observe the changes.

ACTIVITY 1-6

Modify param2.html to include the following message in the alternate HTML section:

```
This browser does not support Java applets.
```

Save the modified source as param3.html to your student disk or folder.

INTRODUCTION TO JAVA PROGRAMMING

LESSON 2

OBJECTIVES

Upon completion of this lesson, you should be able to:

- Explain the structure of a Java program.
- Access the text editor and enter Java source code.
- Compile and run Java programs.
- Describe the basic philosophy of object-oriented programming (OOP).

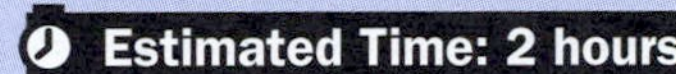

Overview

You have learned that Java source code has to be entered into a text editor, translated by a compiler, and then run by either a standalone interpreter or one included in a World Wide Web browser. Your task in this lesson will be to create an actual Java program on your system. You will first examine the structure of a Java program. Then you will enter a simple program into the text editor, compile it, and run the executable file that is created.

Java Program Structure

Java programs have the basic structure illustrated in Figure 2-1. They are the following:

1. Comments. Comments are remarks that the compiler ignores.
2. Class Definitions. Everything in Java is an object, and a class is the template used to create an object.
3. Main Method. The main method is where every Java application begins.
4. Braces. Braces are special characters used to mark the beginning and ending of blocks of code.
5. Statement. A statement is a line of Java code. Statements end with a semicolon.

Let's examine each part of a Java program in more detail.

FIGURE 2-1
A Java program has several parts.

```
//Simple Java Program
//
//Purpose: To demonstrate the parts of a
//simple Java program.

class HelloWorld
{
    public static void main(String args[])
    {
    System.out.println("Hello World!");
    }
}
```

Comments

When writing a program, you may think that you will always remember what you did and why. Most programmers, however, eventually forget. But more important, others may need to make changes in a program you wrote. They probably will be unaware of what you did when you wrote the program. That is why *comments* are important.

Use comments to:

- explain the purpose of a program.
- keep notes regarding changes to the source code.
- store the names of programmers for future reference.
- explain the parts of your program.

Comments, which are ignored by the compiler, begin with a double slash (//) and may appear anywhere in the program. An entire line can be a comment or a comment can appear to the right of program statements, as shown in Figure 2-2. Because everything to the right of the // is ignored, do not include any program statements to the right of a comment. Be sure to use the forward slash (/) rather than the backslash (\), or the compiler will try to translate your comments and give an error message.

FIGURE 2-2
Comments can follow a statement.

```
int i; // declare i as an integer
```

Class Definition

Java is an object-oriented programming language. For now, you don't need to worry too much about object-oriented programming. However, it will help if you understand that everything in Java is an *object*. Remember the scrolling text applet you worked with in the previous chapter? The applet is an object—a scrolling marquee object.

An object does not exist until it is created. Thus a Java program is not an object. Rather, a Java program instructs the computer on how to create an object. The set of instructions for creating an object is called a *class*. Think of a class as a template or a definition that tells the compiler about an object and how to create it.

Every Java program has at least one class. This class is normally given the same name as the file that it is in. Simple programs can be written entirely within one class. Large programs are divided into several different classes. When a program includes more than one class, execution begins with the class named after the source code's filename.

You will learn much more about classes and objects in future lessons.

Main Method

A *method* consists of one or more statements in a class that performs a specific task within an object. For example, a circle object could have a method written to calculate the area of a circle. That method could be used (or "called") wherever the calculation is needed in the program.

Every Java application has a *main method* (see Figure 2-3). The main method is run first. Just like Java classes, simple programs can be written entirely within the main method, but Java programs are typically divided into multiple methods, which are accessed through the main method.

FIGURE 2-3
Every Java application has a main method.

```
class HelloWorld
{
  public static void main(String args[])        //Main Method
   {
    System.out.println("Hello World!");
   }
}
```

The parentheses that follow the word `main` are required. They tell the compiler that main is a method. All methods have parentheses, although most of them have information inside the parentheses. You will learn how to write your own methods in a later lesson.

Note

All Java applications start running at the main method. However, Java applets use several different methods to take the place of the main method. You will learn about these new methods later in the unit.

Braces

Braces are used to mark the beginning and end of blocks of code. Every opening brace must have a closing brace. Notice in Figure 2-4 that the main method is enclosed in a set of braces. Providing comments after each closing brace helps to associate it with the appropriate opening brace. Also, aligning the indention of opening and closing braces improves readability.

FIGURE 2-4
Braces mark the beginning and end of blocks of code.

```
public static void main(String args[])
{ // This brace marks the start of System.out block of code
  System.out.println("Hello World!");
} // This brace marks the end of System.out block of code
```

Statements

Methods contain *statements* that consist of instructions or commands that make the program work. Each statement in Java ends with a semicolon.

Semicolons

You must have a semicolon after every statement. The semicolon terminates the statement. In other words, it tells the compiler that the statement is complete. Notice, however, method declarations such as `main(String args[])` are exempt from being punctuated by semicolons.

Java and Blank Space

Java allows for great flexibility in the spacing and layout of the code. Use this feature to make it easier to read the code by indenting and grouping statements.

Uppercase or Lowercase

Remember the ASCII codes? In the computer, an A is represented by a different number than an a. The capital letters are referred to as *uppercase*, and small letters are called *lowercase*.

Java is known as *case-sensitive* because it interprets uppercase and lowercase letters differently. For example, to a Java compiler, the word cow is different from the word Cow. Be careful to use the same combination of lettering (either uppercase or lowercase) when you enter source code. Whatever capitalization was used when the command was originally named is what must be used. Most of what you will see in Java will be in lowercase letters. If you key a command in uppercase that is supposed to be lowercase, you will get an error.

From Source Code to a Finished Product

The exact process required to enter source code, compile it, and run it will vary depending on the compiler you are using. Check with your instructor to find out the specifics of compiling and running Java programs on your particular system.

Entering Source Code

The first step in creating a Java program is to enter your Java source code into a text file. Most Java compilers have an integrated programming environment that contains a text editor you can use. An integrated programming environment allows you to enter your source code, compile, and run while your text editor is on the screen. The integrated programming environment runs either the standalone interpreter or a Web browser, depending on your software.

STEP-BY-STEP 2.1

1. Start a new, blank file in your text editor.

2. Enter the Java source code *exactly* as it is shown in Code List 2.1.

3. Save the file as MyFirstProg.java to your student disk or folder, and leave the program on your screen for the next exercise.

CODE LIST 2.1

```
// My first Java program

class MyFirstProg
{
  public static void main(String args[])
  {
  System.out.println("My first Java program.");
  }
}
```

Compiling and Running the Program

Most compilers allow you to compile and run with a single command from the integrated environment.

STEP-BY-STEP 2.2

1. Compile and run the program you entered in Step-by-Step 2.1. If your compiler allows all of these operations to be performed with a single command, use that command. If your program fails to compile or run, check to see if you entered the code exactly as shown in Step-by-Step 2.1 and try again.

2. If your program runs successfully, you should see the text **My first Java program**. on the screen. Otherwise, ask your instructor for help.

3. Leave the source file open for the next exercise.

Making Changes and Compiling Again

You can add, change, or delete lines from a program's source code and compile it again. The next time the program is run, the changes will be in effect.

STEP-BY-STEP 2.3

1. Add the statement from Code List 2.2 to the main function, substituting your name in place of Angela Askins.

   Your program should now appear like the one in Code List 2.3, except your name should be on the new line.

2. Compile and run the program again to see the change.

3. Save and close the source code file.

Note

When executing a Java program in the Microsoft Visual J++ Integrated Development Environment (IDE), the output window may open and close so quickly that the results of executing the program may not be seen. It is possible to keep the window open to view the results of the program execution by changing a Java program to include the following statements.
1.Modify the main method statement as follows:

```
public static void
main(String args[]) throws
java.io.IOException
```

2.Add the following statement after the last System.out.println statement:

```
System.in.read();
```

With these two statements added, the output window will remain displayed until the Enter key is pressed. When the Enter key is pressed, the window will close.

CODE LIST 2.2

```
System.out.println("By Angela Askins");
```

CODE LIST 2.3

```
// My first Java program.

class MyFirstProg
{

  public static void main(String args[])
  {
  System.out.println("My first Java program.");
  System.out.println("By Angela Askins");
  }
}
```

Loading and Compiling an Existing Source File

Often you will load an existing source code file and compile it. Most integrated programming environments have an Open command that can be used to open source files.

STEP-BY-STEP 2.4

1. Start your integrated programming environment.
2. Open the source file Count.java from the student data files.
3. Compile and run the program. The program quickly displays the numbers 1 through 10.
4. Close the source file.

Responsibilities of the Programmer

As you write more advanced computer programs, you should keep certain responsibilities in mind.

1. Privacy. Programmers often have access to databases and other information about individuals. Programmers have a responsibility to protect the privacy of this information.
2. Property Rights. Ideas are not protected by copyright law. Actual program code, however, is. Using software that you do not have legal license to use, or using other programmers' source code without proper permission, is illegal and irresponsible.
3. Impact of Software. Software can do physical damage to computer equipment (in the form of viruses), or have social ramifications. Programmers should not use computers to cause harm to users and should consider the impact of a program on society before writing a program.
4. Reliability. Individuals, schools, businesses, and the government rely on computers more every year. Programmers have a responsibility to produce software that is as reliable as possible and to report and/or repair problems that may affect the reliability of the system.

Congratulations!

You now know the basics of creating and running Java programs. From here you will simply add to your knowledge, which will enable you to write more useful programs. If you feel you need more experience with compiling and running Java programs, repeat the exercises in this lesson or ask your instructor for additional help. Future exercises require that you know how to compile and run Java programs.

First Steps: An Introduction to Object-Oriented Programming

Object-oriented programming (OOP) is more than a programming language. OOP is more of a philosophy of how to solve problems and, more specifically, large-scale problems. Languages such as Java, C++, and Smalltalk are examples of languages that are used to write object-oriented programs. OOP, however, has much more to do with how you think about a program than which language is ultimately used to code the program.

A program that prints out "Hello World!" or adds a few numbers together can be programmed in a simple step-by-step process we call *procedural programming*. However, what do you do when you must develop a program that contains graphical interfaces, such as windows, buttons, or check boxes? What do you do when your company is hired to develop a major software product such as a word processor, a spreadsheet, or a database program? In the software industry, the object-oriented approach to developing software has been the trend for large software projects. In addition, languages such as Java are making OOP a good choice for projects of all sizes.

The OOP County Fair

To understand the difference between procedural programming and object-oriented programming, let's look at two different ways a county fair might be run.

The Procedural Model

In the first approach to running the county fair, each person or family arriving at the fair is met by a guide at the gate. This guide takes the visitors' tickets and stays with the visitors throughout their stay. The same person would strap the visitors into their seats for the roller coaster and then run it; would fix the visitors hot dogs and take their money; and would clean up the streets and sidewalks after the visitors went home.

In this approach, the fair is run like a procedural program. Think of the person who guides visitors through the fair as a procedural program. As a procedural programmer, you would have to think ahead and be prepared at any time for your program to serve the needs of the fair-goers. Your program might be waiting for the next request, and would have code that looked like:

```
if the visitors need cotton candy then .........
if the visitors want to ride the train then .........
if the visitors are ready to leave then .........
```

As long as the fair does not get too large, this procedural approach will work well and be fairly easy to develop. However, if the roller coaster is updated to a newer and faster one, or another new ride is installed, or a new milkshake stand is added, you have to change the parts of the program that address the changes in operating instructions. Of course, you will also have to insert new "if" statements at every point in the program where the visitors might want to ride the roller coaster or drink a milkshake.

Most important, each time you write or rewrite part of the program, you have to make sure that everything still works together without error and that your new code does not have any errors of its own or introduce any further errors to the rest of your program—a process called *debugging*. As you can see, as the fair program becomes larger, developing and maintaining the program is going to become more difficult.

The Object-Oriented Model

The alternative approach to running our county fair is an object-oriented way. By using an object-oriented approach, you have much more room for improvement and growth, and many fewer problems with the programming and debugging process. What you do from the start is write a set of rules on how to take tickets. You write a set of rules for operating a concession or souvenir stand where food and merchandise are sold. You write another set of rules on how to strap people into the roller coaster and run it. You write still another set of rules on how to clean up the streets, sidewalks, and store windows. In OOP, we would call each of these sets of rules the Ticket Taker class, the Retail Outlet class, the Roller Coaster class, and the Facility Maintenance class.

This seems like a nice system, but remember, rules do not get the job done. It takes people following those rules to make the fair really happen. In OOP, we would say that the person following the ticket-taking rules would be a Ticket Taker object, the person running the roller coaster, and following Roller Coaster class rules, would be a Roller Coaster object, and so on. This is a very different approach from using procedural programming. However, if you have ever attended a county fair, you will note that this is how a fair is really run!

Now let's look at how you have improved the programming task. First, if you look at "running the program," you will note that the visitors (called "users" in programming) are now actively involved in the decision-making process. Instead of writing a whole list of "if" statements and trying to guess what the visitors will do next, your user selects an object, and the object knows what to do. This is quite a bit simpler.

But what happens if you upgrade the roller coaster? The answer is, all you have to do is upgrade the roller coaster! You do not have to make any other changes to the program that would take so much time and possibly introduce more problems. The next time a visitor comes to the park, she just goes to the roller coaster object and rides. The process for selecting the roller coaster is the same, but the visitor gets to enjoy the newer and faster ride.

Building Programs Using Objects

Let's consider how an object-oriented approach could help make a county fair easier to create and manage. Suppose we analyze the attractions at the fair and come to the conclusion that those attractions fall into three categories:

- Rides
- Shows
- Retail outlets

Our fair may consist of 18 rides, 7 shows, and 11 retail outlets (stores). Even so, there are things about each of those rides, shows, and stores that are the same. For example, running each of the 11 retail outlets involves taking money, stocking and delivering a product, opening, closing, and other operations common to retail outlets. Whether the retail outlet is a lemonade stand or a souvenir shop, many of the "rules" of operation are the same.

When a milkshake stand is created, the standard operations of a retail outlet are necessary to run the milkshake stand. Other rules and operations that are specific to a milkshake stand (such as how to make a milkshake) are added to the rules and operations of a retail outlet to make a milkshake stand. In effect, the retail outlet is customized to the needs of a milkshake stand.

In Lesson 1 you wrote HTML code that customized the scrolling text applet. What you were actually doing was causing a customized version of the scrolling text applet to be created, much like the milkshake stand would be a customized version of the retail outlet.

With object-oriented programming, you can create all 11 retail outlets, each customized to serve a unique purpose. Rather than writing 11 different programs for 11 different outlets, you can use the same "class" to create all 11 stores.

But the advantages don't stop there. If the standard rules for a retail outlet change, one change to the basic retail outlet class will change all 11 stores. For example, if the rules for a retail outlet change to refuse any bill over $20, the program need only be changed in one place to apply the change to all 11 outlets.

Object-oriented programming is very powerful and very effective. However, it is not the only way to solve programming problems. The important point is that object-oriented programming can simplify many programming tasks—especially large ones.

There is much more to OOP than can be learned from this simple analogy. You are, however, now on your way to an understanding of the philosophy upon which Java is designed. In the lessons to come, you will learn more about object-oriented programming, and you will see why an understanding of OOP is essential to successful Java programming.

Summary

In this lesson, you learned:

- A Java program has several parts.
- Comments are remarks that are ignored by the compiler. They allow you to include notes and other information in the program's source code.
- All Java programs have at least one class definition. A class definition tells the compiler how to create an object.
- All Java programs have a main method. The main method is where the program begins running.
- Braces mark the beginning and end of blocks of code.
- Statements are the lines of code the computer executes. Each statement ends with a semicolon.
- Java allows you to indent and insert space in any way that you want. You should take advantage of this flexibility to format source code in a way that makes programs more readable.
- Java is case-sensitive, which means that using the wrong capitalization will result in errors.
- Java is an object-oriented programming language.
- Object-oriented programming (OOP) is a newer approach to programming that supports large-scale program development and easier, more reliable program maintenance.
- In object-oriented programming, a class is the set of rules that explain what certain things are and how they will be managed or taken care of.
- In OOP, an object is the actual thing that follows the rules and does the job specified by a class.

LESSON 2 REVIEW QUESTIONS

TRUE/FALSE

Circle T if the statement is true, or F if the statement is false.

T F 1. Comments begin with \\.

T F 2. Java is an object-oriented language.

T F 3. The parentheses after the word `main` indicate to the compiler that `main` is a method.

T F 4. Every opening brace must have a closing brace.

T F 5. Java statements end with a colon.

WRITTEN QUESTIONS

Write a brief answer to the following questions.

1. List four uses for comments.

2. What is a class?

3. What is a method?

4. What purpose do braces serve?

5. What does the term “case-sensitive” mean?

6. Which company developed the compiler you are using?

7. Which is the name of the compiler you are using and its version number?

8. Which command or commands are used to run a program with your compiler?

9. Which command opens a source code file from a disk?

10. Which command saves a source code file?

11. What is the name of the method of programming where programs follow a simple, step-by-step process?

12. What is the name of the process where a program is tested for errors and those errors are removed?

13. What approach to programming involves writing a set of rules called a class?

14. Suppose you are designing a class that will include the standard rules and operations of the rides in the fair. One item that would be part of your class would be the length of time the ride runs. List two other items that could be part of your class.

15. Suppose you want to use your ride class to help create a roller coaster ride. What items of information would be specific to a roller coaster that might not be included in your basic ride class?

LESSON 2 PROJECTS

PROJECT 2-1

Enter and run the program shown below, but substitute your name and the appropriate information for your compiler. Save the source code as compinfo.java to your student disk or folder.

```
// COMPINFO
// By Jeremy Wilson

class compinfo
{
public static void main(String args[])
{
System.out.println("This program was compiled using");
System.out.println("Microsoft Visual J++ version 1.1");
}
}
```

PROJECT 2-2

Open the source file Revcount.java from the student data files. Compile the source file and then run it. After you have run the program, close the source file and quit.

PROJECT 2-3

Write a program that prints the message of your choice to the screen. Make the message at least four lines long. Save the source code file as my_msg.java to your course student disk or folder.

LESSON 3

DATA TYPES AND STRINGS

OBJECTIVES

Upon completion of this lesson, you should be able to:

- List different data types used in Java and explain how they are processed in the computer.
- Declare, name, and initialize variables.
- Output variable values to the console.
- Discuss OOP using class wrappers and strings.

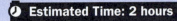

Overview

Computer programs process data to manage and produce information. The job of the programmer, then, is to properly organize data for this storage and use. Most data used by programs is stored in either variables or constants.

A *variable* holds data that can change while the program is running. A *constant* is used to store data that remains the same throughout the program's execution. In this chapter, you will learn about data types used by most computers, and then you will step into the object-oriented data types used by Java.

Data Types

There are eight standard variable types in Java. These data types, shown in Table 3-1, are often called the *intrinsic data types*. The byte, char, short, int, and long data types are for storing integers (whole numbers such as 5 or 27). The float and double data types are for floating-point numbers (numbers having fractional parts such as 7.75 or 92.6).

The char type is used to store single characters such as A. However, because Java uses the Unicode character set, char actually stores the numeric value based on its Unicode equivalent numeric value. That is, A would be stored as 65 (however, when it is displayed, Java converts the 65 back to A). Thus, char is a numeric type. The Boolean type is not numeric. It has a value of either true or false.

TABLE 3-1

DATA TYPE	SIZE (IN BITS)
Boolean	8
byte	8
char	16
short	16
int	32
long	64
float	32
double	64

You may recall from math courses that an integer is a positive or negative whole number, such as –2, 4, or 5133. Real numbers can be whole numbers or decimals and can be either positive or negative, such as 1.99, –2.5, 3.14159, and 4.

Data types are of little concern to the average person. When programming in Java, however, you must select a type of variable, called a *data type*, that best fits the nature of the data itself. Let's now examine the data types that are available for Java variables.

Integer Types

When you are working with either positive or negative whole numbers, you should use integer data types for your variables. There are several integer data types available in Java. Selecting which integer data type to use is the next step.

Table 3-2 lists the variable data types used for storing integers. Notice the range of values that each type can hold. For example, any value from –32,768 to 32,767 can be stored in a short data type variable. If, however, you need to store a value outside of that specific range, you must choose a different data type.

TABLE 3-2

MINIMUM INTEGER DATA TYPES	MINIMUM RANGE OF VALUES	NUMBER OF BYTES OCCUPIED
byte	–128 to 127	1
short	–32,768 to 32,767	2
int	–2,147,483,648 to 2,147,483,647	4
long	–9223372036854775808 to 9223372036854775807	8

Why would you want to use the int type when the long type has a bigger range? Notice the third column of Table 3-2. The variables with the larger ranges require more of the computer's memory. In addition, it may take the computer longer to access the data types that require more memory. Having all of these data types gives the programmer the ability to use only what is necessary for each variable, decrease memory usage, and increase speed.

Characters

Recall from Lesson 1 that characters are stored as numbers in the computer and that, when programming in Java, the computer assigns numbers to the characters using Unicode. Because the computer considers characters to be numbers, they are stored in an integer data type named char. Again, as stated above, this allows the computer, which can hold only numbers, to be able to hold the character data.

Extra for Experts

Earlier you read that floating-point numbers are not as efficient as integers. This is true. But many computer manufacturers include a floating-point unit (FPU) to help with the problem. A floating-point unit is a processor that works with floating-point numbers. FPUs are often called math coprocessors. Microprocessors with an FPU can perform calculations with floating-point numbers much more quickly than a microprocessor without an FPU. Some FPUs are on a chip separate from the microprocessor and some are built into the microprocessor chip.

Floating-Point Types

Integer variables are inappropriate for certain types of data. For example, tasks as common as working with money call for using floating-point numbers.

There are two types of floating-point variables available to Java. The first, simply called the float, has 32 bits or 4 bytes of memory set aside to hold the data. The second, the double, has 64 bits or 8 bytes of memory set aside for the data. In Java, there is also a third quantity defined as either a float or a double. This quantity is called NaN (Not a Number), and may be generated if an attempt is made to divide by zero, or some other mathematical action is taken that does not result in a usable number.

Table 3-3 lists the two floating-point data types and their range of values. The range of floating-point data types is more complicated than the range of integers. Selecting an appropriate floating-point type is based upon both the range of values and the required decimal precision.

TABLE 3-3

FLOATING POINT DATA TYPES	APPROXIMATE RANGE OF VALUES	DIGITS OF PRECISION	NUMBER OF BYTES OCCUPIED
float	3.4×10^{-38} to 3.4×10^{38}	7	4
double	1.8×10^{-308} to 1.8×10^{308}	15	8

When you are choosing a floating-point data type, first look to see how many digits of precision are necessary to store the value. For example, storing π as 3.1415926535897 requires 14 digits of precision. Therefore, you should use the double type in this case. You should also verify that your value will fit within the range of values the type supports. But unless you are dealing with very large or very small numbers, the range is not usually as important an issue as the precision.

Let's look at some examples of values and what data types would be appropriate for the values.

Dollar amounts in the range –$99,999.99 to $99,999.99 can be handled with a variable of type float. A variable of type double can store dollar amounts in the range –$9,999,999,999,999.99 to $9,999,999,999,999.99.

The number 5.98×10^{24} kg, which happens to be the mass of the Earth, can be stored in a variable of type float because the number is within the range of values and requires only three digits of precision.

Boolean Variables

A *Boolean variable* can have only two possible values. One of the values represents true (or some other form of the affirmative) and the other value represents false (or some other form of the negative). In some languages, certain numbers represent the TRUE or the FALSE condition; however, in Java, the only Boolean values allowed are the actual words true and false. Boolean variables are very useful in programming to store information such as whether an answer is yes or no, whether a report has been printed or not, or whether a device is currently on or off.

Note

Boolean variables are named in honor of George Boole, an English mathematician who lived in the 1800s. Boole created a system called Boolean algebra, which is a study of operations that take place using variables with the values true and false.

Using Variables

You are now going to have an opportunity to put your knowledge to work and select the right variable for the job. You must first indicate to the compiler what kind of variable you want and what you want to name it. Then, it is ready to use.

Declaring and Naming Variables

Indicating to the compiler what type of variable you want and what you want to call it is called declaring the variable.

DECLARING VARIABLES

You must *declare* a variable before you can use it. The Java statement declaring a variable must include the data type, followed by the name you wish to call the variable, and a semicolon. An integer variable named `i` is declared below.

```
int i;
```

Table 3-4 shows that declaring variables for other data types is just as easy as the example above.

Java will allow you to declare a variable anywhere in the program as long as the variable is declared before you use it. However, you should get into the habit of declaring all variables at the top of the method. Declaring variables at the top makes your code better organized, makes the variables easy to locate, and helps you plan for the variables you will need.

TABLE 3-4

DATA TYPE	SAMPLE JAVA DECLARATION STATEMENT
char	char Grade;
int	int DaysInMonth;
short	short temperature;
long	long PopulationChange;
float	float CostPerUnit;
double	double DistanceToDeltaQuadrant;

NAMING VARIABLES

The names of variables in Java are typically referred to as *identifiers*. Notice how the variable names in Table 3-4 are very descriptive and consider how they might help the programmer recall the variable's purpose. You are encouraged to use the same technique. For example, a variable that holds a bank balance could be called `balance`, or the circumference of a circle could be stored in a variable named `circumference`. The following are rules for creating identifiers.

- Identifiers must start with a letter, an underscore (_), or a dollar sign ($). You should, however, avoid using identifiers that begin with underscores and dollar signs because the compiler's internal identifiers often begin with underscores or contain dollar signs.
- As long as the first character is a letter, you can use any letters or numerals in the rest of the identifier.
- Use a name that makes the purpose of the variable clear, but avoid making it unnecessarily long.
- Identifiers cannot contain spaces. A good way to create a multi-word identifier is to use an underscore between the words (for example, `last_name`) or to use names with capital letters at the beginning of each word (`LastName`).
- Some Java programmers also identify variable types in the name, for example, `i_numCars`, which identifies numCars as an integer. In addition, you may see some variables start with an m, as in `m_lastname`, which indicates that this variable is a member of a certain class (you will be reading about members later).

The following words, called *keywords* or reserved words, must NOT be used as identifiers because they are part of the Java language. Your compiler may have additional keywords not listed here.

abstract	extends	interface	static
case	final	long	super
catch	finally	native	switch
char	float	new	synchronized
class	for	null	thisboolean
const	goto	package	throwbreak
continue	if	private	transientbyte
default	implements	protected	try
do	import	public	void
double	instanceof	return	volatile
else	int	short	while

Note

Any format that helps you or someone reading your code to understand what the variables represent or what they do will improve your code readability, and therefore maintainability. Professional programmers always write their code to be read by others for exactly this reason.

Recall from the previous lesson that Java is case-sensitive. The capitalization you use when the variable is declared must be used each time the variable is accessed. For example, `total` is not the same identifier as `Total`.

Table 3-5 gives some examples of illegal identifiers.

TABLE 3-5

IMPROPER JAVA VARIABLE NAMES	WHY ILLEGAL
Miles per gallon	Spaces are not allowed
import	import is a keyword
4Sale	Identifiers cannot begin with numerals

DECLARING MULTIPLE VARIABLES IN A STATEMENT

You can declare more than one variable in a single statement as long as all of the variables are of the same type. For example, if your program requires three variables of type float, all three variables could be declared by placing commas between the variables like this:

```
float x, y, z;
```

or

```
double a, b, c;
```

Initializing Variables

The compiler assigns a location in memory to a variable when it is declared. However, a value already exists in the space reserved for your variable. This is because a random value could have been stored when the computer was turned on or the location could retain data from a program that ran earlier. Regardless, the memory location now belongs to your program, and you must specify the initial value to be stored in the location. This process is known as initializing.

To *initialize* a variable, you simply assign it a value. In Java, the equal sign (=) is used to assign a value to a variable. In Figure 3-1, the variables `i` and `j` are initialized to the values of 3 and 2, respectively. Notice that the variable `k` has yet to be initialized because it is to be assigned the sum of `i` and `j`.

Warning

One of the most common mistakes made by first-time programmers is not initializing variables. There may be some conditions where a variable is sure to be given a value, such as a variable that receives data input by the user, and there may be conditions where a variable is only initialized under certain conditions. Your job is to make sure that every variable gets some valid information stored in it before it is used or output.

Extra for Experts

Upon turning on your computer, each byte of memory is filled with a value. The compiler sets up memory locations for your variables, and you must initialize them. When your program is through with a variable, that memory location is once again made available to a different variable or for another purpose. The value you last stored in the variable will remain in that memory location until it is assigned another value.

FIGURE 3-1

This code initializes variables and assigns their sum to another variable.

```
int i = 3; // variable declared and initialized in one statement
int j, k;
j = 2;
k = i + j;
```

STEP-BY-STEP 3.1

In this exercise, you will demonstrate assigning a value to a variable. In addition, you will implement the Java console output method. In a process you will read about later, the java *System* class has a member family of output methods named *out*, and one of the member methods of *out* is *println*. Again, while you will be studying this later in the unit, you can begin your application of object-oriented programming now by giving this output process a try.

1. Enter the program from Code List 3.1 into a blank text editor file:

2. Save the source code file as iDeclare.java to your student disk or folder.

3. Compile and run the program. The program should print Begin Program and then the number 0 (zero) on your screen. If no errors are encountered, leave the program on your screen. If errors are found, check the source code for keyboarding errors and compile again.

4. Next, place the code from Code List 3.2 before the line containing `myVal = 0;` (make sure you place all the code on one line).

   What happens? You can recognize that you are trying to output a value before it has been initialized, so in most cases, you would get inconsistent results (called "garbage" in the programming business). However, you may find that some compilers won't even let you do this—attempting to build a program such as this without variable initialization results in an error. What did your compiler do?

5. Change the initialization statement to set the value of myVal to –40 and run the program again. The number –40 should be shown on your screen. Save the source code again and leave the source code file open for the next exercise.

CODE LIST 3.1

```
// iDeclare.java
// Example of variable declaration.
class iDeclare
{
  public static void main(String args[])
{
  System.out.println("Begin Program\n");
  int myVal;

  myVal = 0;

  System.out.println("Once initialized, myVal is: " + myVal);
  }
}     // end of class iDeclare
```

CODE LIST 3.2

```
System.out.println("Before initialization,
                    myVal is: " + myVal);
```

Exponential Notation

Assigning a floating-point value to a variable works the way you probably expect, except when you need to use *exponential notation*. You may have used exponential notation and called it scientific notation. In exponential notation, very large or very small numbers are represented with a fractional part (called the mantissa) and an exponent. Use an e to signify exponential notation. Just place an e in the number to separate the mantissa from the exponent. Following are some examples of statements that initialize floating-point variables.

```
x = 2.5;
ElectronGFactor = 1.0011596567;
Radius_of_Earth = 6.378164e6; // radius of Earth at equator
Mass_of_Electron = 9.109e-31; // 9.109 x 10^-31 kilograms
```

STEP-BY-STEP 3.2

1. Modify the program on your screen to match the program in Code List 3.3.

2. Compile and run the program. The integer and three floating-point values should print to the screen.

   Why did you have to put the `(float)` in front of two of the variables? Try removing this from in front of the MassOfElectron variable. What happens?

   Some compilers will only recognize floating-point numbers as double types. By inserting `(float)` in front of the number, you are said to be *casting* (or typecasting) the variable to a float. In short, this means you are telling the compiler to treat the quantity as a certain type other than what it looks like to the compiler. In Java, as you will see later, there are several conditions when casting is used.

3. After trying these experiments and seeing your program run successfully, save and close the source code file.

CODE LIST 3.3

```
// iDeclare.java
// Example of variable declaration.
class iDeclare
{
  public static void main(String args[])
  {
  float x, MassOfElectron;
  double Radius_of_Earth;
  int myNewVal;

  System.out.println("Begin Program\n");

  myNewVal = 0;
  x = (float) 2.5;
  Radius_of_Earth = 6.378164e6;
```

continued on next page

CODE LIST 3.3 (continued)

```
    MassOfElectron = (float) 9.109e-31;

    System.out.println("myNewVal = " + myNewVal);
    System.out.println("x = " + x);
    System.out.println("Earth's radius: " + Radius_of_Earth);
    System.out.println("Electron's mass: " + MassOfElectron);
    }
}      // end of iDeclare
```

Object-Oriented Data Types and Strings

The data types you have worked with up to this point are often referred to as *primitive data types* or *intrinsic data types*. The primitive data types are not in an object-oriented format. They are based on similar data types in the C++ language. The designers of Java chose to keep the original primitive types for the simplest of calculations and mathematical manipulations. However, they also chose to develop a group of data type classes that would really be object-oriented data types. These data type classes are called *class wrappers* or *object wrappers*.

Why do you need object-oriented data types? The answer can be found in the OOP county fair analogy. Recall that the objects at the fair each know how to take care of themselves. The Roller Coaster object knows how to get power to operate the roller coaster from the outside, how to strap people into the carts, and how to make the roller coaster go. All objects, by way of obeying their class rules, know how to manage themselves, which is why object-oriented programming is popular. The programmer doesn't have to worry about the details of something that knows how to take care of itself.

One of the most frequent conditions to manage in Java is inputting and outputting data. The fact of the matter is, virtually all data comes into and goes out of Java programs as sets of characters called *strings*. As you may have seen before, strings are just groups of characters, such as your name or a sentence. Figure 3-2 shows several examples of strings. They can contain spaces, commas, and many other characters besides just letters.

When you enter a number as input to a program, you are actually inputting a string of characters. For example, the string "678" does not mean six hundred seventy-eight unless you interpret the string that way. The numerals 0 though 9 are ASCII characters, just like the alphabetic characters. When inputting data into a program, it is easiest to bring in a string and, if necessary, convert the string to a numeric value inside the program.

FIGURE 3-2
These are examples of strings, or groups of characters.

```
"abcdefghijkl"
"123456789"
"Bill Smith"
"K9"
"How now brown cow."
```

Many times, processing all input as strings improves reliability of a program because the computer can take in a series of characters, test them to see if they are numbers, and then work on them if they are, in fact, numbers. In other programming languages, entering the character E when the user should have entered 3 will cause errors or even unpredictable behavior. In Java, you can simply watch for invalid input and deal with it appropriately.

This leads us to an example of why an object-oriented data type may be more useful than a primitive data type. What if we had a data type that could convert itself from a string to a numeric data type (such as an integer) and back to a string? In Java, this is not a problem. Consider the program in Figure 3-3. The program creates two objects: a Double and a String.

FIGURE 3-3
Class wrappers make it possible for data types to behave like objects.

```
class WrapperTest
{
  public static void main(String args[])
  {
  System.out.println("Program Begins");

  // constructing a new Double
  Double myDoubleVal = new Double(4.52);
  // CONSTRUCTING A NEW STRING
  String myStringVal = new String("6.73 abc");

  System.out.println("My String value: " + myStringVal);
  System.out.println("My Double value: " + myDoubleVal);
  System.out.println("My Double value as a string: " +
        myDoubleVal.toString());
  }
}     // end of WrapperTest
```

Note

Class wrappers are called by the same name as their primitive counterparts. Notice, however, that the names of the data types are capitalized when the data type is a class. Remember, Java is case-sensitive. The compiler treats “Double” differently from “double.”

STEP-BY-STEP 3.3

1. Enter the program shown in Figure 3-3, save it as WrapperTest.java to your student disk or folder, compile it, and then run it. Your output should be as follows:

```
My String value: 6.73 abc
My Double value: 4.52
My Double value as a string: 4.52
```

Notice that the string and the double values are interchangeable thanks to being treated the same. Everything in OOP is an object, and it simplifies our programming lives to be able to treat all things with the same actions.

2. Now try to get the integer quantity out of the string value. To do that, add the line in Code List 3.4 to the end of your code.

   What happens? You will now experience your very first Java exception (much like an error—you will study exceptions in Lesson 5). The Integer parser (something that breaks things into smaller parts) gets confused trying to turn a space and some letters into a number. So try a different approach.

3. Remember that a String object should know how to take care of itself, so shouldn't it be able to give you a smaller chunk of its larger self? It does. Replace the code from item 2 with the code in Code List 3.5.

CODE LIST 3.4

```
System.out.println("My String converted back to an int: " +
Integer.parseInt(myStringVal));
```

CODE LIST 3.5

```
String newStringVal = new String(myStringVal.substring(0, 1));

System.out.println("My String converted to an int: "
  + Integer.parseInt(newStringVal, 10));
```

When you run your program with these two lines added, you will get the number 6 as output after the end of the other numbers. It is a little trickier to get a whole float or double value out of a string, but it can be done. This part of the exercise was to show you how a number (an integer) can be pulled from a string.

This exercise should show you something else as well: if you start thinking like an object-oriented programmer, you will begin to make intuitive guesses. If you begin to trust that objects can take care of themselves, you will start to think, "Geez, if that is a Giraffe object, I expect it can see far distances, or I expect it can eat leaves at the tops of tall trees." Think like this—ask yourself what a certain kind of object would be expected to do; in most cases you will be correct.

Let's look back at what you have written. Look at the following code again:

```
// constructing a new Double
Double myDoubleVal = new Double(4.52);
```

The comment states that you are "constructing" a new `Double` object. You will see more discussion of constructors later, but again, using your intuition you can see that it means we are "creating" a new kind of class. Here is how it is done. First, you have to tell the compiler what the name of the object is going to be, and yours is going to be named `myDoubleVal`. To be an object, it needs to know what rules to follow (what kind of class it will represent), and you can see it will be a `Double` object.

Then you use the *new* keyword to get some memory space set up for your object, and then you use the word Double a second time to get the object started. Again, the meanings and uses of these words will be made clearer as the unit progresses; the important thing for you to know at this point is what the declaration format should look like.

The number "4.52" is said to be a parameter that is passed to the method `Double` so it knows what value to give to `myDoubleVal`. Now this can be confusing, but don't let it bother you. With each lesson in this unit, you will be picking up more parts of the whole so that you can slowly build up your understanding of the big picture.

For example, right now you are asking, "Why is there a Double on the left side, and the very same word on the right side?" The answer is, the words on both sides are supposed to be the same, but they do different jobs. The `Double` on the left side is informing `myDoubleVal` what kind of object it will be. The `Double` on the right side, which as we said is a constructor, is getting `myDoubleVal` started up correctly with the number 4.52.

Now look at the first line you added under step 3 of this exercise. Before you read on, see if you can figure out what each part does. Use your intuition. Got it? Check yourself with the following:

1. The first word, `String`, tells the variable what kind of object it will be and what rules the object will have to follow; String is a class name.
2. The second word, `newStringVal`, is going to be the name of the object that will follow the rules of a String class.
3. After the equals sign (the assignment operator) comes the word `new`, which tells the computer to set aside the right amount of memory for a String object.
4. After the word `new` comes the word `String` again, only now this word is acting as a constructor, getting `newStringVal` ready to go with new data.
5. The parameter (or necessary information) that is passed to the String constructor is a whole method or operation of its own. You are passing a substring (a smaller portion) of `myStringVal` starting with the first character (at position 0 [zero]), and ending with the second character (at position 1). Again, `myStringVal`, being a String object, knew how to take out its first character and pass it to another method.

Summary

In this lesson, you learned:

- Most data is stored in either variables or constants.
- There are several types of variables. Some are for integer data and some are for floating-point data.
- Integer data types are selected based on the range of values you need to store.
- Characters are stored in the computer as numbers. The char data type can store one character of data.
- Floating-point data types are selected based on the range of values and the required precision.
- Boolean variables can have only two possible values: true or false.
- Variables must be declared before they are used. Variables should also be initialized to clear any random values that may be in the memory location. When a variable is declared, it must be given a legal name called an identifier.
- Output to the Java console is implemented with the member method `System.out.println`.
- Class wrappers allow primitive data types to be treated and used as objects.
- Groups of characters together are called strings in programming languages.
- Java uses String classes to manage character strings in programs.

LESSON 3 REVIEW QUESTIONS

TRUE/FALSE

Circle T if the statement is true, or F if the statement is false.

T F 1. An integer is a number with digits after the decimal point.

T F 2. The byte data type has a range of values of 0 to 255.

T F 3. A variable of type long can store the number 3,000,000,000.

T F 4. Each char variable can store one character.

T F 5. A float variable has 10 digits of precision.

WRITTEN QUESTIONS

1. What integer data type is necessary to store the value 4,199,999,999?

2. Why is it important to use data types that store your data efficiently?

3. What range of values can be stored in an int variable?

4. What floating-point data type provides the most digits of precision?

5. What is a Boolean variable?

6. What are the words called that cannot be used as identifiers because they are part of the Java language?

7. Why can't "first name" be used as an identifier?

8. Write a statement that declares four int data type variables i, j, k, and l in a single statement.

9. What character is used to assign a value to a variable?

10. If you were to cast a candle as a light bulb, what would the compiler think you were doing?

11. What is the difference between a class and an object?

12. Why should Java have class wrappers?

13. If you had a float quantity, but you wanted it to "look" like an integer, how would you do this?

14. The second line of item 3 of Step-by-Step 3.3 is as follows:

```
System.out.println("My String converted to an int: "
 + Integer.parseInt(newStringVal, 10));
```

What does this line of code do?

LESSON 3 PROJECTS

PROJECT 3-1

1. Enter, compile, and run the following program. Save the source code file as DataType.java to your student disk or folder.

```
// DataType.java
// Examples of variable declaration and
// initialization.

class DataType
  {
  public static void main(String args[])
  {
  // declare a double for the square root of two
  // remember that you cannot declare a constant (final)
```

continued on next page

```
    // unless you are in a unique class
    double SQUARE_ROOT_OF_TWO = 1.414214;

    int i; // declare i as an integer
    long j; // j as a long integer
    long k; // k as a long integer
    float n; // n as a floating point number

    i = 3; // initialize i to 3
    j= -2048111; // j to -2,048,111
    k=40000000021; // k to 4,000,000,002
    // Note: the l suffix above is required by some compilers
    n= (float) 1.887; // n to 1.887

    // output constant and variables to screen
    System.out.println(SQUARE_ROOT_OF_TWO);
    System.out.println("i = " + i);
    System.out.println("j = " + j);
    System.out.println("k = " + k);
    System.out.println("n = " + n);
    }

} // end of class DataType
```

2. Add declarations using appropriate identifiers for the values below. Declare e, the speed of light, and the speed of sound as constants. Initialize the variables. Use any identifier you want for those values that give you some indication as to their purpose.

100	e (2.7182818)
–1000	Speed of light (3.00×10^8 m/s)
–40,000	Speed of sound (340.292 m/s)
40,000	

3. Print the new values to the screen.

4. Save, compile, and run. Correct any errors you have made.

5. Close the source code file.

PROJECT 3-2

Write a program that declares two variables (A and B). Initialize A = 1 and B = 2.2. Next, declare an int named C and a float named D. Initialize C = A and D = B. Write statements to print C and D to the screen. Save the program to your student disk as Project 3_2.java. Compile and run the program. Close the source file.

MATH OPERATIONS

LESSON 4

OBJECTIVES

Upon completion of this lesson, you should be able to:

- Use the arithmetic operators.
- Increment and decrement variables.
- List the order of operations.
- Use mixed data types.
- Demonstrate the ability to avoid overflow, underflow, and floating-point errors.

Estimated Time: 2 hours

Overview

In this chapter, you will learn about Java math operations and demonstrate each concept by compiling and running programs.

First, you will learn about Java operators, some of which have already been mentioned. Next, you will learn how to build expressions using the operators. And finally, we'll talk about shortcuts and how to avoid pitfalls.

The Fundamental Operators

There are several types of operators. In this chapter you will be concerned only with the assignment operator, arithmetic operators, and some special operators.

Assignment Operator

You have already used the assignment operator (=) to initialize variables. The *assignment operator* changes the value of the variable to the left of the operator. Consider the statement below:

```
i = 25;
```

The statement `i = 25;` changes the value of variable i to 25, regardless of what i was before the statement.

STEP-BY-STEP 4.1

1. Start your Java compiler's text editor. In a new blank document, enter the program in Code List 4.1.

2. Save the source code file as iAssign.java to your student disk or folder. Compile and run the program. Notice the difference between the value of i when it is displayed after the first println and after the second.

3. Leave the source code file open for the next exercise.

CODE LIST 4.1

```
class iAssign
{
  public static void main(String args[])
  {
  System.out.println("Program Begins");

  int i = 10000;
  System.out.println("i = " + i);

  i = 25;
  System.out.println("i now = " + i);
  }
}    // end of iAssign
```

Multiple Assignments

Recall from Lesson 3 that you can declare more than one variable in a single statement. For example, instead of

```
int i;
int j;
int k;
```

you can use:

```
int i,j,k;
```

You can use a similar shortcut when initializing multiple variables. If you have more than one variable that you want to initialize to the same value, you can use a statement such as:

```
i = j = k = 25;
```

Multiple assignment is a trick that Java borrows from C++. It can be very handy under some circumstances when more than one variable needs to be assigned the same initial value. However, it is not a good idea to overuse this format. Remember, readability is one of your top goals.

STEP-BY-STEP 4.2

1. Modify the program on your screen to read as shown in Code List 4.2.

2. Compile and run the program. The program's output is:

```
i = 25
j = 25
k = 25
```

3. Close the source code file without saving.

CODE LIST 4.2

```
class iAssign
{
  public static void main(String args[])
  {
  System.out.println("Program Begins");
  int i, j, k;
  i = j = k = 25;

  System.out.println("i = " + i);
  System.out.println("j = " + j);
  System.out.println("k = " + k);
  }
}      // end of iAssign
```

As you have seen demonstrated already, variables may be declared and initialized in a single statement. Both of the following are valid Java statements:

```
  int i = 2;
  float n = 4.5;
```

Arithmetic Operators

A specific set of *arithmetic operators* is used to perform calculations in Java. These arithmetic operators, shown in Table 4-1, may be somewhat familiar to you. Addition and subtraction are performed with the familiar + and - operators. Multiplication uses an asterisk (*), and division uses a forward slash (/). Java also uses what is known as a modulus operator (%) to determine the integer remainder of division. A more detailed discussion of the modulus operator is presented later in this section.

TABLE 4-1

SYMBOL	OPERATION	EXAMPLE	READ AS...
+	Addition	3 + 8	three plus eight
-	Subtraction	7 - 2	seven minus two
*	Multiplication	4 * 9	four times nine
/	Division	6 / 2	six divided by two
%	Modulus	7 % 3	seven modulo three

USING ARITHMETIC OPERATORS

The arithmetic operators are used with two operands, as in the examples in Table 4-1. The exception to this is the minus symbol, which can be used to change the sign of an operand. Arithmetic operators are most often used on the right side of an assignment operator, as in the examples in Table 4-2. The portion of the statement on the right side of the assignment operator is called an *expression*.

The assignment operator (=) functions differently in Java from the way the equal sign functions in algebra. Consider the following statement:

```
x = x + 10;
```

The statement above (`x = x + 10;`) is invalid for use in algebra because the equal sign is the symbol around which both sides of an equation are balanced. The left side equals the right side. But your Java compiler looks at the statement differently. The expression on the right side of the equal sign is evaluated, and the result is stored in the variable to the left of the equal sign. In this statement, the value of `x` is increased by 10.

TABLE 4-2

STATEMENT	RESULT
cost = price + tax;	cost is assigned the value of price plus tax
owed = total - discount;	owed is assigned the value of total minus discount
area = l * w;	area is assigned the value of l times w
one_eighth = 1 / 8;	one_eighth is assigned the value of 1 divided by 8
r = 5 % 2;	r is assigned the remainder of 5 divided by 2 by using the modulus operator
x = -y;	x is assigned the value of -y

STEP-BY-STEP 4.3

1. Retrieve the file Assign.java from the student data files. Save the file to your student disk as Assign.java. Compile the program.

2. Look at the source code and try to predict the program's output.

3. Run the program and see if you were correct in your prediction.

4. Close the source code file.

MORE ABOUT MODULUS

The *modulus operator*, which may be used only for integer division, returns the remainder rather than the result of the division. As shown in Figure 4-1, integer division is similar to the way you divide manually.

When integer division is performed, any fractional part that may be in the answer is lost when the result is stored into the integer variable. The modulus operator allows you to obtain the fractional part of the result as an integer remainder.

FIGURE 4-1
The division operator and modulus operator return the quotient and the remainder.

Quotient — 4r1 — Remainder
2)9

Consider the program in Figure 4-2. Notice the program calculates the quotient using the division operator (/) and the remainder using the modulus operator (%).

STEP-BY-STEP 4.4

1. Enter, compile, and run the program from Figure 4-2. Save the source file as Remain.java to your student disk or folder.

2. Observe the output. Now, change dividend and divisor several times using values that will produce different remainders.

3. Leave the source file open for the next exercise.

FIGURE 4-2
This program calculates the quotient and remainder using variables.

```
// start of Remain.java
class Remain
{
  public static void main(String Args[])
  {
  System.out.println("Program begins");
  int dividend, divisor, quotient, remainder;
  // provide data quantities
  dividend = 37;
  divisor = 5;

  // process data, calculate answers
  quotient = dividend / divisor;
```

continued on next page

FIGURE 4-2 (continued)

```
  remainder = dividend % divisor;

// provide output
  System.out.println("The quotient is: " + quotient);
  System.out.println("and the remainder is: " + remainder);
  }
}    // end of class Remain
```

USING OPERATORS IN OUTPUT STATEMENTS

The program in Figure 4-2 required four variables and eight program statements. The program in Figure 4-3 accomplishes the same output with only two variables and six statements. Notice in Figure 4-3 that the calculations are performed in the output statements. Rather than storing the results of the expressions in variables, the program sends the results to the screen as part of the output.

FIGURE 4-3
This program calculates quotient and remainder in the output statements.

```
class Remain2
{
  public static void main(String Args[])
  {
  System.out.println("Program begins");
  int dividend, divisor;
  // provide data quantities
  dividend = 37;
  divisor = 5;
  // process data, calculate answers and provide output
  System.out.println("The quotient is: " + dividend / divisor);
  System.out.println("and the remainder is: " + dividend % divisor);
  }
}     // end of class Remain2
```

Avoid including the calculations in the output statements if you need to store the quotient or remainder and use them again in the program. But in situations like this, it is perfectly fine to use operators in the output statement. Always remember, though, that readability is one of your top goals.

STEP-BY-STEP 4.5

1. Modify the program on your screen to match Figure 4-3. Save the source file as Remain2.java. Compile it and run it.
2. Test the program to make sure you are still getting the same results.
3. Leave the source file open for the next exercise.

DIVIDING BY ZERO

Dividing by zero in math is without a practical purpose. The same is true with computers. In fact, division by zero always generates some type of error message.

1. Change the program on your screen to set the divisor equal to zero. Compile and run the program again and see what exception message is generated.
2. Close the source code file without saving changes.

SPACES AROUND OPERATORS

Your Java compiler ignores blank spaces. Both of the statements shown below are valid.

```
x=y+z;
x = y + z;
```

The only time you must be careful with spacing is when using the minus sign to change the sign of a variable or number. For example, `x = y - -z;` is perfectly fine. The sign of the value in the variable `z` is changed and then it is subtracted from `y`. If you failed to include the space before the `-z`, you would have created a problem because two minus signs together (--) have another meaning, examined later in this chapter.

Compound Operators

Often you will write statements that have the same variable on both sides of the assignment operator. For example, you may write a statement such as `x = x + 2;` which adds 2 to the variable `x`. In cases like this, you may wish to use special operators, called *compound operators*, available in Java that provide a shorthand notation for writing such statements.

Table 4-3 lists the compound operators, gives an example of each, and shows the longhand equivalent.

TABLE 4-3

COMPOUND OPERATOR	EXAMPLE	LONGHAND EQUIVALENT
+=	i += 1;	i = i + 1;
-=	j -= 12;	j = j - 12;
*=	z *= 5.25;	z = z * 5.25;
/=	w /= 2;	w = w / 2;
%=	d %= 3;	d = d % 3;

If you want to use a compound operator in a statement such as the one below, be careful.

```
price = price - discount + tax + shipping;
```

Because the compound operators have a lower precedence in the order of operations, you may get unexpected results. For example, simplifying the above statement as shown below results in the wrong value because `discount + tax + shipping` is calculated and the sum of those are subtracted from `price`.

```
price -= discount + tax + shipping; // this gives an incorrect result!
```

In this case, you can work around the problem by using parentheses and changing the compound operator to +=. To properly calculate the discount, the unary operator (-) is used to subtract the discount by adding it as a negative value.

```
price += (-discount + tax + shipping);
```

The complexity of dealing with the order of operations in statements with more than one value on the right side of the operator sometimes makes the shorthand notation more trouble than it's worth. Until you are comfortable with the problems presented by the order of operators, you may want to use compound operators with simple statements only. And again, remember that you want people to be able to easily read your program code; don't let these or other shortcuts make your programming difficult to understand.

Counting by One and the Order of Operations

In this section, you will learn about two operators that allow you to increase or decrease the value stored in an integer variable by one. You will also learn the order that the computer applies operators in an expression.

The ++ and - - operators can be used with any arithmetic data type, which includes all of the integer and floating-point types.

Incrementing and Decrementing

Adding or subtracting 1 from a variable is very common in programs. Adding 1 to a variable is called *incrementing*, and subtracting 1 from a variable is called *decrementing*. You will have the need to increment or decrement a variable when a program must execute a section of code a specified number of times, or when you need to count the number of times a process has been repeated.

THE ++ AND -- OPERATORS

The C++ syntax provides Java with operators for incrementing and decrementing. In Java, you can increment an integer variable using the ++ *operator*, and decrement using the -- *operator*, as shown in Table 4-4.

TABLE 4-4

STATEMENT	EQUIVALENT TO...
counter++;	counter = counter + 1;
counter- -;	counter = counter - 1;

You can increment or decrement a variable without the ++ or -- operators. For example, instead of j++ you can use j=j+1. With today's compilers, either way will produce efficient machine code.

STEP-BY-STEP 4.7

1. Retrieve the file Inc_Dec.java from the student data files, and save it under the same name to your student disk.
2. Compile and run the program.
3. Examine the output and leave the source code file open for the next exercise.

VARIATIONS OF INCREMENT AND DECREMENT

At first glance, the ++ and -- operators seem very simple. But there are two ways each of these operators can be used. The operators can be placed either before or after the variable. The way you use the operators changes the way they work.

Used in a statement by themselves, the ++ and -- operators can be placed before or after the variable. For example, the two statements shown below both increment whatever value is in `j`.

```
j++;
++j;
```

The difference in where you place the operator becomes important if you use the ++ or -- operator in a more complex expression, or if you use the operators in an output statement. First, let's look at how the placement of the operators affects the following statement. Assume that `j` holds a value of 10.

```
k = j++;
```

In the case of the statement above, `k` is assigned the value of the variable `j` before `j` is incremented. Therefore, the value of 10 is assigned to `k` rather than the new value of `j`, which is 11. If the placement of the ++ operator is changed to precede the variable `j` (for example `k = ++j;`), then `k` is assigned the value of `j` after `j` is incremented to 11.

STEP-BY-STEP 4.8

1. Add a statement to the Inc_Dec.java file that declares k as a variable of type int.

2. Add the following lines to the program before the closing brace.

```
k = j++;
System.out.println("k = " + k);
System.out.println("j = " + j);
k = ++j;
System.out.println("k = " + k);
System.out.println("j = " + j);
```

3. Save the new source code file as Inc_Dec2.java.

4. Don't forget to change the class name to Inc_Dec2. Compile and run the program to see the new output.

5. Close the source code file.

The increment and decrement operators can be used to reduce the number of statements necessary in a program. Consider the two statements below.

```
attempts = attempts + 1;
System.out.println("This is attempt number " + attempts);
```

Using the increment operator, one statement can do the job of two.

```
System.out.println("This is attempt number " + (++attempts));
// parentheses used around ++ for clarity
```

In both cases, the variable named attempts is incremented and its value is printed to the screen. In the second example, the variable is incremented within the println statement. The ++ operator must come before the variable named `attempts`. Otherwise, the value of the variable will be printed before it is incremented.

Note

Remember, the ++ operator actually changes the variable. If you replaced ++attempts with attempts + 1 in the println statement, the value of the variable would remain the same. The screen, however, would print the result of attempts + 1.

Order of Operations

You may recall from your math classes the rules related to the order in which operations are performed. These rules are called the *order of operations*. The Java compiler uses a similar set of rules for its calculations. Operators in Java are applied in the following order:

1. Minus sign used to change sign (-)
2. Multiplication and division (* / %)
3. Addition and subtraction (+ -)

Java lets you use parentheses to override the order of operations. For example, consider the two statements in Figure 4-4.

FIGURE 4-4
Parentheses can be used to change the order of operations.

```
x = 1 + 2 * 3              x = (1 + 2) * 3
         \ /                      \ /
x = 1 +   6                  x = 3      * 3
     \   /                        \    /
   x = 7                         x = 9
```

STEP-BY-STEP 4.9

1. Open the file Order.java from the student data files.
2. Look at the source code and try to predict the program's output.
3. Run the program and see if your prediction is correct.
4. Close the source code file.

How Data Types Affect Calculations

Java allows you to mix data types in calculations (such as dividing a float value of 125.25 by an integer such as 5). Although you should avoid it whenever possible, this section will show you the way to do it should you need to.

You learned in Lesson 3 that each data type is able to hold a specific range of values. When performing calculations, the capacity of your variables must be kept in mind. It is possible for the result of an expression to be too large or too small for a given data type.

Mixing Data Types

Sometimes you may need to perform operations that mix data types, but doing so is less than desirable. In fact, many programming languages do not allow it. But if you have to mix data types, it is important that you understand how to do it properly.

Java can automatically handle the mixing of data types using a process called *promotion*. Also, remember from Lesson 3 that you can direct the compiler how to handle (or how to treat) the data in your programming by using typecasting.

PROMOTION

Consider the program in Figure 4-5. The variable `numberOfPeople` is an integer. The other variables involved in the calculation are floating-point numbers. Before you mix data types, you should understand the way the compiler is going to process the variables.

In cases of mixed data types, the compiler makes adjustments so as to produce the most accurate answer. In the program in Figure 4-5, for example, the integer value is temporarily converted to a float so that the fractional part of the variable `money` can be used in the calculation. This is promotion. The variable called `numberOfPeople` is not actually changed. Internally, the computer treats the data as if it were stored in a float. But after the calculation, the variable is still an integer.

FIGURE 4-5
The compiler may promote variables used in calculations.

```
// Share.java
class Share
{
  public static void main(String Args[])
  {
  int numberOfPeople;
  float money;
  float share;

  // Number of people with whom to share money
  numberOfPeople = 70;
  // Amount of money to be shared
  money = 7500;
  share = money / numberOfPeople;
  // output results
  System.out.println("Give each person " + share);
  }
}   // end of class Share
```

STEP-BY-STEP 4.10

1. Open the file Share.java from the student data files. The program from Figure 4-5 appears in your editor. Save the program to your student folder or disk.
2. Compile and run the program and observe how the mixed data types function.
3. Close the source file.

Promotion of the data type can occur only while an expression is being evaluated. Consider the program in Figure 4-6. Some compilers may not even allow this code to run without typecasting the calculations.

FIGURE 4-6
Mixing data types can cause incorrect results.

```
// TestPromo.java
class TestPromo
{
  public static void main(String Args[])
  {
  int answer, i;
  float x;
  i = 3;
  x = 0.5;
  answer = x * i;
  System.out.println("answer = " + answer);
  }
}     // end of class TestPromo
```

STEP-BY-STEP 4.11

1. Enter the program shown in Figure 4-6 and save it as TestPromo.java.

2. Compile the program. Was your compiler able to compile the program without errors? If not, what error did you receive?

3. Make the following changes to the program and compile it again.

```
x = (float) 0.5;
answer = (int) (x * i);
```

4. Run the program. Is the answer correct?

The variable `i` is promoted to a float when the expression is calculated, which gives the result 1.5. But then the result is stored in the integer variable answer. You are unable to store a floating-point number in space reserved for an integer variable. The floating-point number is *truncated*, which means the digits after the decimal point are dropped. The number in the answer is 1, which is not correct.

OVERFLOW

Overflow is the condition in which an integer becomes too large for its data type. The program in Figure 4-7 shows a simple example of overflow. The expression `j = (short) (2 * i);` results in a value of 64000, which is too large for the short data type. Note that just to make this code compile, we had to typecast it. Java compilers provide intensive protection against these kinds of mistakes, allowing you to override the compiler only if that is what you really want to do. In your code here, you were trying to make a mistake, so you overrode the expression with a typecast. Be careful how you use this when you are writing code in which you do not want mistakes.

FIGURE 4-7
The result of the expression will not fit in the variable j.

```
// start of class OverFlow.java
class OverFlow
{
  public static void main(String args[])
  {
  short i, j;

  i = 32000;
  j = (short)(2 * i);

  System.out.println("j = " + j);
  }
}      // end of class OverFlow
```

STEP-BY-STEP 4.12

1. Enter, compile, and run the program in Figure 4-7. Notice that the calculation resulted in an overflow and an incorrect result.

2. Change the data type from short to long. Compile and run again. This time the result should not overflow.

3. Save the source file as OverFlow.java and then close the file.

UNDERFLOW

Underflow is similar to overflow. Underflow occurs with floating-point numbers when a number is too small for the data type. For example, the number 1.5 x 10^{-44} is too small to fit in a standard float variable. A variable of type double, however, can hold the value.

Floating-Point Rounding Errors

Using floating-point numbers can produce incorrect results if you fail to take the precision of floating-point data types into account. When working with very large or very small floating-point numbers, you can use a form of exponential notation, called *"E" notation*, in your programs. For example, the number 3.5 x 10^{20} can be represented as 3.5e20 in your program.

You must keep the precision of your data type in mind when working with numbers in "E" notation. Look at the program in Figure 4-8. At first glance, the two calculation statements appear simple enough. The first statement adds 3.9 x 10^{10} and 500. The second one subtracts the 3.9 x 10^{10}, which should leave the 500. The result assigned to y, however, is not 500. Actual values vary depending on the compiler, but the result is incorrect whatever the case.

The reason is that the float type is not precise enough for the addition of the number 500 to be included in its digits of precision. So when the larger value is subtracted, the result is not 500 because the 500 was never properly added.

FIGURE 4-8
The precision of floating-point data types must be considered to avoid rounding errors.

```
// start of class UnderFlow
class UnderFlow
{
  public static void main(String args[])
  {
  System.out.println("Program Begins");
  float x,y;
  x = (float)(3.9e10 + 500.0);
  y = (float)(x-3.9e10);
  System.out.println("y = " + y);
  }
}     // end of class UnderFlow
```

STEP-BY-STEP 4.13

1. Enter, compile, and run the program in Figure 4-8. See that the result in the variable y is not 500. Note here that we have to typecast the expressions as floats to conduct this experiment.

2. Change the data type of x and y to double and run again. The increased precision of the double data type should result in the correct value in y, and you should not need to typecast the expressions this time.

3. Save the source code file as UnderFlow.java and close the source code file.

Using the Random Number Class

The ability to generate random numbers has many applications in programming. Random numbers are used in security encryption, games, and mathematical approximations. The Java library has a Random number class that allows you to generate and manage random numbers. Consider the code in Figure 4-9.

FIGURE 4-9
Java has a standard class for generating random numbers.

```
// start of class MakeRandom
import java.util.Random;
class MakeRandom
{
  public static void main(String args[])
  {
  System.out.println("Program begins");

  // GenerateOne seed is present date on computer
  Random GenerateOne = new Random();

  // GenerateTwo seed is the number given
  Random GenerateTwo = new Random(123456789);

  // create first double and output
  double First = GenerateOne.nextDouble() + 2.5e10;
  System.out.println("First = " + First);

  // create second double and output
  double Second = GenerateTwo.nextDouble() * 7.5e10;
  System.out.println("Second = " + Second);

  double Third;
  Third = First * Second;
  System.out.println("Third = " + Third);
  }
}     // end of class MakeRandom
```

There are a few things to notice about the program in Figure 4-9. First, a new line is added at the top of the code. To bring in the Random class, the compiler must be told to import that part of the Java utilities class, since this class is not automatically built into the code like the simple mathematical operations were. Note in addition that you can also write `import java.util.*;`. This will bring in all of the utilities, including the Random class, but it makes your code unnecessarily large if you do not use the other utilities classes.

There are actually two random number generators available to you. One is part of the Math class. A more extensive random number generator is found in the Random class. The Random class offers more ability to change the seed of the generator. The *seed* of the generator gives it a numeric starting point from which to calculate a random number. You can initialize the random number generator with or without a seed. As you can see from the program, if no seed is provided, the compiler provides the seed (from its clock).

The commands used to initialize the random number generator are called *constructors*. A constructor is the function (or part of the program) that constructs the object based on the "rules" of the class. In this case, the same constructor is used in two different ways: one with a seed and one without. This is called function or method *overloading* and makes some operations, such as constructing, very easy. It is possible to have several constructors in a class, which, like the one used here, allows you to construct a new class with different initial conditions. There are some names for the different kinds of constructors, such as "default," "copy," and so on. You will read about these later in this unit.

As you can see, using the class is very easy. Once again, you implement the process of creating a new object of the class—in this case, two new objects were created. Each one has the ability to generate different kinds of random numbers, but this program needed a double, so the method name was `nextDouble`. The term *method* refers to the segments of code that perform an action within an object. The method `nextDouble` is said to be a *member* of the class `Random`, and we used the *dot operator (.)* to identify that the first `nextDouble` was working for the `GenerateOne` object, and the second `nextDouble` was working for the `GenerateTwo` object. Again, remember that an object knows how to take care of itself and do its appropriate work, so `GenerateOne` and `GenerateTwo` both knew how to send back the next available random number using the member method `nextDouble`.

Finally, note that each number is multiplied by a large floating point number. It is common for random number generators to generate fractional quantities (i.e., decimal numbers between 0 and 1), so the program made these numbers much larger from the start. Then, the two numbers are multiplied together and assigned to the third number, cleverly named `Third`. Work your way through this next exercise and make sure you understand what is happening.

STEP-BY-STEP 4.14

1. Analyze the code in Figure 4-9. What is happening when the two new objects are created, and what does each piece of code do? Make sure you can see what the output would contain before you actually try to run it.

2. Now enter the code in your compiler, save it as MakeRandom.java, and run it. What are the results? Are they what you expected?

3. Is there a possibility of overflow here? In a sentence or two, argue why or why not.

Summary

In this lesson, you learned:

- The assignment operator (=) changes the value of the variable to the left of the operator to the result of the expression to the right of the operator.
- You can initialize multiple variables to the same value in a single statement.
- The arithmetic operators are used to create expressions.
- The modulus operator (%) returns the remainder of integer division.
- Expressions can be placed in output statements.
- Dividing by zero generates an exception in Java, or it may generate a NaN (not a number), or it may generate positive or negative #INF (infinity) depending on where it comes into the error.
- Spaces can be placed around all operators but are not required in most cases; however, they can improve readability and should be used where possible.
- The ++ and -- operators increment and decrement arithmetic variables, respectively.
- The placement of the ++ and -- operators becomes important when the operators are used as part of a larger expression or in an output statement.
- Java calculations follow an order of operations.
- Java allows data types to be mixed in calculations. However, because it is not a good idea, the language will commonly require typecasting to override its own protection from making mixed data type mistakes. When Java is allowed to handle mixed data types automatically, variables are promoted to other types.
- Overflow, underflow, and floating-point rounding errors can occur if you are not aware of the data types used in calculations.
- The Random class generates random numbers for use by programs.
- When classes are needed, most commonly they must be imported from the Java library files.
- There may be more than one way for a class to take an action, such as constructing a new object. Java allows for the same member method name to be reused when it is accomplishing the same task—the difference will be in the types and numbers of parameters.
- A member method is simply one that does the work an object needs done. Since there can be more than one object from the same class, they may all use the same method. However, the way to identify which object is in charge of that method at that moment is by noticing the name of the object on the left side of the dot operator (.).

LESSON 4 REVIEW QUESTIONS

WRITTEN QUESTIONS

Write a brief answer to the following questions.

1. What is the assignment operator?

2. What does the modulus operator do?

3. Write a statement that stores the remainder of dividing the variable `i` by `j` in a variable named `k`.

4. Write a statement that calculates the volume of a box (Vol = length x width x depth) given the dimensions of the box. Use appropriate identifiers for the variables. You do not have to declare types.

5. Write a statement that calculates the sales tax (use 7%) for an item given the cost of the item and the tax rate. Store the value in a variable named `tax_due`. Use appropriate identifiers for the other variables. You do not have to declare types.

6. Write a statement that increments a variable `m` using the increment operator.

7. If the value of `i` is 10 before the statement `j = i++;` is executed, what is the value of `j` after the statement is executed?

8. If the value of `i` is 4 before the statement `j = --i;` is executed, what is the value of `j` after the statement is executed?

9. What will the value of `j` be after the statement `j = 3 + 4 / 2 + 5 * 2 - 3;` is executed?

10. What will the value of `j` be after the statement `j = (3 + 4) / (2 + 5) * 2 - 3;` is executed?

11. What is the term that means the numbers to the right of the decimal point are removed?

12. What is the typecast operator that changes a variable to a double?

13. Define overflow.

14. Define underflow.

15. What is "E" notation?

16. How would you write 6.9×10^{8} in "E" notation?

LESSON 4 PROJECTS

PROJECT 4-1

Write a program that uses the statement you wrote in question 4 above in a complete program that calculates the volume of a box. Save the source code file as Volbox.java.

PROJECT 4-2

Write a program that uses the statement you wrote in question 5 above in a complete program that calculates the sales tax for an item given the cost of the item and the tax rate. Save the source code file as Salestax.java.

PROJECT 4-3

1. Write a program that declares an integer named up_down and initializes it to 3.
2. Have the program print the value of up_down to the screen.
3. Have the program increment the variable and print the value to the screen.
4. Add statements to the program to decrement the variable and print the value to the screen again.
5. Save the source code as UpDown.java, compile it, and run it.

PROJECT 4-4

Write a program that evaluates the following expressions and prints the different values that result from the varied placement of the parentheses. Store the result in a float variable to allow for fractional values. Save the source code file as Paren.java.

```
2 + 6 / 3 + 1 * 6 - 7
(2 + 6) / (3 + 1) * 6 - 7
(2 + 6) / (3 + 1) * (6 - 7)
```

PROJECT 4-5

Write a program that calculates the area of an ellipse. Locate the formula for the calculation. Assign variables to appropriate values to test the program and output the area. Save the program as `Project4_5.java` to student disk or folder.

PROJECT 4-6

Write a program that converts degrees to radians using the formula below. Save the program as Project4_6.java.

```
radians = degrees / 57.3
```

PROJECT 4-7

Write a program that converts miles per hour to feet per second. Save the program as Project4_7.java.

I/O AND EXCEPTION HANDLING

LESSON 5

OBJECTIVES

Upon completion of this lesson, you should be able to:

- Explain how to get console input from users.
- Implement the exception-handling process of console input.
- Determine how to develop programs with user input and output.
- Discuss the multilevel exception-handling process.

Estimated Time: 2 hours

Overview

The programs you have worked with up to this point have created output, such as writing text or numeric values to the screen. But getting input from the user is a little more complicated. To properly obtain input from the user, a program must incorporate a special program error management process called *exception handling*. Exception handling is a system to deal with situations that are exceptions to the normal flow of operation. Exception handling is sometimes called *error handling*. Because input and exception handling go together, you will learn about both in this lesson. Keep in mind, however, that the uses for exception handling are many.

Casting for Input

The console input process for Java is not as simple as that of many other languages. However, the Java way has some advantages. For example, many languages can be set to accept certain data and then use that data for the program's calculations. But what happens if your user enters the wrong type of data? For instance, what happens if the user enters a B when the program needs a number? The answer depends on a variety of factors, yet often the program simply cannot handle the wrong type, and an unplanned shutdown occurs. In other words, the program might "crash."

Another problem can occur when a user provides inappropriate or unrealistic data. Suppose you have a program to calculate the distance an airplane can fly. Most commercial airliners do not fly much faster than 500 or 600 miles per hour. However, your user enters 5,000 miles per hour or some other number that is totally inappropriate. This can lead to calculations whose results are much larger than your declared variables can hold. Inappropriate input can also lead to division by zero.

These kinds of problems have always plagued computer programmers. If an error does require a program to halt, the ability to exit gracefully and then restart is important. You probably at some time have been running a program and received a message that an illegal operation or system error has occurred. When this happens, you can usually return to the operating system and restart the program. However, that is not always the case. Sometimes the problem that invoked that message might have crashed the operating system as well. This makes exception handling even more important. The term exception handling is used because we assume that normally the program will run without error, with the exception of certain problems that may arise.

Refer to the code segment in Figure 5-1. This is an example of the simplest kind of input statement that can be used in the Java console environment.

Although this process is longer than what you might have done in some other languages, it is much safer. If anything goes wrong in the course of entering data to this program, Java will protect the user and the program by shutting down and throwing an exception. The phrase *throwing an exception* means that the program will report the exception and try to explain what went wrong if it can.

FIGURE 5-1

The input process brings in characters to form a line of text. When the Enter key is pressed, the line of text is then printed to the screen.

```
import java.lang.StringBuffer;
import java.io.IOException;
class MyInput
{
  public static void main(String Args[])
  {
  System.out.println("Program begins");

  int noMoreInput = -1;
  char enterKeyHit = '\n';
  int InputChar;

  StringBuffer InputBuffer = new StringBuffer(30);

  System.out.println("Please enter a one word name:");
  try
    {
    InputChar = System.in.read();

    while(InputChar != noMoreInput)
      {
      if((char) InputChar != enterKeyHit)
        {
        InputBuffer.append((char) InputChar);
        }
      else
        {
        InputBuffer.setLength( InputBuffer.length() -1 );
        break;
        }
      InputChar = System.in.read();
      }
    }
```

FIGURE 5-1 (continued)

```
    catch(IOException IOX)
      {
      System.err.println(IOX);
      }

    System.out.println("You entered: " + InputBuffer.toString());
    }
}       // end of class myInput
```

STEP-BY-STEP 5.1

1. Start your text editor and enter the program shown in Figure 5-1. Save the program to your course files folder or disk as MyInput.java. Compile and run the program.
2. Provide a variety of characters as input. Run the program a number of times.
3. Enter your first, middle, and last names with spaces between the names and observe what happens.
4. Leave the program on your screen as the code is analyzed below.

The program you ran in Step-by-Step 5.1 handles almost any attempt you make to crash it. Let's analyze the code to see how it works.

First, you copy, or import, the StringBuffer and IOException classes from the Java library so you can use them. We'll use the StringBuffer to hold data coming in from the keyboard. The IOException class will do our error handling.

```
import java.lang.StringBuffer;
import java.io.IOException;
```

Next, you declare your class and your main method.

```
class MyInput
{
  public static void main(String args[])
  {
```

The code below shows that three variables are declared, along with a `StringBuffer` object named `InputBuffer`. At this point, we are most interested in the `StringBuffer` object. A buffer is like an escalator. The escalator holds people while it moves them upstairs where they can get off in a different place than where they got on. A `StringBuffer` object holds data in a line (called a stream) until the data is removed from the buffer. Initially, we have declared the `InputBuffer` to hold up to 30 characters.

```
int noMoreInput = -1;
char enterKeyHit = '\n';
int InputChar;

StringBuffer InputBuffer = new StringBuffer(30);
```

Next, the program prompts the user for some information. In this case, the user is asked to enter a one-word name. The prompt does not cause the program to stop and wait for input. However, the first line of code within the *try* process will pause the program until the Enter key is pressed (see the code below). The majority of the code within the try process will test what the user has entered to make sure it worked. If something does not work, the *catch* process will take the action necessary to deal with the exception. In this case, it will print out a standard error message related to input and output processes because you have not asked it to do anything else. If no error occurs in the try block, the catch block will be ignored.

```
System.out.println("Please enter a one word name:");

try
  {
  InputChar = System.in.read();

  while(InputChar != noMoreInput)
    {
    if((char) InputChar != enterKeyHit)
      {
      InputBuffer.append((char) InputChar);
      }
    else
      {
      InputBuffer.setLength( InputBuffer.length() -1 );
      break;
      }
    InputChar = System.in.read();
    }
  }
catch(IOException IOX)
  {
   System.err.println(IOX);
  }
```

The *try* and *catch* keywords are easy to remember because of how they are used. User input that may generate an exception is placed in the braces under the try keyword because we want to try that input and see if all goes well. If not, we will catch the problem before it causes other problems.

Inside the try block, the program accepts a character. The character is stored in a variable of type int because the input stream stores integers. As the characters are placed into the `InputBuffer`, the data type will be changed without harming the data.

Although you will study the use of *while* and *if* in the next two lessons, you can see roughly what happens next. The code says, "While the incoming character is not equal to –1 (noMoreInput is equal to –1), keep doing what is between the next pair of braces."

The line that begins with the keyword "if" plays the next important role. The code says, "If the incoming character is not the Enter key (meaning the user has not hit the Enter key yet), then take the newest incoming character and add it to the end of the InputBuffer." This is a process called *appending*. The *else* part defines what will happen if the incoming character is the Enter key. The *break* keyword causes the while loop to end when the user presses Enter.

Note

Using an identifier such as noMoreInput to equal –1 is one way to *self-document*, or explain, what the code is doing.

```
while(InputChar != noMoreInput)
  {
  if((char) InputChar != enterKeyHit)
    {
    InputBuffer.append((char) InputChar);
    }
  else
    {
    InputBuffer.setLength( InputBuffer.length() -1 );
    break;
    }
  InputChar = System.in.read();
  }
```

The line that reads `InputChar = System.in.read();` is placed inside the loop so that the loop may continue to accept characters until Enter is pressed.

Note

You can avoid including the statement that reads in the next character twice by rewriting the code. However, to make the code more clear, the program shown here repeats the read statement.

STEP-BY-STEP 5.2

1. Now that you have analyzed the program, run the program again.

2. Enter the entire sentence below as input:

   Exception handling is a concept used in languages other than Java.

3. The sentence entered in step 2 is greater than 30 characters long. This does not crash the program because the InputBuffer protects itself from such problems by resizing itself, if necessary.

Using Methods

As programs get larger, it is a good idea to break the source code into smaller, more manageable, and reusable blocks of code called *methods*. In this section, you will see how the program used to input data in the previous section could be divided into methods. You will learn more about methods in a later lesson. At this time, it is only important to learn how a program can be divided into logical parts using methods.

Separating Code into Methods

A *method* is a block of code that performs some function. In other languages, you may have seen blocks of code referred to as functions or procedures. In Java, methods are often referred to as member functions. The term *member function* comes from the fact that the function is a member of a certain class.

In the exercise that follows, the program from the previous section is divided into two pieces: the main function and a method for getting input from the user. The advantage to separating the latter code into a separate method may not immediately be apparent. By separating the code, however, the input method may be reused in other programs.

STEP-BY-STEP 5.3

1. Open NewMethod.java from the student data files. The source code shown in Figure 5-2 appears.

2. Leave the source code open on your screen as you read the paragraphs that follow.

FIGURE 5-2
Creating an input method can simplify data input in programs.

```
// NewMethod.JAVA
import java.lang.StringBuffer;
import java.io.IOException;

class NewMethod
{
  public static void main(String args[])
  {
  System.out.println("Program begins");

  System.out.print("Please enter a one word name:");

  String InputString = GetConsoleString();
  System.out.println("You entered: " + InputString);
  System.out.println("Program paused, Press the Enter key to continue");
  InputString = GetConsoleString();
  }

  public static String GetConsoleString()
  {
  int noMoreInput = -1;
  char enterKeyHit = '\n';
  int InputChar;
  StringBuffer InputBuffer = new StringBuffer(30);

  try
    {
    InputChar = System.in.read();

    while(InputChar != noMoreInput)
      {
      if((char) InputChar != enterKeyHit)
        {
        InputBuffer.append((char) InputChar);
        }
```

FIGURE 5-2 (continued)

```
      else
        {
        InputBuffer.setLength( InputBuffer.length() -1 );
        break;
        }
      InputChar = System.in.read();
      }
    }
  catch(IOException IOX)
    {
    System.err.println(IOX);
    }

  return InputBuffer.toString();

  }     // end of method GetConsoleString

}     // end of class NewMethod
```

Notice that the code in Figure 5-2 is not any smaller or much different from the code in the previous section. However, the main method is significantly smaller than it was. It now has only six lines, and the input work is being done elsewhere.

Let's look at some of the details of the code in Figure 5-2. Consider the statement below, which appears in the main method. The statement declares an object of type String named InputString. The object is immediately initialized by invoking the `GetConsoleString()` method. The main method is said to "call" the `GetConsoleString()` method.

```
String InputString = GetConsoleString();
```

In the `GetConsoleString()` method (shown below), we see that, like the main method, it is a public and a static method. However, unlike the main method, which returns nothing or void, the `GetConsoleString()` method returns a String.

```
public static String GetConsoleString()
{
int noMoreInput = -1;
char enterKeyHit = '\n';
int InputChar;
StringBuffer InputBuffer = new StringBuffer(30);

try
  {
  InputChar = System.in.read();

  while(InputChar != noMoreInput)
    {
    if((char) InputChar != enterKeyHit)
      {
```

```
        InputBuffer.append((char) InputChar);
        }
      else
        {
          InputBuffer.setLength( InputBuffer.length() -1 );
        break;
        }
      InputChar = System.in.read();
      }
    }
  catch(IOException IOX)
    {
    System.err.println(IOX);
    }

  return InputBuffer.toString();

  }      // end of method GetConsoleString
```

Think of your methods as couriers. You can send them out to get something, or to process something you give them, and then they will come back and hand you whatever you needed from them. Think of the `GetConsoleString` method as a courier who runs from your program out to the keyboard, gathers up whatever comes in, and returns it to your program. Now, look at the code again. At the top of the `GetConsoleString` method, the String keyword tells you that the method will be returning a string. Also, notice the return statement at the bottom of the method. The return statement returns the contents of the InputBuffer to the function that called the method.

Now that the `GetConsoleInput` method has been written as a separate member function, it may be used every time input is required.

Note

Depending on the compiler you are using, the output of your programs may appear in a window and then disappear before you have enough time to read the contents of the window. By placing a call to the GetConsoleString method at the end of the code, you can pause the program so you can see the output while it waits for input. Of course, since there is no variable to receive the data from the GetConsoleString "courier," nothing is transferred when you enter data. However, the desired result of pausing the output before the window closes is achieved. This method will be added to most of the programs in the text after this point.

STEP-BY-STEP 5.4

1. Save the program on your screen as NewMethod.java to your course files folder or disk. Compile and run the program. It should operate exactly like the previously compiled program.

2. When the program terminates, close the source code file.

More About Exceptions

You learned earlier that exception handling is applied to more than just getting input. In this section, you will see an example of another way that exceptions can be used. You will also learn about the concept of inheritance and how the object-oriented programming feature of inheritance can make exception handling easier to "handle."

Another Exceptional Example

Analyze the code segment in Figure 5-3. The program accepts two numbers from the user. Then, using the exception-handling feature, the program "tries" to divide the two numbers. Exception handling is implemented here because of the possibility that the division may be by zero. In most cases, the division will occur without error, with the exception of division by zero.

FIGURE 5-3
Exception handling can be used to trap errors caused by dividing by zero.

```
class DivideEm
{
  public static void main(String Args[])
  {
  System.out.println("Please enter one number:");

  String InputString = GetConsoleString();

  int NumberOne = Integer.parseInt(InputString);

  System.out.println("Please enter another number:");

  InputString = GetConsoleString();
  int NumberTwo = Integer.parseInt(InputString);

  try
    {
    int NumberThree = NumberOne / NumberTwo;
    System.out.println("NumberOne divided by NumberTwo = "
        + NumberThree);
    }
  catch(Exception E)
    {
    System.err.println("General Exception Thrown");
    }
  System.out.println("Press Enter key to continue ");
  GetConsoleString();

  }      // end of main

// DEFINITION OF GetConsoleString goes here

}      // end of class DivideEm
```

STEP-BY-STEP 5.5

1. Enter the source statements for the program shown in Figure 5-3. Enter the `GetConsoleString` definition from Figure 5-2 at the location indicated in Figure 5-3. Add the two statements shown below at the top of the program and save the source file as DivideEm.java:

```
import java.lang.StringBuffer;
import java.io.IOException;
```

2. Compile and run this code, trying different numbers to be divided.

3. Now try dividing a number by zero by entering 0 (zero) at the second prompt. Note the exception that is thrown.

4. Leave the program on your screen for the next exercise.

Sometimes it is desirable to get more specific about what kind of exception was thrown. The current code has a simple catch section (shown below) that catches any exception thrown. This code catches a general exception.

```
catch(Exception E)
  {
  System.err.println("General Exception Thrown");
  }
```

To be more specific, we can add code to catch a specific kind of exception. The code below shows how two catch blocks may be used to give more detailed information about what went wrong. If the exception thrown was an arithmetic exception, the first catch block will catch the exception and provide the more specific message. If the exception was not caused by an arithmetic problem, the general exception catch block will catch the exception.

```
catch(ArithmeticException AE)
  {
  System.err.println("Divide By Zero Exception Thrown");
  }
catch(Exception E)
  {
  System.err.println("General Exception Thrown");
  }
```

When using multiple catch blocks, place the general exception catch block last. The program will use the first catch block that can handle the type of exception that has been thrown. The general exception catch block will handle any kind of exception. Therefore, catch blocks that follow the general exception catch block will never be used. Be sure always to place the specific exception catch blocks ahead of the general exception catch block.

Note

Some Java compilers will produce a warning if you place a general exception catch before the specific ones.

STEP-BY-STEP 5.6

1. Modify the program on your screen to include the two catch blocks: one for arithmetic exceptions and one for general exceptions.

2. Compile and run the program.

3. Provide input that will lead to division by zero. What happens? The `ArithmeticException` recognizes the problem first and catches it before it can get to the general exception.

4. Swap the two catch blocks so that your `ArithmeticException` process, including braces and output, follows the catch block for the general exception.

5. Compile the program again. If your compiler did not report any errors, run the program again and cause a division by zero again. This time the general exception code catches the exception before the specific exception catch block is reached.

6. Swap the two catch blocks again to return them to the proper order.

7. Compile, run, and test the program.

8. Save and close the program.

Exceptions and Inheritance

Now that you have some experience with exception handling, it is a good time to introduce an important topic of object-oriented programming: inheritance. *Inheritance* is the feature of object-oriented programming that allows you to take code already developed and debugged and build on it to create something new. Before we look at how inheritance is at work in exception handling, let's look at some real-world examples of inheritance.

Note

In simple programs such as the one here, finding the cause of the crash is easy to do, with or without exception handling. In more sophisticated programs, however, the causes of the exception could be many, and it might be difficult to determine what conditions caused the crash. Having more specific catch blocks might help determine the cause of the problem.

A good example of how inheritance can make programming easier can be found in the graphical user interfaces in use on most computers today. A window is an important component of a graphical user interface. Therefore, code to create, position, move, and resize windows is an important part of the operating system. When it is time to create a dialog box, there is no need to start from scratch. A dialog box is a particular type of window. Every time a dialog box appears on the screen, you are witnessing an example of inheritance. Therefore, the properties of a window can be inherited and extended to create a dialog box. That is what inheritance is all about.

For another example, let's go back to the OOP County Fair. Suppose you have designed a set of rules (a class) for a retail outlet (a store) at the fair. Once you have designed the RetailOutlet class, you know how to accept cash from a customer, how to work the cash register, how to do the bookkeeping, and so on. But now, someone wants to open up a little ice cream store, with banana splits and milkshakes. Knowing that an ice cream store is a kind of RetailOutlet means that you can use the rules made for RetailOutlets and add some rules specifically addressing how to make banana splits and milkshakes. In fact, in object-oriented programming, we say that the IceCreamStore can be a "child" of the "parent" RetailOutlet store. We would say that the IceCreamStore is a RetailOutlet. The IceCreamStore class inherits the properties of a RetailOutlet.

Notice that this relationship does not go both ways. RetailOutlets can sell practically anything. IceCreamStores, however, sell only ice cream products. Therefore, it is appropriate to say that an IceCreamStore is a RetailOutlet, but it is not appropriate to say that a RetailOutlet is an IceCreamStore.

With this in mind, consider the Exception class and its children in Java. The Exception classes in Java provide the code necessary to handle the different types of exceptions. The Exception classes build on one another using inheritance. Figure 5-4 shows a small sample of the Exception classes. The compiler you are using should have a reference in chart form, or in CD-ROM form or in the paper documentation, that shows how all the Exception classes are tied together. On the basic chart of Java classes, there are more than thirty Exception classes.

FIGURE 5-4

The Exception classes use inheritance to build on code that already exists.

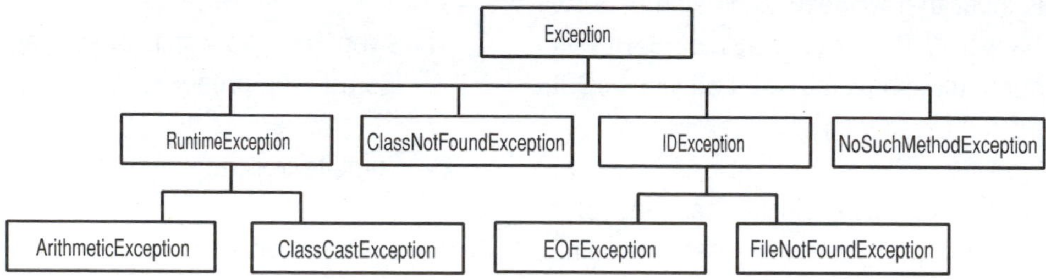

The parent class for handling exceptions is called Exception. Other classes are derived from the Exception class. The RuntimeException class, for example, inherits the properties of the Exception class. The ArithmeticException, which we used in the earlier example, is a RuntimeException, which in turn is an Exception.

The chart also shows that the IOException class, which we used earlier in this lesson to capture input or output problems, is not a RuntimeException. Both the IOException class and the RuntimeException class inherit properties directly from the Exception class.

Note

There is practically no end to the number of levels of inheritance as long as it is appropriate for your new class to use the classes that act as parents.

Summary

In this lesson, you learned:

- Input for Java is more complicated than other languages because Java more completely protects the computer and program against improper data entry.
- For any input operation in Java, you must use the try/catch process to capture any potential input problems.
- Code that may generate an error is placed in a try block. If an error occurs in the try block, an exception is thrown. A catch block catches the exception and deals with it, either by printing a message or in some other way.
- You can have more than one catch block to catch different kinds of exceptions. A general exception catch block will catch any exception.
- There are more than thirty basic Java Exception classes.
- Exceptions, like all other classes in object-oriented programming, are derived, or inherited, from simpler, more general classes in a family-like hierarchy.

LESSON 5 REVIEW QUESTIONS

WRITTEN QUESTIONS

Write a brief answer to the following questions.

1. Why do some of the Java classes have to be imported into your program?
2. Why would you self-document certain variables?
3. Briefly explain how the two keywords *try* and *catch* work together.
4. What does it mean to append a character to a string?
5. Three code lines down from the try in Figure 5-1, the word *char* is in parentheses. What does this accomplish, and why is it done at this point? Hint: the `'\n'` is considered to be a character.
6. From where does the term *member function* come?
7. What is another term for a member function?
8. What was one advantage of separating the `GetConsoleString` code from the rest of the program?
9. What type of data is returned by the `GetConsoleString` method?
10. Why might you place an additional call to `GetConsoleString` at the end of a program before the program terminates?

11. Why is the order of catch blocks important?

12. What type of catch block will catch any exception?

13. If given a bird class and a pelican class, which would be the parent class?

14. Explain why there are so many different kinds of Exceptions available in Java.

15. Explain why the ArithmeticException class is a child of the RuntimeException class.

LESSON 5 PROJECTS

PROJECT 5-1

Write a program that gets the time of day from the user and outputs the number of seconds since last midnight. Save the program to your student disk as Project5_1.java. Compile and run the program. Close the source file.

PROJECT 5-2

Write a program that gets the month and day from the user and outputs the approximate number of minutes since the first of the year. Save the program to your student disk as Project5_2.java. Compile and run the program. Close the source file.

PROJECT 5-3

Write a program that gets from the user a first name, a middle initial, and a last name and outputs all three together as first - middle - last. Try using String objects to do this. Save the program to your student disk as Project5_3.java. Compile and run the program. Close the source file.

DECISION MAKING IN PROGRAMS

LESSON 6

OBJECTIVES

Upon completion of this lesson, you should be able to:

- Describe how decisions are made in programs.
- Understand how true and false are represented in Java.
- Use relational operators and logical operators.
- Describe and program object-oriented comparisons.
- Use the if, if/else, nested if, and switch structures.

Estimated Time: 2 hrs

Overview

One of the most notable powers of computers is that they can do things very quickly. However, computers would not be of significant value to us if they could only do exactly the same thing over and over. One of the more powerful capabilities of computers is the ability to choose from more than one path of action based on some condition (for example, if the left mouse button is clicked, do this, but if the right mouse button is clicked, do that). This is a process called *branching*. In this chapter, you will learn how branching is accomplished in Java programs. You will learn about the building blocks of computer decision making and about programming structures that cause different parts of a program to be executed based on decisions made within the program.

The Building Blocks of Decision Making

When you make a decision, your brain goes through a process of comparisons. For example, when you shop for clothes you compare the prices with those you previously paid. You compare the quality to other clothes you have seen or owned. You probably compare the clothes to what other people are wearing or what is in style. You might even compare the purchase of clothes to other possible uses for your money.

Although your brain's method of decision making is much more complex than the processes a computer is capable of, decision making in computers is also based on comparing data. In this section, you will learn to use the basic tools of computer decision making.

Decision Making in Programs

Every program that is useful involves decision making. Although some algorithms progress sequentially from the first to the last instruction, most algorithms branch out into more than one path. At the point where the path branches out, a decision must be made as to which branch to take.

The flowchart in Figure 6-1 is part of an algorithm in which the program is preparing to output a document to the printer. The user enters the number of copies he or she wants to print. To make sure the number is valid, the program verifies that the number of copies is not less than zero. If the user enters a negative number, a message is printed and the user is asked to enter the value again. If the user's input passes the test, the program simply goes on to whatever is next.

FIGURE 6-1
The decision-making part of this flowchart prevents the program from proceeding with invalid data.

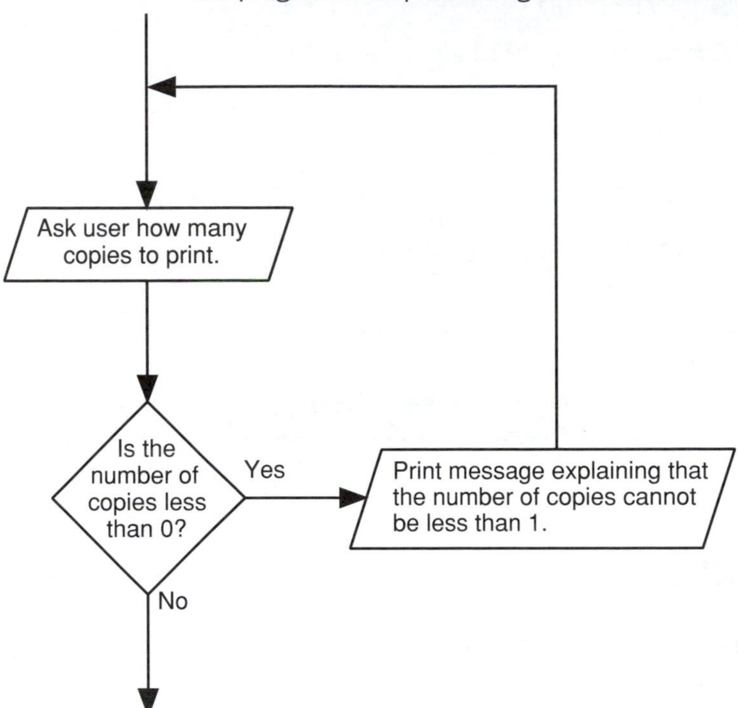

Decisions may also have to be made based on the wishes of the user. The flowchart in Figure 6-2 shows how the response to a question changes the path the program takes. If the user wants instructions printed on the screen, the program displays the instructions. Otherwise, that part of the program is bypassed.

FIGURE 6-2
The path a program takes may be dictated by the user.

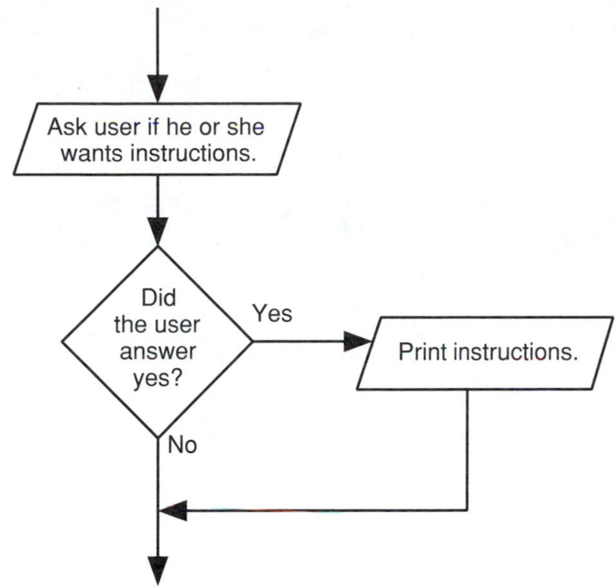

The examples in Figures 6-1 and 6-2 show two common needs for decisions in programs. There are many other instances in which decisions must be made. As you do more and more programming, you will use decision making in countless situations.

Representing True and False in Java

True and false conditions are represented in Java as Boolean type variables with values of true and false. You may be surprised to learn how important the concept of true and false is to programming.

Computers make decisions in a very primitive way. Even though computers make decisions similar to the way the human brain does, computers don't have intuition or "gut" feelings. Decision making in a computer is based on doing simple comparisons. The microprocessor compares two values and "decides" if they are equivalent. Clever programming and the fact that computers can do millions of comparisons per second sometimes make computers appear to be "smart."

Comparison Operators

To make comparisons, Java provides a set of *comparison operators*, shown in Table 6-1. They are similar to the symbols you use in math when working with equations and inequalities.

Extra for Experts

Fuzzy logic is a system that allows more than simply true or false. Fuzzy logic allows for some gray area. For example, instead of simply having a 0 for false and a 1 for true, fuzzy logic might allow a 0.9 as a way of saying "it's probably true." Practical applications of fuzzy logic include the thermostat on your home's air conditioner. A standard thermostat turns the air conditioner on when the temperature goes above the desired comfort level. This causes the temperature in the house to rise and fall above and below the thermostat setting. A fuzzy logic thermostat could sense that the temperature is rising and turn on the air conditioner before the temperature rises above the desired level. The result is a more stable room temperature and conservation of energy.

TABLE 6-1

COMPARISON OPERATOR	MEANING	EXAMPLE
==	equal to	i == 1
>	greater than	i > 2
<	less than	i < 0
>=	greater than or equal to	i >= 6
<=	less than or equal to	i <= 10
!=	not equal to	i != 12

The comparison operators are used to create expressions like the examples in Table 6-1. The result of the expression is true if the data meets the requirements of the comparison. Otherwise, the result of the expression is false. For example, the result of 2 > 1 is true, and the result of 2 < 1 is false.

The program in Figure 6-3 demonstrates how expressions are made from comparison operators. The result of the expressions is to be displayed as either true or false.

FIGURE 6-3
Expressions created using relational operators return either a true or a false.

```
class Compare
{
  public static void main(String Args[])
  {
  System.out.println("Begin Program");
  int i = 2;
  int j = 3;
  boolean true_false;

  System.out.println("i == 2 => " + (i == 2));
  System.out.println("i == 1 => " + (i == 1));
  System.out.println("j > i  => " + (j > i));
  System.out.println("j < i  => " + (j < i));
  System.out.println("j <= 3 => " + (j <= 3));
  System.out.println("j >= i => " + (j >= i));
  System.out.println("j != i => " + (j != i) + '\n');

  true_false = (j < 4);
  System.out.println("true_false = " + true_false);
  }
}     // end of class Compare
```

STEP-BY-STEP 6.1

1. Load the program Compare.java from the student data files and save it to your student disk or folder. The program from Figure 6-3 will appear. Can you predict its output?

2. Compile and run the program.

3. After you have analyzed the output, close the source code file.

Note

Be careful when using the >= and <= operators. The order of the symbols is critical. Switching the symbols will result in an error.

Logical Operators

Sometimes it takes more than two comparisons to obtain the desired result. For example, if you want to test to see if an integer is in the range 1 to 10, you must do two comparisons. In order for the integer to fall within the range, it must be greater than 0 and less than 11.

Java provides three *logical operators* for multiple comparisons. Table 6-2 shows the three logical operators and their meaning.

TABLE 6-2

<table>
<tr><th>LOGICAL OPERATOR</th><th>MEANING</th><th>EXAMPLE</th></tr>
<tr><td>&&</td><td>and</td><td>(j == 1&& k == 2)</td></tr>
<tr><td>||</td><td>or</td><td>(j == 1 || k == 2)</td></tr>
<tr><td>!</td><td>not</td><td>result = !(j == 1 && k == 2)</td></tr>
</table>

Figure 6-4 shows three diagrams called truth tables. They will help you understand the result of comparisons with the logical operators and, or, and not.

FIGURE 6-4
Truth tables illustrate the results of logical operators

AND

A	B	A && B
false (0)	false (0)	false (0)
false (0)	true (1)	false (0)
true (1)	false (0)	false (0)
true (1)	true (1)	true (1)

OR

<table>
<tr><th>A</th><th>B</th><th>A || B</th></tr>
<tr><td>false (0)</td><td>false (0)</td><td>false (0)</td></tr>
<tr><td>false (0)</td><td>true (1)</td><td>true (1)</td></tr>
<tr><td>true (1)</td><td>false (0)</td><td>true (1)</td></tr>
<tr><td>true (1)</td><td>true (1)</td><td>true (1)</td></tr>
</table>

NOT

A	!A
false (0)	true (1)
true (1)	false (0)

Consider the following Java statement.

```
in_range = (i > 0 && i < 11);
```

The variable in_range is assigned the value true if the value of i falls into the defined range, and false if the value of i does not fall into the defined range.

The not operator (!) turns true to false and false to true. For example, suppose you have a program that catalogs old movies. Your program uses a Boolean variable named InColor that has the value false if the movie was filmed in black and white and the value true if the movie was filmed in color. Therefore, if the movie is in color, Black_and_White is set to false.

Note

The key used to enter the or operator (||) is usually located near the Enter or Return key. It is usually on the same key with the backslash (\).

```
Black_and_White = !InColor;
```

STEP-BY-STEP 6.2

1. Start your text editor, and enter the program in Code List 6.1. Save the source code to your student disk or folder as logical.java.
2. Compile and run the program to see the output.
3. After you have analyzed the output, close the source code file.

CODE LIST 6.1

```
public class logical
{
  public static void main (String args[])
  {
  int i = 2;
  int j = 3;
  boolean true_false;

  true_false = (i < 3 && j > 3);

 System.out.println ("The result of (i < 3 && j > 3) is " + true_false);
  true_false = (i < 3 && j >= 3);
  System.out.println ("The result of (i < 3 && j >= 3) is " + true_false);

  System.out.println ("The result of (i == 1 || i == 2) is " + (i == 1 ||
  i == 2));

  true_false = (j < 4);
  System.out.println ("The result of (j < 4) is " + true_false);

  true_false = !true_false;
  System.out.println("The result of !true_false is " + !true_false);
```

continued on next page

CODE LIST 6.1 (continued)

```
    }      // end of method main
  }     // end of class logical
```

COMBINING MORE THAN TWO COMPARISONS

You can use logical operators to combine more than two comparisons. Consider the statement below that decides whether it is OK for a person to ride a roller coaster.

```
ok_to_ride = (height_in_inches > 45 && !back_trouble
          && !heart_trouble);
```

In the statement above, `back_trouble` and `heart_trouble` hold the value true or false depending on whether the person being considered has the problem. For example, if the person has back trouble, the value of `back_trouble` is set to true. The not operator (!) is used because it is OK to ride if the person does not have back trouble and does not have heart trouble. The entire statement says that it is OK to ride if the person's height is greater than 45 inches and the person has no back trouble and no heart trouble.

ORDER OF LOGICAL OPERATIONS

You can mix logical operators in statements as long as you understand the order in which the logical operators will be applied. The not operator (!) is applied first, then the and operator (&&), and finally the or operator (||).

Consider the statement below.

```
dog_acceptable = (white || black && friendly);
```

The example above illustrates why it is important to know the order in which logical operators are applied. At first glance, it may appear that the statement above would consider a dog to be acceptable if the dog is either white or black and also friendly. But in reality, the statement above considers a white dog that wants to chew your leg off to be an acceptable dog. Why? Because the and operator is evaluated first and then the result of the and operation is used for the or operation. The statement can be corrected with some additional parentheses, as shown below.

```
dog_acceptable = ((white || black) && friendly);
```

Java evaluates operations in parentheses first just as in arithmetic statements.

STEP-BY-STEP 6.3

1. Open logical2.java from the student data files and save it to your course folder or disk.

2. Compile and run the program to see the effect of the parentheses.

3. Close the source code file.

SHORT-CIRCUIT EVALUATION

Suppose you have decided you want to go to a particular concert. You can only go, however, if you can get tickets and if you can get off work. Before you check whether you can get off work, you find out that the concert is sold out and you cannot get a ticket. There is no longer a need to check whether you can get off work because you don't have a ticket anyway.

Note

Compilers often have an option to enable or disable short-circuit evaluation.

Java has a feature called *short-circuit evaluation* that allows the same kind of determinations in your program. For example, in an expression such as `in_range = (i > 0 && i < 11);`, the program first checks to see if i is greater than 0. If it is not, there is no need to check any further because regardless of whether i is less than 11, `in_range` will be false. So the program sets `in_range` to false and goes to the next statement without evaluating the right side of the &&.

Short-circuiting also occurs with the or (||) operator. In the case of the or operator, the expression is short-circuited if the left side of the || is true because the expression will be true regardless of the right side of the ||.

THE OOP WAY TO TRUTH

Once again, the object-oriented programming paradigm allows you to look at things almost the same way you did before, but with some small changes. You read earlier that OOP tries to treat all things the same so that programming with ints, floats, buttons, or windows will all have common conditions. This leads to easier programming, because if you know how to test for one of these things, you should know how to test for all of them. While you will be learning more about the use of object-oriented Boolean testing in later lessons, look at Figure 6-5 for your first introduction to this process.

Notice that the program uses the member method equals to accomplish the Boolean test. More importantly, notice that when `IntOne` is compared to `IntTwo`, `IntTwo` is typecast as an Object. While this is a simple example, the implications are large. In object-oriented programming, everything is treated in your code as one common thing: an object. When you are writing large-scale programs, it means you do not have to worry about which kind of type or class or quantity you are working with. You just treat everything the same.

FIGURE 6-5
Objects of any kind can be compared in OOP.

```
class IntegerTest
{
  public static void main(String Args[])
  {
  System.out.println("Begin Program");

  Integer IntOne = new Integer(2);        // Create three integer
```

FIGURE 6-5 (continued)

```
    Integer IntTwo = new Integer(3);        // objects and give
    Integer IntThree = new Integer(3);      // them values.

    boolean true_false;

    // Test to see if IntOne is equal to IntTwo
    true_false = IntOne.equals((Object) IntTwo);
    System.out.println("It is " + true_false + " that IntOne equals
    IntTwo");

    // Test to see if IntTwo is equal to IntThree
    true_false = IntTwo.equals((Object) IntThree);
    System.out.println("It is " + true_false + " that IntTwo equals
    IntThree");

    }      // end of method main
}      // end of class IntegerTest
```

Selection Structures

Programs consist of statements that solve a problem or perform a task. Up to this point, you have been creating programs with sequence structures. *Sequence structures* execute statements one after another without changing the flow of the program. Other structures, such as the ones that make decisions, do change the flow of the program. The structures that make decisions in Java programs are called *selection structures*. When a decision is made in a program, a selection structure controls the flow of the program based on the decision. In this section, you will learn how to use selection structures to make decisions in your programs. The three selection structures available in Java are the *if structure*, the *if/else structure*, and the *switch structure*.

Pitfalls

Remember to be careful not to confuse the == operator with the = (assignment) operator. Usage such as if (i = 3) will cause i to be assigned the value 3 and the code in the braces that follow will be executed regardless of what the value of i was before the if structure.

Using If

Many programming languages include an if structure. Although the syntax varies among programming languages, the if keyword is usually part of every language. If you have used if in other programming languages, you should have little difficulty using if in Java. The if structure is one of the easiest and most useful parts of Java.

The expression that makes the decision is called the *control expression*. Look at the code segment below. First the control expression (i == 3) is evaluated. If the result is true, the code in the braces that follows the if is executed. If the result is false, the code in the braces is skipped.

Note

When only one statement appears between the braces in an if structure, the braces are not actually necessary. It is, however, a good idea always to use braces in case other statements are added later.

```
if (i == 3)
  { System.out.println ("The value of i is 3"); }
```

You can place more than one line between the braces, as in the code segment below.

```
if (YesNo == 'Y')
  {
  System.out.println ("Press Enter when your printer is ready.\n");
  TempIn=5;
  }
```

Figure 6-6 shows the flowchart for an if structure. The if structure is sometimes called a *one-way selection structure* because the decision is whether to go "one way" or just bypass the code in the if structure.

FIGURE 6-6

The if structure is sometimes called a one-way selection structure.

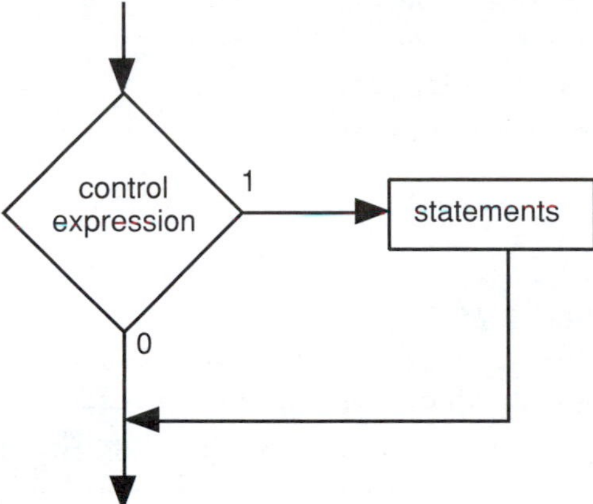

Analyze the program in Figure 6-7. The program declares a String and an integer. The user is asked for the name of her city or town, and for the population of the city or town. The if structure compares the population to a value that would indicate whether the city is among the 100 largest U.S. cities. If the city is one of the 100 largest U.S. cities, the program prints a message saying so.

You have become accustomed to using semicolons to end statements. However, using semicolons to end each line in if structures can cause problems, as shown below.

```
if (i == 3);      // don't do this!!
  { System.out.println ("The value of i is 3"); }
```

The statement in braces will execute in every case because the compiler interprets the semicolon as the end of the if structure.

FIGURE 6-7
This program uses a one-way selection structure.

```
import java.lang.StringBuffer;
import java.io.IOException;

class City
{
  public static void main(String Args[])
  {
  System.out.println("Begin Program");

  String city_name = new String();
  String temp = new String();
  long population;

  System.out.print("Please enter the name of your city or town: ");
  city_name = GetConsoleString();

  System.out.print("Please enter the population of your city or town:
  ");
  temp = GetConsoleString();
  population = Long.parseLong(temp);
  if(population >= 171439)
    {
    System.out.println("According to the 1990 census, " + city_name);
    System.out.println("is one of the 100 largest U.S. cities.");
    }
  System.out.println("Program End - <press a key>");
  GetConsoleString();      // end of program catch
  }      // end of method main

  public static String GetConsoleString()
  {
  // GetConsoleString code here
  }
}      // end of class City
```

STEP-BY-STEP 6.4

1. Open City.java from the student data files. The program from Figure 6-7 appears without the if structure.
2. Add the if structure shown in Figure 6-7 to the program. Enter the code carefully. Save the source file to your course folder or disk as City.java.
3. Compile, link, and run the program. Enter your city or town to test the program.
4. If your city or town is not one of the 100 largest cities, enter Newport News, a city in Virginia with a population of 171,439.
5. Leave the source code file open for the next exercise.

Using if/else

The if/else structure is sometimes called a *two-way selection structure*. Using if/else, one block of code is executed if the control expression is true and another block is executed if the control expression is false. Consider the code fragment below.

```
if (i < 0)
  {
  System.out.println ("The number is negative.");
  }
else
  {
  System.out.println ("The number is zero or positive.");
  }
```

The else portion of the structure is executed if the control expression is false. Figure 6-8 shows a flowchart for a two-way selection structure.

FIGURE 6-8
The if/else structure is a two-way selection structure.

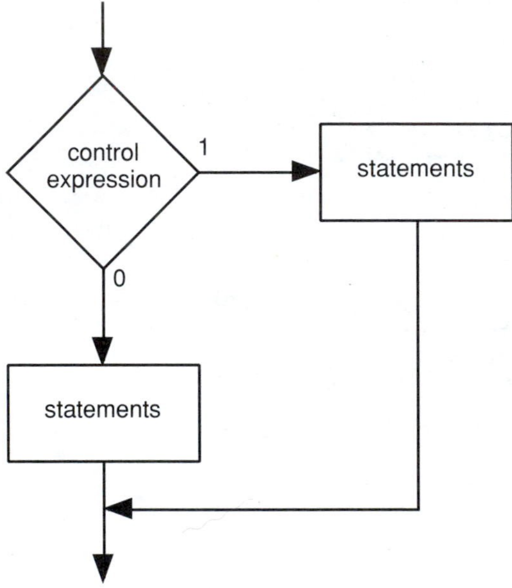

The code shown in Figure 6-9 adds an else clause to the if structure in the program in Step-by-Step 6.4. Output is improved by providing information on whether the city's population qualifies it as one of the 100 largest U.S. cities. If the population is 171,439 or more, the first output statement is executed; otherwise, the second output statement is executed. In every case, either one or the other output statement is executed.

FIGURE 6-9

With an if/else structure, one of the two blocks of code will always be executed.

```
if(population > 171439)
   {
   System.out.println("According to the 1990 census, " + city_name);
   System.out.println("is one of the\n100 largest U.S. cities.");
   }
else
   {
   System.out.println("According to the 1990 census, " + city_name);
   System.out.println("is not one of the\n100 largest U.S. cities.");
   }
```

STEP-BY-STEP 6.5

1. Add the else clause shown in Figure 6-9 to the if structure in the program on your screen. Change the class name to CityElse and save the new program to your course disk or folder as CityElse.java.
2. Compile and run the program.
3. Enter the city of Gary, Indiana (population 116,646).
4. Run the program again using Raleigh, North Carolina (population 212,050).
5. Close the source code file.

Pitfalls

Many programmers make the mistake of using > or < when they really need >= or <=. In the code segment in Figure 6-9, using > rather than >= would cause Newport News, the 100th largest city, to be excluded because its population is 171,439, not greater than 171,439.

Nested If Structures

You can place if structures within other if structures. When an if or if/else structure is placed within another if or if/else structure, the structures are said to be *nested*. The flowchart in Figure 6-10 decides whether a student is exempt from a final exam based on grade average and days absent.

To be exempt from the final, a student must have a 90 average or better and cannot have missed more than three days of class. The algorithm first determines if the student's average is greater than or equal to 90. If the result is false, the student must take the final exam. If the result is true, the number of days absent is checked to determine if the other exemption requirement is met. Figure 6-11 shows the algorithm as a Java code segment.

FIGURE 6-10
This flowchart can be programmed using nested if structures.

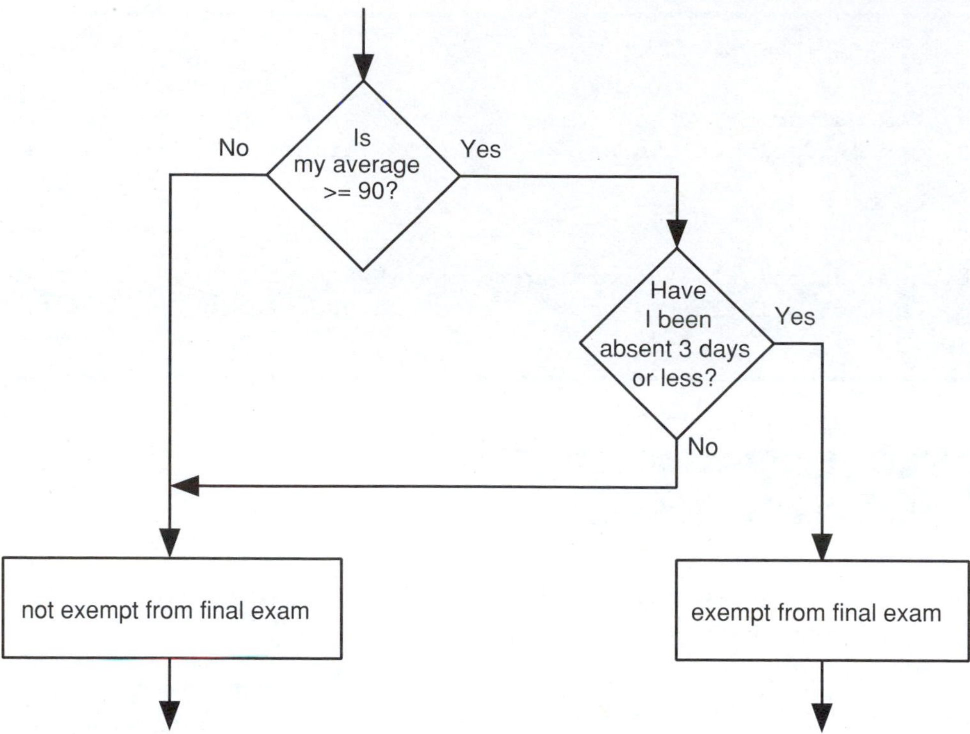

FIGURE 6-11
Nested if structures can be used to check two requirements before making a final decision.

```
exemptFromFinal = false;
if(myAverage >= 90)
  {
  if(myDaysAbsent <= 3)
    {
    exemptFromFinal = true;
    }
  }
```

Note also the use of both indenting and braces in this code segment. It is clear which responses are a result of which decision-making processes. The indenting (horizontally) helps other programmers see what you meant to happen if the condition were true. In addition, the braces provide vertical separation so the code is easy to read. This cannot always be done in textbook examples because of space restrictions, but you should always implement coding formats that support clear understanding of your intentions.

Note

In the code segment in Figure 6-11, the variable that tells whether the person is exempt from the final is set to false. The program assumes that the student fails to meet the exemption qualification and tests to determine otherwise.

Algorithms involving nested if structures can get more complicated than the one in Figure 6-10. Figure 6-12 shows the flowchart from Figure 6-10 expanded to include another way to be exempted from the final exam. In this expanded algorithm, students can also be exempted if they have an 80 or higher average, as long as they have been present every day or missed only once.

FIGURE 6-12
This algorithm provides two paths to exemption from the final.

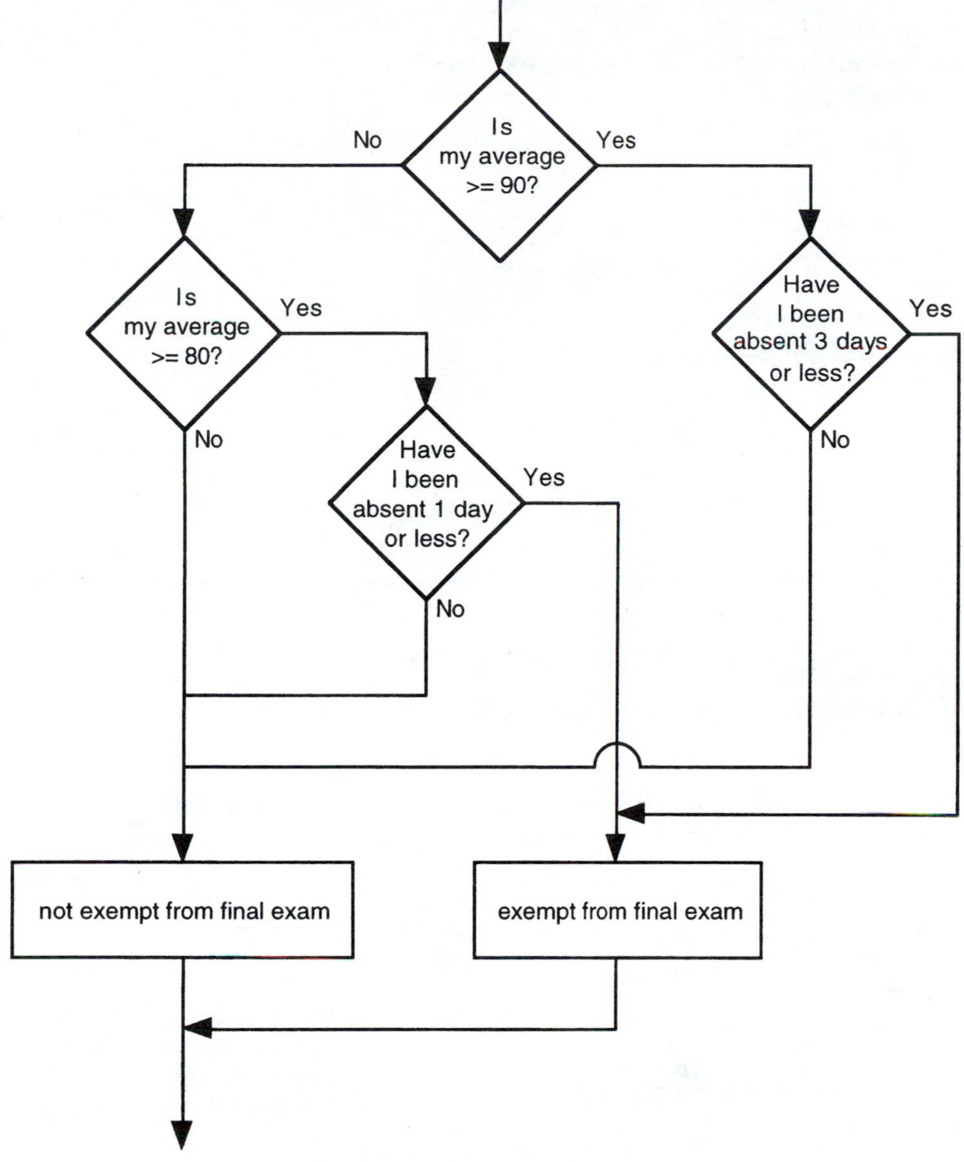

As you can probably imagine, programming the algorithm in Figure 6-12 will require careful construction and nesting of if and if/else structures. Figure 6-13 shows you how it is done.

FIGURE 6-13
Nested if structures require careful construction.

```
if(myAverage >= 90)      // if your average is 90 or better
  {    // and you have missed three days
  if(myDaysAbsent <= 3)  // or less, you are exempt
    {
    exemptFromFinal = true;
    }  // End of if (myDays... clause
  }   // End of if(myAverage... clause
else
  {
  if(myAverage >= 80)    // if your average is 80 or
    {  // better and you have missed
    if(myDaysAbsent <= 1)      // one day or less,
      {      // you are exempt
      exemptFromFinal = true;
      }      // End of if (myDays... clause
    }   // End of if(myAverage... clause
  }
```

STEP-BY-STEP 6.6

1. Open the source for Final.java from the student data files and save it to your student disk as Final.java.

2. Compile and run the program. Run the program several times, testing different combinations of values.

3. When you have verified that the output is correct, close the source code file.

Note

Earlier you learned that it is a good idea to always use braces with if structures. Figure 6-12 illustrates another reason why you should do so. Without the braces, the compiler may assume that the else clause goes with the nested if structure rather than the first if.

Figure 6-14 shows a simple program that includes a nested if structure. The program asks the user to input the amount of money he or she wishes to deposit in order to open a new checking account. Based on the value provided by the user, the program recommends a type of account.

Extra for Experts

The nested if structure in Figure 6-12 is used to set the exempt_from_final variable to true or false. Any type of statements could appear in the nested if statement. However, because the code in this case simply sets the value of the exempt_from_final variable, the entire nested if structure can be replaced with the statement below.

```
exempt_from_final = (((my_average >= 90) && (my_days_absent <= 3)) ||
     ((my_average >= 80) && (my_days_absent <= 1)));
```

Using logical operators, the statement above combines the expressions used in the nested if structure. The result is the value desired for exempt_from_final. To prove it, replace the nested if structure in Final.java with the statement above and run the program again.

Do not be fooled, however, into thinking that statements like the one above make if structures unnecessary. Ordinarily, a selection structure cannot be replaced with a sequence structure and achieve the same result.

STEP-BY-STEP 6.7

1. Open Deposit.java from the student data files. The program shown in Figure 6-14 appears. Save the program to your course folder or disk as Deposit.java.

2. Compile and run the program. Run the program several times using values that are less than $100, between $100 and $1000, and greater than $1000.

3. Leave the source code open for the next exercise.

FIGURE 6-14
The nested if structure can be used to make recommendations.

```
class Deposit
{
  public static void main(String args[])
  {
  String inString = new String();
  float depositAmount;

  System.out.println("Begin Program");
  System.out.print("Enter deposit amount to open account:");
  inString = GetConsoleString();
  depositAmount = toFloat(inString);
  if(depositAmount < 1000)
    {
    if(depositAmount < 100)
      {
      System.out.println("Please consider our EconoCheck account");
      }
    else
      {
      System.out.println("Please consider our FreeCheck account");
      }
    }
  else
    {
    System.out.println("Please consider our InterestMaker account");
    }

  System.out.println("Program End - <press Enter key>");
  GetConsoleString();
  }     // end of main method

  public static String GetConsoleString()
  {
  // CODE FOR GETCONSOLESTRING NOT SHOWN HERE DUE TO SPACE
  }     // end of method GetConsoleString

  public static float toFloat(String inString)
  {
  Float tempFloat = new Float(inString);
  return tempFloat.floatValue();
  }     // end of toFloat method

}     // end of class Deposit
```

Note the addition of another class member method `toFloat`. While this is a fairly simple method, it is an example of modularizing your code so that it is more readable. Remember that virtually all input and output for Java is in the form of a string.

Your program captures the string and then converts it into the float for decision-making use. It does this by passing `inString` to the method, and then returning a float from the method. If you remember from previous lesson discussions, a member method is like a courier that does little chores for you. This courier picks up `inString` and then returns with the value to be placed in the variable `depositAmount`.

There is a way to tighten up your code even more. You can remove the following two lines of code:

```
String inString = new String();
inString = GetConsoleString();
```

and replace the line containing:

```
depositAmount = toFloat(inString);
```

with

```
depositAmount = toFloat(GetConsoleString());
```

Because `GetConsoleString` returns a String, there is no need to temporarily store the String in the object inString. The call to `GetConsoleString` may be placed directly into the line that calls the `toFloat` method.

STEP-BY-STEP 6.8

1. Remove the two lines shown below.

```
String inString = new String();
inString = GetConsoleString();
```

2. Replace the line

```
depositAmount =
  toFloat(inString);
```

with

```
depositAmount =
  toFloat(GetConsoleString());
```

3. Run this program again, testing it with different numbers. You will see that it works just the same as it did.

4. Save and close the source code file.

There are advantages and disadvantages to making methods into parameters for other methods. While doing so does reduce the amount of code, there are times when it makes the code harder to read or more confusing. As you pack more action into a line of code, it is sometimes difficult to grasp all that is going on in the code.

Programmers are always faced with trade-offs. This is an example of a situation where you may give up some readability for more efficient code. Sometimes the more efficient code is necessary. Often, however, the more readable code will reduce development and maintenance costs, which may be more important than a slight increase in efficiency. In most cases, a clearly written program is preferable.

The Switch Structure

You have studied one-way (if) and two-way (if/else) selection structures. Java has another method of handling multiple options known as the switch structure. The switch structure has many uses but may be most often used when working with menus. Figure 6-15 is a code segment that displays a menu of choices and asks the user to enter a number that corresponds to one of the choices. Then, a case statement is used to handle each of the options.

FIGURE 6-15
The switch structure takes action based on the user's input.

```
import java.lang.StringBuffer;
import java.io.IOException;

class Shipping
{
  public static void main(String Args[])
  {
  int shippingMethod;
  double shippingCost;

  System.out.println("SHIPPING PRICE MENU");
  System.out.println("How do you want your order shipped?");
  System.out.println("1 - Ground");
  System.out.println("2 - Two Day Air");
  System.out.println("3 - Over Night Air");
  System.out.print("Please enter desired shipping method: ");

  shippingMethod = Integer.parseInt(GetConsoleString());
  switch(shippingMethod)
    {
    case 1:
      shippingCost = 5.25;
      break;
    case 2:
      shippingCost = 7.75;
      break;
    case 3:
      shippingCost = 10.25;
      break;
    default:
      shippingCost = 0.0;
      break;
    }

  System.out.println("The price for delivery is: $" + shippingCost);
  System.out.println("Press Enter to end program");
  GetConsoleString();
  }     // end of main method
```

FIGURE 6-15 (continued)

```
    public static String GetConsoleString()
    {
    // code not shown due to space limitations
    }     // end of method GetConsoleString

}     // end of class Shipping
```

Let's analyze the switch structure in Figure 6-15. It begins with the keyword switch, followed by the control expression (the variable `shipping_method`) to be compared in the structure. Within the braces of the structure are a series of *case* keywords. Each one provides the code that is to be executed in the event that `shipping_method` matches the value that follows case. The *default* keyword tells the compiler that if nothing else matches, execute the statements that follow.

The *break* keyword, which appears at the end of each case segment, causes the flow of logic to jump to the first executable statement after the switch structure.

Note

A menu is a set of options presented to the user of a program.

Note

In Java, only integer or character types may be used as control expressions in switch statements.

STEP-BY-STEP 6.9

1. Open Shipping.java from the student data files. The program includes the segment from Figure 6-15. Save the program to your course folder or disk as Shipping.java.

2. Compile and run the program. Choose shipping method 2.

3. Add a fourth shipping option called Carrier Pigeon to the menu and add the necessary code to the switch structure. You decide how much it should cost to ship by carrier pigeon.

4. Compile and run to test your addition to the options.

Nested if/else structures could be used in the place of the switch structure. But the switch structure is easier to use and a programmer is less prone to making errors that are related to braces and indentions. Remember, however, that an integer, character, byte, or short data type is required in the control expression of a switch structure. Nested ifs must be used if you are comparing floats and most other objects.

When using character types in a switch structure, enclose the characters in single quotes like any other character literal. The following code segment is an example of using character literals in a switch structure.

```
switch(character_entered)
  {
  case 'A':
    system.out.println ("The character entered was A, as in albatross.");
    break;
  case 'B':
    system.out.println ("The character entered was B, as in butterfly.");
    break;
  default:
    system.out.println ("Illegal entry");
    break;
  }
```

Extra for Experts

Java allows you to place your case statements in any order. You can, however, increase the speed of your program by placing the more common choices at the top of the switch structure and less common ones toward the bottom. The reason is that the computer makes the comparisons in the order they appear in the switch structure. The sooner a match is found, the sooner the computer can move on to other processing.

Summary

In this lesson, you learned:

- Computers make decisions by comparing data.
- Comparison operators are used to create expressions that result in a value of true or false.
- Logical operators can combine comparison expressions.
- Selection structures are how Java programs make decisions.
- The if structure is a one-way selection structure. When a control expression in an if statement is evaluated to be true, the statements associated with the structure are executed.
- The if/else structure is a two-way selection structure. If the control expression in the if statement evaluates to true, one block of statements is executed; otherwise another block is executed.
- The switch structure is a multi-way selection structure that executes one of many sets of statements depending on the value of the control expression. The control expression must evaluate to an integer, character, byte, or short value.

LESSON 6 REVIEW QUESTIONS

WRITTEN QUESTIONS

Write a brief answer to the following questions.

1. List two comparison operators.

2. Write an expression that returns true if the value in the variable `k` is 100 or more.

3. Write any valid expression that uses a logical operator.

4. Write an expression that returns false if the value in the variable `m` is equal to 5.

5. What is the value returned by the following expression?

```
(((2 > 3) || (5 > 4)) && !(3 <= 5))
```

6. What is the purpose of the *break* keyword?

7. Write an if structure that prints the word *help* to the screen if the variable `need_help` is equal to 1.

8. Write an if/else structure that prints the word *Full* to the screen if the float variable `fuel_level` is equal to 1, and prints the value of `fuel_level` if it is not equal to 1.

9. What is wrong with the if structure below?

```
if (x > y);
        { System.out.println ("x is greater than y"); }
```

10. What is wrong with the if structure below?

```
if (x = y)
        { System.out.println ("x is equal to y"); }
```

LESSON 6 PROJECTS

PROJECT 6-1

In the blanks beside the statements in the program below, write a T or F to indicate the result of the expression. Fill in the answers beginning with the first statement and follow the program in the order the statements would be executed by this method in a running program.

```
public class Prob711
{
  public static void main (String args[])
  {
  int i = 4;
  int j = 3;
  boolean true_false;


   true_false = (j < 4);                                   ______

   true_false = (j < 3);                                   ______

   true_false = (j < i);                                   ______

   true_false = (i < 4);                                   ______

   true_false = (j <= 4);                                  ______

   true_false = (4 > 4);                                   ______

   true_false = (i != j);                                  ______

   true_false = (i == j || i < 100);                       ______

   true_false = (i == j && i < 100);                       ______

   true_false = (i < j || true_false && j >= 3);           ______
```

```
true_false = (!(i > 2 && j == 4));          ______

true_false = !true;                         ______
```

PROJECT 6-2

Write a program that asks for an integer and displays for the user whether the number is even or odd. *Hint:* Use if/else and the modulus operator. Save the source code file to your student disk or folder as evenodd.java.

PROJECT 6-3

Rewrite the code in the Final.java file that you saved earlier in this lesson so that it begins with the assumption that the student is exempt and makes comparisons to see if the student must take the test. Save the revised source code to your student disk or folder as Final2.java.

PROJECT 6-4

1. Open lengths.java from the student data files, save it to your student disk using the same name, and analyze the source code.
2. Compile and run it several times and try different conversions and values.
3. Add a conversion for miles to the program. Use 0.00018939 for the conversion factor.
4. Test the program.

PROJECT 6-5

Obtain the exchange rates for at least three foreign currencies. Write a program similar in form to lengths.java that asks for an amount of money in American dollars and then prompts the user to select the currency into which the dollars are to be converted. Save the program to your student disk as Project6_5.java. Compile and run the program.

PROJECT 6-6

Write a program that asks the user a multiple-choice question on a topic of your choice. Test the user's answer to see if the correct response was entered. When the program works for one question, add two or three more. Save the program to your student disk as Project6_6.java. Compile and run the program.

LESSON 7

LOOPS

OBJECTIVES

Upon completion of this lesson, you should be able to:

- Explain the importance of loops in programs.
- Write a program that uses for loops, while loops, do while loops, and nested loops.
- Demonstrate the use of the *break* and *continue* keywords.

Overview

You have probably noticed that much of the work a computer does is actually repeated over and over. For example, a computer can print a personalized letter to each person in a database. What happens, of course, is the basic operation of printing the letter repeats for each person in the database. When a program repeats a group of statements a given number of times, the repetition is accomplished using a *loop*.

In Lesson 6 you learned about sequence structures and selection structures. The final category of structures is *iteration structures*. Loops are iteration structures; each "loop" or pass through a group of statements is called an *iteration*. A condition specified in the program controls the number of iterations performed. For example, a loop may iterate a set number of times or until a specific condition occurs, such as a variable reaching the value 100.

In this lesson you will learn about the three iteration structures available in Java: the for loop, the while loop, and the do while loop.

The for Loop

The *for loop* repeats one or more statements a specified number of times. A for loop is difficult to read the first time you see one. Like an if statement, the for loop uses parentheses. In the parentheses are three items called *parameters* that are needed to make a for loop work. Each parameter in a for loop is an expression. Figure 7-1 shows the format of a for loop.

FIGURE 7-1
A for loop repeats one or more statements a specified number of times.

```
for(initializing expression; control expression; step expression)
  {
  statement or statement block
  }
```

Look at the main method in Figure 7-2. The variable i is used as a counter variable. Notice that the counter variable is used in all three of the for loop's expressions. The first parameter, called the *initializing expression*, gives the counter variable a starting value. The second parameter is the expression that will end the loop, called the *control expression*. As long as the control expression is true, the loop continues to iterate. The third parameter is the *step expression*. It changes the counter variable, usually by adding to it.

FIGURE 7-2
A for loop uses a counter variable to test the control expression. Here the statements in the for loop will repeat three times.

```
class ForLoop
{
  public static void main(String Args[])
  {
  int i;
  for(i = 1; i <= 3; i++)
    System.out.println("i = " + i);
  }      // end of method main
}     // end of class ForLoop
```

Let's look at each part of the loop in Figure 7-2.

- **initializing expression: `i=1`** The variable i, which was declared as an integer, is initialized to 1.
- **control expression: `i<= 3`** The control expression tests to see if the value of i is still less than or equal to 3. When i exceeds 3, the loop will end.
- **step expression: `i++`** The step expression increments i by one each time the loop iterates.

Pitfalls

Placing a semicolon after the closing parenthesis of a for loop will prevent any lines from being iterated.

STEP-BY-STEP 7.1

1. Start your text editor and key the program from Figure 7-2.
2. Save the source code file to your student disk or folder as ForLoop.java.
3. Compile and run the program.
4. Close the source file.

Counting Backward and Other Tricks

A counter variable can also count backward by having the step expression decrement the value rather than increment it.

STEP-BY-STEP 7.2

1. Key the program from Code List 7.1 into a blank editor screen.
2. Save the source file to your student disk or folder as BackWard.java.
3. Compile and run the program. Figure 7-3 shows the output you should see.
4. Close the source code file.

CODE LIST 7-1

```
class BackWard
{
  public static void main(String Args[])
  {
  int i;
  for(i = 5; i >= 0; i--)
    System.out.println(i);
  System.out.println("End of loop.\n");
  }     // end of main method
}     // end of class BackWard
```

FIGURE 7-3
A for loop can decrement the counter variable.

```
5
4
3
2
1
0
End of loop.
```

The output prints numbers from 5 to 0 because i is being decremented in the step expression. The phrase "End of loop." is printed only once because the loop ends with the semicolon that follows the first System.out statement. Note that the line to be repeated by the loop is clearly indented.

The counter variable can do more than step by one. In the program in Figure 7-4, the counter variable is doubled each time the loop iterates. In the next exercise, you will see the effect of this for loop.

STEP-BY-STEP 7.3

1. Key the program from Figure 7-4 into a blank editor screen.
2. Save the source file to your student disk or folder as DblStep.java. Can you predict the program's output?
3. Compile and run the program to see if your prediction was right.
4. Close the source file.

FIGURE 7-4
The counter variable in a for loop can be changed by any valid expression.

```
class DblStep
{
  public static void main(String Args[])
  {
  int i;      // counter variable
  for(i = 1; i <= 100; i = i + i)
    System.out.println("i is now: " + i);
  }     // end of main method
}     // end of class DblStep
```

The for statement gives you a great deal of flexibility. As you have already seen, the step expression can increment, decrement, or count in other ways. Some more examples of for statements are shown in Table 7-1.

TABLE 7-1

for STATEMENT	COUNT PROGRESSION
for (i = 2; i <= 10; i = i + 2)	2, 4, 6, 8, 10
for (i = 1; i < 10; i = i + 2)	1, 3, 5, 7, 9
for (i = 10; i <= 50; i = i + 10)	10, 20, 30, 40, 50

Using a Statement Block in a for Loop

If you need to include more than one statement in the loop, use braces to make a statement block below the for statement. If the first character following a for statement is an open brace ({), all of the statements between the braces are repeated. The same rule applies as with if structures.

STEP-BY-STEP 7.4

1. Key in the source code from Code List 7.2.
2. Compile and run the program to see that the phrase beginning with "This" is in the loop that prints on every line. The second println statement is now part of the loop because it is within the braces.
3. Close the source file without saving changes.

CODE LIST 7-2

```
class BackWard2
{
  public static void main(String Args[])
  {
  int i;
  for(i = 10; i >= 0; i--)
    {
    System.out.println (i);
    System.out.println ("This is in the loop.\n");
    }
  }      // end of main method
}      // end of class BackWard2
```

Extra for Experts

Earlier in this lesson, you learned that placing a semicolon at the end of the parentheses in a for statement will cause the loop to do nothing. While it is true that the statements that follow will not be iterated, there are cases where you might actually want to do just that.

Suppose you are given an integer and asked to calculate the largest three-digit number that can be produced by repeatedly doubling the given integer. For example, if the given integer is 12, repeatedly doubling the integer would produce the sequence 12, 24, 48, 96, 192, 384, 768, 1536. Therefore, 768 is the largest three-digit number produced by repeatedly doubling the number 12. The program segment below uses an empty loop to achieve the result outlined above.

```
public static void main(String args[])
{
long i;
i = Integer.parseInt (GetConsoleString());
for(; i <= 1000; i = i * 2);
  System.out.println (i/2);
}
```

The first parameter of the for statement is left blank because i is initialized by the user in the GetConsoleString statement. Even though the loop is empty, the stepping of the counter variable continues and the value is available after the loop terminates. The value of i is 1000 or more when the loop ends. The println statement then divides the counter by two to return it to the highest three-digit number.

while Loops

A while loop is similar to a for loop. Actually, while loops are sometimes easier to use than for loops and are better suited in many situations. With a for loop, the parameters in the parentheses control the number of times the loop iterates; in a while loop, something inside the loop triggers the loop to stop. While loops are often called "conditional" because they will continue to repeat until a certain condition occurs. For example, a while loop may be written to ask a user to input a series of numbers until the number 0 is entered. The loop would repeat until 0 is entered.

There are two kinds of while loops: the standard while loop and the do while loop. The difference between the two is where the control expression is tested. Let's begin with the standard while loop.

The Standard while Loop

The *while loop* repeats a statement or group of statements as long as a control expression is true. Unlike a for loop, a while loop does not use a counter variable. The control expression in a while loop can be any valid expression. The program in Figure 7-5 uses a while loop to divide a number by 2 repeatedly until the number is less than or equal to 1.

FIGURE 7-5
A while loop may not use a counter variable.

```
public static void main(String args[])
{
float num;
System.out.println("Please enter the number to divide:");
num = toFloat(GetConsoleString());
while(num > 1)
  {
  System.out.println("num is: " + num);
  num = num / 2;
  }
}      // end of method main
```

In a while loop, the control expression is tested before the statements in the loop begin. Figure 7-6 shows a flowchart of the program segment in Figure 7-5. If the number provided by the user is less than or equal to 1, the statements in the loop are never executed.

Something else to know about while loops is that, like the if statements, while loops can work with objects as well as the basic data types. In other words, the following code segment is possible (but not commonly used):

```
while(! FloatObject.equals((Object) floatVariable))
  {
  // do some action
  }
```

The value that might be gained by using object-oriented programming here is lost in having to write additional code to manage the Float object, so this operation will not be used often. However, you will see some conditions that work in this manner.

Pitfalls

As with the for loop, placing a semicolon after the closing parenthesis of a while loop will prevent any lines from being iterated.

FIGURE 7-6
A while loop tests the control expression before the loop begins.

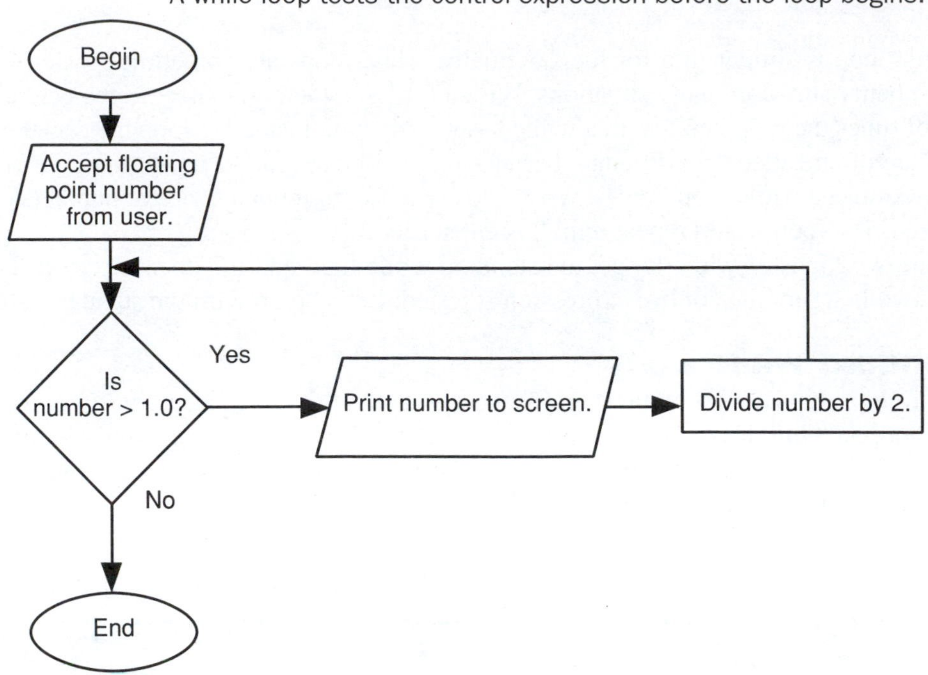

STEP-BY-STEP 7.5

1. Enter the program segment shown in Figure 7-5 into a blank editor screen. Copy in the `toFloat` and `GetConsoleString` methods from a previous file (don't forget the import statements) and make your own While1 class.

2. Save the source file to your student disk or folder as While1.java.

3. Compile and run the program. Run the program several times. Try the following numbers as input: 8, 21, 8650, 1, 2.1, 0.5.

4. Close the source file.

Note

At this point, you should be able to develop a program on your own. Many of the code segments given from here forward will be just that—segments that most commonly will show the main method of a program. Using the given main method, and the supporting methods toFloat and GetConsoleString, you can develop your own programs. If you need a reminder, refer back to your previous programming examples.

In order for a while loop to come to an end, the statements in the loop must change a variable used in the control expression. The result of the control expression must be false for a loop to stop. Otherwise, iterations continue indefinitely in what is called an *infinite loop*. In the program you compiled in Step-by-Step 7.5, the statement `num = num / 2;` divides the number by two each time the loop repeats. Even if the user enters a large value, the loop will eventually end when the number becomes less than 1.

A while loop can be used to replace any for loop. So why have a for loop in the language? Because sometimes a for loop offers a better solution. Figure 7-7 shows two program segments that produce the same output. The program using the for loop is better in this case because the counter variable is initialized, tested, and incremented in the same statement. In a while loop, a counter variable must be initialized and incremented in separate statements.

However, the opposite is not always true; that is, a for loop cannot always replace a while loop. That's because many while loops iterate until a particular condition exists. Often you will not know how many times the loop will repeat until that condition occurs (as when asking a user to enter 0 when he or she has no more data to enter). In those instances, a while loop must be used.

FIGURE 7-7
Although both of these programs produce the same output, the for loop gives a more efficient solution.

```
public static void main(String args[])
{
{int i;
for(i = 1; i <= 100; i++)
  System.out.println("i = " + i);
}     // end of method main


public static void main(String args[])
}
int i = 1;
while(i <= 100)
  {
  System.out.println("i = " + i)
    i++;
  }
}     // end of method main
```

The do while Loop

The last iteration structure in Java is the *do while loop*. A do while loop repeats a statement or group of statements as long as a control expression is true at the end of the loop. Because the control expression is tested at the end of the loop, a do while loop is executed at least one time. Figure 7-8 shows an example of a do while loop.

FIGURE 7-8
In a do while loop, the control expression is tested at the end of the loop.

```
class DoWhile
{
  public static void main(String args[])
  {
  float num, squared;

  do
    {
    System.out.println("Enter a number (Enter 0 to quit):");
    num = toFloat(GetConsoleString());
    squared = num * num;
    System.out.println("The number " + num + " squared is: " + squared);
    }while(num != 0);
  }      // end of method main
```

To help illustrate the difference between a while and a do while loop, compare the two flowcharts in Figure 7-9. Use a while loop when you need to test the control expression before the loop is executed the first time. Use a do while loop when the statements in the loop need to be executed at least once.

FIGURE 7-9
The difference between a while loop and a do while loop is where the control expression is tested.

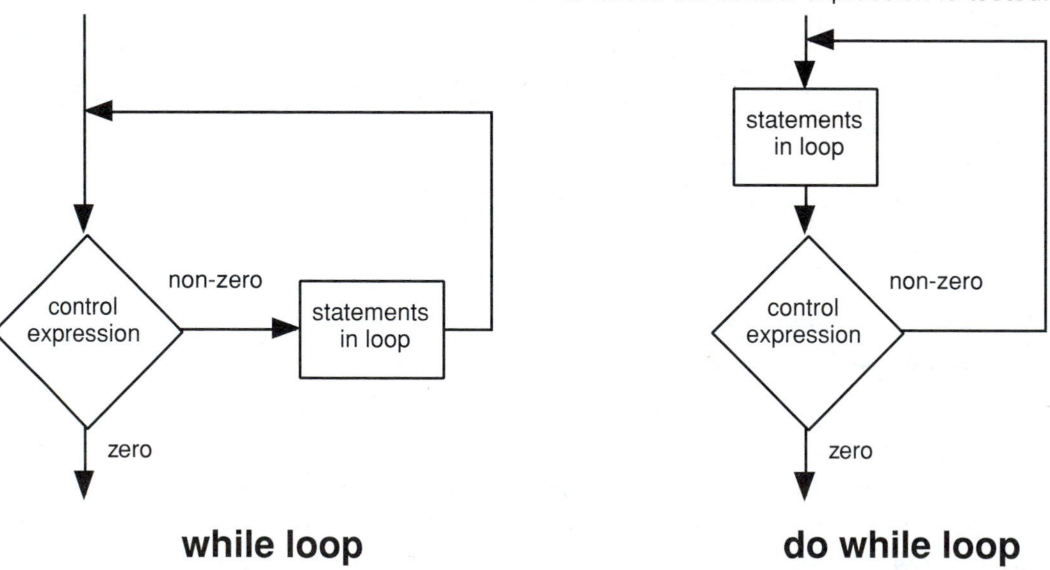

STEP-BY-STEP 7.6

1. Enter the main method from Figure 7-8 into a blank editor screen, and add the `GetConsoleString` and `toFloat` methods to your DoWhile class.

2. Save the source file to your student disk or folder as DoWhile.java.

3. Compile and run the program. Enter several numbers greater than 0 to cause the loop to repeat. Enter 0 to end the program.

4. Close the source file.

Note

You should allow the control expression to end an iteration structure whenever practical. When you are tempted to use a break statement to exit a loop, make sure that using the break statement is the best way to end the loop.

Stopping in the Middle of a Loop

The keyword *break*, also utilized with switch statements, can be used to end a loop before the conditions of the control expression are met. Once a break terminates a loop, the execution begins with the first statement following the loop. In the program you ran in Step-by-Step 7.6, entering zero caused the program to end. But the program squares zero before it ends, even though the step is unnecessary. The program segment in Figure 7-10 uses a break statement to correct the problem.

In the program in Figure 7-10, the value entered by the user is tested with an if statement as soon as it is input. If the value is zero, the break statement is executed to end the loop. If the value is any number other than zero, the loop continues. The control expression can remain `num == 0` without affecting the function of the program. In this case, however, the break statement will stop the loop before the control expression is reached. Therefore, the control expression can be changed to true to create an infinite loop. The true creates an infinite loop because the loop continues to iterate as long as the control expression is true (which is represented by the value true). The loop will repeat until the break statement is executed.

FIGURE 7-10
The break statement ends the loop as soon as the value of zero is input.

```
public static void main(String args[])
{
float num, squared;

do
  {
  System.out.println("Enter a number (Enter 0 to quit):");
  num = toFloat(GetConsoleString());
  if(num == 0)
    {
    break;
    }
  squared = num * num;
 System.out.println("The number " + num + " squared is: " + squared);
  }while(num != 0);
}     // end of method main
```

The *continue statement* is another way to stop a loop from completing each statement. But instead of continuing with the first statement after the loop, the continue statement skips the lines below it in the loop and starts over with the next iteration of the loop. Figure 7-11 shows an example of how the continue statement can be used to cause a for loop to skip an iteration.

FIGURE 7-11
The continue keyword eliminates the number 5 from the outputted list of numbers.

```
public static void main(String args[])
{
int i;
for(i = 1; i <= 10; i ++)
  {
  if(i == 5)
    continue;
  System.out.println("i = " + i);
  }
}      // end of method main
```

The continue statement in Figure 7-11 causes the statements in the for loop to be skipped when the counter variable is 5. The continue statement also can be used in while and do while statements.

STEP-BY-STEP 7.7

1. Open the source code file Continue.java from the student data files and save it to your student disk or folder using the same name.
2. Compile and run the program. Notice that the number 5 does not appear in the output because of the continue statement.
3. Close the source file.

Nesting Loops

In Lesson 6 you learned how to nest if structures. Loops can also be nested. In fact, loops within loops are very common. You must trace the steps of the program carefully to understand how *nested loops* behave. The program in Figure 7-12 provides output that will give you insight into the behavior of nested loops.

FIGURE 7-12
Even though this program has little practical use, it illustrates what happens when loops are nested.

```
public static void main(String args[])
{
int i, j;
System.out.println("Program Begin");
for(i = 1; i <=3; i++)
  {
  System.out.println(" Outer loop:  i = " + i);
  for(j = 1; j <= 3; j++)
    {
    System.out.println("      Inner loop:  j = " + j);
    }
  }
System.out.println("Program End");
}
```

The important thing to realize is that the inner for loop (the one that uses j) will complete its count from 1 to 3 every time the outer for loop (the one that uses i) iterates. That is why in the output, for every loop the outer loop makes, the inner loop starts over (see Figure 7-13).

FIGURE 7-13
The output of the program in Figure 7-12 illustrates the effect of the nested loops.

```
Program Begin

Outer loop:  i = 1
  Inner loop:  j = 1
  Inner loop:  j = 2
  Inner loop:  j = 3
Outer loop:  i = 2
  Inner loop:  j = 1
  Inner loop:  j = 2
  Inner loop:  j = 3
Outer loop:  i = 3
  Inner loop:  j = 1
  Inner loop:  j = 2
  Inner loop:  j = 3
Program End
```

STEP-BY-STEP 7.8

1. Open NestLoop.java from the student data files.

2. Compile and run the program.

3. Close the source file without saving it.

Note

If you know how to use your compiler's debugger, step through the program to trace the flow of logic.

Nesting may also be used with while loops and do while loops, or in combinations of loops. The program in Figure 7-14 nests a do while loop in a for loop.

FIGURE 7-14
This program has a do while loop nested within a for loop.

```
public static void main(String Args[])
{
CHAR PARTY;
char ERROR = '\0';
int i, numReps;
int democrats = 0, republicans = 0, independents = 0;
String tempVal = new String();

System.out.println("\nHow many U.S. representatives does your state have?");
numReps = Integer.parseInt(GetConsoleString());

System.out.println("Enter the party affiliation for each representative");
System.out.println("Enter D for Democrat, R for Republican,");
System.out.println("and I for Independents or other parties");

for (i = 1; i <= numReps; i++)
  {
  do
    {
    System.out.println("Party of representative #" + i);
    tempVal = GetConsoleString();
    party = tempVal.charAt(0);

    switch(party)
      {
      case 'D':
      case 'd':
        democrats++;
        break;
      case 'R':
```

FIGURE 7-4 (continued)

```
        case 'r':
          republicans++;
          break;
        case 'I':
        case 'i':
          independents++;
          break;
        default:
          System.out.println("Invalid entry.  Enter D, R, or I.");
          party = ERROR;
          break;
        }      // end of switch statement
      }while(party == ERROR);  //  end of do . . while loop
    }      // end of for loop
  System.out.println("Your state is represented by:");
  System.out.println("      " + democrats + " Democrats");
  System.out.println("      " + republicans + " Republicans");
  System.out.println(" and " + independents + " Independents");
  }      // END OF MAIN METHOD
```

The program segment in Figure 7-14 asks the user for the number of U.S. representatives in his or her state. A for loop is used to ask the user to identify the party of each representative. The do while loop is used to repeat the prompt if the user enters an invalid party choice.

STEP-BY-STEP 7.9

1. Open Reps.java from the student data files and save it to your student disk using the same name.

2. Study the program carefully before you run it.

3. Compile and run the program. Enter some invalid data to cause the nested loop to iterate. If you have trouble understanding the program, study the source code and run it again.

4. Close the source code file without saving.

Summary

In this lesson, you learned:

- A loop is a group of statements that is repeated a number of times. A loop is an iteration structure.
- A for loop causes one or more statements to be repeated a specified number of times. The three parameters of a for loop are the initializing expression, the control expression, and the step expression.
- A while loop executes one or more statements as long as the control expression is true. The control expression is tested before the statements in the loop begin. A do while loop works like a while loop except the control expression is tested at the end of the loop.
- A break statement can be used to exit a loop before the control expression ends the loop. The continue statement causes the loop to skip to the next iteration of the loop.
- A loop within a loop is called a nested loop. The more deeply nested the loop, the more times the loop will be executed.

LESSON 7 REVIEW QUESTIONS

WRITTEN QUESTIONS

1. What category of structures includes loops?
2. What is the name of the for loop parameter that ends the loop?
3. What for loop parameter changes the counter variable?
4. What happens if you key a semicolon after the parentheses of a for statement?
5. How many statements can be included in a loop?
6. Write a for statement that will print the numerals 3, 6, 12, 24.
7. Write a for statement that will print the numerals 24, 12, 6, 3.
8. Where does a do while loop test the control expression?
9. What is the term for a loop without a way to end?

10. What is the loop control expression in the code segment below?

```
while (!done)
{
  if(i < 1)
    {
    done = true;
    }
  i--;
}
```

11. What is the error in the code segment below?

```
do;
  {
  if(i < 1)
    {
    done = true;
    }
  i--;
  }
while(!done);
```

12. Write a loop that prints your name to the screen once and then asks you to enter 0 (zero) to stop the program or any other number to print the name again.

13. Write a for loop to print the odd numbers from 1 to 999.

LESSON 7 PROJECTS

SCANS

PROJECT 7-1

Write a program that uses a for loop to print the odd numbers from 1 to 21. Save the source file to your course disk or folder as OddLoop.java.

PROJECT 7-2

Write a program that implements the flowchart in Figure 7-15. Save the source file to your student disk or folder as Sumitup.java.

FIGURE 7-15
Write a program to implement this flowchart.

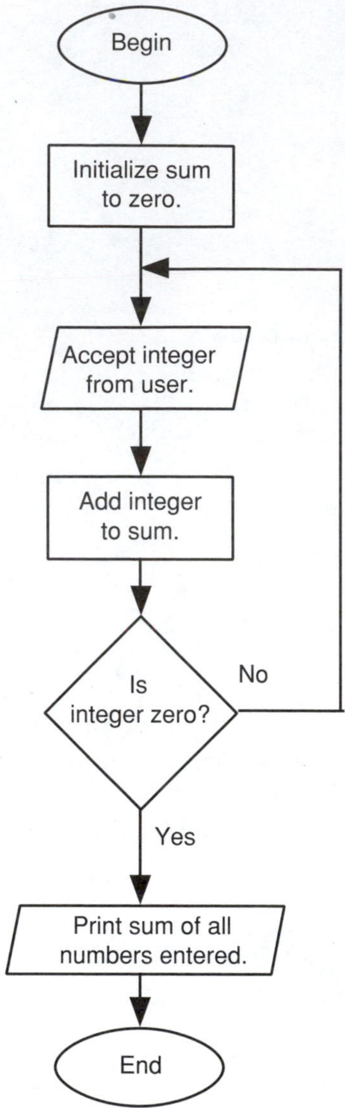

PROJECT 7-3

Write a program that prints the numbers 1 to 20, but skips the numbers 15, 16, and 17. Save the source code file to your student disk or folder as Skipthem.java.

PROJECT 7-4

Modify the program from Step-by-Step 7.9 (Reps.java) so that it calculates the percentage of your state's representatives that belong to each party. Save the modified source code to your student disk or folder as Reps2.java.

PROJECT 7-5

1. Write a program that asks the user for a series of integers one at a time. When the user enters the integer 0, the program displays the following information:
   _ the number of integers in the series (not including zero)
   _ the average of the integers
   _ the largest integer in the series
   _ the smallest integer in the series
   _ the difference between the largest and smallest integer in the series

2. Save the source file to your course disk or folder as Ints.java.

PROJECT 7-6

1. Draw a flowchart for a simple program of your own design that uses a while loop.

2. Write the Java source code for the program. Save the program to your student disk as project7_6.java.

3. Enter the source code into a blank editor screen and give it an appropriate filename.

4. Compile and run the program.

PROJECT 7-7

Write a program that asks the user to think of a number between 1 and 100, then attempts to guess the number. The program should make an initial guess of 50. The program should then ask the user if 50 is the number the user has in mind, or if 50 is too high or too low. Based on the response given by the user, the program should make another guess. Your program must continue to guess until the correct number is reached. Save the source file to your student disk as Hi_Lo.java. Compile and run the program, and close the source file.

PROJECT 7-8

1. Open Binary.java from the student data files. The program uses four nested loops to print the binary equivalent of 0 to 15 to the screen. Study the source code, save it to your student disk, compile, and run the program to see its output.

2. Modify the program to generate an additional column of digits. The resulting output should be the binary equivalent of 0-31. Save the modified source file to your student disk as Binary31.java.

3. Close the source code file.

LESSON 8

DATA FILE BASICS

OBJECTIVES

Upon completion of this lesson, you should be able to:

- List the uses for data files.
- Discuss the difference between sequential-access and random-access data files.
- Open and close data files.
- Write to data files.
- Read from data files.
- Add data to the end of a file using random-access techniques.
- Use multiple data files at the same time.
- Prompt the user for filenames.

Estimated Time: 2 hours

Overview

Many useful programs collect all input from the keyboard and print all output to the screen. However, the ability to input data from a disk file and send output to a disk file opens the door to many more possibilities. For example, a program that organizes names and addresses of all students would probably never be run if the user had to first type everyone's name and address from the keyboard each time it was executed! In addition, the output for such a program is almost useless if it's just flashed up on the screen or stored temporarily in RAM memory.

In this lesson, you will learn about sequential-access and random-access data files. You will see how to open and close a sequential-access file, write data to a file, read data from a file, and how to add data to the end of an existing file using random-access techniques. You will also learn how to use multiple files at the same time and how to prompt the user for filenames.

File Concepts

Data files are not difficult to understand. Storing data in a file simply involves taking data from your computer's RAM and copying it to a disk. Retrieving data from a file is just the opposite. Data stored on disk is copied into RAM and then can be placed into variables or other data structures.

Why Use Data Files?

Recall that your computer's random access memory (RAM) holds data only as long as the computer is on. Furthermore, data in RAM is lost as soon as your program ends. Disks and other forms of secondary storage hold data even after the computer is turned off. Therefore, any data that your program needs again should be stored on disk so that it can be reloaded into your program.

For example, suppose you have a program that prints mailing addresses on labels and envelopes. Unless a data file is used to store the addresses, the user has to enter the data from the keyboard every time the program runs.

Another reason to use data files is the amount of space available on a disk as compared to RAM. In the example of the program that prints addresses, a data file could store hundreds or even thousands of addresses—many times the number that could fit in RAM.

Sequential-Access vs. Random-Access Files

There are two types of data files: sequential access and random access. The difference between the two is in how they access the data that is stored in them.

SEQUENTIAL-ACCESS DATA FILES

A *sequential-access file* works like an audio cassette tape. When you put a cassette tape in a tape deck, you must fast forward or rewind to get to a specific song. Thus, you must move through the songs sequentially—one after the other—until you reach the song you want to hear. Blocks of data stored in a sequential-access data file are placed one after the other like songs on a cassette tape. To retrieve specific data from a sequential-access data file, you must start at the beginning of the file and search for the data you want.

Sequential-access files are the most widely used data files. Word processors save documents in sequential-access files. Spreadsheets, graphic files, and some databases are also stored as sequential-access files.

A sequential-access file can contain data of mixed types and sizes. For example, a word processor file may begin with general information about the document, followed by the text of the document itself. There may even be codes that control formatting mixed in with the document's text. The programmers who developed the word processor program created rules for the way data would be placed in the file. When the program loads the document from disk, those same rules are followed in order to correctly interpret the data file.

Figure 8-1 represents a sequential-access file storing a list of names. Notice that the names vary in length. To find the fourth name in the list (Beau Chenoweth), the three names that precede it must be read first.

FIGURE 8-1
A sequential-access file requires that data be read from the beginning of the file each time it is accessed.

Shelley Neff	James MacCloskey	Kim Fan	Beau Chenoweth	Sarah Boyd	Britney Sooter

RANDOM-ACCESS DATA FILES

A *random-access file* works like an audio compact disc (CD). With the touch of a button, you can immediately access any song on the CD. You can play the songs on a CD in any order, regardless of the order in which they appear on the CD. Like an audio CD, a random-access data file allows you to move directly to any data in the file.

Random-access files are most often used to store databases. A database with a large number of records is more efficiently managed with a random-access file because you can move quickly to any desired record in the database.

The secret to a random-access file is that data is written to the file in blocks of equal size. In reality, the file appears on the disk as a sequential-access file. Because the file is made up of equal-sized blocks, a program can predict how far to move forward from the beginning of the file in order to get to the desired data.

Figure 8-2 represents a random-access file. Regardless of the length of the person's name, the data occupies the same amount of disk space. While the random-access file allows almost instant access to any data in the file, the disadvantage is that random-access files often occupy more disk space than sequential-access files.

FIGURE 8-2
A random-access file allows any data to be accessed directly.

Shelley Neff	James MacCloskey	Kim Fan	Beau Chenowe

In this lesson, you will write programs that primarily use sequential-access data files. However, you will also run a program that uses a random-access data file.

Using Sequential-Access Files

Using sequential-access files requires that you complete a few simple but important steps. First, the file must be opened. Data can then be stored or retrieved from the file. Finally, the file must be closed.

Opening and Closing Files

Like everything else in Java, files are treated as objects. Two basic classes exist for using sequential-access files: FileInputStream and FileOutputStream. The class you use depends on whether you will be retrieving data from the file or storing data in the file. After you create an object using one of these two classes, other Java classes can be used to make file input and output easier and more robust.

> **Extra for Experts**
>
> The examples in this unit are primarily limited to sequential-access files. Java provides one class, RandomAccessFile, for random-access file input and output. This unit will provide a short exposure to these types of files.

As you learn how to use files, you will notice that the term *stream* comes up quite often. Streams are an abstract way of thinking about the data inside a computer. If you think about it, data flows from one component to another inside your computer. Data flows from the keyboard to the CPU and from the CPU to any number of peripherals, including the screen, a printer, or a modem. Using this concept, to get information from the keyboard, you simply attach your program to the stream of data coming from the keyboard. When working with files in Java, you use *file streams.*

DECLARING AND OPENING FILE STREAMS

Depending on how you intend to use the file stream, the way you declare it will be different. If you want to open the file input.dat and retrieve data from it (input), you would use the FileInputStream class.

```
FileInputStream fileInputStream = new FileInputStream("input.dat");
```

This statement creates a new object called fileInputStream, modeled after the FileInputStream class, which will let the program read data in from the file input.dat.

If you want to write data (output) to the file ouput.dat, you would use the FileOutputStream class.

```
FileOutputStream fileOutputStream = new FileOutputStream("output.dat");
```

This statement creates a new object called fileOutputStream, modeled after the FileOutputStream class, which will let the program write data to the file output.dat.

USING ADVANCED INPUT/OUPUT CLASSES

The FileInputStream and FileOutputStream classes have a few very limited methods for *reading* data from files and *writing* data to files. It is better to use some of Java's more advanced input/output classes for file input and output. The type of data that you are inputting and outputting determines which set of classes you use. For inputting and outputting primitive data types, use the DataIntputStream and DataOutputStream classes. If you are reading and writing text data (String objects) or numerical data that you want to remain in a readable form, you should use the BufferedReader and PrintWriter classes.

Note

When outputting data to a file that already exists, the data in that file will be overwritten.

CLOSING FILE STREAMS

After a file has been opened, you will want either to read data from it or to write data to it. When you complete your work with a file, you must close it. Both the FileInputStream class and the FileOuputStream class have a method for closing the stream.

```
fileInputStream.close();
fileOuputStream.close();
```

Only the file stream objects need to be closed. The other advanced input and output objects will be closed and destroyed by the Java Virtual Machine when the file streams are closed.

Reading and Writing Data Using Files

READING AND WRITING NUMERICAL DATA

As stated earlier, when reading and writing Java's primitive data types, you should use the DataOutputStream and DataInputStream classes. The DataOutputStream class has several different methods for outputting data. Each of these methods corresponds to one of the basic data types. The DataInputStream class has several different methods for inputting data. Just like the DataOutputStream, each of these methods corresponds to one of the basic data types in Java.

Before the DataInputStream and DataOutputStream objects can be used for file input and output, they must be associated or "hooked" to a file stream object. This is done by referencing the appropriate file stream in the constructor of the DataIntputStream or DataOutputStream.

Warning

In a paper filing system, a folder or drawer left open might result in important information getting misplaced or lost. Closing a computer file might be even more important. A data file left open by a program can be destroyed if a power failure or a program crash occurs. A closed file is generally protected from such occurrences.

Figure 8-3 is the source code to the TestIO class. Notice that the bulk of the source code is in the main method. The program starts by opening a FileOutputStream named fileOutputStream. A DataOutputStream object is then created to output data to the fileOutputStream object. The integers zero through nine are then written to the file TestIO.dat. Then the fileInputStream is closed. Next, the data file is reopened as a FileInputStream. The dataInputStream object is created using the fileInputStream object, and the integers are read in from the file and printed to the screen. Then, the fileInputStream is closed and the program finishes.

FIGURE 8-3

A simple Java program that writes integers to a file and then reads them back in.

```
DataInputStream dataInputStream = new DataInputStream(fileInputStream);
DataOutputStream dataOutputStream = new DataOutputStream (fileOutputStream);

import java.io.*;
public class TestIO
{
  public static void main(String args[])
  {
     boolean endOfFile = false;     int i = 0;

  try
    {
    System.out.println("Opening file for output");

    FileOutputStream fileOutputStream = new FileOutputStream("TestIO.dat");
    DataOutputStream dataOutputStream = new DataOutputStream(fileOutputStream);

    System.out.println("Writing data to the file");

    for(i = 0; i < 10 ; i++)
      {
      dataOutputStream.writeInt(i);
      System.out.println("" + i);
      }

    System.out.println("Closing the file");

    fileOutputStream.close();
    }
  catch(IOException e)
    {
    System.out.println("An Error Occurred");
    e.printStackTrace();
    }

  try
    {
    System.out.println("Opening the file for input");

    FileInputStream fileInputStream = new FileInputStream("TestIO.dat");
    DataInputStream dataInputStream = new DataInputStream(fileInputStream);

    System.out.println("Reading data from the file");

    while(!endOfFile)
```

FIGURE 8-3 (continued)

```
      {
      try
        {
        i = dataInputStream.readInt();
        System.out.println("" + i);
        }
      catch(EOFException e)
        {
        endOfFile = true;
        }
      }

    System.out.println("Closing the file");
    fileInputStream.close();
    }
  catch(IOException e)
    {
    System.out.println("An Error Occurred");
    e.printStackTrace();
    }
  }
}
```

STEP-BY-STEP 8.1

1. Open the TestIO.java program from the student data files, and save it to your student disk or folder using the same name. Compile and run the TestIO.java program. Notice that the TestIO.dat file is always overwritten whenever the program is run.
2. Modify the for loop at the beginning of the program so that the program only outputs the numbers zero through four.
3. Save the program, compile, and run it. Then, close the program.

Exceptions and File Errors

Notice that all of the code in the main method of Figure 8-3 is inside a try statement. At the end of the try statement is a catch statement. If any problems occur while the files are being opened, written to, read from, or closed, an IOException will be thrown and the catch statement will catch it. Several different problems can cause an IOException to occur: the file may not exist, the file cannot be created, the storage device may be full, the storage device may be write protected, or the end of the file may have been reached unexpectedly.

Exceptions are not always errors. The different I/O classes use different exceptions for different reasons. In the second part of the program in Figure 8-3, the try statement is nested inside of another. The inner try statement watches for the EOFException to be thrown, indicating that the end of the file has been reached. When the EOFException is thrown, the endOfFile variable is set to true, so the program knows not to read any more data from the file.

When writing Java programs, you have to read the documentation concerning the methods that you are using. The documentation will help you to use the method to its fullest and to understand when an error has occurred.

Note

A *buffer* is a temporary holding area for data while it is transferred from one place to another. Buffers help data flow more smoothly. For instance, your computer uses a buffer between the keyboard and your programs. The keyboard buffer can store keys when your program is not ready to accept them. When the program is ready, the program gets the characters out of the buffer.

READING AND WRITING TEXTUAL DATA

The BufferedReader and PrintWriter classes, which are used for text and String-based input and output, are more complicated than the DataInputStream and DataOutputStream classes that were used in the previous section. Specifically, these classes use a large amount of buffering. This buffering allows these classes to operate more quickly and efficiently than other, simpler classes. However, this buffering requires that some additional settings be indicated and that some other methods be used.

Three steps are required when using the BufferedReader class for file input:

1. Open a FileInputStream.
2. Create an InputStreamReader object and associate it with the FileInputStream.
3. Create a BufferedReader object and hook it to the InputStreamReader object.

```
FileInputStream fileInputStream = new FileInputStream("Test.dat");
InputStreamReader inputStreamReader = new InputStreamReader(fileInputStream);
BufferedReader bufferedReader = new BufferedReader(inputStreamReader);
```

The method that you will use most in the BufferedReader class is `readLine()`. If the `readLine` method comes to the end of the file or streams, it will return a String that is equal to null.

```
String input = bufferedReader.readLine();
```

The PrintWriter class is a bit simpler than the BufferedReader class. The declaration and initialization requires only two steps, just like the DataOutputStream class.

```
FileOutputStream fileOutputStream = new FileOutputStream("Test.dat");
PrintWriter printWriter = new PrintWriter(fileOutputStream);
```

The important thing to remember about the PrintWriter class is that it is a buffered class. This means that when you use a PrintWriter object to output data, the data is not always immediately written to the stream. The data is kept in a buffer and emptied into the stream when the buffer becomes full. Therefore, if you are using a PrintWriter to output data to a file and the buffer does not fill up, no data will be written to the file. The process of forcing an object to empty its buffer is called *flushing*. PrintWriter objects have a method called `flush()` for performing this action. So, whenever you use the PrintWriter object, you always have to flush it when you are done with it.

Figure 8-4 contains a short program that shows how the PrintWriter and BufferedReader classes are used for file output and input. The program begins by opening the file TestStringIO.dat and attaching a PrintWriter object named printWriter to it. Then the program writes several lines of text to the stream.

The stream is flushed and the file is closed. Remember, the stream must be flushed before you close the file or the data remaining in the buffer will be lost.

The second part of the program reopens the file TestStringIO.dat, attaches an InputStreamReader to it, and then attaches a BufferedReader object, bufferedReader, to the InputStreamReader object. Strings in the file are read in using the `readLine` method, which is nested inside a while loop. This while loop makes the program continue to read data until the end of the file is reached, indicated by the `readLine` returning a null. Finally, the file is closed and the program ends.

The same classes and methods can be used to write Java's basic data types to a text file. The file would remain readable and the data could be used by other programs or read by a person.

FIGURE 8-4
The BufferedReader and PrintWriter classes are used for String-based file IO.

```
import java.io.*;

class TestStringIO
{
  public static void main(String args[])
  {
  String inputString;

  try
    {
    FileOutputStream fileOutputStream = new FileOutputStream ("TestStringIO.dat");
    PrintWriter printWriter = new PrintWriter(fileOutputStream);

    printWriter.println("Who is cooler, Einstein or Todd?");
    printWriter.println("Einstein had more brains...");
    printWriter.println("Todd has more trains...");

    printWriter.flush();

    fileOutputStream.close();
    }
  catch(IOException e)
    {
    System.out.println("An Error Occurred");
    e.printStackTrace();
    }

  try
    {
    FileInputStream fileInputStream = new FileInputStream("TestStringIO.dat");
    InputStreamReader inputStreamReader = new InputStreamReader(fileInputStream);
    BufferedReader bufferedReader = new BufferedReader (inputStreamReader);

    inputString = bufferedReader.readLine();
    while(inputString != null)
```

FIGURE 8-4 (continued)

```
            {
            System.out.println(inputString);
            inputString = bufferedReader.readLine();
            }

          fileInputStream.close();
          }
        catch(IOException e)
          {
          System.out.println("An Error Occurred");
          e.printStackTrace();
          }
      }
  }
```

STEP-BY-STEP 8.2

1. Open the file TestStringIO.java from the student data files, and save it using the same name to your student disk or folder. Examine the program and determine what the program should do and what the program's output should look like.
2. Compile and run the program. Does the output look like you thought it should? When you are done, close the program.

Using Random-Access Files and Multiple Files

As with sequential-access files, a random-access file must be opened before the data can be accessed, and it should always be closed when done using it. Random-access files can be opened for read-only processing or for read/write processing.

There are sure to be occasions when you will need to have more than one file open in a program. This is very easy to do in Java, as you will learn in this section.

Opening and Closing Random-Access Files

As with sequential-access files, random-access files are treated as objects. The Java IO class for using random-access files is RandomAccessFile. This class is used for both reading and writing data to the file. When opening a random-access file, you must specify the filename as well as an open mode. Random-access files can be opened in read-only mode, which allows the file data to be accessed but not modified. A random-access file can also be opened in read/write mode, which allows the file to be both read and updated.

DECLARING AND OPENING RANDOM-ACCESS FILE STREAMS

Declaring a file stream for a file that is to be opened for read-only access can be accomplished by using the statement below. A file opened using this stream can be read but cannot be modified.

```
RandomAccessFile fileOutputStream =
new RandomAccessFile("Random_out.txt", "r");
```

The following statement would be used to declare a file stream for a random-access file that is to be read and/or updated.

```
RandomAccessFile fileOutputStream =
new RandomAccessFile("Random_out.txt", "rw");
```

In both statements, the mode parameter is specified following the name of the file to be opened. In the first example, the "r" mode specifies read-only access. In the second example, the "rw" indicates read/write access.

CLOSING RANDOM-ACCESS FILE STREAMS

As with a sequential file, any file opened for random access should always be explicitly closed when processing of the file is finished. The RandomAccessFile class has a method for closing the file that looks the same as for a sequential-access file.

```
fileOutputStream.close();
```

Reading and Writing Random-Access Files

Reading data from and writing data to a random-access file is quite simple because of the variety of methods defined for the RandomAccessFile class. Methods are defined for reading and writing all of Java's primitive data types, as well as for accessing string data. In this unit, we will cover only the methods used to read and write string data.

READING TEXTUAL DATA FROM A RANDOM-ACCESS FILE

After the file has been opened, the `readLine` method can be used to read a line of text from the file. The program shown in Figure 8-5 is a simple Java program that opens a file using a RandomAccessFile stream, reads each line of data from the file, and displays it on the screen.

FIGURE 8-5
This program reads a file using the Random AccessFile class.

```
import java.io.*;

class Random_in
{
  public static void main(String args[])
  {
  String inputString;

  try
    {
    RandomAccessFile fileInputStream =
```

FIGURE 8-6 (continued)

```
        new RandomAccessFile("Random_out.txt", "r");

    inputString = fileInputStream.readLine();
    while(inputString != null)
      {
      System.out.println(inputString);
      inputString = fileInputStream.readLine();
      }

    fileInputStream.close();
    }
  catch(IOException e)
    {
    System.out.println("An Error Occurred");
    e.printStackTrace();
    }

  }      // end of main method
}     // end of class Random_in
```

This program opens the file Random_out.txt in read-only mode, as indicated by the "r" mode specifier in the RandomAccessFile declaration statement. It then uses the `readLine` method to read the first line of text from the file, which is then displayed within the while loop before reading the next line of text from the file. When the end of the file is reached, the program closes the file before exiting.

APPENDING TEXTUAL DATA TO A RANDOM-ACCESS FILE

One of the advantages of a random-access file is the ability to add new information to the file without destroying the data currently in the file. This is done by appending data to the end of the file. The program shown in Figure 8-6 opens the file used by the Random_in program shown in Figure 8-5 and adds a new line of text to the end of the file. It then reads the file again and displays the old text data as well as the new line of text.

FIGURE 8-6
This program uses RandomFileAccess to add a text string to the end of an existing file.

```
import java.io.*;

class Random_out
{
  public static void main(String args[])
  {
  String inputString;

  try     // open the file for read/write access
    {
    RandomAccessFile fileOutputStream =
        new RandomAccessFile("Random_out.txt", "rw");
```

FIGURE 8-6 (continued)

```
        fileOutputStream.seek(fileOutputStream.length());
        fileOutputStream.writeBytes("The silver fox is smart.");

        fileOutputStream.close();
        }
      catch(IOException e)
        {
        System.out.println("An Error Occurred");
        e.printStackTrace();
        }

      try      // open the file for read-only access
        {
        RandomAccessFile fileInputStream =
            new RandomAccessFile("Random_out.txt", "r");

        inputString = fileInputStream.readLine();
        while(inputString != null)
          {
          System.out.println(inputString);
          inputString = fileInputStream.readLine();
          }

        fileInputStream.close();
        }
      catch(IOException e)
        {
        System.out.println("An Error Occurred");
        e.printStackTrace();
        }
      }      // end of main method
  }      // end of class Random_out
```

The Random_out class shown in Figure 8-6 opens the Random_out.txt file in read/write mode, as shown by the "rw" mode specifier when the file stream is declared. The following two statements, which are shown below, then position the file pointer to the end of the file and add a new text string to the file.

```
fileOutputStream.seek(fileOutputStream.length());
   fileOutputStream.writeBytes("The silver fox is smart.");
```

The `seek` method is used to set the offset from the beginning of the file at which the next read or write operation will take place. In this case, the current length of the file is specified as the offset value passed to the method, which positions the file pointer at the current end of the file. The `writeBytes` method is then passed a text string that is to be added to the file at the location set by the `seek` method.

The file is then closed and reopened in read-only mode. Each record in the file is read and displayed on the screen, and the file is again closed before exiting.

STEP-BY-STEP 8.3

1. Open the file Random_in.java from the student data files and save it to your student disk or folder using the same name. Copy the file Random_out.txt from the student data files and save it to your student disk or folder. Compile and run the Random_in.java program. The output should look like the following:

```
The red fox is sly.
The brown fox is quick.
The gray fox is sleek.
```

2. Change the class name to Random_out and save the program to your student disk or folder as Random_out.java. Refer to Figure 8-6 and modify the program on your screen by inserting the try and catch statements that declare the file as a random-access file and open the file in read/write mode. Save, compile, and run the program. The output should now look like the following:

```
The red fox is sly.
The brown fox is quick.
The gray fox is sleek.
The silver fox is smart.
```

3. Close the program.

Opening Multiple Files

As mentioned earlier, you can have more than one file open at a time. Just declare and use a separate file stream for each file. Why would you want more than one file open at a time? There are many reasons. Let's look at a few of them.

Suppose you need to add some data to the middle of a file. Since you cannot insert data in a file, you must read the data from the original file and write it to a new file. At the position where the new data is to be inserted, you write the data to the new file and then continue writing the rest of the data from the original file.

Large database programs, called *relational database* systems, use multiple database files. For example, a program for an animal clinic might use one database file to store the information about the owners of pets and another file for the information about the pets themselves. The database of pets would include a field that linked the pet to its owner in the other database file. The term relational database comes from the fact that multiple database files are related or linked by certain fields.

Another example of when more than one file may be necessary is when performing a conversion process on a file. Suppose you need to convert all of the lowercase alphabetic characters in a file to uppercase letters. The program in Figure 8-7 reads the text in one file one line at a time, converts where necessary, and writes the converted characters to another file.

FIGURE 8-7
This Java program takes in one file and capitalizes all the letters.

```
import java.io.*;

public class Capital
{
  public static void main(String args[])
  {
  String inString;

  try
```

FIGURE 8-7 (continued)

```
      {
      FileInputStream fileInputStream = new FileInputStream ("lower.dat");
      InputStreamReader inputStreamReader =
          new InputStreamReader(fileInputStream);
      BufferedReader bufferedReader = new BufferedReader(inputStreamReader);

      FileOutputStream fileOutputStream = new FileOutputStream("upper.dat");
      PrintWriter printWriter = new PrintWriter(fileOutputStream);

      System.out.println("Reading a line");
      inString = bufferedReader.readLine();

      while(inString != null)
        {
        printWriter.println(inString.toUpperCase());
        System.out.println("Reading a line");
        inString = bufferedReader.readLine();
        }

      printWriter.flush();

      fileInputStream.close();
      fileOutputStream.close();
      }
    catch(IOException e)
      {
      System.out.println("An Error Occurred");
      e.printStackTrace();
      }
  }      // end of main method
}
```

STEP-BY-STEP 8.4

1. Open the Capital.java program from the student data files and save it to your student disk or folder with the same name. Compile and run the program. An IOException Error should occur. The error occurs because the lower.dat file does not exist.

2. Use a text editor to create the lower.dat file. Fill it with lowercase strings. Save it in the same directory with the Capital.class file.

3. Run the Capital program again. Verify that the upper.dat file was created and contains the contents of the lower.dat file converted to uppercase.

Prompting for Filenames

Up to now we have used filenames that are *hard coded* into the program, meaning that the names cannot be changed when the program runs. This was done by putting the filenames in the form of string literals. To make a program like the one in Figure 8-7 more flexible, you can *prompt* the user for filenames. The code segment below prompts the user for two filenames and opens them.

```
System.out.print("Enter the name of the input file: ");
String inputFile = GetConsoleString();
System.out.print("Enter the name of the output file: ");
String outputFile = GetConsoleString();

FileInputStream fileInputStream = new FileInputStream(inputFile);
FileOutputStream fileOutputStream = new FileOutputStream(outputFile);
```

STEP-BY-STEP 8.5

1. Open the Capital.java file from your student disk and replace the hard-coded filename code with the source code from the code segment shown above.

2. Add the `GetConsoleString()` method to the Capital class below the `main` method. Change the class name to Capital2 and save the modified program as Capital2.java.

3. Compile and run the program. Enter lower.dat as the input file and upper2.dat as the output file.

4. Check the output file (upper2.dat) to make sure that the conversion took place.

5. Close the source code file and the output file.

Summary

In this lesson, you learned:

- Data files allow for the storage of data prior to a program's ending and the computer being turned off. Data files also allow for more data storage than can fit in RAM.
- A sequential-access file is like an audio cassette tape. Data must be written to and read from the file sequentially.
- A random-access file is like a compact disc. Any record can be accessed directly.
- The first step to using a file is declaring a file stream. Some file streams are for writing data and some are for reading data.
- After a file stream has been declared, the next step is to open the file. Opening a file associates the file stream with a physical data file.
- After data is written or read, the file must be closed.
- Data can be added to a random-access file anywhere in the file by positioning the file pointer to the desired spot.
- You can use more than one file at a time by declaring multiple file pointers.
- You can prompt the user for input and output filenames.

LESSON 8 REVIEW QUESTIONS

TRUE/FALSE

Circle T if the statement is true or F if the statement is false.

T F 1. Storing data in a file involves taking data from RAM and copying it to a disk.

T F 2. Disks store data only until the computer is turned off.

T F 3. Typically, more data can be stored on disk than in RAM.

T F 4. Sequential-access files allow instant access to any data in the file.

T F 5. Random-access files are the most widely used data files.

T F 6. A file must be opened before data can be written to it or read from it.

T F 7. In Java, files are treated as objects.

T F 8. To write to a file, a FileInputStream is used.

T F 9. The FileInputStream class closes automatically when the stream becomes empty.

T F 10. The flush method is used to force a PrintWriter object to empty its buffer.

WRITTEN QUESTIONS

Write a brief answer to the following questions.

1. List three reasons to use data files.
2. What are the two types of data files?
3. List some types of files stored as sequential-access files.
4. Describe an advantage of using random-access data files.
5. Describe a drawback of using random-access data files rather than sequential-access files.
6. What are the two basic Java classes for working with sequential-access files?
7. What is the danger of leaving a file open?
8. What happens if you open a sequential file for output that already exists?
9. Describe a condition that may cause an error when opening a file.
10. What are the two main classes used for sequential-access file input and output?
11. What function is performed by the RandomAccessFile `seek` method?
12. What is required to work with more than one file at a time?
13. What are databases called that use multiple files linked together by certain fields?
14. What is the advantage of having a program that prompts the user for a filename?
15. Write a statement that opens a file for output, assuming the filename is stored in a String object named outfile.

LESSON 8 PROJECTS

PROJECT 8-1

Write a program that asks the user's name, address, city, state, and ZIP code. The program should then save the data to a data file. Save the source code to your student disk as Addrfile.java.

PROJECT 8-2

Modify the program you saved in Step-by-Step 8.4 to convert uppercase letters to lowercase, rather than lowercase to uppercase. Save the modified source code to your student disk as upperlow.java.

PROJECT 8-3

Write a program that copies a text file. The program should remove any blank lines and spaces between words as it writes the new file. Save the Java program to your student disk as Project8_3.java.

PROJECT 8-4

Write a program that prompts the user for the name of a text file, reports the number of characters in the text file, and reports the number of end-of-line characters in the text file. Save the Java program to your student disk as Project 8_4.java.

PROJECT 8-5

Write a program that prompts the user for his or her full name. The program should check the first character of each name to make sure it appears in uppercase, making conversion where necessary. For example, if the user enters *jessica hope baldwin*, the program should output *Jessica Hope Baldwin*. Save the Java program to your student disk as Project8_5.java.

LESSON 9

DEVELOPING AND INHERITING CLASSES

OBJECTIVES

Upon completion of this lesson, you should be able to:

- Organize and create a complete Java class.
- Develop the data and methods for a class.
- Explain the need for private and public class members.
- Derive new classes through inheritance.

Estimated Time: 2 hours

Overview

Up to this point, you have been working with different parts of the Java language. Since Java uses an object-oriented style, you have already been using OOP along the way. In fact, you were introduced to OOP all the way back in Lesson 2, and you have been exposed to the uses and applications of this programming method in almost every lesson since. It is not possible to learn about the pieces of an object-oriented programming language without learning about OOP in parallel.

However, all you have done up to this point is use OOP; you have not developed or created your own classes. As you remember from Lesson 2, OOP is basically about the classes that represent the set of rules for how something works, and objects are the actual things that do the work. When you set up an ice cream stand at the OOP County Fair, you had to have the rules for how to run the store. This is like the class.

When you ran the store using those rules, your ice cream store was said to be an object of the class IceCreamStore. In addition, since the OOP County Fair covers a large area, there is plenty of room for other IceCreamStore objects, so other IceCreamStore objects around the fair are implemented. In object-oriented terminology, they are said to be *instantiated*. One set of rules (the class) will decide what one or more actual things (the objects) will be and what they will do.

In this lesson, much of what you have already seen will be brought together using both the philosophy and the actual code to support your learning of OOP.

Charging the Process

Credit cards have developed from a simple device with minimal services to a financial device that many consider to be a necessity. OOP classes often follow a similar course. A well-conceived idea can begin as a simple class and grow to become a multifeatured part of a program. In this section, we will develop a simple credit card class that will later be extended to provide additional functionality.

A Credit Card as a Class

When the concept of a credit card was invented, the developers decided what a credit card would be and what it would do. Interestingly enough, since OOP tends to follow real-world approaches, creating a class requires you to decide what the object will be and what it will do. Let's consider how we would define what a credit card is and what it does.

A credit card is an object that allows people to borrow money for a short term to purchase products or services, charges them a percentage to use the money, and requires monthly repayment of a percentage of the present balance. Table 9-1 summarizes some of the characteristics of a credit card.

TABLE 9-1

What it is:	It is an object that has an account number. It is an object that has a balance (how much money the customer owes). It is an object that has a credit limit (how much money the customer can borrow). It is an object that has an interest rate to charge the customer for use of the money.
What it does:	It allows the customer to purchase products or services. It maintains a balance for the customer. It charges the customer an interest rate every month. It sends the customer a bill every month.

People today know that credit cards can do much more than what is outlined in Table 9-1, but when they were first invented, they were pretty simple. Like objects in the real world, objects used in programs may evolve. As you will see, there will be plenty of room and opportunity for the credit card class to grow.

By defining what a credit card is and what it does, you have created a set of rules. A set of rules qualifies as the class. No specific credit card has actually been created here, so no objects exist as of right now. An object of this simple credit card class might be a basic oil company credit card.

The Credit Card Class

In Java, defining a class is simple and looks like the code below:

```
class CreditCard
{
  // CreditCard class contents
} // end of class CreditCard
```

The class declaration has the keyword *class*, followed by the name of the class, and then an opening brace, the contents of the class, and a closing brace. The first item to go into the contents of the class is data.

Note

The keyword *class* may be preceded by the keyword *public* to allow other classes to access this in a file or elsewhere.

DEFINING THE DATA

The necessary data has already been defined in the rules above. The code needed to implement the data is shown in Figure 9-1.

Take a quick look at the code. The `accountNumber` variable will be a long type so it can handle multiple-digit account numbers. Next, we will hold the balance, the credit limit, and the interest rate in double variables, as they are the most easily managed in calculations. The one other item to notice is that these variables have all been declared public. This means that other programs and member methods can access this data from outside the class, as you will see shortly.

FIGURE 9-1
The data is to be used by the CreditCard class.

```
class CreditCard
{
  public long accountNumber;      // account number
  public double balance;      // balance
    //  (how much money the customer owes)
  public double creditLimit;      // credit limit
    //  (how much money the customer can borrow)
  public double interestRate;     // interest rate to charge
    // the customer for use of the money

    // remainder of class goes here

}    // end of class CreditCard
```

DEFINING THE METHODS

Now that you have the "what it is" questions answered, you need to tackle the "what it does" problem. This will take a little longer than the data development, because the actions will need to be defined. Notice as the member methods are developed, however, that it is very easy to solve each little problem one at a time rather than trying to write a whole program full of methods at once.

MAKING A PURCHASE

Let's begin by creating the method for making a purchase. Look at the code in Figure 9-2.

FIGURE 9-2
The makePurchase method adds functionality to the CreditCard class.

```
public boolean makePurchase(double purchaseAmount)
{
if((balance + purchaseAmount) < creditLimit)
  {
  balance = balance + purchaseAmount;
  return true;
  }
else
  {
  return false;
  }
}     // end of member makePurchase
```

The method shown in Figure 9-2 first makes sure the `purchaseAmount` plus the balance is not greater than the `creditLimit`. If the purchase does not cause the credit limit to be exceeded, then the purchase is approved and the balance is increased. The method returns a value of true if the purchase is within the limit. If the purchase attempts to go over the limit, then the method returns a false value and the balance is not changed.

ADDING FINANCE CHARGES AND BILLING

Figure 9-3 shows two additional methods that the CreditCard class needs: one to add finance charges to the balance and one to produce a bill for the customer.

FIGURE 9-3
The makeBill method calls the addInterest method.

```
public double addInterest ()
{
balance = balance + (balance * interestRate);
return (balance * interestRate);
}       // end of member addInterest
public void makeBill ()
{
double interest, payment;
interest = addInterest ();
System.out.printIn("Your interest for this month is: $" + interst);
System.out.printIn("Your balance now is: $" + balance);
Payment = .05 * balance;
System.out.printIn("Your payment (due on the 20th) is: $" + payment);
} // end of member makeBill
```

The second of the class rules was that a CreditCard class would maintain the customer's balance. Since the balance is changed by only certain transactions, you will not need a separate method for this action. However, to add interest to the account, the method simply does the calculation and updates the balance. Finally, the `makeBill` method actually implements the `addInterest` method, which both adds interest to the account and returns the interest value back to `makeBill`. Here, `makeBill` is said to be the *calling method*, and the `addInterest` method is to be *called*. These terms go back to the days of "calling" subroutines in other programming languages.

The user of the program calls `makeBill` at the end of the month, and `makeBill` goes off to do its work. But then `makeBill` calls `addInterest`, sending that courier off to its work. Then, `addInterest` adjusts the balance and returns the actual amount of interest that is then stored in the variable `Interest`, and then used by `makeBill`'s printing process. Finally, when `makeBill` is finished, the program action goes back to whatever method called `makeBill`. This is not a difficult process as long as you take the time to follow the program process through its different steps.

CONSTRUCTING OBJECTS

Completing these methods responds to all the requirements of "being" and "acting like" a credit card. However, there is a little problem. Our CreditCard class knows how to do and be all things it is supposed to, but it does not know how to be created. How will it ever know its account number, or its initial balance, or its initial credit limit if it is not given that information up front? Actually, you have already seen and used the answer to this question. In object-oriented programming, we use a *constructor*. As you know from previous use, the constructor gets everything started correctly.

A new credit card needs an initial balance, an initial credit line, an initial interest rate, and an account number. The constructor must set up this information. Below is an example of a constructor.

```
public CreditCard()
{
accountNumber = 0;
balance = 0.0;
creditLimit = 500.0;
interestRate = .12;
}     // end of default constructor
```

THE DEFAULT CONSTRUCTOR

This first constructor is called a *default constructor* because if nothing else is stated, the default is to set everything at the above conditions. As you can see, each of the variables is initialized to some quantity. If they were not initialized, they would still have the "garbage" left from when the same memory location was used before. This construction process must be done. Note two more things about the constructor. First, the constructor must always have the same name as the class itself; this is required. Second, as you may have noticed, the constructor, unlike other methods, does not return any values; it doesn't even return a void. Constructors do not return any values; their only job is to get the new object on its feet.

CONSTRUCTORS THAT INITIALIZE

Now look at the next constructor below, which will also have the name CreditCard. This means there will be two (and later three) constructors with the same name. Having member methods with the same name is called *method overloading*. As you should know by now, you can write a method that will do anything you want it to. The rule is, however, if you overload a method, any or all of the methods should do the same thing. In this case, any methods named CreditCard should initialize, or construct, the class CreditCard.

```
public CreditCard(double newCreditLimit, double newInterestRate)
{
accountNumber = 0;
balance = 0.0;
creditLimit = newCreditLimit;
interestRate = newInterestRate;
}     // end of initializing constructor
```

This constructor could be called an *initializing constructor*, because it will take in information and initialize the class with values other than the defaults. Like the couriers that have been discussed before, this one takes the parameters `newCreditLimit` and `newInterestRate` and uses them to set up the class.

One point to note with this initializer method is that it has two *local* variables. The `newCreditLimit` and `newInterestRate` variables are said to be local in scope. The word *local* means these variables are only "alive" inside this method. They cannot be accessed or used anywhere else or at any time other than when this method is doing its work. The word *scope* is a fancy term that means the program code location where the variable is alive. The two variables mentioned are said to be *in scope* when this method has been called, and *out of scope* at any other time.

Notice that the class data members are said to be in scope during all the time the class itself is "alive." The variable balance, for example, is said to be *global* to the CreditCard class methods, because any of the class methods can use it; but it is still local to the CreditCard class, meaning it will not be "alive" if there are no CreditCard objects instantiated, and it is not accessible to another class, such as your HelloWorld class.

THE COPY CONSTRUCTOR

The third constructor that is shown is called a *copy constructor*. This is a constructor that will take all the information from another object and place it in a newly created object. This is usually used to make a duplicate object when necessary in a program. The copy constructor looks like this:

```
public CreditCard(CreditCard InComingCard)
{
this.accountNumber = InComingCard.accountNumber;
this.balance = InComingCard.balance;
this.creditLimit = InComingCard.creditLimit;
this.interestRate = InComingCard.interestRate;
}      // end of copy constructor
```

The action here is fairly obvious. All of the information from the incoming object, called InComingCard, is transferred to the local object. Next, as you have seen before, the *dot operator* has been used here to identify which data member belongs to which class. Since both the InComingCard object and the local object are of the same class, and both have access to the same kinds of data (but not exactly the same data), the dot operator identifies which data item is being used.

THE this KEYWORD

The next item of discussion is the *this* keyword. However, to explain how *this* is used, the actual code to instantiate the class will need to be shown. Figure 9-4 shows the way all of the constructors would be used, and then the following discussion explains the *this* keyword.

FIGURE 9-4
This program example shows the use of the different constructors.

```
class MyClass
{
  public static void main(String args[])
  {
  // the default constructor
  CreditCard firstCard = new CreditCard();

  // the initializing constructor
  CreditCard secondCard = new CreditCard(2000.0, 0.08);

  // the copy constructor
  CreditCard thirdCard = new CreditCard(secondCard);
  }      // end of main method
}      // end of MyClass
```

In Figure 9-4, you can see what you have seen several times previously in this text. Having gone through class development, you now know what goes on "underground." What looks like a single line, such as the statement below, actually creates a class, initializes any class *member* data (the data local to that class), and sets aside the memory for that class to do its job.

```
// the default constructor
CreditCard firstCard = new CreditCard();
```

The firstCard object has been set up with the default conditions given above. The secondCard object has been set up with the default account number and balance, but the credit limit has been set at $2000 and the interest rate has been set at 8% (this person has a good credit history). Finally, the thirdCard object has been initialized with the secondCard conditions using a copy constructor.

Now look at the transaction between the secondCard and the thirdCard during the copy constructor process. The object actually doing the action is the thirdCard object—*this* is the object that is being constructed and receiving the new information. The object doing the action is thought to be *this* object, and any other objects are just supporting the process. Getting back to the fundamentals, remember that the class is the framework, or the set of rules with which all objects of that class must abide. However, since there can be more than one object of the same class, there are times when a programmer needs to discriminate, literally, between this object and any of the others. The *this* keyword takes care of that business.

FIGURE 9-5
A copy constructor is used to make thirdCard a duplicate of secondCard.

```
// the copy constructor
CreditCard thirdCard = new CreditCard(secondCard);
```

Look again at the code segment copy constructing thirdCard in Figure 9-5. Since both secondCard and thirdCard have access to this member method, the compiler (and the programmer) need to know which side holds which. Again, the *this* keyword takes care of that business.

```
public CreditCard(CreditCard InComingCard)
{
this.accountNumber = InComingCard.accountNumber;
this.balance = InComingCard.balance;

// etc
```

One final note on this issue. Since it is implicitly assumed that the object on the left (in the class method and in the program code using the class) is the *this* object and the one on the right is not, the method code can be written as follows:

```
public CreditCard(CreditCard InComingCard)
{
accountNumber = InComingCard.accountNumber;
balance = InComingCard.balance;
creditLimit = InComingCard.creditLimit;
interestRate = InComingCard.interestRate;
}     // end of copy constructor
```

In this code segment, the *this* keyword is left out entirely; it is implicitly assumed to be there. *Implicit* simply means that even though something is not shown, it is still assumed to exist or act.

FIGURE 9-6
The main component of the CardEx program is shown.

```
public static void main(String args[])
{
// the default constructor
CreditCard FirstCard = new CreditCard();

// the initializing constructor
CreditCard SecondCard = new CreditCard(2000.0, 0.08);

// the copy constructor
CreditCard ThirdCard = new CreditCard (secondCard);

if(FirstCard.makePurchase(750.0))
  {
  System.out.println("Transaction accepted, First Card balance is: "
        + FirstCard.balance);
  }
else
  {
  System.out.println("Transaction not accepted, amount goes over "
        + "First Card's limit");
  }

if(ThirdCard.makePurchase(750.0))
  {
  System.out.println("Transaction accepted, Third Card balance is: "
        + ThirdCard.balance);
  }
else
  {
  System.out.println("Transaction not accepted, amount goes over "
        + "Third Card's limit");
  }

System.out.println("\nFor the First Card:");
FirstCard.makeBill();
System.out.println("\nFor the Second Card:");
SecondCard.makeBill();
System.out.println("\nFor the Third Card:");
ThirdCard.makeBill();
}     // end of method main
```

STEP-BY-STEP 9.1

1. Open CardEx.java from the student data files and save it to your course folder or disk. The main component is in Figure 9-6. Look through the code and make sure you can identify each action. Note that you now have two classes, the CreditCard class and the CardEx class.

2. Compile the file and then run the CardEx program. Look at the responses. Notice how the `makePurchase` transaction is tested for success. If the person does not have a high enough credit limit, the transaction is denied.

3. Try adding other transactions for each of the CreditCard objects. Always make sure your `makeBill` and output methods stay at the bottom, so you can see how the new transactions affect the behavior of the CreditCard object.

4. Leave the file open for the next exercise.

Completing the Class

In the last section, we created a simple credit card class. There are a couple of problems, however, that make the credit card class incomplete. In this section, you will address these problems and complete the basic credit card class.

Paying the Bills

To be complete, the credit card class needs a method that accepts money into the credit card account, reduces the debt, and returns the new balance. Figure 9-7 shows two possible ways such a method could be written.

FIGURE 9-7
One of these two forms of the payBill method is a necessary addition to the CreditCard class.

```
Option 1:

public double payBill(double payment)
{
balance = balance - payment;
return balance;
}     // end of method payBill

Option 2:

public double payBill(double payment)
{
return (balance -= payment);
}     // end of method payBill
```

STEP-BY-STEP 9.2

1. Add one of the methods in Figure 9-7 to the CreditCard class. Save the source file to your student disk or folder as CardEx2.java, and modify the class name to CardEx2. Modify the CardEx2 class so that one of the cards receives a payment before the bills are processed.

2. Save the source code, compile, and run the CardEx2 program again.

3. Notice that since the method returns the balance, that amount can be output in the main with a message such as "Thank you, your new balance is: $xx.xx," because you have access to that data.

4. Leave the source code open for the next exercise.

Using the static Keyword

As you should know at this point, every time you instantiate a new object, you create a brand new set of data variables with the object. In other words, in the CreditCard class, for all three CreditCard objects you instantiated, each one has four data variables. However, Java has the ability, using the *static* keyword, to allow just one variable to be instantiated and hold just one piece of data for all the objects.

For example, suppose all credit cards were to have the same interest rate. To accomplish that, you could use the *static* keyword to cause all CreditCard objects to share the same `interestRate` variable, as shown below.

```
public static double interestRate;
```

Let's use the *static* keyword to fix another small problem with the credit card class. You may have noticed that there is no mechanism for assigning a unique account number to each credit card. We can add a static data member to the CreditCard class that holds the most recently assigned account number. Each time a new credit card is instantiated, the last account number used can be incremented to become the account number for the new credit card.

The code below shows the new declarations with the static variable `NewAccountNumber` declared and initialized to zero.

```
public static long NewAccountNumber = 0;
public long accountNumber;
public double balance;
public double creditLimit;
public double interestRate;
```

Now, the constructors will have to be changed as well so that they can place an appropriate (and different) account number in each new object. The following code shows how this is done.

```
public CreditCard()
{
accountNumber = NewAccountNumber;
NewAccountNumber++;       // increase account number
balance = 0.0;      // for next use

// etc
```

By making the change above in all of the constructors, it would seem that the program should work well; and it does. But there is still another refinement that can be made.

STEP-BY-STEP 9.3

1. In the CardEx2 program, add the static data element `NewAccountNumber` to the CreditCard class.

```
public static long NewAccountNumber
   = 0;
```

2. Change the constructors as shown in the text to have them provide a new account number to each new object. Do not change the copy constructor.

3. Leave the source code open for the next exercise.

Data Hiding and Encapsulation

As you can see, and as you have noted when you worked with the code in Step-by-Step 9.1, any of the data members can be brought up, used, and changed. However, a much smarter design would require that all accesses and changes to the data in your object be handled through special functions that are created to safely access and change the data in the object.

One of the major advantages to object-oriented programming is the ability to control access to the data in the object. These features of OOP are known as *data hiding* and *encapsulation*. Data hiding, just as it sounds, is a way to keep programmers from accessing some variables or accidentally accessing others. Encapsulation is maintaining data in a format that allows data to be accessed and modified only by methods designed to handle those operations.

THE private KEYWORD

To hide the data in an object, the *private* keyword is used, as shown in the code below. Trying to access any of these private variables from your main method will result in an error.

```
private static long NewAccountNumber = 0;
private long accountNumber;
private double balance;
private double creditLimit;
private double interestRate;
```

Accessors

Because data in an object does have to be accessed from outside the object, you will need to generate a set of methods called *accessors*. The method below is an example of an accessor.

```
public double returnBalance()
{
return balance;
}
```

The method above could be called a pure accessor. It simply returns the balance to the calling method. In the case of the balance, it should never be changed except as part of a transaction. The accessor function controls how the data is accessed, and no modifications can be made through this function. An accessor function might do more than simply return a value. For example, it might calculate a value based on data in the object.

An accessor fits into the object-oriented philosophy that says we don't look inside the object and get the data we need. Instead, we ask the object (using an accessor) to provide us with the information for which we are looking. We don't care what the object does internally to come up with the data. We just want the data.

Modifiers

Because there are appropriate times to change items such as the credit limit, accessing data in an object is not always enough. You may need to modify the data in an object. A type of method called a *modifier* (sometimes called a *mutator*) is used to make changes to data inside an object.

Remember, we have discussed communicating with objects in terms of sending messages. A modifier handles messages that request a change be made to data inside an object. Rather than going to the data stored in the object and changing it, we send a message to the object asking it to change itself.

The method below is a modifier. It accepts a new credit limit and sets the credit limit inside the object to the new credit limit. As an added convenience, the method returns the new credit limit to the calling method.

```
public double setCreditLimit(double newCreditLimit)
{
if(newCreditLimit > 0)
  creditLimit = newCreditLimit;
return creditLimit;
}
```

Notice that the credit limit will not be changed unless the new credit limit is more than zero. Because a credit limit cannot be negative, the modifier protects the object by rejecting any requests to set the credit limit to a negative value.

STEP-BY-STEP 9.4

1. Add an accessor method to the CreditCard class that returns the credit card's balance to the program on your screen.

```
public double returnBalance()
{
return balance;
}
```

2. Add an accessor method that returns the credit card's account number.

3. Add a modifier from Code List 9.1 that sets the credit limit and returns the new credit limit.

4. Add a modifier that sets the interest rate and returns the new interest rate. Have the modifier check to make sure the new interest rate is positive.

5. Save the program, compile, and test the new methods.

6. Close all open source code files.

CODE LIST 9-1

```
public double setCreditLimit(double newCreditLimit)
{
if(newCreditLimit > 0)
  creditLimit = newCreditLimit;
return creditLimit;
}
```

Children of Java: Inheritance

Object-oriented programming has broken down many of the barriers to developing high-quality, large-scale, robust programs. As stated earlier in the book, OOP is more of a style or philosophy of program development than it is a language. You have seen this since the programs you have written throughout the unit have sometimes been procedural (step-by-step) and sometimes object-oriented.

One of the benefits of OOP has been the development of classes and then objects from those classes. A class that has been developed and then debugged and extensively tested can be trusted to work as well as it possibly can in every foreseeable environment. This is called *robust* code. Robust code should handle not only all the work it is supposed to do, but also recover from unusual conditions such as the wrong data entered, necessary files missing, or a myriad of other unusual events.

The downside of this is that if the class does not do exactly what another programmer needs it to do, then this programmer must either rewrite the class or develop a new one. In either case, the programmer is back in the developing, debugging, and testing stage all over again. All of the work applied to the previously developed class may be lost as new programming code adds opportunity for bugs to creep back into the program. The object-oriented solution to this is called *inheritance*.

Once class code has been developed and tested, it should not be changed or modified again. However, in OOP, programmers are allowed to take the previously developed classes and "extend" them to do the unique job on which the programmer is working. This extending process is called inheriting, and it is a very powerful tool for creating powerful and robust programs quickly. For example, Java has a class that provides a graphical user interface. A programmer simply extends a Java window to hold whatever the programmer wants to put in it. All the code and development (and debugging) of writing a nice-looking window-like program is done. You only extend it to accomplish your tasks.

In Java, the original class is called the Object class. From this class, there are a multitude of inherited classes. For example, the OutputStream class is inherited from Object; then the FilterOutputStream class is inherited from OutputStream; and then DataOutputStream, a class we used in the previous lesson, is inherited or derived from OutputStream. Each new class gets to use all the things the other classes before it bring with them. The result is that programs look better, work better, and go together faster.

Having developed a basic credit card class, you might now be asked to develop a credit card system for an automobile gas company, such as GoFast Gas. The program in Figure 9-8 shows how a gas credit card class might be used.

FIGURE 9-8
The class used in this program (GasCoCard) inherits properties from the CreditCard class.

```
class GasCardEx
{
  public static void main(String args[])
  {
  int gasStops;
GasCoCard MyGasCard = new GasCoCard(2000, 0.10);
  for(gasStops = 0; gasStops < 4; gasStops++)
    {
    MyGasCard.buyGas(30.0);
    }     // end of for loop

  System.out.println("\nFor the Gas Card:");
  MyGasCard.makeBill();
  }     // end of method main
}     // end of class GasCardEx
```

Now that we have a simple program that shows how the gas card will be used, we can get started on the inheritance process. As you can see from the code above, the new class will be called GasCoCard, but it will inherit methods and attributes from the CreditCard class using the *extends* keyword.

```
class GasCoCard extends CreditCard
{

}     //  end of class GasCoCard
```

Before we create the new GasCoCard class, we need to know its specifications. This new GasCoCard starts out life a little different from a credit card. The specifications are as follows:

- All clients start with a $2,000 credit limit and 10% interest rate.
- All clients start with 5 bonus points for signing up on the credit card.
- Bonus points are given every time a client makes a purchase, and clients who purchase a minumum amount or get a certain number of bonus points get a discount on their credit card bill.

With these specifications in mind, the following code will be added inside the GasCoCard brackets:

```
private int gasPoints;

public GasCoCard(double credit, double interest)
{
super(credit, interest);
gasPoints = 5;
}     // end of initializing constructor
```

Notice that the value `gasPoints` is declared as a private integer, and then it is initialized to 5 when the GasCoCard is constructed. In addition, note the method that appears to be called *super*. By itself, super is a Java keyword that means "the name of my parent class." With the parentheses immediately beside it, it acts like one of your parent class constructors; in this case it is the initializing constructor. The compiler knows that because it has two type double parameters.

What happens is that the parent class constructor is called, which then constructs everything about the basic credit card. Then the only thing new to initialize is to give the client 5 bonus gasPoints, and you are done. Thanks to inheritance, you only have to write code that changes or extends the parent code.

Next, the following member method will be added to the code under the constructor:

```
public boolean buyGas(double gasPrice)
{
if(makePurchase(gasPrice) == true)
  {
  System.out.println("Gas purchase: " + gasPrice);
  gasPoints++;
  return true;
  }
else
  {
  return false;
  }
}      // end of method buyGas
```

Again, since all you have to do is extend the previously written code, you use the `makePurchase` method from the parent, and then add the additional code. Here, you print to the screen that a gas purchase has been made, and then you give your client another gasPoint. This assumes that the client had enough credit to do this. Remember that the `makePurchase` method will return false if the client is over the credit limit.

There are two notes to make here. First, the `makePurchase` method could have been written `super.makePurchase` to identify it as the parent method. You might do that (as we will in a moment) if there was a possibility that the compiler was unclear on which method to call. In this case, since it is clear which method is being called, the *super* keyword is not necessary. It is said to be implicit.

Next, as you should remember from earlier lessons, the code could have been written as shown below, instead of having the == `true`.

```
if(makePurchase(gasPrice))
```

Since `makePurchase` returns a Boolean, it "looks like" a Boolean (true or false) and would work just fine by itself. The code is written the way you see it to make sure you understand the process.

The next step is to add the following code under the `buyGas` method.

```
public void giveCredit()
{
double presentBalance, bonusCredit = 0;

presentBalance = returnBalance();
if(presentBalance > 100)
  {
    if(gasPoints > 10)
      {
      bonusCredit = presentBalance * .04;
      }
    else
      {
      bonusCredit = presentBalance * .02;
      }
```

```
            System.out.println("Bonus Credit Given: " + bonusCredit);
            payBill(bonusCredit);
        }
    }       // end of method giveCredit
```

As you can see, this method gives the customer a discount if he or she buys quite a bit of fuel. There are two benefits: If the customer buys more than $100 worth of gas in a month, she gets at least a 2 percent discount; and if she gets more than 10 gasPoints, she gets 2 percent more, for a total of 4 percent discount. Go back up to the top of the code and look at the transactions (the buyGas activities). From the code, see if you can figure out what kind of discount she will get.

The last step is to add the following method:

```
    public void makeBill()
    {
    giveCredit();
    super.makeBill();
    }       // end of makeBill
```

This is obviously a simple method, but you notice it has the same name as the parent method. Writing a method in a child class that has the same name as a method in the parent class is called *overriding* the parent method. This is acceptable if the child method does basically the same thing as the parent method with whatever modifications are added.

Notice the *super* keyword again here. In this case, you cannot be assured that the compiler will know the difference between the child method and the parent method. In fact, the compiler would probably call the child `makeBill` method, which would call itself in a repeated process called *recursion*. While recursion can be a good thing in some cases, it would be a bad thing here because there would be nothing to stop the self-calling process. For that reason, the word super must be placed with the dot operator in front of the parent method `makeBill`. As you can see, the `giveCredit` method is called first to modify the balance as appropriate, then the super method `makeBill` is called. The GasCoCard class has now been completely developed.

STEP-BY-STEP 9.5

1. Open the CreditCard.java file from the student data files, save it to your student disk or folder, and compile it. Open the CardEx3.java file from the student data files, save it to your course disk or folder, and compile it. The CreditCard.java file contains the source code for the CreditCard class. The CardEx3.java file contains the source code for the GasCoCard class that was constructed in this section and a class named CardEx3, which uses the GasCoCard class.

2. Run the CardEx3.class program.

3. Close all open files.

Accomplishing the tasks in this lesson makes you much more capable of developing the real classes and programs of which Java is capable. As mentioned before, you are not limited to inheriting and extending your own code; you have dozens of classes provided by the Java language, of which most are inheritable. From here forward, you can find yourself extending classes that will make your own programs effective and impressive.

Extra for Experts

Java also has the ability to develop *packages*. Packages are groups of classes that have been placed in a separate directory for access by the compiler. When you use the import keyword, you are reaching into some packages that Java has developed. It is not particularly difficult to develop packages, but it is also not necessary for the scope of this text. If you find yourself building large enough groups of classes that should be organized in certain ways, look in the documentation of your software on how to develop a package. You will find the process fairly simple.

Summary

In this lesson, you learned:

- All Java programs are encapsulated in classes, and it is common to use more than one class when writing larger programs.
- The object-oriented method of programming requires that you analyze what an item should be and what it should do. From there, the class development is a matter of following these specifications.
- All Java programs implement constructors. If you do not write one, the compiler will generate a simple "do-nothing" or default constructor. However, you should make sure to initialize all the necessary and appropriate data in the constructor. You may do this with default constructors, initializing constructors, and/or copy constructors.
- Method overloading is a way to let programmers develop more than one method that does basically the same thing, but takes different parameters in order to change the action slightly.
- The *this* keyword identifies the object taking the action. The dot operator shows the object to which each member method or member data belongs.
- Java allows private data members to "hide" or encapsulate data that may be harmed by inappropriate use in the main method.
- Accessors are methods that return data from an object to a calling method.
- Java modifiers or mutators are methods that actually change data.
- Most classes in Java can be inherited. This means that the class data and methods can be used and then extended to make a more unique program. The *super* keyword is the way that Java classes access their parents' methods or data.

LESSON 9 REVIEW QUESTIONS

TRUE/FALSE

Circle T if the statement is true or F if the statement is false.

T F 1. Objects are instantiated from classes.

T F 2. The *object* keyword is used when creating a new class.

T F 3. Methods perform the "what it does" properties of an object.

T F 4. Default constructors require at least one argument.

T F 5. A copy constructor is used when copying an object of the same type.

T F 6. A variable defined as static creates a copy of the variable for all objects.

T F 7. Data hiding prevents programmers from accessing some variables.

T F 8. Data in an object can be accessed from outside the object by means of an accessor method.

T F 9. Data defined in an object cannot be modified.

WRITTEN QUESTIONS

Write a brief answer to the following questions.

1. When developing a new class, what two questions should you ask?
2. Write a simple class declaration for a class named MyClass.
3. What is a constructor?
4. What is a global variable?
5. Data available only inside a particular method is called what?
6. What is the keyword that creates a single copy of a variable that can be shared by all objects in the class?
7. What is data encapsulation?
8. What is a modifier method used for?
9. What is the term for program code that should do everything it is supposed to do but can also recover from unexpected conditions or events?
10. What is inheritance?
11. What does the keyword *super* stand for?
12. What does it mean to override a class?
13. What is a Java package?

LESSON 9 PROJECTS

PROJECT 9-1

Construct a simple class and save the source to your student disk or folder as Project9_1.java. This class should have a variable to store the radius of a circle and methods to return the radius and area of the circle. Try to use a static variable to hold the value of pi, so that all the instances of the Circle class use the same value. Then, build a Cylinder class that inherits the properties of the Circle class. Make methods for the Cylinder class that return the height, volume, and surface area of the cylinder.

PROJECT 9-2

In Lesson 2 we began discussing the OOP County Fair. Design a base class that all the attractions in the park can inherit properties from and save it to your student disk as Project9_2.java. This class should include the number of operators required to run the attraction, the number of people who can use or ride the attraction, and the minimum height requirement for the attraction. Add other properties that you think are needed.

LESSON 10

ARRAYS AND VECTORS

OBJECTIVES

Upon completion of this lesson, you should be able to:

- Discuss the concept of arrays and why they are needed.
- Use the basic arrays of primitive data types.
- Use the Java Vector class to manage a set of organized objects.

Estimated Time: 2 hours

Overview

By now, you are comfortable with the concept of storing data in a computer program. You have already had the opportunity to use variables and, in many cases, have even invented and named some variables of your own. You now know how easy it is to put a variable to work. If, for example, you need a variable to hold a person's age, you understand that an integral number is required and that you can create an integer called personsAge.

You may, however, be aware of a limitation to using variables as only standalone values. Suppose you are writing a program to track grades. One of the specifications of this program is that it has to hold 45 homework grades, 15 quiz grades, and 5 major exam grades. Creating and naming individual variables for each of these required pieces of data is obviously inconvenient. Writing code to use those variables is even more of a pain.

In this lesson, you will learn about Java features that allow you to store data in collections of variables of the same type, called *arrays*. Arrays allow programmers to work with lists of data using one name and a numerical subscript that indicates which item in the list to reference. You will also learn about *vectors*. Vectors are arrays of objects that provide programmers with flexible storage of almost any kind of data.

Introduction to Arrays

Consider the grade example given above. If storing collections or lists of data required declaring each variable independently, code like that shown below would only be the beginning of the problems.

```
int HomeWorkGrade1, HomeWorkGrade2, HomeWorkGrade3 . . .;
float QuizGrade1, QuizGrade2 . . .;
float MajorExamGrade1, MajorExamGrade2 . . .;
```

Not only would your hands be sore from typing before your program had all the variables declared, but imagine all the code that would be needed to use these variables! You would be thinking to yourself, "There has to be a better way to do this!" And, of course, you are right. In this section, you will learn how to use basic Java arrays.

Arrays in Real Life

If you stop by your local hardware store, you will see different kinds of screws organized in little cups, called bins. The "array" of bins will be arranged from top to bottom and left to right to make the screws easy to find. You might discover that each row holds a different type of screw (sheet metal, wood, etc.), and that smaller screws are on the left, while larger ones are on the right.

Suppose you need to buy screws to fix your back door. You know that you need wood screws, and you know that they should probably be about 1 ¼ inches long. Rather than begin with the first bin and search each one, you find the row with wood screws and begin searching about halfway across the row. A similar, logical method of storage can be developed in computers through arrays.

Because arrays are common in real life, they are often a required part of a computer program. In the grade record program discussed earlier, you need a row of "bins" to hold the homework grades, another to hold the quiz grades, and so on.

Using Java Arrays

For your first introduction to Java arrays, let's stick with the concept of bins. The statement below declares 50 floating point variables in an array named `myBins`.

```
float [] myBins = new float[50];
```

Let's consider what is happening in the statement above. The first word tells the compiler that the object being created is of type float. Between the *float* keyword and the variable name (`myBins`) is a set of square brackets, indicating that `myBins` is going to be an array of objects. All of that taken together tells the compiler that `myBins` is going to be an object of type float.

Next, the statement instructs the computer to make space for the `myBins` object using the new operator. The new operator allocates space for 50 elements.

Extra for Experts

Java allows arrays to be declared in two ways. The first way was shown above. The other method of declaring arrays corresponds with other languages such as C++.

```
float myBins[]=new float[50];
```

ACCESSING ELEMENTS OF THE ARRAY

Accessing elements on an array is actually very straightforward. The name of the array is used in conjunction with a number, called a *subscript*. Java arrays are accessed beginning with the number zero (0). This is often hard for beginning programmers to get used to. For example, a ten-element array is accessed using the values 0 through 9. The statement below will initialize the first element of the `myBins` array with the number 3.6.

```
MyBins[0] = 3.6;
```

The code below could be used to prompt the user for 45 homework grades, storing each response in the array. Notice that the array stores the values using subscripts 0 through 44.

```
for(i = 0; i < 45; i++)
{
  System.out.println("Please enter homework grade number " + (i+1) + ": ");
  myBins[i] = toFloat(GetConsoleString());
}
```

To output the 45 homework grades, a loop like the one below could be used.

```
int i = 0;

while(i < 45)
{
  System.out.println("Homework item number " + (i+1) + " is: " + my Bins[i]);
  i++;
}
```

UNDERSTANDING SUBSCRIPTS

It is at this point that many people start to ask, "Why does Java use subscripts beginning at zero?" Believe it or not, there is a reason. The subscript (also known as the *index*) is actually an offset from the original element. For example, the name `myBins` points to the first element of the array. The second element, however, is offset from the beginning by one space.

Suppose you had a 20-mile stretch of road and you wanted to place a trash barrel at the beginning of each mile. The first barrel would be at the zero-mile marker, the second at the one-mile marker, etc. The last barrel would be placed at the 19-mile marker, because the 19-mile marker is the beginning of the 20th mile. The same concept applies to arrays. Think of the subscript of the array as a distance that the element is offset from the beginning.

Note

In almost all cases, your last element will have a subscript one less than the real total. For example, in an array of five elements, your last subscript will be four. If you do try to use five as a subscript, you are said to be out of the array bounds. Some languages do not handle this very well and may cause problems by overwriting the wrong areas of memory (where your program code resides, for example). Java keeps a close watch on subscripts, and if a program does attempt to use incorrect subscripts, Java generates an ArrayIndexOutOfBoundsException and shuts down the program. This goes along with the general Java approach, which is to create programs that do not harm the computers on which they are running.

STEP-BY-STEP 10.1

1. Open the source file HighTemp.java from the student data files. The main method is shown in Figure 10-1. Copy the `GetConsoleString` and the `toFloat` methods from a previous program and insert them into the HighTemp.java program. Save HighTemp.java to your student disk or folder.

2. Compile and run the program. Test the program by providing five or more temperatures as input.

3. Run the program again. When prompted for the number of days for which you have data, enter a value less than 1 or greater than 31. The program should prompt you to enter a valid value. Enter a valid value and complete the session with the program.

4. Close the source code file.

FIGURE 10-1
This program uses an array of integers to store high temperatures for a series of days.

```
import java.io.IOException;
class HighTemp
{
  public static void main(String args[])
  {
  int ARRAYSIZE = 32;           // array size value
  int numValues;                // number of days to enter values
  int index;                    // index for loop counter and arrays
  float averageHigh;            // calculate average high temperature
  int total = 0;   // total temps before averaging

  int [] dailyTemp = new int[ARRAYSIZE];      // the temperature array

  // Use a do . . while loop to get valid input of the number of days
  do
    {
    System.out.println("Enter the number of data items to be input:");
    numValues = Integer.parseInt(GetConsoleString());
    if((numValues < 1) || (numValues >= ARRAYSIZE))
      {
      System.out.println("Please enter a number between 1 and "
        + (ARRAYSIZE - 1));
      }
    }     // end of do while loop
  while((numValues < 1) || !(numValues < ARRAYSIZE));

  // The following loop gets the high temperature from the user for as
  // many days as the user specified in numValues. The subscript 0 is
  // not used so that the subscript will correspond with the day number.
  for(index = 1; index <= numValues; index++)
```

FIGURE 10-1 (continued)

```
        {
        System.out.println("Please enter the high temperature for day "
            + index);
        dailyTemp[index] = Integer.parseInt(GetConsoleString());
        }     // end of for loop

      // Print the values from the array to the screen
      System.out.println("The array contains high temperatures for "
            + numValues + " days.");
      System.out.println("The values are as follows:");
      for(index = 1; index <= numValues; index++)
        {
        System.out.println("Day " + index + ": " + dailyTemp[index]);
        total = total + dailyTemp[ index ];
        }     // end of for loop

      // Calculate the average by dividing the total by the numValues
      // and assigning to averageHigh
      averageHigh = (float) total / (float) numValues;

      // Print the results to the screen
      System.out.println("The average high temperature during the");
      System.out.println("      " + numValues + "-day period was "
            + averageHigh + " degrees");
      }     // end of main method

      public static String GetConsoleString()
      {
      // code for GetConsoleString
      }     // end of method GetConsoleString

      public static float toFloat(String inString)
      {
      // code for toFloat
      }     // end of toFloat method

  }     // end of class HighTemp
```

Multidimensional Arrays

Now that you have used one-dimensional arrays, you can see how easy it is to store and access a group of data figures. This is much like dropping each number (or object) into a bin and then counting which bin it is in. You are just holding a list of data in an organized fashion. However, sometimes it might be better to organize your data in a different way. Take a look at the hardware store bins again. If we were to have just one long row of bins of screws, we could certainly find the screws we need if we can walk far enough down the rows.

Rather than make one long row, however, the hardware folks chose to make several rows one on top of the other. This is called a *two-dimensional array* in computer science. Now you can go down each row to get to the kinds of screws you want, and you can go from left to right (by columns) to get the size of the screw you want. This is much easier and more manageable as long as all the data is of the same type. Note that it is possible to hold different kinds of data in some Java array conditions. Basic arrays—if they are declared as type float—can contain only type float.

You should also note that you could have whole sets of rows and columns of bins going back in a direction away from you so as to have depth. This would be a three-dimensional array. Any array having more than just one dimension is called a *multidimensional array*. There are uses for two- and three-dimensional arrays. However, it can get very confusing for the programmers reading your code if the arrays have too many dimensions. Make sure you really need the number of dimensions you are planning to develop, and make sure your indices (indexes) are properly self-documented to make your intentions clear to others who will read your code.

Two-dimensional arrays are also commonly referred to as tables. A table of data might look much like Figure 10-2, which shows a table of individual shipping prices based on weight and distance ("Shipping Zones"). A person can weigh a package and locate the correct row, and then he or she can identify the Shipping Zone and identify the proper column. As an example, a package weighing 19 pounds and traveling to Shipping Zone 6 would cost $7.39. The computer would find the data as follows:

```
shippingPrice = shippingRate[3][5];     // this would place the value of the
  // fourth row and the sixth column in the
  // output variable
```

FIGURE 10-2
The rates in this table are a good candidate for a two-dimensional array.

Shipping Rates

Weight (up to)	Shipping Zones 1	2	3	4	5	6	7	8
5 lbs.	2.65	2.75	2.87	3.06	2.65	3.35	4.73	6.13
10 lbs.	3.05	3.18	3.35	3.84	4.60	5.58	7.68	9.33
15 lbs.	3.25	3.40	3.63	4.24	5.08	6.13	8.46	10.38
20 lbs.	4.10	4.28	4.59	5.34	6.20	7.39	9.93	11.85
25 lbs.	4.65	4.95	5.35	6.23	7.25	8.66	11.55	13.58
30 lbs.	5.25	5.49	5.99	6.90	8.03	9.69	12.69	15.49

Remember that your subscripts are going to be one less than the location you are looking for. The table process is easy for people to use, but it is even easier for a computer to look up; and as the table gets larger, it becomes much easier for the computer to look up than for a human to do so. In Figure 10-3, look at the program segment showing a simple lookup process for this Shipping Rate table.

FIGURE 10-3
This code segment looks up shipping costs in a two-dimensional array.

```
public static void main(String args[])
  {
  double shipRate[ ] [ ] = {
  { 2.65, 2.75, 2.87, 3.06, 2.65, 3.35, 4.73, 6.13 },
  { 3.05, 3.18, 3.35, 3.84, 4.60, 5.58, 7.68, 9.33 },
  { 3.25, 3.40, 3.63, 4.24, 5.08, 6.13, 8.46, 10.38 },
  { 4.10, 4.28, 4.59, 5.34, 6.20, 7.39, 9.93, 11.85 },
  { 4.65, 4.95, 5.35, 6.23, 7.25, 8.66, 11.55, 13.58 },
  { 5.25, 5.49, 5.99, 6.90, 8.03, 9.69, 12.69, 15.49 } };

  float weight; // weight of package
  int weightCategory;    // weight category in table
  int zone;   // zone of package destination

  weight = getPackageWeight();

  zone = getPackageZone();

  weightCategory = (int) (weight / 5);

  System.out.println("Shipping price is: "
        + shipRate[ weightCategory ] [ zone ]);
  }     // end of main method
```

While this is a fairly simple program, you can see the power of a *lookup* table such as this one when, out of several million automobiles registered in a state, a law enforcement official needs to find out who owns the red car parked on the side of the highway. You can also see how the shipping agency can have several hundred combinations of weights and zones; and if you think about it, this might be a job for a three-dimensional array that also holds information on how fast the customer wants some package delivered. If `deliveryMethod` were coded as 0 = normal, 1 = two-day air, and 2 = overnight, then your code segment might look like:

```
shippingPrice = shipRate[deliveryMethod][weightCategory][zone];
```

Remember that more than two dimensions can be hard to understand, but if you self-document your variables, this is very usable.

Take one more look at the code in Figure 10-3. While you have seen most of this code before, there is a little change when ShipRate is first initialized. Normally, you have to provide the words *new* and *float* to tell the compiler how much room to set aside in the computer. However, since you are giving the compiler the information up front, it can figure out how much memory is needed and therefore does not need the extra keywords.

STEP-BY-STEP 10.2

1. Open the source for ShipRate.java from the student data files. Save the program to your student disk or folder as ShipRate.java.

2. Study the source code to see how the program is divided into segments using supporting methods to make the main method process clearer. Notice the error checking performed in the methods that get the values from the user.

3. Compile and run the program. Give the program a weight of 35 pounds or greater. Then enter a valid weight.

4. Give the program a zone number that is outside of the allowable range of 0 to 7. Then enter a valid zone number.

5. Check the shipping cost provided by the program against the table in Figure 10-2 to make sure the program provided the output you expected.

6. Now change the zone input method so that it allows numbers higher than 7 to be input. Run the program and enter a larger number. What happens? What kind of exception did Java generate?

7. Close the source file.

Using Vectors to Store Objects

As mentioned earlier, the Vector class can hold virtually any kind of computer data, much like the little bins can hold different kinds of hardware. The difference is that a Vector class can change its own size and provide other information about itself while you are using it. For example, if you have a *capacity* of 15 bins, and you are about to add the 16th item, the program will double the memory quantity to 30 bins and accept the new data. A Vector can self-adjust; it can provide other information, such as returning the first item or the last item; and it can report on its capacity (how many bins are presently set aside) or its size (how many items are in the bins at present)—just to name a few of its abilities. This removes all the burden of managing the data storage from the programmer, who can concentrate on getting the data management job done.

A good way to demonstrate the Vector class would be to show how the class manages a class that has already been developed. The credit card class that was developed in Lesson 9 will be used, but a new data member will be added so that the class can contain a customer name. A few more changes will be made to the class as well, some of which will be demonstrated in the code. For now, look at the format used for implementing a new Vector class.

```
Vector CCVector = new Vector(2, 2);
```

The CCVector (credit card vector) object is instantiated using one of three possible constructors. This constructor takes two parameters: a size parameter and a size incrementing parameter. The size parameter decides how many bins to set aside initially; the size incrementing parameter decides how many bins to add whenever more space is needed. The way this is set up, you start with two bins, and every time you need more space, the program adds two more bins to the end of your Vector. If you had implemented a constructor "Vector(3, 5)", you would have started with three bins, and each memory increment would add five more bins.

One of the other constructors, a default constructor, simply opens an empty Vector, and the other constructor can pass a single parameter telling the Vector how many bins to start with. Both these constructors will cause the available capacity to double each time more memory is needed. The practice of doubling memory for data management is fairly standard, but in some programs this practice consumes too much memory. For that reason, Java offers the option to decide how many bins can be added with each capacity increase, which we will use for this example.

To add a new item, or *element*, to the Vector, you use the following code. It is simple and intuitive enough to be clear. It is required that a Vector accept an Object type to be added, so we will be adding a CreditCard object. We could have set it up this way:

```
// ansString gets card holder name from user in the variable "ansString"
CreditCard newCard = new CreditCard(ansString, 2000, 0.09);
CCVector.addElement( newCard );
```

This is perfectly legal and proper, but unnecessary. Java allows you to create one class inside the parameter of a method, like the following:

```
CCVector.addElement(new CreditCard(ansString, 2000, 0.09));
```

This process saves computer time and memory resources to make a new object that is just passed to another method and then discarded. Note at this point that the CreditCard class constructor has been slightly modified to take in a name, the credit limit, and the interest rate.

Figure 10-4 shows the data entry part of the VectorClass program, and there are a few things to point out. The user is asked for the cardholder name, and then the new CreditCard Object is placed in the Vector by way of the `addElement` method. Having done this, some information is presented back to the user about the size and the capacity of the Vector. This will be of value when you run the program. Note also the do while loop operation asks the user if he wants to add any more data. The `GetConsoleString` gets the character, which is just one char. This char is compared to both upper- and lower-case N to see if the program should end. The while evaluation process reads as follows: "If the returned char is not equal to little n AND it is not equal to capital N, THEN continue running the program."

FIGURE 10-4
The data input segment of the VectorClass program is shown.

```
// Enter the data
do
  {
  System.out.print("Please enter name of client: ");
  ansString = GetConsoleString();
  CCVector.addElement(new CreditCard(ansString, 2000, 0.09));
  System.out.println("New Cardholder is: " + ansString);
  System.out.println("Number Items in Vector: " + CCVector.size());
  System.out.println("Present Capacity: " + CCVector.capacity());
  System.out.println("\nWould you like to continue? (y / n): ");
  ansString = GetConsoleString();
  System.out.println("");
  }
while((ansString.charAt(0) != 'n') && (ansString.charAt(0) != 'N'));
```

The next process to be evaluated is the program's output, shown in Figure 10-5, which basically dumps the newly acquired data to the screen. It is easy enough to run a for loop from 0 (the lowest Vector index) to one less than the size of the Vector, a value returned by `CCVector.size()`. A CreditCard Object, which was declared prior, is used to capture a CreditCard Object from the `elementAt` member function.

FIGURE 10-5
This is the output process of the VectorClass program.

```
for(index = 0; index < CCVector.size(); index++)
  {
  CreditCardItem = (CreditCard) CCVector.elementAt(index);
  System.out.println("Item No " + (index + 1) + " name: " +
  CreditCardItem.clientName);
  System.out.println("Account Number: " +
  CreditCardItem.accountNumber);
  NumString = doubleToString(CreditCardItem.creditLimit, 6, 2);
  System.out.println("  Credit Limit: $" + NumString + "\n");
  }     // end of for loop

  ansString = GetConsoleString();
```

Remember that Vectors can only hold Objects, so they do not know what to return unless you inform them by way of casting the returning data. This must always be done. It should be pointed out that you could put a CreditCard Object in the array (using the `addElement` method), and then you could put a String Object in right behind it. In fact, a Vector, unlike an array, can hold heterogeneous (different) types of Objects in the same data container. The downside is that you have to take the different Objects out in exactly the same order you put them in, or your output will be garbage. Unless there is a well-developed management system for getting the order right in your program, this is a power of Java that might be better left alone.

The only other new part of the code in Figure 10-5 is the use of another utility method, called `doubleToString`. This method converts double numbers to a formatted String quantity so that your output will look nicer. The parameters used by the method are the double number itself, the width of the whole number including the decimal, and then the number of digits on the right of the decimal point. The method for this code is simply added inside the class VectorClass braces along with the methods `GetConsoleString` and `toFloat`. `DoubleToString` returns a formatted double number preceded by blank spaces if the width parameter is larger than the number of digits with the decimal point.

Although the code for this utility method will not be discussed in the text, it will be given as a project at the end of the lesson. However, a Java constant, called a final value, is used in this code, and that should be pointed out. Immediately after the class statement you will see the definition of a variable by the name of `MAX_SHIFT`, as follows:

```
static final int MAX_SHIFT = 12;
```

This variable is a constant, meaning it can never be changed in the program. It is used to implement the algorithm for turning a double into a formatted String.

This is a judgment call. When you develop programs, you should use constant quantities instead of just placing numbers into the decision-making parts of your code. This significantly increases readability of the code and reduces the chance that a wrong number might be entered where the constant belongs. Many times when a number has to be inserted in code in several different places, like a tax rate for instance, it is safer to declare a constant TAX_RATE so that you don't mistype the number 0.87675 in one of the places it is used. It is also much easier to change the number in one place (at the beginning of the program) than it is to find and replace it in several places.

However, for some utility methods you may choose to encapsulate these quantities as variables inside their own methods, even though as variables they can be changed. Finally, you will notice that the constants are all capital letters; this also is a standard practice that increases clarity in your programming.

STEP-BY-STEP 10.3

1. Open the file CreditCard2.java from the student data files, and save it to your student disk or folder as CreditCard2.java. Compile the CreditCard2 class. Open the source file VectorClass.java from the student data files and save the program to your student disk or folder as VectorClass.java.

2. Compile and run the program, entering names into the Vector.

3. Note that each time you enter a name, the item is added. Since the array was made small to start with, and increases by only two bins at a time, you will have a chance to watch the array resize itself as you continue entering data.

4. After having entered five to seven names, enter an N at the "Continue?" query, and observe the data printed to the screen. Note the client names, the increasing account numbers, and the format for the credit limit printout. The `doubleToString` format is set at 6 wide with 2 digits after the decimal point; this makes the output more professional looking and more vertically aligned.

5. This program has one more little option that may help with some compilers. If you are running your programs using Microsoft's Visual J++ jview from the command line, you are able to see your output when your program finishes. However, in some compilers, the output screen may not stay up after the

STEP-BY-STEP 10.3 CONTINUED

program finishes. By placing the following code at the end of the program, you cause the computer to wait for more String data input and keep the screen open for you. Here is the code segment; it can be removed if you do not need it:

```
ansString = GetConsoleString();
```

In this situation, ansString is said to be a "dummy" variable in that it captures data that will not be used.

6. Close all open source code files.

Finishing this lesson with the Vector class project is evidence of how large a fairly simple program can become as some of the parts of the program are improved and refined. At the same time, notice that the `GetConsoleString` method was reused and has been used for a few lessons now. Good programming requires code reuse and developed code that can continue to be effective as the conditions surrounding the code change. At this point in your work, you are beginning to see the larger scale of the Java programming language.

Summary

In this lesson, you learned:

- Arrays are like bins that hold a group of homogenous or like things. In Java, you can have arrays of integers, floats, Strings, and almost any other kind of object.
- Arrays may be one-, two-, three-dimensional, or more. If it is appropriate, multidimensional arrays are very useful. However, they can be difficult to understand if they are not well-documented.
- The actual data quantity in an array is called an element. The number used to access the element, much like its address, is called either an index or a subscript.
- If a program attempts to access an element that does not exist in an array (e.g., the program tries to access element 9 in an array 7 elements wide), the subscript is said to be out of the array bounds, and Java will return an exception.
- Vectors are special self-adjusting and self-reporting data containers that act as arrays of Objects. Virtually any Object list can be maintained by a Vector.
- Unlike arrays, Vectors can hold heterogenous, or unlike groups of data. However, except in certain circumstances, this may lead to some data management problems that will cause incorrect return of items.
- Constants in programs are like variables, but cannot be changed in the program. They support clarity and readability in the code, such as using the quantity NO_MORE_INPUT instead of the less clear –1 quantity that is returned from the method. Constants in Java are declared using the *final* keyword. It is also easier to set and change one constant variable than to find all the numbers in your program when the time comes to change the value.

LESSON 10 REVIEW QUESTIONS

WRITTEN QUESTIONS

Write a brief answer to the following questions.

1. Define *array*.
2. Other than the ones mentioned in this lesson, give an example of an array that exists in the real world.
3. Explain why arrays are indexed beginning with zero.
4. Write a statement that declares an array of 25 doubles.
5. What does the *new* keyword do for arrays?
6. Give an example of a kind of data that might be stored using a two-dimensional array.
7. Give an example of a kind of data that might be stored using a three-dimensional array.

8. What kind of tables do you use on a day-to-day basis?

9. Write a statement that places the value from the second row and fourth column of an array named `lookupTable` into a variable named `value`.

10. Write a loop that initializes all values in the first row of a 10 x 10 array named `lookupTable` to zero.

11. Why is a Vector more flexible than an array?

12. Why is the ability to resize dynamically important?

13. Can you create a vector of primitive data types? Why or why not?

14. What is the danger of mixing object types in a vector?

15. Describe the function of the `doubleToString` method.

LESSON 10 PROJECTS

PROJECT 10-1

Look at the code in the `doubleToString` method in the VectorClass.java file. Write the algorithm in English to describe how this process works. Try writing the specifications for this method, meaning all the things it can do or conditions it can deal with.

Answer the following questions:

1. Can it deal with the number zero?

2. Can it deal with both positive and negative numbers?

3. How does it do this?

4. How does it accomplish making preceding spaces before the number?

PROJECT 10-2

Write a program that uses a one-dimensional array to hold an item number for a product line sold by a small retail store. The items are held in bins, and each item number should be stored in the array element representing the bin number the item is held in. There are 10 bins in the store and each item number must be between 1000 and 2000. (Note: Remember the array items will be addressed as a range 0 through 9, but these addresses really represent bin numbers 1 through 10.) The program should prompt the user to enter each item number for the bin number currently displayed on the screen. Each successive item number must be of a greater sequential value than the item number before it, and no duplicate item numbers are allowed. When all 10 items have been entered, display the item numbers that were entered and the corresponding bin number each item is stored in. Save the program to your student disk or folder as Project10_2.java.

PROJECT 10-3

Create a program that uses a vector class to store address book objects. Each object should include at least a name and phone number for someone you know. Initially, the vector should hold at least six entries and should expand by three entries every time it reaches capacity. The program should prompt for input and should report its current capacity and number of entries as each item is entered. It should also display a message every time it expands indicating its new capacity and current number of objects stored. Save the program to your student disk as Project 10_3.java, compile the program, and run it. Enter new objects until the initial capacity is full, and then force it to expand by adding additional entries.

APPLETS

LESSON 11

OBJECTIVES

Upon completion of this lesson, you should be able to:

- Describe what an event is and how it is processed.
- Explain the difference between an applet's and an application's class structure.
- Understand the restrictions placed on applets.
- Create an applet that can change font characteristics.

Overview

Other than a quick stop in applets and Web pages in Lesson 1, this unit has focused almost entirely on Java programs, also called applications. As you know, all Java programs must run on some kind of platform that knows how to act like a Java virtual machine. One of those platforms is the Microsoft "jview" Java interpreter or other console interpreter you have used up to this point. The other platform that will be addressed in this lesson is a Web browser. While Java is a developer's language that can put together significant applications to be run on jview, it is most famous for its ability to bring dynamic interaction to users of the World Wide Web. In this lesson, you will explore the basics of how an applet is constructed and how to get one started.

Applications vs. Applets

The simplest distinction between applications and applets is that applications run through a Java interpreter (usually text-based) and applets run through a Web browser or other graphical Java interpreter. The central part of an application is the main method. When an application is run, the main method is called, and from there, the other classes, methods, and associated components are called or implemented. An applet is a little different in that no main method is required. The class constructor(s) are implemented and the program is initialized through a method called `init`, and then things are off and running.

Events

In applets, there is no procedural or step-by-step process like the one followed in the main method; instead, *events* control the actions and happenings from that point forward.

Events are defined in computer science as any interaction that could happen to or with the computer. A mouse motion or click is an event; a keyboard keystroke is an event; even opening or closing a program is an event. And, rather than taking one procedural step at a time, an *event manager* (or *event handler*) waits for events to come in and then passes the events to one or more different running programs depending on the kind of event.

Think of an event manager like a dispatcher for truckers. Suppose a load of cabbage needs to go to a particular city. The dispatcher looks for trucks going to the destination, and then among the trucks found, the dispatcher finds one with a refrigeration unit that can haul cabbage safely. The job is then passed to the identified trucker.

The computer event manager does the same thing. It will pass an event to the most likely program (or applet) that can handle the event. If the event can be handled, then it is; if it cannot be handled, then the event is passed on to the next most likely candidate. You will implement some of these actions in code later, but right now just be aware that the event-handling process is how the applets know what to do next.

Applet Methods

While applets do not have a main method, they do tend to have several more methods for getting their tasks completed. When you write an applet program, you simply develop the class with the necessary methods in it; and when your Web page tells the class to make an object of itself, the event manager sees to it that everything is done in the right place.

Figure 11-1 contains the complete source code for the MyApplet applet. We will use this simple example to show how the different methods in a Java applet are used.

FIGURE 11-1
MyApplet.java is a complete Java applet.

```
import java.applet.Applet;
import java.awt.Graphics;
public class MyApplet extends Applet
{
  int constructCount;
  int initCount;
  int startCount;
  int stopCount;
  int paintCount;


  public MyApplet()
  {
  constructCount = 0;
  initCount = 0;
  startCount = 0;
  stopCount = 0;
  paintCount = 0;
  constructCount++;
```

FIGURE 11-1 (continued)

```
    }      // end of constructor MyApplet

    public void init()
    {
    initCount++;
    }      // end of method init

    public void start()
    {
    startCount++;
    }      // end of method start

    public void stop()
    {
    stopCount++;
    }

    public void paint(Graphics graphOut)
    {
    paintCount++;
    graphOut.drawString("Number of construct actions: "
          + constructCount, 50, 50);
    graphOut.drawString("Number of init actions: " + initCount, 50, 75);
    graphOut.drawString("Number of start actions: " + startCount, 50, 100);
    graphOut.drawString("Number of stop actions: " + stopCount, 50, 125);
    graphOut.drawString("Number of paint actions: " + paintCount, 50, 150);
    }      // end of method paint
}      // end of class MyApplet
```

As we go through each part of the MyApplet applet, pay special attention to the method names and when and why they are called. Each of these methods plays a special part in making the applet function correctly.

IMPORTING THE REQUIRED CLASS

The source code of an applet must always begin with an import statement for the Applet class and the Graphics class. All applets are subclasses of the class Applet, so you must import the java.applet.Applet class. In addition, because applets run inside of World Wide Web browsers, they are completely graphics-based. This graphics-based context requires that all applets import the java.awt.Graphics class (see below). As you go through the remainder of the lesson, notice how there is very little reference to printing an object. Instead, all objects are either drawn or painted.

```
import java.applet.Applet;
import java.awt.Graphics;
```

THE APPLET CLASS DEFINITION

The class definition should always resemble the one shown below. The correct style is, first, the keyword *public* (making the class usable by anyone), followed by the keyword *class*, the class name, and the statement text *extends Applet*. This makes the class public so the browser can run it and makes the class a subclass of Applet.

```
public class MyApplet extends Applet
{
}     // end of class MyApplet
```

THE CONSTRUCTOR AND init METHOD

Inside of the class definition several different methods are defined. Among these are the applet's constructor and the `init` method.

```
public MyApplet()
{
  constructCount = 0;
  initCount = 0;
  startCount = 0;
  stopCount = 0;
  paintCount = 0;
  constructCount++;
}     // end of constructor MyApplet

public void init()
{
   initCount++;
}     // end of method init
```

The constructor and the `init` method are both run when the applet is loaded. The methods can be used to create new objects, set up variables, and load other files that might be required. In most cases, only one of the two methods needs to be used. The constructor, however, can be used to initialize the data values in the program and the `init` method can be used to initialize the user interface of the applet, including the window, buttons, labels, etc. The constructor and the `init` method are each only run once, with the constructor being run first and the `init` method being run next. The `init` method is only called once for an applet, normally when its home page is loaded. Even if the user of the Web browser goes to another page and then returns, the `init` method is not called again.

The constructor for the MyApplet class initialized all the variables and increments the constructor Count variable by one.

THE start METHOD

The `start` method is called after the `init` method has been called. The `start` method will also be called if the user returns to the page that contains your applet. Therefore, the `start` method for an applet can be called several times while it is loaded.

```
public void start()
{
  startCount++;
}     // end of method start
```

THE stop METHOD

The `stop` method is called whenever the user leaves the page that contains an applet. Keep this in mind when you create your applets. You do not want an applet to be using valuable processor time when the user is not viewing the applet. The `start` method is used to start a method that has been stopped. The `start` and `stop` methods can be called several times while an applet is loaded.

```
public void stop()
{
  stopCount++;
}
```

THE paint METHOD

The `paint` method has the job of repainting the screen any time the event manager updates the program; therefore, it is called several times during an applet's lifetime. This can happen for several reasons, such as pulling down a window on top of the applet, minimizing or maximizing the browser window, or other actions that can occur. Interestingly, in programs that use the `paint` method, the method is not called directly from the program. Instead, the event manager (which knows when to do these things) calls an update method that then will call the `paint` method.

```
public void paint(Graphics graphOut)
{
  paintCount++;
  graphOut.drawString("Number of construct actions: "   + constructCount, 50, 50);
  graphOut.drawString("Number of init actions: " + initCount, 50, 75);
  graphOut.drawString("Number of start actions: " + startCount, 50, 100);
  graphOut.drawString("Number of stop actions: " + stopCount, 50, 125);
  graphOut.drawString("Number of paint actions: " + paintCount, 50, 150);
}     // end of method paint
```

THE destroy METHOD

The Applet class has one more method that can be overridden. The `destroy` method is called just before the browser exits. The `destroy` method can be used to do any cleanup that the programmer feels is necessary. This is especially useful for stopping threads or other objects that may be using computing resources.

THE REQUIRED HTML

Like the applets you worked with in Lesson 1, you will need HTML documents in order to test your applet in a Web browser. To test the MyApplet applet, we will use two HTML documents. Figure 11-2 contains the HTML necessary to load the applet. The document in Figure 11-3 will be used to test the `stop` method.

FIGURE 11-2
The MyApplet.html document references the MyApplet applet.

```
<HTML>
<HEAD>
<TITLE>My Applet</TITLE>
</HEAD>
<BODY>
<HR>
<applet
code=MyApplet
width=200
height=200>

</applet>
<HR>
</BODY>
</HTML>
```

FIGURE 11-3
The stop.html document will be used to test some of the features of an applet.

```
<HTML>
<HEAD>
<TITLE>Stopapplet</TITLE>
</HEAD>
<BODY>
<HR>
MyApplet should be stopped when this page is loaded.
<HR>
</BODY>
</HTML>
```

STEP-BY-STEP 11.1

1. Enter the HTML code from Figure 11-3 into a document and save it to your student disk or folder as stop.html.

2. If your development environment can construct Web pages for you, open your editor and enter the source code from Figure 11-1 into an empty file. Save the source code to your student disk as MyApplet.java. Compile the MyApplet.java class, and then run the MyApplet applet. If you don't have a development environment that constructs Web pages for you, enter the HTML code from Figure 11-2 into an empty text file and save it to your student disk as MyApplet.html. Run the MyApplet.html document in a Web browser.

3. Notice the counters next to each of the method names. Resize the window a few times and watch which counters change.

STEP-BY-STEP 11.1 CONTINUED

4. Open the stop.html document in the same browser window, and then return to the MyApplet.html document. Notice which methods were called when you opened the stop.html document.

5. Try and find other ways to make the different method counters change.

6. When you have finished testing the applet, close all windows.

Applet Restrictions

In order to prevent Java applets from causing any kind of damage to a computer system, several restrictions have been put in place. First, Java applets cannot read or write to the client's file system. In some cases when an applet can read or write to the file system, the access is limited to specific directories. Second, applets can only communicate with the server from which they were downloaded. Finally, applets cannot run any other programs on the client's computer. Each of these are high-level security restrictions. The Java language and Java compilers and interpreters also have many features that keep an applet from doing any harm to a computer system.

Java Gets Fancy

In getting started with applets, one of the first things you want to get familiar with is how to make the output look good to the user. In this section, we will study the classes that manipulate the fonts, which are themselves classes.

Working with Fonts

In using the object-oriented approach to font management, it is logical to have a class called Font. Java does have such a class. The class Font knows everything about being a font. Yet, when you think about it, fonts don't actually do much. Likewise, Font methods do little more than tell you about themselves. These methods are given names such as `getStyle`, `getSize`, and `isBold`—they give a description of what this class does. So, if a Font is just a font, then programmers need some Font management.

The Graphics class, which paints the screen with various things, actually takes charge of using the Font class to its own ends. You may have noticed that the Graphics class is not really declared in the program. This is because it is initialized by other methods used by the event manager, so that it is ready to go to work when the `update` method calls the `paint` method. Once a Font object has made up its mind what to be like, the Graphics method can then call the `setFont` method, and the work is done.

As you see in Figure 11-4, the `init` method starts by resizing itself. This simply makes the working box a little smaller, but the size of your applet will also depend on how large you allowed it to be in the HTML file as well. Next, three of the conditions that make a font unique are set in their own variables and then placed in a new Font object. Later, in the `paint` method where the Graphic object `graphOut` is in scope, the method `graphOut.setFont` is called, which actually places the font information into the Graphics object.

The message, as you have seen before, is sent to the screen. However, note that it is not printed on the screen but is actually painted or drawn on the screen. Once you start working in the *GUI (graphical user interface)* environment, everything that goes to screen is graphical, including text. After the message has been painted on the screen, a new object of the FontMetricsClass (a class that understands font measurements and conditions) is instantiated, and it is asked to collect all the information it can about the font related to "Hi Mom!" After doing this, the font is changed in style and size, and the "Hi Mom!" font information is output to screen.

The myFontMetrics object "learns" all about the "Hi Mom" string in the method called `getFontMetrics`, and then the object is asked to provide that information to the screen in the two output statements at the end of the code.

FIGURE 11-4
This applet outputs different types, styles, and sizes of fonts.

```
import java.applet.Applet;
import java.awt.*;

public class FontChange extends Applet
{
  Font myFont;
  FontMetrics myFontMetrics;

  public FontChange()
  {
  }      // end of constructor FontChange

  public void init()
  {
  resize(200, 200);

  myFont = new Font("Times New Roman", Font.Italic, 36);
  }      // end of method init

  public void paint(Graphics graphOut)
  {
  String momString = new String("Hi Mom!");
  graphOut.setFont(myFont);

  graphOut.drawString(momString, 50, 50);

  myFont = new Font("Arial", Font.BOLD, 14);
  graphOut.setFont(myFont);
  myFontMetrics = getFontMetrics(myFont);

  graphOut.drawString("String width is: "
        + myFontMetrics.stringWidth(momString), 50, 100);
  graphOut.drawString("String height is: "
        + myFontMetrics.getHeight(), 50, 125);
  }      // end of method paint
}      // end of class FontChange
```

STEP-BY-STEP 11.2

1. Start your text editor and open FontChange.java from the student data files. Save it to your student disk or folder as FontChange.java. Create an HTML document named FontChange.html to run the applet and save it to your student disk.

2. Compile and run the program.

3. Change the attributes of the `myFont` constructor. Notice what this does to both the output string and the metrics, or measurements, of the string. The font style can be set at BOLD, PLAIN, or ITALIC. The font type will vary with your computer, but you can usually try any of the more popular fonts such as Times New Roman, Arial, etc. Some fonts, such as Courier, may not be resizeable. Give that one a try as well.

4. Change the text, but remember you will have to change the size of the applet window as well. To do this, change the numbers in the method `resize` in your `init` method. You will also have to change the height and width parameters in your HTML page that calls your applet.

5. Save your changes, and close the file.

Applets are actually kind of easy when you already understand the underlying Java language and terminology. You should be able to develop simple applets and try out new ideas with applets as you finish this lesson.

Summary

In this lesson, you learned:

- Java applets are fully functional programs written in the Java language that can be "placed" in a Web page.
- Like all Java programs, a Java applet is comprised of at least one class that will be instantiated.
- Events in Java are any action that happens with the computer. An event manager (or handler) identifies the event and passes it to the program most likely to use it. If that program does not or cannot use it, it is passed to the next likely process.
- Since Java applets work in an event-driven environment, there is no main method to tell the program what to do next. Note, however, that Java applications can also work as event-driven programs if they are developed a bit differently.
- All font information and management is conducted by objects interacting with each other. A wide range of font attributes can be used in a Java program.

LESSON 11 REVIEW QUESTIONS

WRITTEN QUESTIONS

1. What is the primary difference between an applet and an application?
2. What are the methods `start` and `stop` commonly used for?
3. What does an event manager (or handler) do?
4. What is an event?
5. When are the constructor and `init` methods of an applet called?
6. How is the `paint` method called in a Java applet?
7. What class manages fonts for the Java language?
8. What class measures and reports on font objects?
9. What member function almost always does the output-to-screen process in an applet?
10. What class and method are used to draw the text characters on the screen?
11. Why is the Graphics class not declared in a program that uses fonts?

LESSON 11 PROJECT

PROJECT 11-1

Write an applet that paints your name to the screen in the font of your choice. Using the `paint` method to increment a variable, have the program increase the point size of the font in which your name is written each time the applet repaints the screen. Begin with a small font size and build in a safety check that stops incrementing the point size when the name is too large to fit within the bounds of the applet. Save the file to your student disk or folder as Project 11_1.java. Compile and run the program. Close the source file. Remember to set the height and width parameters in your HTML file to match the size specified in your applet.

Java Review

UNIT REVIEW

TRUE/FALSE

Circle T if the statement is true or F if the statement is false.

T F 1. Every Java program must have at least one class.

T F 2. In Java, multiplication and division have the highest order of operations.

T F 3. The if/else structure is called a sequence structure because the result returned from evaluating the control expression determines in what sequence the code will be executed.

T F 4. The records in a sequential access file are all the same length.

T F 5. The elements within an array are accessed using a numeric variable called a subscript to address a particular location.

FILL-IN-THE-BLANK

1. Java's __________ data type requires 8 bytes of storage and can be used to store very large whole numbers.

2. Incorporating special logic into your Java programs to trap any errors that may occur is called __________ handling.

3. Any iteration structure can be terminated before the conditions of the control expression are met by coding the __________ keyword to exit the loop.

4. Variables in a class that are declared as __________ can be accessed from outside the class by other programs and methods.

5. As with other Java programs, a Java applet is comprised of at least one __________ that will be instantiated.

PROJECTS

PROJECT 5-1

In this project, you will create a program to declare several variables. The program will attempt to display the variables before they are initialized, then initialize them, then display them again.

1. If necessary, start your text editor or Java IDE application. Create a new program file, and save it as **varbtest.java**.

2. Declare at least **three variables** of any type that you wish, but only one variable for each type. Do **NOT** initialize any of the variables.

3. Add Java statements to **display** each of the **variables** that were declared.

4. Add Java statements to **initialize each variable** to some value of your choice.

5. Add Java statements to **display** each of the **variables** after they have been initialized.

6. Depending on the compiler you are using, you may wish to add statements to the program to force the user to press a keyboard key to end the program so it does not end before you can view the output.

7. Save the program and compile it. Did your compiler compile it without errors? If so, run the program. Did your compiler display the un-initialized variables, or did you receive an error? If you received an error message, comment out the lines that print the variables before they are initialized, and then recompile and rerun the program.

8. Close your text editor or IDE application when the program runs without errors.

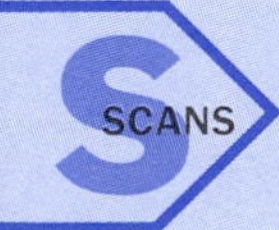

PROJECT 5-2

In this project you will use declared variables to receive information input by the user from the keyboard. You will use selection structures to process the user input, and then use a string variable to display the results to the user. The program will ask the users what type of sandwich they want and have them select from a menu of choices. They will also be asked if they want cheese for their sandwich, and asked to select the type. You will process these input values and display a message telling the user what sandwich and which cheese they requested.

1. If necessary, start your text editor or Java IDE application. Open the **delimenu.java** skeleton program from the Unit Review Data File folder. This program includes everything you will need except the main function code itself. It has the header files you will need, and the `GetConsoleString` function you will use.

2. Declare two **integers** and one **String** variable within the **main** function. The **integer** variables will be used to hold a **sandwich type** and a **cheese type** to be input from the user. The **String** variable will be used to **display** the final sandwich type to the user.

3. Add the Java statements to **display a menu** of **sandwich types** to the user, and each type should have an **associated number** that the user will enter to correspond to that type. The types should be **Roast Beef**, **Ham**, **Turkey**, or **Veggie**. Add a call to the `GetConsoleString` function to get the user's preference and store it in the **sandwich type** variable.

4. Add the Java statements to **display a menu** of **cheese types** to the user, and each type should have an **associated number** that the user will enter to correspond to that type. The types should be **American**, **Swiss**, **Cheddar**, or **No Cheese**. Add a call to the `GetConsoleString` function to get the user's preference and store it in the **cheese type** variable.

5. Add Java **selection structure** statements to process the **sandwich type** and the **cheese type** input by the user. You can use if statements, if/else statements, or the switch structure to process the user's choices. How you prefer to do it is your choice. However you do it, the **String** variable should first be initialized to **display some text indicating the sandwich type** selected by the user, and **then have the cheese type concatenated to the message** to show the overall sandwich the user chose. If the user entered an invalid sandwich type, display a message to that effect. If the user entered an invalid cheese type, you can indicate that, or use the No Cheese option as the default option.

6. Compile and test the program. Correct any errors until the program runs as expected. Then close your text editor or IDE application.

PROJECT 5-3

In this project you will create a program that uses the main menu to ask the user if they want to write data to, or read data from, a file. The program will make sure they enter a proper option, and call a method to either write the output to the file, or read input from the file.

1. If necessary, start your text editor or Java IDE application. Create a new Java program class and save it to your student folder as **NameProg.java**.

2. In the `main` method, create a loop to **display a menu** that asks the user if they want to **write data to a file**, **read data from a file**, or **exit** the program. Read the user's response and verify that the value entered is correct. If users want to write data to a file, call a method named `writeMyFile()` to process the output file. If they want to read input from the file, call a method named `readMyFile()` to read an input file. Check the return codes from the functions to write and read data. If they completed successfully, indicate that in a message. If an error occurred, indicate that also. If the user wants to exit, terminate the program. If the user entered an invalid option, show a message to that effect. Remain in this loop until the user indicates he wants to terminate the program.

3. Create a function called `writeMyFile()` to write data to a file. **Prompt** the user for the **name of the file to be created**, and open the file for output. Create a loop that asks the user for a name, address, and city/state/zip. Append each of the user's input values to a string and write it to the file. Continue looping and asking for input until the user wants to stop writing data. Close the file and return a code of **zero** if no errors occurred. Add try and catch logic to catch any errors, and return a code of **-1 (minus one)** if an error occurs.

4. Create a function named `readMyFile()` to read input from a file and display it to the user. **Prompt** the user for the **name of the file** to open, and open it. Create a loop to read all records in the file, and display each record as it is read. If no errors occur, return a code of **zero**, or else return a code of **-1 (minus one)**.

5. Copy the `GetConsoleString` and `toFloat` methods from an earlier Java program, and use them for console input and conversion functions.

6. Save your changes, and compile and run the program. Correct any errors if necessary, and close your IDE or text editor when the program runs as it should.

PROJECT 5-4

In this project you will create a program that prompts a user to enter an item number, an item description, and an item price. Each value input by the user will be put into an array for that element type.

1. If necessary, start your text editor or Java IDE application. Create a new Java program class and save it to your student folder as **ItemArray.java**.

2. In the `main` method, define **three arrays**, for any size you wish, but they all must be of the same capacity. One array will be for **integer** values, another for **string** values, and the third for **float** values.

3. Write a loop that **prompts** the user to **input an item number**. If it is not the first item for the array, check all existing item numbers to be sure it is not already present in the array. If it is, display an error message and have the user reenter the number. If it is not already present, **prompt** the user to enter a **description** of the item and store it in the array for the descriptions at the same offset as the item number is located in its array. **Prompt** for an item **price** and store it in the same way as you did the description.

4. After all items have been entered, create a loop that displays the item number, its location, and its corresponding description and price.

5. Add an instruction to **pause** before ending the program. Compile and run the program and correct any errors if necessary.

SIMULATION 

SIMULATION 5-1

A small manufacturing company has asked you to create an order processing program to be distributed to their own salespeople, as well as to a number of independent sales agents that represent the company in areas where there is no permanent sales representative. The program should write the order information to a file that the sales rep can then mail or send to the home office via an Internet transfer. The company has issued all its permanent salespeople laptops running the Windows operating system, but the independent agents use their own laptops, which do not all necessarily run the same operating system. Would you most likely use Visual Basic, C++, or Java to create this program? Explain why you would choose the language you select.

SIMULATION 5-2

Create a Java class to hold a description of an item similar to Project 5-4 above. The class should consist of an item object that includes an item number, a description, a cost, the name of the vendor from whom the item was purchased, and the quantity of this item currently in stock. At the least the class should have a default constructor, an initializing constructor, and modifier methods to alter the values in the item. There should also be a method to display all fields and contents of a given item. Save the program source code as **ItemClass.java**, and compile it.

SIMULATION 5-3

Create a test driver program to test the ItemClass class created in Simulation 5-2. The program should declare at least two item objects. Instantiate one of the item objects using the default constructor and the other using the initializing constructor. Display both item objects after they have been created. Use the class modifiers to set new values for the item created using the default constructor, and redisplay that item. Compile and run the program.

GLOSSARY

-- operator An operator used to decrement a variable.

++ operator An operator used to increment a variable.

A

accessor A method that allows data in an object to be accessed from outside the object.

ActionListener An event handler that is invoked when an event occurs for an object.

action method An event handler for events generated by key press operations.

actual parameter The name of a parameter that a method uses when calling another method.

alternate HTML HTML code that will be displayed by a Web browser that does not support Java.

American Standard Code for Information Interchange (ASCII) A standardized set of numeric values used to represent letters, symbols, and numeric values in a computer.

analog A device that uses quantities that are variable or exist in a range.

appending Adding new data characters to the end of an existing buffer.

applet A small Java program that can be included in Web pages to enhance the appearance or functionality of a Web page.

<APPLET> tag A tag that tells a Web browser a Java applet is included in the HTML document.

arithmetic operators Operators used in mathematical calculations, such as addition, subtraction, division, or multiplication.

array An area of storage holding multiple variables of the same data type.

assembler A program that converts a programmer's statements into machine language code.

assembly language A programming language that is very close to machine language.

assignment operator Used to change the value of a variable to the left of an equal sign to the value on the right side of the equal sign.

B

binary number system A number system that uses the digits 0 and 1 to represent data values.

bit A binary digit that can contain either a 0 or a 1.

Boolean variable A variable that has only two states, true or false.

BorderLayout A Java interface layout that divides the screen into five areas where objects can be placed.

braces Characters used to mark the beginning and end of blocks of code.

branching A method a program uses to test a condition and jump to the appropriate function.

break A keyword that can be used to stop processing of a loop or a switch structure.

buffer An area used to temporarily store data while it is being processed.

bus Electronic circuits used to move data and instruction between the microprocessor chip and RAM, ROM, and peripheral devices.

byte A combination of 8 bits used to represent a single character.

byte codes Java instructions that have been partially compiled and can then be interpreted by a Java virtual machine.

byte variable An 8-bit area used to hold an integer value.

C

called method A method that is called by another method.

calling method A method that originates a call to another method.

capacity The maximum size or quantity an object can hold.

case A keyword used to handle a specific condition in a switch structure.

case sensitive Interpreting characters differently based on the case (upper or lower) of the characters.

casting Indicating to the compiler that a variable should be treated as a certain data type even if it looks like a different type to the compiler. Also called *type casting*.

catch process A block of code that catches program exceptions and reports them.

char variable A 16-bit area used to hold a single character.

character An alphabetic letter, symbol, or numeral that can be processed by a computer.

check boxes An interface object that can be checked to indicate it is selected.

CheckBoxGroup A set of checkboxes that only allows one box to be checked at a time.

class A set of instructions that create an object.

class wrapper An object-oriented data type. Also called *object wrapper*.

client computer A computer running a Web browser and requesting Web pages.

close A process used when finished working with a file.

comments Nonexecutable statements in a program that can be used to document the purpose of the program or to track changes to the program.

comparison operators Operators used to create expressions to evaluate data or variables.

compiler A program that translates a high-level language into machine language code.

components Things that can make up a program, such as buttons, check boxes, etc.

compound operators Special operators that provide a shorthand notation for modifying variables.

constant A storage area that retains its value for the duration of the program's run.

constraint Conditions that an object must abide by.

constructor A function that creates an object based on the rules of the object's class.

containers An object derived from a component that can hold things.

context An environment, or theoretical place.

continue A keyword that stops the processing of a loop pass but continues the loop with the next iteration.

control expression An expression that makes a decision.

copy constructor A constructor that takes the information from an object and puts it in a newly created instance of the object.

D

data A computer's representation of something that exists in the real world, such as names and addresses, dollar amounts, letters, spreadsheets, etc.

data hiding A means of preventing programmers from accessing some variables.

data type A way to specify what type of data is held in a variable or a constant.

debugging A step-by-step method of testing a program and correcting programming errors.

decimal number system A number system that uses the digits 0 through 9 to represent data values.

declare The process of telling a compiler the name of a variable or constant and the type of data it will contain.

decrementing Subtracting 1 from the value of a variable.

default constructor A constructor that sets a class to its default values.

destroy method A method within an applet called when the Web browser exits.

digital A device that uses switches (or digits) in combination to represent something in the real world.

do while loop A loop that always executes at least once and continues to execute until a condition is met.

dot operator A period used to associate a member with a method or class.

double buffer A method of reducing on-screen flicker when animating objects.

double variable A 64-bit area used to hold floating point values.

E

"E" notation A method for expressing very large and very small numeric values.

element An entry in an array.

encapsulation Hiding data and code within a class.

event An interaction that requires a computer program to perform processing.

event listener An object in a program that waits for another object to generate an event.

event manager (handler) A program that is given control when an event occurs and transfers control to a program capable of processing the event.

event source An object in a program that generates, or initiates, an event.

exception A situation contrary to the normal flow of processing.

Exception classes Java programs that provide the code necessary to handle various types of exceptions.

exception handling A system designed to deal with program exceptions.

executable file A program file that can be run repeatedly without having to translate the program each time.

exponential notation Also called *scientific notation*, a method of specifying very large and very small values.

expression The portion of a programming statement on the right side of an assignment operator.

F

file stream A method of accessing files using Java.

float variable A 32-bit area used to hold floating-point values.

floating-point unit The area of a computer where math operations are performed.

floppy disk A storage device containing a magnetic disk used to hold small quantities of data and/or programs.

FlowLayout A simple Java interface layout where objects placed on the screen flow from left to right, top to bottom, as they are placed.

flush The process of forcing all data for a file from a buffer.

for loop A loop that repeats one or more statements a specific number of times.

formal parameter The name of a parameter as it is defined in the method processing the parameter.

fuzzy logic A system that allows for more than a true or false condition.

G

garbage collection The process of retrieving memory and resources no longer being used.

global variable A variable that is in scope as long as the class is active.

graphical user interface (GUI) A method of communicating with a computer by manipulating pictures and icons.

GridBagLayout A Java interface that allows objects of different shapes and sizes.

GridLayout A Java interface that must hold equally shaped objects in rows and columns.

H

handleEvent An event handler that handles any event not handled by a specific event handler.

hard coded A value, string, or expression coded into a program that can be externally changed when the program runs.

hard disk A storage device consisting of one or more magnetic platters used to permanently store programs and data files.

hardware The physical devices and components that make up a computer.

high-level language An English-like or easy-to-write language that uses instructions that do not necessarily correspond one-to-one with a computer's instruction set.

HTML (Hypertext Markup Language) A programming language used to create Web pages.

HTTP (Hypertext Transfer Protocol) A communications protocol used by Web servers to transmit HTML and other document types to a Web browser.

I

identifier A name given to a variable or a constant.

if structure A structure that executes one or more programming statements if a condition is true.

if/else structure A structure that executes one or more programming statements if a condition is true, or a different statement or statements if the condition is false.

image A graphic representation of an object.

implicitly An inference, or assumption, based on the most likely possibility.

incrementing Adding one to the value of a variable.

infinite loop A program loop that executes indefinitely.

inheritance A term that refers to a child object inheriting the properties of its parent object.

init method An applet method that is given control when the page containing an applet is loaded.

initialize The process of setting a variable to its starting value.

initializing constructor A constructor that initializes a class with values other than the default values.

initializing expression A loop parameter that sets a counter to a starting value.

inner class A class defined within a class that has access to all objects within the primary class.

input data Data that is to be processed by a computer.

instantiate To declare an object.

interact The process of getting information and providing a response.

interface Classlike groups of methods that can work with a program by inheriting from their parent classes.

interpreter A program that translates a program's source code or byte codes into machine language while the program is being executed.

intrinsic data types The eight standard data types supported by Java.

int variable A 32-bit area used to hold integer values.

iteration A single loop through a block of program statements.

iteration structure A series of structures that perform loops.

J

Java A programming language originally created for specific-purpose computers that has now found widespread acceptance in general-purpose computers.

Java virtual machine (JVM) Interprets Java byte codes into a machine language instruction that can be executed on the platform running the Java program.

K

keyword A word reserved for use by the Java language.

L

linker A program that links multiple software object files into a single executable module.

local variable A variable that is only in scope within the method it is defined in.

logical operators Operators that allow the use of and, or, and not in an expression.

long variable A 64-bit area used to hold integer values.

lookup A portion of a program that is used to find a specific entry in an array.

loop A process where a program repeats a series of statements a specific number of times.

low-level language A programming language that is very precise and non-English-like, such as machine language or assembly language.

lowercase The non-capital letters of the alphabet.

M

machine language A series of numeric values that a computer interprets as program instructions and addresses.

main method The primary method, or routine, in a Java application program.

math coprocessor The area of a computer's processor where math operations are performed.

member A method defined as part of a class of objects.

member function A method that is a member of a class.

menu A means of selecting from more than one option or function.

method One or more statements in a class performing a specific task within an object.

method overloading Creating multiple methods with the same name within a class.

microprocessor A circuit board that controls all processing within a small computer.

modem A device that connects a computer to a telephone line and can be used for sending and receiving data.

modifier Also called a *mutator*, a method of modifying data within an object.

modulus operator An arithmetic operator that returns the remainder value in a divide operation.

multidimensional array An array that can hold items in a two- or three-dimensional grid.

mutator A modifier used to make changes to data inside an object.

N

nested loop A loop contained within another loop.

nested structure A programming structure contained within another structure.

new A keyword used to allocate space for an object or variable.

O

Oak The original name for the Java language.

object An instance of a class containing data and the functions that manipulate the data.

object code Machine language code that results from assembling or compiling a source code program file.

object file The result of processing a program source file through a compiler.

object-oriented programming (OOP) Building programs by creating, controlling, and modifying one or more objects.

object wrappers A set of object-oriented data types within Java.

one-way selection structure A structure that allows to go only one way if a tested condition is met.

open The first step required to use a file for input or for output.

open mode A means of specifying if a random-access file is to be used for input or for output.

operating system Computer software that controls the operation of a computer.

order of operations The order in which a mathematical expression is evaluated.

output The data resulting from the processing of input.

overflow A condition that occurs when a variable becomes too large for its defined type.

overloading Using a constructor in more than one way.

overriding A method in a child class that has the same name as a method in a parent class.

P

packages Groups of classes that are available for use by a compiler.

paint method A method within an applet that repaints the screen each time the program is updated.

panel A container and an object that can hold containers.

<PARAM> tag An HTML tag that can be used to pass parameters to a Java applet.

parameters Information that can be passed to a Java applet that can be used to customize the applet.

pixel A very small dot printed on a computer screen representing a chunk of information about some object.

primary storage Internal memory called RAM that is the place where the computer stores active programs and data being processed.

primitive data types Basic data types, such as Boolean, int, float, etc.

procedural programming Creating a program by using a step-by-step process to perform specific tasks.

process A task being performed in a multitasking environment.

programming language A means of providing processing instructions to a computer without having to learn machine language.

promotion A process of temporarily changing a variable of one type to another type to perform a math operation.

prompt A method for asking a user for input.

R

radio button Another name for a CheckBoxGroup check box.

RAM (random access memory) The primary storage area in a computer used to hold programs and data being processed.

random-access file A file consisting of equal length records or data that can be read in any sequence.

reading data The process of retrieving data from a file used as an input file.

relational database A collection of multiple files containing various types of information related to each other by some common field or data.

robust program code Code that does everything it is supposed to do and also attempts to handle any unusual conditions.

ROM (read-only memory) Memory circuits that have data and programs permanently stored on them, normally used to start up the computer.

S

scope A term that describes the location where a variable is alive.

secondary storage Storage devices that retain data even when power is turned off, such as hard disks, floppy disks, or CD-ROMs.

seed A value given to a randomizing class to use as a starting point when generating a random number.

selection structures Structures in a Java program that make decisions.

self-document Using variable names to indicate the purpose or content of a variable or constant.

sequence structures Structures that execute one program statement after another without changing the program's flow.

sequential-access file A method of reading a file whereby data is read or written from the beginning of the file to the end of the file.

short-circuit Evaluation terminating processing of an expression if a required condition fails its test.

short variable A 16-bit area used to hold integer values.

size How many items are contained in an array or vector class.

source code A program in its native form, before being assembled or compiled.

start method A method within an applet that is called after the init method completes and every time that the page containing the applet is loaded.

statements Instructions or commands within a method that make a program work.

states The conditions that an object can exist in, such as on or off.

static A keyword that causes only one variable to be created and hold one piece of data for all the objects.

step expression The part of a for loop that modifies a counter variable.

stop method A method within an applet that is called every time a user leaves the page containing the applet.

stream A place where data is contained during processing, or the flow of data within a program.

string A group of characters representing data.

subscript A numeric value or set of values used to reference a particular entry in a array.

substring A smaller portion, or segment, of a string.

super A keyword that allows a Java class to access its parent's methods or data.

switch structure A structure capable of handling multiple options.

T

tags A word to describe the delimiters used in the HTML language.

text editor A program that can be used to create a program by entering text strings and values.

text file A file saved by a text editor.

this A keyword that implicitly tells Java which object is being referenced.

thread A portion of a process that can function independently.

throwing an exception A program's method of reporting an exception and an attempt to explain the exception.

truncate The loss of precision or data values because a variable is larger or smaller than the field defined for the value.

truth tables A means of illustrating the results of logical operators.

try process A block of code that examines data to see if it is valid.

two-way selection structure A structure that allows two ways to proceed if a condition is met, or not met.

U

underflow A condition that occurs when a variable is too small for its defined type.

Unicode A standard that defines how charcters and symbols are represented in a computer.

uppercase The capital letters of the alphabet.

V

variable An area that holds data that can be modified during program execution.

vector A Java class that can hold multiple objects and is dynamically expandable.

volatile A term used to describe a computer component, such as RAM, that cannot retain its contents when power is shut off.

W

Web server A computer connected to the Internet that hosts Web pages and transmits requested pages to client computers.

while loop A loop that continues to execute until a specified condition is met.

writing data The process of placing data in a file being used as an output file.

APPENDIX A

ASCII Table

TABLE A-1

ASCII CHARACTER	DECIMAL	HEXADECIMAL	BINARY
NUL	0	00	000 0000
SOH	1	01	000 0001
STX	2	02	000 0010
ETX	3	03	000 0011
EOT	4	04	000 0100
ENQ	5	05	000 0101
ACK	6	06	000 0110
BEL	7	07	000 0111
BS	8	08	000 1000
HT	9	09	000 1001
LF	10	0A	000 1010
VT	11	0B	000 1011
FF	12	0C	000 1100
CR	13	0D	000 1101
SO	14	0E	000 1110
SI	15	0F	000 1111
DLE	16	10	001 0000
DC1	17	11	001 0001
DC2	18	12	001 0010
DC3	19	13	001 0011
DC4	20	14	001 0100
NAK	21	15	001 0101

TABLE A-1 (continued)

ASCII CHARACTER	DECIMAL	HEXADECIMAL	BINARY
SYN	22	16	001 0110
ETB	23	17	001 0111
CAN	24	18	001 1000
EM	25	19	001 1001
SUB	26	1A	001 1010
ESC	27	1B	001 1011
FS	28	1C	001 1100
GS	29	1D	001 1101
RS	30	1E	001 1110
US	31	1F	001 1111
space	32	20	010 0000
!	33	21	010 0001
“	34	22	010 0010
#	35	23	010 0011
$	36	24	010 0100
%	37	25	010 0101
&	38	26	010 0110
‘	39	27	010 0111
(	40	28	010 1000
)	41	29	010 1001
*	42	2A	010 1010
+	43	2B	010 1011
,	44	2C	010 1100
-	45	2D	010 1101
.	46	2E	010 1110
/	47	2F	010 1111
0	48	30	011 0000

TABLE A-1 (continued)

ASCII CHARACTER	DECIMAL	HEXADECIMAL	BINARY
1	49	31	011 0001
2	50	32	011 0010
3	51	33	011 0011
4	52	34	011 0100
5	53	35	011 0101
6	54	36	011 0110
7	55	37	011 0111
8	56	38	011 1000
9	57	39	011 1001
:	58	3A	011 1010
;	59	3B	011 1011
<	60	3C	011 1100
=	61	3D	011 1101
>	62	3E	011 1110
?	63	3F	011 1111
@	64	40	100 0000
A	65	41	100 0001
B	66	42	100 0010
C	67	43	100 0011
D	68	44	100 0100
E	69	45	100 0101
F	70	46	100 0110
G	71	47	100 0111
H	72	48	100 1000
I	73	49	100 1001
J	74	4A	100 1010

TABLE A-1 (continued)

ASCII CHARACTER	DECIMAL	HEXADECIMAL	BINARY
K	75	4B	100 1011
L	76	4C	100 1100
M	77	4D	100 1101
N	78	4E	100 1110
O	79	4F	100 1111
P	80	50	101 0000
Q	81	51	101 0001
R	82	52	101 0010
S	83	53	101 0011
T	84	54	101 0100
U	85	55	101 0101
V	86	56	101 0110
W	87	57	101 0111
X	88	58	101 1000
Y	89	59	101 1001
Z	90	5A	101 1010
[	91	5B	101 1011
\	92	5C	101 1100
]	93	5D	101 1101
^	94	5E	101 1110
_	95	5F	101 1111
`	96	60	110 0000
a	97	61	110 0001
b	98	62	110 0010
c	99	63	110 0011
d	100	64	110 0100

TABLE A-1 (continued)

ASCII CHARACTER	DECIMAL	HEXADECIMAL	BINARY
e	101	65	110 0101
f	102	66	110 0110
g	103	67	110 0111
h	104	68	110 1000
i	105	69	110 1001
j	106	6A	110 1010
k	107	6B	110 1011
l	108	6C	110 1100
m	109	6D	110 1101
n	110	6E	110 1110
o	111	6F	110 1111
p	112	70	111 0000
q	113	71	111 0001
r	114	72	111 0010
s	115	73	111 0011
t	116	74	111 0100
u	117	75	111 0101
v	118	76	111 0110
w	119	77	111 0111
x	120	78	111 1000
y	121	79	111 1001
z	122	7A	111 1010
{	123	7B	111 1011
|	124	7C	111 1100
}	125	7D	111 1101
~	126	7E	111 1110
DEL	127	7F	111 1111

APPENDIX B

THE BINARY NUMBER SYSTEM

Overview

Data is a computer representation of something that exists in the real world. For example, data can be values such as money, measurements, quantities, or a high score. Data can also be alphabetic, such as names and addresses, or a business letter.

In a computer, all data is represented by numbers, and the numbers are represented electronically in the computer. To understand how electrical signals become numbers, let's begin by looking at a simple electric circuit that everyone is familiar with: a switch controlling a light bulb.

From Circuits to Numbers

When you think of an electric circuit, you probably think of it being either on or off; for example, a lightbulb is turned on and off by a switch. The lightbulb can exist in two conditions: on or off. In technical terms, the lightbulb has two states.

Imagine you had two lightbulbs on two switches. With two lightbulbs there are four possible states, as shown in Figure B-1. You could assign a number to each of the states and represent the numbers 0 through 3.

FIGURE B-1
There are four light combinations possible with two lightbulbs.

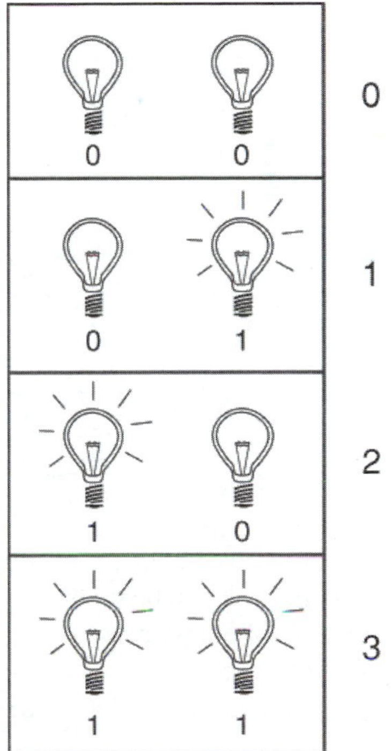

You cannot do much using only the numbers 0 through 3, but if more circuits are added, the number of states increases. For example, Figure B-2 shows how three circuits can represent the numbers 0 through 7 because there are eight possible states.

FIGURE B-2
There are eight light combinations possible with three lightbulbs.

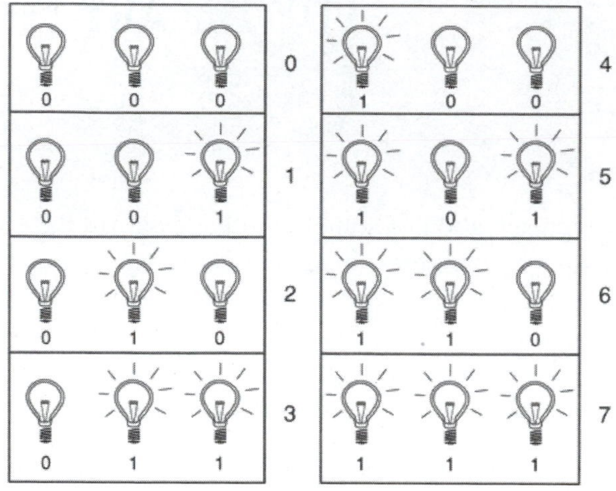

If you are the mathematical type, you may have noticed that the number of states is determined by the formula 2^n, where n is the number of circuits (see Table B-1).

TABLE B-1

NUMBER OF CIRCUITS	NUMBER OF STATES	NUMBERS THAT CAN BE REPRESENTED
1	$2^1=2$	0,1
2	$2^2=4$	0...3
3	$2^3=8$	0...7
4	$2^4=16$	0...15
5	$2^5=32$	0...31
6	$2^6=64$	0...63
7	$2^7=128$	0...127
8	$2^8=256$	0...255

Now instead of lights, think about circuits in the computer. A single circuit in a computer is like a single light; it can be on or off. A special number system, called the binary number system, is used to represent numbers with groups of these circuits. In the binary number system each binary digit, called a bit for short, is either a 0 or a 1. As shown in Figure B-3, circuits that are off are defined as 0, and circuits that are on are defined as 1. Binary digits (bits) are combined into groups of 8 bits called bytes.

FIGURE B-3
In the computer, signals that are off are defined as 0 and signals that are on are defined as 1.

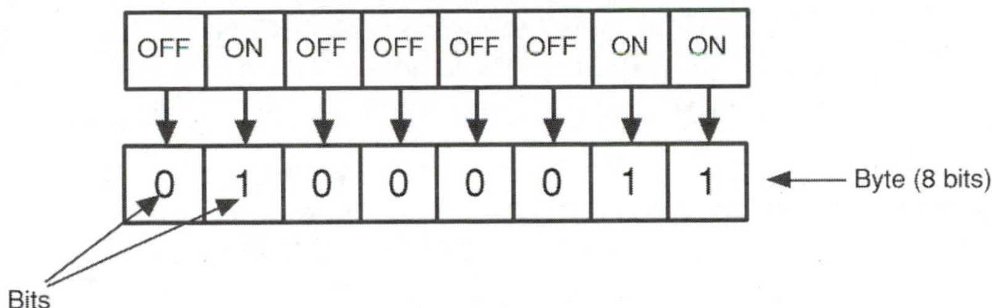

If a byte is made up of 8 bits, then there are 256 possible combinations of those 8 bits representing the numbers 0 through 255 (see Table B-1). Even though 255 is not a small number, it is definitely not the largest number you will ever use, so to represent larger numbers, computers group bytes together.

Binary versus Decimal

The binary number system may seem strange to you because you count using the decimal number system, which uses the digits 0 through 9. Counting in the decimal number system comes very naturally to you because you probably learned it at a very young age. But someone invented the decimal number system just like someone invented the binary number system. The decimal number system is based on 10s because you have 10 fingers on your hands. The binary number system is based on twos because of the circuits in a computer. Both systems, however, can be used to represent the same values.

FIGURE B-4
Each digit of the decimal number 3208 represents a power of 10.

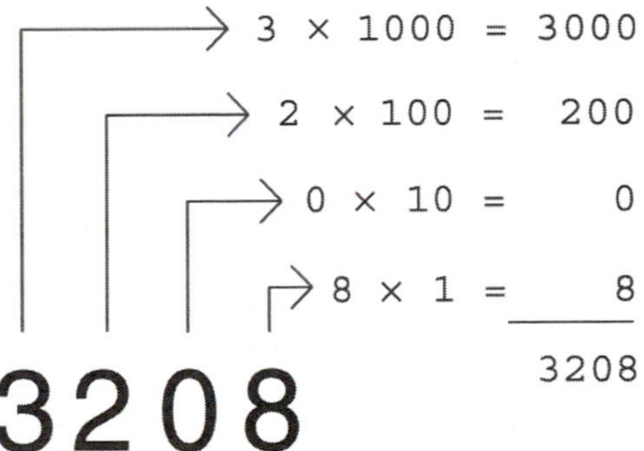

In the decimal number system, each digit of a number represents a power of 10. That is why the decimal number system is also called the base 10 number system. Consider the number 3208, for example. When you read that number, you automatically understand it to mean three thousands, two hundreds, no tens, and eight ones. Represented mathematically, you could say (3 x 1000) + (2 x 100) + (0 x 10) + (8 x 1) = 3208, as shown in Figure B-4.

In the binary number system, each digit represents a power of 2, as you saw in Table B-1. Working with powers of 2 is not as natural to you as working with powers of 10. But with a little practice you will see that base 2 numbers are not so mysterious. Consider the binary number 1101. Even though the number is four digits long, its value is nowhere near a thousand. The powers of 2 are 1, 2, 4, 8, 16, 32, and so on. So for this number, its decimal equivalent is (1 x 8) + (1 x 4) + (0 x 2) + (1 x 1) = 13, as shown in Figure B-5. So the binary number 1101 is equivalent to 13 in the decimal number system.

FIGURE B-5
Each digit of the binary number 1101 represents a power of 2, so conversion to the decimal system is easy.

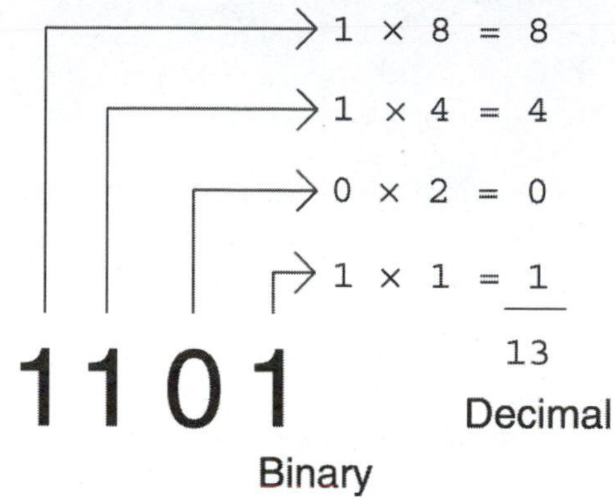

Decimal Points and Binary Points

You have used decimal points for a long time. Did you know there is a binary point? A decimal point divides the ones place and the tenths place, or 10^0 from 10^{-1}. There is an equivalent in the binary number system called the binary point. It divides the 2^0 place from the 2^{-1} place.

With a binary point, it is possible to have binary numbers such as 100.1, which in decimal is 4.5. Can you convert the binary number 10.01 to decimal? If you got 2.25 as the answer, you are correct. Try converting the binary number 11.001001 to decimal.

REVIEW QUESTIONS

1. Define data.
2. How many bits are in a byte?
3. How many combinations of bits are possible with 3 bits?
4. How many combinations of bits are possible with 4 bits?
5. How many combinations of bits are possible with 5 bits?
6. How many combinations of bits are possible with 6 bits?
7. Convert the binary number 1010 to decimal.
8. Convert the binary number 10001 to decimal.
9. Convert the binary number 101111 to decimal.
10. Convert the binary number 11111111 to decimal.

APPENDIX C

THE PROGRAMMING PROCESS

Overview

Programmers are always tempted to immediately begin writing code to solve a problem. There is a better way. Sure, if you are writing a program to print your name on the screen a million times you might get by with just sitting down and keying in a program. But most programs are more complicated, and a more structured and disciplined approach to programming is necessary.

Although different programmers use different approaches, most good programmers follow five basic steps when developing programs:

1. Define the problem.
2. Develop an algorithm.
3. Code the program.
4. Test and debug the program.
5. Document and maintain the program.

Defining the Problem

Defining the problem to be solved requires an understanding of what the program is to accomplish.

For example, a program that calculates interest on a loan is fairly easy to define. Start by identifying the inputs and outputs. As input, the program needs the loan amount, the interest rate, and the number of months that the money is to be borrowed. A specific known formula can be applied to the data, and the amount of interest is the output.

Many programs are more difficult to define. Suppose you are defining a game program that involves characters in a maze. In your definition, the abilities of each character must be defined. In addition, the maze and how the characters interact with the maze and each other must also be defined. The list goes on and on.

Imagine how much there is to define before writing a program to handle airline reservations for a worldwide airline or the software that controls the launch of the space shuttle. Before any part of the program is written, the programmer must know exactly what the goal is.

Defining the problem does not take into consideration how the program will do the job, just what the job is. Exactly how a program accomplishes its work is addressed in the second step of the process.

Developing an Algorithm

The second step in the programming process is to develop an algorithm. An algorithm is a set of sequential instructions that are followed to solve a problem. Algorithms have been commonly used for years. A recipe for baking a cake, instructions for assembling a bicycle, and directions to a shopping mall are all examples of algorithms. The directions to a mall, shown in Figure C-1, are a set of steps that you execute sequentially.

FIGURE C-1
This algorithm leads you to a shopping mall.

```
Drive south on University Avenue to 50th Street.
Turn right (west) on 50th.
Drive west on 50th to Slide Road.
Turn left (south) on Slide Road.
Drive south on Slide Road until you see the mall entrance on the right.
```

FIGURE C-2
Some steps in an algorithm may be repeated many times.

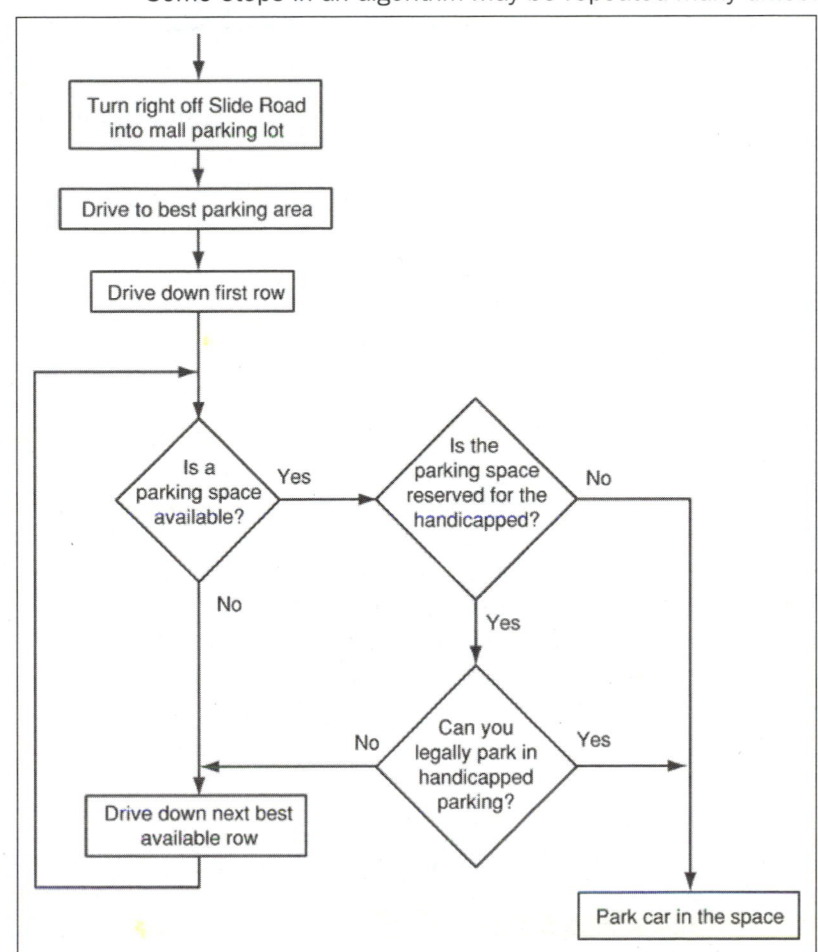

Some algorithms involve decisions that change the course of action or cause parts of the algorithm to be repeated. Consider the algorithm for parking the car once you reach the mall. A more complicated algorithm is best illustrated with symbols in a flowchart as shown in Figure C-2.

Programming a computer requires that you create an algorithm. The instructions the program gives the computer must tell the computer exactly what steps to do and in what order to do them. The computer executes each instruction sequentially, except when an instruction causes the flow of logic to jump to another part of the program.

When first developing an algorithm, you should avoid the temptation of initially writing in a programming language. A better method is to use pseudocode. Pseudocode expresses an algorithm in everyday English, rather than in a programming language. Pseudocode makes it possible for you to describe the instructions to be executed by the program. The precise choice of words and punctuation, however, is less important. Code List C-1 is an example of pseudocode for a mathematical program that prompts the user for an integer (a whole number without any decimal places) and squares it.

CODE LIST C-1

```
declare j and k as integers
prompt user for j
l = j * k
print l
```

Depending on the complexity of your program, developing algorithms can be a quick process or the most time-consuming part of developing your program.

Coding the Program

An algorithm's pseudocode is next translated into program code. This book teaches you the commands and structures you need to translate algorithms into actual programs.

Errors can be made during coding that can prevent the program from successfully compiling and linking. So part of the coding step involves resolving errors that prevent the program from running.

A common error is called a syntax error. A syntax error occurs when you key a command or some other part of the program incorrectly. Computers must be told exactly what to do. If someone leaves you a note that reads "Lock the back dore before you leave," you will be able to figure out what the instruction is. When the computer recognizes a syntax error, the programmer is notified immediately. Everything has to be just right or the computer will not accept it.

There are other errors that the computer may detect when compiling. Most of them are easily resolved. When all of those errors are resolved, the program will compile, link, and be ready to run. Even if a program runs, it may still fail to do its job correctly. That is where the next step of the programming process comes in.

Testing and Debugging

Testing and debugging is an important step that is too often ignored. Programs typically fail to operate 100% correctly the first time they are compiled or interpreted. Logic errors and other hidden problems called bugs must be located. Software must be tested and "debugged" to make sure the output is correct and reliable.

One way to test a program is to provide input for which the results are known. For example, a program that converts meters to feet can be easily tested by giving the program input values for which you know the output. Carefully select a wide variety of inputs. Use values that are larger or smaller than those which are typical. Use zero and negative numbers as inputs when allowable.

You should also test every part of a program. Make sure you provide input that tests every line of your code. Test each part of the program repeatedly to make sure that consistent results are obtained.

Did You Know?

Back when computers used vacuum tubes, the heat and light generated by the tubes sometimes attracted bugs such as moths. The bugs sometimes caused short circuits, resulting in the need to "debug" the computer.

A type of error that can cause your program to stop running (or crash) is called a run-time error; it occurs when a program gives the computer an instruction that it is incapable of executing. A run-time error may lead to a program "crash." For example, if your program tries to divide a number by 0, a run-time error will occur on most systems. A run-time error could also occur if the system runs out of memory while your program is running.

You will experience lots of bugs and errors as a programmer. They are a part of every programmer's day. Even the best programmers spend lots of time testing and debugging. Throughout this book you will be warned of possible pitfalls and bugs so that you can avoid as many as possible. But the best way to learn how to avoid bugs is to experience them.

Documenting and Maintaining the Program

This step applies mostly to programs used in the real world. But since you may someday write such programs, you should be aware of this step as well. Programmers must document their work so that they and other programmers can make changes or updates later. Documentation may also have to be written for the program's users.

You should document your programs while you are programming and avoid saving the task for last. The time to write documentation for a program is while you are programming. By the time you finish the programming, you may have already forgotten some of what you did.

You may also be less likely to write proper documentation once a program is complete. You may think your time is better spent on another project, but you will be pleased to have the documentation when it is needed.

Documentation in the Program

Documentation that is included in the program itself is very important. Virtually all programming languages allow comments to be included in the source code. The comments are ignored by the interpreter or the compiler; therefore, the programmer can include notes and explanations that will make the program easier for people to read.

Documentation Outside of the Program

Many times a program is complex enough that documents should be written that explain how the programming problem was solved. This documentation might be diagrams, flowcharts, or descriptions.

Documentation for the User

You have probably already been exposed to user documentation. Programs that are to be used by more than a few people usually include user documentation that explains the functions of the software.

Program Maintenance

Maintenance is an important part of the programming process. Most programs are written to help with a task. As the task changes, the program must also change. Users are likely to request additions and changes be made to the program. Maintaining a program is an important part of the process because it keeps the programmer's work up to date and in use.

During the maintenance phase of the programming process, bugs may be found that were not uncovered during the testing and debugging phase. It is also possible that better ways to accomplish a task in the program may be discovered. It is important to understand that the steps of the programming process may be repeated in order to refine or repair an existing program.

REVIEW QUESTIONS

1. List the five basic steps in the programming process.

2. Give an example of an algorithm used in everyday life.

3. Define the term bug as it relates to programming.

4. What is the purpose of documentation inside a program?

5. Write an algorithm that gives directions from one location to another. Choose a starting point (your home, for example) and give detailed, step-by-step directions that will lead anyone who might be reading the algorithm to the correct destination.

6. Draw a flowchart that describes the steps you follow when you get up in the morning and get ready for your day. Include as many details as you want, including things such as hitting the snooze button on your alarm clock, brushing your teeth, and eating breakfast.

Appendix D

Order of Operations

In both the Java and C++ units of this book, the order of operations for math operators has been discussed. This Appendix provides more in-depth information on the order of operations for C++ and Java.

C++ Math Operators

The chart below is a more complete table of the order of operators of all types. The operators shown in each group have the same precedence level. The group with the highest precedence appears at the top of the table. Under the Associativity heading, you can see whether the operators are evaluated from right to left or left to right. If the operator you are looking for does not appear in the table below, check your compiler's documentation for a complete list. Note: Some of the operators in this table were not covered in the C++ unit in this book. They are included for completeness.

TABLE D-1
C++ Operators

GROUP	SYMBOL	DESCRIPTION	ASSOCIATIVITY
Scope resolution	::	scope-resolution operator	left to right
Structure operators	->	structure pointer operator	left to right
	.	dot operator	
Unary operators	!	logical negation	right to left
	+	unary plus	
	-	unary minus	
	&	address of	
	*	dereferencing	
	++	increment operator	
	--	decrement operator	
	(typecast)	typecasting	
	sizeof	sizeof operator	
	new	memory allocation	
	delete	memory deallocation	

TABLE D-1 (continued)

GROUP	SYMBOL	DESCRIPTION	ASSOCIATIVITY
Multiplicative operators	*	multiplication	left to right
	/	divide	
	%	modulus	
Additive operators	+	addition	left to right
	-	minus	
Relational operators	<	less than	left to right
	<=	less than or equal to	
	>	greater than	
	>=	greater than or equal to	
Equality	==	equal to	left to right
	!=	not equal to	
Logical AND	&&	logical AND	left to right
Logical OR	||	logical OR	left to right
Assignment	=	assignment operator	right to left
	*=	compound assign product	
	/=	compound assign quotient	
	%=	compound assign remainder	
	+=	compound assign sum	
	-=	compound assign difference	

Java Operators

In Unit Five, several of the operators defined in Java were introduced. Following are two tables showing those operators and others not covered in the unit. The first table lists the operators by their Java group, shows the symbols for each operator, and provides a description of their use. The second table lists the order of precedence Java uses to evaluate expressions containing the operators.

TABLE D-2
Java Operators

GROUP	SYMBOL	DESCRIPTION
Assignment	=	assignment operator
	*=	compound assign product
	/=	compound assign quotient
	%=	compound assign remainder
	+=	compound assign sum
	-=	compound assign difference
Arithmetic	+	addition
	-	subtraction
	*	multiplication
	/	division
	%	modulus
Unary	++	increment
	- -	decrement
	-	negation
	~	bitwise complement
Comparison	==	equal to
	!=	not equal
	>	greater than
	>=	greater than or equal
	<	less than
	<=	less than or equal
Logical	!	unary negation (not)
	&&	logical and
	||	logical or
Bitwise	~	ones complement
	&	bitwise and
	|	bitwise or

TABLE D-2 (continued)

GROUP	SYMBOL	DESCRIPTION
	^	bitwise xor
	>>	shift right
	<<	shift left
	>>>	shift right, zero fill
Other	?:	ternary
	instanceof	instanceof comparison operator

In the following table, the operators are arranged top to bottom, highest to lowest precedence. Operators on the same line have equal precedence.

TABLE D-3
Precedence of Java Operators

ROW NO.	OPERATOR SYMBOLS				
1	.	[ ]	( )		
2	++	—	!	-	instanceof
3	*	/	%		
4	+	-			
5	<<	>>	>>>		
6	<	>	<=	>=	
7	==	!=			
8	&				
9	^				
10	|				
11	&&				
12	||				
13	?:				
14	=	op=			
15	,				

Appendix E

The bool Data Type

The bool data type (discussed in the C++ unit) was not originally in the C++ language. Before the bool data type, programmers used integers for all true and false values. As you learned, false is represented by 0 and true is represented by 1.

Some older C++ compilers do not support the bool data type. If your compiler is among those compilers, there is an easy fix. On the Electronic Instructor CD for this book is a file named bool.h. The contents of the file are shown below. If your compiler does not automatically support the bool data type, simply include bool.h in your program and an equivalent data type will be defined for you.

```
#ifndef _BOOL_H
#define _BOOL_H

typedef int bool;
const int FALSE = 0;
const int TRUE = 1;

#endif
```

The string class requires the bool data type. The oostring.h file includes the following statement.

```
//#include "bool.h"
```

By default, the `#include "bool.h"` statement is commented out of the string class. However, if your compiler does not support the bool data type, simply remove the slashes and the bool.h file will be included.

INDEX

A

B

C

D

M

N

O

P

R

S